The Pinter Review

NOBEL PRIZE/EUROPE THEATRE PRIZE VOLUME: 2005 – 2008

The Pinter Review

NOBEL PRIZE/EUROPE THEATRE PRIZE VOLUME: 2005 – 2008

Edited by
FRANCIS GILLEN
with
STEVEN H. GALE

THE UNIVERSITY OF TAMPA PRESS
TAMPA, FLORIDA
2008

The Pinter Review: Nobel Prize/Europe Theatre Prize Volume is published by The University of Tampa Press. Editorial correspondence should be addressed to Francis Gillen, *The Pinter Review,* Box 11F, The University of Tampa, Tampa, Florida 33606. The annual invites articles, notes, production reviews, queries, bibliographical, and other information which furthers the appreciation of the work of Harold Pinter. Manuscripts should be sent in duplicate, double-spaced, in current MLA style, or the style appropriate to the author's country, accompanied with return postage. Requests for library standing orders and purchase of past volumes should be sent to The University of Tampa Press, 401 W. Kennedy Blvd., Tampa, FL 33606. Hardcover, $35; softcover, $25—add $10 per book for International postage.

Cover: Conclusion of Nobel Address in Harold Pinter's handwriting.

ISBN 978-1879852-19-8 (hardcover)
ISBN 978-1879852-20-4 (softcover)
ISSN 0895-9706

Printed and bound by Thomson Shore.

For Marie Gillen—in loving memory

For Harold Pinter: Always Remembered

ACKNOWLEDGMENTS

The on-going publication of *The Pinter Review* has been made possible in large part by the generosity of The University of Tampa, its Board of Trustees, and the Dana Foundation at The University of Tampa. In particular, the belief in the value of this scholarly journal by then president Bruce Samson, provost David Ford, and J. Leonard Levy of Hillsboro Printing enabled us to begin publication of something more than a mere newsletter, and we will always be grateful. The production of this current volume has enjoyed the generous support provided by UT's president, Dr. Ronald Vaughn, as well as that of Provost Janet McNew; Dean of Arts and Letters, Dr. Donald Morrill; Dr. Andy Solomon and Dr. Judy Hayden, past and present chairpersons of English and Writing; and Dr. Richard Mathews, director of The University of Tampa Press, Sean Donnelly, and Ana Montalvo. My thanks, too, to Charles Grimes, Marilyn Gillen, and my UT library colleagues for their invaluable help.

Several of the essays published here were presented in Turin, Italy, on the occasion of the awarding of the Europe Theatre Prize. My thanks to Alessandro Martinez, Michela Giovannelli, Michael Billington, and all associated with the Europe Theatre Prize for inviting me to speak there, and to Maria Helena Serodio, Maria João Brilhante, and Rui Pina Coelho for publishing that talk in Portuguese in their outstanding journal, *Sinais de Cena*.

The Pinter Review

NOBEL PRIZE/EUROPE THEATRE PRIZE VOLUME

Contents

PINTER IN PRODUCTION

BOOK REVIEWS

BIBLIOGRAPHY

INTRODUCTION: CELEBRATION

This volume is dedicated to the loving memory of my wife, Marie C. Gillen, in particular to all the times Marie listened to me talk about Harold Pinter and this journal, to the invaluable, often publicly unnoticed part she played in its existence, design and publication, and, most importantly, to what, beyond words, she was, is, and will always be in my life and the lives of our daughters, Marilyn Gillen and Kathy Gillen Pohl. It is also dedicated to Harold Pinter—in celebration.

"Celebration despite..." has always been a quiet motif in Harold Pinter's work, one that I feel very close to as I write this brief introduction. Good writers give us the truth of our precarious human existence; the best give us that truth with at least a glimmer of hope, even if it exists only in the consciousness of the universality of human suffering, in the celebration of mystery that is Pinter's theatre. If we can laugh only to a point in Pinter's world, we can still laugh. If life is unsolvable, we can still drink to it, as we recall Pete's broken "Stan, don't let them tell you what to do!" or Rebecca's breakthrough down into the sea of human cruelty. Pinter's theatre is about seeing, point of view on stage, and so even in the face of ultimate state power we can never be hopeless because there is always the possibility of seeing differently. Power, sexual roles, conventional expectation, our relationships to one another, to the state: all are malleable though not easily, as in ordinary stage endings, for that would mean the eternal polarity between what is and what might be had stopped. As power takes new forms, so must resistance. Our dignity is in resistance. Let us celebrate resistance.

And so I see Harold Pinter giving his Nobel speech practically from his hospital bed, gaining a more powerful voice as he goes along, gaining strength from his words, from imagination rooted in the truth that is, but not enslaved by it, for the "room" that is our world shifts as perception changes. I see Harold Pinter on stage in Turin, Italy, before the cultural ministers of the European countries. I see him lifting the stick he had used to walk on stage, shaking it at them and at the audience, demanding that we all be accountable for not seeing the powerlessness of power. Provided we resist. This volume celebrates such resistance. Let us drink to it. Let our last words be those of resistance. Of the "determination," written so boldly on our cover in Harold Pinter's own hand, not to cease until the dignity of man, even when that person now seems the "other," becomes realized in our political system.

As for the contents of this volume, the many brilliant and differing perspectives on Pinter, what I wrote in the first *Pinter Review* in 1987, what I said to him over our first lunch together, remains so today. Its value lies in the bridges it builds to Harold Pinter's work. The work is all. And yet students I teach today, and audiences generally, come to the theatre with far different sensibilities and mindsets than the students that I taught when I first began to write and publish on Pinter, now nearly forty years ago. So new bridges for new sensibilities are perennially helpful, as are different appreciations for staging, comparisons to other writers, worldwide cultural contexts, compilation and discussion of new trends. All are here in the work of our distinguished contributors.

Like most scholarly journals, *The Pinter Review* does not pay for itself, and I express my profound thanks to the University of Tampa and its promotion of independent scholarship for making possible its original and continuing publication.

Francis Gillen

EDITOR'S NOTE:

While this volume was going to press, the world received the sad news of Harold Pinter's death on December 24, 2008. The sincere sympathies of all our editors and readers go out to Lady Antonia Fraser and all the rest of Harold's family. My personal grief is deep beyond words.

At the suggestion of the family, a poem by his grandson, Simon Soros, is included in this volume in memoriam. Even though it ends with "And now I live," I have decided to keep Harold's poem "To My Wife" which was to open the volume with a celebration of Harold's love. Harold Pinter lives indeed in our memories, on stage as long as there is theatre, and in the world's memory as long as there are conscience and courage of conviction.

I invite all who would like to join in celebrating Harold's life in the next *Pinter Review* to send me their manuscripts within the next few months.

F. G.

Grandpa

SIMON SOROS

A lot of people die out there everyday
But there's one I can single out
This one very close
And I'm not gonna boast
Yeah, yeah, uh uh, yeah
His name is Harold
Or Grandpa as known to me
I'm gonna say this
But definitely not carolled
There's no easy way
To put this as a sunshine ray
I'm gonna say "adios", bye-bye
I'm gonna miss you
I remember when I last saw you
You were looking as good as can be
You may have been unconscious
But your heart was filled with dances
All of them saying
"You're gonna live longer
But if you don't
In heaven you'll grow stronger".

You were born on the tenth of October
In the year of nineteen thirty
But you didn't have a father called Bertie
Yeah, Yeah, Uh Uh, Yeah
You definitely were a great playwright
And believed in civil rights
Also were an actor
And I thought you had the "I can do it" factor
I'm gonna say "adios", bye-bye
I'm gonna miss you
I'm sorry you had to go so soon
When you won the Nobel Prize
You were definitely going to rise
When I last saw you and kissed your hand
Everyone in the land
All of them saying
"You're gonna live longer
But if you don't
In heaven you'll grow stronger".

To My Wife

I was dead and now I live
You took my hand

I blindly died
You took my hand

You watched me die
And found my life

You were my life
When I was dead

You are my life
And so I live

Harold Pinter
June 2004

Presentation Speech for the 2005 Nobel Prize in Literature

by Per Wästberg,
Member of the Swedish Academy, Chairman of its Nobel Committee,
December 10, 2005

Your Majesties, Your Royal Highnesses, Esteemed Nobel Laureates, Ladies and Gentlemen,

Harold Pinter is the renewer of English drama in the 20th century. "Pinteresque" is an adjective listed in the Oxford Dictionary. Like Kafka, Proust and Graham Greene he has charted a territory, a Pinterland with a distinct topography.

With his twenty-nine plays and about a hundred that he has directed or acted in, he has made the theatre his own domain. His figures barricade themselves in unpredictable dialogues. Between the lines of unresolved threats, it roils and stings. What we hear are signals for everything we do not hear.

The abyss under chat, the unwillingness to communicate other than superficially, the need to rule and mislead, the suffocating sensation of accidents bubbling under the quotidian, the nervous perception that a dangerous story has been censored—all this vibrates through Pinter's drama.

His characters are at the mercy of each other on the periphery of life. They are also prisoners in the limbo of class divisions, set phrases and solidified habits. Their identities, backgrounds and histories are vague, and different versions exist depending on who is remembering. They seldom listen to each other but it is precisely their mental deafness that makes us listen. Not a word passes unnoticed, nor can we relax a single minute. Atmospheric pressure fluctuates as secrets unroll and shift the distribution of power.

Memories—invented, manipulated or real—flow as a hot undercurrent through Pinter's plays. We model the past to respond to the demands of the present and to form our future.

As closed rooms open to an international community, Pinter redefines romantic love as a more resilient love that includes friendship and the exigency to promote justice through action. In *Mountain Language*, love takes the form of an unconditional generosity missing in his earlier works.

To survive, we must do good deeds and stand up for the enslaved in this age of terror and spiralling violence.

It is usually said that Pinter's political commitment came late. But Pinter himself describes even his first period—*The Dumb Waiter*, *The Birthday Party*, *The Hothouse*—as political. In these "comedies of menace," language is a weapon of aggression, evasion and torture. The early works can be seen as metaphors for authoritarian intervention on several levels: the power of the state, the power of the family, the power of religion—all undermining the individual's critical questions. Pinter uncovers the reasons for wanting to destroy the identity of others and the fear disguised as violence against those who stand outside the party, club or nation.

Pinter's work has neither winners nor losers. In the power game between characters, we seldom know who has the upper hand; they change places, growing and sinking through lines that seldom seem deliberate. The characters have sides invisible to the eye, exposed in the ultraviolet rays of ambiguity. They grope forward between invisible walls and stratify into different levels of reality. In defending themselves against intrusion, they blockade themselves in spaces mined like alien terrain.

Pinter has perforated conventionally realistic drama with taciturnity's mystery, and has equipped his overblown figures with so many outlets that we can live with the characters and see them age and decay as we do. The solid and impenetrable figures of public life disintegrate in disastrous incoherence. They send messages that never seem to arrive, yet we leave the theatre less righteous than on entering.

For systematists, the world exists to put in order. For Harold Pinter it is for dissembling, through which the good and the humane find a way to seep out through the bureaucratic cage of ingrained reflexes. In a ruthless analysis of the totalitarian, he illuminates the pain of the individual.

Throwaway lines sting, little words corrode, what is half-said crushes, what is tacit forebodes catastrophe. Pinter, the tailor's son, scissors language, allowing the action to originate from the voices and rhythms of the characters. Thus, there is no given plot. We do not ask: "What will happen next?" Rather, "What is happening?"

The words are instruments of power. Words are repeated until they resemble truth. In a time of over-information, Pinter frees words from describing reality and makes them reality itself, at times poetic, more often oppressive. At the end, it is only through language that we can erase our destiny and recreate it.

Dear Harold Pinter,

In its choice of a Nobel Laureate the Swedish Academy recognises only the creative power of a single individual regardless of nation, sex and literary genre. This needs emphasising. However British you may appear in the eyes of many, your international and inter-human impact in the field of drama has been uniquely strong and inspiring for half a century. If someone thinks your prize is late in coming, we may reply that at any given moment somewhere in the world your plays are reinterpreted by new generations of directors and actors.

In your works, seductively accessible and frighteningly mysterious, the curtain rises on dense life-landscapes and harrowing confinement. In poetic images, you illuminate an existence where fantasy and the nightmare of reality clash.

In the absence of this year's Nobel Laureate in Literature, I request his publisher Mr. Stephen Page to come forward and receive Mr. Pinter's Prize from the hands of His Majesty the King.

Nobel Literature Lecture 2005
Art, Truth and Politics

In 1958 I wrote the following:

'There are no hard distinctions between what is real and what is unreal, nor between what is true and what is false. A thing is not necessarily either true or false; it can be both true and false.'

I believe that these assertions still make sense and do still apply to the exploration of reality through art. So as a writer I stand by them but as a citizen I cannot. As a citizen I must ask: What is true? What is false?

Truth in drama is forever elusive. You never quite find it but the search for it is compulsive. The search is clearly what drives the endeavour. The search is your task. More often than not you stumble upon the truth in the dark, colliding with it or just glimpsing an image or a shape which seems to correspond to the truth, often without realising that you have done so. But the real truth is that there never is any such thing as one truth to be found in dramatic art. There are many. These truths challenge each other, recoil from each other, reflect each other, ignore each other, tease each other, are blind to each other. Sometimes you feel you have the truth of a moment in your hand, then it slips through your fingers and is lost.

I have often been asked how my plays come about. I cannot say. Nor can I ever sum up my plays, except to say that this is what happened. That is what they said. That is what they did.

Most of the plays are engendered by a line, a word or an image. The given word is often shortly followed by the image. I shall give two examples of two lines which came right out of the blue into my head, followed by an image, followed by me.

The plays are 'The Homecoming' and 'Old Times'. The first line of 'The Homecoming' is 'What have you done with the scissors?' The first line of 'Old Times' is 'Dark.'

In each case I had no further information.

In the first case someone was obviously looking for a pair of scissors and was demanding their whereabouts of someone else he suspected had probably stolen them. But I somehow knew that the person addressed didn't give a damn about the scissors or about the questioner either, for that matter.

'Dark' I took to be a description of someone's hair, the hair of a woman, and was the answer to a question. In each case I found myself compelled to pursue the matter. This happened visually, a very slow fade, through shadow into light.

I always start a play by calling the characters A, B and C.

In the play that became 'The Homecoming' I saw a man enter a stark room and ask his question of a younger man sitting on an ugly sofa reading a racing paper. I somehow suspected that A was a father and that B was his son, but I had no proof. This was however confirmed a short time later when B (later to become Lenny) says to A (later to become Max), 'Dad, do you mind if I change the subject? I want to ask you something. The dinner we had before, what was the name of it? What do you call it? Why don't you buy a dog? You're a dog cook. Honest. You think you're cooking for a lot of dogs.' So since B calls A 'Dad' it seemed to me reasonable to assume that they were father and son. A was also clearly the cook and his cooking did not seem to be held in high regard. Did this mean that there was no mother? I didn't know. But, as I told myself at the time, our beginnings never know our ends.

'Dark.' A large window. Evening sky. A man, A (later to become Deeley), and a woman, B (later to become Kate), sitting with drinks. 'Fat or thin?' the man asks. Who are they talking about? But I then see, standing at the window, a woman, C (later to become Anna), in another condition of light, her back to them, her hair dark.

It's a strange moment, the moment of creating characters who up to that moment have had no existence. What follows is fitful, uncertain, even hallucinatory, although sometimes it can be an unstoppable avalanche. The author's position is an odd one. In a sense he is not welcomed by the characters. The characters resist him, they are not easy to live with, they are impossible to define. You certainly can't dictate to them. To a certain extent you play a never-ending game with them, cat and mouse, blind man's buff, hide and seek. But finally you find that you have people of flesh and blood on your hands, people with will and an individual sensibility of their own, made out of component parts you are unable to change, manipulate or distort.

So language in art remains a highly ambiguous transaction, a quicksand, a trampoline, a frozen pool which might give way under you, the author, at any time.

But as I have said, the search for the truth can never stop. It cannot be adjourned, it cannot be postponed. It has to be faced, right there, on the spot.

Political theatre presents an entirely different set of problems. Sermonising has to be avoided at all cost. Objectivity is essential. The characters must be allowed to breathe their own air. The author cannot

Raymond Seitz had a very good reputation as a rational, responsible and highly sophisticated man. He was greatly respected in diplomatic circles. He listened, paused and then spoke with some gravity. 'Father,' he said, 'let me tell you something. In war, innocent people always suffer.' There was a frozen silence. We stared at him. He did not flinch.

Innocent people, indeed, always suffer.

Finally somebody said: 'But in this case "innocent people" were the victims of a gruesome atrocity subsidised by your government, one among many. If Congress allows the Contras more money further atrocities of this kind will take place. Is this not the case? Is your government not therefore guilty of supporting acts of murder and destruction upon the citizens of a sovereign state?'

Seitz was imperturbable. 'I don't agree that the facts as presented support your assertions,' he said.

As we were leaving the Embassy a US aide told me that he enjoyed my plays. I did not reply.

I should remind you that at the time President Reagan made the following statement: 'The Contras are the moral equivalent of our Founding Fathers.'

The United States supported the brutal Somoza dictatorship in Nicaragua for over 40 years. The Nicaraguan people, led by the Sandinistas, overthrew this regime in 1979, a breathtaking popular revolution.

The Sandinistas weren't perfect. They possessed their fair share of arrogance and their political philosophy contained a number of contradictory elements. But they were intelligent, rational and civilised. They set out to establish a stable, decent, pluralistic society. The death penalty was abolished. Hundreds of thousands of poverty-stricken peasants were brought back from the dead. Over 100,000 families were given title to land. Two thousand schools were built. A quite remarkable literacy campaign reduced illiteracy in the country to less than one seventh. Free education was established and a free health service. Infant mortality was reduced by a third. Polio was eradicated.

The United States denounced these achievements as Marxist/Leninist subversion. In the view of the US government, a dangerous example was being set. If Nicaragua was allowed to establish basic norms of social and economic justice, if it was allowed to raise the standards of health care and education and achieve social unity and national self respect, neighbouring countries would ask the same questions and do the same things. There was of course at the time fierce resistance to the status quo in El Salvador.

I spoke earlier about 'a tapestry of lies' which surrounds us. President Reagan commonly described Nicaragua as a 'totalitarian dungeon'. This was taken generally by the media, and certainly by the British government, as accurate and fair comment. But there was in fact no record of death squads under the Sandinista government. There was no record of torture. There was no record of systematic or official military brutality. No priests were ever murdered in Nicaragua. There were in fact three priests in the government, two Jesuits and a Maryknoll missionary. The totalitarian dungeons were actually next door, in El Salvador and Guatemala. The United States had brought down the democratically elected government of Guatemala in 1954 and it is estimated that over 200,000 people had been victims of successive military dictatorships.

Six of the most distinguished Jesuits in the world were viciously murdered at the Central American University in San Salvador in 1989 by a battalion of the Alcatl regiment trained at Fort Benning, Georgia, USA. That extremely brave man Archbishop Romero was assassinated while saying mass. It is estimated that 75,000 people died. Why were they killed? They were killed because they believed a better life was possible and should be achieved. That belief immediately qualified them as communists. They died because they dared to question the status quo, the endless plateau of poverty, disease, degradation and oppression which had been their birthright.

The United States finally brought down the Sandinista government. It took some years and considerable resistance but relentless economic persecution and 30,000 dead finally undermined the spirit of the Nicaraguan people. They were exhausted and poverty stricken once again. The casinos moved back into the country. Free health and free education were over. Big business returned with a vengeance. 'Democracy' had prevailed.

But this 'policy' was by no means restricted to Central America. It was conducted throughout the world. It was never-ending. And it is as if it never happened.

The United States supported and in many cases engendered every right wing military dictatorship in the world after the end of the Second World War. I refer to Indonesia, Greece, Uruguay, Brazil, Paraguay, Haiti, Turkey, the Philippines, Guatemala, El Salvador, and, of course, Chile. The horror the United States inflicted upon Chile in 1973 can never be purged and can never be forgiven.

Hundreds of thousands of deaths took place throughout these countries. Did they take place? And are they in all cases attributable to US foreign policy? The answer is yes they did take place and they are attributable to American foreign policy. But you wouldn't know it.

It never happened. Nothing ever happened. Even while it was happening it wasn't happening. It didn't matter. It was of no interest. The crimes of the United States have been systematic, constant, vicious, remorseless, but very few people have actually talked about them. You have to hand it to America. It has exercised a quite clinical manipulation of power worldwide while masquerading as a force for universal good. It's a brilliant, even witty, highly successful act of hypnosis.

I put to you that the United States is without doubt the greatest show on the road. Brutal, indifferent, scornful and ruthless it may be but it is also very clever. As a salesman it is out on its own and its most saleable commodity is self love. It's a winner. Listen to all American presidents on television say the words, 'the American people', as in the sentence, 'I say to the American people it is time to pray and to defend the rights of the American people and I ask the American people to trust their president in the action he is about to take on behalf of the American people.'

It's a scintillating stratagem. Language is actually employed to keep thought at bay. The words 'the American people' provide a truly voluptuous cushion of reassurance. You don't need to think. Just lie back on the cushion. The cushion may be suffocating your intelligence and your critical faculties but it's very comfortable. This does not apply of course to the 40 million people living below the poverty line and the 2 million men and women imprisoned in the vast gulag of prisons which extends across the US.

The United States no longer bothers about low intensity conflict. It no longer sees any point in being reticent or even devious. It puts its cards on the table without fear or favour. It quite simply doesn't give a damn about the United Nations, international law or critical dissent, which it regards as impotent and irrelevant. It also has its own bleating little lamb tagging behind it on a lead, the pathetic and supine Great Britain.

What has happened to our moral sensibility? Did we ever have any? What do these words mean? Do they refer to a term very rarely employed these days—conscience? A conscience to do not only with our own acts but to do with our shared responsibility in the acts of others? Is all this dead? Look at Guantanamo Bay. Hundreds of people detained without charge for over three years, with no legal representation or due process, technically detained forever. This totally illegitimate structure is maintained in defiance of the Geneva Convention. It is not only tolerated but hardly thought about by what's called the 'international community'. This criminal outrage is being committed by a country which declares itself to be 'the leader of the free world'. Do we think about the inhabitants of Guantanamo Bay? What does the media say about them? They pop up occasionally—a small item on page six. They have been consigned to a no man's land from which indeed they may never return. At present many are on hunger strike, being force-fed, including British residents. No niceties in these force-feeding procedures. No sedative or anaesthetic. Just a tube stuck up your nose and into your throat. You vomit blood. This is torture. What has the British Foreign Secretary said about this? Nothing. What has the British Prime Minister said about this? Nothing. Why not? Because the United States has said: to criticise our conduct in Guantanamo Bay constitutes an unfriendly act. You're either with us or against us. So Blair shuts up.

The invasion of Iraq was a bandit act, an act of blatant state terrorism, demonstrating absolute contempt for the concept of international law. The invasion was an arbitrary military action inspired by a series of lies upon lies and gross manipulation of the media and therefore of the public; an act intended to consolidate American military and economic control of the Middle East masquerading—as a last resort—all other justifications having failed to justify themselves—as liberation. A formidable assertion of military force responsible for the death and mutilation of thousands and thousands of innocent people.

We have brought torture, cluster bombs, depleted uranium, innumerable acts of random murder, misery, degradation and death to the Iraqi people and call it 'bringing freedom and democracy to the Middle East'.

How many people do you have to kill before you qualify to be described as a mass murderer and a war criminal? One hundred thousand? More than enough, I would have thought. Therefore it is just that Bush and Blair be arraigned before the International Criminal Court of Justice. But Bush has been clever. He has not ratified the International Criminal Court of Justice. Therefore if any American soldier or for that matter politician finds himself in the dock Bush has warned that he will send in the marines. But Tony Blair has ratified the Court and is therefore available for prosecution. We can let the Court have his address if they're interested. It is Number 10, Downing Street, London.

Death in this context is irrelevant. Both Bush and Blair place death well away on the back burner. At least 100,000 Iraqis were killed by American bombs and missiles before the Iraq insurgency began. These people are of no moment. Their deaths don't exist. They are blank. They are not even recorded as being dead. 'We don't do body counts,' said the American general Tommy Franks.

Early in the invasion there was a photograph published on the front page of British newspapers of Tony Blair kissing the cheek of a little Iraqi boy. 'A grateful child,' said the caption. A few days later there was a story and photograph, on an inside page, of another four-year-old boy with no arms. His family had been blown up by a missile. He was the only survivor. 'When do I get my arms back?' he asked. The story was dropped. Well, Tony Blair wasn't holding him in his arms, nor the body of any other mutilated child, nor the body of any bloody corpse. Blood is dirty. It dirties your shirt and tie when you're making a sincere speech on television.

The 2,000 American dead are an embarrassment. They are transported to their graves in the dark. Funerals are unobtrusive, out of harm's way. The mutilated rot in their beds, some for the rest of their lives. So the dead and the mutilated both rot, in different kinds of graves.

Here is an extract from a poem by Pablo Neruda, 'I'm Explaining a Few Things':

And one morning all that was burning,
one morning the bonfires
leapt out of the earth
devouring human beings
and from then on fire,
gunpowder from then on,
and from then on blood.
Bandits with planes and Moors,
bandits with finger-rings and duchesses,
bandits with black friars spattering blessings
came through the sky to kill children
and the blood of children ran through the streets
without fuss, like children's blood.

Jackals that the jackals would despise
stones that the dry thistle would bite on and spit out,
vipers that the vipers would abominate.

Face to face with you I have seen the blood
of Spain tower like a tide
to drown you in one wave
of pride and knives.

Treacherous
generals:
see my dead house,
look at broken Spain:

from every house burning metal flows
instead of flowers
from every socket of Spain
Spain emerges
and from every dead child a rifle with eyes
and from every crime bullets are born
which will one day find
the bull's eye of your hearts.

And you will ask: why doesn't his poetry
speak of dreams and leaves
and the great volcanoes of his native land.

Come and see the blood in the streets.
Come and see
the blood in the streets.
Come and see the blood
in the streets!

Let me make it quite clear that in quoting from Neruda's poem I am in no way comparing Republican Spain to Saddam Hussein's Iraq. I quote Neruda because nowhere in contemporary poetry have I read such a powerful visceral description of the bombing of civilians.

I have said earlier that the United States is now totally frank about putting its cards on the table. That is the case. Its official declared policy is now defined as 'full spectrum dominance'. That is not my term, it is theirs. 'Full spectrum dominance' means control of land, sea, air and space and all attendant resources.

The United States now occupies 702 military installations throughout the world in 132 countries, with the honourable exception of Sweden, of course. We don't quite know how they got there but they are there all right.

The United States possesses 8,000 active and operational nuclear warheads. Two thousand are on hair trigger alert, ready to be launched with 15 minutes warning. It is developing new systems of nuclear force, known as bunker busters. The British, ever cooperative, are intending to replace their own nuclear missile, Trident. Who, I wonder, are they aiming at? Osama bin Laden? You? Me? Joe Dokes? China? Paris? Who knows? What we do know is that this infantile insanity—the possession and threatened use of nuclear weapons—is at the heart of present American political philosophy. We must remind ourselves that the United States is on a permanent military footing and shows no sign of relaxing it.

Many thousands, if not millions, of people in the United States itself are demonstrably sickened, shamed and angered by their government's actions, but as things stand they are not a coherent political force—yet. But the anxiety, uncertainty and fear which we can see growing daily in the United States is unlikely to diminish.

I know that President Bush has many extremely competent speech writers but I would like to volunteer for the job myself. I propose the following short address which he can make on television to the nation. I see him grave, hair carefully combed, serious, winning, sincere, often beguiling, sometimes employing a wry smile, curiously attractive, a man's man.

'God is good. God is great. God is good. My God is good. Bin Laden's God is bad. His is a bad God. Saddam's God was bad, except he didn't have one. He was a barbarian. We are not barbarians. We don't chop people's heads off. We believe in freedom. So does God. I am not a barbarian. I am the democratically elected leader of a freedom-loving democracy. We are a compassionate society. We give compassionate electrocution and compassionate lethal injection. We are a great nation. I am not a dictator. He is. I am not a barbarian. He is. And he is. They all are. I possess moral authority. You see this fist? This is my moral authority. And don't you forget it.'

Apart from That

Two people on mobile phones.

GENE: How are you?

LAKE: Very well. And you? Are you well?

GENE: I'm terribly well. How about you?

LAKE: Really well. I'm really well.

GENE: I'm so glad.

LAKE: Apart from…oh you know…

GENE: I know.

LAKE: Apart from…oh you know…

GENE: I do know. But apart from that…?

LAKE: How about you?

GENE: Oh you know…all things considered…

LAKE: I know. But apart from that…?

Silence.

GENE: Sorry. I've lost you.

LAKE: What do you mean?

GENE: I lost you.

LAKE: No you didn't. I'm right here. Where I was.

GENE: Anyway, where were we?

LAKE: Sorry?

Pause.

GENE: I mean apart from all that, how are you really?

LAKE: Terribly well.

GENE: Well you certainly sound well.

LAKE: I am. Apart from...oh you know...

GENE: Yes. I know.

LAKE: But *you're* well anyway.

GENE: I'm wonderfully well, to be honest.

LAKE: I'm really glad.

GENE: Apart from...you know...

LAKE: But apart from that?

Silence.

GENE: What?

LAKE: Apart from that, how are you really?
Apart from that?

Harold Pinter
May 2006

thinking, perhaps in order to avoid those feelings, those thoughts. Because he was not afraid of silence or letting his characters lapse into stuttering or inscrutability or mystery. Because he understood that if you push reality hard enough, desperately enough, it will end up exposing under its surface another dimension, fantastic, absurd, delirious. Because he suggested that the worst hallucinations of fear are not immune from the pendulum of humor. But all of these lessons in dramatic craftsmanship paled in comparison to what he taught me about human existence, about—dare I say the word—politics.

From the very start, I was visited by the intuition that Harold Pinter was unfolding a world that was deeply political. Not in the overt sense (as would happen later, in several of his plays written from the early Eighties onwards) that his creatures were affected by who governed them, whether this man or that one controlled the Army, gave orders to the police, held sway over the State. No, these figments of Pinter's psyche, at least back in the Sixties, did not care about disputing the public arena, about changing the world for better or for worse, were not interested in ruling a land or resisting tyranny. They were, on the contrary, sad citizens of intimacy, obsessed only with their very own private survival.

And yet, by trapping us inside the lives of those men and women, Pinter was revealing, I felt, the many gradations and degradations of power with a starkness I had not remarked before in other authors. All power, all domination and liberation started there, he seemed to be saying, in those claustrophobic rooms where each word counts, each slight utterance needs to be accounted for, is paid for in some secret currency of hope or suffering. You want to free the world, humanity, from oppression? Look inside, look sideways, look at the hidden violence of language. Never forget that it is in that language where the other parallel violence, the cruelty exercised on the body, originates.

Two men waiting in a basement to kill somebody. An old tramp laying claim to a derelict room. A birthday celebration interrupted by intruders. A woman afraid of being evicted.

Primal scenes of betrayal which could be transpiring anywhere on our planet, embodiments of a vast and disquieting landscape of dread, the precarious condition inhabited by most of contemporary humanity, the neglected narrative of the twentieth century. It was perhaps natural that I should have projected onto those stories born in England the disturbing shadows of my own Latin America. How many Davies crossed our Santiago streets? How many Peruvian Roses feared and desired that visitor from her past? How many killers took their time in the Buenos Aires cellars of yesterday, how many would soon await us in the Sao Paolo cellars of tomorrow?

And how to tell those stories, how to respect the uncertainty of those existences on the rim of extinction, how to mercilessly strip the masks forged out of the lives we made for ourselves and yet be gentle, be oh so tender with these victims of their own delusions?

Pinter knew how.

And I was haunted by his knowledge, by my need to understand.

So haunted that my first book—started in 1965, when I was twenty-three, and finally published in 1968—was an examination of his theatre: *El Absurdo entre cuatro paredes: el teatro de Harold Pinter*.

So haunted that, many years later, when I began to write for the theatre, it was his influence and his aesthetics that guided me. In fact, my dramatic works can be read, in part, as a conversation with Pinter. Not only *Death and the Maiden*, which is dedicated to a Harold who is now one of my dearest friends, but many of the other plays as well: *Widows* and *Reader* and, most recently, *Purgatorio* and *The Other Side*. Affected by the way in which Pinter uses language, troubled by the way in which Pinter deals with memory, peopled by characters who, in an entirely different setting, recall their genesis in the Pinter universe, distant cousins, half-sisters, illegitimate sons and daughters of those men and women I first glimpsed on a Chilean stage more than forty years ago.

I insist that I cannot pinpoint the moment, cannot say when and where and how and what play, but at that moment in the early Sixties there was something I did know and did not say, something I feel compelled to convey now all these decades later.

His characters may not have been communicating with one another and were undoubtedly lost in the swamp of their own words and solitude, but Pinter himself is another matter. He spoke to me on that inaugural occasion with unmistakable clarity, set about dispelling the terror of my loneliness. And I knew then in a flash what I know now in a more mature and meditative way: that Harold Pinter was the elder brother I had been looking for and that even if he had been born by some accidental contingency in faraway England, he was, and continues to be, profoundly, irresistibly, maddeningly Latin American.

one kisses the fist of power, or rips a child from a mother's arms. And that act for Rebecca, as the light dims and the landscape of the play becomes clearly interior, is not remote or past but here, now, all history from Aeschylus to Pinter become, as Borges wrote, a single act—child taken from mother in what Mark Taylor-Batty describes so accurately as "our primal urge to attain self-definition through 'possession' of another" (Batty, 55).

As we turn to Sophocles we think obviously of Oedipus, certain in his self-contained purity that the curse he pronounces upon the killer of Laius does not affect him, of his scorn for those who would reason with him, of Jocasta's mockery of the oracles—all just before they know the truth. We think of Creon who in his pride of power declared to his son Haemon with the tyrant's arrogance: "Am I to rule by other mind than mine?" to which his son replies: "You'd rule a desert beautifully alone" (I, 206). Creon, who can see an adversary only as inhuman, other. Antigone, who recognizes the same humanity in all, a brother who is more than foe, another of the dead who must be buried with the respect worthy of all persons who share our common fate. Centuries later Harold Pinter writes in words so reminiscent of *Antigone*:

> Who was the father or daughter or brother
> Or uncle or sister or mother or son
> Of the dead and abandoned body?
>
> Was the body dead when abandoned?
> Was the body abandoned?
> By whom had it been abandoned?
>
> Was the dead body naked or dressed for a journey?
>
> . . .
>
> Did you wash the dead body
> Did you close both its eyes
> Did you bury the body
> Did you leave it abandoned
> Did you kiss the dead body
>
> from *Death* in *War* (ellipsis is mine)

Instead in his *hubris*, Creon, prepares for his enemy, Antigone, the sealed and hollow cave that will also be the place of his son's death, the cause of his wife's demise, and following upon this, of his own life, as he describes it, "warped past cure" (I, 225). As the chorus declares in the final words of the play: "Great words by men of pride/bring greater blows upon them" (I, 226).

Though Pinter's world is not peopled with kings, it is certainly one which weighs questions of *hubris* and power. In *The Birthday Party* Goldberg appears to have all the power to deal with Stanley, yet in the opening scene of Act Three, we see that his supposed power is a sham consisting of nothing he can internalize, only bits and pieces of a culture whose words he has absorbed, but whose meaning and coherence, if there are any, wholly escape him.

> ... That's why I've reached my position, McCann. Because I've always been as fit as a fiddle. All my life I've said the same. Play up, play up, and play the game. Honour thy father and thy mother. All along the line. Follow the line, the line, McCann, and you can't go wrong. What do you think, I'm a self-made man? No! I sat where I was told to sit. I kept my eye on the ball. School? Don't talk to me about school. Top in all subjects. And for why? Because I'm telling you, I'm telling you, follow my line? Follow my mental? Learn by heart. Never write down a thing. And don't go too near the water.
>
> And you'll find—that what I say is true.
>
> Because I believe that the world ... (*Vacant.*) ....
>
> Because I believe that the world ... *(Desperate.)*....
>
> BECAUSE I BELIEVE THAT THE WORLD ... *(Lost.)*....
>
> *He sits in chair.*
>
> (*Complete Works: Two*, 77–78)

In Pinter's silences are the pure fragmentation of coherent meaning—power without the wisdom the Greeks so admired.

Similarly, in the moment that Davies feels safe in his supposed alliance with the slippery, evasive Mick, he overreaches and destroys his safe place with the kindly brother, Aston, in *The Caretaker*.

> DAVIES *takes the bag and presses the contents down.* All right ... I been offered a job here ... you wait ... *(He puts on his overcoat.)* You'll be sorry you called me that... you ain't heard the last of this ... *(He picks up his bag and goes to the door.)* You'll be sorry you called me that....
>
> *He opens the door,* ASTON *watching him.*
>
> Now I know who I can trust.
>
> (*Complete Works: Two*, 78)

What follows is his expulsion, his loss of whatever safety and shelter he may have had. Similarly in *The Homecoming*, at the very moment when male possessiveness and authority appear securely triumphant, Ruth undermines the seemingly ascendant patriarchy with her counter demands:

> RUTH. How many rooms would this flat have?
>
> LENNY. Not many.

then or for liquid gold today is not popular politics, war must be made mythological, and fought for "honor" or "love" or "democracy" at the tip of a smart bomb.

In *Hecuba*, Euripides, through the mouth of the herald Talthybius, casts doubts on the gods used to justify war and death.

> What shall I say, Zeus,—that thou look'st on men?
> Or that this fancy false we vainly hold
> For naught, who deem there is a race of gods,
> While chance controlleth all things among men?
>
> (406)

In *Iphigeneia in Tauris*, the story used to justify so much death is again false. Iphigeneia had not been killed at Aulis, but rescued by Artemis and made a priestess of Artemis among the savage Tauri. There, eighteen years later, Orestes, seeking peace, and his companion, Pylades, arrive there, are captured and set to be sacrificed in the prime of their youth at the very temple over which Iphigeneia presides. As she sees them, she thinks:

> To none is given
> To know the coming nor the end of woe;
> So dark is God, and to great darkness go
> His paths, by blind chance mazed from our ken.
>
> (410)

Like Euripides, Pinter uses myth to play against myth which in our modern world is produced by the media, popular culture, and the increasing power of government to manipulate both. *The Birthday Party* plays against the media-generated myth of the strong-minded emissary sent on a mission, only, as we have seen, to reveal Goldberg as a finally vacant follower. *The Homecoming* demolishes the myth of the close-knit family. Ben and Gus are in a sense mythic knights on a mission, except that, in Pinter's version in *The Dumb Waiter* they don't understand it and it proves self-destructive. *Betrayal* undermines the myth of romantic love existing in a realm apart from other realities such as male friendship, children and work. Jerry's words, expressed brilliantly at the conclusion of the play carry in their absolute romantic assertion all the irony of what has gone before:

> JERRY
>
> ... I'm madly in love with you. I can't believe that what anyone is at this moment saying has ever happened. Nothing has ever happened.
>
> Nothing. This is the only thing that has ever happened.
>
> (*Complete Works: Four*, 266–277)

But the myth that is most relevant to us today, that which Pinter exposes, as did Euripides in his political plays, is that of the self-exonerating, all-powerful state and the supposed immunity from all other law its service confers under the name of patriotism. In *Mountain Language* he does this, as Euripides does in *The Trojan Women*, by showing the suffering of those destroyed by the myth, refusing to allow them to remain abstractions. In both plays the women tremble for family, for what was and is now senselessly destroyed. Listen to the lament of Hecuba and the chorus:

Chorus

Our city fallen to the spear
fades as smoke winged in the sky

. . .

Hecuba

O soil where my children grew

Chorus

Alas

Hecuba

O children, hear me; it is your mother who calls

Chorus

They are the dead you cry to. This is a dirge.

(II, 293)[3]

In *Mountain Language*, in the middle of all the brutality and arbitrary use of power for power's sake, the stage goes to half-light and our sense of what is lost comes from the Young Woman and her prisoner husband, voice over because it can never be in this reality, speaking from memory, love, longing for what humanly was, ought to be and, by the State's action, cannot be.

MAN'S VOICE

We are out on a lake

YOUNG WOMAN'S VOICE

It is spring

MAN'S VOICE

I hold you—I warm you

YOUNG WOMAN'S VOICE

When my eyes open I see you above me and smile

Sensing, though, that giving play to the broad scope of the state with its uniforms, mass movements, parades and music may actually reinforce the very myth a play or a film may seek to oppose, as, for example, so many films about Hitler's Germany have done, Pinter reduces the militaristic state to its simplest elements, the torturers, the human shells who must be filled with the state's power in order to have any identity at all, and its profiteers who gladly repress all humanity to maintain their status. The macro picture is exposed in the micro picture; the cruelty, sadism and lust for power in the state is seen and demythologized through the dramatization of that power in the individual. In the four separate scenes of *One for the Road* what the torturer Nicolas exploits is the vulnerability of those one loves, even as the state today demands conformity through its professed power to protect one's loved ones. The power of life and death over those one loves is the same in Nicolas and the state, for Nicolas finds himself in his state-conferred power mythologized as patriotism. And, as Pinter pointed out in the "Conversation with Nicolas Hern," the audience, painfully, must identify with such power:

> It is also, however, true that many of the natural sadistic qualities, which we all possess, are given free reign in the play. The audience felt fear—but what was it fear of? Fear not only of being in the position of the given victim, but a fear also born of recognition of themselves as interrogator. Because think of the joy of having absolute power (16–17).

In *The Bacchae*, under the influence of bacchic orgy, the women, the inner circle so to speak, tear apart the outsider, Pentheus, who has dared look upon their orgies. For those in the Greek audience who accept the myth, Pentheus is rightly punished for violating their seclusion and maligning the worshippers of Bacchus. But those who knew Euripides' plays must have had other thoughts as they watched Agave, Pentheus' mother, wrenching off one of his shoulders, finally impaling his head on her ivy wreathed wand, and racing back to the city in triumph with her "trophy of my hunt," (III, 246) asking her father Cadmus to "Glory in my kill and invite your friends to share/the feast of triumph" (III, 247–8).

At the opening of the play the chorus had intoned a ritual cleansing on the celebrants: "Blessed, blessed are those that know the mysteries of god" (III, 196).

In both *Party Time* and *Celebration*, Pinter stages similar bacchanals for our time. The celebrants too revel in their own mysteries which accord them, by God's grace, presumably, privilege made clean and sanctified, joined as they are in a "holy band" which likewise punishes outsiders who threaten their privilege. Once again, by not locating the situation in absolute historical place or time, Pinter echoes all of us who prefer not to know the pain of "other" or the cost to "others" of using most of the world's resources while 30,000 children worldwide die daily of poverty-related causes. In *Party Time*, Dusty endangers the celebratory mood by worrying about her brother who is outside where a roundup of dissidents is presumably taking place. Her husband Terry warns:

TERRY

> ... You come to a lovely party like this, all you have to do is shut up and enjoy the hospitality and mind your own fucking business. How many more times do I have to tell you? You keep hearing all these things. You keep hearing all these things spread by pricks about pricks. What's it got to do with you? (8)

But Pinter exposes the violence at the heart of this "cast-iron peace." Having "let down" her husband by relating to the "other" who has been marginalized into being expendable by words such as "prick" or today "insurgent," "terrorist," Dusty asks, ironically, if he will kill her: "Do you think that if you put an end to me that would be the end of everything for everyone?" And for a moment Terry revels in sadistic fantasy that presages universal destruction:

> We've got dozens of options. We could suffocate every single one of you at a given signal or we could shove a broomstick up each individual arse at another given signal or we could poison all the mother's milk in the world so that every baby would drop dead before it opened its perverted bloody mouth (24–25).

The final word in *Party Time*, though, is that of the outsider, the marginalized, ever present at the door. As opposed to the dismissive "prick," he insists on name:

> I had a name. It was Jimmy. People called me Jimmy.
>
> That was my name (37).

Jimmy, the outsider at the door of our luxury, Jimmy the expendable, the embodiment of those whom we consign to death to keep our party going. What an absolutely perfect theatrical image, this ending of *Party Time*! An icon across the ages, the outsider at our door, the dead whose death we do not feel or weep for because they are "the other." My name was Hecuba. My name is Paul. I was from Dahfar. People called me Paul. That was my name. Across time, Pinter lets us fill in the blanks.

In *The Bacchae*, as in *Party Time* and Pinter's other political plays, revelers momentarily lose identity, and with it personal responsibility. For Euripides this takes place in the orgy, for Pinter in the all-excusing service of the nation-state. Their victims too are threatened with loss of identity—"prick," "man," "insurgent," "intruder." In both instances, the tragic moment occurs when name is reasserted and the victim becomes human again, one of us whom we have destroyed—when the intruder becomes again Pentheus—son, father—destroyed by his own mother and her uncriticized beliefs.

> I am in anguish now, tormented, who walked in triumph minutes past, exulting in my kill. And that prize I carried home with such pride was my own curse. (III, 253)

As when the "insurgent" becomes just another mother's son.

So too with Jimmy who, as outsider, somehow bears in himself all those deaths so lightly spoken of inside the privileged, superficial party.

> The dark is in my mouth and I suck it. It's the only thing I have. It's mine. It's my own. I suck it (38).

And I cannot help but think that what Pinter said about the audience in *One for the Road* is true here as well. Some part of us is ashamed and discomforted, for we too identify at some level with the desire for power and the luxury.

In *Celebration*, certain code words unite the privileged "us," just as they continue to identify the "outsiders." Unlike *Party Time*, however, there seem to be no immediate outside threats, so that Pinter here exposes the need for constant grave outside threat, even if it is largely non-existent, to maintain and justify privilege linked to power: "Taking charge. Keeping the peace. Enforcing the peace" (43). To continue the link with Euripides, we might say that one always needs a Pentheus to tear apart, to keep the celebration going, and the real purpose of the myth is to destroy real time and real history until, at the height of the orgy, there is nothing left but "us" and "them," "we" and, sadly, a word as old as history, "our enemy." At the moment Agave rips apart her son, there is no real history past or future, there's only the created, mythic history of the moment which justifies the act, even as today we ratchet up the colors of a threat and turn a real but relatively minor one into an all-encompassing, all-justifying binary one. But even in the claustrophobic *Celebration,* history *is* present but ineffective in the interjections of the waiter. For the play's metaphors of incest, womb, claustrophobia not only comment ironically on the shallowness of the celebration, but define its insularity. Only the waiter, when all the rest have left, stands alone commenting indirectly on our real, historical situation. "I can't find the door to get out."

In discussing Harold Pinter's theatre and that of the Greek tragic theatre, what I've hoped to call attention to is the broad humanity of Harold Pinter's work. Both take the measure of our human place in the world. Both excoriate us when we as individuals or states are bloated-up with arrogance and pride, and both see such *hubris* as ultimately destructive. Both require that we identify with the whole of humanity that, like us, is born and dies, a common humanity that extends beyond states, gender, and certainly ideologies. A lot has been written lately about the "angry" Pinter, but that anger, I truly believe, like that of Euripides especially, is born out of dismay at our capacity for self-deceit and our denial of that common humanity. It is born finally, then, out of love. Obviously, as I noted at the opening, there are many differences of time, the referentiality of language, perhaps of *catharsis*, but it seems clear to me, as I hope I have shown, that the Greek tragedians and audience alike would recognize Harold Pinter as one of their own, a kindred spirit. Rightly Harold Pinter takes his place, not only with the greatest dramatists of our time, but across the ages as well.

NOTES

[1] In *Where Laughter Stops: Pinter's Tragicomedy*, Bernard F. Dukore writes that tragicomedy "establishes a basic affinity to one of the two major genres, tragedy or comedy, but its development denies the exclusive characteristics of the tragic or comic genre with which it is primarily associated—characteristics of plot, audience response, or both—and its conclusion denies the exclusiveness of the type of change associated with that genre" (3). Pinter himself has called *The Caretaker* "funny, up to a point. Beyond that point it ceases to be funny, and it was because of that point that I wrote it" (*Sunday Times*, London, August 14, 1960). I am not arguing here that Pinter's works are "tragedy" only that they bear certain affinities to the works of the Greek tragedians.

The classical scholar, H.D. Kitto, uses the term tragic-comedy to describe Euripides' *Helen* and *Iphigeneia in Tauris*. He claims the plays have only "a theatrical reality" and therefore the audience's emotions are "limited to the play and to the moment" instead of being related to an external reality, as in traditional Greek tragedy (315).

[2] Moses Hadas writes in this vein of a complexity of character in Greek tragedy similar to that usually associated with Pinter. "For discussion and reflection there is always room, for Greek tragedy never presents a white hero as opposed to a black villain—the spectacle of virtue always triumphant could only corroborate smugness; the spectacle of flawless virtue crushed to earth would only be shocking, as Aristotle points out" (*A History of Greek Literature*, New York, Columbia UP, 1962, p.75).

[3] In his adaptation of the play, Jean-Paul Sartre gave the final words to Poseidon:

Idiots!
We'll make you pay for this.
You stupid, bestial mortals
Making war, burning cities,
violating tombs and temples,
torturing your enemies,
bringing suffering on yourselves
Can't you see
War
Will kill you:
All of you? (80).

WORKS CITED

Batty, Mark. *Harold Pinter*. Devon: Norcote House, 2001.

Dukore, Bernard F. *Where the Laughter Stops: Pinter's Tragicomedy*. Columbia and London: U of Missouri Press, 1976.

Durant, Will. *The Life of Greece*. New York: Simon and Schuster, 1939.

Grene, David and Lattimore, Richmond, eds. *Greek Tragedies*. Three volumes (listed I, II, or III in citations). Chicago and London: U of Chicago Press, 1960.

Hadas, Moses. *A History of Greek Literature*. New York and London: Columbia U Press, 1950.

Kitto, H.D.F. *The Greeks*. Harmondsmith: Penguin, 1963.

Murray, Gilbert. *A History of Ancient Greek Literature*. New York: Ungar, 1966.

Pinter, Harold. *Celebration and The Room*. New York: Grove Press, 2000.

—. *Complete Works: One*. New York: Grove Press, 1977.

—. *Complete Works: Two*. New York: Grove Press, 1977.

—. *Complete Works: Three*. New York: Grove Press, 1978.

—. *Complete Works: Four*. New York: Grove Press, 1981.

—. *Mountain Language*. New York: Grove Press, 1988.

—. *One for the Road*. New York: Grove Press, 1985.

—. *War*. London: Faber and Faber, 2003.

Sartre, Jean-Paul. *The Trojan Women: Euripides*. English version by Ronald Duncan. New York: Knopf, 1967.

Gertrude Stein on Harold Pinter: An Impossible Analysis

KATHERINE H. BURKMAN

Writing is such a condition of my living that I have continued to write here in the afterwards.

Words Words Words.

I find the writer Harold Pinter very interesting. The English writer. The playwright and poet. The one who was born of working class parents in 1930, his father a Jewish tailor—well I, of course, am Jewish too. I wonder if he knows that I am responsible for his 2005 Nobel Prize for literature. After all, without my genius, where would be his? Am I not the quintessential modernist and is he not following following following in the directions that I have given to the young to follow. Not to mention post-modernists. I know I know Harold is 78, but he is young at heart and that is what I like about him. Have we not each, in our own way, taken language out of its realistic prison and extended its boundaries, its uses. It is true that I have been called repetitious and even long-winded in my time, and that Harold is very stingy with his words, and that he is famous for his pauses and his use of silence, which is not of course my way but he also repeats as a way to approach the real. He repeats repeats yes repeats.

Have you read Ernest's story, "The Killers"? If not you really must. Ernest Hemingway? Ernest was quite good when he was young (alas, he did not get along with Alice so our friendship waned, although the flowers remain, always the flowers). Well, I had a most tremendous influence on Ernest when I took to writing short sentences and repeating and Harold Pinter certainly has been rewriting "The Killers" all of his writing life his writing his life. I mean look at the two killers in his play *The Dumb Waiter* or his Goldberg and McCann in *The Birthday Party*, a reincarnation of Ernest's characters. It's true that Ernest sent me a note once saying "A bitch is a bitch is a bitch" but that only meant he understood me and that was fine. And I think that Margaret Atwood is an interesting writer and that she has some words about Harold that are probably relevant: "Prickly, bothersome, mordant and dour. Always unexpected: coming up on you sideways with an alarming glare." It must be all that

Hitchcock that he watched as a child. He has denied the significance of his own remark that his plays are about the weasel under the cocktail cabinet but then who is he to deny the significance of his own remark, his own remark, his remark.

Of course with Harold a rose is not always a rose and that is a fault. He has followed that Russian Anton Chekhov and insists on his characters hiding what they are saying underneath what they are saying or hiding it in silence. There is the text, the text, the text, and then there is the subtext, yes the subtext, the subtext in other words whatever is underneath the text. Always Harold says, beneath the thing said, another thing is being said another thing is being said beneath the thing said so that, for example, in his very first play, *The Room*, written in 1957, when Rose keeps talking about how safe she feels in her room and noting what a good room it is, she is actually telling us how frightened she is about being ousted from the room. I am surprised at Harold for this part of his style. He was after all a Shakespearean actor in his youth; indeed that is where he met his first wife Vivian Merchant who was also an actress, but Shakespeare, like me, said what he meant to be saying on the line, not under it. But then I was never one to be believing in Freud.

The room, the room, the room. Until recently, Harold always wrote about what was happening in a room. Usually there is a threatening event or person and usually that person who invades the space ousts the person hiding hiding in the room. Or destroys that person. In *A Slight Ache*, a matchseller who seems to be blind and smells haunts the back gate of a middle-aged English couple and without saying a single word is kept by the wife, who replaces her husband with him. In his 1965 masterpiece *The Homecoming*, a seemingly perfectly nice professor who has been teaching in America brings his wife home to England to meet the family, the family being an ex butcher, a demolition worker studying to be a boxer, a pimp and a chauffeur. The family decide with Ruth's permission to keep her and send Teddy the professor back to America. In *The Caretaker*, a person has taken an old man into his room, but his brother is always taunting him, the old man, and he finally throws him out.

Now of course Harold is not writing a realistic play and he is always very funny I mean his characters are usually very funny so that even in his early play *The Birthday Party* as two henchmen of some unknown power seek out Stanley who is hiding out in a boarding house, another room, yes, even as they destroy him with words yes you can be destroying another with words even at the worst moments the audience is laughing. And then they are no longer laughing. And like me he turns things around so that if we look closely at the professor in *The Homecoming* we see that he is not worthy of Ruth and that there is much more hope for life for Ruth with his family despite their shocking language and lower class activities and possibly even their brutality. And that Teddy who is being detached all the time and even watches Ruth on the couch with his brother is really being quite dead dead dead. "You wouldn't understand my works," he tells his family, referring to his philosophical works as he is a philosophy teacher. "You wouldn't have the faintest idea of what they were about. You wouldn't appreciate the points of reference. You're way behind. All of you. There's no point in my sending you my works. You'd be lost. It's nothing to do with the question of intelligence. It's a way of being able to look at the world. It's a question of how far you can operate on things and not in things.... You're just objects. You just ... move about. I can observe it. I can see what you do. It's the same as I do. But you're lost in it. You won't get me being.... I won't be lost in it." Of course his brother Lenny who is a pimp is a true philosopher as he knows how to ask questions.

And Edward in *A Slight Ache* is just such another academic you see so that even if the Matchseller smells and seems hopelessly, wordlessly an impossible creature, he does seem to be a better choice than Edward because he seems to be a part of nature and Flora who is Edward's wife prefers nature well all you have to do is look at her name and it is not surprising really that she is choosing him the Matchseller. Pinter never did go to college well he went to acting school for a time but he dropped out and he does seem to be finding academics disposable and he has this habit of calling them Edward or Teddy which is just the same. And if we look closely at *The Caretaker* we can be seeing that the old man whom the older brother is throwing out is not pathetic but aggressive and secretive and trying always to turn the brothers against one another and that the brothers are learning to talk to each other finally. So that despite the terrible things that are occurring all the time in Harold's plays and the shocking things because it is shocking to see Ruth's behavior with her husband's family these things are perhaps necessary if some of the people are to grow. Or change. I of course don't think people do change, but Harold does he does Harold does. He even says that *The Homecoming* is about love, which I think is a very nice thing to be saying. And of course Harold may not know it, but like me he is a feminist and it is usually the women who grow. That is just the way it is. Of course it is not surprising that he makes his most disposable character an Englishman who has become an American. Wasn't it in the English playwright John Osborne's *Look Back in Anger* that a character lamented that all our children will be American? "Perhaps all our children will be Americans. That's a thought," his Jimmy says in that play. It does not seem to be so very different when Pinter's own Jimmy in his *Party Time*, who has apparently been arrested with all other dissidents, feels that all he has left is to "suck on the dark." If you look at Harold's Nobel Prize speech you will find that he only talks briefly about his plays because he wants to scold Americans, well Britans too of course, but especially Americans for what he considers their terrible policies and their terrible presidents and their terrible behavior. Scold is perhaps too mild a word for the castigation of what some called a political rant. He says in his speech that he would like to be President Bush's speechwriter and this is what he would write.

> God is good. God is great. God is good. My God is good. Bin Laden's God is bad. His is a bad God. Saddam's God was bad, except he didn't have one. He was a barbarian. We are not barbarians. We don't chop people's heads off. We believe in Freedom. So does God. I am not a barbarian. I am the democratically elected leader of a freedom-loving democracy. We are a compassionate society. We give compassionate electrocution and compassionate lethal injection. We are a great nation. I am not a dictator. He is. I am not a barbarian. And he is. They all are. I possess moral authority. You see this fist? This is my moral authority and don't you forget it.

Now I have read a critic who shall be nameless here who likes Pinter's politics—I neither like them nor do I dislike them as I am not much interested in politics—but this critic says and she shall be nameless here that she does disagree with the way Pinter says in his Nobel speech that there is no truth in art where nothing is verifiable but there is in politics because there are facts. Harold even gave up writing plays saying that 29 was enough so that he could spend more time working on stopping torture and other political things. He and his second wife Antonia Fraser have been activists throughout many many many years.

Harold has often insisted in interviews that what happens in life and in art is not verifiable verifiable verifiable. We can see that very clearly in his play *Old Times* in which three characters remember their pasts in very different ways. But this critic I have been reading has said that it doesn't matter what the truth is because the truth in the play is what is happening now in the present as the three characters battle over their memories and again it is a power thing and there is a winner and there are losers. Harold learned this from me of course, of course he did that there is only the present and that is where there is truth only in the present and that is art making the past the present so this critic says that if the past is not verifiable as Harold says it doesn't matter because there is something verifiable in the present and that is what he writes about so he is writing the truth. "There are some things one remembers even though they may never have happened," Anna says in Pinter's *Old Times.* "There are things I remember that may never have happened but as I recall them, so they take place." Rebecca in Harold's gut-wrenching as opposed to heartwarming play *Ashes to Ashes* may never have been in the Holocaust, but as she remembers herself in it, so she claims her guilt and her self.

This unnamed critic even thinks Harold is writing that truth in ways that echo important myths and rituals which shape his structures—such as *The Homecoming* being based on The Book of Ruth in the Bible which is the bible not a myth and that the ousted husbands in Harold's plays are dying kings that is James Frazer's *Golden Bough* types of the king must die but he must be replaced with a new king who is united with the old king's wife. But I don't wish to go into all of that what or to give you footnotes or references which are very hard to come by in the afterwards. What I wish to do is say that Pinter's plays have been political from the beginning because power is what politics is about, well money too, but that involves power and power is an interesting thing and Harold is very interested in it and he is opposed to it when it is used to destroy other people. But I happen to think he is also attracted to it. I do think it is interesting that Harold has remained an actor most of his life and what characters has he played, yes, the Interrogator in *One for the Road*, who enjoys using words to torture his victim, and yes Goldberg in *The Birthday Party* who enjoys tormenting Stanley with words and Harold knows how to play these roles very well and I just find that interesting.

I don't take anything this critic says too seriously because she seems to find me more interesting as a character or a person than as a writer and I have struggled with that all my days and even in the afterwards. But I am my writings I am being my writings and she should understand that even as she seems to understand that Pinter's plays are his politics and his politics are part of his plays. She does find him the most important living playwright and since I am not living I will give her that and since Samuel Beckett is not living I will give her that. But important is an interesting word and what might she be meaning by using it well I think she is finding him a great seer into the human mind and feelings and a great critic of society and a great dramatist of the agony of growth and also very funny which of course is always nice. And mostly she likes his anger which she thinks we all should be feeling feeling feeling … feeling because only it can fuel the changes that also mean growth. And she likes the mystery that is never being solved. She particularly likes the Waiter in Harold's last real play, *Celebration*, because he is in the mystery and can't get out and she is pretty sure Harold likes him too.

On my deathbed I am reported to have said What is the answer, no what is the question. Or perhaps Alice said what is the answer and I said no what is the question. That is very interesting and very important because people who go to plays and people who read plays often want answers and they are often asking the wrong questions when they read my work or see Harold's work. If you want to know what really happened in the past, you may never find that out in a Pinter play, you may need to read Arthur Miller or Eugene O'Neill to find answers. Even in Harold's play *Betrayal*, which moves backwards in time, one never finds out what one is finding out in Miller or O'Neill. You may be seeing what happened in the past but that does not mean you know what is happening. But if you are going to read a Pinter play what has happened is the wrong question, that is the wrong question. The right question is always, what is happening now. And that is all I am saying about Harold Pinter today.

The Nobel Prize Festivities: Stockholm, December 2005. A Joyous Report

CHRISTOPHER C. HUDGINS

My Stockholm adventure began early one morning, about 6:30, with a call from a friend on the East Coast to my residence in Las Vegas. Said friend had the kindness to restrain himself (??) until 9:30 a.m. his time, busting with the news that the Swedish Academy had just announced that the 2005 Nobel Prize in Literature would be awarded to Harold Pinter. Ecstatic, I called a few other friends and headed to my office at the University of Nevada, Las Vegas, where I am Chair of the English Department.

Soon after I downed my first cup of coffee, Wole Soyinka dropped by. As you may recall, Soyinka, the Nigerian playwright and poet, received the Nobel Prize in Literature for 1986. A faculty member at UNLV for several years as the Elias Ghanem Chair of Creative Writing, Soyinka was just beaming with the news, his eyes a-twinkle with joy and just a bit of mischief. Harold Pinter and Wole have been friends for years, as one might expect given their mutual interest in human rights and political justice. Soyinka came by that morning to share what he knew would be our mutual excitement at the Academy's announcement.

We made a tentative date for dinner and a toast to Harold's success, and Wole told me that we must go to Stockholm. Various e-mails sped back and forth among Pinter Society members. As various political situations heated up in Nigeria, Wole regretfully decided that he could not go to Stockholm after all. Still, I was terribly excited and pleased to receive first an e-mail message, then a formal notice, from Ulrika Kjellin, the Assistant to the Permanent Secretary of the Swedish Academy, inviting me to attend. I booked a flight for Monday, December 5, and accepted her generous offer to reserve a room for me at the Grand Hotel, where all of the Nobel Laureates and a large number of Nobel Guests were staying. I wrote Harold Pinter a note of congratulations, telling him that I was coming to Stockholm. And just a few days later, Harold Pinter's assistant sent me a note with both good and bad news—"Harold is thrilled that you will be making the trip to Stockholm … but his doctor has insisted he cut short his Stockholm trip." She went on to extend Pinter's invitation to me for a drinks reception for family and friends, adding that Harold would give his lecture on the 7th but not attend the presentation ceremony on the 10th of December.

At this stage, I wrote a number of friends, hoping some of them would be going to Stockholm as well. Susan Hollis Merritt would attend, as would Donald and Patty Freed, longtime friends of Harold. As news came that Harold's health would not allow him to attend at all, Susan and I determined to go anyway. Our purpose, after all, was to honor Harold Pinter and his career.

I rolled into the Grand Hotel in Stockholm about 7:00 p.m. on December 6, a Tuesday. Susan and I agreed to meet in the lobby to take a cab to the Swedish Academy that Wednesday evening for the screening of Pinter's Nobel Lecture, planning to arrive early to secure good seats. The hall had been configured differently for this event, with the three very large screens placed across the length of the large third-floor, gorgeously furnished room. As we debated where to sit, Ulrika Kjellin, who had so generously helped us both in making our plans, approached us with what we were to learn was her usual good humor and escorted us as representatives of *The Pinter Review* to the section she had reserved for publishers. The event began to feel a bit like a reunion as Susan and I greeted Donald and Patty Freed, Eric Price, of Grove Press, and Stephen Page, Pinter's publisher at Faber and Faber, who would accept the Award for Pinter at the ceremony to follow.

As the crowd waited expectantly, Ulrika pointed us out to Harold and Heather Goodman, who came up to Susan and me, anxious to meet "the *Pinter Review* people." Harold Pinter and Harold Goodman have been friends since their teenage years, cricket teammates for years after that, and, when Pinter was successful enough to need one, Harold Goodman had been and continues to be Pinter's accountant.

I escorted the Goodmans to the two lovely display cases, filled with a selection of some twenty-eight works by and about Pinter. Among the books the Swedish Academy's Literature Committee had chosen to include in this display were FIVE volumes of *The Pinter Review*, 1990, 1992-93, 1995-96, 1997-98 and 2001-2002. Harold Goodman told me that he had spoken to Harold Pinter very recently via phone from his hospital room and gave us some of the details, in advance, of his speech. Goodman told me that Harold had thought his delivery focused and strong and that he was pleased with the editing, despite the fact that he'd had to give the speech from a wheelchair. Best of all, though, Harold Goodman set our minds at ease about Harold Pinter's health. While serious, painful and debilitating, this illness was NOT the return of the esophageal cancer as many of us had feared. Excitedly, I passed the good news to our little party, and Harold Goodman reiterated and provided a few more details. He assured us that Harold Pinter was going to recover. And that news, of course, let us all look forward to the speech itself with even greater anticipation and excitement.

Finally, Horace Engdahl stepped to the podium to introduce the Nobel Laureate Lecture in Literature for 2005. Permanent Secretary of the Swedish Academy, a writer and a specialist in comparative literature, he introduced Pinter in Swedish, so we didn't catch much of it, though the tone was respectful and enthusiastic, perhaps even joyous is not too strong.

Then the screens glowed into life, with Harold Pinter towering over us now, though seated, larger than life, in a dark blazer and black shirt, strong of voice, his color apparently good, against a light blue backdrop or lighting. In short, despite his apparent weakness, we were encouraged by his appearance.

It's not my purpose, here, to analyze Pinter's wonderfully effective, politically and aesthetically powerful speech. Other writers for this issue of *The Pinter Review* will do that in some detail. I'll merely try to capture for you some of the tenor of the audience's response on this wonderful evening. As Harold concluded his talk, *in absentia*, applause began to ring out. Susan and I were perhaps the first to rise to our feet, and a goodly number of the audience joined us in our enthusiastic standing ovation, including all of our little band. It was certain to be a controversial speech, especially given what some construe to be Sweden's tilt toward the U.S.A.'s foreign policy positions. When I congratulated Horace Engdahl on his introduction a bit later, he told me, seemingly pleased at the notion, that no Nobel Laureate had *ever* done what Harold Pinter did with his speech on this evening of December 7; in short, Engdahl thought the speech a significant, historic event. He repeated that same phrase after the Nobel Banquet on December 10th during another conversation in the Golden Hall of Stockholm's City Hall, with the dancing going on around us underlining both of our pleasurable responses to this uniquely powerful Nobel Laureate Lecture in Literature.

I discovered the next day that Harold Goodman had gone "straight way" to his cell phone and called Harold Pinter in his hospital room to report on the enthusiastic reaction of the audience in Stockholm. Pinter could see the broadcast of his speech in London and listen to the commentators' remarks, but there was no feed for the event itself. Pinter had no way, in short, of knowing how his Nobel Lecture had been received that evening. That's what good friend Harold Goodman provided for Harold Pinter that historic night. Goodman reported back to the Pinter entourage, soon to expand as he met more of us, that Harold Pinter was just delighted at the reception of his Lecture, especially given that standing ovation, and that there were no "boos" or other displays of discontent. Harold Goodman told me, eyes twinkling, that he'd told Pinter that the Americans were the first on their feet.

We celebrated with an improvised drinks and dinner party at The Golden Peace, honoring Harold's smashing success as a Nobel Laureate Lecturer. Den Gyldene Freden has had a very long, colorful history as an establishment where artists and writers congregated, including the much beloved Carl Michael Bellman, an 18th-century poet and *bon vivant*, and, more recently, Evert Taube and his "Friends of the Troubadour Society." Gradually, the spot has become the chief haunt of the Swedish Academy. The group gathers regularly in a private dining room, both to hold business meetings and discussions and to nourish body and spirit. Once each year, so we were told by a wondrously hospitable staff, the members dine in the public rooms, the night of the Nobel Literature Lecture. As fortune and the troubadour tradition would have it, we were seated next to the Nobel Committee as they were winding down their meal. Donald Freed proposed a toast to the Committee and the wisdom of their choice, and the Freeds, Susan, Eric Price, Stephen Page, and I, along with several other friends, sat down to a marvelous meal. After several more toasts to Harold Pinter and his work, we called it a night.

December 9, Friday, included the Nobel Foundation Reception in the Nordic Museum. Several of us began our day with a canal boat tour of the city. We were glad, I think, not to be in Stephen Page's shoes as he lunched with the British Ambassador, Mr. Anthony Cary, that afternoon at the British Embassy. As Harold's publisher at Faber and Faber, the man who would accept Pinter's award for him, Stephen was certainly the logical person to attend the traditional gathering at the Ambassador of the Nobel Laureate's country, but, given the harsh criticism Pinter included in his Lecture of Tony Blair and British foreign policy, we all worried that this meeting might be awkward. At the Nobel Reception that evening, though, Stephen reported that the luncheon had been a pleasant affair, for the most part. Ambassador Cary is fortunately an admirer of Pinter's plays, and so the conversation, diplomatically, dwelt on that literary area rather than on the political, with which the Ambassador, of course, could not agree—or at least that's the secondhand summary I can provide, with thanks to Stephen Page.

The Saturday morning of the 10th of December, as promised, dawned clear and without much breeze in Stockholm, perfect weather for the actual Nobel Prize Awards Ceremony and Banquet. Susan and I met in the lobby, by the Nobel Desk, and vamped for a few pictures of our elegant selves, gown, white-tie and tails, and all. Guests at the Grand Hotel not attending the event happily watched the proceedings. The mood of the crowd seemed so joyous as to be highly contagious. When we arrived at the Concert Hall, I was surprised to find mobs of people behind police tape barriers, for all the world as if they were watching celebrities going into the American Academy Awards. With the occasional top hat or evening cape for the men, the occasional luxe furs for the women, and the sea of white tie and tails and elaborate gowns and coiffeurs, we were a pretty impressive looking group, I suppose. People in the crowds were snapping off pictures as we filed in. Up in the balcony area the mood was festive. As an early arrival, it was easy for me to meet folks as they came in, and the seating committee, or Ulrika, had done a grand job of arranging for many of the Pinteristas to sit together, translators, theatrical impresarios, publishers, scholars, and Pinter friends. Stephen Page, of course, was going to be on stage to accept the Nobel Prize for Harold Pinter.

The Programme began with the seating of the Royal Party, the audience standing as the King and Queen and their family made their entrance to the Royal Stockholm Philharmonic Orchestra's *March in D Major, KV 249* by Amadeus Mozart. After the Nobel Laureates took their seats on the elaborate stage, the Chairman of the Board of the Nobel Foundation, Marcus Storch, made a brief speech, followed by another musical interlude. The first two Nobel Prizes were awarded in Physics and in Chemistry, to two men in each category, again with brief speeches to introduce each of the two awards. After the speech, the ritual entails the Nobel recipients coming forward, bowing to the King, bowing to the Nobel Foundation members, shaking the King's hand and accepting the Nobel Prize, then bowing to the audience, which erupts in applause. Another musical interlude followed these first two categories, this time from *La Bohème*, with the very talented Swedish soloist, Erika Sunnegardh. The presentation of the Nobel Prize in Physiology or Medicine again went to two recipients, with another operatic interlude featuring Sunnegardh preceding the "Presentation of the 2005 Nobel Prize in Literature to Mr. Harold Pinter."

Pinter's award was presented by Per Wästberg, Member of the Swedish Academy and Chairman of its Nobel Committee. The prize citation: "*who in his plays uncovers the precipice under everyday prattle and forces entry into oppression's closed rooms.*" Mr. Wästberg began his address this way: "*Your Majesties, Your Royal Highnesses, Esteemed Nobel Laureates, Ladies and Gentlemen.*" At the conclusion of his brief but insightful remarks, Mr. Wästberg included these words:

> Dear Harold Pinter,
> In its choice of a Nobel Laureate the Swedish Academy recognizes only the creative power of a single individual regardless of nation, sex and literary genre. This needs emphasizing. However British you may appear in the eyes of many, your international and inter-human impact in the field of drama has been uniquely strong and inspiring for half a century. If someone thinks your prize is late in coming, we may reply that at any given moment somewhere in the world your plays are reinterpreted by new generations of directors and actors.

After a brief concluding summary, Mr. Wästberg finished his introduction: "In the absence of this year's Nobel Laureate in Literature, I request his publisher Mr. Stephen Page to come forward and receive Mr. Pinter's Prize from the hands of His Majesty the King." Stephen Page stepped forward and received with great dignity the Nobel Prize for Harold Pinter. As he turned from the King, bowing to the audience, now, thunderous applause echoed through the hall. The memory still gives me chills.

I love the irony of the title of the musical interlude which followed Pinter's award: *Allegro di molto* from Symphony no. 94 in G major, "Surprise," by Joseph Haydn. The final Nobel Award, in Economic Sciences, seemed to float by; the Orchestra played the Swedish National Anthem as the Royal Party exited the stage, and then Hugo Alfven's *The Queen of Sheba's Festivity March* from *The Prodigal Son.*

Filing out of the hall, again through throngs of celebrating Swedes, we once more boarded the buses and moved on to The City Hall for the Nobel Foundation Banquet. How wonderful to be in a country where the populace celebrates intellectual and artistic achievement so enthusiastically. Greeted at the entrance by a living entryway of children holding burning torches on high, we moved into the reception area of the hall where we could find our seats through the *Bordsplacering*, the Seating List, with its maps of the banquet room, its alphabetical list of dinner guests, and its seating chart for the ancillary tables, numbers 1 through 65. The dining hall was vast, of course, with flowers and color everywhere, the tables set with fine china and crystal and silver, and with row upon row of gold- foil-wrapped chocolates in the shape of the Nobel Medal scattered over each table. A long table down the middle of the hall served as the "Head Table" for 88 guests, the Royal Party, the Nobel Laureates and other special guests of the Academy; the other tables were arranged perpendicularly to the long Head Table, with the result being that no one felt quite so far-removed from the awardees as one might have imagined. To great pomp and circumstance, the Royal Party and the Nobel Laureates entered the Hall in a processional moving along the balcony surrounding the Hall and down the ornate stairway. Once the Royal Party and guests were seated, the Chairman of the Board of the Nobel Foundation proposed "His Majesty's Toast," which the guests drank with the fine champagne (Pommery Grand Cru Vintage 1995 for you wine buffs) poured by the choreographed wait staff, students we were told, who had competed for the honor of serving the Banquet. His Majesty the King then proposed a toast to Alfred Nobel's memory. The dinner itself then began with coquilles Saint-Jacques and langoustines and continued for several similarly wonderful courses, accompanied by fine wines, again elegantly poured. In between courses, the multitude was entertained by a "Divertissement," titled "Floral Transformations," with a chorus of perhaps forty voices, in various floral costumes, making a joyful and very beautiful noise. The leisurely pace of the dinner and the interludes allowed some conversation between the various tables, as we greeted old friends.

As the banquet concluded, with desserts, cognac and cordials and coffee, as the program foreshadows, "Students from Swedish universities and colleges, bearing the standards of their student unions, pay homage to the Laureates." That doesn't quite capture the ceremonial grandeur of the actual event, with the students and their banners lining the balcony around the giant hall, dipping their colors, one after one, in tribute. At this point, one Nobel Laureate from each of the prize categories ascended the stairway, roughly halfway, and presented a brief speech, often humorous, in thanks, and in tribute to his colleague who shared the prize. Once this portion of the program concluded, again with a grand flourish which makes the term "pomp and circumstance" live a bit beyond its usual associations, "The guests of honour rise from the table and leave in procession," up that grand staircase and around the balcony to what apparently is an exit.

As the Programme suggests, though, what appears to be an exit actually leads into another portion of City Hall, "The Golden Hall," where a band, 14 pieces I seem to recall, played good swing music, with yet another hall off the Golden Hall providing libations to fuel the dancers. As the Royal Party and the Nobels concluded their exits, we milled about a bit, toasting Harold Pinter once more, wishing he had been here. Donald Freed pulled me over to introduce me to a few of his and Patty's tablemates, including Erika Sunnegardh. As I congratulated her on her wondrous voice and afternoon's operatic performance, Freed teasingly suggested that neither Erika nor I had an escort nor a dance partner. All of us headed up the stairs together, and, in between conversation, champagne and general festivities, we ourselves danced the night away and marveled at the spectacle of Nobel Laureates cutting a rug with glee.

As the evening continued, we spoke again with our friends from the Nobel Committee, thanked them once more, and, at about 1:00 a.m., my pumpkin coach arrived and I headed back to the Grand Hotel, dreading just a bit my early morning flight to Las Vegas via London. Three final Stockholm events brightened my weary morning: as I waited for the elevator, the Nobel Laureate in Economics, after a night of his own energetic dancing, was energetically debating some fine points of world finance with one of his colleagues; as I entered my cab, the staff person who had helped me on my way told me that the television coverage of the banquet and dancing certainly revealed that I too had had a wonderful time on that dance floor; and, at the airport, I picked up three Swedish tabloids which featured wonderful color photographs of the Awards Ceremony and the Banquet. Those photographs, given the quality of the paper, are bound to fade. I don't think that the memories will of this magnificent series of events that, in toto, honored Harold Pinter's work and its place in the world. Hermetically sealed, one of those foil-wrapped chocolate Nobel Medals is framed, sitting in a prominent place, with several other Nobel Prize mementos on my office shelves. It daily reminds me of how truly delightful I found it to be in Stockholm to help honor the man, Harold Pinter, and his work, which so many of us have treasured for so many years.

Thank goodness Harold Pinter was able to attend the Turin 10th Annual Europa Theatre Awards just a few months later, which he so enjoyed. I wish he, and all of you, could have been in Stockholm. This narrative, then, has been an attempt to share some of that joy.

Las Vegas
April 2006

Nobel Week 2005–The Experience of a Lifetime: Homage to Harold Pinter

SUSAN HOLLIS MERRITT

On October 13th, 2005, around 8:30 a.m. EST, my husband (who arrives at work very early) came home unexpectedly. A night owl, perpetually on European time from earlier travel, I was still just waking up. "Harold Pinter has won the Nobel Prize!" he announced. He had been at his work desktop checking his home page, which happens to be the *New York Times* news site, and the headline had just been posted. Thrilled, I jumped up and down and danced around the kitchen a few times. I waited until 9 a.m. to call Frank Gillen, in Tampa, Florida, on my cell phone to share the news. Frank hadn't yet heard it, and, of course, he too was thrilled. "Congratulations!" I exclaimed to him. "Congratulations to you too," he kindly replied. Friends, family, and colleagues started to e-mail and mail me congratulatory messages and cards. Sometime after 1 p.m. London time, surmising that his assistant would answer (as she did), I called London, to leave a telephone message of congratulations for Harold Pinter, who of course is the one who actually deserves them! Indeed, as all the world would learn, Pinter spent the rest of his day receiving phone calls, telegrams, flowers, and various other congratulatory missives, emerging from his Campden Hill Square home briefly to answer questions and to wave happily to journalists gathering outside the door.

Dedicated Bibliographical Editor of *The Pinter Review* that I am, I began checking online news sites and blogs and started collecting what would amount eventually to perhaps hundreds (from hundreds of thousands) of notices, reports, and comments over the next couple of months. When I checked the online BBC News website, I discovered a comments page already begun. Privately, I e-mailed its editor. I got a reply back, asking if he could "ring me up" for an interview for an online article that he was writing. I received a telephone call from Neil Smith, "BBC News Entertainment Reporter," who interviewed me for his article "Political Element to Pinter Prize" (<http://news.bbc.co.uk/2/hi/entertainment/4339096.stm>), quoting my comment that it would be "simplistic" to claim that Pinter had been selected "only" because of his political activism; rather, "he was chosen to honour [sic] his entire body of work in the over 50-year span of his career," and I was "very pleased" about that recognition.

In mid-November, I began to plan to go to Stockholm, to attend the Nobel Week 2005 festivities. The details became complicated by alarming changes in Harold Pinter's health, forcing him to cancel his plan to give the Nobel Lecture in person in Stockholm; suffice it to say that—with the welcome assistance of Ulrika Kjellin (Samuelsson), Assistant to Horace Engdahl, the Permanent Secretary of the Swedish Academy, and the Publicity Office of the Nobel Foundation—everything did work out. During the two weeks from November 15th through the 30th, I completed all the necessary arrangements to attend Harold Pinter's Nobel Lecture (Wed., Dec. 7th), the Nobel Concert featuring Yo-Yo Ma (Thurs., Dec. 8th), the Nobel Foundation Reception at the Nordic Museum (Fri., Dec. 9th), and the Nobel Award Ceremony Rehearsal, the Nobel Award Ceremony, and the Nobel Banquet (Sat., Dec. 10th). I had applied for and been granted press credentials (which were very limited in number—just 30 for the entire international press for the Lecture, Rehearsal, and Ceremony and just 12 for the Banquet), representing *The Pinter Review*. Subsequently, the Swedish Academy invited me to attend both the Banquet and a reception hosted by the Nobel Foundation at the Nordic Museum. Harold Pinter had also invited me to a private reception for family and friends to be held directly after his Nobel Lecture at the Swedish Academy; on December 1st, the day after he canceled his trip to Stockholm, Ulrika informed me that it would not be held. Faced with the prospect of Harold's absence, I felt even more compelled to "pay homage" to him in Stockholm. A mutually-encouraging conversation with Chris Hudgins furthered our determination to go to Stockholm to honor Harold Pinter and to have what we both expected would be a "once-in-a-lifetime experience." Chris and I looked forward to each other's company.

On Monday, December 5th, I flew to Stockholm, arriving the next morning at the Grand Hôtel (<http://www.grandhotel.se/english/hotell/index.php>)—which was indeed *grand*. I marveled at the elegant lobby (beautifully decorated for Christmas) and tried to look as though I belonged there while registering for my room. The room, though small by American standards, was very comfortably appointed; trimmed with Scandinavian wood veneers, it featured a bath almost entirely of marble, and included some other luxurious amenities that came with my special "A Nobel Stay" package.

One of the most exciting aspects of staying in the Grand Hôtel was being among so many Nobel Laureates. There was a wonderful feeling of anticipation and comradery in the air as the Laureates and their families and other guests arrived. A special bonus was overhearing and even participating in so many intriguing conversations with the Nobel Laureates and their family and guest colleagues in elevators, in the lobby, and at breakfast in the Grand Veranda, where everyone (dressed casually) was treated with the same deference. The Grand Hôtel became a great leveler in reverse—elevating more ordinary people to the heights of the Nobel Laureates. At breakfast every day, I particularly enjoyed overhearing Dr. J. Robin Warren (from Adelaide, South Australia) enthusiastically telling and retelling the story about how his colleague (the youngest 2005 Laureate, at 54 years old) Barry J. Marshall (from Western Australia), with whom he shared the 2005 Nobel Prize in Physiology or Medicine "for their discovery of the bacterium *Helicobacter pylori* and its role in gastritis and peptic ulcer disease," had intentionally drunk a potion infecting himself with that bacterium to produce such stomach inflammation (which could have become fatal), as a means of testing their hypotheses. Marshall's bravery led them to prove that these diseases were bacterial in nature and could be cured with "a short regimen of antibiotics and acid secretion inhibitors," a "pioneering discovery." During the Nobel Banquet, when Barry Marshall spoke on behalf of himself and Dr. Warren, he was wittily self-deprecating (in a manner more "Down Under" than British).[1] "Harold Pinter would love hearing this," I recall thinking.

Throughout Nobel Week, the Nobel Laureates and their families and guests attended a series of activities, celebrations, and related events, beginning on Monday, December 5th, through the rest of that week, including a sightseeing bus trip to the exhibition The Dutch Golden Age. Rembrandt, Frans Hals and their contemporaries (<http://www.nationalmuseum.se/NMTemplates/NMSingleExhibition____3769.aspx>) at the Stockholm National Art Museum, Sunday, December 11th; a Royal Banquet at the Palace, Monday, December 12th, along with individual visits to the Nobel Foundation; and visits to Swedish and other Nordic universities beginning Tuesday, December 13th.

In the early afternoon of December 6th, after I had a chance to relax and unpack before his arrival. Early afternoon the supremely-organized Ulrika Kjellin (Samuelsson) very kindly came to meet me downstairs in the hotel lobby, where she gave me an elegant Nobel Week package, containing formal letters of invitation, all embossed with a tiny version of the gold Nobel Medal®. (Various quantities of miniature facsimiles of the Nobel Medal® stamped on gold-foil enclosed chocolate coins are offered for sale at the Nobel Museum, I learned later; liberally sprinkled on every table at the Banquet, they would also be presented to each of us that night, along with a long-stemmed red rose by wandering minstrels.) Ulrika also gave me my press credential badge, and the various tickets and related information that had been arranged for the rest of the week. Given all that she had to do, I was surprised and pleased that she took so much time to chat with me. It was a very pleasant way to begin. I felt comfortably oriented.

On Wednesday, December 7th (the day of Harold Pinter's evening Nobel Lecture), Chris Hudgins and I got together for lunch in The Grand Veranda to bask in what was to come. After getting in touch with Harold Pinter's good friends Donald and Patty Freed, who were staying at the Hotel Esplanade (a small privately-owned pension across the bridge), all four of us planned to get together for lunch there on Thursday, December 8th, after which we visited the Strindberg Museum, located on the top floor of the building housing Strindberg's furnished apartment. It was filled with Strindberg memorabilia; his office was intact, with his wire spectacles atop his desk; his bedroom featured a little bed (reminding me of Keats's bed in Keats House in Hampstead); and, in the hall, there was even a telephone and a telephone book, as we were informed that Strindberg was among the first in Stockholm to have such advanced technology! We looked at his manuscripts in his office and lots of programs of productions of his plays on display. Although I have taught Strindberg's major plays, such as *The Father*, *Miss Julie*, *A Dream Play*, and *The Ghost Sonata*, I was struck by how much more there is to know about Strindberg. The Strindberg Museum is a scholarly resource, as well as a novelty for tourists and students (who seemed to disappear as instantly as they had appeared).

At Harold Pinter's Nobel Lecture, Wednesday, December 7th, as illustrated by the photograph published on the front page of the *New York Times* on December 8th, I was seated, alongside Chris and the Freeds, in a section reserved for "Mr. Pinter's publishers," located a few rows behind the Swedish audience members with a slight gap between these sections. Directly opposite the screen to the farthest left, I was sitting between Chris Hudgins (on my left) and Patty and Donald (on my right) in the first row, and we all met Pinter's other good friends, Heather and Harold Goodman, who sat in the second row. (One can see only the backs of our heads in the *New York Times*photo.) Before we spoke with Harold Goodman (who would assure us, after the lecture, that he expected imminent improvement in "the other Harold's" health), I think that we were all feeling quite nervous for Harold Pinter. How would he appear? Would he be able to give his address as forcefully as he wanted to do? The room darkened ominously. But, as the streaming video featured on the Nobel Foundation website and the DVD produced from the Channel 4 broadcast document, Harold gave the performance of a lifetime. Even though he was sitting in a wheelchair, he looked elegantly handsome in his usual all-black attire. His legs were covered loosely with a rust-varicolored wool lap blanket (which perhaps Antonia had brought from home). While Harold looked quite frail at first, speaking somewhat softly as it was clearly painful for him to speak at all, and while his voice was still quite hoarse, there were clearly intense fire in his eyes and increasing passion in his strengthening demeanor. Fascinated, indeed totally absorbed, we all relaxed into it. He was doing exceptionally well. Pinter's voice gained in volume with heightened concentration, as he made smooth transitions from talking as an "author" about composing some of his plays to talking as a "citizen" about the state of the world vis-à-vis American and British foreign policy and, finally, to the poems by Pablo Neruda and himself that he read so clearly and movingly. It was a great speech. One aspect that no photograph or streaming video can convey, however, is how much "larger than life" Harold appeared on those three big screens to all of us. We could see where he might have been standing at a podium had he been there in person, and he would have been merely a normal-sized man in that high-ceilinged venue. But on each screen the close ups of his head, showing the expressions playing in his eyes accompanying ironies in his speech, exaggerated his size relative to us. Harold Pinter was a literary giant that night.

Given the critique of American foreign policy and the current war in Iraq that Harold Pinter presented, we Americans were aware of the significance of our public response. I recall bumping into Chris as we were both the first to rise, joined by the entire rest of the audience, giving Harold a very extended standing ovation. We wanted the world to know that we fully supported Harold Pinter and his critique of Bush and Blair. We Americans (Chris Hudgins, the Freeds, Grovel Atlantic Vice President Eric Price, Eric's guest Carl Bazil, and I), as well as the Brits (Faber and Faber President Stephen Page and the Goodmans), were also among the last to sit down. We were very intrigued by the revealing references that Harold made to composing his plays in the first and last parts of the speech. As Donald suggested right afterward, "We could listen to Harold talk about his work all night."

Immediately after the Lecture, a Swedish televison crew briefly interviewed me on camera. I am not sure whether that footage has actually been broadcast, however. While the others looked on, the interviewer focused on my being an American and my views of what Pinter said, which, of course, I supported whole-heartedly. That seemed to surprise her. She may have expected me to be offended by his vigorous "attack on America." After I expressed my thoughts and feelings about what I had just witnessed, I handed her my card, which identifies me as the Bibliographical Editor of *The Pinter Review*. She did a bit of a double take, perhaps realizing that I am not just an American member of the general audience, but a Pinter scholar who had already read and heard Harold express parts of his critique before and that I share and endorse it.

Next I had an opportunity to chat with Fred Olav Johannessen, a Scandinavian agent representing the Nordiska Literary Agency in Copenhagen, Denmark, who was also very enthusiastic about Pinter's performance, and with Odd Zschiedrich, administrative coordinator of the Swedish Academy, who was greatly impressed by Pinter's speech and by his dramatic delivery.

Odd singled out Harold Pinter's significant pause indicated by the comma between "*Sweden*" and "*of course*": "The United States now occupies 702 military installations throughout the world in 132 countries, with the honourable exception of Sweden, of course." That emphasis, Odd said, would endear him to Swedish audiences.

For dinner, after the Lecture, Donald and Patty Freed, Chris Hudgins, Eric Price, Carl Bazil, Stephen Page, Faber Drama Editor Dinah Wood, and I went to Den Gyldene Freden (The Golden Peace), a classic Swedish and French restaurant selected for us by Patty Freed, who has a wonderful knack for choosing exactly the perfect place and even selecting in advance the perfect menu. A book about the restaurant written by Henrik Johannes Alm was published by Bonnier Books in 1948. Built in 1721 and opened in 1722, it is considered "Stockholm's oldest tavern" and one of its most famous restaurants. It was restored by Anders Zorn, who then donated it to the Swedish Academy. Its members dine there in a private room every Thursday night, except for the night after the Nobel Lecture in Literature. That night they dine in public.[2] As we were sitting at a table next to members of the Nobel Committee, after Donald went to their table to toast them, convivially commending their choice of Harold Pinter for the Nobel Prize in Literature, I snapped a photo of that lofty group. Then a waiter snapped one of our more humble group. High on Harold Pinter's success (and a few drinks and some fine wine!), we reveled in the food and the company.

On Thursday evening, December 8th, while Chris planned to dine again with the Freeds, I attended the inaugural Nobel Concert at Stockholm Concert Hall. In August 2005, months before I had learned that Harold Pinter was to be awarded the Nobel Prize in Literature, I had coincidentally encountered a news report announcing a new special "Nobel Concert" to be inaugurated in 2005 and to feature world-renowned cellist Yo-Yo Ma.[3] Being a longtime lover of classical music for the cello and of Yo-Yo Ma particularly, I imagined how wonderful it would be to attend that concert. Little did I know then that I would actually have the opportunity.

My seat mate was a charming Swedish woman from Stockholm; we delighted in each other's company, joining each other for our champagne interval, as we marveled at the tender power of Yo-Yo Ma's performance. (During the interval, Stephen Page and I bumped into each other again, so he got to enjoy the concert as well.) Yo-Yo Ma announced that just that morning he had decided to add more to the program. Perched high above each side of the stage, two young female Swedish folk singers performed an eery indigenous chant *a capella*. The program (as printed), performed by the Royal Stockholm Philharmonic Orchestra, conducted by Sakri Oramo, Chief Conductor of the Finnish Radio Symphony Orchestra and the City of Birmingham Symphony Orchestra, also included: *Legend of Herlen* (2000), by Byambasuren Sharav, "a contemporary version of the

Mongolian tradition of telling a story through music" commissioned by the Silk Road Project; *The Firebird Suite* (1919), by Stravinsky, and *Cello Concerto B minor op 104*, by Dvořák. Between his solo performances with the Orchestra, Yo-Yo Ma left the main stage to climb stairs to a mezzanine overhanging the stage, where he (on horse head fiddle) and other members of the "boundary-breaching Silk Road Project" performed the piece by Sharav, augmented by two trombonists from the Stockholm Philharmonic Orchestra, along with the female Mongolian soloist, Khongorzul Ganbaatar, whose "long song" was utterly haunting. The entire program thrilled everyone, occasioning five standing ovations, not including each time the full audience and those on stage had to stand when Her Royal Highness Crown Princess Victoria entered and left her box. Yo-Yo Ma played several solo encores to the audience's great delight. As I floated back to the Grand Hôtel on the bus with the others, I deeply regretted that Harold Pinter and members of his family could not also experience such a marvelous concert. When I disembarked, I found myself standing right behind Yo-Yo Ma, who was just as sweet in person as he had appeared on stage interacting (mostly through his eyes and body language) with his musical colleagues. He posed for photographs taken by one of the Nobel guests while he waited for the elevator taking him to the "VIP" dinner being held in his honor that night.

On Friday, December 9th, Chris Hudgins, Patty Freed, and I took a very relaxing winter canal cruise, departing from the harbor across from the Grand Hôtel, while Donald Freed had his tails fitted for Saturday's Nobel gala. Later that evening, still very much missing Harold Pinter, Antonia Fraser, and their extended family, we all went to a truly sumptuous Smörgåsbord and champagne reception, hosted by the Nobel Foundation at the Nordic Museum, a palatial structure built in the style of the Danish Renaissance, and featuring elegant chamber music in the vast center hall. Chris and I spoke with the Permanent Secretary of the Nobel Foundation, Horace Engdahl (Chris recounts their conversation in some detail), and also spent quite a bit of time talking individually again with the Swedish Academy administrator Odd Zschiedrich. Odd offered that when Harold Pinter's health improves, the Swedish Academy and the Nobel Foundation would love to have him visit Stockholm, that they would host an entire theater festival in his honor, adding that they would treat him like "a returning king." (At Saturday's Nobel Banquet, I introduced Odd to Michael Billington, so that Odd could repeat that "open invitation" in case Michael could perhaps convey it in person to Harold Pinter later in London; I would mention it in my own e-mail to Harold after I returned home.) I spoke also with the calligrapher of Harold's Nobel Prize Diploma, Annika Rücker, who designed it as a tribute to Pinter's own writing style (<http://nobelprize.org/literature/laureates/2005/pinter-diploma.html>).

Following the Nordic Museum reception Friday evening, the Goodmans graciously joined Donald, Chris, and me for dinner at Wedholms Fisk, "one of the classic—and one of the best—[seafood] restaurants in Stockholm" (according to *Frommer's Guide*), which Patty Freed had so generously selected and reserved for us (though, unfortunately, she was unable to come too). The display of modern paintings by Swedish artists was as "riveting" as *Frommer's* claims," and our various assorted smoked herring appetizers, cheeses, and fresh fish entrées were superb. The Goodmans related their first date, about fifty years earlier, which consisted of Harold Goodman taking Heather to see Harold Pinter in an out-of-town rep play (he was "very good in it"); they had to give Pinter a ride back to London because he had no car. Heather laughingly described how she had to sit on "the other Harold's" lap, because Goodman's car had only two seats. Out of her husband Harold's earshot, Heather related that, on Wednesday, when he had reported the audience response to the Nobel Lecture to Pinter, who asked him how it went, he had returned from their cell phone conversation with "tears in his eyes ... though he would never admit it." The poignancy of that moment struck us all again: while his friends were privy to the Stockholm audience's response, writer/deliverer Harold Pinter lay in hospital watching himself on Channel 4 but still "in the dark" about how his decidedly-controversial speech was being received by a largely Swedish but still international audience. Tears of joyful commiseration welled up all around.

Since I also had a press credential badge and a ticket, I had the opportunity to attend and to observe the Nobel Prize Award Ceremony Rehearsal, scheduled for 10:30 on the morning of Saturday, December 10th, at the Stockholm Concert Hall; the Nobel Prize Award Ceremony was scheduled to begin at 4:30 p.m. at the Concert Hall, followed by the Nobel Banquet at 7 p.m. in Blue Hall of Stockholm City Hall. Buses were arranged for the Nobel Laureates, their family members, and all the guests for the two major events later that day. In the morning, however, I took a taxi back to the Concert Hall and entered the "Stage Door" as directed. There was only a handful of journalists at the Rehearsal; I sat in on some of the taped interviews, asked a few questions of my own, and took notes. Spouses of the Nobel Laureates joked about their husbands and recounted tales of their learning of their Nobel Prizes and their experiences thus far of Nobel Week that would become family legends—"The American Dream meets Nobel Week,"quipped Lindy (Mrs. John L.) Hall, the wife of one of the three 2005 Nobel Laureates in Physics. While bemoaning his lack of wardrobe *savoir faire*, Mrs. Hall spoke admiringly of the accomplishments of her "federal scientist" husband, who is U.S.A. Senior Scientist at the National Institute of Standards and Technology. She cited his being "famous for his integrity" and training scores of government scientists, and shared anecdotes, as she and the other wives looked on as "their guys," now casually dressed in jeans, sweaters, sport shirts, athletic shoes or Hush Puppies, and, yes, sometimes white socks (but soon to be in tails and white tie), were choreographed. They were to process on stage to take their special seats, and, when announced, get up, step forward to receive their Nobel Prize Diploma and Medal, shake hands with (the stand in for) His Royal Majesty King Carl XVI Gustaf, bow first to him, then turn back to bow to the Nobel Committee, past Laureates, and other dignitaries on stage, and finally step forward again to face and then bow to the audience (while receiving applause). Stephen Page was instructed to bow only to the King and not to those on stage and not to turn to the audience, but to return to his seat after bowing to the King, since he himself was not actually being awarded Pinter's Prize. (The ensuing applause would be for Pinter, of course, not for him.) The guys all practiced a number of times. Professor Robert J. Aumann (Economic Sciences) could not attend due to the Rehearsal being scheduled on the Jewish Sabbath. While there should have been eleven Nobel Laureates on stage, if Harold Pinter had also been there, at the Rehearsal there were only nine instead of ten.[4]

As I would do later during the actual Ceremony, during the Rehearsal, I imagined Harold Pinter and Lady Antonia Fraser there, in the midst of his Nobel colleagues and their spouses, who all share in the special distinction of belonging to the Nobel club, over a hundred years of recipients of the most prestigious honors in the world in their fields. I thought, "Lady Antonia really should be here" to chat with the other Nobel spouses. While still enjoying myself, it did sadden me that Pinter and his wife could not enjoy what should have been their own "Nobel experience." Yet, I felt that Chris and I and his other guests were representing him in our own unique ways and that, eventually, supplementing published news accounts and video footage, Nobel Laureate Harold Pinter would get to read about and hear our impressions, and, most especially, how he was foremost in our minds throughout our own "Nobel stay."

Just getting ready for the Nobel Award Ceremony took hours. Nobel Laureates' spouses and adult daughters and granddaughters had appointments at the Grand Hôtel spa and hair salon throughout the day in preparation for the evening. Chris and I in our respective formal attire each strove to present ourselves appropriately. The throngs of Swedish well-wishers lining our red-carpeted paths to the Stockholm Concert Hall and the cobblestones leading into medieval Blue Hall at Stockholm City Hall did take us by surprise. Not being citizens of a country with royalty, as Chris also suggests, our comparison is Hollywood's Academy Awards night, which most of us get to experience only vicariously on television. (Harold Pinter was nominated for an Academy Award for Best Writing [Screenplay Based on Material from Another Medium] for his film script of *Betrayal* in 1983; he did not attend the award ceremony, and he did not win that year, but he has certainly received his share of accolades at major award ceremonies throughout the world.) Perhaps, just as bombarded by American popular culture as the rest of the world, we felt a bit like movie stars for a few moments, but the image of hundreds of Swedes braving the December chill to honor the recipients of the highest awards given in the sciences and literature "ennobled" our Nobel academic spirits even more. No performing arts, movie, or music awards ceremony holds a candle to the Nobels.

The Nobel Award Ceremony, from the "Opening Address" by Dr. Marcus Storch, Chairman of the Board of the Nobel Foundation, through the presentation of the 2005 Nobel Prize in Literature to Harold Pinter by writer Per Wästberg, member of the Swedish Academy and Chairman of its Nobel Committee, is already described in some detail by Chris Hudgins.[5]

As instructed in our program, I did not take a camera with me to either event. But I have many audiovisual images stored in actual (not just virtual) memory. Among them: the black-and-white spectacle of those processing on the colorful floral-decorated stage and being seated in very specific order, with a great vantage point on the Royal party (from my seat in the fifth row), especially of The King's beautiful elder daughter and the next in line of succession, Her Royal Highness Princess Victoria, was especially striking. Dressed in a gorgeous ice-blue gown with a train, she sat always erect throughout the ceremony, prescribed inches from the back of her chair, perfectly parallel to Queen Silvia, looking on with interest and smiling with appreciation.

The musical program of the Royal Stockholm Philharmonic Orchestra is listed in full for those interested in such details. Prior to the presentation of Harold Pinter's Nobel Prize by Mr. Wästberg, fourth in order of the awards, soloist Soprano Erika Sunnegårdh, a tall, beautiful blonde Swedish-American with a warm voice, who made her operatic debut in Sweden and sings both in the United States and in Europe, performed "Quando m'en vo' soletta, Musetta's Waltz" from *La Bohème*, by Puccini, and "Anch'io dichiuso" from *Nabucco*, by Verdi. (Just over a month later, Ms. Sunnegårdh would be making her debut as Leonore in *Fidelio* with the Metropolitan Opera in New York.[6])

In his presentation of Harold Pinter's Nobel Prize in Literature, Mr. Wästberg offered some insightful descriptions of Pinter's work, so it is worth reading the whole speech. In the final part, he added the word "regrettable" to the phrase "In the absence of ..." in the printed English text (which he spoke in English), saying "In the *regrettable* absence of this year's Nobel Laureate in Literature ... ." Then Stephen Page (though "somewhat nervous," his wife Caroline Hird, who was sitting to my right, whispered in my ear), rose and walked stage center, and, very dignified, gracefully accepted

Pinter's Nobel Prize Diploma and Medal from His Royal Majesty King Carl XVI Gustav, shaking his hand and bowing only to the King (but neither to the Nobel Committee nor to the audience), returning to his seat more quickly than the actual Nobel Laureates, as he had practiced during the Rehearsal, while the audience, still standing as for all the Nobel Laureates' awards, resoundingly applauded Harold Pinter. After the Ceremony, as the Nobel Laureates congratulated one another and received congratulations from their beaming family members all converging on stage, the rest of us Banquet guests began filling buses conveying us to Stockholm City Hall (<http://www2.stockholm.se/cityhall/eng_tittain.htm#>).

Spectacular floral arrangements "dominated by lilies, roses, calla lilies and carnations in yellow, white and red for the sixth consecutive year" adorned the cavernous Blue Hall, "in its winter best with 10,000 white flowers, silver fir and eucalyptus." The details of the Nobel Banquet's musical and flower "Divertissement," like the menu, kept secret until the event, are now listed on the Nobel Foundation website. After the trumpet fanfares announcing the procession of "the guests of honor," the Nobel Laureates themselves, and their moving and often witty speeches (especially by Nobel Laureate in Physiology or Medicine Barry J. Marshall), the most striking highlights were the precisely stage-managed "Floral Transformations" ("Floating Flower Fieldtrip," "Decoration Delivery Dangerously Delayed"—long-stemmed red roses "delivered" to each woman with fabulous fanfare—and "Princess Primavera's Plantation Parade"). Looking up at the chorus in the galleries, then down at the parading flower deliverers, I savored every image, every sound, every flower, every morsel of food and sip of drink.[7]

I marveled at the student flag bearers, the dancers and singers from all over Sweden, and the precisely-trained serving staff, weaving in total unison and harmony among 65 tables seating 1,350 guests (<http://nobelprize.org/nobel/events/photos/2005_sthlm/images/14_sthlm.jpg>) placed tightly together and set at right angles to the left and right of the enormously-long Table of Honor (<http://nobelprize.org/nobel/nobel-foundation/press/2005/table-of-honor.html>) seating 92 current and former Nobel Laureates, significant others, the Swedish Royal Family, and other "Very Important Persons"; at opposite ends of it sat Professor Bo Sundqvist (Member of the Board of the Nobel Foundation) and Professor Michael Nobel (one of Alfred Nobel's great grandnephews and Chairman of the Nobel Family Society). At our table (23), we all felt intimately connected and convivial, as we ooh-ed and ah-ed and chatted back and forth with our dinner partners. I was sitting between Chris Hudgins (directly opposite Eric Price) and Carl Bazil (directly opposite Michael Billington). Opposite me sat Solveig Allén, the wife of Swedish Academy member Professor Sture Allén, and on her left Weini Kahsai Nobel, who works in the office of the

Swedish Ombudsman against ethnic discrimination (first held by Peter Nobel from 1986 to 1991).

By the end of the Banquet, my feet (strapped all night into high-heeled dress sandals) were no longer "made for dancing." Bravely, I negotiated back up the slippery marble white stairs, dodging small groups being photographed partway up, and made my way slowly across the width of The Gallery of the Prince, into The Golden Hall, looking for Chris. When I finally saw his head above most of the rest of the crowd of dancers and how much fun he was having, I knew that his dancing partnership with Erika Sunnegårdh would probably last the rest of the night! Along the way, quite content just watching those with hardier feet jitterbugging the night away, I chatted over the music with Eric Price and Carl Bazil, Fred Olav Johannessen, Stephen Page and his wife, Caroline Hird (next to whom I had sat during the Nobel Award Ceremony), Odd Zschiedrich and his girlfriend, Annika Schildt (who soon swirled off together dancing), and Michael Billington (who was rather tired from his trip from London that very day and decided to retire early). Eric mentioned that Morgan Entrekin, the president and publisher of Grove/Atlantic (Pinter's American publisher), had not been able to come to Stockholm, because his wife was about to give birth to their first child.[8] Entrekin's Grove/Atlantic business partner Joan Bingham was there, however, and she seemed to be loving the event, though she had begun losing her voice during dinner. Skipping the after-Banquet nightcap (!), I got my coat and tote bag, stowed my black-beaded evening clutch and high heels, switched to my more-sensible, low-heeled winter boots, and, with Eric, Carl, and Joan, shared a taxi back to the Grand Hôtel. Very hoarse, Joan went off to bed right away, and, soon afterward, so did I, quite exhausted but happy and very glad that I did not have to pack, since, given my preparations, my room looked as if a cyclone had hit it.

Unlike those who had to pack and rush off early that Sunday morning, I stayed on an extra day to visit the Nobel Museum (<http://nobelprize.org/nobel/nobelmuseum/>), an easy walk from the Grand Hôtel. In the Museum's center foyer, I snapped photos of Harold's crystal obelisk engraved with the Nobel citation, part of a special tribute to the 2005 Nobel Laureates. Then I explored the Centenary Exhibition "Cultures of Creativity," viewed another special exhibition "Albert Einstein 'for his discovery of . . .'" and collected brochures and postal cards, noting down titles of various books about Einstein to get later for my husband, who is a professor of chemistry and physics and for whom I brought back the posters of the 2005 Nobel Laureates in Chemistry and Physics, along with my own poster featuring the 2005 Nobel Laureate in Literature: Harold Pinter, all of which I had collected earlier in the week from the Nobel Desk in the Grand Hôtel. (The Nobel Museum gift shop had not yet unveiled Pinter's portrait postal card, though it should be available by now. I bought the gift shop's postal card of Beckett for myself and one of Wole Soyinka for Chris Hudgins, which I gave to Chris at the MLA Convention in Washington, DC, later in December.) When I left the Nobel Museum at its closing time of 5 p.m., it was already very dark, but the clear air outside was just a bit nippy not bone-chilling. I walked down the Museum steps straight into a Christmas street fair of makeshift booths strung with bright multi-colored lights, bought a small paper cup of Swedish Glögg, a chocolate-covered marzipan "cigar" (which I brought home with me), and a small paper bag of just-roasted and sugar-coated California (!) almonds, and happily sipped and munched my way down the hill and over the bridge back to the Grand Hôtel. What a lovely evening!

Sunday night I packed and the next afternoon, Monday, December 12th, I flew back home via Frankfurt and Washington, DC, fully satisfied that I had just had a "once-in-a-lifetime" experience (a phrase that both Chris and I would use frequently in talking about it). It was an experience that I and all the others attending would, of course, have preferred to have shared personally with Harold Pinter in Stockholm. Chris and I have tried to share it in words, hoping that in some way we can convey to Harold Pinter and the other readers of *The Pinter Review* our wondrous enjoyment of Nobel Week 2005.

NOTES

[1] Here is the relevant excerpt from Barry Marshall's Banquet Speech:

> Let me clarify here, while it is true that [Sir Frank] MacFarlane Burnet [Australia's most famous scientist and the 1960 Nobel Laureate in this field] injected himself with the rabbit myxoma virus, and I did actually infect myself with *Helicobacter pylori*, I don't suggest to other aspiring Aussie scientists that this process will guarantee a Nobel Prize. But to young people listening tonight I would say, find passion in your work—whatever it is. If, like me, you are working in the area of science, I can promise you that it can be the most exciting and rewarding of careers.

(Cf. <http://nobelprize.org/medicine/laureates/2005/marshall-speech.html>; <http://nobelprize.org/medicine/laureates/1960/index.html>.)

A full length-video of the 2005 Nobel Banquet, recorded by Sveriges Television (75 mins.) is accessible from the official Nobel Prize website (<http://nobelprize.org/medialayer/index.pp?id=811>).

[2] According to *Frommer's Guide*,

> The cozy dining rooms are named for Swedish historical figures who were patrons. Today it's popular with artists, lawyers, and poets. You get good traditional Swedish cooking, especially fresh Baltic fish and game from the forests. Herring is a favorite appetizer. More imaginative appetizers include a creamy artichoke soup, Jerusalem artichokes with a dollop of caviar, and an especially intriguing consommé of oxtail with tiny ravioli stuffed with quail breast. Notable main courses are fried breast of wild duck in Calvados sauce, and roast of reindeer in juniper-berry sauce. A particular delight is

> homemade duck sausage with three kinds of mushrooms in black pepper sauce. Want something different for dessert? How about warm rose hip soup with vanilla ice cream? Of course, if you order that, you'd be denying yourself the "symphony" of lingonberries or the longtime favorite: Stockholm's best chocolate cake.
>
> (cf. <htt;://www.gyldenefreden.sel>.)

[3] See, e.g., "NobelMedia," posted on the Nobel Foundation website:

> In 2005, Nobel Media is launching the Nobel Prize Concert, an annually recurring classic concert concept of the finest international class, following in the tradition of the Jubilee Concert held in the 1990s and the Centennial Concert in 2001 on the occasion of the 100th anniversary of the Nobel Prize. To be held at the Stockholm Concert Hall, the event honors the year's Nobel Laureates, in the presence of the Laureates and their parties, Sweden's Royal Family and the Nobel Foundation's guests. The general public is also invited to attend. World-renowned cellist Yo-Yo Ma, famous interpreter of the classic cello repertoire and Founder-Artistic Director of the boundary-breaching Silk Road Project, and who performed the music for Ang Lee's film "Crouching Tiger, Hidden Dragon," is the first soloist of this newly-established Nobel programme.
>
> (<http://nobelprize.org/nobelmedia/index.html/>)

[4] In "Only Men … .: If you thought that women had finally won their place in the host of penguin-clad celebrities, you were grievously mistaken," Ewa Stenberg observes:

> This year's Nobel Day coincided with the Jewish sabbath, which meant that the deeply religious professor Aumann went to the synagogue on Saturday morning instead of practising his bows at the dress rehearsal for the prize-giving. He caused a problem for the security service—as Jews are not allowed to use a limousine on the sabbath, Bob Aumann walked from the Grand Hotel to the Concert Hall.
>
> (<http://www.dn.se/DNet/jsp/polopoly.jsp?d=554&a=501055>)

Being a smart man (!) and being toward the end, though not at the Rehearsal, Professor Aumann could just mimick the procedure of those receiving awards before him (when to bow, etc.). Stenberg observes significantly:

> If the British dramatist and son of a tailor, Harold Pinter, had not been seriously ill, he would probably have found himself beside one of the Economics laureates, Robert Aumann, on the podium. Just imagine what they might have whispered to each other! Harold Pinter used his Nobel lecture for an intense and incandescent critique of the USA and Great Britain and their war in Iraq. Professor Aumann, an Israeli, thinks that disarmament has made the world less secure.

[5] The English text of Mr. Wästberg's full speech is reproduced on the Nobel Foundation website, and one can watch his approximately-ten-minute presentation in the video of the entire ceremony in RealPlayer featured on the Nobel Foundation website "Events" section. It begins approx. 46 mins., 25 secs. into the program, which lasted approx. an hour and fifteen minutes. Specific details of the full program are posted in pdf files linked on that website, as well as in other linked documents. There are some wonderful high-quality digital still photographs created by the pool photographers of both the Ceremony and the Banquet posted in the "photograph collection" as well. (Cf. <http://nobelprize.org/nobel/events/video/

ceremony-banquet-05/sthlm-prizeaward-hi.ram> and <http://nobelprize.org/nobel/events/photos/2005_sthlm/index.html>.) It is also printed in full in this volume.

[6] See the Metropolitan Opera webpage on *Fidelio*, listing the dates of performances (first two weeks of April) and her debut on April 1, 2006 and the related feature article about Erika Sunegårdh: (<http://www.metoperafamily.org/metopera/season/production.aspx?id=8097>; <http://www.operainfo.org/broadcast/operaBio.cgi?person=50000000000581&language=1>)

[7] According to a Nobel Foundation Press Release (1 Dec. 2005), a team of five chefs, consulting with three other chefs, devised "this year's concept ... characterized by Nordic winds." The three-course menu (presented in French and translated into both English and Swedish, now accessible on the Nobel Foundation website) was also "kept secret" until 7 p.m., the starting hour of the Nobel Banquet, coordinated by the general manager and head chef of Stockholm City Hall's Stadshuskällaren restaurant. Being very partial to scallops, lobster, and other shellfish, and ignoring my "elevated cholesterol" for the night, I appreciated the first course of Coquilles Saint-Jacques et Langoustines ("Crayfish panna cotta with fennel-backed Arctic char, scallops and Norwegian lobster on bay lettuce"). Puzzled at first at the identity of the second, meat course (Poitrine de Perdrix des Neiges en Robe Forestière et Sa Garniture), I discovered later that it was the "breast" of a game bird in the grouse family called "Tarmigan" [or "Ptarmigan"], "baked in 'horn of plenty' mushrooms with caramelised apples, poached onions and broad beans, served with Sauce Normandy" ("Calvados sauce"), and "accompanied by Gâteau de Pommes de Terre" ("potato cake"). The third and final course was a deliciously-tart, not-too-sweet dessert, Mousse Citronée Garnie de Framboises ("a lemon and yoghurt mousse with Arctic bramble marmalade, fresh raspberries and raspberry-Arctic bramble sauce"). In addition to Pommery Grand Cru Vintage 1995 Champagne beginning the toasts and throughout the dinner, we also were served both red and white wines (Penfolds RWT 2001, Barossa Valley and Le Dauphin de Guiraud 2002, Sauternes), followed by coffee, cognac (Rémy Martin VSOP), and Cointreau, as well as a fine Swedish mineral water, Ramlösa, first produced in 1707. "The Food, and the People" (*Dagens Nyheter* 11 Dec. 2005) provides an interesting review of the menu in English ("Nobel in English" sec.). (<http://nobelprize.org/nobel/events/menus/menu-2005.html>; <http://www.finewaters.com/Bottled_Water/USA/Imported/Ramlosa.asp>; <http://www.dn.se/DNet/jsp/polopoly.jsp?d=554&a=501103>.)

Also now accessible online are the full details of the "Divertissement" (<http://nobelprize.org/nobel/nobel-foundation/press/2005/divertissement-05.html>).

[8] Their son, Allan Ervin Entrekin, was born 13 Feb. 2006, I learned from a telephone conversation with Eric Price in June 2006.

From Stockholm

Chris Hudgins and Susan Hollis Merritt (right) at some of the Nobel festivities.

Display cases at the Nobel Ceremony include four volumes of The Pinter Review *published by The University of Tampa Press.*

Mind the Gap: Perception and Cognition in Harold Pinter's Confrontation Scenes

LUC GILLEMAN

Mind the Gap

Like his friend and mentor Samuel Beckett, Harold Pinter has now received the Nobel Prize for Literature. In a videotaped acceptance speech, he talked about the function of truth in drama and in civic life. While its delivery was effective, the content of the speech was not original. Pinter had been making similar statements in interviews since the late Sixties. The war in Vietnam then demanded an unambiguous response, and Pinter seems to have worried that the suspension of judgment that characterizes his art would be mistaken for moral relativism or a postmodern suspicion of factual truth. In the Eighties, the Nicaraguan contra revolution and Thatcherism awakened the political activist in Pinter, and the man who had confessed to "detest soapboxes" mounted them at every occasion (Bensky 63). He became an active member of PEN, Amnesty International, and Arts for Nicaragua; he even created a political discussion group referred to as 20th June Society. He spoke out often and always with moral outrage. One could no longer invite Pinter the playwright without having to listen to Pinter the enraged world citizen—even though, much like Noam Chomsky, he insists that the professional and the activist speak in distinct voices. To some people's dismay, his Nobel lecture too erupted into a vehement diatribe against the United States, its lying President, and its invasion of Iraq. America, he contended, is responsible for hundred of thousands of deaths, which it not only ignores ("we don't do body counts") but has convinced others to ignore as well: "It never happened. Nothing ever happened. Even while it was happening it wasn't happening."[1] People who associated Pinter mainly with artistic subtlety and minimalism were taken aback by the rancor behind these political views.

When Pinter talks about politics, his language can be breathtakingly ferocious, as here in an interview given in 1966:

> I'll tell you what I really think about politicians. The other night I watched some politicians on television talking about Vietnam. I wanted very much to burst through the screen with a flame-thrower

> and burn their eyes out and their balls off and then inquire from them how they would assess this action from a political point of view. (Bensky 27)

In his Nobel lecture, he refers to politics as "a vast tapestry of lies"; underneath is the truth—and that truth is base and abject. "You have the rhetoric of the free, the Christian, the democratic," he said to Mel Gussow in a 1988 interview with reference to America's involvement in Nicaragua, "but underneath the rhetoric what you have is excrement, vomit, urine, blood, mutilation, horror, deprivation, poverty" (73). The loftier America's talk about freedom and democracy, the viler the reality of its actions. So Pinter's verbal crudeness is meant to close the gap between ideology and reality—its savagery a measure of the distance between the two.

Incidentally, this view of reality agrees with the two-tiered approach of plays that assume the demonstrable existence of a common and often unpleasant truth, awaiting discovery during a climactic confrontation scene. Plot progression in such plays often revolves around observation, around issues of vision and visibility. This is most obviously so in plays where the confrontation scene involves a prop whose physical presence represents the visibility of truth. In Arthur Miller's *Death of a Salesman* (1949), the confrontation scene between father and son starts off with Biff slapping a piece of rubber tubing onto the table:

> BIFF: Leave it there! Don't move it!
>
> WILLY [*not looking at it*]: What is that?
>
> BIFF: You know goddam well what that is.
>
> WILLY [*caged, wanting to escape*]: I never saw that.
>
> BIFF: You saw it. The mice didn't bring it into the cellar! What is this supposed to do, make a hero out of you? This supposed to make me sorry for you?
>
> WILLY: Never heard of it.
>
> BIFF: There'll be no pity for you, you hear it? No pity!
>
> WILLY [*to* Linda]: You hear the spite!
>
> BIFF: No, you're going to hear the truth—what you are and what I am! (2. 104)

This short and effective dialogue argues for an unambiguous relationship between knowing ("You know goddam well what that is") and seeing ("You saw it")—a relationship Biff refers to as "the truth." And the truth represented by the rubber tube is unpleasant and shameful, associated with death and obscenity: Willy uses it to inhale gas in an attempt at suicide, while its ridiculous phallic appearance reminds us of his pathetic, secret sexual life.

In other words, the confrontation scene is an attempt to close the gap between what is seen and what is said through the articulation of a judgment. This is how David Hare expresses it in "A Lecture" (1976):

> Judgement is at the heart of the theatre. A man steps forward and informs the audience of his intention to lifelong fidelity to his wife, while his hand, even as he speaks, drifts at random to the body of another woman. The most basic dramatic situation you can imagine; the gap between what he says he is and what we see him to be opens up, and in the gap we see something that makes theatre unique; that it exposes the difference between what a man says and what he does.

In this exposure lies the insight the dramatist is seeking to offer us. In the political drama in which Pinter has cast the later part of his life, this is essentially the scene he is playing out over and over again. In his artistic work, however, this is precisely the kind of confrontation scene he is known for refusing to write. We "see" things happening in his plays, often dismal, sometimes brutal: a room is invaded, a man is taken away—but the gap between what happens and what is spoken remains an unhealed wound: we never get "to hear the truth."

"Mr. Pinter's buses really run"

In a Pinter play, the abrogation of the customary link between what is happening and what is articulated leads to a particularly unnerving suspense of judgment that has led to the appellation "comedy of menace." At first this was seen as a largely aesthetic gesture, a sort of stylistic peculiarity that linked Pinter with the Absurdists. But it is remarkable how soon that style, which at first was thought to be strange and rather off-putting, was recognized as in some ways "realistic." The term makes its first appearance early in Pinter's career, a few years after the production of *The Birthday Party* in 1958. In his influential *The Theatre of the Absurd* (1961), Martin Esslin bestowed a degree of respectability on the young Pinter by discussing his work among that of Samuel Beckett, Eugène Ionesco, and Arthur Adamov. Yet Esslin immediately conceded that, in comparison to these absurdist playwrights, Pinter is looking for "a higher degree of realism in the theatre." Pinter, he explained, possesses a "clinically accurate ear for the absurdity of ordinary speech" in all "its repetitiveness, incoherence, and lack of logic or grammar." "The dialogue of Pinter's plays," Esslin continued, "is a casebook of the whole gamut of *non sequiturs* in small talk" (206-207). This was confirmed by Pinter, who in a 1961 essay "Writing for Myself" confirmed the mimetic quality of his art:

> I'm convinced that what happens in my plays could happen anywhere, at any time, in any place, although the events may seem unfamiliar at

first glance. If you press me for a definition, I'd say that what goes on in my plays is realistic, but what I'm doing is not realism. (11)

In other words, while Pinter's drama does not follow the dictates of conventional realism, it nevertheless claims to reflect some aspects of lived experience.

The term "realistic" crops up equally early in the writings of other scholars and critics attempting to define Pinter's theatre: in 1962, Arthur Ashworth claimed that Pinter's plays "belong more to the realist theatre. He creates a nucleus of realistic and very lifelike characters in the style of the realist theatre, and puts them in situations which can be explained in terms of real life" (153). And around the same time, John Bowen pointedly remarked that we only had to "compare the dialogue of *The Birthday Party* or any of Mr. Pinter's revue sketches with that of *The Bald Prima Donna* or the scene with the logician in *Rhinoceros*" to see the essential difference: "Mr. Pinter's buses really run; his observation may be appalled, but it is exact. His characters do not use language to show that language doesn't work; they use it as a cover for fear and loneliness" (162). If Pinter's dialogues seem strange, these critics are implying, it is because they do not follow established conventions of dramatic speech. They do however imitate the absurdity of much of what we persist in calling conversation in daily life. As a retired professor of English once said to me: "'Pinteresque' is what goes on over dinner with my wife."

Around the same time that Pinter wrote his tantalizingly recognizable yet bewildering dialogues, psycho- and sociolinguistics were codifying some of the same properties of language that Pinter made use of in his plays. From the 1950s onwards, linguistics, catching up with insights gained by language philosophy in the 1920s, moved beyond the study of what language says (semantics) towards theories about what language does (pragmatics). The prolonged, empty chatter about the cornflakes in Pinter's *The Birthday Party* (1958) apparently had a name. Sociolinguists, reviving a term coined in the 1930s by anthropologist Bronislaw Malinowski, called it phatic communication (or "communion" as Malinowski preferred to call it), "a type of speech in which ties of union are created by a mere exchange of words" (Laver 215). Nothing much, or nothing essential, is said during phatic communion, but a relationship is nevertheless being established. Similarly, in speech-act theory, J. L. Austin recognized that even descriptive statements in the final instance are "performatives" that act upon the world.[2] Communication theory in the meantime had validated another Pinter device, silence, by depriving speech of its hitherto unchallenged status as sole object worthy of investigation: "every act, every pause, every movement in living and social systems is also a message; silence is communication; short of death it is impossible for an organism or a person not to communicate" because "in a communications system, nothing never happens" (Wilden 124). In shifting its attention from written to spoken language, and from spoken language to communication in general, just when drama was emancipating itself from its subservience to plot, linguistics offered new concepts that helped critics recognize the mimetic quality of Pinter's dialogues.

Analyses of Pinter's drama began to appear in language and communication journals. Kripa K. Gautam, for instance, proved the usefulness of various dynamic linguistic paradigms, such as H. P. Grice's conversational maxims of cooperation, J.M. Sinclair's, R.M. Coulthard's, and Harvey Sacks's analysis of exchange and conversational structure, for an understanding of *The Caretaker.*[3] Role analysis and game theory proved equally illuminating to rationalize what was happening in a Pinter play. Lois G. Gordon's *Pinter Stratagems to Uncover Nakedness* (1969) was an early attempt to supplement Freudian assessment of personality with Eric Berne's transactional analysis theory. And in a number of articles and books, Deirdre Burton used discourse analysis of, among others, William Labov, Gail Jefferson, and John Laver to examine in detail the language structures that Pinter's dialogues share with real-life conversation.[4] As is the case with Watzlawick, Beavin, and Jackson's pragmatic analysis of Edward Albee's *Who's Afraid of Virginia Woolf,* the assumption seems to have been that drama provides a concise and purified sampling of "real" dialogue that researchers can use to demonstrate "real" patterns of human interaction.

The Quigley Problem

Until the early seventies, one could either propose a linguistic analysis of Pinter's plays or a normative literary reading of the text. A linguistic analysis used Pinter's dialogues as examples of certain recently codified principles; a literary analysis proposed an interpretation of a whole play. The combined effect was disconcerting because the former would come to the conclusion that Pinter was a most masterful writer of realistic dialogue, while the latter would often point to the obscurity of that same language as impeding the communication of the play's message. The two approaches seemed mutually exclusive until Austin Quigley united them in *The Pinter Problem* (1975). The thrust of Quigley's argument was that while claiming to leave language philosophy and linguistics to their respective specialists, conventional drama criticism had in reality (and for far too long) been wedded to a philosophy centered on the subject and to a linguistics based on the correspondence theory of meaning and reference. Quigley pointed out that "as long as criticism is handicapped by an implicit belief that language is primarily referential, that it is mainly concerned with the transfer of verifiable facts, we will continue to be puzzled by the connective thread which links successive statements in Pinter's plays" (50).

Quigley's own interpretations of Pinter's major plays were so elegant and rational that one could only wonder why these plays had ever caused such frenetic exegetic activity. In the rational glare of Quigley's critical spotlight, there were no longer any dark areas in Pinter's work. Everything in Pinter made supreme sense. Quigley could now look back on the misguided efforts of previous critics. And his verdict was scathing: "The unanalyzed in Pinter's work is a product of temporary critical failure, not of some metaphysical, ultra-valuable, un-analyzable characteristic located behind, above, or beneath the text of the plays" (29). Quigley's interpretive key was disarmingly simple: it seemed that one only had to look at what Pinter's characters *did* with their language for the meaning of his confusing plays to emerge. Once this was understood, it was no longer necessary to escape the play's apparent unresolved incongruities in the notion of a mysterious subtext, the "real" story that Pinter refused to tell. The theoretical backbone of Quigley's work was the language philosophy of Ludwig Wittgenstein and J. R. Firth. Quigley's pragmatic reading of the plays was primarily inspired by Wittgenstein's belief that the meaning of a sentence is determined by its use.[5] With this simple stratagem, Quigley was able to transcribe Pinter's plays in ways that brought out their commonsense meaning.

The Pinter Problem clearly defined the unique properties of a Pinter play. Whereas conventionally realistic plays build towards a climactic confrontation scene, each scene in a Pinter play is organized as a verbal or nonverbal sparring match between characters. And instead of resulting in the discovery of a problematic truth and the gaining of valuable insight (known as "recognition" or *anagnorisis*), confrontations in a Pinter play deepen rather than clarify the initial conflict. When the curtain falls on *The Birthday Party* (1958), we still do not know who Stanley is and what crime he has committed. This is frustrating; it is also interesting because it suggests a philosophy of truth and identity until then not commonly associated with any but absurdist drama. Character in a Pinter play is no longer a given either; it is, as Quigley argues, created dynamically, the result of "negotiations" with other characters. From that point of view, it makes little sense to discuss character in isolation, as Lucina Gabbard does in her Freudian analysis or Elizabeth Sakellaridou in her evaluation of Pinter's portrayal of women. Neither does it hold much promise for further insight into the "Pinter problem" to say with Harold Bloom that the characterization of Davies in *The Caretaker* is "flawed" because of his lack of redeeming qualities. Such criticism refuses to acknowledge that Pinter's drama no longer depends on the "rounded" characterization of conventional realism. Discussion of character, Quigley claims, has to make way for discussion of the interactive self, the self-concept that comes into being during the dynamics of the interaction. This is what is so precarious about the world that Pinter creates:

> Unless others act upon the fact that a character's identity is what that character believes or wants it to be, the identity lacks corroboration and is of uncertain value. [....] Yet as soon as external confirmation is required, the self-concept that exists unchallenged in a private reality is put at risk. Relationships thus become major battlegrounds as characters attempt to negotiate a mutual reality. [....] In an important sense, then, the "personality" of a particular character, the kind of identity with which he can operate, is a function of a compromise in a particular relationship. (54)

Quigley no longer assumes the well-roundedness of characters, referring instead to "operative identities," and he replaces a supra-individual, "given" reality by a "mutual reality" in constant flux and redefinition.

Martin Esslin, who is perhaps most responsible for making Pinter research academically respectable, was not impressed. Quigley, he said, had merely "discover[ed] the obvious at enormous length" (*Review* 105). He seemed to suggest that Quigley's labor amounted to not much more than a beat-by-beat analysis of a play—the way actors study it, as a chain of transactions. Esslin overlooked the important implications of Quigley's rejection of the more customary literary analysis, namely that Pinter had created not only a new dramatic idiom but also new structural conventions. However, by referring to the "obvious" quality of Quigley's work, Esslin unwittingly put his finger on a problematic point that is left unattended in *The Pinter Problem*. The Pinter problem, as Quigley formulates it, is "how to reconcile belief in the obscurity of the plays with the widespread recognition of Pinter's mastery of his form" (16). By not treating the plays as poorly constructed conventionally realistic stories, Quigley's analysis had confirmed "Pinter's mastery of his form." Pinter, Quigley affirms, does not withhold the real story. Everything we need to know in order to interpret the play is present; it only requires a pragmatic reading. But after reading Quigley's interpretations, which demonstrate so eloquently how commonsensical Pinter's dialogues are, it becomes hard to understand how the plays earned their reputation for "obscurity" in the first place. The feelings of menace, uncertainty, and of sense continuously deferred appear to be misplaced reactions to a superbly rational composition. Esslin's critique of the "obviousness" of Quigley's analysis draws attention to what Quigley had left unexplained, namely the distance between the obvious and its rationalization which is responsible for that feeling of uncertainty which we call "the Pinter effect."

That Quigley was not unaware of the problem appears from the first pages of his study where he states that "the capacity to respond to a play in performance is not wholly dependent upon the ability to conceptualize that response for the purpose of communicating it to others" (18). He also remarks that

> [a] considerable burden is placed on the audience, which must be able to infer something of the previous joint experience of the characters if it is to understand the context in which current events are operating. [....] In other plays, in which truths about the central concerns demonstrably exist independent of an individual character's construction of them, it is possible to organize a conversation on stage in which explicit statements will convey the "reliable" version to the audience. But in a Pinter play the dominant interrelational function obviates this possibility. (69)

Quigley here is referring to a convention typical of the well-made play whereby some speech remains privileged, its "truth" not subordinated to the give and take of interaction. Moments when speech articulates truth tend to be clearly marked. In *Death of a Salesman,* Biff confronts his father with an angry, "No, you're going to hear the truth, what you are and what I am!" (2.130). The explicit statements that then follow confirm or negate the audience's conjectures about the ultimate meaning of the dramatic action—conjectures based on evidence provided in the scenes leading up to the climactic confrontation.

Quigley suggests that there is no such privileged speech in a Pinter play, where language can never be detached from interaction, and because no statement can be taken at face value, structural indicators acquire paramount importance (37).[6] As Pinter puts it in his Nobel lecture: "Truth in drama is forever elusive. You never quite find it but the search for it is compulsive. The search is clearly what drives the endeavour. The search is your task." Quigley took on that challenge, and by equating meaning with use solved the "Pinter problem." Quigley's problem, however, is that he succeeds almost too well. Conflating experience and understanding, Quigley closes the gap, the very basis of the famous Pinter effect. If what typifies Pinter's drama is not the absence but the distance of truth, what is needed now is a way to measure the intellectual burden the search for truth places upon an audience.

"That way madness lies"

The solution to the problem of visualizing the sense-making process that a Pinter dialogue requires comes from an unexpected direction. Reviewing *The Pinter Problem* for *TLS,* the sociologist Liam Hudson repeated Esslin's taunts about Quigley's lengthy "approximations to common sense" but added the valuable remark that Quigley had rigged the wrong horses to his carriage. Ludwig Wittgenstein and J. R. Firth were not the right team to pull into motion an interpretive mechanism that relied so heavily on existential-phenomenological analyses of "mutual experiences." Instead, Quigley ought to have read "psychiatrists, psychologists and sociologists like R. D. Laing, Eric Berne and Erving Goffman; the first of these especially."

These specialists of the sense behind "broken patterns of communication" were closer to Quigley's chosen field, which, as Hudson pointed out, was, despite the references to Wittgenstein and Firth, psychology rather than philosophy. And, as if this proved his point, Hudson reminded his readers that both Pinter's *The Caretaker* and Laing's *The Divided Self* "came out in the same year."

With that last remark, Hudson referred to a period "in the late 1950s and early 1960s," characterized by a "preoccupation with loneliness and despair" and, more specifically, by an interest in the schizoid condition. Hudson was not the only, and certainly not the first, commentator to hint at the striking similarities between dialogues quoted in postwar case studies of schizophrenia and those prevalent around the same time in modern literature and drama. In 1964, Steven Marcus, discussing Michel Foucault's *Madness and Civilization* (1961) and Milton Rokeach's study of schizophrenia, *The Three Christs of Ypsilanti* (1964), said that "we must recognize that [...] insane speech is tapping the same resources of psychic energy and impulse as some of the most characteristic expressions of modern literature" (143). Marcus was particularly struck by the poetic suggestiveness of "schizophrenese" which he compared to similarly expressive passages in Beckett's work (142).

Commenting on the demented quality of Pinter dialogue was commonplace even before then. In 1958, reviewing *The Birthday Party*, *The Times* noted the play's "off-beat note of madness, a sort of delirium," and *The Manchester Guardian* thought that "the characters speak in non-sequiturs, half gibberish, lunatic ravings" and added petulantly, "what all this means only Mr. Pinter knows" (qtd. by Toynbee 24). More recently, in 1990, John Peter reanimated this cliché in a most interesting way, claiming that "to experience one of these plays is like dealing with certain types of mental illness in which another person's truth becomes inaccessible because its logic rests on a different matrix." So, critical orbits constantly touched upon the similarities between schizophrenese and Pinter dialogue, only to regain the safer space of critical "common sense" after giving off the first promising sparks.

None of these sparks caught fire. Although the comparison of Pinter's dialogues with schizophrenese is striking, such similarities hardly seem to promise a better understanding of Pinter's plays. Admittedly, certain thematic concerns of Pinter confirm the importance of madness in his oeuvre. *The Birthday Party* (1958) and *Tea Party* (1965) demonstrate the process of mental breakdown; Lenny in *The Dwarfs* (1960) experiences a psychotic break during which he suffers from hallucinations; Aston in *The Caretaker* (1960) talks about the electroshock treatment he received in a mental hospital; and a power struggle in a mental institute forms the subject of *The Hothouse* (written in 1958; produced in 1980). However, in none of these works does Pinter engage in a romantic exploration of a pathological mental condition, the way Tennessee Williams does in *The Glass Menagerie* (1945) or *A Streetcar Named Desire* (1947), for instance. Neither does he pursue madness in the form of a docudrama as David Edgar does in *Mary Barnes* (1978), nor explore the topic politically, to attack the constraints imposed by normalization, as Peter Weiss does in *Marat/Sade* (1959). It is clear from his "Letter to Peter Wood" that Pinter does not intend his audience to feel estranged from his characters, to think of them as weird or abnormal. "Nothing salutary for the audience to identify itself with," Pinter conceded with regards to Stanley, the protagonist of *The Birthday Party*. "And yet, at the same time, I believe that a greater degree of identification will take place than might seem likely" (5).

Pinter's characters may behave strangely, but his drama is clearly not about strangeness. The "madness" of his dialogues lies in its disconnected quality, in the way characters refuse to keep the dialogue on track. This is both a familiar and a strangely unsettling phenomenon. As Ronald Hayman remarks,

> [n]obody's behaviour seems to be affected by anyone else's behaviour. [....] In *The Homecoming*, the relationship between action and reaction is not even one of opposites. Almost nothing seems to happen as a reaction to anything else that happens. Everyone's behaviour consists of a series of unexpected, separate actions, each one either disconnected from the last or at a tangent with it, and the actions are separate, not only from each other, but from the personality of the protagonist. (66)[7]

Thomas Van Laan talks in this respect of the "dizzying dislocations" of Pinter's dialogues, and H. R. Hayes remarks on the deceptively simple world of appearances in Pinter which "conceal[-] a world of chaos and madness" and in which characters refuse to behave "according to a predictable pattern" (33). Hinchliffe similarly states that "It is not so much the lack of logic as the madness of logic that informs [Pinter's] plays" (26). In view of all this, John Peter's remark that Pinter's language may well be built on an unusual "matrix" merits closer attention, especially since his suggestion is based on a feeling, shared by many others, that the alienating effect of Pinter's language resembles that produced by the language of "certain forms of mental illness" in the listener who searches for sense.

Schizogenic Dialogues

What is needed then is a theory that applies the notion of "insanity" not to people but rather to the interaction they are engaged in. In the 1950s and 1960s, a number of psychiatrists rebelled against the stereotyping and policing of mental illness. The work of these "anti-psychiatrists" complemented that of social theorists such as Herbert Marcuse and Michel Foucault who questioned and blurred the difference between the normal and the abnormal. After all, "normal" people, using "normal" reasoning, had created the absurdities of the Cold War, according to which other "normal" people were supposed to live "normal" lives against the backdrop of a looming nuclear war and mass extermination. What if the schizophrenic were the hapless scapegoat and schizophrenia the general pathology we call modern existence? Attention shifted from individuals to the maddening "systems" in which they were trapped. At a time when the two superpowers were engaged in a particularly dangerous form of lingering stalemate, communication theorists such as Gregory Bateson studied deadlocks in human interaction, calling them "double binds."

While critics and reviewers complained about Pinter's mad and unpredictable dialogue, anti-psychiatrists were composing a matrix of madness to bring the apparently unpredictable within range of comprehension. For this, they found help in the work of communication theorists. To the latter, there is no essential difference between noise and information. What is meaningful to one may be meaningless to another. Once one ceases to equate information with meaning, disconnected, skewed dialogue structures become interesting. Incongruities, illogicalities, contradictions, paradoxes increase the potential for information and thus enhance the listener's "amount of freedom of choice" (Shannon and Beaver 8-13). From that perspective, the language of the schizophrenic is more entropic and thus more informative than the accurate language of the rocket scientist.

Consider, for instance, the following highly dramatic interaction between a hospitalized, "schizophrenic" son and his parents that follows the therapist's question of why the patient thinks he is selfish:

SON: Well, when my mother sometimes makes me a big meal and I won't eat it if I don't feel like it.

[*Pause.*]

FATHER: But he wasn't always like that, you know. He's always been a good boy.

MOTHER: That's his illness, isn't it, doctor? He was never ungrateful. He was always most polite and well brought up. We've done our best by him.

SON: No, I've always been selfish and ungrateful. I've no self-respect.

FATHER: But you have.

SON: I would have, if you respected me. No one respects me. Everyone laughs at me. I'm the joke of the world. I'm the joker all right.

FATHER: But, son, I respect you, because I respect a man who respects himself. (Laing, *Self and Others* 142-43)[8]

The dialogue revolves around the son's alleged selfishness. Every potential line of reasoning on which the successful conclusion of this issue would depend is abrogated by the insidious way in which dichotomies (grateful vs. ungrateful; respect vs. disrespect; accusation vs. self-condemnation) are subverted. The son, for instance, readily admits to being selfish and ungrateful, but with an example of such triviality that his self-condemnation turns into an accusation of parents who demand of their son nothing less than complete self-abnegation. The father not only remains impervious to the son's disqualification of his selfishness but also actually confirms it by saying that "he wasn't *always*" so selfish and ungrateful (my emphasis). He immediately disqualifies this accusation in the next sentence; the son apparently has "*always* been a good boy" (my emphasis). The mother then defines her son's ungratefulness not as a chosen behavior but as his illness. Her son is not what they both think he is and what he, following their logic, admits he is: he "was never ungrateful." Then, in case this would sound like a compliment to her son and a confirmation of his ego, she makes it the fruit of a successful education. Following on this, the son now paralogically defines selfishness as the opposite of self-respect. He has no self-respect because he is selfish, and, as he stated before, he is selfish because he does not deny himself the right of refusing the dinner his mother cooks for him. The father's reaction to this is similar to the mother's in that it denies the correctness of the son's self-image. The son now defines lack of self-respect as an attitude towards himself inspired by the attitude of others to him, whereas previously he had connected his lack of self-respect with his own ungrateful attitude to others defined as an unwillingness of total self-abnegation. The father's response is to deny the son's views. The son, he claims, is both respected and respected by others. The logical disjunctions in the dialogue engender an impressive amount of information; a short verbal exchange has given dramatic shape to a complex world of affective and relational problems in which both parents and son are entangled.

Laing called this kind of dialogic pattern "schizogenic," believing it typical of families in which someone was sooner or later labeled as "schizophrenic." In his view, and in that of other anti-psychiatrists, schizophrenia is a social phenomenon, though only one person, the scapegoat of the family, gets officially designated as "sick." The story of madness, as told by anti-psychiatrists, is the story of modernity, with characters imprisoned by the rules of their own interaction, fighting desperately to preserve a precarious status quo with the language of silence, paradox, and tangential response—a fight that in the absence of any conceivable solution also becomes its own end. "Madness," at that stage, feeds on itself, and the partners constitute a perfect machine kept in motion by an ingenious system of checks and balances that every participant has developed over the course of many years.

This existential-phenomenological account of schizogenic dialogues suggests a possible worldview in which Pinter's plays make sense. In Pinter's radio play *A Night Out* (1960), the mother's constant disconfirmation of her son's desires is matched by the latter's inability to choose resolutely for his own freedom. His one gesture of open defiance, when he threateningly lifts that emblem of the family's oppressive domesticity, the kitchen clock, against his old mother, only strengthens the chains that bind him to her by increasing his feelings of guilt. In the final confrontation scene, the mother disqualifies the son's gesture of rebellion by insisting that despite everything he is "really" good, not really bad at all.[9] Her magnanimity puts him into her debt. Albert's final silence allows his mother to entertain hopes of keeping her son from ever escaping her influence, yet is also sufficiently ambiguous to introduce a degree of doubt:

> *She strokes his hand.*
>
> We'll go away ... together.
>
> [*Pause.*]
>
> It's not as if you're a bad boy ... you're a good boy ... I know you are ... it's not as if you're really bad, Albert, you're not ... you're not bad, you're good ... you're not a bad boy, Albert, I know you're not ...
>
> [*Pause.*]
>
> You're good, you're not bad, you're a good boy ... I know you are ... you are, aren't you? (3.3.247)

The final question mark indicates continuation of the same old pattern: the mother, driven by uncertainty, not so much about her son's feelings as about his willingness to hide them from her, will continue to hold him in check with a mixture of wheedling and stubborn refusal to acknowledge the deep-seated resentment that motivates his occasional waywardness.

The same dialogue also draws attention to Pinter's play with dichotomies (here of "good" and "bad"), a feature reminiscent of Laing's "schizogenic" dialogues. It returns in other early Pinter plays, as in the following dialogue from *Night School* (1960):

> MILLY. I don't want the milk hot, I want it cold.
>
> ANNIE. It is cold.
>
> MILLY. I thought you warmed it up.
>
> ANNIE. I did. The time I got up here it's gone cold.
>
> MILLY. You should have kept it in the pan. If you'd brought it up in the pan it would have still been hot.

ANNIE. I thought you said you didn't want it hot.

MILLY. I don't want it hot.

ANNIE. Well, that's why I'm saying it's cold.

MILLY. I know that. But if I had wanted it hot. That's all I'm saying. (*She sips the milk.*) It could be colder. (216).

One could easily dismiss such dialogue as an instance of verbal tomfoolery; Pinter, after all, writes masterful comedy, often based on music hall routines. Traditionally, comedians have been as much alive to the bewildering absurdities of interaction as R. D. Laing and other anti-psychiatrists are. Yet, the alternation of "hot" and "cold" in this passage is not just comical; it occurs within a context of mutual disqualification that is presented for its tragic, existential reality. Pinter shares with Laing the conviction that a truly shared experience, based on mutual trust and the belief in a common truth, is out of most people's reach. Locked into ourselves, each of us peers out anxiously for a confirmation of our self-image and our understanding of the world, while the same anxiety prevents us from granting it willingly to others.

Mirror Palace

The schizogenic conversation between father, mother, and son—quoted earlier on—is as dramatically effective as a Pinter dialogue and for similar reasons. Its dramatic quality results from the contrast between its appearance of simplicity and its actual relational complexity, structurally present in the form of contradiction and disqualification. In other words: it simultaneously promises and resists sense—the latter because of its structural density. Its promise of sense calls for the outsider's participation in constructing the meaning of what appears temptingly meaningful, but its structural obscurity frustrates and confuses. In *Self and Others* (1961), and later in *Interpersonal Perception: A Theory and a Method of Research* (1966), R. D. Laing (in the second work, in collaboration with H. Phillipson and A. R. Lee) outlines schematically what is involved in making sense of incongruent interaction patterns. The method, as he explains in *Reason and Violence* (1964), is based on Jean-Paul Sartre's *Critique of Dialectical Reason* (1960), an existential-phenomenological account of the individual in group (159). In that work, Sartre attempts to totalize the fragmented views of individuals with which existentialism customarily deals. Like Sartre, R. D. Laing insists on the crucial role of empathy: "One has to be able to orientate oneself as a person on the other's scheme of things rather than only to see the other as an object in one's own world, i.e. within the total system of one's own reference" (*Divided Self* 25). Laing, Phillipson, and Lee developed a simple notation system to represent the process of reciprocal monitoring whereby each partner in an interaction anticipates the other's moves and that accounts for the dialogues' apparent disconnectedness.

Each person not only tries to guess what the other is thinking of her, but also of what the other is thinking that she is thinking of the other, and even what the other is thinking that she is thinking that the other is thinking of her, and so on. This increasing complexity of speculative empathetic insight is presented as an ascending series of logical "levels," intimating the interactional superiority of the one who achieves the highest level of insight. The obvious analogy here is that of two people engaged in a game of poker or chess, where the best player is the one able to forecast the greatest number of scenarios, consisting not only of every possible move, but also of responses to an antagonist's responses to each of those moves. *Interpersonal Perception* proposes the following formulaic notations to represent the various levels of empathetic insight:

A (B)	how A sees B	direct perspective
A (B (A))	how A sees B seeing A	metaperspective
A (B (A (B)))	how A sees B seeing A seeing B	meta-metaperspective

The B character is engaged in a similar series of theoretically open-ended conjectures, resulting in a view of interaction as a "vortex" or system of interlocking spiral perspectives. Interaction, in that view, is a hazardous venture in which each participant tries to foresee not only the other's next move, but also the other's knowledge of his own moves and of what he thinks the other knows about his knowledge of the other's moves, and so on.

Since no one has immediate access to the other's experience, all knowledge revolves around close observation. Laing, Phillipson, and Lee conjure up the gaze's theoretically limitless reciprocal refractions in the eyes of two people facing each other. In their vision, "the human race is a myriad of refractive surfaces staining the white radiance of eternity. Each surface refracts the refraction of refractions of refractions. Each self refracts the refractions of others' refractions of self's refractions of others' refractions ..." (3). Such a dizzying mirror palace is also Len's haunted world in Pinter's *The Dwarfs* (1960): "What you are, or appear to be to me, or appear to be to you," he says to Mark,

> changes so quickly, so horrifyingly, I certainly can't keep up with it and I'm damn sure you can't either. But who you are I can't even begin to recognize, and sometimes I recognize it so wholly, so forcibly, I can't look, and how can I be certain of what I see? You have no number. Where am I to look; where am I to look, what is there to locate, so as to have some surety, to have some rest from this whole bloody racket? You're the sum of so many reflections. How many reflections? Whose reflections? Is that what you consist of? (112).

Laing explored the poetic potential of what he called the "spiral of interpersonal perception" in a well-known little work *Knots*. For Pinter characters it is often a source not of wonder but of anxiety—and it is not by accident that the one character who professes such keen awareness of identity as endless reflections, namely Len, is also the most distinctly schizophrenic one.

It is this philosophy of uncertainty about the other's intentions that made Pinter declare that "communication is too alarming. [....] To disclose to others the poverty within us is too fearsome a possibility" and that made him characterize speech as "a necessary avoidance, a violent, sly, anguished or mocking smoke screen which keeps the other in its place" ("Writing for the Theatre" 14-15). Laing and his collaborators suggest a possible rationale for such a view by stating that "[h]uman beings are constantly thinking about others and about what others are thinking about them, and what others think they are thinking about the others, and so on. One may be wondering about what is going on inside the other. One desires or fears that other people will know what is going on inside oneself" (23). When the sense of self becomes so vulnerable to the vicissitudes of human interaction, language indeed becomes, as Pinter phrases it, a "continual evasion, desperate rearguard attempts to keep ourselves to ourselves" ("Writing for the Theatre" 15).

Panoptical Delirium

Of course, Pinter is not the only one who writes plays that involve games of intense mutual awareness; the difference is that Pinter takes these games one or two steps further than others. The dynamics of an emotionally charged play such as O'Neill's *Long Day's Journey into Night* (1956) are based on the fairly straightforward, empathetic paradigm, "I know that you know." The play emphasizes the examining, scrutinizing "stare," both of the accuser and accused. Husband and sons watch Mary for proof of her drug use, and Mary, as Jamie puts it perhaps best, "watches us watching her—" (1.38). And it is a character's knowledge of the knowledge of others that motivates attempts at evasion or escape. "I knew you knew," says Mary (M), explaining to Edmund (E) why she, at one point, preferred him to stay away from home. Edmund's presence is unbearable to Mary because she believes she understands how he sees her:

$$M (E (M) = E (M)$$

It is guilt that drives each character to superb feats of self-revealing and self-justifying rhetoric, the main attraction of O'Neill's drama. And spectators become involved because, though the dialogue meanders between the desire to uncover and the desire to conceal, its circuitous path eventually leads towards some kind of revelation, an uncovering of the past, an unveiling of an identity.

Pinter's characters never even attempt such an exposure. As Ronald Knowles explains, Pinter cuts out expositions and resolutions (16-17).

And indeed, in his short essay, "Writing for the Theatre," Pinter admits he is not keen on "the last act 'resolution,'" and refuses to satisfy our desire for proof and verification (12). Trapped in a panoptical machine of greater sophistication than that of O'Neill, the watcher remains the prisoner of his own gaze. Unable not to look in the mirror of each other's eyes, each character falls victim to his or her own reflection. The result is a paralyzing guardedness or a self-conscious strutting and prancing—neither of which elicits the least acknowledgement from the interlocutor, whose evasions are motivated by similar reasons. Or as Trilling Ossia remarked in an early essay on Pinter, "statement and counter-statement endlessly revolv[e] around a central core of dissension without ever achieving resolution" (190).

For a spectator, the pleasure of watching a Pinter play lies not in discovering the truth but in following the complex games of matching or mismatching perspectives. In *The Caretaker* (1960) this mechanism of incessant mutual monitoring adds depth to an otherwise trivial exchange between Mick and Davies about Mick's brother, Aston. For Davies, who depends on the hospitality of others, a good relationship with Mick, the owner of the room, could give him better footing in his dealings with Aston. When he thinks to have rightly judged Mick's disappointment in his brother's lack of efficiency, he seizes the opportunity to side up with Mick against Aston:

> DAVIES: Well ... he's a funny bloke, your brother.
>
> MICK: What?
>
> DAVIES: I was saying, he's ... he's a bit of a funny bloke, your brother.
>
> Mick *stares at him.*
>
> MICK: Funny? Why?
>
> DAVIES: Well ... he's funny ...
>
> MICK: What's funny about him?
>
> *Pause.*
>
> DAVIES: Not liking work.
>
> MICK: What's funny about that?
>
> DAVIES: Nothing.
>
> *Pause.*
>
> MICK: I don't call it funny.
>
> DAVIES: Nor me. (2.58-59)

Calling Aston "a funny bloke" is the closest Davies (D) comes to revealing his direct perspective of Aston (A), and he does this only because he believes

Mick (M) shares his view. Using Laing, Phillipson, and Lee's notation, the situation can be represented as follows:

$$D(M(A)) \overset{?}{=} M(A)$$

The scene derives its momentum from the uncertain matching of Mick's direct perspective with Davies's meta-perspective of Aston. Simply put, the initial problem is whether the way Davies thinks Mick sees his brother, Aston, is correct. In the course of the dialogue, Davies doubts whether this is actually the case and retracts. Mick's superiority at this point—and throughout the play—is based on his ability to seduce Davies into venturing a direct perspective so that he can reproach him for his views. This suggests that Mick possesses a higher level of mutual awareness than Davies—which can be formulated as follows:

$$M(D(M(A))) = D(M(A))$$
$$D(M(A)) \neq M(A)$$

Whether Mick's view of Aston is correct or not is immaterial. The tension revolves around higher perspectives. Mick's insight in this interaction is superior to that of Davies because his meta-meta-perspective matches Davies's meta-perspective, whereas Davies's meta-perspective does not correspond to Mick's direct perspective of Aston. As Laing, Phillipson, and Lee point out, the matching or mismatching of one person's meta-perspective with the other's direct perspective determines their *understanding* or *misunderstanding* and that of "the one person's meta-metaperspective and the other person's metaperspective on the same issue [signifies] *realization* or *failure of realization* [of understanding or misunderstanding]" (62). Alternatively and more elegantly put, Mick understands Davies, but Davies does not understand Mick; and Mick realizes this, whereas Davies does not. The algorithm is useful because it visually demonstrates the required depth of empathetic insight a spectator needs in order to achieve a basic understanding of this deceptively simple exchange.

Some Pinter plays articulate the game of interlocking spiral perspectives more emphatically. This is the case, for instance, with *A Slight Ache* (1959) that takes place at high summer, when luscious abundance signals pending decay. Edward has just reassured himself he is still in control of his surroundings by killing a wasp, an exercise to which he brings all the cunning and resolve of a battle commander. Yet his all too easily gained self-confidence is shattered by the unmoving presence of an old man at the back gate, apparently a match seller. Edward's wife Flora is quick to notice her husband's growing apprehension. He resents her solicitude, however, as it confirms his fears that she knows of the insecurity beneath his assurance. He turns on her fiercely, denying she possesses any knowledge while firmly asserting his own:

> EDWARD: No, you're a woman, you know nothing. [*Slight pause.*] But he [the match seller] possesses other faculties. Cunning. The man's an imposter and he knows I know it.
>
> FLORA: I'll tell you what. Look. Let me speak to him. I'll speak to him.
>
> EDWARD [*quietly*]: And I know he knows I know it.
>
> FLORA: I'll find out all about him, Edward. I promise you I will.
>
> EDWARD: And he knows I know.
>
> FLORA: Edward! Listen to me! I can find out all about him, I promise you. I shall go and have a word with him now. I shall ... get to the bottom of it.
>
> EDWARD: You? It's laughable. (189)

The paradigm, explicitly referred to here, requires the audience to match Edward's meta-meta-perspective—in this case one that Edward explicitly articulates:

$$M(E(M)) = E(M)$$
$$E(M(E(M))) = M(E(M))$$

The match seller (M) understands how Edward (E) views him, but Edward claims superiority because he realizes that the match seller understands him whereas the match seller presumably does not know this. Edward's identity revolves around his control over his immediate environment; his masculinity is dependent upon his ability to maintain the myth of his superior insight—namely, that he knows the other knows he knows. And yet, this superior insight renders him particularly vulnerable. To be valid, it has to be verified: it requires an unspoken counterstatement, "I know that you know that I know that you know," in other words, a recognition of that second order putative insight.

$$M(E(M(E(M)))) \stackrel{?}{=} E(M(E(M)))$$

And it is in an attempt to gain this recognition that Edward finally exposes his ignorance. He invites the mysterious match seller into his house to demonstrate his greater insight and self-assurance, but in the end, the old man's silence is so unnerving that it forces Edward to reveal his lack of knowledge. He ventures into a series of increasingly improbable conjectures until he is finally driven to concede his ignorance, asking the match seller, "who are you?" (199). With this simple question, revealing the hollowness of his understanding, he collapses and loses house and wife to the invader.

Smarter Pinter characters use a more circumspect method to assert their superiority. In *Betrayal* (1978), Jerry meets Robert, thinking the latter has only the night before been informed of his wife's affair with him. Since Robert is his best friend, he is understandably nervous. In the movie version, Ben Kingsley's—that is, Robert's—blankly staring eyes offer little comfort to the miserable Jerry, who finally musters up the courage to tackle the difficult issue. His starting point is the usual "I know that you know":

JERRY: I know about last night. She told me about it. You were up all night, weren't you?

ROBERT: That's correct.

JERRY: And she told you ... last night ... about her and me. Did she not?

ROBERT: No, she didn't. She didn't tell me about you and her last night. She told me about you and her four years ago.

Pause.

So she didn't have to tell me again last night. Because I knew. And she knew I knew because she told me herself four years ago.

Silence

JERRY: What?

ROBERT: I think I will sit down.

He sits.

I thought you knew.

JERRY: Knew what?

ROBERT: That I knew. That I've known for years. I thought you knew that.

JERRY: You thought I knew?

ROBERT: She said you didn't. But I didn't believe that.

Pause.

Anyway I think I thought you knew. But you say you didn't? (2. 181-82)

Jerry (J) wonders whether he understands how Robert (R) sees him:

$$J(R(J)) \stackrel{?}{=} R(J)$$

He clearly does not. Robert has the superior insight because his meta-meta-perspective is correct.

$$R(J(R(J))) = J(R(J))$$

The scene is pleasantly confusing because of the repetition of the verbs "to think," "to tell," and "to know" in various combinations and tenses. Of crucial importance here is knowledge that characters hold or claim to hold over one another. The meaning of the scene depends on whether Robert truly thought Jerry knew he knew or whether he preferred to think so in order not to have to inform Jerry and thus preserve the superiority of his own knowledge: I know that he does not know that I know. If Robert knew about the affair all these years, who in the end was cheating whom? Jerry, who thought he was cheating on Robert by having an affair with his wife, has been cheated by the man he is deceiving; and Robert together with his wife Emma, who knew that Jerry did not know that Robert knew about the affair, have been the knowing observers of Jerry's deceptive displays of friendship. Whenever the two men meet, Emma watches her husband fooling Jerry who, in his innocence, thinks he is fooling Robert. So a sort of conspiracy came into being between husband and wife that leaves Jerry out in the cold, while Jerry was all along convinced that he had established a conspiracy with Emma that excluded his friend Robert. Emma here plays an ambiguous role. The two men indeed do not need to play squash. They are involved in a much more intricate game in which Emma is the "ball." And it seems that Robert is the better player, especially since all that time he himself has been having numerous affairs and thus is also cheating on Emma. Rather than moving forward towards a disclosure of some ultimate truth, the action in *Betrayal* moves backward in time, juxtaposing scenes so as to demonstrate the deceptions wrought by memory.

Smashing the Mirror

The algorithms cited above trace the many levels of reflections that Quigley's pragmatic analyses of Pinterian confrontation scenes take into account, visualizing their logical complexity. It appears then that confrontations in Pinter revolve no longer around "truth" but around matching or mismatching perspectives. Knowledge is no longer of someone but rather of someone's perception. And this distinguishes Pinter's drama from O'Neill's. The correctness of Edmund's view of Mary is confirmed when we learn that Mary is indeed back on drugs; and so we also know that Mary is correct when she knows that Edmund knows. In Pinter, knowledge consists rather of a correct guessing and successful parrying of another's knowledge of one's own perceptions.[10] Yet while a Pinter play is a mirror palace, truth is not absent. It is the monster lurking behind the mirror. When it pounces, the consequences are disastrous: a room is invaded, a man is kidnapped, a friendship is betrayed, a man is murdered.

Instead of mirroring the soul, eyes mirror other eyes that serve as mirrors to their own mirroring. Characters who follow the adage, "I know it when I see it" rarely fare well in Pinter plays. In *The Collection* (1961), James insists on seeing the man, Bill, with whom his wife claims to have had a recent affair: "I want to see what he's like. It'll be instructive, educational," he tells his wife Stella. "He'll know me when he sees me," says James to Harry, refusing to reveal his identity over the phone (121). He repeats the phrase when Bill finally answers the phone: "You'll know me when you see me" (126). And when James suddenly appears at their door, Harry reports to Bill, "You'd know him if you saw him" (140). But the more James gets to see, the less he knows. Instead of uncovering the truth, James only becomes more deeply entangled in deceptions. Bill at one moment claims not even to know his wife: "Wouldn't know her if I saw her. Pure fantasy" (154). Ironically, the one who thinks he knows is in the weakest position. James, the bearer of what he believes to be the truth, is trapped between two realities or perhaps fantasies, that of his wife and that of her alleged lover. At the end of the play we learn that nothing at all happened, or rather that Bill and Stella just fantasized about what they could have done if they were to be unfaithful to their partners ... or perhaps they did nothing of the kind; perhaps they never even met. James, who so brazenly confronted Stella and Bill with his superior knowledge, is left at their mercy:

> You just sat and talked about what you would do if you went to your room. That's what you did.
>
> *Pause.*
>
> Didn't you?
>
> *Pause.*
>
> That's the truth ... isn't it?

As the final stage direction reads, "Stella looks at him, neither confirming nor denying. Her face is friendly, sympathetic" (157). She wins this game because, unlike James, she does not depend on anyone: "I don't need to look, do I? I know what I've got" (139).

It finally boils down to what James knows about himself—for instance, about the intentions behind his desire to make the acquaintance of the homosexual Bill. As Bill points out, you may think you know what you look like, but you see yourself only in mirrors. And mirrors are "deceptive" (146). Knowledge that depends on perception is vulnerable to the distortions of the senses. "When we look into a mirror we think the image that confronts us is accurate," Pinter says in his Nobel lecture, returning to an image that haunts his dramatic work. "But move a millimetre and the image changes. We are actually looking at a never-ending range of reflections." Given the distortions of the senses, discovering the truth requires no negotiations. It is mainly a matter of conviction, requiring an energetic sweeping away of subtleties and a refusal to be caught in the web of reflections. Exploring the range of reflections is what Pinter does best as a dramatist, but "sometimes," he explains, "a writer has to smash the mirror —for it is on the other side of that mirror that the truth stares at us."

I believe that despite the enormous odds which exist, unflinching, unswerving, fierce intellectual determination, as citizens, to define the real truth of our lives and our societies is a crucial obligation which devolves upon us all. It is in fact mandatory.

NOTES

[1–2] Austin's *How to Do Things With Words* was published in 1962. The lectures on which it is based were delivered in 1955.

[3] Other examples are R. P. Murphy, "Non-Verbal Communication and the Overlooked Action in Pinter's *The Caretaker," Quarterly Journal of Speech* 58 (1972): 41-47, and I. Müller-Zannoth's "Der Dialog in Harold Pinters Dramen: Aspekte seiner kommunikativen Funktion," *Angelsächsische Sprache und Literatur* 48 (Bern, Frankfurt a.M.: Europäische Hochschulschriften, Reihe XIV, 1977). These two references are mentioned in another similar approach by Ewald Mengel, "Das Sozialpsychologische Konzept des Self-Monitoring als Schlüssel zum Verständnis von Harold Pinters Dramen," *Poetica: Zeitschrift für Sprach- und Literaturwissenschaft* 17 (1985): 131-148.

[4] Other examples include Burton's *Dialogue and Discourse: A Sociolinguistic Approach to Modern Drama Dialogue and Naturally Occurring Conversation* (London: Routledge and Kegan Paul, 1980); "Making Conversation: On Conversational Analysis, Stylistics, and Pinter," *Language and Style* 12 (1979): 188-200. See for a discussion of this approach Susan Hollis Merritt's *Pinter in Play: Critical Strategies and the Plays of Harold Pinter* (Durham and London: Duke UP, 1990) 164-66.

[5] This belief is expressed in different ways in Wittgenstein's *Philosophical Investigations*, as, for instance, in 421: "Look at the sentence as an instrument, and at its sense as its employment" [trans. G.E.M. Anscombe, 3d Ed. (New York: Macmillan, 1989)].

[6] Quigley further pursues this inquiry elsewhere, for instance, in "The Temporality of Structure in Pinter's Plays," *Pinter Review* 1 (1987): 7-21.

[7] The passage is also quoted in Ewald Mengel, "Das Sozialpsychologische Konzept des Self-Monitoring als Schlüssel zum Verständnis von Harold Pinters Dramen." *Poetica: Zeitschrift für Sprach- und Literaturwissenschaft* 17 (1985):131.

[8] This dialogue is also quoted in R. D. Laing's *The Politics of Experience* (1967). The analysis is mine, not Laing's.

[9] Terms such as disqualification, disconfirmation, imperviousness, as distinct negative responses in an interaction, appear in many types of pragmatic analyses and are explained in Paul Watzlawick et al. (1968).

[10] Pinter finds it quite irritating when critics point out the occasional moment in his plays when a character's knowledge seems to be confirmed by a self-revealing monologue, as happens in *The Caretaker* when Aston talks to Davies about his history of mental problems. But, as Pinter explains, "the one thing that people have missed is that it isn't necessary to conclude that everything Aston says about his experiences in the mental hospital is true" (Bensky 28). In other words, the interrelational function of that monologue is important, not its possible truth. Davies believes he now possesses a trump card he can play out in his dealings with Mick. In communicating what

he thinks to be his correct knowledge of Aston, he discloses his own intentions—a mistake that Mick is keen to exploit.

WORKS CITED

Ashworth, Arthur. "New Theatre: Ionesco, Beckett, Pinter." *Southerly* 22 (1962).

Austin, J. L. *How to Do Things With Words.* Cambridge: Harvard UP, 1962.

Bensky, Lawrence M. "Harold Pinter: An Interview." *Pinter: A Collection of Critical Essays.* Ed. Arthur Ganz Englewood-Cliffs, N.J.: Prentice Hall, 1972. 19-33. Reprinted from: George Plimpton, ed. *Writers at Work: The Paris Review Interviews.* Third Series. (1967).

Billington, Michael. *The Life and Work of Harold Pinter.* London: Faber, 1996.

Bloom, Harold. Introduction. *Harold Pinter.* Ed. Harold Bloom. Modern Critical Views. New York: Chelsea House, 1987.

Bowen, John. "Accepting the Illusion." *Twentieth Century* 169 (1961).

Burton, Deirdre. "Conversation Pieces." Carter and Burton 86-115.

Carter, Ronald and Deirdre Burton. *Literary Text and Language Study: Explorations in Language Study.* London: Arnold, 1982.

Esslin, Martin. Review of *The Pinter Problem,* by Austin E. Quigley. *Journal of Beckett Studies* 2 (1977).

—. *The Theatre of the Absurd.* Anchor Books. Garden City, N.Y.: Doubleday, 1961.

Gabbard, Lucina P. *The Dream Structure of Pinter's Plays: A Psychoanalytic Approach.* Rutherford, N.J.: Fairleigh Dickinson U.P., 1976.

Gautam, Kripa K. "Pinter's *The Caretaker:* A Study in Conversational Analysis." *Journal of Pragmatics: An Interdisciplinary Bi-Monthly of Language Studies* (1987) 49-59.

Gordon, Lois G. *Stratagems to Uncover Nakedness: The Dramas of Harold Pinter.* Missouri Literary Frontiers Series 6. Columbia: U of Missouri P, 1969.

Gussow, Mel. "Stan, don't let them tell you what to do." Interview with Harold Pinter December 1988. *Conversations with Pinter.* New York: Limelight Editions, 1994.

Hayman, Ronald. *Harold Pinter.* Contemporary Playwrights. London: Heinemann, 1968.

Hays, H. R. "Transcending Naturalism." *Modern Drama* 4 (1962).

Hinchliffe, Arnold P. *Harold Pinter.* Revised edition. Boston: Twayne, 1981.

Hudson, Liam. "Intimate War Games." *TLS* 9 April 1976: 415.

Kendon, Adam, Richard M. Harris, and Mary Ritchie Key. *Organization of Behavior in Face-to-Face Interaction.* The Hague: Mouton, 1975.

Knowles, Ronald. *Understanding Harold Pinter.* Columbia: U of South Carolina P, 1995.

Laing, R. D. *The Divided Self: An Existential Study in Sanity and Madness.* London: Tavistock, 1969.

—. *The Politics of Experience.* New York: Pantheon, 1967.

—. *Self and Others.* London: Tavistock, 1961.

Laing, R. D. and D. G. Cooper. *Reason and Violence: A Decade of Sartre's Philosophy 1950-1960.* London: Tavistock, 1964.

Laing, R. D., H. Phillipson, and A. R. Lee. *Interpersonal Perception: A Theory and a Method of Research.* London: Tavistock; New York: Springer, 1966.

Laver, John. "Communicative Functions of Phatic Communion." Kendon, Harris, and Key.

Marcus, Steven. "Madness, Literature, and Society" (1964). *Representations: Essays on Literature and Society.* New York: Random House, 1975.

Miller, Arthur. *Death of a Salesman.* New York: Penguin, 1998.

O'Neill, Eugene. *Long Day's Journey into Night.* New Haven: Yale UP, 1989.

Ossia, Trilling. "The New English Realism." *Tulane Drama Review* 7 (1962).

Peter, John. "Harold Pinter: The Poet of No-Man's Land." *The Sunday Times* 7 October 1990: 7/16.

Pinter, Harold. *Betrayal. Complete Works: Four.* New York: Grove Weidenfeld, 1981. 155-268.

—. *The Caretaker. Complete Works: Two.* New York: Grove Weidenfeld, 1977. 16-87.

—. *The Collection. Complete Works: Two.* New York: Grove Weidenfeld, 1977. 119-157.

—. *The Dwarfs. Complete Works: Two.* New York: Grove Weidenfeld, 1977. 89-117.

—. "A Letter to Peter Wood" (1958). *Drama* 142 (1981).

—. *A Night Out. Complete Works: One.* New York: Grove Weidenfeld, 1976. 201-247.

—. *Night School. Complete Works: Two.* New York: Grove Weidenfeld, 1977. 197-233.

—. *A Slight Ache. Complete Works: One.* New York: Grove Weidenfeld, 1976. 167-200.

—. "Writing for Myself." *Complete Works: Two.* New York: Grove Weidenfeld, 1977. 9-12.

—. "Writing for the Theatre." *Complete Works: One.* New York: Grove Weidenfeld, 1976. 9-16.

Quigley, Austin E. *The Pinter Problem.* Princeton: Princeton UP, 1975.

Sakellaridou, Elizabeth. *A Study of Female Characters in the Plays of Harold Pinter.* Totowa, N.J.: Barnes & Noble, 1988.

Shannon, Claude E. and Warren Beaver. *The Mathematical Theory of Communication.* Urbana: U of Illinois P, 1964.

Toynbee, Polly. "The Master of Strident Silences." *Guardian Weekly* 14 October 1990:2 4.

Van Laan, Thomas. "*The Dumb Waiter:* Pinter's Play with the Audience." *Modern Drama* 24 (1981): 494-502.

Watzlawick, Paul, Janet Helmick Beavin, and Don D. Jackson, *Pragmatics of Human Communication: A Study of Interactional Patterns, Pathologies, and Paradoxes.* Mental Research Institute, Palo Alto, Cal. London: Faber, 1968.

White, Kenneth S. *Savage Comedy: Structures of Humor.* Amsterdam: Rodopi, 1978.

Wilden, Anthony. *The Rules Are No Game: The Strategy of Communication.* London: Routledge & Kegan Paul, 1987.

The Homecoming to *No Man's Land*

JOHN PETER

I saw the premiere production of *No Man's Land*, starring John Gielgud and Ralph Richardson, four times. On the last occasion, I took two very senior *Sunday Times* colleagues with me. One was a leading music critic, the other a most distinguished literary critic and editor who had been a friend of Virginia Woolf and was one of the last survivors of the Bloomsbury circle. The two old men were both known for being opinionated and having sharp tongues. The three of us together were just over two hundred years old.

Walking away from the theatre afterwards, my guests were silent for a while. Finally, one of them said: "That was a most interesting play. Most interesting. Fascinating. I've no idea what it was about but it was absolutely riveting."

This was an extraordinary admission from a cultivated and notoriously opinionated old man who was still a practising critic. Normally, he would have thought that a play he could not understand was simply rubbish. But perhaps he felt, and perhaps on some level he knew, that *No Man's Land* was something else. It had something that held him, riveted his attention, and perhaps disturbed him. It was not rubbish.

Such reactions are an enigma and a warning. What a play is about and what it means are not the same thing; and in one sense it would be a mistake to talk about the "meaning" of a play. Can a play, strictly speaking, "mean" anything, in the sense that a word or a sentence "mean" something? I am not qualified to tackle this subject, except to say that the nearest we can come to a play's meaning is to say that all plays are conflicts, and then to discover, if we can, an intention, conscious or unconscious, by the dramatist to reveal the nature of that conflict and the forces that caused it.

On one level, *No Man's Land* is about two elderly men in a room, trying to form a relationship, compelled to form, unable to form, resisting the compulsion to form a relationship which is mutually suspicious, mutually belligerent, reluctantly desired, compulsively needed. That is what the play is "about." What it "means," what drives the play, the emotional-psychological atom of enriched uranium at its centre is what had brought these two elderly literati together in the first place.

Spooner never calls Hirst by his name. Hirst never calls his guest Spooner. In Act Two, after waking from a nap, or perhaps a good night's sleep, he calls him Charles. Later again, he calls him Charles Wetherby. Spooner doesn't protest. Foster and Briggs, Hirst's manservants, introduce themselves to Spooner who returns the compliment, calling himself Spooner, not Charles. That is in Act One. In Act Two, Hirst addresses Briggs as Denson. Briggs doesn't protest either; nor does anyone else.

The point is that names do "mean" something. The name Hirst "means," certainly refers to, the person who bears it. In *No Man's Land*, identities shift, or remain obscure, as they sometimes do in dreams. Hirst and Spooner clearly have shared experiences. The two men appear to be mysteriously bonded to each other. Spooner notices that there are two mugs on the shelf in Hirst's drawing room; the second, Hirst says, is for Spooner. Spooner, who had clearly never been here before, nor indeed met Hirst before, does not react. Hirst seems to know things about Spooner; he can predict what Spooner is going to say and what he can or cannot remember. They talk about Spooner's wife, who had apparently left him, almost as if she could have been the wife of either of them. The erotic past of each man seems to resemble, to overlap, to echo the other's. There is almost a suggestion of wife-swapping or mistress-swapping which causes tension and indignation between them, but no breach. Hirst threatens Spooner with horse-whipping, but he does nothing; neither does he throw Spooner out of the house. The language of middle-class Englishmen of a certain age, a language which can be both blunt and evasive, heightens the sense of obscurity and uncertainty. Again, you are reminded of dreams in which objects or persons can stand out with unnatural clarity, but their relation to each other remains unexplained. An obscure past seems to be haunting an obscure present. "I have known this before" is a phrase which recurs like a musical motif, reminding you that dreams often feel like reincarnations of memories.

My reading of the play is that it is a drama of a shared dream. Spooner and Hirst are aspects of the same man. Hirst is the man Spooner had once longed to become: wealthy, confident, commanding, at ease. Spooner is the man Hirst might once have been, if success and prosperity had not arrived: anxious, insinuating, restless, insecure, pushy. Hirst's language is bluff, compact, imperious, icily polite; the language of a man who employs staff, lives expensively and belongs to select clubs. Spooner's language is flowery, elaborate, insinuating itself like an unwanted guest; it speaks of the anxiety of a man who has spent his life trying to make an impression.

Spooner's dream is the dream of resentment and anxiety, the kind that can torment the unfulfilled. Look at this, the dream says, I could have become this. Perhaps I can stay with him and be him. Hirst's dream is the dream of uneasy conscience, of the retrospective insecurity which nags those who are fulfilled. Look at this, Hirst's dream says. I was this once. I could have remained the same. I need to see and know what I was and what I could have remained; it validates the man I have become. There is also a sense of shame here which explains the visions of the former self being dead and so relieving the conscience of the present self from having to acknowledge it as a part of himself. And so, the two dreams collide, overlap, enrich each other and cancel each other out. The two men who are one man, are in no man's land, where the dreamer and the one he dreams of are one and the same. The dream will never end, and its subject, which is The Other, the one who haunts The Self, will never be changed.

No Man's Land is, among other things, about anxiety, fear, and the fending off of fear. No other dramatist, not even Strindberg, has written about anxiety and fear with Pinter's insight, clarity and compassion, about the psychology of anxiety and fear, the dynamics of anxiety and fear, the sinister attraction of anxiety and fear. Pinter's work has often been discussed in terms of territorial imperatives, the invader and the invaded. It is more complex than that. Take Davies in *The Caretaker*. His presence irritates Mick, and seems to endanger the safety of his brother Aston. But it was Aston who befriended Davies in the first place, invited him home, offered him shelter. Mick threatens Davies, but never throws him out, which he could easily do. In *A Slight Ache*, The Matchseller is a passive presence whose very passivity is seen as incomprehensible and therefore threatening. But it is Flora and Edward who invite him in, as if fear was an object of fascination, almost of desire. *The Homecoming* is an ironical title. Max's house had once been Teddy's home, but his unexpected homecoming, with an unexpected wife, looks to his father like an invasion until she becomes, materially and erotically, the dominatrix of the family. In *Old Times*, Anna's arrival does turn out to be an invasion of Deeley and Kate's marriage, but it was they who had invited her, and Deeley's attitude to her imminent arrival is one of curiosity and cautious hospitality. And of course, in *No Man's Land* it was Hirst who picked up Spooner on Hampstead Heath, brought him home, and is now offering him whisky, absolutely as it is.

Amateur psychology is a dangerous tool to use in criticism, as it is in life; but I have always wondered whether either or both of my octogenarian guests had a subconscious reaction to *No Man's Land*. They were both the Hirsts of their day. Could they have remained Spooners? Could it have had an obscure fascination for them to see a man of achievement needing to recall the anxieties of past failure, and at the same time consoling itself by the reassurance that failure is only a dream of a memory, a recollection of what could have been but never was?

Some of Pinter's best plays are, in fact, not so much about invasion as about the way the fear of it is transformed into curiosity and desire; the way we try to disarm evil, the way we are fascinated by it, the way we try to neutralize it by offering it our cautious friendship, our conditional protection, and our whisky.

No Man's Land contains one of the most haunting lines Pinter has written. "There are," Hirst says, "places in my heart ... where no living soul ... has ... or can ever ... trespass." Hirst and Spooner are both night visitors, each haunting the other as if trying to trespass his secret heart, each invading the other's past and present, each inviting the invasion, but fearing the encroachment: a mutual homecoming which hurts and is desired.

Fear is a symptom of need. The Self has need of The Other but fears its arrival. The presence of The Other is the price The Self pays for filling up the vacuum of insecurity. In the end, we need both ourselves and each other. No man is an island. Every man is two islands.

I'll drink to that.

Two Ways to Melt with Ruth: Pinter's *Homecoming* and Stoppard's *Night and Day*

RICHARD CORBALLIS

Stoppard and Pinter both began writing plays in the late 1950s, when the English theatre was enjoying a renaissance inspired not only by the work of Osborne, Wesker and other "kitchen sink" realists, but also by influences from abroad, including the Berliner Ensemble's visit to London in 1956 and the London premiere of *Waiting for Godot* in 1955. Pinter got into his stride at once. *The Room* was written and performed (by amateurs in Bristol) in 1957; a professional London production (which opened at the Hampstead Theatre before transferring to the Royal Court) followed in 1960. In the meantime, his first full-length play, *The Birthday Party,* also written in 1957, had opened at the Lyric Theatre, Hammersmith (after a preview at the Arts Theatre, Cambridge) in 1958. These two plays immediately established a hallmark "Pinteresque" style, for which Irving Wardle (in the September/October 1958 issue of *Encore*) coined the title "comedy of menace", [1] though Martin Esslin was almost as quick to enlist Pinter as a fringe exponent of the "theatre of the absurd" (231–57). The style, however we define it, has remained fairly consistent over the years, though the nature of the subject-matter, most critics would agree, has changed at least twice.

Stoppard took much longer to develop a distinctive style. In 1958 he began a play for *The Observer's* playwriting competition, but, in his own words, "it petered out after a dozen pages that were not unlike *Look Back in Anger*" (Stoppard, "The Definite Maybe" 18). A subsequent one-acter, "The Gamblers", eventually staged by amateurs in Bristol in 1965, was, he records, "not unlike *Waiting for Godot*" (*ibid*) or (almost ten years later) "*Waiting for Godot in the Condemned Cell*" (Stoppard, "Ambushes" 4). And "A Walk on the Water", completed in 1960 but subsequently revised and given the title by which it is now known (*Enter a Free Man*), owes much to Arthur Miller and Robert Bolt; Stoppard refers to it diffidently as "Flowering Death of a Cherry Salesman" (Amory 67) or, more simply (to avoid any association with Chekhov, perhaps), as "Flowering Death of a Salesman" (Stoppard, "Ambushes" 4). *Rosencrantz and Guildenstern Are Dead* (1966) is still a very derivative play. Assiduous critics have found echoes of Albee, Genet, Pirandello, Pinter, and James Saunders, as well as the pervasive presence of Beckett's *Godot* (and Shakespeare's *Hamlet,* of course). Not until *Jumpers* did he fully establish his hallmark "high comedy of ideas".

While Stoppard was cultivating other men's flowers in his writing (and, in everyday life, contriving to look like Mick Jagger, whom both he and Pinter subsequently befriended), he was also imitating others in the way he talked about his plays. His early interviews were, as Kenneth Tynan once observed, "worked out beforehand" (54); certain aphorisms recur continually, including one—"I should have the courage of my lack of convictions" (Hayman 2)—that seems to derive from a line in Christopher Hampton's *The Philanthropist*: "I'm a man of no convictions. At least I think I am." But the person that Stoppard imitated most assiduously in his early statements about his craft was Pinter.

Pinter seldom speaks about his writing (or anything else), and when he does, his remarks—at least until recently—have generally been as opaque as those of his characters, who, he has claimed, "tell me so much and no more, with reference to their experience, their aspirations, their motives, their history" (*Plays: One* 13)—and even, we might reasonably add, their names. An oft-quoted refusal to attach any meaning to his plays features in the transcript of a 1961 conversation with Richard Findlater, published as "Writing for Myself":

> I start off with people, who come into a particular situation. I certainly don't write from any kind of abstract idea. And I wouldn't know a symbol if I saw one.... I'm not committed as a writer, in the usual sense of the term, either religiously or politically. And I'm not conscious of any social function. I write because I want to write. (Pinter, *Plays: Two* 10, 12)

In his speech to the 1962 National Student Drama Festival in Bristol he likewise insisted that "what I write has no obligation to anything other than itself" and that "I've never started a play from any kind of abstract idea or theory and never envisaged my own characters as ... allegorical representations of any particular force...." (Pinter, *Plays: One* 10–11). And in his 1970 speech accepting the German Shakespeare Prize, he was still maintaining that:

> where a writer sets out a blueprint for his characters, and keeps them rigidly to it, where they do not at any time upset his applecart, where he has mastered them, he has also killed them, or rather terminated their birth, and he has a dead play on his hands. (Pinter, *Plays: Four* xii)

Stoppard, though always readier than Pinter to discuss his craft, was no less equivocal about the content and genesis of his plays. And he often appeared to mimic Pinter, as when he insisted that "I've written what appealed to me" (Hayman 5), and that "the most widespread misapprehension about playwrights ... is that they set out to say something and then say it, in short that a play is the end product of an idea" (Stoppard, "But for the Middle Classes" 677). It is hard to decide whether this mimicry was conscious or unconscious. Stoppard had evidently admired Pinter from the early 1960s, and botched an opportunity to get to know him while he was still a journalist in Bristol (Nadel 215). Then, in 1967, Pinter sent Stoppard a telegram congratulating him on the success of *Rosencrantz and Guildenstern,* but Stoppard was evidently baffled by the fact that it was signed "PINTA" (Delaney 187).

According to Ira Nadel, "their friendship flourished ... by 1969", when they began playing cricket together (215). Thereafter they attended each other's parties, and offered comfort in times of stress. When Stoppard and Felicity Kendall parted in 1990, for example, Pinter's wife, Antonia Fraser, wrote to Stoppard, assuring him that "we're your pals (I hope) and we're *here* (I know). Also: one does survive, as you may have noticed. Tuesday is our 10th wedding Anniversary. Unbelievable! Or it would have been in July 1975" (Fraser to Stoppard 24/11/90). But, on Pinter's side at any rate, the friendship was not unconditional; when (in 1974) Joeph Losey tried to persuade him to play the Doctor in *The Romantic Englishwoman* (scripted by Stoppard), Pinter turned him down, and Losey had to inform Stoppard that:

> Harold Pinter thinks the script greatly improved but no longer finds the Doctor scene interesting for himself.... Previously found it amusing—now finds it factual and not amusing for himself. (Losey to Stoppard 21/8/74)[2]

In the late 1970s Stoppard's take on his own plays suddenly became less Pinteresque. The erstwhile evasiveness was, he now confessed, "a sort of 'travelling pose'" that "has the overstatement of most epigrams". In fact, he went on, his previous insistence that "the ideas are the end-product of the play, not the other way round ... stopped being applicable round about the time I started writing *Jumpers*" (*Gollob and Roper* 10–11). At about the same time he responded thus to Joost Kuurman's query about the genesis of his plays: "It's an idea.... It starts off with an idea.... Usually one has an idea for a play and then works out some kind of form for it..." (Kuurman 45, 52–3). Of course, he was by now writing overtly political plays, beginning with *Professional Foul* (1977). He was also publicly supporting Amnesty International.

So was Pinter. But, while his political activism goes back at least as far as his protest against the overthrow of Chile's President Allende in 1973, his shift to overtly political plays[3]—"from dialogue to denunciation", as

Alan Franks puts it (4)—post-dated Stoppard's by several years: "Precisely" was first performed in 1983, followed by *One for the Road* in 1984, and the more substantial *Mountain Language* in 1988. By now he had cautiously begun to talk more frequently and frankly about his work, beginning with the 1980 interview with Miriam Gross. So what began as the younger playwright's adulation of the older one (in the late 1960s) had become something of a mutual admiration society by the late 1970s, with Pinter sometimes following Stoppard's lead.

To what extent did the admiration extend to their respective plays? Neither seems to have commented publicly on the other's work, except when exchanging tributes on their respective fiftieth birthdays (Nadel 363–4).[4] Critics have often depicted them as rivals, especially when they produced new plays at about the same time (*Night and Day* and *Betrayal* in 1976, *Arcadia* and *Moonlight* in 1993). But I wonder if a curious similarity between Stoppard's *Night and Day* and Pinter's *The Homecoming* may be read as an oblique tribute from the younger playwright to the older one, just at the moment, oddly enough, when Stoppard began to set the pace with respect to political plays and constructive interviews. At least, I believe, a comparison between the two plays will clarify certain aspects of their oft-contrasted styles, and cast light on a curious detail of *The Homecoming*.

Though Peter Hall assigns *The Homecoming* (1965) to Pinter's "great middle period" (147), it is more commonly associated with that earlier phase of Pinter's output to which the labels "realism" and "naturalism" have sometimes been applied (e.g. by Knowles 74, 79). The former label, which Pinter himself tentatively endorsed when he told Findlater that "what goes on in my plays is realistic, but what I'm doing is not realism" (Pinter, *Plays: Two* 11), acknowledges the play's "kitchen sink" setting and its oblique structural affinities with the well-made plays in which Pinter, *alias* David Baron, so often acted before he became a successful playwright (and began acting under his real name). The term "naturalism", on the other hand, links Pinter with Zola, Strindberg and other post-Darwinian playwrights of the late nineteenth century who bleakly endorsed the survival of the fittest and its attendant animal imagery. John Lahr, for one, argues that "Harold Pinter … uses the conventions of Naturalism to … chart mankind's evolving sense of its own boundaries" ("Pinter and Chekhov" 61). What both labels fail to acknowledge, however, is the quasi-expressionistic elements that continually disrupt the pervading realism of *The Homecoming* and several of the other early plays, and all but displace it in the "memory plays", beginning with *Landscape*.

The urgent rockings of Rose in *The Room* constitute the earliest example of Pinter's dramatic expressionism. As Rose rocks, she fervently asserts—sometimes to her taciturn husband Bert, sometimes to herself—the superiority of her room (which has a window) to the building's basement (which has no window, and a "ceiling right on top of you"). In her mind Rose converts her tawdry surroundings into a light and spacious area where "You stand a chance" (Pinter, *Plays: One* 105).[5]

In Pinter's subsequent plays the characters' dreams take them through the window to outdoor settings, which are generally near water. In *The Birthday Party* the possibility that Stanley might evade his persecutors by abandoning Meg's boarding house for the nearby beach remains implicit, though Lulu does her best to persuade him to leave the house: "Come out and get a bit of air.... It's lovely out. And I've got a few sandwiches" (*Plays: One* 36).

The longing for a watery outdoors first becomes explicit in *A Slight Ache* (1958), towards the end of which the housebound Edward paints a "*nostalgic*" picture of an outdoor setting where he "could stand on the hill and look through my telescope at the sea" (*Plays: One* 195). This motif is more explicit still in "The Basement". In 1963 Pinter revisited his early prose-poem "Kullus" and its offshoots, "The Task" (a poem) and "The Examination" (a short story), and reinvented them as a film script called "The Compartment". In 1967 a revised version of "The Compartment", now called "The Basement", screened on BBC Television. Pinter retained the basic theme of two men's struggle for control of a room (and a woman, in the case of "Kullus"), but fragmented the plot, juxtaposing indoor and outdoor settings, summer and winter, night and day, and (for the indoor scenes) radically different furnishings for the basement initially owned by Law, but eventually ceded to Stott.

Most critics agree that these frantic juxtapositions are "taking place in Law's mind" (Billington 191). Dohmen, for example, argues that:

> The dizzying alternations of setting, of decor in the room, and of time from winter to summer, night to day, defy any effort to impose chronology on the action.... Such deliberate disruption of time suggests the workings of the subconscious, and in fact the play can readily be interpreted as Law's fantasy, rather like an enactment of Len's verbalised visions in *The Dwarfs* (189).

I would refine this diagnosis slightly by adding that "Law's fantasy" is conveyed primarily in the exterior scenes, which are generally relaxed and summery—and often located at a beach. The interior scenes, on the other hand, tend to be tense, bleak and wintry; they reflect the reality of Law's situation.

Landscape uses a more coherent version of the same formula. Duff, the realist, sits at the table, talks (on the whole) about mundane things (including inclement weather), and "*refers normally to Beth*", who sits apart, "*never looks at Duff, and does not appear to hear his voice*" (*Plays: Three* 175). That her speeches are dream fantasies is suggested by a number of factors in addition to her apparent failure to hear Duff or to be heard by him. Prominent among these factors is an obsession with the beach. She shares this obsession with Law, with Rebecca in *Ashes to Ashes* (where the dream turns into a nightmare—*Plays 4* 416), with the waiter in *Celebration* (*Celebration & The Room* 72), and with the dreamy characters of *Old Times,* all of whom live by the sea.

Aspects of Beth's style and syntax also suggest her dreaminess. For example, she refuses to ground her discourse in a particular tense; future, present and past (simple and perfect) jostle with each from the play's first two lines:

> I would like to stand by the sea. It is there.... I have. Many times. It's something I cared for. I've done it. (177)

Another telling stylistic quirk is her fondness for ellipses and sentence fragments. Pinter does not always use these to signify dreaminess, of course. In the case of Davies, in *The Caretaker,* for example, they often signify panic. But Beth—like Aston and Ruth, as we shall see shortly—seems to belong to a breed that is impervious to panic. She is not afraid to pause and correct herself ("Two women looked at me, turned and stared. No. I was walking, they were still"—178), and she likewise enjoys the opportunity to repeat herself ("So that I never lost track"—196). In short, unlike Pinter's power-hungry characters (including Duff, I would suggest), she seems to relish indecision, pauses, and silences.

For most of Pinter's characters the "pause" is terrifying—for reasons outlined in his oft-quoted speech at the 1962 National Student Drama Festival:

> When true silence falls we are ... nearer nakedness. One way of looking at speech is to say that it is a constant stratagem to cover nakedness.... I think that we communicate only too well, in our silence, in what is unsaid, and that what takes place is a continual evasion, desperate rear-guard attempts to keep ourselves to ourselves.... To disclose to others the poverty within us is too fearsome a possibility. (*Plays: One* 15)

Austin Quigley draws attention to the power of silence in *The Caretaker*, where "Aston's mode of non-participation, silence, remains a potent threat to Davies, who consistently assumes that Aston is resisting and seeing through the web of fabrication that he profusely spins" (123–4). The character who breaks the silence of a Pinter "pause" (almost always Davies, in *The Caretaker*) is generally the person who is losing the current power struggle: "The ones that keep silent are the best off", as the Man remarks in "Monologue" (*Plays: Four* 125). Those who nonchalantly ride out the pauses are either in control or else blissfully unaware that a struggle is going on. Beth (in *Landscape*) falls into the latter category. So does Aston, who is happy to play around quietly with a toaster or a plug while Davies directs a torrent of anxious language in his direction. When Aston does deliver speeches of any length, they are in the languid, elliptical style of Beth. The first of these is his account (shortly before Mick's first entrance) of the woman in the café who talked about her holiday on "the south coast" before suggesting that she might "have a look at [his] body" (33–35). Here is the sea imagery again—albeit at one remove from the dreamer. In the big monologue that closes Act 2 there are no references to the sea, but, like the slightly earlier speech about the shed that he hopes to build (49–50), it depicts the outdoors (in this case "the garden") as a refuge from the claustrophobia (and worse) of what Pinter elsewhere calls *The Hothouse*. The hallucinatory quality of this speech is enhanced by an unusual lighting cue: "*During Aston's speech the room gets gradually darker. By the close of the speech only Aston can be seen clearly.*" As I shall suggest presently, Stoppard manipulates the lighting in a similar way in *Night and Day.*

In *The Homecoming* it is Joey who most closely resembles Aston. Although he purports to be a boxer, his prospects in the ring would appear to be limited, if Max is correct in his claim that "you don't know to defend yourself, and you don't know how to attack" (*Plays: Three* 33)—a claim that Max substantiates when he floors Joey at the end of Act 1. Unlike Max and Lenny—and, in their more covert fashion, Teddy and Sam—Joey eschews power games and is happy to acknowledge the gentler side of life, most famously when, returning from a long but unconsummated off-stage liaison with Ruth, he insists that "sometimes you can be happy without going the whole hog. Sometimes you can be happy without going any hog" (84). Paul Rogers, who played Max in the inaugural production, maintains that "Joey is the one person in that family whom they all really rather love.... Joey's in a way a very balanced character. Almost sweet" (Lahr, "Interview" 158–9). Rolf Fjelde adds that Joey is "the only one who neither shares nor needs the ritual cigar" (102).

Like Pinter's other "sweet" characters (including Aston and Beth), Joey lets his thoughts stray from time to time to the world outside, though Lenny is quick to convert the most extended of these dreams into a sordid account of sexual bravado (without "contraceptive protection") in the neighbourhood of Wormwood Scrubs (82–4).[6] In the *Maestà* (or *Pietà*?) that closes the play, it is Joey who plays Christ (or Saint John?) to Ruth's Madonna. This closeness is appropriate, since she too is, in a rather different way, impervious to the aggression of the play's "three bears": Max, Lenny and Sam.[7] Part of her strength derives from the fact that, like Pinter's other female characters with four-letter names (Beth, Kate and Anna), she is happy to dream about a watery outdoors. Shortly after arriving at Teddy's family home in London she actually has the temerity to physically venture outside in the dead of night. Then, in the second act, in the course of explaining to Lenny her former career as "a model for the body" (whatever that may mean, exactly),[8] she adopts the more familiar tactic of conjuring up a sunlit scene beside water—not this time the sea, but a lake:

> Once or twice we went to a place in the country, by train. Oh, six or seven times. We used to pass a … a large white water tower. This place … this house … was very big … the trees … there was a lake, you see … we used to change and walk down towards the lake … we went down a path … on stones … there were … on this path. Oh, just … wait … yes … when we changed in the house we had a drink. There was a cold buffet.
>
> *Pause.*
>
> Sometimes we stayed in the house but … most often … we walked down to the lake … and did our modelling there. (73)

Ruth's claim that she modelled in a big house by a lake is as dubious as Beth's account of a tryst on a lonely beach. The languid prose suggests that both may be imagining something that never was. Pinter generally incorporates little semiotic clues in the staging to indicate the commencement of dream sequences such as these. In *The Room* it is Rose's retreat to her rocking chair; in *Landscape* it is Beth's distance from the table, which is firmly grasped by the down-to-earth Duff. In *The Homecoming* the clue is the stage direction that introduces Ruth's account of her lakeside modelling:

> *She closes her eyes.*
>
> LENNY *appears from* U.L.
>
> *He walks into the room and sits near her.*
>
> *She opens her eyes.*
>
> *Silence.* (72)

The fact that Ruth closes her eyes may be enough—at least in a small theatre—to indicate to the audience that a dream sequence is about to begin. The film version shows in close-up this closing of the eyes, and when Ruth reopens them, a longer shot reveals that, without any aural or visual clue, Teddy has vanished and Lenny has appeared beside Ruth. It is as if she has conjured him up. On a big stage the mysterious, dream-like nature of Lenny's entrance has to be suggested by other means. Three pages earlier (69) Lenny left the house to go to the gym with Joey and Max. They must have exited through "the front door U.R."—the only outside door specified in the opening description of the set (21) and the only one used by characters exiting the house. The opening description also specifies "a staircase ascending U.L., well in view". Early in Act 1 Lenny's first exit involves "turning to his right" (30). This takes him away from the front door, which is "U.R." (and therefore to Lenny's left as he leaves the main stage). This exit presumably takes him not to the street, but to his bedroom, whence he reappears two pages later before leaving the house (through the "front door"—33). The existence and location of this downstairs bedroom is explained a little later, when Lenny confronts Teddy for the first time: "I sleep down here now. Next door. I've got a kind of study, workroom cum bedroom next door" (41)—presumably under the stairs, up left.[9] So when Ruth "*closes her eyes*" and "*Lenny appears from U.L.*", he must come from his bedroom. But how did he get there, given the fact that his last exit was through "the front door U.R."? Somehow he has got into his bedroom without re-entering the house.[10] As in the film (but by much subtler means) we get the impression that Ruth has conjured him up. The word "*appears*" (72—in place of the customary "*enters*") reinforces this impression. Ruth then embarks on her dreamily asexual seduction of Lenny pending Joey's return from the gym, for which the standard door to the street ("*U.R.*") is used (74).[11]

Before examining the implications of this interpretation, let us look at a very similar episode at about the same point in Stoppard's *Night and Day*. Here a different Ruth, as bored and dissatisfied with her life in Kambawe (a former British colony in Africa) as Pinter's Ruth is in the American mid-West ("all rock. And sand", with "lots of insects"—69), also conjures up a dream-lover.

The stage-direction that initiates this dream sequence (at the very beginning of Act 2) exists in at least two versions. I quote the revised one from the second edition of the play: "MILNE *stands at the edge of the room, but is at first invisible in the darkness*" (*Night and Day* 1979, 64). The stage-direction goes on to explain that "*he becomes visible as he begins to join in the conversation*", probably as the result of a subtle lighting change, since no move is specified.[12] The ethereal nature of his entry is probably meant to suggest that this Milne is an imaginary character conjured up by Ruth's words—or, as it transpires, her thoughts. The first edition provides an additional clue when it stipulates that "*[Milne] is dressed the way we first saw him*" (*Night and Day* 1978, 64)—i.e. not in the clothes he was wearing when we *last* saw him, at the end of Act 1 as he set out on his ill-fated attempt to interview the leader of Kambawe's rebels. This anomaly—if we are smart enough to recognise its significance—reinforces the impression that this Milne is a figment of Ruth's imagination.

As in Ruth's dream in *The Homecoming*, a curiously asexual seduction ensues, leading to a climax in which Milne and Ruth "*kiss on the mouth, but not passionately, and not holding each other*" (69). The ensuing stage-direction then establishes that the whole episode has been a dream:

> *She lets herself fall over backwards on the sofa. Only her calves and feet are visible....* MILNE *turns and walks upstage into the dark and dis-*

> *appears.* RUTH'*s feet disappear out of sight behind the sofa and then "she" (double) stands up with her back to the audience looking towards where* MILNE *disappeared, undoes her dress and steps out of it (she has nothing on underneath) holding on to the dress with one hand and trailing it after her as she follows* MILNE *into the dark. Before she has disappeared* CARSON *has walked unhurriedly, relaxed, into the room from the study. He lights a cigarette and stands thoughtfully watching as* RUTH *moves into the dark. After a moment or two, behind him,* RUTH'*s voice.... She is lying on the sofa behind* CARSON. (1979, 69–70)

The Ruth who speaks from "*the sofa behind CARSON*" is the "real" Ruth; the one who "*moves into the dark*" is a figment of this "real" Ruth's imagination. The elaborate stage business involving the two Ruths was no doubt designed to "ambush" the audience—a favourite pastime of Stoppard's; we think we are watching the real Ruth and the real Milne, and then he makes us realise that we have been conned. What we have been watching is Ruth's dream about a man who—we soon discover—is already dead.

At least that is what we are *supposed* to realise, but this "ambush" has proved too subtle for many; Stoppard himself has acknowledged that "one found that ... some people weren't quite sure ... afterwards whether it was a fantasy or not. Although there was no way it couldn't be one" (Hardin 160). Those who did not construe the episode as fantasy may have been influenced by the stage direction indicating that Carson "*stands thoughtfully watching as [the dreamt]* RUTH *moves into the dark*". The word "*watching*" suggests that Carson can see this departing "Ruth" (the dreamt Ruth), whereas Stoppard's "ambush" relies on the assumption that she is invisible to all but the "real" Ruth (Ruth the dreamer). Had the literalists been able to see this "real" Ruth "*lying on the sofa*" before the double's exit, they might have realised that Carson was simply staring into space, and thus made sense of the "ambush". But Stoppard keeps the dreaming Ruth out of sight until after the dreamt Ruth's departure. Of course, the replacement of the latter by the former is very difficult to effect, given the fact that—except for the moment when the double takes over the role of the imagined Ruth—both are played by the same actor. Getting her on to the sofa (from her position "*out of sight behind [it]*") without the audience seeing the transfer is technically challenging, and Stoppard (and/or Peter Wood, the director) probably needed Carson's gaze after the departing "Ruth" to draw the audience's attention away from the relocation of the "real" Ruth.[13]

Those of us who pick up all the clues (as perhaps we should, so soon after refreshments during the interval) will understand the cleverly contrived "ambush", and smugly congratulate both Stoppard and ourselves. Those who don't will feel mystified. Mystification was surely not what Stoppard intended, but it is a risk that he often runs in his determination to push our mental dexterity to its limits.

Pinter, on the other hand, often seems to delight in mystification. So his early critics felt, at any rate. A.P. Hinchliffe, for example, noted that audiences were "baffled by *Tea Party* and confounded by *Homecoming*" ("Mr Pinter's Belinda" 173), and Richard Schechner described the early plays as "conceptually incomplete" (177). It was Quigley who came to Pinter's rescue, arguing that there are "different ways in which language can carry information" (26), and that viewers who were "baffled ... and confounded" were approaching Pinter's language in the wrong way. What was needed, he insisted, was not "an implicit belief that language is primarily referential, that it is mainly concerned with the transfer of verifiable facts" (50), but a recognition of "the interrelational function" of Pinter's dialogue (55). By dispensing with "the reference theory of reading" (52) and acknowledging instead this "interrelational function" of the words in a "sequence-oriented interpretation" (74), Quigley argued, we shall find "the connective thread which links successive statements in Pinter's plays ... anything but obscure" (50).

Quigley's thorough and rigorous analyses of the early stage-plays generally prove his point. I have only one misgiving about his "interrelational" approach. It assumes (as naturalistic plays generally do) that every speech, every action is an attempt to establish dominance; there is no room for disinterested dreaming. For example, Quigley sees the duet between Ruth and Lenny in the second act of *The Homecoming* as an attempt to establish a somewhat unlikely alliance:

> Ruth openly seeks approval from Lenny for her clothes, and Lenny, for once, shows no sign of the habitual mockery that characterizes his relationship with everybody else. A tentative mutual sympathy is exhibited here, and with it an embryonic mutual trust.... Encouraged by Lenny's sympathetic response, Ruth begins to explore a further potential common ground between them: a shared professional interest.... This halting recollection is evidence of the gradual recreation of an experience whose value to Ruth can only be judged by the context in which she is now raising it. (213–5)

In fact this episode hardly qualifies as dialogue. Lenny may be present on stage as Ruth muses about her past as "a model for the body", but he contributes little more than Ophelia does to Hamlet's "To be or not to be"; at best, he serves simply to prompt the elaboration of Ruth's monologue. To my mind this scene works best when Ruth—like Beth in *Landscape*—speaks without making any contact with the other character on stage. She is in a world (not a room) of her own. Gillen sagely observes that "most of the characters are using language for something they do not know and may not want" (46), and, in his analysis of the changes made to the first draft of the modelling episode, he notes how "Pinter ... adds poetic lines which capture with brilliant indirection Ruth's longing for a completeness of being which seems to have eluded her in her life with Teddy" (38).[14]

This and Pinter's other monologues are moments of stasis, not unlike Joyce's epiphanies. In Ruth's case, I think that her languid account of the big house by the lake may trigger her determination to recover her old independence and self-esteem. Of course, I offer this hypothesis in defiance of Quigley's insistence that any assessment of Pinter's meaning (or the lack of it) must be "a product of the linguistic data" (14). There is, however, a degree of intertextuality in the play that might be seen to legitimise such flights of fancy. The play's Oedipal pattern has been done to death by critics, but not all have acknowledged how far back it goes. The ingeniously layered structure traces the pattern through three generations: Max and Sam (sons of a "bed-ridden" mother) and their "adopted" sibling Mac are succeeded by another set of three boys (sons of the dead Jessie), and when Ruth opts to desert Teddy in the course of the play, she leaves three more sons with a harsh father and a lost mother. [15] There is evidently something more than "interrelational" dialogue going on in this play.

Still less attention has been paid to the allusion to the fairy tale of "Goldilocks and the Three Bears" when Teddy and Ruth first step into the house and speculate on the ownership of various chairs and beds (36–7). A little later, after Teddy has gone to bed, Lenny tries to wrest a glass of water from Ruth (49–50), but—unlike Goldilocks, who runs off, leaving the porridge behind when the bears return to the house—she refuses to be bullied. This house is indeed a bear-pit, but Ruth is tougher (and—at least when played by Vivien Merchant—darker) than Goldilocks, and she eventually makes the bears dance to her tune.[16] The play's fluid mix of realistic and expressionistic elements, I would suggest, supports these hints of a mythic dimension, which lifts the play out of the jejune formula imposed by Quigley's "interrelational" reading of the dialogue.

Just how fluid the relationship between realism and expressionism can be in Pinter's plays becomes apparent when we attempt to define the moment at which Ruth's dream ends. Just three lines after it began, perhaps, when Ruth "*opens her eyes*" once more? But the dreamy, elliptical syntax continues for several pages, to be succeeded by equally dreamy dancing and kissing (with Lenny) and a curiously asexual embrace (with Joey), first on the sofa ("JOEY *lies heavily on* RUTH. *They are almost still*"), and then—still passive—on the floor (75–6).

In the film version the switch back to realism seems to occur when Ruth pushes Joey aside, gets up from the floor, demands a whisky (in a tumbler rather than a wine-glass) and "something to eat" (76), insists that the music be turned off, and "*walks around the room*" as if she owns the place (77). There is, to be sure, one more dreamy moment—in the following scene, when Joey, having revealed that he and Ruth "didn't get all the way" during a two-hour tryst upstairs (82), gently insists that "Now and again ... you can be happy ... without going any hog" (84). This speech confirms Joey's Aston-like imperviousness to the struggle going on around him, but it does not revive Ruth's dreams. She reinstates the law of the jungle—even "more explicitly" in the first draft than in the published text (Gillen 40)—before taking Joey upstairs, and while she is off-stage with him, the bears mercilessly bait Teddy (who, not to be completely outdone, contrives to swap Ruth for a cheese roll) before setting about planning a lurid future for Ruth. Once she reappears in the room, Joey's speech notwithstanding, she joins in the tussle, and easily beats the bears at their own game, bargaining successfully with Lenny, dismissing Teddy, and reducing Max to a crawling, quivering heap. By the end, Teddy has disappeared, Max and Sam are more or less comatose on the floor, Lenny remains—but at a distance—while Joey kneels at Ruth's feet, perhaps ready, like Caliban, "to dream again".

Joey (continually) and Ruth (intermittently) help us to see that *The Homecoming* is more than just a study in "interrelational" dialogue. They provide glimpses of a world beyond the jungle (or the room). R. F. Storch defines what Pinter is "doing" in terms similar to mine:

> By dislocating our attention from the common sense view of things he makes us alive to primitive fears, destroys the rational façade of the adult mind, and lays bare repressive fantasies. (137)[17]

When Pinter enlarged the expressionistic ingredient in his memory plays, beginning with *Landscape*, he seems to have intensified his audiences' bafflement, but the delicate balance of realism and expressionism in *The Homecoming* and, to a lesser extent, the other early plays was by then keeping most viewers intrigued; it is, in fact, a crucial aspect of what we have come to call the "Pinteresque" style.

While Stoppard's plays occasionally use childish instinct to make a point,[18] they are generally designed to appeal to "the rational façade of the adult mind". So in Act 2 of *Night and Day* there is—or was intended to be—no doubt as to exactly where Ruth's dream begins and ends. Such military precision deprives the episode of any visceral elements; this Ruth's dream stirs in the audience no "primitive fears" or "repressive fantasies". At best, Stoppard manages to arouse a gently melancholy, as when Ruth—sadder, but evidently no wiser, after hearing of Milne's death—ruefully settles for a second night in bed with the boorish Dick Wagner. Like Pinter's Ruth, she leaves us wondering whether she is about to become a "tart" (a word used in both plays), but again the two playwrights approach this issue in very different ways. In the case of Pinter's Ruth, we are left unsure whether she will accede to the family's wish that she should become a prostitute. In the case of Stoppard's, the issue is simply semantic. Does committing adultery twice with the same man make a woman a "tart"? And how can she know until she has tried it?

So far the comparison between the two Ruths seems to endorse the conventional view of the playwrights' contrasting styles, which Nadel (focusing on 1993, when Pinter's *Moonlight* and Stoppard's *Arcadia* were first staged) defines thus:

> Pinter spare and modernist; Stoppard postmodern and rococo; Pinter the minimalist, hard and obscure; Stoppard the classicist, cerebral and subtle; obscenities in one, wit in the other; Pinter produced on the fringe, Stoppard in the subsidized theatre.... Pinter's *Moonlight* succeeds as a play without words, desolation and loss poised on the stage; Stoppard's *Arcadia* triumphs by its time shifts as chaos theory supplements art theory and politics, as in the early *Travesties*. Humour, gaiety, quips and puns challenge the audience.... Pinter, however, takes over where Stoppard leaves off; when the party is over, the characters must confront the mess—in silence. (446)

But, as Nadel is well aware, this conventional view ignores Stoppard's "new emotional energy that first surfaced in *The Real Thing*" (Nadel 444) and—helped initially by Carl Thoms's evocative set and lighting designs, particularly in the case of *Hapgood*—has been increasingly evident in the plays that have followed. Billington (in a review of *The Invention of Love*) goes so far as to claim that "Stoppard, for all his cerebral qualities, is at his best when he endorses private passion"; he "always writes best when he writes from the heart" ("Passion" 33).

In hindsight one might be so bold as to suggest that Stoppard's heart was beginning to challenge his head as early as the second act of *Night and Day*. Could Pinter's Ruth play have facilitated this development? At first glance, this may seem an unlikely proposition. For one thing, Pinter generates emotion from dreams and memories, whereas Stoppard derives it from the disappointments of reality. Still, cricket—the sport that both men revere—allows contrasting styles and techniques to work together towards a common goal. I think we should desist from stressing the differences between Pinter and Stoppard. The early similarities may have been largely factitious, but a degree of overlap can be discerned from 1978 or thereabouts. In their different ways, both have come to acknowledge that a play may be "the end product of an idea", and that truth is an essential element of all but the most farcical (Stoppard's *On the Razzle* and *Rough Crossing*) and the most polemical (Pinter's "Precisely" and *One for the Road*) forms of drama. These two giants of the contemporary stage should, I think, be regarded as complementary—rather than contrasting—playwrights.

NOTES

[1] Hinchliffe notes that Wardle borrowed this phrase from the subtitle to David Campton's 1957 play *The Lunatic View* (*Harold Pinter* 38).

[2] There may have been other reasons for Pinter's rejection of the role; Losey proceeded to inform Stoppard that "Vivien Merchant likes the script but wants to discuss it". By 1974, Pinter would almost certainly have baulked at the prospect of playing alongside Merchant. In the end Glenda Jackson played the title role, and Michael Lonsdale the Doctor.

[3] Pinter is evidently unhappy about such a distinction between his early and late plays; in 1995 he told Michael Billington that "*The Dumb Waiter*, *The Birthday Party* and *The Hothouse* are doing something that can only be described as political" (Billington 286–7).

[4] Nadel (216, 363–4, 449–50) notes some general comments by Pinter on Stoppard's work, and there is a tribute to Pinter in Kalem's interview with Stoppard. An enigmatic undated note from Pinter to "Tom and Miriam", consisting simply of the words "I love W.G.", is probably a cricketing reference (to W. G. Grace).

[5] One of Pinter's own comments about the play implies that Rose's wish-fulfilment is misguided, and that her spiritual home is the basement: "I've always seen Riley as ... her potential saviour who is trying to release Rose from the imprisonment of the room and the restrictions of her life with Bert. He's inviting her to come back to her spiritual home..." (Billington 69). Quigley has it both ways: "To Rose, the room is a haven", but "she is also fascinated by and drawn toward the mysterious life that she has cut herself off from.... The most frequently recurring manifestation of her ambivalence is her fascination with the basement of the house..." (82–3).

[6] Gillen (41) notes that in the transition from the first draft to the published version "some of Joey's lines become Lenny's, making it more obvious that it is he who is directing this story of superior sexual power at Teddy."

[7] It is hard not to associate Teddy and Ruth's arrival at the family home (with its emphasis on the ownership of chairs and beds) with the story of Goldilocks and the Three Bears.

[8] In the first draft of the play Susan (as Ruth is called at this stage) defines her role more specifically: "I modelled in the nude. Or in underwear. With other models" (Pinter, "First Draft" 18).

[9] Eileen Diss's design for a recent production provides space for a bedroom door between the main room and the staircase, but it is U.R. (and the front door is U.L.).

[10] In the first draft of the play Lenny does not leave for the gym with Joey and Max; he stays in the house for a few more skirmishes with Teddy. Then—somewhat discomforted—"he goes", leaving Teddy with Susan (as Ruth is called in this draft), whom he tries to persuade to return with him to America. When "he goes" to pack, Lenny immediately comes "in at kitchen door" (which suggests that he never left the house, and was probably eavesdropping). A direction in the typed draft that 'he slips upstairs, back again' has been cancelled by hand, leaving only the words "he sits by her". Susan is evidently surprised that he has stayed in the house: her first remark to him is "I thought you were boxing." Lenny then has to distinguish himself from Joey before Ruth's modelling monologue can proceed (Pinter, "First Draft" 17–18). The simplification of Lenny's re-entry may mark the moment when Pinter decided to locate Lenny's bedroom downstairs.

[11] In his December 1971 interview with Mel Gussow, Pinter confirms that, after *The Homecoming,* he "couldn't go on with those damn doors". As noted above, the description of the set specifies only one door. It may be the door to Lenny's room—hidden from the audience by the stairs—that prompted this use of the plural "doors" (Gussow 18).

[12] Stoppard' s handling of Milne's entry here is very similar to Pinter's introduction of Anna early in *Old Times.* Pinter reverses the process at the end of Act 1 of *The Caretaker,* gradually dimming the lights as Aston delivers his long monologue.

[13] Stoppard probably envisaged a dimming of the lights at this point, sufficient to black out the sofa while the transfer takes place. In the event, as a note in the second edition explains, "in the first production she went behind the tree growing in the room, and her double came from behind the tree" (1979, 69).

[14] Gillen also notes that Ruth's account of the house where she did her modelling "is more detailed, making Ruth more emotional about her past"; indeed he finds Ruth "more sentimental" in the draft, which leads to an undesirable "closing" of "the distance between the audience and Ruth" (39). Moreover, in the draft Teddy knew—and loved—the house, and Gillen remarks that his "moving" description of it serves to "remind us ... of how clearly Teddy is rejecting not simply Ruth but his own sensual being" (42).

[15] Max's query, "All yours Ted?" raises the possibility that one of the sons in each generation may be illegitimate; as Paul Rogers suggests (Lahr, "Interview" 158), the most likely candidate from the middle generation is Joey—the son of MacGregor perhaps, who in turn may have been dreamier than both Max and Max's father. Quigley, however, identifies Lenny as the odd man out (199), while Gillen (commenting on the first draft) suggests Teddy (40).

[16] For subtler accounts of Ruth's status at the end of the play, see Ann Hall (70–71) and Gillen (44–45).

[17] According to John Russell Taylor, "Pinter has said that the play came to him all of a piece, with the shattering force of a dark dream" (65).

[18] These appeals (up to and including *The Real Thing*) are discussed by Corballis (*passim*).

WORKS CITED

Amory, Mark. "The Joke's the Thing." *Sunday Times Magazine* 9 June 1974: 65–75.

Billington, Michael. *The Life and Work of Harold Pinter.* London: Faber, 1996.

—. "Passion amid Scholarship." *Guardian Weekly* 12 October 1997:33.

Corballis, Richard. "Tom Stoppard's Children." *Tom Stoppard: A Casebook.* Ed. John Harty. New York: Garland, 1988. 261–79.

Delaney, Paul, ed. *Tom Stoppard in Conversation.* Ann Arbor: U of Michigan P.

Diss, Eileen. "*The Room* and *The Homecoming,* Set Designs." *The Pinter Review: Collected Essays 2001 and 2002.* Ed. Francis Gillen and Steven H. Gale. Tampa, Florida: U of Tampa P, 2002. 143.

Dohmen, William F. "Time after Time: Pinter Plays with Disjunctive Chronologies." *Harold Pinter: Critical Approaches.* Ed. Stephen H. Gale. London and Toronto: Associated University Presses, 1986. 187–201.

Esslin, Martin. *The Theatre of the Absurd*. 3rd ed. London: Eyre Methuen, 1974.

Fjelde, Rolf. "Plotting Pinter's Progress." *A Casebook on Harold Pinter's* The Homecoming. Ed. John Lahr. New York: Grove, 1971. 87–107.

Franks, Alan. "The Unmellowing of Harold Pinter." *Times Saturday Review* 19 October 1991: 4–6.

Gillen, Francis. "Pinter at Work: An Introduction to the First Draft of *The Homecoming* and Its Relationship to the Completed Drama." *The Pinter Review: Collected Essays* 1997 *and* 1998. Ed. Francis Gillen and Steven H. Gale. Tampa, Florida: U of Tampa P, 1999. 31–47.

Gollob, David and David Roper. "Trad Tom Pops In." *Gambit* 37 (1980): 5–17.

Gross, Miriam. "Pinter on Pinter." *The Observer* 5 October 1980: 25, 27.

Gussow, Mel. *Conversations with Pinter.* New York: Grove, 1994.

Hall, Ann C. *"A Kind of Alaska": Women in the Plays of O'Neill, Pinter and Shepard.* Carbondale and Edwardsville: Southern Illinois U P: 1993.

Hall, Peter. "Directing the Plays of Harold Pinter". *The Cambridge Companion to Harold Pinter.* Ed. Peter Raby. Cambridge: Cambridge U P, 2001. 145–154.

Hardin, Nancy Shields. "An Interview with Tom Stoppard." *Contemporary Literature* 22 (1981): 153–66.

Hayman, Ronald. *Contemporary Playwrights: Tom Stoppard.* London: Heinemann, 1977.

Hinchliffe, A.P. *Harold Pinter.* 2nd ed Boston: Twayne, 1981.

—. "Mr Pinter's Belinda." *Modern Drama* 11 (September 1968): 173–9.

Kalem, T.E. "Ping Pong Philosopher." *Time* 6 May 1974: 55.

Knowles, Ronald. "Pinter and Twentieth-Century Drama." *The Cambridge Companion to Harold Pinter.* Ed. Peter Raby. Cambridge: Cambridge U P, 2001. 73–86.

Kuurman, Joost. "An Interview with Tom Stoppard." *Dutch Quarterly Review of Anglo-American Letters* 10 (1980): 41–57.

Lahr, John. "An Actor's Approach: An Interview with Paul Rogers." *A Casebook on Harold Pinter's* The Homecoming. Ed. John Lahr. New York: Grove, 1971. 151–75.

—. "Pinter and Chekhov: The Bond of Naturalism." *Pinter: A Collection of Critical Essays.* Ed. Arthur Ganz. Englewood Cliffs, N.J.: Prentice Hall, 1972. 60–71.

Nadel, Ira. *Tom Stoppard: A Life.* New York: Palgrave Macmillan, 2002.

Pinter, Harold. *Celebration* & *The Room.* London: Faber, 2000.

—. "First Draft, *The Homecoming.*" *The Pinter Review: Collected Essays* 1997 *and* 1998. Ed. Francis Gillen and Steven H. Gale. Tampa, Florida: U of Tampa P, 1999. 1–30.

—. *Plays: One.* London: Methuen, 1976.

—. *Plays: Two.* London: Methuen, 1977.

—. *Plays: Three.* London: Methuen, 1978.

—. *Plays Four.* London: Methuen, 1981.

—. *Plays* 4. Expanded edition. London: Faber, 1998.

Quigley, Austin. *The Pinter Problem.* Princeton: Princeton U P, 1975. Schechner, Richard. "Puzzling Pinter." *Tulane Drama Review* 11 (Winter 1966): 176–84.

Stoppard, Tom. "Ambushes for the Audience: Towards a High Comedy of Ideas." *Theatre Quarterly* 4 (1974): 3–17.

—. "But for the Middle Classes." *Times Literary Supplement* 3 June 1977: 677.

—. "The Definite Maybe." *The Author* 78 (Spring 1967): 18–20.

—. *Night and Day.* London: Faber, 1978.

—. *Night and Day* 2nd ed. London: Faber, 1979.

Storch, R.F. "Harold Pinter's Happy Families." *Pinter: A Collection of Critical Essays.* Ed. Arthur Ganz. Englewood Cliffs, N.J.: Prentice Hall, 1972. 136–46.

Taylor, John Russell. "Pinter's Game of Happy Families." *A Casebook on Harold Pinter's* The Homecoming. Ed. John Lahr. New York: Grove, 1971. 57–65.

Tynan, Kenneth. *Show People: Profiles in Entertainment.* New York: Simon and Schuster, 1979.

Interactive Space and Virtuality on the Pinter Stage

ELIZABETH SAKELLARIDOU

In the present state of immense crisis in global politics Pinter's growing political activism in both his later dramatic output and his public profile seems to be the most evident and welcome topic to talk about—and justifiably so. Even the Nobel Prize ceremony in Stockholm echoed heavily the strongly political content of his speech. However, the unduly insistent critical focus on the political aspect of his work eclipses other, perhaps less topical but equally exciting new perspectives on his oeuvre. One such challenging new reading is Pinter's potential relationship with digital technology and the intelligent stage. I want to suggest that in Pinter's dramatic work there are inherent perceptual notions and images that have been successfully materialized only through the recent development of interactive media technology.

There are some memorable passages in Pinter's early play *The Dwarfs* (1960), which refer to a very strange perception of an enclosed space, a room, not as a stable locus with given boundaries but as a moving, ever changing entity with an independent will:

> This is my room. This is a room. There is wall-paper, on the walls. There are six walls. Eight walls. An octagon. This room is an octagon. [...] This room moves. This room is moving. It has moved. (Pinter 1977: 96)

At a later stage this partial view is amplified into a generalized statement about the erratic behaviour of walls and rooms:

> The rooms we live in ... open and shut. [*Pause.*] Can't you see? They change shape at their own will. I wouldn't grumble if only they would keep to some consistency. But they don't. And I can't tell the limits, the boundaries, which I've been led to believe are natural. (Pinter 1977: 99)

Within the context of the play the experience that the speaking character, Len, is narrating is undoubtedly hallucinatory. Tested against his companions, Len seems to have a defective perception of the world and spends some time in an unspecified kind of hospital. That he may be suffering from a mental or a psychic illness is highly probable, though it is never verified nor denied in the course of the play. Beyond the possibility of a clinical interpretation, however, Len's strange vision can now also be interpreted as exposure to a virtual environment generated through digital media. In her recent book, *Virtual Theatres,* Gabriella Giannachi refers convincingly to the ability of "virtual theatre" to offer the subject the possibility to see itself as "out of joint" (Giannachi 12).

Pinter's plays abound in such bizarre images and experiences, which we might now describe and name but also effectively represent by recourse to the language and practice of the new digital technology. Writing in the 1960s, the father of contemporary media theory Marshall McLuhan had already picked out existential philosophy and the Theatre of the Absurd as discourses that create "anti-environments" compatible to the ones generated by the new media (Ben-Zvi 473). More recently, Giannachi concludes her introductory study on "virtual theatres" by stressing the basic characteristic of virtual reality "to allow access to a *different universe* [...] where the real can be seen inside out" (Giannachi 159, my emphasis). Giannachi further familiarizes us with such new terms as "telematic dreaming" and the "biologization of technology" which suggest the productive crossing of electronic technology with contemporary life experiences (Giannachi 107 and 111). Many of Pinter's characters are agents of a virtual reality via memory, fantasy, desire, or some kind of mental or psychological disturbance. Notwithstanding the origin of their supra-natural vision, these characters are able to perceive other virtual or semi-virtual beings or to construct a virtual environment regarding the perception of both temporality and spatiality and the objects and bodies inhabiting them. Thus, Len in *The Dwarfs* lives with some spectral beings, the "dwarfs," who remain throughout invisible to the other characters as much as to the spectators of the play. In *A Kind of Alaska* (1982) Deborah has an extraordinary experience of moving space, similar to the one quoted from *The Dwarfs.* In one of her poetic monologues she describes this staying memory from the period of her illness:

> Oh yes. The most crushing spaces. The most punishing spaces. That was tough going. Very difficult. Like dancing with someone dancing on your foot all the time[...] But sometimes the space opened and became light, sometimes it opened and I was so light [...]. (Pinter 1982: 25-26)

Once again it is the contemporary media theory and practice that have made us familiar with the new hybrid notions of "organic" or "liquid" architecture, which—in Giannachi's words—"liberate[s] architecture from Cartesian space and Euclidean form" (97). Such definitions and reported experiments correspond most suitably to the hallucinations described by Pinter's characters.

Even in an earlier play, *A Slight Ache* (1958), the protagonist, Edward, feels threatened by the currents, shades, and shapes of space, which "carried their bodies on [him]" (Pinter 1976: 198). Another character in the same play, the Matchseller, is on the borderline between reality and unreality, at the point of disappearance. Likewise, Anna in *Old Times* (1970) may well be an im-material presence, a memory or a reality or both at the same time, in a play which conflates real and virtual space and time incessantly. A similar situation unfolds in *Ashes to Ashes* (1996), where a mythified Holocaust experience overlaps in various ways with the characters' here-and-now situation. *Moonlight* (1993) is inhabited by real and virtual characters, who move in real and virtual time and space accordingly but also cross over and meet in a liminal zone with no logical explanation. In *The Basement* (1966) we are faced with an ever-changing space, as the action incessantly moves from an unstable interior environment to a protean exterior landscape and back again into the room, whose furnishing keeps altering as if through magic. What is more, one of the characters, Stott, is objectified, in the consciousness of the other two characters, and his body reaches the vanishing point. The liminal position of bodies between reality and unreality, appearance and disappearance, which is so frequent in Pinter's plays, has a lot in common with the practice of interactive media technology, where "immersion" lies at the bottom of their function (Giannachi 5). What is more, contemporary theorists like Philip Auslander have affirmed and specified the close relationship between live performance and the performance of mediatization in that they are both "predicated on disappearance" (Auslander 45).

What all the above mentioned Pinter plays share in common is the concept of constant movement, change, and potential disappearance. All these notions and experiences interestingly lie at the very heart of contemporary digital media technology. The lack of stability and the ever-lasting motility that these three concepts designate are certainly what, in a theatre situation, constitute dramatic tension and ensure stage interaction. I want to highlight this last word, *interaction*, because its derivative, *interactivity*, has become the new technology's key word for denoting its basic dynamic as movement which crosses between real and projected space and its contents, bodies and things (Birringer 1999: 7 and 2002: 26).

Interactive digital systems have already been successfully used in dance, which is a purely performance art, but in the case of scripted performance such as theatre, the situation is more risky and complicated and such compound technological application is still in a lab state. As theorists and practitioners in this new domain of research inform us, the area on which to focus our theoretical and practical investigation is on the one hand the new "aesthetics of disappearance" (Causey) and on the other hand the dramatic potential of digital interaction with the live stage (Saltz).

As we live in a culture strongly habituated to digital services and experience—Causey suggests—"the option to return to things as they were [...] is not available. [...] The traditional subject position [is] impossible" (Causey 60 and 61). In this new field of theatre research, generated by our recent digital cultural experience, avant-garde dramatists like Beckett and Handke have already been considered in the light of a possible digital interactivity.[1] I want to argue that Pinter also provides for such technological speculation. It is no accident that all these three writers—Beckett, Handke and Pinter—present fragmented subject positions and they share a multi-perspectival phenomenological view of the world and, consequently, they have been subject to phenomenological studies of their work.[2] Phenomenology, especially the model offered by Maurice Merleau-Ponty, seems to supply a satisfactory theoretical coverage for the versatile consciousness, the multiple perspectivalism, engendered in the work of these dramatists. However, it is the digital media experiments that have managed to make accessible to us such "metaphysical" visions so far restricted mainly to the minds of artists and philosophers.

Pinter's stage plays repeatedly anticipate hyper-real sensations, which for the most part remain locked in the narratives of the characters because of the representational limitations of the traditional stage. Pinter seems to consider the nakedness of the stage a major challenge to his art. Nonetheless he has repeatedly acknowledged, in his interviews, the flexibility of other media such as film and television[3] and has worked for them. His two television plays, in particular, reveal how aware he is—just like Beckett—of the high potential of the TV screen to represent the unrepresentable. *Tea Party* (1965), which focuses on the gradual disintegration of the protagonist's personality, makes ample use of the camera to contrast his erring vision to the "reality" of his environment, thus managing to represent invisible states of the psyche, of the human unconscious. Likewise, *The Basement* (1967) manages to record images of fantasy and desire, in other words to represent subjective sensations which project bodies and objects in hyper-real spaces and activities.

The appropriateness of television for such psychic close-ups had already been spotted by McLuhan in his groundbreaking book *Understanding Media* in 1964. Despite his own anticipation of such potential Pinter chose not to pursue his experimentation with the TV camera any further. The virtual aspects of his characters' universe were reported on stage as imaginary or hallucinatory constructs. Their "anomalous" perception can now be reread as futuristic experiences of electronic virtuality, which is already in the process of becoming naturalized in our everyday life. Pinter's foresight of virtual reality can now be mediated to the spectators through the use of an interactive intelligent stage.

We could tentatively distinguish four domains in Pinter's virtual perception. The first is concerned with spatiality, a basic concept in theatre performance, where all meaning, even temporality, is spatially perceived. As examples from various plays can illustrate (from early ones such as *A Slight Ache*, *The Dwarfs* and *The Basement* or later ones such as *Old Times* and *A Kind of Alaska* or more recent ones such as *Moonlight* and *Ashes to Ashes*), Pinter often provides an "elastic" space (Pinter 1977: 100), which can open and shut at its own will, can change shape and can allow "any amount of permutation" (Pinter 1981: 44)—as his own stage directions in *Old Times* explicitly claim. In other words this is a space that acquires agency, becomes *interactive*, assuming a protagonist's role along with the roles embodied by live actors. This feature of space "liveness" can only be fully effected in stage production through the use of three-dimensional digital image projection. Giannachi reports a number of artistic experiments with a media-contaminated architecture, a hybrid form that creates a dialectic between physical space and a psychic one (Giannachi 96). In Pinter's theatre such spatial dynamism and motility are only partially *seen*, for example, in the incessant permutation (real and narrated) of the position and function of the divans in *Old Times* and in the dispensable scenography of *The Basement*, which—it must be remembered—owes its cinematic agility to the initial inception of the piece as a TV play. It is worth mentioning that in the language of technologized theatre such stage environmental phenomena are ambiguously dabbed "scenographic apparition[s]" (Birringer 1999: 10). There may be a certain amount of playfulness in this concept of a virtual animation of the environment but there is also alarm in the possibility of an autonomized, embodied space—a bizarre feeling of insecurity that Pinter had sensitively captured in Edward's monologue in *A Slight Ache*:

> It was not so much any deficiency in my sight as the airs between me and my object [...] the change of air, the currents obtaining in the space between me and my object, the shades they make, the shapes they take, the quivering, the eternal quivering [...] things happened upon me [...] the shades, the petals, carried themselves, carried their bodies upon me (Pinter 1976: 198)

Edward's description does not refer to physical space any longer but to a metaphysical one, which can only materialize fully on stage through digital mediation in which the viewing subject is immersed. It is the technologized space that can acquire agency comparable to that of the live actor's body (Salzt 107). The idea of interaction between virtual and real space can certainly have a strong psychological impact on our understanding of the world and reality and Edward's unease may point both to an unexpected existential experience he is facing but also, simultaneously, to the spectator's unprecedented experience of attending an interactive media performance. Edward's hyperreal experience may indeed be emblematic of the destabilization of the self, a kind of "schizophrenia," that recent commentators have spotted as major negative symptoms of our technologized age.[4]

Another domain where Pinter's metaphysical vision is comparable to and perhaps preempts—figuratively at least—the effects generated by digital media technology is that of temporality. The majority of his characters are seldom anchored in present-day reality; they systematically slip into the past, which in itself is a terribly slippery ground as it is never firmly constituted. It may be stolen from their own stored experience or somebody else's or it may be a mere fictive invention with no real referent at all. Anna's enigmatic statement in *Old Times,* "There are things I remember which may never have happened but as I recall them so they take place" (Pinter 1981: 28) is an excellent description of virtual temporality spreading out in an equally virtual locality. As phenomenology has shown us, the concept of subjective time on stage, as in life, is translated into spatial terms. Movement and change in space give us also a clue to the passage of time. At this point again computer generated effects can enhance the sensation of interactive temporality for the spectators of plays such as *Landscape*, *Old Times*, *Moonlight,* and *Ashes to Ashes*, where reality, memory and desire produce a nexus of spatio-temporal virtuality. The projection of still and moving images from the past can be made to interact with the present situation enacted by the live stage.

A third domain in our investigation of virtual Pinterland involves fantastic characters like Bridget, Maria and Ralph in *Moonlight* and the Woman in *Ashes to Ashes*, who belong to the imaginary of the real characters in these plays but who are actually incarnated by live actors on the conventional stage or are identified with the visible characters. Pinter's technique of providing a virtual environment for these non-existent characters is—especially in the case of Bridget—a special use of lighting, which actually "sculpts" her space. "Sculpting" space is a term currently used in the language of the architectonics of space on the intelligent stage (Birringer 2002: 22). The particular use of the moonlight in Pinter's play, as I have argued elsewhere,[5] gathers around it a thick materiality that turns lighting almost into an interactive partner to the live actors themselves.[6] What a computer-generated lighting effect could do here is to heighten the interactivity by arranging digital emission through sensors attached to the body of the performer(s).

Concerning the stage representation of the imaginary characters as such, the contribution of digital intervention would be greater through the creation of virtual bodies—or "video ghosts" (Birringer 1999: 10)—projected into real space and able to interact in real time with the on-stage flesh characters. The advantage would be, as Birringer explains, to create a sense of "free floating," of loss of gravity, of "crossovers to an impossible body aesthetic" (1999: 10, 15).

All these are very essential sensations for the full appreciation of the inherent liminality of many Pinter plays, not only *Moonlight* and *Ashes to*

Ashes, where there are ipso facto non-existent or at least non-present characters (who should therefore stay invisible like the mysterious "Dwarfs" in the eponymous play), but also in others, where some characters are on the border of non-existence, non-presence or disappearance. I am referring to Anna in *Old Times*, the Matchseller in *A Slight Ache*, and Stott in *The Basement*, who are all on the vanishing point of existence and who could most effectively be doubled by virtual figures, interacting with their live-stage embodiments. Here we need to recall again that Pinter first conceived of such liminal characters as the Matchseller and Stott not for the theatre stage but for other media, the radio and television respectively, which have different methods and techniques of mediating absence or unreality than stage theatre.

One last point where Pinter's imaginative thought intersects with the performance dynamics of interactive digital systems concerns the "unnatural" behaviour of things. Len's self-parodic proclamation in *The Dwarfs*—"I'm all for the natural behaviour of rooms, doors, staircases, the lot. But I can't rely on them" (Pinter 1977: 99)—hints most prominently at sensory analogies between these two different systems of representation. In several Pinter plays various objects transgress all "natural" laws imposed by the solipsistic human subject and acquire phenomenological agency that turns them into live entities in an intersubjective relationship with the human characters of the play. For example, Len in *The Dwarfs* is terrified at the thought that the cheese he has eaten "*didn't die*. It only *began to live* when you swallowed it [...] *it got me*" (Pinter 1977: 108, my emphasis). He is equally alarmed by the "change[s] in the *posture* of the room" (109, my emphasis). In both cases Len, through the language he uses, confers organic agency to lifeless things, being in a perceptual state that phenomenology would term *animism*. From the idea of *animism* to the practising of virtual *animation* that digital technology has made accessible to us it is not such a big leap any longer.

There are other instances of "performing objects" (Causey 68) in Pinter's plays, which confirm the correspondence of his prophetic imagination with the effects of an interactive intelligent stage. In *Ashes to Ashes* this type of object animism becomes self-parodic without losing its alarming grip. On the contrary, it enhances the liminal nature of the play oscillating between materiality and virtuality. The specific incident concerns the peculiar behaviour of a pen that rolls off the table where it had been placed. The question then arises whether it is "innocent" (that is, with no intention or will of its own), until it is further loaded with human features; it acquires "parents" and a personal "history" (Pinter 1996: 35). In *Old Times* Anna expresses a peculiar sensation that Kate's and Deeley's house "would be gone" (Pinter 1981: 15) as if in disobedience to human volition. Anna's fancy of the arbitrary disappearance of a material object comes as a response to Kate's earlier doubt of the materiality of London itself as an urban complex (14). This is another case of potential object interactivity but as in all other instances of Pinter's anticipated animism or animation it is trapped once again in discourse because the only way it can be visually represented on stage to real effect is through the current achievements of digital technology. Giannachi's exciting accounts of hypersurface architecture experiments, talking of "building[s] refus[ing] to take root" and virtual houses conceived as a "potential field of vectorial relationships" (Giannachi 97), give the measure of the fantastic dimensions of such advanced technological achievements. Beckett had also played with the idea of "performing objects" in his twin mime shorts *Act Without Words I* and *Act Without Words II*, which he wrote in the 1950s, but his view of a "technologized" stage was actually that of mechanical, not of digital compound equipment.

My aim in this paper has not been to advocate a "post-human" stage that would diminish the function or the power of Pinter's "peopled" theatre.[7] On the contrary, I am suggesting a cross-reading of his theatre with the stage potential of contemporary interactive media in order to prove that the two can be mutually enriching. Pinter, on his part, has dramatized experiences of exposure to the invisible and the unpresentable most discernibly. Digital technology, on the other hand, is now offering high possibilities of materialization of Pinter's dramatic anticipation of virtuality. It seems to me that the intelligent stage can be a very useful collaborator for a new mise-en-scène of Pinter's dramaturgy, in visualizing for the first time fully the writer's poetics of disappearance. In that sense, and contrary to the intrusive and disruptive nature of the linear media so far used on stage, the interactive media can come to life as a true dramatic partner, in mutual dialogue with Pinter's "peopled," live theatre.

NOTES

1 See Causey and Saltz. Linda Ben-Zvi also turns her recent article "Beckett and Television: In a Different Context" to a similar direction, claiming that Beckett uses television technology "to say the unsayable" (473).

2 See Garner and Sakellaridou. Causey also acknowledges the relevance of phenomenology to his own research within digital technology and the stage.

3 See interview with Jacky Gillot (BBC4, 13 June 1971) and interview with Melvyn Bragg (The South Bank Show, ITV, 25 Sept. 1981)

4 See Manuel Castells, *The Information Age*. Also Ben-Zvi (op. cit.)

5 See Sakellaridou, "Pinter's Phenomenological Mise-en-Scène" (2002).

6 Bridget's poetic description of the moonlight stresses the substantial texture it acquires: "When I got to the house it was *bathed* in moonlight. The house, the glade, the lane, were all *bathed* in moonlight" (Pinter 1993: 80, my emphasis).

7 I am curiously reminded here of the moving title of Martin Esslin's early study of Pinter's plays, *The Peopled Wound* (1970).

WORKS CITED

Beckett, Samuel. *Act Without Words I*. In *Collected Shorter Plays*. London and Boston: Faber, 1984. 41-46.

—. *Act Without Words II*. In *Collected Shorter Plays*. London and Boston: Faber, 1984. 47-51.

Ben-Zvi, Linda. "Beckett and Television: In a Different Context." *Modern Drama*. 49.4 (2006): 469-490.

Birringer, Johannes. "Contemporary Performance/Technology." *Theatre Journal*. 51.4 (1999): 361-381.

—. "Dance and Interactivity." *Gramma*. 10 (2002): 19-40.

Causey, Matthew. "The Aesthetics of Disappearance and the Politics of Visibility in the Performance of Technology." *Gramma*. 10 (2002): 59-85.

Esslin, Martin. *The Peopled Wound: The Plays of Harold Pinter*. London: Methuen, 1970.

Giannachi, Gabriella. *Virtual Theatres: An Introduction*. London and New York: Routledge, 2004.

McLuhan, Marshall. *Understanding Media: The Extensions of Man*. London: Routledge, 1964.

Pinter, Harold. *Ashes to Ashes*. London and Boston: Faber, 1996.

—. *The Basement*. In *Plays: Three*. London: Eyre Methuen, 1978. 149-172.

—. *The Dwarfs*. In *Plays: Two*. London: Eyre Methuen, 1977. 89-117.

—. *A Kind of Alaska*. In *Other Places*. London: Methuen, 1982.

—. *Landscape*. In *Plays: Three*. London: Eyre Methuen, 1978. 173-198.

—. *Moonlight*. London and Boston: Faber, 1993.

—. *Old Times*. In *Plays: Four*. London: Eyre Methuen, 1981. 1-71.

—. *A Slight Ache*. In *Plays: One*. London: Eyre Methuen, 1976. 167-200.

—. Interview with Melvyn Bragg. ITV. "The South Bank Show." 7 November 1981.

—. Interview with Jacky Gillott. BBC Radio 4. 13 June 1971.

Sakellaridou, Elizabeth. " Pinter's Phenomenological Mise-en-Snène." *The Pinter Review* (2002): 106-120.

Saltz, David Z. "Live Media: Interactive Technology and Theatre." *Theatre Topics*. 11.2 (Sept. 2001): 107-130.

Pinter: Compiling the Record

WILLIAM BAKER

I'd like to begin with some preliminary remarks about the by no means comfortable relationship between a writer and the bibliographer, the documenter of achievement. Then I'll move into Harold Pinter and his bibliographical history.

The object of my current bibliographical sleuthing wrote to me: "the idea of disinterring my journalism and juvenilia fills me with horror." I'd rather not at this stage put my foot in it and ask what is being covered up, what is being hidden! But a few tales told by other sleuths might not go amiss. Rick Gekoski proposed that he should do an authorized bibliography of William Golding's work. The proposal met with neither encouragement nor refusal. This is exactly the same response I have received from the present object of my Sherlock Holmes activities. If we wish to do such a foolish thing, we can certainly go ahead, but neither Gekoski nor I can expect to receive help or encouragement.

According to Golding, "it would be like drinking my own bathwater" and he added that it made him "feel posthumous." In his *Foreword* to Gekoski and Grogan, *William Golding: A Bibliography 1934–1993* (London: Deutsch 1994), Golding writes: "Bibliographers … they are an awesome crew … they will go to any length to make their list complete in a positive perfection of assiduity. I took the steps of making things easy for my bibliographers, not realizing that by doing so I had deprived them of half their fun. But they and this present book constituted an eye-opener to one who doesn't know an apostrophe from a colophon." He added, "How can they do it? Scholars are mysterious beings, a breed to whom the shuffles, cobblings-up, adjustments, tricks, sleights-of-hand of your novelist [and I must add in the present context dramatists] are quite unknown.… Unless you are a scholar you invent your autobiography simply because research is too much trouble and invention, not just a concealment of the dirty bits or dishonest or shamming or criminal bits. It is quite simply fun; and more highly paid than research."

Especially, I might add, if the film rights accompany the novel or play or if the dramatist is writing film scripts. To quote Golding again: "When my putative autobiography is finished, it will be lies from beginning to end;

and it will contain a bibliography—a bibliography of the books I never wrote. To adapt some lines by (I think) Nicholas Bentley, "'Bibliography is about books,/Autobiography is about crooks.'"

Golding did conclude by making almost a positive comment about his sleuths. He "must place on record [his] own astonishment that people should be not just meticulous, for God's sake, but exhaustively inclusive with not a white lie in sight" (xii–xiii).

When asked to see some papers relating to early publications, he answered testily and suggestively, "I'm not letting anyone into *my* drawers!"

Some people may think that doing bibliographical research is achingly dull and requires enormous discipline. Golding said to Gekoski, "Who cares a damn about it?" The reply was, "It will be useful to anyone who wants to know the scope of your work, what you have written and when or who it was published by" (Rick Gekoski, *Tolkien's Gown and Other Stories of Great Authors and Rare Books*, London: Constable, 2005, 27). I would add it is amazing but many of us forget what we have written: our own productions somehow almost deliberately slip from the memory. Further, given the present occasion, the Nobel and the Europe Drama Prize are given for lifetime achievement, not for a single work.

To date, I have not to my knowledge received the fate of Gekoski who is transformed into Rick Turner in Golding's *The Paperman* (1984), rooting around rubbish bins in the hope of carrying away some significant biographical data. I have not appeared in one of Harold's plays: received no such distinction, unlike Sussex cricketers and medium-fast bowlers of yesteryear. The Don Bateses, for instance, of this world (Bates, over 6'5" tall and angular, with an enormous run-up, opened the bowling for Sussex in the late 1950's and early 1960's).

The relationship between the recorder and the subject has not always been a hostile one. T. S. Eliot greatly assisted Don Gallup. The late B.C. Bloomfield in his "Foreword" to his bibliography of Philip Larkin relates how the great poet initially encouraged him and liked the idea. Larkin, a professional librarian, had greatly admired Bloomfield's Auden bibliography: "He rather liked the thought of his work being commemorated in this fashion and thought it deserved such treatment; and ... because he had, I believe," Bloomfield writes, "formed the opinion that he could trust me not to be too enquiring about his personal as opposed to his literary life."

The bibliographer has self-respect. Bloomfield demanded of Larkin that "COMPLETE HONESTY must prevail between subject and bibliographer.... In the end he accepted the idea of the bibliography and inscribed his *Oxford Book of Twentieth Century English Verse* 'To Barry, mine own executioner'" (*Philip Larkin: A Bibliography, 1933–1994*, London: British Library, 2002, x).

But what about unpublished materials, personal papers, etc., unpublished poems or plays? These are very sensitive areas. All this is preliminary: what about Harold Pinter? As will emerge from what I'm going to say, his attitude to the sleuth slushing around in the bath water has transformed over a period of thirty or so years.

The opening of his Nobel Prize speech runs as follows:

> "In 1958 I wrote the following:
>
> There are no hard distinctions between what is real and what is unreal, nor between what is true and what is false. A thing is not necessarily either true or false; it can be both true and false."
>
> Pinter adds, "I believe that these assertions still make sense and do still apply to the exploration of reality through art. So as a writer I stand by them but as a citizen I cannot. As a citizen I must ask: What is true? What is false?
>
> Truth in drama is forever elusive. You never quite find it but the search for it is compulsive. The search is clearly what drives the endeavour. The search is your task."

These wise words apply to the bibliographical historian. Shortly after the publication in August 2005 of *Harold Pinter: A Bibliographical History*, by the British Library [published in USA by Oak Knoll] Harold Pinter wrote in the black felt tip pen—so characteristic of his manuscripts and working drafts—to his bibliographical historians: "Dear William Baker & John Ross. What a piece of work! I'm staggered. Apart from anything else, it gives shape to my own life! Thank you very much. Sincerely, Harold Pinter."

What then is the bibliographical history, what is true? What did the compulsive search conducted over a forty year period since the late 1950s uncover? It is based on my personal collection of material by and about Pinter. This began when I was a schoolboy on the south coast of England. It must have been (but here there is "no hard distinction between what is real and what is unreal") a response to the broadcast on the BBC Third Programme on 29 July 1959 of *A Slight Ache*. Or the search, the endeavour, may really have been triggered by a Saturday afternoon matinee early in 1960 at the Theatre Royal Brighton and to the pre-London run of *The Caretaker*. Mick's smashing of pieces of Aston's Buddha still haunts the memory. Shortly after the theatrical visit, I managed to obtain a copy of *The Caretaker*—which I still have. Not the Encore first edition, difficult to find, but the first Methuen paperback edition in the blue covers, of which 7,500 copies were initially printed—or so I am told. Still I remember that the scene of the Buddha smashing lacked the detail found in the theatrical experience. But the theatrical performance changes with each performance depending on the director, the actors, and the audience and so on. Printed texts of the play have undergone revisions: the four printings of *The Caretaker* before

1966 contain verbal changes; a revised hardback edition appeared in 1962, less than a year after the first Methuen edition. A revised Methuen issued in hardback and paperback was published in 1967.

The memories and the printed data intertwine: the latter, the data, the factual record is documented in the bibliographical history. *Harold Pinter: A Bibliographical History*, for convenience, in order to "give shape to my own life" is divided into eleven sections. These take into account Pinter's published juvenilia from 1947 until the terminus *ad quem*, October 2004. In other words 57 years of a creative career. A second edition is already in the works. This would have to include, for instance: his Nobel Prize acceptance Speech with manifold incarnations; the interview with the freelance journalist found on the Nobelprize.org website dated October 13, 2005 [a big assumption here which I'm going to return to is that the website is maintained and does not disappear into an ethereal graveyard]; *Voices*, Text by Harold Pinter, Music by James Clark, broadcast on BBC Radio 3 on Monday October 10, 2005; *Various Voices Prose, Poetry, Politics 1948-2005*, a continuation of the same title *1948-1998*, both published in the UK by Faber; and, to take one other instance, Grove Press, New York *Death etc.* not published in the UK. This includes Pinter's "Wilfred Owen Award" Speech, given on March 18, 2005, not accidentally included in the *Various Voices* latest incarnation.

The eleven sections of the *Bibliographical History* are: "A. Plays, and Sketches for the stage, Radio and Television", "B. Screenplays", "C. Poetry", "D. Fiction", "E. Prose Nonfiction: Essays, Articles and Published Speeches", "F. Published Letters to Newspapers, Magazines, etc", "G. Interviews Printed in Newspapers or Magazines", "H. Miscellaneous: Minor Pieces, Collaborative Writings, Editing, etc.", "I. Editions of Collected or Selected Works", "J. Sound Items", "K. Audio-Visual Materials".

A1.1 is the Encore first edition of *The Birthday Party* published on 1 December 1959 in a print run of 1,000 copies. Chronologically by date of publication the first item is in fact C.1 "Dawn", a poem published in the *Hackney Downs School Magazine*, no. 161 (Spring 1947) on page 27. No, I am wrong; there are in fact eight Pinter contributions to his school magazine. There is another poem, "O beloved maiden" in the Summer 1947 issue on page 14 and six other prose items. The first of these, an essay on "James Joyce" appeared in No. 160 (Christmas 1946), pp. 32–33, and is E1. According to this essay, by the time he was 16, Pinter had "read *Portrait* and *Ulysses* ... and was deep into *Finnegan's Wake*" [a volume I believe the now defunct Hackney Public Library allowed its borrower an overdue amnesty on many decades later. In his "A Speech of Thanks" for the David Cohen Award, Pinter admits to having "on a extended loan, as it were," the Bermondsey Public Reserve Library copy of Beckett's first novel *Murphy* hanging around since 1938!]. The youthful Pinter's words on *A Portrait* are worth recalling. It is "typical of Joyce, startlingly honest, true and forthright ... a work of great lyrical beauty." Of *Ulysses* Pinter writes,

> This enormous work, which depicts a day in the life of a Dubliner, stands supreme among twentieth-century literature. It is outstanding as a feat of narration, relating to streams of consciousness the innumerable thoughts that flit to and fro across the screen of the subconscious mind. Joyce omits nothing whatever, describing every thought, every word of this man. *Ulysses* is one of the most complete works of art ever written ... Joyce has always had great feelings for words ... no modern writer has used them to such effect.

And the description of *Finnegan's Wake* pinpoints and anticipates his artistic development:

> A nocturnal adventure, in which Joyce combined all languages to form an exquisite 'Joycean' prose. Here we are in a dream world, having as its main axis, the River Liffey, which flows through Dublin. All the Rivers of the world meet it, and with them come all their past river-side connections. Great personalities are vaguely introduced, and beyond these runs the chatter of Irish charwomen washing clothes in the Liffey. Many fantastic characters appear.... Joyce stands out ... as a very great humourist. At length the whole dream world falls asleep, and the words become drowsy and sleepy, and slowly the words subside into softness, softly drifting, and the work ends where it begins, in the middle of a sentence.

Pinter begins his schoolboy essay by exalting Joyce as the artist in exile who "As a very sensitive young man ... experienced seething discontent with his life in Dublin." Pinter notes how Joyce "rebelled against his narrow, Catholic environment, his home, his religion and his country, and left Ireland to return but once. Even though he spent most of his life abroad, all his work was about Dublin, which was the one great influence of his life—a great Irish Catholic shadow that for ever lay over him." Many autobiographical parallels connect the London poet with his admired Irish predecessor. Pinter still lives in London, but far from Hackney: his has been the voyage from Hackney to Chiswick, Worthing, Regent's Park via Stratford-upon-Avon and now Campden Hill Square, W8.

What is *not* recorded in *Harold Pinter: A Bibliographical History,* as it is largely confined to "published writings", are the telegrams received from Pinter, some of which were contradictory. The words I quoted at the beginning of this essay seem pertinent here. I will repeat them. They are not Harold's: "The idea of disinterring my journalism and juvenilia fills me with horror." When I wrote to Harold for permission late in 1972 I wished to publish extracts from the early writings and to itemize them and

Pinter's school activities as recorded from his school magazine. He was at Hackney Downs Grammar School from September 1942 to July 1948. It is my belief that Pinter's early work, his juvenilia, represented, for instance, by his comments on *Ulysses* and *Finnegan's Wake*, reveal his genius as well as Joyce's. They are some of the most insightful, helpful observations that I know on those two great works. Over the years my students have agreed with me.

Pinter has acknowledged in prose and in poetry the debt to his English Master, "Joseph Brearley 1909–1977". Here is his poem of that name first published in *Soho Square* edited by Ian Hamilton in 1982 (my C. 25):

Joseph Brearley 1909–1977
(Teacher of English)

Dear Joe, I'd like to walk with you
From Clapton Pond to Stamford Hill
And on,
Through Manor House to Finsbury Park,
And back,
On the dead 653 trolleybus,
To Clapton Pond,
And walk across the shadows on to Hackney Downs,
And stop by the old bandstand,
You tall in moonlight,
And the quickness in which it all happened,
And the quick shadow in which it persists.

You're gone. I'm at your side,
Walking with you from Clapton Pond to Finsbury Park,
And on, and on.

Following the tribute published in *Soho Square* is a three-line, eleven-word "Poem." Another tribute by Pinter:

I saw Len Hutton in his prime
Another time
another time

The first mention of Pinter in the *Hackney Downs School Magazine* I can find is in the "School Sports. Christmas 1946" section: He came 3rd in 220 yards for the under 16's. In the summer 1948 he was awarded school cricket and football colours. In the Spring 1947 he had opposed the motion "That a United States of Europe would be the only means of preventing war" in the School Literary and Debating Society.

Why the contradictory telegrams? In late 1972 and early 1973 Harold was undecided whether to give permission for publication of such information. This was included eventually in my first book, *Harold Pinter* (Oliver and Boyd, Barnes & Noble, 1973). The focus of the monograph was that the key to understanding Pinter lay in his ethnicity. One telegram said "Don't publish, Harold" and another "Publish if you must", and there were others now in my archive. Incidentally, in the autumn of 1947 he spoke to his schoolmates on "Realism and Post-Realism" focusing on Marcel Carne's *Les Enfants du Paradis*. This focuses on the relationship between art and life, fantasy and reality. It captures the Pinteresque poetry of dreams on the edge of destruction and chaos, the whiff of betrayal during the Nazi occupation of France, and the weasel underneath the cocktail cabinet.

Back however to "What is true?" *Harold Pinter: A Bibliographical History* "paints an extraordinary, detailed picture of a lifetime in print" (Angus O'Neill, *Bookdealer*, 17 November 2005, p. 16) of one who, to quote the Nobel citation, "In his plays uncovers the precipice under everyday prattle and forces entry into oppression's closed rooms."

The two appendices largely describe Pinter's manuscripts loaned by him to the British Library. "Appendix I: Individual Literary Works" (W. 1-67) presents the record of Pinter's more substantial or significant literary works and orders them in terms of the estimated order of their composition, that is of the completion of their composition. "Appendix II: Textual Revisions and Prompt Books" (A.1-7; B.1-8) largely describes print variants. Unfortunately, over one hundred and fifty pages of description of variants had to be cut at a late stage due to the insistence of the author's agent, Judy Daish, that the *Bibliographical History* include only published materials. There isn't space here to discuss the sensitive issues of the relationship between: (1) the author, (2) the agent—the agent's role and the evolving relationship with the author—and (3) the sleuth, the bibliographer. Nor is there time to investigate the complex relationship between the creator, his publisher or publishers, and the sleuth, except to note that Faber & Faber have a notable, commendable history of understanding the importance of the documentary record. For instance in the cases of Ezra Pound, T. S. Eliot, Larkin, and Pinter, they generously place no obstacles in the way. In fact, on the contrary, they were very helpful, providing, for example, important data, such as the number of copies printed of each title with the exact date of publication and so on.

To return to Pinter's bibliographical record, amongst the fascinating items uncovered is a poster for Janus Films, *The Guest*, the American title for *The Caretaker* (W.14.6.b), and details of an unpublished sketch, "Getting Acquainted" (W.11.2.b). These are listed in the comprehensive "Index" divided into "Index I: Works by Harold Pinter" and "Index II: General Index." Careful scrutiny of the first index reveals, for instance, under *Family Voices* a play for Radio (1981), "a series of silk screen prints designed and signed by Guy Vaesen and countersigned by Harold Pinter in a limited edition of forty, each signed and numbered in Pencil by Pinter and Vaesen. They measure 55 x 38.5 cms" (A.40.a). Four were offered on the Internet; this writer managed to obtain one for his collection.

The second index reveals that Harold Pinter, in a single sentence on the back cover of Anne Wilkinson's *Heresies: The Complete Poems of Anne Wilkinson, 1924-1961*, published in Montreal in 2003, endorses the work of the great Canadian poet: "Poised, spare, delicate, poignant, Anne Wilkinson's verse reveals rare poetic sensibility" (A.69.a).

In conclusion, *Harold Pinter: A Bibliographical History* records a career of enormous artistic longevity. During the period of nearly 60 years, Pinter has produced at least 30 plays, 14 sketches, 24 screenplays (4 of them adaptations for film of his own stage plays), many poems (a form he is now concentrating on), at least 12 published short stories, one novel, at least fifty-seven essays, articles, and published speeches, over fifty letters to newspapers. There are 125 interviews printed in newspapers and magazines, 70 miscellaneous items—endorsements, introductions, selections (for instance, of Larkin's poems) and other creative work. Not to mention the fact that he has acted in more than one hundred plays.

The period of his working life has witnessed extensive technological transformations, with print technology moving from linotype to computer by resetting and other media being transformed, as with the advent of colour TV, or completely new media coming into being. For example, the textual version of some speeches and poems has so far been published ONLY on the website www.haroldpinter.org. How long the website will be maintained is open to question. We live in an age of disappearing information. Websites are impermanent, they can be removed or disappear in the electronic never-never land. Scripts transformed into cassettes or discs may not be able to be played or even re-transcribed if the hardware cannot read the software. Technology becomes all too quickly obsolescent: indeed, it contains built-in obsolescence. Hence the even more urgent need for bibliographical history. This will ensure that somewhere the record is preserved and does not disappear. "My name is Ozymandias, King of Kings: Look upon my works, ye Mighty, and despair!" Also the lines about the sands of the desert and "The darkness drops again" don't seem too inappropriate in this context!

Harold Pinter: A Bibliographical History records and describes Pinter's creative output. It provides the context for the political, sociological and also aesthetic changes which its subject is responding to. It is a tribute to genius. To repeat, as Harold Pinter wrote in a most moving letter to its authors following publication, "it gives shape to my own life!"

Three Unpublished Harold Pinter Filmscripts: *The Handmaid's Tale, The Remains of the Day, Lolita*

CHRISTOPHER C. HUDGINS

My fascination with the unpublished filmscripts of Harold Pinter began with my first interview with Pinter, in that wonderful London study of his, in the spring of 1984. Anticipating my first sabbatical, I spent a considerable bit of time composing my very first letter to Harold Pinter, letting him know that I'd published a few pieces on his work and that I would be delighted if he could find the time to sit for an interview during my time in London when I would be researching his film and television work at the BBC and British Film Institute Archives. Generously, he spent about 90 minutes with me in very pleasant conversation. Soon after I returned to Las Vegas, Pinter sent me typescripts of two then-unpublished scripts, his still unproduced adaptation of Joseph Conrad's *Victory* and his adaptation of Russell Hoban's *Turtle Diary*. I was thrilled, of course, eventually publishing what I think was the first essay on Pinter's adaptation of *Victory*.

In the fall of 2000, Faber and Faber's wondrous three-volume collection of Harold Pinter's screenplays appeared. Not surprisingly to those who know their Pinter filmscript history, Pinter elected not to publish three of his completed filmscripts, *The Handmaid's Tale, The Remains of the Day,* and *Lolita*. Therein lies this tale, the reasons behind Pinter's decision not to publish these masterful filmscripts and their demonstrable superiority to the shooting scripts that were eventually used to make the films. We can thank our various lucky stars, though, that these Pinter filmscripts are now available not only in a few private collections but also in the Pinter Archive at the British Library. I've previously written at some length on both *Handmaid* and *Lolita,* but more succinctly examining all three unpublished filmscripts in conjunction with one another provides several interesting insights about Pinter's adaptation process.

Between 1987 and 1991, Pinter wrote three intensely "political" filmscripts, *Reunion, The Handmaid's Tale* and *The Remains of the Day.* During a two-hour interview in October of 1994, Pinter spoke with

Steven H. Gale and me about, among other things, how pleased he was with his filmscript adaptation of Fred Uhlman's *Reunion* and the film that resulted, particularly with its success at showing the effects of a period of horrific history through the personal vision of one man whose life has been destroyed by those historical forces and by too many of his fellow citizens' failing to resist them. Konraden, whose resistance has proved fatal, we understand as a man of moral courage, of a nobility that is spine-tingling in its selflessness and rightness. Hitler executed him, as one of the central figures involved in the assassination attempt, all hung with piano wire. All of Pinter's most obviously political works, including his script for *The Handmaid's Tale*, derive a worldview through the central perspective of one individual rather than attempting a more epic, sweeping vision. They are all the more effective because of that "personalization," avoiding the most serious aesthetic defect of "social" works of art, overt didacticism and self-satisfied superiority or condescension. Many of his works, too, for screen and stage embody tales of women's struggle against male or societal oppression, or religious oppression, and of their triumph.

I find Pinter's summary line about Josef K., in reference to his filmscript for Kafka's *The Trial*, perhaps his most revealing comment to consider as we think about his central figure in Pinter's filmscript adaptation of Margaret Atwood's *The Handmaid's Tale*. The thing he admires about Kafka's Josef K., Pinter says, is "The important thing ... that he fights like hell all the way along the line" (Gussow 73).

In Atwood's novel and in Pinter's adaptation, Kate exhibits some of that same courage. Much of her struggle to find it in the novel emerges through internal monologues. In his script, Pinter invents imaginative equivalents for that internal voice, and focuses on the horrors of Atwood's dystopia with specific reference to our own culture, society, and governance, worldwide. Unfortunately, during the "collaborative" film-making process, the director and others jettisoned or revised large chunks of Pinter's script. Pinter very kindly sent me some years ago a copy of his script for *Handmaid*, final typescript, dated February 1987. During our 1994 interview, Pinter told me that in the spring of 1987 he informed director Volker Schlondorf that he did not have the energy nor the time to do more with the script, suggesting that Schlondorf consult with Margaret Atwood about any revisions to Pinter's script he thought necessary. In retrospect, intensely regretting letting the film go, he told me, and later Mel Gussow, that he was surprised that the author "fucked up her own work," and that Schlondorf let actors revise a good bit of his dialogue. Pinter tells Michael Billington that the "thing became a hotchpotch" (299).

The film itself is an uneven, structural and pedestrian disaster put together by a committee of the director, the actors, and Margaret Atwood herself. While Pinter had honed and restructured the novel for the film medium, inventing dramatically rendered scenes to work toward the effect of most of the internal monologues, Atwood replaces some of Pinter's inventions with her own scenes and reinserts some of the material he has excised. That meddling destroyed the structural cohesiveness of Pinter's script and obliterated much of our understanding of Kate's moral or identity-seeking journey. The final scenes the collaborative process provides, at the expense of Pinter's very effective, coherent ending, add a layer of melodrama and claptrap which is even anti-feminist and which destroys any possibility of considering the film seriously.

At the end of the novel's narrative, Kate steps into that rescuing van, irresolute, musing to herself, "Whether this is my end or a new beginning I have no way of knowing. I have given myself over into the hands of strangers, because it can't be helped. And so I step into the darkness within; or else the light" (378). In essence, Atwood provides an ending where a prince in shining armor rescues the helpless lady fair. In his filmscript, Pinter improves upon that ending, capturing the spirit of the novel as a whole, which Atwood's ending ironically weakens. In Pinter's script, and in the finished film, Kate finally *acts*, no longer waiting, and kills the Commander in his study, a Pinter invention, with a knife hidden in her room by the Mayday resistance movement. Unfortunately, though the "Committee Script" keeps this element of Pinter's conclusion, it also reverts to Atwood's initial notion that Kate's child has been adopted by the elite and adds one of the soppiest voice-over wrap-ups I've ever endured, one which makes Kate appear weak, unsympathetic, and living for the purposes of the *men* of the rebellion. In contrast, the Pinter script, after Kate has been rescued by Mayday, provides a three-part coda. First we see a shot of the underground railroad, represented by a house in the country, at dawn, a new beginning. Kate gets out of an anonymous car as it pulls up, dressed in a short leather jacket and skirt, no longer obscured by the Handmaid's garb. We see and hear the owners of the house tell Kate that it's set for tomorrow at dawn, and watch a television broadcast about her lover Nick's successfully fooling the authorities. The second part of the coda, a recitative of the filmscript's first scene, shows Kate skiing off across the valley, a dangerous journey, but one potentially freeing.

Part three of the coda begins with shot 180, a Canadian country street, an ice cream wagon, girls in short skirts, boys riding bicycles. In the midst of this scene of normalcy, we hear "Sounds of children" as Kate discovers her daughter in the schoolyard and goes into the building to reunite with Jill. The scene evokes Kate's courage, her willingness to risk capture to regain her daughter, *and* the fact that she does this on her own, not as a recipient of a man's largesse. Providing a pleasing formal unity with the film's beginning image, this coda completes a pattern of suggestions that

Kate has achieved a type of growth, a renewal of moral courage in spite of adversity, which no longer leaves her "waiting" or despairing. That's remarkably superior to the film's ending, where Kate pleads with Nick, "Please don't leave me." In contrast, Pinter's Kate strikes a blow against the forces of patriarchal theocracy *and* embodies an emblem of motherhood and familial and sexual love. Pinter's script is much better than a work that merely says "Patriarchal Theocracies are bad." It's a very great shame that the filmmakers did not use it.

But in this instance, Pinter's contract did not allow him to remove his name from the film. By the time *The Remains of the Day* emerged, he had remedied that problem. Pinter had bought the rights to Kazuo Ishiguro's Booker Prize-winning novel, which he eventually sold to Mike Nichols, who had planned to direct the film using the script Pinter provided. When Nichols' schedule prevented him from directing the project, he sold the rights to Columbia, which set up Ismail Merchant and James Ivory to make the film with their scriptwriter, Ruth Prawer Jhabvala (Billington 324). In his letter to me of March 13, 1995, about his *Lolita* screenplay, Pinter writes: "My contract states that the film company can bring in another writer but that in such a case I can withdraw my name, which is exactly the case with 'The Remains of the Day.'"

I'll concentrate on what I think are the two most illogical, aesthetically unjustified revisions Jhabvala imposed on Pinter's far-superior script. As Edward T. Jones has suggested, the central problem with the finished film is that it emphasizes the frustrated love story implicit in the novel's narrative at the expense of "the political content that Ishiguro and Pinter underscore, most notably in the social criticism found in the novel" (100). Though Jhabvala retains much of Pinter's script, she destroys its aesthetic wholeness, its *quiditas,* by eliminating the character of the American industrialist, Mr. Farraday, who is the new owner of Darlington Hall in the novel. Instead, she has the new lord of the manor be former Pennsylvania Congressman Lewis, the American who has attacked Lord Darlington as a dangerous amateur trying to ameliorate the English government's hostility to Hitler's Nazi Germany. All sort of silliness mars the Jhabvala script, but this is perhaps the worst bit of illogical structuring, for her decision to have the former congressman purchase the Hall obviates the fact that he has been right in his political analysis and obviates the reversal of the Henry James theme, the American Innocent at the mercy of the sophisticated Europeans. As Stanley Kauffmann observes, in the novel, we see through Stevens', the Butler's, "eyes, more clearly than he does, what is happening around him. Ishiguro means this, I believe, as a comment on England. The film fractures his intent" (33).

The second worst bit of silliness in the Jhabvala script is its lack of faithfulness to the spirit of the novel at the film's conclusion. In the film, after an elaborate tea, Stevens and Miss Kenton, now Mrs. Benn, go to the pier together, where the crowd awaits the lights' switching on as dusk approaches. Miss Kenton utters the lines to Stevens about the evening being the best part of the day, and we watch, supposedly moist of eye, as the pair wave goodbye in the rain. Miss Kenton is at the open back of the bus as it draws away from Stevens, who doffs his hat and returns to his repressed life, measuring out his final days with coffee spoons.

In Pinter's script, which echoes the novel, after the couple have said their much less soppy goodbyes, Stevens ventures alone out onto that pier, a bit of courage in itself, emblematically, where he meets another of Pinter's surprising strangers, a retired bus driver in the Pinter script, who tells Stevens, "Take my tip. Stop looking back. Looking back'll get you nowhere. Why don't you look forward? Look forward to the evening. Believe me, it's the best part of the day" (164). The lights go on. We hear the crowd, laughing and calling to one another. Stevens suddenly gets up from that bench, pays his entry fee, and goes into the crowd. He and we in the audience have learned something about the dangers of retreat from both the political and the personal. As Jones concludes, the Pinter script, like the novel, "permits the English gentleman/butler to glimpse ... the evanescent and disturbing forms of twentieth-century politics and history, and then to go about his business, if he can" (107). No wonder Pinter removed his name from a film which emerged as a corny historical, romantic melodrama *posing* as serious.

The history of Adrian Lyne's *Lolita* is the most bizarre of the lot. In my 1994 interview with Pinter, he told me that he had thoroughly enjoyed writing a filmscript based on Nabokov's *Lolita,* which, at the time, he fully expected Lyne to use as the shooting script. Lyne, the director of *9 1/2 Weeks, Fatal Attraction* and *Indecent Exposure,* for pity's sake, had originally employed James Dearden, the writer for *9 1/2 Weeks,* to write the adaptation. Soon after my return from London, Pinter sent a copy of his version, suggesting that he'd enjoy reading my comments on it. In response to my lengthy reply, I was delighted to get back from Pinter a gracious letter of thanks, but disappointed to read this line: "I gather that David Mamet has been brought in, whether this means he will start afresh I have no idea" (Letter, 23 Jan. 1995). David Mamet very kindly sent me his *Lolita* script, and, through circuitous routes, I received a copy of the Dearden script and of the shooting script by Stephen Schiff, a staff writer for *The New Yorker* whom Lyne hired once the Mamet script was rejected. Pinter, of course, refused to publish this script as well, and his name is most certainly not on the film itself.

The Dearden script is remarkably ham-handed; the Mamet script is remarkably moralistic, missing much of Nabokov's subtlety; and the Schiff script, incorporating elements of the other three, and, as Lyne suggested, trying to "punch-up" the comic and the sexual elements of this masterpiece novel (Brennan, F-14), appears to have been written by committee. The Pinter script, a manuscript dated Sept. 26, 1994, in contrast, is one of his most masterful, again, fortunately available now in the Pinter Archive at the British Library. In one of the best commentaries on *Lolita,* David Rampton argues that the book calls on the reader both to condemn Humbert and to sympathize with him, recognizing in the central scene where Humbert meets the now pregnant and married Lolita that both Humbert and Lolita have grown morally. He finds that the novel's dramatic scenes, those without narrative comment, are central to the fruitful ambiguity of the novel, and it is precisely these scenes in which the strength of Pinter's adaptation lies, along with its beautifully structured use of Humbert's memory sequences.

Pinter's script includes a number of references to Humbert's recognition of his horrific destruction of the young girl he has loved and tried to nurture, but the central one is indeed their final meeting. In contrast to the other three scripts, too, Pinter does not allow his audience to ignore nor laugh at the truly despicable sexual behaviors that Humbert has pursued—there is nothing in Pinter's script like the nymphette eating a banana and pulling out her retainer.

After Lolita's letter pleading for Humbert's help arrives under the caption, "Three Years Later," we return to the beginning scene of Pinter's script, Humbert's driving toward this meeting, gun and reverently handled bobby pin in hand. Pinter has prepared us, subtly and ambiguously, to recognize Humbert's growth in his scene with Lolita Schiller, which is very faithful to the novel. Pinter chooses not to use in voice-over Humbert's interior monologue in the novel about not just adoring the nymph but loving the mature Lolita. But Pinter's precise dialogue and imagery, Humbert's clear despair at his recognition that Lolita, even pregnant and unkempt, will not come with him, are enough to make the point. Humbert's willingness to give Lolita the large sum of money to try to ensure her happy married life, despite her refusal of the favors she used to offer him for money, underlines that Humbert has grown morally; Lolita's refusal to go into detail about her debauches with Quilty, given the "presence" of that baby in her womb, points toward her own moral growth, as does her faithfulness to her husband and his promise of only a working class life—and her rejection of Quilty.

After Humbert has murdered Quilty, in pursuit of his "redemption," in the novel Humbert awaits the police. He remembers a day soon after Lolita's leaving him when he has contemplated a valley from a similar hill. Humbert recognizes, now, that the sound that accompanies his contemplation of a glorious natural setting "was but the melody of children at play, nothing but that, and so limpid was the air that within this vapor of blended voices, majestic and minute, remote and magically near, frank and divinely enigmatic—one could hear, now and then, as if released, an almost articulate spurt of vivid laughter, or the crack of a bat, or the clatter of a toy wagon.... I stood listening to that musical vibration from my lofty slope.... And then I knew that the hopelessly poignant thing was not Lolita's absence from my side, but the absence of her voice from that concord" (280).

More evocative than Dearden's truncated version of this miraculous passage in his adaptation, and more concise than Schiff's, Pinter's direction for this scene reads: "A growing sound from the valley. The sound consists of a melody of children at play. It is distant. It vibrates, murmurs, sings. Humbert stands still." This last direction suggests contemplation, and, then, in voice-over, Humbert whispers, "Light of my life, fire of my loins. My sin, my soul. Lo–lee–ta" (188). That juxtaposition of sin and soul points us toward our cumulative recognition that Humbert is aware that he has wronged Lolita by robbing her of her childhood; he is also aware that, in part, that selfish theft has occurred because of his own loss of childhood, both of mother and first love, scenes which Pinter includes in his script—but *also* that his "sin" has been his inability to overcome, through strength of will, that traumatic experience for many years, to his own detriment, as well as to Lolita's.

At its core, Pinter's *Lolita* adaptation, like his others, is so successful because his ear for language results in an intelligent echoing and fruitful reshaping of Nabokov's descriptions of Humbert's interior musings and memories, *and* because his restructuring of the novel so aptly fits it to the film medium. Coupled with a marvelous facility at invention, which echoes the spirit of these novels, and at compression, Pinter unerringly centers on what is best about these novels, and most essential. All three films would have been much better had they not violated the scripts produced by our most intelligent, sensitive, and evocative writer of adaptations of complex novels for the screen.

NOTE

This paper was presented at the 10th Annual Europe Theatre Awards, Turin, Italy, March 2006. My thanks to Michael Billington and to Susan Hollis Merritt for their help in arranging my invitation to participate in this wonderful event, sponsored this year by the Italian Ministry of Culture and Sport.

WORKS CITED

Atwood, Margaret. *The Handmaid's Tale*. Boston: Houghton Mifflin, 1986.

Billington, Michael. *The Life and Work of Harold Pinter*. London: Faber, 1996.

Brennan, Judy. "Not Your Average Nymphet." *Los Angeles Times*. 14 July 1995, F1, F14.

Dearden, James. *Lolita.* Unpublished screenplay. Christopher C. Hudgins Collection. The script is labeled "Third Draft," and dated Oct. 21, 1991.

Gussow, Mel. *Conversations with Pinter.* New York: Grove, 1994.

Hudgins, Christopher C. "Harold Pinter's *The Handmaid's Tale:* Freedom, Prison, and a Hijacked Script." *Captive Audience: Prison and Captivity in Contemporary Theatre.* Ed. Thomas Fahy and Kimball King. New York: Routledge, 2003, 81–108.

— "Harold Pinter's *Lolita:* 'My Sin, My Soul.'" *The Films of Harold Pinter.* Ed. Steven H. Gale. Albany: State University of New York Press, 2001, 123–46.

— "*Victory:* A Pinter Screenplay Based on the Conrad Novel." *The Pinter Review: Annual Essays 1991.* Ed. Francis Gillen, Steven H. Gale. Tampa: U of Tampa P, 1991, 23–32.

Ishiguro, Kazuo. *The Remains of the Day.* London: Faber, 1989.

Jones, Edward T. "On *The Remains of the Day:* Harold Pinter Remaindered." *The Films of Harold Pinter.* Ed. Steven H. Gale. Albany: State University of New York Press, 2001.

Kauffmann, Stanley. "An Elegy." *New Republic,* Dec. 6, 1993, 32–33.

Mamet, David. *Lolita.* Unpublished screenplay. Christopher C. Hudgins Collection. The script is dated March 10, 1995.

Nabokov, Vladimir. *Lolita.* New York: Berkeley, 1982, rpt. New York: Random House, 1955; rpt. New York: Vintage, 1989.

Pinter, Harold. *The Handmaid's Tale.* Unpublished screenplay. Christopher C. Hudgins Collection. The script, labeled "Final Typescript," carries the date Feb. 1987.

— Interview with Christopher C. Hudgins, May 15, 1984.

— Interview with Christopher C. Hudgins and Steven H. Gale, October 26, 1994.

— Letter to Christopher C. Hudgins, Jan. 23, 1995.

— Letter to Christopher C. Hudgins, March 13, 1995.

— *Lolita.* Unpublished screenplay, Sept. 26, 1994. Christopher C. Hudgins Collection.

— *The Remains of the Day.* Unpublished screenplay, 1991. Christopher C. Hudgins Collection.

Rampton, David. "*Lolita.*" *Lolita: Modern Critical Approaches.* Ed. Harold Bloom. New York: Chelsea House, 1987. Rpt. *Vladimir Nabokov:* A *Critical Study of the Novels.* London: Cambridge U P, 1984.

Schiff, Stephen. *Lolita.* Unpublished screenplay. Christopher C. Hudgins Collection. The script carries the notations "Second Revised Draft" and "8/22/95 Rev. Blue." The date at the lower right is July 6, 1995.

(Anti-)Global Pinter[1]

SUSAN HOLLIS MERRITT

(With apologies and thanks to Harold Pinter and Len Hutton)

I knew Harold Pinter in his day
Another play, another play

> I travel the globe in my job. [....] My work took me to Sicily. My work concerns itself with life all over, you see, in every part of the globe. With people all over the globe. I use the word globe because the word world possesses emotional political sociological and psychological pretensions and resonances which I prefer as a matter of choice to do without, or shall I say to steer clear of, or if you like to reject. How's the yacht?
>
> – Deeley to Anna, in *Old Times* (1971)

> I'm in an odd position because in a sense I'm undoubtedly an outsider in society because I simply use my critical intelligence.... But at the same time, I have to face the fact—it's not a bad thing—that I'm very much part of the world in which I live because I've been part of it for such a long time and I've done an awful lot of work and my work is performed, and done, and I'm part of all that. So that I think I'm also accepted generally as an idiosyncratic, you know, bloke, who nevertheless is part of contemporary drama—my plays have been done for the last 45 years or whatever it is.... I think [for some] it's a question of securing your uneasy and precarious place in the world: the best thing to do is not ask too many questions.... I think that with some people there's a terrible fear of being unpopular, but somehow I've always been vaguely unpopular, so I'm used to it.
>
> – "Unthinkable Thoughts—An Interview with Harold Pinter —August 1999" (Edwards)

The official Web site for "the international playwright Harold Pinter" (www.haroldpinter.org) was launched in September 2000. A few years later, in 2003, Vivienne Jabri (Director of the London Centre of International Relations, at the Department of War Studies, King's College, University of London) contemplated Pinter's entrance into "the fray in the scene of the international": "Pinter is a powerful voice in the British public sphere. He carries with him social capital that few others possess, for his is a voice not just of protest but of a form of legitimacy that comes with being a member of the British establishment. He is a dissident who has access to the public sphere" (2).

The prestige of the Nobel Prize has expanded Pinter's "access to the public sphere," assuring a vast worldwide audience for his Nobel Lecture, "Art, Truth and Politics." Technological advances propelling mainstream media online and alternative voices "chattering" throughout the burgeoning "blogosphere" give Pinter's words and images unprecedented reach. Beyond "Pinter's various public pronouncements against tyranny and war"—which he reiterates and expands in his Nobel Lecture—and beyond "political theatre"—which he also addresses in it—Pinter's theater itself now functions even more as, what Jabri calls, "a location of dissent." Pinter's political impulses are deeply personal and passionately felt by Pinter himself and others. Charles Grimes posits that "all of Pinter's work emerges from his political views," while Michael Billington establishes its biographical contexts, how Pinter's political views emerge from the author's life experiences. Pinter's double focus on personal and political aspects of power relations throughout his life and work generates "a complex, interactive, social space" (Jabri 4). As this "space" extends into *virtual space*, Pinter's influence grows exponentially in complexity and interactivity.[2]

While an "international" playwright, citizen Pinter is not "global." He is anti-*globe* or pro-*world*; reversing Deeley's priorities, he prefers to use "the word world" to "the word globe." He dramatizes and confronts world-related "emotional political sociological and psychological pretensions and resonances" in multiple media and venues. He opposes the petrochemical, military-industrial complex and corporate privatization of public utilities reducing health, education, and other social services; supports nuclear disarmament; opposes war; exposes deceits catapulting thugs toward world hegemony and descries their violence. Anti-globalization, pro-world, living and working in the theater—outside/inside global politics, Harold Pinter is pro-human rights, pro-humanity—*for* "all these people" whom politics puts at risk. He understands what endangers our human species.

Truth in Play

> As long as art is searching and unafraid, it has to be seen as a positive force.
>
> –Harold Pinter, interview conducted by Isabel Hilton, 11 May 2004 (Andrews)

> Political theater does not mean putting on a play about politics; it means putting on a play by Václav Havel. That is a deliberate

act. That is a political act. You can put Havel in prison, but you can't put Vaněk in prison.

–Achim Benning, Artistic Director of the Burgtheater in Vienna (9 Oct. 2002)

In the state theaters we are doomed to be insincere.

–Oleg Chidorchik, actor with the Belarussian Army Theater (Feb. 2006)[3]

In "Art, Truth and Politics," juxtaposing his earlier statements on "truth" and "reality" featured on his Web site and offering fascinating details about his creative processes in composing *The Homecoming* and *Old Times*, Pinter speaks as an author about "truth" in "dramatic art":

> Truth in drama is forever elusive. You never quite find it but the search for it is compulsive. The search is clearly what drives the endeavour. The search is your task. More often than not you stumble upon the truth in the dark, colliding with it or just glimpsing an image or a shape which seems to correspond to the truth, often without realising that you have done so. But the real truth is that there never is any such thing as one truth to be found in dramatic art. There are many. These truths challenge each other, recoil from each other, reflect each other, ignore each other, tease each other, are blind to each other. Sometimes you feel you have the truth of a moment in your hand, then it slips through your fingers and is lost. (*Art, Truth & Politics* 5-6)[4]

Echoing his own words "Language ... is a highly ambiguous business" from his speech at the National Student Drama Festival in Bristol in 1962 ("Writing for the Theatre" 23), but adding striking new imagery, Pinter concludes: "So language in art remains a highly ambiguous transaction, a quicksand, a trampoline, a frozen open pool which might give way under you, the author, at any time" (8). Despite such insecurity, such lack of certitude, and however transitory dramatic truth may be, Pinter is quite clear about the need for its search to go on unimpeded: "But as I have said, the search for the truth can never stop. It cannot be adjourned, it cannot be postponed. It has to be faced, right there, on the spot" (8).

When Pinter turns his scrutiny from truth in art and in drama in general to "political theatre," he observes that political theater "presents an entirely different set of problems" (8). In his 1985 interview with Nicholas Hern about *One for the Road* (1984), "A Play and Its Politics," Pinter admits, "I always find agit-prop insulting and objectionable. And now, of course, I'm doing exactly the same thing. There's very little I can say about it. I'm aware of that great danger, the great irritant to an audience" (18). Early in his career, in 1962, Pinter complained about people's expectations for "the playwright to be a prophet":

> There is certainly a good deal of prophecy indulged in by playwrights these days, in their plays and out of them. Warnings, sermons, admonitions, ideological exhortations, moral judgements, defined problems with built-in solutions; all can camp under the banner of prophecy. The attitude behind this sort of thing might be summed up in one phrase: '*I'm* telling *you*!' ("Writing for the Theatre" 22).

Forty-three years later, in his Nobel Lecture presented at the Swedish Academy, he begins with the same stance, then deviates from it significantly:

> Sermonising has to be avoided at all cost. Objectivity is essential. The characters must be allowed to breathe their own air. The author cannot confine and constrict them to satisfy his own taste or disposition or prejudice. He must be prepared to approach them from a variety of angles, from a full and uninhibited range of perspectives, take them by surprise, perhaps, occasionally, but nevertheless give them the freedom to go which way they will. This does not always work. And political satire, of course, adheres to none of these precepts, in fact does precisely the opposite, which is its proper function. (8)

Thus, Pinter provides a rationale for his own political satires: *The Hothouse* (1980); *Precisely* (1983), *One for the Road* (1984), *Mountain Language* (1988), *The New World Order* (1991), *Party Time* (1991/1992), *Press Conference* (2002), and aspects of *Ashes to Ashes* (1996) and *Celebration* (2000)—and for political satires of recent decades by other playwrights whom he admires, such as Ariel Dorfman, Václav Havel, and David Hare, and newer playwrights like the late Sarah Kane (1971-1999) and Martin McDonagh (1970-), whose work Pinter supported or influenced.[5]

One for the Road, *Mountain Language*, *Party Time*, and *Ashes to Ashes* are plays to which Pinter may be referring when, after learning of his Nobel Prize, he told Michael Billington that "the world has had enough of my plays" and that in his native England especially, where he perceives "a bit of a silence," the audience does not seem to "like" his "later plays" particularly ("'They said'"). "More than any other contemporary playwright," Jabri observes, "Pinter reveals to an audience the complexity of power and how power operates upon the body of the subject. An audience comes to be witness to its own vulnerability as its visceral corporeality is made all too evident" (2).[6] In these "later plays," Pinter is "engaged in exposing the present and the power relations contained therein" (Jabri 6); yet, as in his earlier plays, he also dramatizes that dimension of power over minds through the use of power over bodies.

In *One for the Road*, Nicolas breaks down his victims' mental resistance and bodily resilience with threatening words and gestures, backed up by his "soldiers" who carry them out. Victor—ironically no victor—is Nicolas' prisoner, subject to whatever he says and does. Frightened, he is mostly silent as Nicolas taunts him:

> What do you think this is? It's my finger. And this is my little finger. I wave my big finger in front of your eyes. Like this. And now I do the same with my little finger. I can also use both ... at the same time like this. Like this. I can do absolutely anything I like. (*One for the Road* 33)

Citing this passage in "A Play and Its Politics," his February 1985 interview with Nicolas Hern, Pinter observes:

> [Nicolas] has all power within those walls. He knows this is the case, he believes that it is right, for him, to possess this power, because, as far as he's concerned, he's acting for his country legitimately and properly. When he refers to the country's values, those are his values. And because of those values, he will kill, allow rape, everything he can think of. And torture. In order to protect the realm, anything is justified.

He adds:

> It is also ... true that many of the natural sadistic qualities, which we all possess, are given free rein in the play. The audience felt fear—but what was it fear of? Fear not only of being in the position of the given victim, but a fear also born of recognition of themselves as interrogator. Because think of the joy of having absolute power. (16-17)[7]

In the last scene Victor speaks but is barely audible, as his tongue has been mutilated offstage between scenes. He "*mutters*" something indecipherable, which Nicolas makes him repeat, clarifying that he is asking after his son—"My son" (75-77). Nicolas responds, nonchalantly—"Your son? Oh, don't worry about him. He was a little prick" (79). From this cruelly-casual use of the past tense ("was"), Victor and the audience learn that Nicky—ironically a diminutive of Nicolas—is dead. Shocked speechless, all Victor can do is "*straighten ... and stare at* NICOLAS" (80).

During the Lincoln Center Festival's Harold Pinter Festival in New York, in the summer of 2001, performing Nicolas in *One for the Road*, Pinter began with a long pantomime, potently projecting how Nicolas' "joy" in having such power is mitigated by doubts and insecurities (assuaged by alcohol), paralleling his violent precursors, Goldberg and McCann in *The Birthday Party* (1958), Roote in *The Hothouse* (1958/1980), and Ben and Gus in *The Dumb Waiter* (1959). These early plays are more "metaphorical" than his later "overtly-political plays."[8]

Mountain Language, Jabri observes, "is not simply about an oppressed minority whose language is forbidden. Above all else, it is, like others of Pinter's plays, about the language games that contain relations of domination; between men and women in the most intimate relations to the most overtly political encounters in the prison cell" (5). Alluding to *The Birthday Party* in his Nobel Lecture, Pinter says: "I think I allow a whole range of options to operate in a dense forest of possibility before finally focusing on an act of subjugation" (8). In contrast, he asserts, "*Mountain Language* pretends to no such range of operation. It remains brutal, short and ugly" (8). Pinter puts the relatively few comic moments of such violent plays into context: "But the soldiers in the play do get some fun out of it. One sometimes forgets that torturers become easily bored. They need a bit of a laugh to keep their spirits up" (8-9). After a brief dramatic pause, Pinter observes dryly: "This has been confirmed of course by the events of Abu Ghraib in Baghdad" (9). Once critical of viewing "the playwright as a prophet," Harold Pinter the playwright has indeed been prophetic.

Death

> We are encouraged to be cowards. We can't face the dead. But we must face the dead because they die in our name. We must pay attention to what is being done in our name.
>
> –Harold Pinter, "Oh, Superman" (Broadcast for *Opinion* Channel 4, 31 May 1990)

> I have referred to death quite a few times this evening. I shall now quote a poem of my own called 'Death.'
>
> –Harold Pinter, "Art, Truth & Politics" (7 Dec. 2005)

Mountain Language "lasts only 20 minutes, but," Pinter emphasizes in the Nobel Lecture, like real-life torture, "it could go on for hour after hour, on and on and on, the same pattern repeated over and over again, on and on, hour after hour" (9).[9] "*Ashes to Ashes*, on the other hand," he adds, "seems to me to be taking place under water" (9). This metaphorical description of *Ashes to Ashes*, a play written a decade ago, whose language and subject are at times tortuous and torturous, seems informed by Pinter's own personal near-death experiences following his cancer surgery in 2002, his frightening fall on rain-slicked pavement in Dublin, resulting in a head injury, the weekend before his 75th birthday (10 Oct. 2005, just three days before the Nobel announcement, on the 13th), and hospitalizations preventing him from attending the Nobel Prize Ceremony and from giving his Nobel Lecture in person in Stockholm in December. Later, in March 2006, most fortunately recovered enough to travel to Turin, Italy, where he accepted the Europe Theatre Prize, Pinter repeated his personal associations between dying and drowning, recalling movingly how his inability to breathe in the hospital in December 2005 reminded him of a boyhood experience of nearly drowning.

Throughout his work, increasingly over the past two decades, Pinter reveals how much "the dead" and dying have "haunted" him and, since late 2001/early 2002, how this much-heightened sense of his own mortality has preoccupied him: "the one thing that I can say [...] is that having escaped death, by the skin of my teeth by the way, I'm much much more aware of what mortality is and I know I didn't think about death before I had cancer. I mean, I thought about death but not from right in the pit of my stomach, you know, and now I realise that having escaped once I am not going to escape twice" (Batty 92).[10] In his videotaped Nobel Lecture Pinter echoes not only imagery of *Ashes to Ashes* but also imagery that he used in August 2002, when speaking with Ramona Koval at the Edinburgh International Book Festival, his first public appearance since his cancer surgery. Describing his post-operative experience to Koval, he said: "I'll give another image, an ocean in which you can't swim. You've no idea how to get out of it and you simply float about and bob about and are hit by terrible waves and so on, and it's all very dark, really."[11] In November 2002, upon accepting his honorary degree from the University of Turin, he repeated these metaphors but connected the personal with the political:

> The operation and its after-effects were something of a nightmare. I felt I was a man unable to swim, bobbing about under water in a deep dark endless ocean. But I did not drown and I am very glad to be alive. However, I found that to emerge from a personal nightmare was to enter an infinitely more pervasive public nightmare—the nightmare of American hysteria, ignorance, arrogance, stupidity and belligerence: the most powerful nation the world has ever known effectively waging war against the rest of the world. ("University of Turin Speech" 241)

Pinter's metaphorical description of *Ashes to Ashes* as "taking place under water" alludes to his character Rebecca's account of a purportedly hitherto-unmentioned "lover" to Devlin, who appears to be her husband. Rebecca describes this torturer/lover (who may actually be her phantasmagorical projection of Devlin himself) as a "guide" who "led me down the alleys between the rows of workpeople" in "a kind of factory" (reminiscent of Nazi slave laborers) whose workers "would follow him over a cliff and into the sea, if he asked them, he said" (25). Later, Rebecca envisions a scene outside a garden window in Dorset: "a whole crowd of people" (evocative of refugees fleeing the Nazis) "walking through the woods, on their way to the sea," into which they escape with their suitcases, apparently drowning themselves.[12]

As Pinter is "haunted" by these particular "images" that he could not have experienced himself, so is his character Rebecca; it is *as if* these images *were* memories (for both Pinter and his character).[13] In that sense,

Rebecca is a projection of the author, Harold Pinter, and reflects his own vicarious experiences of various media (books, films, television programs, etc., including his research about the Nazis and the Holocaust for various projects, as Grimes suggests as well): what Begley refers to as "culture" and "cultural representation" (184); cultural memory (in a Jungian sense). In that millions of people died as a result of the Holocaust and other "atrocities" to which *Ashes to Ashes* alludes, survivors' testimonies and cultural artifacts based on them and embellished by our own imaginations are really all the rest of us ("survivors" by default of history) can experience vicariously in order to understand and to try to envision and to come to terms with what "happened" to them. We relate to their personal histories in our own unique ways, in terms of our own unique life experiences.

Rebecca's images of "all these people" carrying suitcases through the woods on their way to the sea recall visual scenes from the film *A Day in October* (1992), a fictionalized account of an historical event which occurred in October 1943. During the Nazi occupation of Denmark, "some 7,200 Jews," threatened with deportation to death and concentration camps, were successfully rescued in fishing boats across the sea to neutral Sweden in the chilly dark of night.[14] In recounting a "memory" (as it were) to Devlin, Rebecca reverses that fortunate historical outcome to a horrific mass suicide ("death by water" [T. S. Eliot, Part IV of *The Wasteland*]) incongruously set on a warm summer day:

> Oh yes, there's something I've forgotten to tell you. It was funny. I looked out of the garden window, out of the window into the garden, in the middle of summer, in that house in Dorset, do you remember? Oh no, you weren't there. I don't think anyone else was there. No. I was all by myself. I was alone. I was looking out of the window and I saw a whole crowd of people walking through the woods, on their way to the sea, in the direction of the sea. They seemed to be very cold, they were wearing coats, although it was such a beautiful day. A beautiful, warm, Dorset day. They were carrying bags. There were ... guides ushering them, guiding them along. They walked through the woods and I could see them in the distance walking across the cliff and down to the sea. Then I lost sight of them. I was really very curious so I went upstairs to the highest window in the house and I looked way over the top of the treetops and I could see down to the beach. The guides ... were ushering all these people across the beach. It was such a lovely day. It was so still and the sun was shining. And I saw all these people walk into the sea. The tide covered them slowly. The bags bobbed about in the waves. (47-49)

Unlike the actual rescue effort of the Danish Jews, which resulted in transporting several thousand people to safety by boats (at night), in Rebecca's account "all these people" (who leave during the day) drown themselves in "the sea" and thus perish. The changes of such details would seem to reflect (and be a gauge of) Rebecca's own preoccupations and fantasies (fears and wishes). As Pinter suggests, she seems to want to "die."[15] In his Nobel Lecture Pinter alludes rather cryptically to this monologue—which, in the Roundabout Theatre Company American première, Lindsay Duncan performed, without affect—a depressive helplessly haunted by memory, both real and fantasized, both mesmerized and mesmerizing (Merritt, "*Ashes to Ashes* in New York" 157-58). Pinter reverses Rebecca's projection onto "all these people," duplicating his character's (and his own) introjection of their experiences imagined vicariously from accounts and cultural representations of the Holocaust and other atrocities that he (and presumably she) has read and seen in films. Rebecca is a symbol ("a lost figure") for these "others"; no longer a "sole survivor," she herself becomes a victim succumbing to the fate that she describes, one who suffers deeply from (however imagined) "survivor's guilt." Whatever "suffering" she may have endured in her real-life experience with Devlin, whom she calls a "fuckpig" (*Ashes to Ashes* 9), causes her to retreat into her own state of mind, so that, by the play's end, she is totally absorbed in it, becoming "a lost figure in a drowning landscape," a configuration of her own imagination:

> A drowning woman, her hand reaching up through the waves, dropping down out of sight, reaching for others, but finding no one there, either above or under the water, finding only shadows, reflections, floating; the woman a lost figure in a drowning landscape, a woman unable to escape the doom that seemed to belong only to others. (*Art, Truth & Politics* 9)

In that passage of his Nobel Lecture, Pinter elaborates on the metaphor used by Rebecca to describe the "condition known as elephantiasis" as becoming engulfed—drowning—in a "vast sea of gravy" in *Ashes to Ashes*:

> This mental elephantiasis means that when you spill an ounce of gravy, for example, it immediately expands and becomes a vast sea of gravy. It becomes a sea of gravy which surrounds you on all sides and you suffocate in a voluminous sea of gravy. It's terrible. [… .] (51)

Though not *directly* responsible for the deaths of the victims of the Holocaust and other "atrocities" that she appears to "remember," nevertheless Rebecca assumes such responsibility:

> But it's all your fault. You brought it upon yourself. You are not the *victim* of it, you are the *cause* of it. Because it was you who spilt the gravy in the first place, it was you who handed over the bundle [with the baby wrapped up in it]. (51).[16]

Retrospectively, in his Nobel Lecture, it seems to me, one with his character, Pinter identifies with Rebecca, who he interprets to be identifying with these "others" described in *Ashes to Ashes*: with Holocaust victims and survivors such as Bessie K., whose videotaped and transcribed testimony Rebecca echoes later in her echoing monologues. Rebecca denies their connection—"nothing has ever happened to me … I have never suffered" (41). But such "atrocities" *have* "happened" to "all these others" however much they are denied ("It never happened"). "But as they died, she must die too," Pinter explains. But as they died, he must die too. But as they died, we must die too. Rebecca is "all these people," Harold Pinter is Rebecca, Rebecca is Harold Pinter, we are they, and they are we. Such *comradery* in death, such mutual "responsibility" for "the dead," is one of "many truths" in Pinter's dramatic art.

Yet another "truth" may prevail, as Pinter is also not Rebecca, and neither are we. If he succeeds in "estrang[ing]" us from Rebecca's "disabling awareness of guilt," as Grimes suggests Pinter "attempts" to do in *Ashes to Ashes* (204), then he may be enabling and even directing us to embrace a personal, political, and social activism that his isolated character's cultural and personal repression prevents her from achieving. Pinter may direct us toward a different kind of responsibility, *civic responsibility*—a pre-requisite for the kind of "civil society" advocated by Václav Havel.[17]

The Politics of Deception/The Politics of Death

> I see myself not only as an actor and an entertainer, but … I'm also a citizen of the world in which I live, and I take responsibility for that, I really *insist* on taking responsibility and *understand* my responsibility quite precisely as *actually* trying to find out what *the truth* is. And what actually happens. And so [what] I've found is that we're really at the bottom of a *blanket* of lies which unfortunately we are either too indifferent or too frightened to question.
>
> –Harold Pinter, "Language and Lies" (1988)

Making his transition from "truth" in art to lack of truth or "lies" in politics, Pinter observes that

> Political language, as used by politicians, does not venture into any of this [artistic] territory since the majority of politicians, on the evidence available to us, are interested not in truth but in power and in the maintenance of that power. To maintain that power it is essential that people remain in ignorance, that they live in ignorance of the truth, even the truth of their own lives. What surrounds us therefore is *a vast tapestry of lies, upon which we feed.* (*Art, Truth & Politics* 9; italics added.)

This phenomenon—living in "lies"—is the antithesis of what Václav Havel calls "living in truth." Deploying a similar mixture of metaphors, in *The Politics of Truth: Inside the Lies that Led to War and Betrayed My Wife's CIA Identity: A Diplomat's Memoir* (2004), Ambassador Joseph Wilson documents "the fabric of lies, distortions and misinformation that [the Bush administration] had woven and fed the world to justify its war" (414-15).[18] As Wilson documents throughout his book, Harold Pinter recognizes: "The truth is something entirely different. The truth is to do with how the United States understands its role in the world and how it chooses to embody it" (9). Pinter continues:

> As every single person here knows, the justification for the invasion of Iraq was that Saddam Hussein possessed a highly dangerous body of weapons of mass destruction, some of which could be fired in 45 minutes, bringing about appalling devastation. We were assured that was true. It was not true. We were told that Iraq had a relationship with Al Quaeda and shared responsibility for the atrocity in New York of September 11th 2001. We were assured that this was true. It was not true. We were told that Iraq threatened the security of the world. We were assured it was true. It was not true. (9)

Before chronicling this "vast tapestry of lies, upon which we feed" in "the present," Pinter reviews "the recent past … United States foreign policy ['low intensity conflict']" (10-15), charging that, on its way to world domination, the U.S. dismantled democratically-elected governments "throughout the world" and "supported and in many cases engendered … every right-wing military dictatorship in the world after the end of the Second World War."[19] Echoing as a refrain his 1996 essay "It Never Happened" and several of his other essays and speeches, now for a vast world-wide audience, he adds, "And it is as if it never happened":

> Hundreds of thousands of deaths took place throughout these countries. Did they take place? And are they in all cases attributable to US foreign policy? The answer is yes they did take place and they are attributable to American foreign policy.
>
> But you wouldn't know it.
>
> It never happened. Nothing ever happened. Even while it was happening it wasn't happening. It didn't matter. It was of no interest. (15)

Continuing to echo his earlier polemical writings, Pinter declares:

> The crimes of the United States have been systematic, constant, vicious, remorseless, but very few people have actually *talked* about them. You have to hand it to America. It has exercised a quite

> clinical manipulation of power worldwide while *masquerading* as a force for universal good. It's a brilliant, even witty, highly successful act of *hypnosis.* (15; italics added)

Returning to the present, Pinter refers graphically to the "criminal outrage" and "torture" being committed by the detentions in Guantanamo Bay, resulting from "[t]he invasion of Iraq," which (as he has done consistently in other speeches and essays), Pinter considers "a bandit act, an act of blatant state terrorism, demonstrating absolute contempt for the concept of international law," "an arbitrary military action inspired by a series of lies upon lies and gross manipulation of the media and therefore of the public," and "an act intended to consolidate American military and economic control of the Middle East masquerading—as a last resort—all other justifications having failed to justify themselves—as liberation" of the Iraqi people from the dictatorship of Saddam Hussein (16-17). Contrary to the Bush administration's rhetoric, as Ambassador Joseph Wilson and so many others have pointed out and as Pinter charges, the U.S.-Coalition led War in Iraq is, in actual practice: "A formidable assertion of military force responsible for the death and mutilation of thousands and thousands of innocent people" (17). But Pinter also goes beyond "It Never Happened" and his earlier writings to wonder rhetorically: "What has happened to our moral sensibility? Did we ever have any? What do these words mean? Do they refer to a term very rarely employed these days—conscience? A conscience to do not only with our own acts but to do with our *shared responsibility* in the acts of others? Is all this *dead*?" (16; italics added). We must acknowledge our own "shared responsibility" for the casualties of the politics of deception: we must "actually *talk* … about them," as Pinter does in his Nobel Lecture:

> Death in this context [war] is irrelevant. Both Bush and Blair place death well away on the back burner. At least 100,000 Iraqis were killed by American bombs and missiles before the Iraq insurgency began. These people are of no moment. Their deaths don't exist. They are blank. They are not even recorded as being dead. "We don't do body counts," said the American general Tommy Franks.
>
> ....
>
> The 2,000 [4,113 as of 26 June 2008] American dead are an embarrassment. They are transported to their graves in the dark. Funerals are unobtrusive, out of harm's way. The mutilated rot in their beds, some for the rest of their lives. So the dead and the mutilated both rot, in different kinds of graves. (*Art, Truth & Politics* 18).[20]

We must renounce cowardice ("It never happened") and become brave comrades" of "all these people" whom Rebecca ("a drowning woman") imagines drowning in a sea of lies. We must "always remember" the victims and "never forget" the murderers, lest we join them either in perpetrating or in being victims of the same "doom."[21]

Harold Pinter reads an "extract" from Pablo Neruda's poem "I'm Explaining a Few Things" (19-20), published by Jonathan Cape in 1970, calling it the most "powerful visceral description of the bombing of civilians" in "contemporary poetry" that he knows (20). Its harrowing refrain "Come and see the blood in the streets" recalls the "bumpy" icy streets that Rebecca describes in *Ashes to Ashes* and may even have inspired them.[22] Pinter returns to United States military policies (10) and asserts more emphatically than he has done in earlier speeches:

> Many thousands, if not millions, of people in the United States itself are demonstrably sickened, shamed and angered by their government's actions, but as things stand they are not a coherent political force—yet. But the anxiety, uncertainty and fear which we can see growing daily in the United States is unlikely to diminish. (21).[23]

Pinter offers facetiously to "volunteer" for "the job" of President Bush's speech writer, scripting a scene in which this "man's man" lays claim to his "moral authority" (21-22), sounding perhaps more like Nicolas in *One for the Road* as played by himself or Alan Bates—or like Rebecca's torturer/lover and presumed husband Devlin in *Ashes to Ashes*: "Kiss my fist" (3 & 73-75)—than like President Bush: "'You see this fist? This is my moral authority. And don't you forget it'" (*Art, Truth & Politics* 22). In casual "photo ops" and "sound bytes," most often President Bush dons the disguise and drawl of a bashful, awkward Texas cowboy (even though he comes from Maine and went to Yale). Yet his actions taken "in our name" *are*, as Pinter charges, precisely those of a thug. Pinter *uncovers* true human suffering camouflaged by the self-serving, self-righteous political rhetoric of such global "gangsters" as Bush and Blair (Wark)—dangerous outlaws whom he believes should be indicted as "war criminals."

Coming full circle, Pinter segues back to his major contrast between the life of a writer, whose pursuit of truth is "a highly vulnerable, almost naked activity," who is "open to all the winds, some of them icy indeed," and the life of a politician, whose "protection" comes from living in lies: As an author, "You find no shelter, no protection—unless you lie—in which case of course you have constructed your own protection, and, it could be argued, become a politician" (22). Then Pinter reads his own poem—initially occasioned by the death of his father but incorporating allusions to the "The Disappeared" of the world—simply called "Death" (22-23).

Projected onto the three large screens at the Swedish Academy, Harold Pinter reading both these poems was enormously moving; his "presence" palpably powerful. Empowered by his own physical frailty then occasioning his actual absence, death becomes a *vital* central motif of his Nobel Lecture. Our perceptions of "truth" and "beauty" of life are ultimate consequences of art. But actual deaths (not simply awareness of mortality) are ultimate consequences of misuse and abuse of power in the politics of deception. Death is truth—the true outcome of lies. To tell the truth is to talk about "death etc.": to unravel the "politics of death."

Freedom

> When you can't write you feel you've been banished from yourself.
>
> –Harold Pinter, "On Being Awarded the German Shakespeare Prize in Hamburg" (1970)
>
> Being thrown out of the US embassy in Ankara [Turkey] with Arthur Miller—a voluntary exile—was one of the proudest moments of my life.
>
> –Harold Pinter, "Arthur Miller's Socks" (1985)
>
> I am belonged.
>
> –Jack Mapanje, *This Prison Where I Live*

International PEN congratulated Pinter on his Nobel Prize in Literature in a press release recalling: "in addition to his prolific and ground-breaking body of work," Harold Pinter "has long been a champion for freedom of expression and has worked on behalf of persecuted writers around the world. He has signed petitions, picketed at embassies, visited countries to speak out for writers who were imprisoned and persecuted by their governments."[24] It cites a touching anecdote, linking prisoners of conscience with other writers around the world:

> In the anthology *This Prison Where I Live* Malawian poet Jack Mapan[je] tells of having a news clipping from the *British Guardian* smuggled into him in prison. "Lord Almighty! A picture of Ronald Harwood, Harold Pinter, Antonia Fraser, and other members of English PEN reading from my book of poems in protest at the Malawi High Commission in London! It must sure have an effect I thought. Ten thousand miles away, among the cockroaches of the prison where I lived I felt utterly humbled. Shattered. Such generosity, such warmth I surely did not deserve. All for one slim volume of poems?... Despair was vanquished. 'I am belonged,' I heard myself whisper." ("International PEN")

Freedom is a human right. Concerns about where one lives and with whom one lives, how and about what one speaks and in what language, whether one lives at all—the importance of freedom and its loss—reverberate throughout Pinter's work. Death is the ultimate exile; as Joseph Brodsky writes in his foreword to *This Prison Where I Live*: "the ultimate in the unknown and in the deprivation of freedom." Entertaining and inspiring while taking on the "known and the unknown" with supreme comic wit, Pinter compels us to *talk* about how we can deter, or at least defer as long as possible, death and deprivation throughout the world. Dramatizing complexities of power relations often resulting in this ultimate death (of body and mind), "the international playwright Harold Pinter" imparts truths about creativity and life.

The Dissonant Dissident in Dramatic "Retirement": Prospective Activism

> I think I've stopped writing plays now, but I haven't stopped writing poems.... I think I've written about 29 plays. Isn't that enough? I think it's enough for me. I think I've found other forms now. You see my energies are going into different directions, certainly into poetry.... But also, as you know, over the last few years I've made a number of political speeches at various locations and at various ceremonies.... I'm using a lot of energy ... more specifically about political states of affairs, which I think are very worrying as things stand.
>
> –Harold Pinter, interview with Mark Lawson, BBC Radio 4 (28 Feb. 2005)

> Incidentally, I didn't say I wouldn't *ever* write any more drama. I haven't written a play for six years, and I'm writing more and more poetry. ... [T]here is a side of me which is optimistic, otherwise I wouldn't be writing poetry at all. I wouldn't be doing anything. To write something is to be positive and, to a certain degree, optimistic. So ... I'm like most other people actually, I'm both very pessimistic [*He chuckles*] and a *little* optimistic.
>
> –Harold Pinter, interview with James Naughtie, BBC Radio 4 (18 Mar. 2005)

Audience Question 3: I wondered what it was that had drawn you to the conclusion that you'd written yourself out.

Harold Pinter: Well I recently did have a holiday in Dorset and I took a couple of yellow pads with me (which I've been writing on all my life. I have to say they do tend to come from New York, these pads...) But I didn't write a damn word. I looked at these pads every day and thought, well, go on, what does this mean? Finally I turned them over and put them in a drawer. It reminded me somewhat of... there's a line in Scott Fitzgerald's *The Last Tycoon*,

> I don't know if you know it, about...I once wrote a screenplay of when a New York lawyer goes to Hollywood and looks into the Writers' Building and reports, 'You know, today I looked in the window of the Writers' Building. There were all these writers in this building and not one of them was writing a damn word.' The same thing applies to me.
>
> –Harold Pinter, interview with Ramona Koval (25 Aug. 2006)

For over five decades, Harold Pinter has performed roles as "a man of the theater" and the cinema (actor, playwright, screenwriter, director, and even stage designer [under a pseudonym "Gomez"]), living and working for about half that time mostly outside global politics. With growing frequency, Pinter has taken a leading role as political activist, endorsing global calls to action and other humanitarian campaigns, writing and publicly reading speeches and his own and others' poetry, becoming "profoundly engaged" (Drake 6). "Harold Pinter the man" is "the sum" of all these roles.

Len's concern about mirrors in *The Dwarfs* ("I can't see the mirror I have to look through. I see the other side. The other side. But I can't see the mirror side. [*Pause.*] I want to break it, all of it. But how can I break it? How can I break it when I can't see it?" [95-96]) extending into his monologue ("The point is, who are you? ... You're the sum of so many reflections ... . What have I seen, the scum or the essence?" [104-5]), resonates in Pinter's final Nobel Lecture imagery:

> When we look into a mirror we think the image that confronts us is accurate. But move a millimetre and the image changes. We are actually looking at a never-ending range of reflections. But sometimes a writer has to smash the mirror—for it is on the other side of that mirror that the truth stares at us. (23)

Current world calamities compel citizen Pinter to "smash the mirror" so as to confront this truth:

> I believe that despite enormous odds which exist, unflinching, unswerving, fierce intellectual determination, as citizens, to define *the real truth* of our lives and our societies is a crucial obligation which devolves upon us all. It is in fact mandatory. If such a determination is not embodied in our political vision we have no hope of restoring what is so nearly lost to us—the dignity of man. (23; italics added)

In a memorial tribute to Québécois political activist Charles Gagnon (1939-2005), Mordecai Briemberg quotes Pinter's conclusion, extending the contrast between negative versus positive possibilities:

> Without such political vision [as Pinter's] our voices are muffled—when they need to be heard clearly; our passions are stilled—when

> they need to be vibrant; our motion is frozen—when it needs to be focused; and our capacities to change the world are crippled—when they need to be enhanced. ("Personal Memories" 45).[25]

Determined "to define the *real* truth of our lives and our societies"—to live in truth—we must retain hope that, with champions of human rights and dignity like Václav Havel, Orhan Pamuk, Jack Mapanje, the late Ken Saro-Wiwa and Charles Gagnon, and Harold Pinter—"all these people" (too numerous to name) unjustly imprisoned, mistreated, and/or murdered while in custody and all those speaking on their behalf—we will prevail over "powerful" voices who imprison "others" for their difference and who make them—like Jimmy in *Party Time*—"suck" the "dark" (47-48). As Rose says, in *The Room*, "It's murder" (91), "It's murder out" (101) there. It's murder inside as well: deception, destruction, mayhem, mutilation, and death inside this "New World Order."

Charles Grimes ends his book *Harold Pinter's Politics* observing that "[t]he unnamed and incapacitated victim in *The New World Order* stands only for opposition per se" and concluding that "[t]he sketchy nature of oppositional values in Pinter's writing reveals his distance from other committed playwrights and emphasizes his vast political pessimism" (220). Grimes argues:

> It is a familiar idea that political theater need only ask the right questions; it does not have to answer or solve them. Pinter's unique, even paradoxical style of political drama separates as far as possible the act of questioning from the existence of solutions. Pinter ends his political theater in silence because he has no answers to afford us.

But both inside and outside of his plays, like Jimmy's sister Dusty, who keeps asking about what has happened to her brother, citizen Harold Pinter is not "silent." He writes from a "courageous fierce determination" in "pursuit" of his own developing "political vision," with perhaps at least "a *little*" or even "quite a big streak of optimism" offsetting his pessimism.

In his Nobel Lecture "Art, Truth and Politics," in his interviews conducted before and after he delivered it, and in the letters and petitions that he signs as a political activist, Pinter clarifies that he does not regard himself as a "black pessimist" and that he does have at least *some* "answers to afford us." On 25 August 2006, at the Edinburgh International Book Festival, in response to an audience member's comment that "there is hope that the people can change and oust the leaders who take these unpopular positions," Pinter said:

> Well let's damn well hope so. I agree with you. Let's hang on to that hope. You see I don't think—speaking for myself—I've often been called a pessimist, you know? But I couldn't write

> anything at all if I didn't have quite a big streak of optimism in me. Otherwise there'd be absolutely no point. If I was a black pessimist I might as well lie down and that's it. So I agree with you. One has to live with that hope. And, you know, on we go. (Koval, "The Book Show")

"That hope" appears to be Pinter's "answer" to the abuses of power relations and structures of power that his plays critique. Speaking truth to power, Pinter responds that we must keep the faith and work non-violently and determinedly to change the status quo. We must reshape the future of our one and only world (Kyriakou). Pinter's—our—legacy to future generations is no less than the preservation of humanity, of human kind. Preserving our humanity is, of course, the hope that "springs eternal"—that keeps us all going. Without it, we *would* be lost. With it, as Rose says, in *The Room*, we might have "a chance" at survival.

The Beatles sing "All You Need Is Love." But, of course, while Lennon and McCartney's lyrics proclaim "It's easy," as everyone knows, it (life, love) is not easy. There is no "easy" answer to the problems that Pinter's plays pose, the problems of life and love. As his early plays *The Caretaker* and *The Homecoming* dramatize, in the real world, love is fraught with conflicts of epic proportions, with all sorts of "emotional political sociological and psychological pretensions and resonances." Paradoxically, while Pinter's plays expose the powerful, often political, forces which humans must surmount to survive the battle against injustice, they also reveal the crucial positive value of loving one another in creating justice (Prentice). While selfishness and competitiveness motivate negative aspects of human nature (the "evil" or "unethical") which create and enable malevolence, in the opposite, positive aspects of human nature, love and compassionate understanding (the "good" or "ethical"), Pinter indicates wherein "no-easy answers" may lie. Given this potential for a *double perspective* in and on Pinter's plays—encompassing "both-and" rather than "either-or"— how one regards his work depends on one's own nature: the classic conundrum of whether one perceives "the glass half empty or half full." Whether or not one appreciates Pinter's work may depend on the degree to which one is attuned to and tolerant of potential complexities and ambiguities ("truths") of life and literature.

Though Harold Pinter lives in the same complex and ambiguous world as the rest of us, his own increasing emphasis on his "very happy personal life" (e.g., Batty 92) underscores the importance of developing such "happy" personal relationships on the microcosmic or local level of life and art as a basis for developing "happier" political ones on the macrocosmic or global level, both throughout our lives and throughout our work. Crucial to the "global" ability to do so (throughout the "world," or across the "globe," so to speak) is the universal human right (the "freedom") *of all human beings* to seek such happiness. In his perseverance in seeking and revealing "truth" in art and politics, Harold Pinter's life and work dramatize the personal, social, and political values and benefits of such freedom through—to borrow from Simone de Beauvoir— his own (anti-)global "ethics of ambiguity."

NOTES

[1] I presented an earlier version of this essay, entitled "(Anti-)Global Pinter: Living and Working in the Theater—Outside/Inside Global Politics (An Intersubjective, Inter(con)textual Reading of Harold Pinter's Nobel Lecture 'Art, Truth & Politics')," at the symposium "Pinter: Passion, Poetry and Politics," held during the 10th edition of the Europe Theatre Prize, in Turin, Italy, from 10-12 Mar. 2006. (See Merritt, "Europe Theatre Prize Celebration.") I thank Michael Billington for inviting me and Michela Giovannelli for her assistance and hospitality in Turin. (Following the title as printed in the Turin program, I have omitted the subtitles for publication here.)

[2] After the announcement of his Nobel Prize in Literature and before Harold Pinter delivered "Art, Truth and Politics," people from all over the world posted over a thousand news items and comments about the award electronically; these items now number in the millions. There were over 10,200 citations of the speech by 25 Feb. 2006, as I mentioned to Pinter in Turin in March. He shared that with others but also said that he had received correspondence from an American saying that there had been no U.S. television coverage of his Nobel Lecture (December 8 or afterward). As I was in Stockholm that week, I was not in New York to watch television news then; subsequently, though I have found that National Public Radio (NPR) did cover it briefly, I have not found evidence that American TV did so as well. Pinter's Nobel Prize and Nobel Lecture have been cited in commentaries and campaigns, including global calls to action organized on the World Wide Web, such as "A Global Call for Nonviolent Civil Resistance to End the U.S.-Led Military Occupation of Iraq" (*Global Call Iraq*), which he endorsed. On 21 Feb. 2006, *Common Dreams Progressive Newswire* issued a press release about it headlined "Nobel Laureates and Religious Leaders Call on World to Resist Iraq Occupation," featuring Pinter's signature and prominently citing Pinter's words about the U.S. "invasion of Iraq." Cf. Kyriakou.

[3] Interview with Benning, as qtd. in Rocamora 353. See the context for Chidorchik's remark:

> "A writer can write a manuscript and put it in the desk, like Bulgakov," he said after performing here [in Moscow, with the Free Theater of Belarus,] in "We. Self-Identification," referring to Mikhail Bulgakov, the Soviet-era author whose works were banned. "A composer can do it. But theater is here, now. In the state theaters we are doomed to be insincere." (Qtd. in Myers E7)

[4] Batty offers an interesting perspective on "the two facets of 'truth' which Harold Pinter justifies as his legitimate preoccupations, and it is an investigation of what constitutes 'truth' that marks all of his activity as both artist and citizen" (2-3). This perspective informed the title of the conference Artist and Citizen: 50 Years of Performing Pinter, which Batty organized at the University of Leeds from 12 to 15 April 2007, on which occasion Pinter was awarded his seventeenth Honorary Degree of Doctor of Letters.

[5] On the influence of Pinter on McDonagh, see O'Toole 44. Billington observes that Pinter "became a keen admirer of Sarah Kane's explosive *Blasted*" (*Harold Pinter* 132), and Raby comments on Pinter's "unequivocal support, together with Edward Bond, for Sarah Kane, when her first play *Blasted* was viciously dismissed by the London critics" (2).

[6] Jabri suggests that

> Pinter's work relates to how the most everyday aspect of lived experience can be violently penetrated by the most unimaginable cruelty. That the very act of speech and communication can be rendered an impossibility. Over and above the capacity to speak, Pinter's vision is one that portrays [untrammeled] power through the reduction of the self to what Giorgio Agamben [*Remnants of Auschwitz: The Witness and the Archive*, trans. Daniel Heller-Roazen (New York: Zone Books, 1999)] would refer to as "bare life", the corporeal self, the embodied self reduced to its sheer corporeality, exposed in all its vulnerability. (2)

[7] "Citing an Israeli production of *One for the Road* (where the torturer character was depicted as an Israeli as opposed to a Palestinian), [Pinter] said that this decision showed a willingness to 'share the joy and disgrace of being human'" (Andrews 2).

[8] See Merritt, *Pinter in Play* 171-209; cf. Grimes 13-100, et passim.

[9] Throughout his dramatic career, Pinter's plays use such patterns of repetition and continuity, featuring verbal repetitions, repeated motifs and cadences, reversals of the characters' positions, cyclical plots, and the sense of no definitive ending, or a lack of resolution: e.g., *A Slight Ache* (1959); *The Dumb Waiter* (1957); *The Caretaker* (1960); *The Dwarfs* (1960); A *Night Out* (1961); *The Lover* (1964); *The Homecoming* (1965); *The Basement* (1968); *Old Times* (1971); *No Man's Land* (1975); *Betrayal* (1978); *One for the Road* (1984); *Mountain Language* (1988); *Party Time* (1991, 1992); *Moonlight* (1993); *Ashes to Ashes* (1996); and *Celebration* (2000).

[10] Pinter was responding to a question posed to him by Mark Batty, in an interview conducted on 16 Sept. 2004, inquiring as to "*what effect having to face something as final as [having cancer] might have had*" on him and how it may have "*changed*" his "*perspective*": "*Have you relaxed in terms of your political engagement or has it made you consider your artistic output in any different way? Or do you just simply go on as before now that you're free from it?*"(91). Adding to his comments already quoted in my text, Pinter clarified:

> All I'm saying is, all I can say is, that I'm more aware of death since the operation than I was ever before, and I sometimes look back on the operation, which was a grisly experience, the whole damn thing, and wonder in heaven's name how I survived it really. Quite apart from the surgeon's brilliance, the whole experience was so … it was like a nightmare really. So I've really been through the valley of the shadow, that's what it is. (91-92)

Two previously-unpublished poems added to the 2005 ed. of *Various Voices* (179-80) emanate from Pinter's brush with death, following "Cancer Cells" (Mar. 2001): "To My Wife" (June 2004) and "Death May Be Ageing" (April 2005).

[11] In speaking with the interviewer, Australian National Radio journalist Ramona Koval, Pinter read his poem "Cancer Cells" (Mar. 2002) and described the ordeal that led to his writing it:

> I wrote the poem when I was having chemotherapy. And you know in chemotherapy you sit there where the nurse just puts the thing into your arm.

The chemo. And she suddenly said this, this particular nurse said, Cancer cells are those which have forgotten how to die. I was so struck by this statement that I went away and wrote that poem. Because at the time I didn't know whether I was going to die or not. And that poem, I think, represents precisely, I hope, what I felt at the time. I had no idea what was going to happen, and in fact it's been quite a year from that point of view. The stanza there says, "I need to see my tumour dead / A tumour which forgets to die / But plans to murder me instead." And in fact I'm happy to say that I have seen my tumour dead. [applause]

....

[T]he whole thing, honestly, Ramona, remains a kind of dark dream, for me. It was like being in a pretty impenetrable forest in which you literally couldn't see the wood for the trees. In other words, I had no idea what was going on half the time, during this operation, and coming out of the operation—you see I'd never been ill in my life before, really—so it was quite extraordinary at the age of seventy-one to suddenly find myself in hospital facing a very severe cancer and a major operation. And it was something I hadn't even considered. I found myself, as I say, in a very dark world which was impossible to interpret. I couldn't work it out. So for two or three weeks I was somewhere else. I was in another place altogether. Not very pleasant, I must say.

Ramona Koval: Do you mean post-operatively?

Harold Pinter: Post-operatively, yes. I didn't quite know where I was. And certainly not what I was—if I was anything at all. And it was really only very, very gradually—I don't know if anyone here has had this kind of experience, I'm sure there are one or two people who have—it's like being plunged into, well, I'll give another image, an ocean in which you can't swim. You've no idea how to get out of it and you simply float about and bob about and are hit by terrible waves and so on, and it's all very dark, really. Anyway, the thing is, here I am. (Koval, "Books and Writing")

[12] Batty observes:

The 1996 play *Ashes to Ashes* brought genocide explicitly to British shores in the questionable remembrances of Rebecca, who talks of having seen refugees herded out off the beach and into the sea in Dorset. Whilst this account serves to undermine the authenticity of some of her memories, the painfully genuine attribution she has made of Holocaust atrocities to her own present childless state is emotionally potent (she repeatedly recalls having her baby taken away from her at a train station, in a scenario reminiscent of William Styron's novel *Sophie's Choice*). (74)

As I have already documented in "Harold Pinter's *Ashes to Ashes*" (80-84) and in "'HURRY UP PLEASE IT'S TIME'" (70-71, 77n23), Pinter's (uncredited) source for some of Rebecca's "memories" and the "echoes" in *Ashes to Ashes* appears to be excerpts from transcripts of a videotaped testimony of Bessie K., an actual Holocaust survivor, whose words are quoted in several versions of work by Lawrence Langer and a PBS TV documentary based on it. See "Bessie and Jacob K.," the videotaped testimony (HVT-206) in the Fortunoff Video Archive for Holocaust Testimonies at Yale University. Though I have discussed this connection with Harold Pinter during a lunch (15 Feb. 2001), when he said that my pointing it out in my *Pinter Review* article was a "surprise," and although we engaged in subsequent e-mail correspondence about possible published sources that I later proposed (which I have shared with Charles Grimes prior to his book's publication), Pinter has not confirmed when, where, or how he may have first read or otherwise encountered Bessie K.'s testimony or excerpts from it. It appears that he may simply not recall having done so. Nevertheless, portions of Rebecca's monologues are almost exactly the same as Bessie K.'s videotaped testimony and, from my perspective, far more "authentic" than Batty, Begley, and some other observers appear to have recognized.

[13] Having seen documentary film footage of and read published transcripts of excerpts of Bessie K.'s videotaped testimony and seen the Danish film *A Day in October*, I must say that I perceive and appreciate the figurative "authenticity" of Rebecca's "memories" despite their historical or literal impossibility. The stage directions defining her age and that of Devlin as "Both in their forties" and the time as "Now" (at least 1996) do establish that, born no earlier than 1947, Rebecca is too young to have actually experienced, on the coast of England, what actual Holocaust survivors like Bessie K. (who had already borne and lost a child during the Holocaust) and the rescued Jewish Danes did. The disparity between such "facts" heightens the compelling "truth" of what Rebecca imagines in conflict with Devlin's relative literal-mindedness, a conflict of attitudes that Pinter dramatizes emphatically in *Ashes to Ashes.*

[14] According to "Rescue," an article in the United States Holocaust Memorial Museum's *Holocaust Encyclopedia* hyperlinked in the Web site *The Rescue of the Jews of Denmark*:

> Despite the indifference of most Europeans and the collaboration of others in the murder of Jews during the Holocaust, individuals in every European country and from all religious backgrounds risked their lives to help Jews. Rescue efforts ranged from the isolated actions of individuals to organized networks both small and large. German-occupied Denmark was the site of the most famous and complete rescue operation in Axis-controlled Europe. In late summer 1943, German occupation authorities imposed martial law on Denmark in response to increasing acts of resistance and sabotage. German Security Police officials planned to deport the Danish Jews while martial law was in place. On September 28, 1943, a German businessman warned Danish authorities of the impending operation, scheduled for the night of October 1-2, 1943. With the help of their non-Jewish neighbors and friends, virtually all the Danish Jews went into hiding. During the following days, the Danish resistance organized a rescue operation, in which Danish fishermen clandestinely ferried some 7,200 Jews (of the country's total Jewish population of 7,800) in small fishing boats, to safety in neutral Sweden.

Cf. "A Tribute to Danish Rescuers," commemorating "the 60th anniversary of this historic effort ... through an evening of film and music" held at the United States Holocaust Memorial Museum, 10 Dec. 2003: "In the Fall of 1943, citizens of Denmark learned that the German occupation authorities in their country were planning to deport Danish Jews [to concentration camps] in a matter of days. In response, the Danes launched a massive rescue operation, ferrying their Jewish neighbors by boat to Sweden under cloak of night." *The Rescue of the Jews of Denmark* adds: "Thanks to this remarkable mass rescue effort, at war's end Denmark had one of the highest Jewish survival rates for any European country." The "Tribute" included a screening of the documentary film *The Danish Solution: The Rescue of the Jews in Denmark*, "written and directed by Karen Cantor and Camilla Kjaerulff... presented in English and Danish with English subtitles ... [which] tells the story of how Danish citizens managed to secure the safety of 95 percent of their country's Jewish population during the Nazi occupation."

[15] After having her child taken away from her by a Nazi guard at a train station on the way to a concentration camp (after "losing" the "bundle"—"the baby"—"what baby?"), in denial, Bessie K. describes herself as "dead" even though she "survived." Many people say that losing a child is worse than dying. "Survival" for such victims of real atrocities as Bessie K. describes her own experience becomes a "numbness," "death in life" or "living death" (Merritt, "Harold Pinter's *Ashes to Ashes*" 81-82 and "'HURRY UP PLEASE IT'S TIME'" 70-71; 77n23; cf. Grimes 213). Rebecca's "memory" about "all these people" drowning also echoes the imagery of Primo Levi's *The Drowned and the Saved*. After observing that "Acts of recollection and witness are themselves conditioned by the fact of silence" in Holocaust literature, Grimes points out that Pinter "has expressed admiration" for Levi's book, which argues that "the true witnesses of what happened in the concentration camps paradoxically cannot and could never utter testimony—both before and after their deaths a particular kind of Nazi victim was condemned to silence. In contemplating such a true witness, Levi evokes the *Muselmänner* of the concentration camps—those who endured a living death, a death in life, seemingly resigned to or unaware of their fate. These are the 'drowned' of Levi's book title" (213). Grimes considers the "final silence" of Rebecca vis-à-vis Holocaust literature and several of Pinter's other plays as "the paradoxical, ultimate statement of Pinter's political theater" (214-20). Levi testifies to how the Nazis attempted to annihilate all witnesses of the "frightful atrocities being committed" in order to "silence" them, and thus to obliterate all "knowledge" of "the truth about the Lagers," the death camps (15).

[16] In his concluding chapter on "*Ashes to Ashes*: Morality and Politics after the Holocaust" (195-220), Grimes observes that "Rebecca's remarks [about having "never suffered"] reflect society's (or human beings') efforts to deny historical atrocities, even in the case of individuals who do try to 'admit' them into consciousness" (202). He speculates that "Pinter may have gathered the basis for this image from a Sereny anecdote[:] When Nazi official Hans Fritzsche was forced to watch movies of the death camps at the Nuremberg trials, he responded to his personal guilt with a description of his own horror, saying with a mixture of remorse and self-pity, 'I have ... the feeling ... I am drowning in filth ... I'm choking in it. ... I cannot go on. ... It is a daily execution'" (Gitta Sereny, *Albert Speer: His Battle with Truth* [New York: Knopf, 1995] 341, as qtd. in Grimes 237 [204n9]). Grimes states that "Pinter attempts to estrange us from Rebecca's historical sympathy by associating it ... with death and, in the passage on 'mental elephantiasis' (51), with a disabling awareness of guilt" (Grimes 204n9).

[17] Havel stated in his telegram congratulating Pinter on his Nobel Prize: "You have no idea how I happy I am that you have won the Nobel Prize for Literature. I think you absolutely deserve it" (Qtd. in the London *Independent* of 14 Oct. 2005, following Pinter, "Torture and Misery," in "'A Colossal Figure'"). Billington cites Pinter's "friend" Havel as an example of how "Not everyone, even on the liberal left, shared Pinter's point of view" about the NATO bombing of Serbia in 1999 (*Harold Pinter* 402).

[18] Pinter's subsequent account of U.S. policy and actions in foreign affairs parallels Wilson's historical accounts in *The Politics of Truth* (412-15).

[19] Cf. Wilson, "Republic or Empire?" *The Nation* 3 Mar. 2003, rpt. in *Politics of Truth* 470: "The underlying objective of this war [in Iraq] is the imposition of a Pax

Americana on the region and installation of vassal regimes that will control restive populations. ... Hegemony in the Arab nations of the Gulf."

[20] See Baker, et al., *The Iraq Study Group Report*, published in December 2006. For current figures on Iraqi civilian deaths caused by the U.S.-Led Coalition War in Iraq, Pinter and others consult the Web site *Iraq Body Count*, which is "run by academics and peace activists, based on reports from at least two media sources" (Reuters, "FactBox—Military and Civilian Deaths in Iraq"). The updated figure within brackets derives from the U.S. Department of Defense Confirmation List as documented in *Iraq Coalition Casualty Count.*

[21] Former Israeli Prime Minister Ariel Sharon used imagery of drowning at a Holocaust Remembrance ceremony at Auschwitz in 2004: "Always remember the victims, never forget the murderers. Do not forget how millions of Jews were marched to their deaths while the world stood silent, *how thousands of Jews floundered in stormy waters searching in vain for sanctuary*," Sharon said. "*Do not let (the world) forget—remember the silence of the world*" ("'Never Forget'"; italics added). Cf. Grimes:

> "Never forget" is one famous purported lesson of the Holocaust. Pinter's play is a testament to the impossibility as well as the necessity of commemorating the dead. Rebecca's isolation indexes profound loss and gestures to the irremediable absence that both provokes, and concludes, engagement with atrocity's legacy. ... *Ashes to Ashes* summons us to make the past meaningful in our present as it simultaneously demonstrates how attempting to obey such a calling has complex, threatening, and self-destructive consequences. (217)

[22] After hearing Pinter read the excerpt from Pablo Neruda's poem, I believe even more strongly than I have already developed in "Harold Pinter's *Ashes to Ashes*" that the cause of "bumps" in the "icy" streets imagined by Rebecca (*Ashes to Ashes* 53, 69-71) is fluids flowing from wounded and dead bodies prior to their chilling in cold weather (79), paralleling Neruda's refrain "blood in the streets" (from which Rebecca's images may originate). Rebecca's reference to "veins" seems to be a metonymy for blood. Cf. Begley 177-85 on Pinter's particular usage of "metaphor and metonymy" in *Ashes to Ashes.*

[23] Cf. Pinter, "University of Turin Speech": "Many Americans, we know, are horrified by the posture of their government but seem to be helpless" (243). Pinter repeated and updated this perspective in his June 2006 *Newsnight Review* interview with Wark televised on BBC Two.

[24] Pinter has been signing such petitions and demonstrating and protesting against human rights abuses and other injustices since about 1963, when he supported the anti-Apartheid movement in South Africa, signing a "declaration," along with other British playwrights, refusing to allow his plays to be produced professionally or commercially in South Africa.

[25] Briemberg goes on to describe his departed friend and colleague Charles Gagnon as another man whose "courage was just that: his fierce determination to embody in a political vision the truth of our lives and our societies, for the purpose of securing the human dignity of people everywhere" ("Personal Memories" 45). In analogizing the "courageous, fierce determination" in Pinter's and Gagnon's "pursuit of political vision," he observes that Gagnon's "courage ... encompassed the willingness to evaluate his own political vision no less critically than the political vision of others." Pinter's critics have at times questioned whether he possesses that same willingness.

WORKS CITED

Andrews, Tanya. "Harold Pinter–Freedom & Independence." Report on interview of Harold Pinter conducted by Isabel Hilton. Freedom and Independence Section. Brighton Festival. In association with English PEN and the Universities of Sussex and Brighton. The English Centre of International PEN. 11 May 2004. Web. 24 Feb. 2006. <http://www.englishpen.org/events/>. (2 pages.)

Baker, James A., III, Lee H. Hamilton, et al. *The Iraq Study Group Report.* New York: Vintage Books, 2006. Web. <http://www.bakerinstitute.org/Pubs/iraqstudygroup_findings.pdf>.

Batty, Mark. *About Pinter: The Playwright and the Work.* London: Faber, 2005.

Begley, Varun. *Harold Pinter and the Twilight of Modernism.* Toronto: U of Toronto P, 2005.

Bessie and Jacob K. "Holocaust Testimony." Interviewed by Laurel Vlock. 20 May 1983. HVT-206. New Haven: Fortunoff Video Archive for Holocaust Testimonies, 1983. Yale U Library, Manuscripts and Archives Call Number: MS1322. (Videorecording; 3 hrs., 38 mins.)

Billington, Michael. *Harold Pinter.* 1996. London: Faber, 2007.

—. "'They said you've a call from the Nobel committee. I said, why?'" *Guardian* 14 Oct. 2005: 1. Updated 6 July 2006. Web. 30 June 2008. http://www.guardian.co.uk/uk/2005/oct/14/books.nobelprize>.

Briemberg, Mordecai. "Introduction" and "Personal Memories." 42 and 45 in Raymond Legault, and Marie-Jose Nadal. "The Political Journey of Charles Gagnon." *Relay* Nov.-Dec. 2006: 42-45.

"Casualties in Iraq: The Human Cost of Occupation." Ed. Michael Ewens. *Anti-War.com.* Web. 29 June 2008. <http://www.antiwar.com/casualties/>.

Dardagan, Hamit, John Sloboda, and Josh Dougherty. "Reality Checks: Some Responses to the Latest Lancet Estimates." Iraq Body Count Press Release. *Iraq Body Count.* 16 Oct. 2006. Web. 29 June 2008. <http://www.iraqbodycount.net/press/pr14.php>.

A Day in October (*En Dag i oktober*). Screenplay by Damian F. Slattery. Dir. and prod. Kenneth Madsen. Perf. Daniel Benzali (Solomon Kublitz), Tovah Feldshuh (Emma Kublitz), D.B. Sweeney (Niels Jensen), and Kelly Wolf (Sara Kublitz). Denmark & US: Det Danske Filminstitut & Kenmad/Panorama Film International, 1992.

Drake, Sylvie. "Acting Is Just Like 'Old Times' for Pinter." *Los Angeles Times* 29 Oct. 1985, sec. 6: 1, 6.

Edwards, David. "Unthinkable Thoughts – An Interview with Harold Pinter – August 1999. *Medialens.* 19 Dec. 2005. Web. 29 June 2008. <http://www.medialens.org/forum/viewtopic.php?p=4799>. (11 pages.)

"Global Call for Nonviolent Civil Resistance to End the U.S.-Led Military Occupation of Iraq." English version. *A Global Call.* 10 Feb. 2006. Web. 22 Feb. 2006. <http://globalcalliraq.org/en/call>. (Harold Pinter is among the first group of signatories.)

Grimes, Charles. *Harold Pinter's Politics: A Silence Beyond Echo.* Rutherford and Cranbury, NJ: Fairleigh Dickinson UP and Associated UP, 2005.

Havel, Václav. *Living in Truth: Twenty-two Essays Published on the Occasion of the Award of the Erasmus Prize to Václav Havel.* Ed. Jan Vladislav. London: Faber and Faber, 1990.

"International PEN Congratulates Harold Pinter on Nobel Prize." 27 Oct. 2005. Web. 29 June 2008. <http://internationalpen.mindunit.co.uk/index.php?pid=33&aid=391&return=33>.

Iraq Body Count: The Worldwide Update of Reported Civilian Deaths in the Iraq War and Occupation. 3 Mar. 2006. Web. 29 June 2008. <http://www.iraqbodycount.net/>. Reuters. "FactBox – Military and Civilian Deaths in Iraq." *Reuters.* 30 Apr. 2008. Web. 29 June 2008. <http://www.reuters.com/article/topNews/idUSL30638800200804 30 >.

Iraq Coalition Casualty Count. 26 June 2008. Web. 30 June 2008. <http://icasualties.org/oif/>.

"Iraq Death Toll 'Soared Post-War.'" *BBC News.* 29 Oct. 2004. Web. 29 June 2008. <http://news.bbc.co.uk/2/hi/middle_east/3962969.stm>.

Jabri, Vivienne. "Pinter, Radical Critique, and Politics." *Borderlands e-journal* 2.2 [2003]). (8 pages.) Web. 29 June 2008. <http://www.borderlandsejournal.adelaide.edu.au/vol2no2_2003/jabri_pinter.htm>.

Koval, Ramona. "Books and Writing with Ramona Koval: Harold Pinter." Summary and edited transcript of interview with Harold Pinter. Provocations: The David Cohen British Literature Prize Event. Edinburgh International Book Festival. Edinburgh, Scotland. 25 August 2002. Broadcast 15 Sept. 2002. Australian National Radio. Web. 29 June 2008. <http://www.abc.net.au/rn/arts/bwriting/stories/s671912.htm>.

—. "The Book Show: Harold Pinter, Nobel Prize-Winning Playwright and Poet, at Edinburgh International Book Festival (Transcript Available)." Edited transcript of interview with Harold Pinter. Edinburgh International Book Festival. Edinburgh, Scotland. 25 Aug. 2006. Australian National Radio. 25 Sept. 2006. Web. 6 Nov. 2006. <http://www.abc.net.au/rn/bookshow/stories/2006/1746077.htm#>.

Kyriakou, Niko. "Nobel Laureates Join Call to End Iraq Occupation." *One World United States.* 23 Feb. 2006. Web. 29 June 2008. <http://us.oneworld.net/article/view/128238/1/>.

Lawson, Mark. "Pinter 'to give up writing plays'." Interview with Harold Pinter. *Front Row.* Broadcast on BBC Radio 4. Last updated 28 Feb. 2005. "Pinter on Front Row." *BBC News.* (RealPlayer audio.) Web. 11 Nov. 2006. <http://news.bbc.co.uk/1/hi/entertainment/arts/4305725.stm>. (My transcription.)

Lennon, John, and Paul McCartney. "All You Need Is Love." *Magical Mystery Tour.* Recorded 27 Nov. 1967. Web. 7 Nov. 2006. <http://www.allspirit.co.uk/allyouneed.html>. Rpt. from *The Beatles Complete Chord Songbook.* Milwaukee, WI: Hal Leonard Corp., 2000.

Levi, Primo. *The Drowned and the Saved.* 1988. New York: Vintage (Random House), 1989.

Merritt, Susan Hollis. "*Ashes to Ashes* in New York." *The Pinter Rev.: Collected Essays 1997 and 1998.* Ed. Francis Gillen and Steven H. Gale. Tampa: U of Tampa P, 1997. 156-59.

—. "Europe Theatre Prize Celebration–Turin, Italy." *The Harold Pinter Society Newsletter* (Autumn 2006): 2-3.

—. "Harold Pinter's *Ashes to Ashes*: Political/Personal Echoes of the Holocaust." *Pinter Rev.: Collected Essays 1999 and 2000.* 73-84.

—. "'HURRY UP PLEASE IT'S TIME': Pinter Past, Pinter Present, and Pinter Future." *Pinter Rev.: Collected Essays 2003 and 2004.* 61-82.

—. *Pinter in Play: Critical Strategies and the Plays of Harold Pinter.* 1990. Durham & London: Duke UP, 1995.

Myers, Steven Lee. "A Troupe Is a Potent Force in Belarus's Underground." *New York Times* 9 Feb. 2006: The Arts: E1, 7.

Naughtie, James. Interview with Harold Pinter. *Today.* Broadcast on BBC Radio 4. 18 Mar. 2005. RealPlayer audio. (5 mins., 58 secs.) 28 Feb. 2006. Web. <http://www.bbc.co.uk/radio4/today/listenagain/ram/today5_pinter_20050318.ram>. (My transcription.)

"'Never Forget,' Participants of Auschwitz Holocaust March Urged.'" Online Posting. *The All I Need.* 2004. 4 Mar. 2006 <http://www.theallineed.com/news/0505/054547.htm# >. (Reposted from AFP.com news agency.)

One for the Road. Dir. Robin Lefevre. Perf. Rory Corpus (Nicky), Lloyd Hutchinson (Victor), Harold Pinter (Nicolas), & Indira Varma (Gila). Set & Décor Liz Ascroft. Lighting Mick Hughes. The Gate Theatre, Dublin. New Ambassador's, London. 3-7 July 2001. Transferred, as part of a double bill with *A Kind of Alaska*, to the Lincoln Center Festival 2001: Harold Pinter Festival, New York. 16-31 July 2001. 16, 17, 20, & 21 July 2001.

O'Toole, Fintan. "Life and Letters: A Mind in Connemara: The Savage World of Martin McDonagh." *New Yorker* 6 Mar. 2006: 40-47.

Pinter, Harold. "Arthur Miller's Socks." 4-5 in *Arthur Miller and Company.* Ed. Christopher Bigsby. Rpt. as "Happy Birthday, Arthur." *Guardian* 17 Oct. 1995, Guardian Features Page: T12. Web. 30 June 2008. <http://www.haroldpinter.org/politics/politics_torture.shtml>.

—. "Art, Truth and Politics: The Nobel Lecture." Delivered at the Swedish Academy, Stockholm, Sweden, on 7 Dec. 2005. Photocopy courtesy of the Swedish Academy. *Harold Pinter: The Nobel Prize in Literature 2005.* Web. 29 June 2008. <http://nobelprize.org/nobel_prizes/literature/laureates/2005/pinter-lecture.html>.

—. *Art, Truth and Politics: The Nobel Lecture.* London: Faber, 2005. (Private printing of 1,000 copies.)

—. *Ashes to Ashes.* New York: Grove P, 1997.

—. The Birthday Party *and* The Room: *Two Plays by Harold Pinter.* Rev. ed. 1961. New York: Grove P, 1968.

—. *Death etc.* New York: Grove P, 2005.

—. *HaroldPinter.Org.* Web. 1 July 2008. <http://www.haroldpinter.org/home/index.shtml>. (Hyperlinked menu: >"Forum: The Harold Pinter Community.")

—. "It Never Happened." London *Guardian* 4 Dec. 1996. *ZMagazine.* Feb. 1997. Web. 25 Feb. 2005. <http://www.zmag.org/zmag/zarticle.cfm?Url=articles/feb97pinter.html>. Rpt. in Harold Pinter, *VV* 214-17.

—. "Language and Lies." *Index on Censorship* 17.6 (1988): 2.

—. "Oh, Superman." Broadcast for *Opinion.* Channel 4. 31 May 1990. Transcript published in *VV* 190-200.

—. *Old Times.* New York: Grove P, 1971.

—. "On Being Awarded the German Shakespeare Prize in Hamburg." 1970. 39-43 in *VV*.

—. *One for the Road. With Production Photos by Ivan Kyncl and an Interview on the Play and Its Politics.* Incl. "A Play and Its Politics: A Conversation between Harold Pinter and Nicholas Hern" (Feb. 1985) and Pinter's "Postscript" (May 1985). New York: Grove P, 1986.

—. Party Time *and* The New World Order*: Two Plays by Harold Pinter.* New York: Grove P, 1993.

—. *Three Plays:* A Slight Ache, The Collection, The Dwarfs. New York: Grove P, 1962.

—. "Torture and Misery in the Name of Freedom." London *Independent* 14 Oct. 2005. Web. 30 June 2008. <http://www.independent.co.uk/news/world/politics/pinter-torture-and-misery-in-name-of-freedom-510906.html>. [Followed by series of reactions headed "'A Colossal Figure'."]

—. "University of Turin Speech: On the Occasion of the Award of an Honorary Degree 27 November 2002." *VV* 241-43. Also rpt. in *War*.

—. *Various Voices: Prose, Poetry, Politics 1948-2005.* Rev. ed. 1998. London: Faber, 2005. (*VV*)

—. *War*. London: Faber, 2003. (N. pag.)

—. "Writing for the Theatre." *VV* 20-26.

Prentice, Penelope. *The Pinter Ethic: The Erotic Aesthetic.* Garland Reference Library of the Humanities, Vol. 2237. Rev. ed. 1994. New York: Routledge, 2000.

Raby, Peter. "Introduction." 1-3 in the Cambridge Companion to Harold Pinter. Ed. and introd. Peter Raby. Cambridge Companions to Literature. New York and Cambridge, England: Cambridge UP, 2001.

"Rescue." *Holocaust Encyclopedia. United States Holocaust Memorial Museum.* Updated 30 May 2008. Web. 30 June 2008. <http://www.ushmm.org/wlc/article.php?lang=en&ModuleId=10005185>.

Rocamora, Carol. *Acts of Courage: Václav Havel's Life in the Theater.* Hanover, NH: Smith and Kraus, 2004.

This Prison Where I Live: The PEN Anthology of Imprisoned Writers. Ed. Siobhan Dowd. Fwd. Joseph Brodsky. Afterword Jack Mapanje. New York: Cassell, 1996.

"A Tribute to Danish Rescuers." Public program to commemorate the 60th anniversary of the rescue of the Danish Jews (Oct. 1943). In "Public Programs." *The Rescue of the Jews of Denmark* . United States Holocaust Memorial Museum, Washington, D.C. 10 Dec. 2003. Web. 29 June 2008. <http://www.ushmm.org/museum/exhibit/focus/danish/>. <http://www.ushmm.org/museum/exhibit/focus/danish/pdf/TributeDanishRescuers.pdf>.

Wark, Kirsty. "Harold Pinter on *Newsnight Review.*" Broadcast on BBC Two. 23 June 2006. Web. 29 June 2008. <http://news.bbc.co.uk/2/hi/programmes/newsnight/5110060.stm>. "Interviews: Harold Pinter." RealPlayer streaming video. Web. 29 June 2008. <http://news.bbc.co.uk/1/hi/programmes/newsnight/review/default.stm>.

Wilson, Joseph. *The Politics of Truth: Inside the Lies that Led to War and Betrayed My Wife's CIA Identity: A Diplomat's Memoir.* New York: Carroll & Graf, 2004.

Pinter's Mise-en-Scène: *Party Time* as Television Drama

ROBERT GORDON

The television production of *A Kind of Alaska* in 1984, two years after its London stage première, established a pattern in which the stage production of each of Pinter's subsequent one-act plays was given a prestigious television production, usually based on the first or second stage production.[1] Two months after the première of *Mountain Language* (October 1988) at the National Theatre, a production directed by Pinter especially for television but with the cast of his own stage production, was broadcast by the BBC. Pinter's television production of *Party Time* employed the cast of his own première production—that had been presented in a double bill with *Mountain Language* at the Almeida Theatre (1991)—to recreate the play in a way which in many respects seems to me to be even more effective than the stage production.

In some obvious ways, *A Kind of Alaska*, *One for the Road*, and *Party Time* is in each case perfectly adapted to the format of studio-based television drama. Each play takes between forty and fifty minutes to perform, conforming to the conventional length of the one-off TV drama. At twenty-five minutes, *Mountain Language* is the length of an average episode in a drama series. Too short for a full-length evening in the theatre, any of these plays could be successfully programmed into an evening television schedule and receive appropriate attention from an intelligent viewer. *Ashes to Ashes* (1996) and *Celebration* (2000) could be effectively transposed to the medium of television without much adaptation. Although regarded as a full-length play, Pinter's *Moonlight*, first presented at the Almeida Theatre in 1993 before being transferred to the West End, only runs for eighty minutes in performance.

Since his earliest days as a playwright Pinter has explored the diverse range of dramaturgical possibilities offered by theatre, radio, film, and television. However, the masterly productions of *Mountain Language* and *Party Time* that he created for television suggest that his directorial experiments with the aesthetic possibilities of television drama had an impact on his approach to dramaturgical structure. The fact that the stage plays from *A*

Kind of Alaska onwards do not lose anything in the translation from theatre space to television screen—if anything they gain by the transposition—may reveal something about the terms of their artistic conception.

As impressive as *Party Time* was at the Almeida, the breadth of the spatial focus was the least successful aspect of the production, groups of characters being obliged to sustain unheard background conversations in order to maintain the continuous action of a party while the dialogue of the speaking characters was being foregrounded. One could understand why Pinter had decided against spotlighting those whose conversation the audience was overhearing while leaving the remaining characters in semi-darkness. Such an approach would have undermined the quasi-naturalistic representation of Gavin's chic party, substituting a starkly expressionistic representation of souls bared and secrets shared, for the accurate evocation of milieu suggested by Pinter's brilliant representation of the London argot of the Nineties.

Yet it is precisely in the tension between the class attitudes exposed through the social posturing of the partygoers and the mental landscapes glimpsed through intimate exchanges that the television production locates the crux of the drama. Where the optics of stage performance tended in the first production to restrict the free interplay of verbal and visual images, blurring the focus of the spare and elegant text, the potential of television to juxtapose medium shots of two, three, and four characters with close-ups on individual faces, provides a technique perfectly suited to articulating the ebb and flow of inter-cut conversations that are so strikingly satirical on the page. The television version creates a tightly focused field of attention that highlights a scenographic dialectic of bodies and faces in order to articulate its core drama of power and exclusion as a struggle for corporeal well-being.

The repeated attempts of the characters at the party to join or construct groups and subgroups through which they might identify and gain access to society's locus of power are emblematised in the image of the club introduced by Terry at the opening of the play. His repeated attempts to return conversations with his betters to this topic exposes the ordinary experience of mixing with guests at a party as a struggle for inclusion in the society of insiders from which Dusty's brother Jimmy has been forcibly excluded—along with the many others who are victims of the 'bit of a round-up' to which Gavin refers near the end of the play. The opening action of the party establishes Gavin as the suave host engaged in conversation with the insecure and somewhat obsequious Terry who is extolling the virtues of the exclusive new club. The social pleasantries are disrupted by the entrance of Terry's wife Dusty, whose urgent question, 'Did you know what happened to Jimmy?', introduces an apparently inappropriate note of personal anxiety that causes the guests to freeze for a moment, disturbing the poised complacency of the social occasion. Terry's momentarily angry response is another socially inappropriate expression of genuine emotion: 'Nobody's discussing this. Nobody's discussing this, you follow? If you're not a good girl, I'll spank you.' Terry immediately attempts to re-establish social decorum by forcing Dusty to conform to the etiquette of cocktail party chit-chat: 'Tell him about the club'. In an attempt to contain her fear and anger she somewhat sarcastically complies, but the unease introduced by Dusty's question is compounded by Dame Melissa's more urbane but nonetheless perplexing entrance speech:

> 'What on earth's going on out there? It's like the Black Death … The town is dead, there's nobody on the streets, there's not a soul in sight apart from some… soldiers. My driver had to stop at a … you know, what d'you call it? A roadblock. We had to say who we were. It really was a trifle …'

In its opening minutes the play not only maps the emblematic divide between the insiders and the excluded, the scene (a luxurious apartment) and the unseen (the contiguous off-stage world of the street outside), but in parallel also exposes the contrast between the manners of the Establishment figures (Gavin and Melissa) and those privileged outsiders whose acts of service and obsequy earn them the right to participate in the Establishment's rituals of social self-approbation. In contrast with the demand made at the roadblock to 'say who we were', the true identities of the characters are never explicitly revealed. For the whole duration of the play the viewer is therefore led to decipher clues about the precise nature of the network of power relationships that lie below the surface of the characters' behaviour. The play effects a progressive deconstruction of the significance of the naturalistic code of meaning, exposing the factitious emptiness of its conventional semiological relationships.

The motif of inside/outside (scene/unseen) is visually indicated by recurring shots of the corridor and front door of the apartment that break the flow of action at roughly equal intervals. These shots are of varied duration and are underscored by stings of music which follow a cessation of speech. The hauntingly atmospheric quality of this quasi-expressionistic device undermines the seemingly realistic representation of party behaviour, implying that the significance of the observed action requires deeper levels of explication than that allowed by the hermeneutic conventions of naturalism. The disturbing speech and starkly contrasting visual presence of the excluded Jimmy framed in the open doorway at the end of the play is the climax of the series of shots of the corridor and door. As a coda to the main action of the play, his appearance in immaculately white clothes, backlit by a glow of stark white light identifies his body in direct visual opposition to the sleek bodies of the partygoers—conspicuous consumers whose fashionable black evening dress fetishises the power and glamour of their 'designer' bodies. His significant absence from the plenitude emblematised by the party defamiliarises the games of social competition and conformity represented by the unceasing attempts of the party guests to avoid social ostracism and to enhance their social status.

As director, Pinter effectively exploits the aesthetics of television studio drama in order to express this desparate struggle to avoid social exclusion. Eighteen basic groupings of characters in various parts of the elegantly furnished apartment are used to construct the mise-en-scène, the camera alternating between medium shots and close-ups to vary the point of view during each of these eighteen segments of action/conversation. The mise-en-scène thus highlights as visual leitmotif the relationship between the performers' fashionably clothed bodies and the cool neo-classicism of the environment. As the action progresses the viewer's chief hermeneutic challenge is to interpret the setting as milieu. The plot unfolds simply as a series of constantly re-forming conversation groups in which guests jockey to establish their positions within the supposed hierarchy of the social group (emblematised by the idea of joining 'the club'). The snippets of gossip and chatter are juxtaposed as fragmented narratives that repeatedly provoke unanswered questions about who the speakers are and what their relationship is with the unexplained 'round-up' that is apparently occurring in the streets outside.

In the theatre there is a danger that the saturated conventions of naturalistic acting might render some of the ambiguities invisible, obliging actors to play them too knowingly. The ability of the camera, on the other hand, to create a continually changing series of frames for groups of bodies and faces, permits the director to concentrate on the most subtle nuances of behaviour, exploring the full expressiveness of the vocabulary of naturalistic acting with its repertoire of facial and gestural reactions or non-reactions. Camera work also explicitly invites the viewer to compare the reaction of one character with another. In such a brief and elliptical play as *Party Time* this is a great gain. Having emphasised the idiosyncratic use he is making of the medium, Pinter proceeds to indicate the constructed quality of the television image by visually foregrounding the symmetry of the pseudo-classical architecture and decor, at times grouping waiters and guests in geometrically balanced couples, thus enhancing the viewer's self-consciousness with respect to the act of viewing.

In *Mountain Language* he had composed beautiful but flat tableaux of suffering victims and sadistic torturers, normal televisual conventions being subverted by a slow and regular rhythm of cutting from one face to another, to very tight close-ups on eyes and mouths. Groups of actors were placed so as virtually to eradicate the sense of three-dimensionality. Such tableaux are occasionally staged in *Party Time* (e.g. the framing of Jimmy in the doorway and the very slow zoom into close-up all the way through his speech) but more often than not the symmetries are emphasised by way of contrast with the more angled views of character groups, the composition of which highlights violent movements within a fairly tight frame and a more conventional rhythm of cutting from one face to another which reinforces the power play being enacted among the various individuals within each group.

In the television version of *Party Time* Pinter has made explicit the connection between the ethos and education of the upper class Establishment and its ruthless commitment to the use of force as a means of preserving its privileged way of life. His exploitation of the medium itself creates a self-reflexive stylistic discourse on the way in which the human body is inscribed in the systems of consumer culture. The relationship between camera/editing technique and mise-en-scène dramatises the discourse on consumer culture that Pinter's choice of setting emblematises. By creating a series of images of the objectified human body (the miniature sculpture of a dancer that the camera picks up on occasions, the formalised grouping of flunkeys—or are they henchmen?—framing the door at the end of the corridor and facing directly into the camera, the pair of waitresses standing with drinks, and the static conversational groups whose decorum is broken by Dusty and Terry's socially inappropriate domestic brawling) the television production presents the body as both source and object of power. Gavin and Melissa's behaviour perfectly matches the cool elegance of the decor. As representatives of the power of the Establishment, their behaviour is in complete harmony with their social environment. By contrast, Liz and Terry are desperately eager to adopt the trappings of this lifestyle and therefore each attempts to play the role of appreciative guest. In this context 'becoming a member of the club' involves keeping one's body trim enough to fit easily into the sleek surroundings which represent the accoutrements of naked power. The decor itself wittily alludes to the cool style of interior decoration typical of the Thatcherite 1980s and early 1990s, its postmodernist visual culture eclectically mixing neo-classical and modern minimalism so that the décor of expensive sports clubs in the City seems to mimic that of exclusive homes in Knightsbridge—or vice versa!

The visual discourse of the body is expressed in Liz and Charlotte's gossip about the romance of sex in the fifth section of the play. Their language provides a surreal echo of the previous speech of Terry ('You keep hearing all these things spread by pricks about pricks...'), amplifying the objectification of the body through a fetishising of male body parts:

LIZ So beautiful. The mouth, really. And of course the eyes.

CHARLOTTE Yes

LIZ Not to mention his hands

....

LIZ But that bitch had her legs all over him

....

CHARLOTTE That's why you're in such pain

LIZ Yes, because that bigtitted tart—-

CHARLOTTE Raped the man you loved.

In an absurdly comic inversion of the traditional sexual conquest of the passive woman by the lustful man, Liz and Charlotte speak of Liz's female rival as a rapist, appropriating conventions of masculine sex-talk in order to assert the force of Liz's own desires. At the same time her own apparent aggressiveness is contradicted by her adoption of an incompatibly sentimental romantic posture: 'You're right. I fell in love. I am in love. I haven't slept all night. I'm in love.' Such a conflation of pornographic fantasies and sentimental love reflects the psychological clichés of women's magazines of the Eighties and Nineties, representing the pervasive sexualisation of culture for commercial profit. The conversation clearly introduces a psycho-sexual dimension into the discourse of power and privilege that the situation embodies.

The television version adds six new characters and six short episodes to the original stage script—a donnish older woman, Pamela; two apparently well-heeled younger women, Emily and Suki; Sam, a man in his fifties, whose speech suggests he is not one of the public school elite; and Harlow and Smith—two taciturn and sinister young men who are identified as public school types but seem to be seriously involved in whatever military or paramilitary operation is 'going on in the street'. One obvious function of these scenes is to focus and enhance the representation of the new Establishment as it was conceived in Thatcher's Britain. The behaviour of the characters seems to suggest that Gavin White and Dame Melissa are at the apex of a hierarchy determined by social status, with Fred, Douglas, Charlotte and Liz below them, and Pamela, Emily, Suki, Sam, Harlow, and Smith on the lowest rung of the ladder. Terry and Dusty's comparative lack of urbanity and Terry's working-class London dialect indicates that they are part of a class of ambitious 'servants' given privileged access to the social rituals of the ruling class in order to do its dirty work. The precise nature of the hierarchy is never directly revealed, and is complicated by the co-existence of a shadowy nexus of power relationships dominated by Gavin, in which men have unquestioned power over women and all the men other than Jimmy are Gavin's assistants and henchmen. In one respect *Party Time* represents the way in which the new Thatcherite Establishment of the late Eighties constituted a re-alignment of privilege and power, effecting the rapprochement between new money and the old ruling elite (aristocracy and the Oxbridge-educated upper-middle class).

Douglas and Fred are agents of power, seeming to be party to the political manoeuvring of the elite, and certain l y implicated in the use of force to protect the interests of people like Gavin. Though their style is urbane, Douglas and Fred as portrayed by Gawn Grainger and Roger Lloyd Pack, are not aux fait with the full repertoire of public school mannerisms. Their *arriviste* manners at times hint menacingly at the physical brutality alluded to in speech but never literally manifest on the screen. It is their yoking of glib generalities with crude expletives that alerts one to the repressiveness of their instincts.

FRED: We've got to make it work

DOUGLAS: What?

FRED: The country.

....

DOUGLAS: All this fucking-about has got to stop.

In their first exchange (the sixth segment, approximately a third of the way into the play), they are placed in the central corridor framing the door at the end of the passage behind them, echoing the later positioning and stance of Harlow and Smith, sinister ex-public school types who appear as silent henchmen at various moments on screen. The heads and shoulders of Douglas and Fred are framed square-on to the camera. Their clenched fists ('A bit of that') almost threaten the viewer by virtue of the characters' fully frontal position and the proportion of screen space they occupy. The image implies that the physical fitness which Charlotte later admires in Fred is put to brutal use in the work which is required by the 'regime' to which she punningly alludes. Yet for all their assumed upper-class *savoir faire*, Fred and Douglas cannot attain the cool and elegant poise of Gavin, who never needs to raise his voice in order to communicate the complete authority he assumes as the true representative of hegemonic power. The iconic presence of these (and other) menacingly healthy men in immaculate black suits signifies the way in which the shadowy forces of authoritarian violence may be hidden just below the polite surfaces of a democratic society.

Douglas and Fred's conversations elliptically allude to the reasons for the military activity that seems to be taking place in the street. They attempt to justify it in the threatening language of military or police strategy—without any concern for justice or human rights:

DOUGlAS: We want peace and we're going to get it. But we want that peace to be cast iron.... Tight as a drum. That's the kind of peace we want. And that's the kind of peace we're going to get. A cast iron peace. *(He clenches his fist)* Like this.

FRED: You know, I really admire people like you.

DOUGLAS: So do I.

On the surface, their mutual admiration comically evokes the type of homoerotic *frisson* of young sportsmen, but the smug self-righteousness of these middle-aged men is horrifying in its narcissistic intimation of the attractiveness of brute force as a proto-fascist means of maintaining social harmony.

As television director, Pinter amplifies these intimations of unseen repression and violence with remarkable economy. No shot seems gratuitous. In section 11, he makes sophisticated use of the convention of the close-up reaction shot in order to highlight the sinister nature of the euphemistic discussion of the death of Charlotte's husband. The camera cuts from the medium shot of Douglas, Fred, Liz and Charlotte to a reaction shot on Charlotte during the silence after Fred's line, 'You married someone. I've forgotten who it was.' Nicola Pagett's studied and glamorous lack of facial expression during the silences that precede and follow her flat delivery of the words, 'He died', implies a series of seemingly contradictory subtextual possibilities, prompting the viewer to imagine a number of alternative scenarios, each of which might help to comprehend the battle ambiguously referred to by Charlotte in section 15 when she twice says 'I think there's something going on in the street.'

The fact that the viewer cannot know what Charlotte is thinking or feeling whenever she refers to her husband's death ('Oh by the way, he wasn't ill') becomes integral to the dialectical relationship between text and subtext that is critical in the television production. Television camerawork reinforces the effectiveness of Nicola Pagett's acting. Where her deadpan playing in the stage production occasionally appeared as mannerism, the television production brilliantly focuses the significance of her failure to express her feelings about the murder of her husband. The implication is that she has in the past experienced what Dusty is suffering in the present moment with respect to her brother Jimmy. Here as in other aspects, the television production powerfully conveys the idea that society conditions and coerces individuals to fit the fashionable trappings of consumer culture.

CHARLOTTE Oh my husband. Oh yes. That's right. He died.

FRED Was it a long illness?

CHARLOTTE Short.

FRED Ah.

Pause.

Quick then

CHARLOTTE Quick, yes. Short and quick.

....

FRED ... A quick death must be better than a slow one. It stands to reason -

CHARLOTTE No it doesn't.

Pause.

CHARLOTTE Anyway, I'll bet it can be quick and slow at the same time. Oh by the way, he wasn't ill.

Pause.

FRED You're still very beautiful.

The conversation rather disturbingly implicates Fred and Charlotte in some kind of previous sexual liaison, compressing unemotional references to what must have been the political execution of her husband in a cool line of cocktail party chatter wholly unsuited to the discussion of such a grave matter. The rhythm of the conversation exposes an unconscious voyeurism in their pre-occupation with the victim's experience of dying that is psychologically consistent with the narcissistic impulses that provoke their flirtation. Their behaviour here reveals the substitution of a sexualised consumer culture in which other people are objectified as potential playthings in place of a coherent moral order. The masculine desire for power that exults in its ability to torture and kill Charotte's husband is the same impulse that derives pleasure from the contemplation of possessing her sexually.

Charlotte has learned to repress her human sensitivities in order to become an attractive sex object who in her turn views the men who oppress her as sex objects. While Dusty is still reacting spontaneously in voicing her anger at being pressured to become an elegantly sexualized object in a world of expensive consumer artifacts, Charlotte has become accustomed to the futility of challenging the brutal repressiveness of the system. In the process of accommodating herself to it she has seemingly been obliged to transform the instinctive resistance to being repressed into a masochistic pleasure in being dominated by the masculine power of her oppressors. The perverse erotic thrill that Charlotte derives from her collusion with masculine brutality is emphasised in her punning use of 'regime'.

CHARLOTTE: God, your looks! No, seriously. You're still so handsome! How do you do it? What's your diet? What's your regime? What is your regime, by the way? What do you do to keep yourself so... I don't know... so trim, so fit?

FRED I lead a clean life.

The discourse on the psychosexual nature of power is amplified in three other sections of the play—Liz and Charlotte, Emily and Suki and Dusty and Terry. Conversations about horse trials and tennis remind one of the specific ethos of the English upper classes—their obsession with the kind of prowess demonstrated in equestrian sports and the kind of social accomplishments symbolised by tennis and golf. References to sport metaphorically reinforce the corporeal presence and visual play of bodies in the mise-en-scène.

In describing the island which he and Liz take for the summer, Douglas further elaborates notions that have been entertained about the romance of sex as bodily well-being. There is an ironic echo of *The Heart of Darkness* in Douglas' colonialist idyll of being at one with nature tended by the few locals who 'do' for them, and an absurdly sexual implication in the fact that they have their own generator. The various images of the fetishised body as a locus of power contrast directly with the statuette of the lithe dancer—an emblem of the beauty of the body as an expressive instrument.

The legitimation of the use of force to repress and exclude dissidents by apparently democratic societies is alluded to in more abstract terms in the series of conversations between Pamela, Sam, Harlow and Smith. Threaded through the play is a line of argument about a generalised topic concerning social values, pursued by Pamela with a donnish assumption of philosophical rigour that she might have learned while studying at Oxford: 'We can't afford to beat about the bush. We have to ask direct questions. "What is valuable? What is of value?" That is my question. "What are the values we choose to protect—and why?"' In context, this constitutes a spurious rationalisation of the ethics of using force to crush those who do not share the interests and values of those in government. In Segment 12, Sam, Harlow and Smith present a degraded version of Pamela's attempts to offer a philosophical justification for state repression that echoes the banal instrumentalism of pub small-talk:

SAM: What is right is right, that's what I say.

HARLOW Exactly.

SAM I mean if a thing works, if a thing is right, respect that. Acknowledge it, respect it and hold to it.

SMITH Hold on to it.

SAM Hold to it—we're talking about principle.

Sam speaks in tautologies, with the stereotypical respect for the status quo characteristic of authoritarian societies and institutions like the army. The human implications of such respect for order are spelt out in a more sinister way a few minutes later.

SAM I mean—I met a man at a party the other day. I couldn't believe it. He was talking the most absolute, bloody crap. His ideas about the world and that kind of thing. He was a complete and utter and total arsehole. A musician or something.

SMITH	Stoddard.
SAM	That's it. Now you see, these kind of people, they're an infection.
SMITH	Don't worry about Stoddard. We've seen him off.
HARLOW	We've had him for breakfast.

As in *The Birthday Party*, the artist (musician) is considered by the Establishment as the social non-conformist whose threat to authority must be ruthlessly repressed. As they quaff champagne, Smith and Harlow's thuggish euphemisms extend the metaphor of conspicuous consumption, while their coarse laughter is grimly reminiscent of the school bully's pleasure at hurting the sensitive child. The exchange echoes the motif of the pyscho-sexual dynamics of power repeated in various ways throughout *Party Time*.

Pamela apprears smugly indifferent to the party's atmosphere of grossly narcissistic materialism. The intention of her seemingly disinterested philosophical question is to justify the strong-arm tactics of those in power. For the viewer, however, the question ironically implies the arbitrariness of authority, exposing the lack of any moral justification for the force used by the Establishment to protect the material interests which the party displays with ostentatious understatement.

The party ends with Melissa and Gavin being warmly applauded for their self-congratulatory speeches in celebration of the selfish and narcissistic ethos institutionalised by the 'club'. Melissa's references to the tennis and swimming clubs of her youth having been replaced by the new club represents the way in which the old Establishment re-constituted itself in a less traditionally class-based form in the Thatcher period to accommodate and exploit the new money created by the deregulation of the London Stock Market. Melissa's membership of the new club demonstrates the conjunction of the authority of the traditionally aristocratic Establishment with the consumerist Darwinism of the New Right, her casual dismissal of her old friends ('they weren't my friends, anyway') revealed as a ruthlessly pragmatic betrayal of old loyalties.

Excluded from the comfortable world of the power elite—outside the door to Gavin's elegant apartment—are those like Jimmy. The many shots of the corridor with the door at the end of it, either closed or open with white light spilling through the doorway, repeatedly foreshadow the appearance at the end of the play of this young man dressed in loose white trousers and white vest, only his face standing out vividly from the white light behind him. Although he has been denied access to the trappings of consumer culture, his body is nevertheless located within the system of material objects. Filmed directly from the front, his image is distinct though two-dimensional, his neutral white garments reflecting his status in this society as a non-person, a body that has no value except insofar as it might be refashioned by violent means into a human object fit for service in Gavin's apartment.

The close-up of Harry Burton's face as Jimmy adds another dimension to the staging of this moment. The youthful openness and vulnerability of the face make a startling contrast with the consciously composed faces of the party guests. Towards the end of the speech a tear trickles down the actor's cheek, apparently caused by the glare of light in his eyes, for he is not sobbing. Although the performance stresses Jimmy's vulnerability, there is no literal representation of the physical torture he must have endured. His oppression is implied by his words, suggesting that he has been deprived of light, that he lives in a world of sounds and that his identity has been negated by his isolation from human society:

> I had a name. It was Jimmy. People called me Jimmy. That was my name.... Sometimes, a door bangs. I hear voices, then it stops. Everything stops. It all stops. It closes down. It shuts. It all shuts. It shuts down. It shuts. I see nothing at anytime any more. I sit sucking the dark. It's what I have. The dark is in my mouth and I suck it. It's the only thing I have. It's mine. It's my own. I suck it.

In the hermeneutic order of the television production Jimmy's complete deprivation is the inverse of the material plenitude which the party represents. The political theme of the drama is thus articulated through the contrast between the plenitude of here and the void of an unlocated and terrifying elsewhere. Exclusion becomes the definitive modern form of oppression. The battle taking place 'in the street' involves the protection of such locations of conspicuous consumption from the have-nots, those excluded by accident of birth or by political choice from the material power of plenty.

NOTES

1. The exceptions are *Victoria Station* and *Celebration*.

The Birthday Party

Directed by Lindsay Posner, the play opened at Birmingham Repertory Theatre on 11 March 2005, transferring to the Theatre Royal, Bath, from 28 March to 2 April, with a London opening at The Duchess Theatre, on 25 April 2005.

Geoffrey Hutchings (Petey), Dame Eileen Atkins (Meg), Paul Ritter (Stanley), Sinead Matthews (Lulu), Henry Goodman (Goldberg), Finbar Lynch (McCann).

The word that springs to mind in relation to this highly acclaimed production is 'intelligent.' Michael Billington (*Guardian*) uses it, describing the production as 'probing, intelligent and very well acted', and so does Robert Hanks (*Independent*), who notes the 'intelligence and elegance' of the production. Charles Spencer (*Telegraph*) calls it 'superb', capturing 'all the familiar unease, the disconcerting pauses' in 'a production without a weak link'. Victoria Segal (*The Times*) praises Posner's direction, and the cast 'who seem to have sprung whole from the post-war clutter of the Boles's home', in creating a production that 'bears a vivid freshness.' Alastair Macaulay (*Financial Times*) describes the cast as 'superb', and critics have particularly singled out Henry Goodman's performance as Goldberg and Dame Eileen Atkins' 'totally dippy but oddly sensual' Meg (Sid Langley, *Birmingham Post*). Much praise also went to Peter McKintosh's 'marvellous design' (Segal), and the set which captures the 'drab, pinched atmosphere of the 1950s' (Spencer). The only dissenting voice was that of Kate Kellaway (*Observer*), who notes the 'freshness of the writing', but describes the production as 'vintage Pinter' and 'pined for something riskier.' But if this is vintage Pinter, it is more like the restoration of an 'old master', since Posner re-balances, through direction and design, a whole range of nuances at play within the writing from the political to the existential, and brings it to fresh new life.

Pinter's great comic gift and the play's debt to radio shows of the 1950s (already noted by Ronald Knowles)[1] was evident from the start with Meg's repeated 'Is that you?' getting full laughter. And the audience was quick to respond to other moments, such as the exchange between Meg and Petey over the birth announcement in the newspaper, and later,

Goldberg's many variations on his own name. In contrast to the humour, Posner brings out the inherent sense of menace, beginning with Goldberg and McCann's first silent materialisation, and building through their patently false bonhomie, until by Act III their threat achieves full force. For example, when Petey, overhearing them, helpfully offers Sellotape for Stanley's broken glasses, they turn slowly, menacingly, to look at him, giving Pinter's stage directions a chilling authenticity. Another particularly chilling moment comes in the game of blind man's buff, when McCann catches Stanley, placing his finger not on Stanley's glasses, but in the centre of his forehead, as if marking the spot where a bullet will go. Other moments also disturb, such as the pathetic image of Stanley isolated centre stage at his own party, or sobbing into his hands after asking Meg just who she thinks she is talking to. Then there is the disturbing vision of this Meg, tall, gangling, middle-aged, effecting a slinky promenade in her green silk party dress, and the long, lingering kiss she gives Stanley after wishing him 'Happy Birthday.'

It is the strength of Eileen Atkins' Meg, 'dim, vulnerable, and with a terrifying amorousness about her' (Spencer) which has helped to shift the balance slightly away from Stanley's central predicament. Yet each member of the cast has their own innate strength. Sinead Matthews' fluffy, sexy Lulu is particularly convincing as a not-so-dumb blonde. She does, after all, note Stanley's lack of air, and opens a door to the outside world, ironically increasing the sense of claustrophobia within. Henry Goodman as Goldberg has been justly praised, Billington noting the way that his smile is allowed to 'linger too long as if it had been refrigerated.' And yet, 'in the last act [...] he reveals the sweat-stained panic of the organisation man perpetually in thrall to some higher authority.' Billington also notes how Finbar Lynch's 'dour, buttoned-up, very funny McCann' reminds us that he is 'a recently unfrocked priest.' As for Paul Ritter's Stanley, there is far less of the catatonic about him than in previous productions. He appears to be a perfectly ordinary bloke, albeit a bit depressed, nervous, and tending to fantasy. When he is taken away, neat and tidy, but sightless and speechless, we are concerned—but his is only one part of the tragedy, and is balanced by Meg and Petey's response to the event. As Alastair Macaulay says, with the 'odd strength of character that Geoffrey Hutchings brings to Petey' this is '[p]erhaps the most surprising twist of the production.' And it is that characterisation, carefully balanced with that of Stanley and Meg, that allows a refreshing rereading of the whole. When Petey attempts to stop Goldberg and McCann taking Stanley away ('Leave him alone!'), they '(*insidiously*)' invite him to come with them—repeating the invitation three times. Whereupon 'Petey (*broken*)' calls 'Stan, don't let them tell you what to do!' (pp. 79-80). Billington suggests that this broken cry comes from one who has himself been broken by the system. Hutchings delivers the line with a crushed quietness, not as one who has suffered the trauma experienced by Stanley, but as one who has come to acknowledge his own helplessness against such overwhelming power. Facing the wings, and thus avoiding any eye contact, he drops his head as he speaks, showing himself defeated. When he later tells Meg that Stanley is 'still asleep' upstairs, we understand that he is putting off the moment not only when Meg must face the truth, but when he too must face the truth of his own moral frailty. We are therefore left at the end of the play with a balance between victim and onlookers that amounts to a social mirror. Pinter, speaking in April 2005 on BBC 2's *The Culture Show*, refers to the play as making 'more and more sense' today in a political climate where 'an establishment [is] trying to dominate or dictate' to 'a dissenting individual.'[2] And through Meg and Petey we have the response of the average person to that situation. Just like Meg, there are those of us who are too wrapped up in ourselves to notice anything wrong, and then there are those of us like Petey who know there is something utterly wrong, and yet, believing ourselves helpless, do nothing.

This fine reading of a great play is given added depth by Peter McKintosh's superb design. For Kate Kellaway the setting has 'the effect of situating the play within a sepia photograph, a time warp.' But this is not the case, because here too, Posner's production gives a refreshing rereading of the play, returning the play to the notion of room as an extension of the self, and a sense of the existential. In his reading of the play, L. A. C. Dobrez points to the palpable unease created by Pinter's 'characteristic [...] juxtaposition of normality and the abnormal', which is all there in the dialogue of the play, in 'Meg's breakfast cereals and the sense of underlying horror' and where 'A toy drum becomes a mysterious object.' This 'surreal juxtaposition' is, says Dobrez, a '*simultaneous* presentation of inner and outer reality'.[3] And it is this 'presentation' of both 'inner and outer reality' that is underscored in Posner and McKintosh's collaboration.

First of all, there is the realistic detail of the room. Charles Spencer describes how this example of a 'squalid boarding house' is so precise 'that you can almost smell the unrefrigerated milk.' It is a point echoed by Victoria Segal, who finds that the design creates such a 'physical specificity' of set and characters that they make 'the enigmatic details of plot and personality all the more disturbing.' The 'air stagnates', and the walls, were they on 'a Dulux colour chart [..] would be called "Nicotine Eternity".' The scene brings to mind Walter Sickert's painting 'Ennui' (c. 1914),[4] where a man and a woman stare vacantly into space. But for the spectator, the focus is a blank wall in centre frame, a drab yellow-brown which lowers the spirit to that of the two figures in the picture. This is the effect of McKintosh's drab brown room, which darkens toward the ceiling where grease and dust and lives have coagulated. This is setting as affect, the same mix of inner and outer reality that Dobrez has defined. The room is both a precisely realised period setting and an emotional correlative for Stanley's state of mind, an insight into his stasis that the audience is led to share. Dobrez describes how in these early plays 'the room represents one's identity, always a precarious possession in Pinter', linking it to Heidegger's concept of '*dasein* or being-there.' In *The Dwarfs,* for example, Pinter places his audience 'in the same situation' as the central character, 'that is, in the situation of *dasein* which gazes at its world as one already *in* it, as one whose objective viewpoint is necessarily grounded in subjectivity'[5]. And a similar viewpoint operates here, not just for Stanley but for the audience as well, since the setting reinforces our participation in Stanley's subjective vision.

One more element of the design brings it even closer to an existential reading. Critics appear to have overlooked the importance of an earlier image, one which faces us as we take our seats. This image, scanachromed onto a gauze in front of the safety curtain[6], fills the stage, and this is the scene we become familiar with while waiting for the play to begin. It shows two huge deckchairs on a shingled bank, each chair holding a different shaped emptiness, and before them, facing us, a cold, bright mist, obscuring all vision. This scene forms a sharp contrast to the one revealed when the curtain rises. As it rises a tinny pub piano plays 'Around the World I've Searched For You' and brings us in from that nebulous white space to the claustrophobic brown hole of the Boles's living room. A hatch at the back of the main room allows us to see through to the kitchen, but the overall effect is still one of claustrophobia. An open door to the left of the hatch allows another view into the kitchen, and a back wall hung with various shabby domestic objects. Their worn appearance creates a sense of time hanging heavily. People are trapped here. When Lulu complains to Stanley about the stuffiness inside and opens the back door, a shaft of light cuts across black and white tiles on the kitchen floor. The open door, the chequered tiles suggest the domestic interiors of Dutch old masters; the domestic still life. The open door increases the sense of claustrophobia because it hints at a world outside—one that is light and bright—pointing up the gloom inside. But in this case the quality of the light suggests that if you step outside this door, you step into the nebulous white space of that earlier scene, unpeopled, empty, surrounded by mist. This is the 'nowhere' into which Stanley invites Lulu, the 'nowhere to go' of the real Stanley whom Pinter encountered in his seaside boarding house (p. 20).[7] There is only the room—a 'precarious possession' as Dobrez suggests—because there is also always the door, 'avenue for the entry of the Other', and which in Heidegger's terms 'represents oneself as *mitsein* or being-with.'[8] It is this unknown quantity of 'being-with' that creates a constant threat.

For Meg too, there is only the room; she appears not to be able to see outside ('Is it nice out?', p. 4) , and gives the impression of rarely going out. But as Pinter says, 'She does go out', she just 'doesn't go very far. She's certainly frightened of the outside world. She feels there's a lot of threat out there.'[9] In *The Birthday Party* the Other takes the form of the intruders, Goldberg and McCann. But there is another threat which runs throughout Pinter's work, and which is suggested by the first image we encounter, that dense white mist. From Bert's ride in his van in the formless dark (in *The Room)* to the cold, unmoving vistas of *A Kind of Alaska* and *No-Man's Land*, characters struggle against an internal and externalised formlessness. When Stanley asks for the second time, 'Tell me, Mrs Boles, when you address yourself to me, do you ever ask yourself who exactly you are talking to?' (p. 15), it suggests that he too, would like to know the answer, and his story of the job offer in Berlin, and the concert in Lower Edmonton, appear to be efforts to cover over that void by creating a persona he can cling to. In the same way, Meg's closing statement constructs herself as 'belle of the ball.' 'Oh, it's true, I was. *Pause*. I know I was.'

Posner must be commended for this production. Nothing has been imposed on the play, but the resonances within it have been brought to life. Stanley is both political victim and average man, the intruders actual threats or, as Dobrez suggests, perhaps figments of his imagination, representing the relationship between Stanley and his world. Posner and his designer have gone much further with this production to place the audience inside Stanley's 'room', so that we share his mind-set, and the situation in which he finds himself, faced with the nebulous threat from outside. In this way the production supports an existential reading. At the same time, the carefully balanced playing of the three central characters, Stanley, Meg and Petey, illuminates a political reading, showing the apparent helplessness of the individual against the powerful institutions at work in the world.

NOTES

[1] Ronald Knowles suggests that 'the comedy double act of [Jimmy] Jewel and [Ben] Warriss, famous in the 1950s on music-hall and radio, was the prototype of Goldberg and McCann.' Noted by Michael Billington, *The Life and Work of Harold Pinter*, (London: Faber, 1996) p. 77.

[2] Harold Pinter interviewed by Lawrence Pollard, *The Culture Show*, BBC 2, 21 April 2005.

[3] L. A. C. Dobrez, *The Existential and its Exits: Literary and Philosophical Perspectives on the Works of Beckett, Ionesco, Genet and Pinter* (London: Athlone Press; NY: St. Martin's, 1986), pp. 325, 330. I am greatly indebted to Ronald Knowles, who, some years ago, recommended a reading of Dobrez.

[4] Walter Richard Sickert, *Ennui,* (c.1914), Tate Britain, London.

[5] Dobrez, 323.

[6] Conversation with member of production team, Birmingham Rep, 26 August 2005.

[7] Interviewed by Mark Lawson on *Front Row,* BBC Radio 4, 28 February 2005, Pinter tells the story of his encounter with a ghastly seaside boarding house in which were 'Meg' the landlady, and the man who became Stanley. When Pinter asked this man "Why do you stay here?" he said, "There's nowhere else to go."

[8] Dobrez, p. 323.

[9] Pinter, *Front Row,* 28 February 2005.

WORKS CITED

Michael Billington, *Guardian Unlimited*, 26 April 2005: http://www.guardian.co.uk/arts/reviews/story/O,,1470591,00.html

Michael Billington, *The Life and Work of Harold Pinter* (London: Faber, 1996).

L. A. C. Dobrez, *The Existential and its Exits: Literary and Philosophical Perspectives on the Works of Beckett, Ionesco, Genet and Pinter* (London: Athlone Press; New York: St. Martin's, 1986).

Robert Hanks, *Independent,* 27 April 2005: http://enjoyment.independent.co.uk/theatre/reviews/story.jsp?story=633410

Kate Kellaway, *Observer,* 1 May 2005, p.9.

Sid Langley, icBirmingham, 17 March 2005: http://view.atdmt.com/SCH/iview/trntymsh0050000024shc/direct/01?cache=6729433

Alastair Macaulay, *Financial Times,* 27 April 2005.

Harold Pinter, *The Birthday Party, Plays One* (London: Faber, 1991).

Harold Pinter, interviewed by Lawrence Pollard, *The Culture Show,* BBC 2, 21 April 2005.

Harold Pinter, interviewed by Mark Lawson, *Front Row,* BBC Radio 4, 28 February 2005.

Victoria Segal, *The Times, Arts,* 1 May 2005.

Walter Sickert, *Ennui* (c.1914), Tate Britain, London.

Charles Spencer, *Telegraph Arts,* 26 April 2005.

Linda Renton

Pinter's *Zanni*: Using a *Commedia dell' arte* Approach to *The Dumb Waiter*

MARDIA BISHOP

As a playwright, Harold Pinter is consistently praised for his use of language. Two comments from the back cover of his recent play *Celebration* highlight this fact. John Lahr writes in *The New Yorker*: "In Pinter's plays, words are probes launched into the world, variously, to mask, to mystify, to mock, or to murder. He sets out his entire smorgasbord of gorgeous verbal moves...." John Peters echoes his comment in *The Sunday Times*, London: "One of the finest comic writers in the language ... Pinter's dialogue has a sense of ebb and flow, of bursting out and retreating in defeat, of self-abasement and evasion, of attack and tactical withdrawal. The result is that the most prosaic passages can have a musical quality; harsh minor keys, perversely accurate rhythms, heady crescendos that take you headlong into pauses pregnant with knowledge."

As these passages describe, Pinter creates dialogue that not only has meaning, but a definite rhythm or movement to it. For a directing project, I wanted to see if it were possible to capture the rhythms of Pinter's language in movement. Only recently has the potential of movement in producing Pinter plays been examined, most notably Richard Allen Cave's "Body Language in Pinter's Plays." Cave's emphasis, however, is on the meaning of gestures and movement once in production, not on how movement in the rehearsal process could inform a production. As I further contemplated my directing concept, I decided I wanted to go further—not only to try to match the movement inherent in the language to actual physical movement, but to investigate a work by a playwright known for agility with language through neither linguistic nor literary approaches. What happens when we apply a non-literary, non-text-based, actor-centric, physical performance style to a literate, text-based, verbal text that is usually governed by the director's and playwright's interpretation? How would this approach dictate/inform the performance of the text? What would this approach do to the comedy, the tone, the characters' relationships, and those instantaneous transitions in tone?

The movement-centered performance style I chose was *commedia dell'arte*. Primarily, I chose it because *commedia* developed through an oral tradition in which language is passed down, susceptible only to the subtle evolutions of memory and speech. Although Pinter is praised for his mastery of dialogue, his dialogue, like all of his craft, is richly informed by literary antecedents and traditions. The choice of *commedia* was also driven by the recognition that the main language of all the Masks, the stock characters, is action.

I chose Pinter's *The Dumb Waiter* for several reasons, but principally for its accessibility to student actors[1] and because its basic plot premise—two *zanni* wait for orders from their master—mirrors a standard *commedia* scenario. These Pinter protagonists are puppets of an unseen master, just as *commedia zanni* are puppets of their masters and their own desires for food. In England, in fact, *commedia* characters eventually evolved into actual puppets—Punch and Judy.

The Dumb Waiter, like Pinter's other early plays, has already been dissected for its music hall or vaudevillian type of humor and performance style.[2] Although *The Dumb Waiter* has already been recognized and played as vaudeville, I wanted to explore what would happen to the play if we pushed the comedic movement itself into a much more heightened and critical aspect of the play's interpretation and production.

On the comedy continuum, *commedia* is a more emphatically physical and caricatured style of comedy than vaudeville. Vaudeville encapsulates a number of comedic and entertainment routines, from the Laurel and Hardy style double-teaming and repartee to acrobatic acts to stupid people tricks. For the most part, however, vaudeville is based on short skits or sketches, while a true *commedia* performance inhabits a different world—it is fuller, having a storyline, narrative, and an ensemble of specific, interactive stock characters, each of whom has its own signature movement styles. Although it is argued that vaudeville/musical performers employ *commedia* techniques, particularly Laurel and Hardy, in terms of shtick and character types, vaudeville is not full-blown *commedia*.[3]

There are many resources available on the *commedia dell'arte*'s history and performance style. Two of the most popular for actors and directors are Mel Gordon's *Lazzi* and Ducharte's *Commedia dell'Arte*. However, I chose to use John Rudlin's *Commedia dell'Arte: An Actor's Handbook* because, according to Angus Whyte, professional actor and director of *commedia*, Rudlin's "book is the first of its kind that has 'real practical value' to an actor or a director. Other books on commedia [are] consulted and used, [but] it is the first one that is any real help, in that it acts as a how-to guide to performing the characters" (Whyte, email to author).

For those not conversant with it, the term *commedia dell'arte* translates as "comedy of the artists," implying performances by professionals. Although the term was not used until the 18th century by Goldoni, the term refers to a professional, masked, and initially publicly improvised performance on temporary outdoor platforms that became prominent during the Italian Renaissance. Although many scholars trace the *commedia* characters to Atellan farces that achieved their highest popularity in the 1st century BCE, Rudlin traces the origin of the *commedia* to the mid-16th-century Italian market place and carnival. Working from scenarios (or plot outlines), actors playing stock characters would improvise performances based on these well known plots. A typical story line consisted of a dirty old man trying to marry a pretty ingénue who would, of course, be in love with the dirty old man's son. Through the help of clever servants, the dirty old man is humiliated and outwitted and the young lovers are united. Non-improvised elements were included as well, such as *lazzi* (sight gags), *battute* (stock repartees), and *concetti* (stock rhetorical passages). *Commedia dell'arte* quickly spread throughout Europe and was the leading form of public entertainment there for approximately 200 years.

Commedia dell'arte was performed by professional troupes, usually consisting of family members. The parts would be taught and passed down from generation to generation. One family who began a troupe in 16th-century Venice still operates today. The performance style was usually big, loud, and physical since *commedia* was an outdoor performance where actors had to attract, interest, and hold an audience while competing with the clamor of the piazza. Voices were loud and coarse and the overall performance was extremely physical, featuring many beatings, sight gags, sword play, acrobatics, and other extremes of physicality.

There were three levels of stock characters in *commedia dell'arte* which Rudlin calls Masks or comic prototypes. Traditionally, theatre historians discuss *commedia* characters in terms of the young lovers or *innamorati*, the masters, and the *zanni* or servants. According to Rudlin, the term "*zanni*" is both singular and plural. When the "Z" is in lower case, *zanni* refers to all servant characters, and when in upper case, Zanni refers to an actual Mask, or comic stereotyped character.

The Dumb Waiter's Ben and Gus, who are hit men waiting for instructions regarding their current assignment, can easily be classified as *zanni* characters. For the purposes of this directing project, the actors, in consultation with the director, chose specific *zanni* as comic prototypes for Ben and Gus. The *zanni* selected for Ben was Brighella and for Gus, Zanni.

As a Mask, or comic stereotyped character, Zanni's status is that of the servant character, "that regrettably eternal unfortunate, the bottom of the pecking order" (Rudlin 67). The Zanni character was based on the Bergamese peasants who were immigrant workers in northern Italian towns. They were "coarse fellows, simple and good natured enough, who come down from the mountains of Bergamo to fetch and carry for the rest of mankind" (T. Garzoni, *Piazza Universale*, 1585, quoted in Lea: 55). Zanni's characteristics include a strong survival instinct, a constant, gargantuan hunger, ignorance (the very act of thinking is alien to him), and the willingness and ability to dish out heavy thwacks with his slapstick. In addition, he is intolerant of discipline and authority, but very faithful. Zanni is everyone's "gofer," and for the audience, he is the most sympathetic character.

We chose Zanni as the prototype for Gus's character because of his many characteristics that were similar to Gus's personality. Like Zanni, Gus is the subordinate partner in his relationship with Ben. He is at the "bottom of the pecking order." He is very much the "gofer" character being told by Ben to "light the kettle," "pick it [the envelope of matches] up," and "Fetch one of those plates." In addition, Gus is always hungry, desiring crisps or Eccles cakes, and lamenting that he had to give all his food to the dumb waiter—"I'm thirsty too. I'm starving ... We send him up all we've got ... Why did I send it up?" (Pinter 1119). Moreover, Gus's strong sense of survival drives him relentlessly to try to figure out what is going on. Unlike Ben, who initially doesn't question the odd occurrences and inconsistencies that had never occurred in their past jobs, Gus immediately pounces on the discrepancies and is worried and wondering what could happen to him and Ben. Gus also questions authority—he's constantly trying to figure out who is the boss and why they are there, yet he is faithful to the organization and when it is time to prepare for the hit, he has no problem performing his job. Finally, Gus is the most sympathetic character in *The Dumb Waiter* because of his subordinate status, his comic attempts at figuring out what is going on, and because he "allies himself with the wrong side of the aggressor-victim conflict"—Gus has allied himself with the victim they are supposed to hit (Coppa 49).

The Mask that was most similar to the Ben character is Brighella. Brighella's status when appearing with other *zanni* is that of the boss. He is only a little boss, the keeper of an inn or the proprietor of a shop, but in the *commedia* world, the very fact that he has managed to better himself gives him high status. In addition, he is never a victim and always maintains his status.

Brighella's characteristics include exploiting whomever he has a scene with, being astute and ready for anything, and being a criminal who is amoral rather than evil. In addition, he appears relaxed and calm until the action's tension increases and then he becomes more urgent in his voice and movement. Brighella's props consist of a dagger and a mandolin/guitar. In *The Dumb Waiter*, Ben's dagger is a revolver and the mandolin/guitar on which a Brighella would sing stories becomes a newspaper from which he reads stories—another difference in an oral versus literate tradition.

As with Gus and Zanni, we chose Brighella as the prototype for Ben because of the many similarities between them. Ben's status in his relationship with Gus, another *zanni*, is that of boss. Early on in the play, he asks Gus, "Who's the senior partner here, me or you?" asserting his position. Ben always tells Gus what to do and seems to know more about the organization and their current assignment than Gus. In addition, Ben is never the victim—at the end of the play, Gus is the intended victim, not Ben.

Ben, like Brighella, tends to exploit others. With Gus, Ben is the boss and has Gus do the majority of the grunt work. When reading from the paper, Ben chooses stories to demonstrate the stupidity of other human beings, such as the 87-year-old man that crawls under a lorry to cross the road. Ben uses his storytelling choices to affirm his own superiority.

Ben also appears confident and in charge of the action. He doesn't question his situation; he appears to be in control and in alignment with the organization. It is Gus who asks Ben for information about the organization. Ben seems unfazed by the apparent strangeness of the things that Gus brings up, such as the absence of gas or the kitchen stove having only three rings when the apartment supposedly used to be a café. Ben appears relaxed throughout all the strange incidents until toward the end of the play. After being continuously questioned by Gus regarding who is upstairs operating the dumb waiter and who is challenging them—questions that Ben cannot answer—Ben starts to beat Gus.

After identifying appropriate Masks, the actors then researched and practiced the specific physical traits associated with Zanni and Brighella. Those traits included stances, walks, gestures, and vocal qualities. Again we turned to John Rudlin's descriptions of the Masks to guide us. Zanni's movements in general are dynamic, exaggerated, and always urgent. He appears nervous, constantly moving his head from side to side and using his hands to illustrate whatever he is saying. His stance features a low center of gravity, an arched back, one leg bent and the other extended. Never staying still, he changes feet repeatedly (Rudlin 69). Zanni's walk features "shoulders down, elbows forward, feet pointed with knees coming high off the ground and to the side and a two-time rhythm in even beats with the head pecking like a chicken" (Rudlin 69-70). And his speech is loud, open-mouthed, and coarse. Brighella's movement, on the other hand, is more lithe or cat-like. His stance features "flat feet, ballet first position, with knees slightly bent and belly forward" (Rudlin 73). His walk is more of a strut with the chest pushed forward and the arms pushed back.

As we began the rehearsal process our goal was to use a *commedia* performance style to see where it would lead us. However, I had specific issues to explore. For example, I was curious how Ben and Gus would be fleshed out if approached from a *commedia* style and whether or not the style would interfere with the stark tone and seriousness of the play (*commedia* is harsh as well, but does its style constitute a "comedy of menace"?). Moreover, I was curious whether or not the style would interfere with the flow or substance of the dialogue.

In beginning this experiment, I had misgivings right away. The approach was antithetical to Sir Peter Hall's text-centric suggestions for directing Pinter. Hall's productions of Pinter have been seminal and his approach to a Pinter work is a four-step process that reifies Pinter's linguistic complexity and includes: 1) an in depth study of the text, including the rhythms of the language and the types of pauses; 2) rehearsal in which the psychological processes of the characters are explored (Hall comments that Stanislavsky techniques are used 'cautiously' "because this process cannot result in improvisation, or alteration of the dialogue, or the pauses, or the shape of the text" (Hall 152); 3) releasing the melodrama that lies underneath the text and then hiding it; and, 4) staging, which needs restraint because "too much movement blurs the text" (Hall 152).

In contrast, our approach emphasized movement and began with improvisation. Basically our rehearsal process was to first identify appropriate *zanni* characters. Then, the actors explored the physicalities of these characters. They practiced the walks, the stances, and the gestures. We then added typical emotional traits of the *zanni*—Zanni/Gus's overwhelming hunger, Brighella/Ben's desire to always be in charge—and conducted improvisations to allow the actors to get a sense of how the practiced movement would play out when the character had an objective. Then we added the basic relationship between the *zanni*, i.e. Gus and Ben, and conducted improvisations to solidify their movement in relation to each other. Next, we went to the text, but just the conflicts in each beat, not the dialogue. We divided the text into beats and the actors performed their objectives with movement and the commedia *grummelot* or gobbledygook. Finally, we added Pinter's dialogue.

Approaching *The Dumb Waiter* with a *commedia dell'arte* performance style had several significant consequences. These will be discussed from the perspective of the actors and their process first. Then, I will address how the *commedia* approach affected the text and the production values for the audience.

Using the *commedia* approach probably produced its most positive outcomes for the acting process: our actors were college theatre majors who were talented but not professionals nor experts in *commedia* technique. Consequently, as a director I was extremely conscious of how a *commedia* approach might help or hinder them and made directing choices accordingly. The *zanni* movements helped the actors get a handle on Pinter's oblique characters— characters for whom the traditional "fleshing out" or psychological profiling can be difficult or impractical. For the actor playing Gus, Zanni's walk provided a sense of urgency in exploring/questioning his situation. The walk also gave him a sense of the goofiness needed for Gus. The actor who played Gus is an intellectual actor who tends to have stiff movement. The physical preparation loosened up the actor and gave him a feel for comedic movement and timing—and in some instances he even used his own stiffness of movement to advantage. The actor playing Ben (another intellectual actor) was also helped by the *zanni* movements. Brighella's movement gave him more control over and understanding of Ben. Brighella's walk and stance forced the actor to fill up space and become bigger. The actor playing Ben described the character as someone who is insecure about not knowing everything but who pretends to expertise in every situation. In order to accomplish the masquerade, this actor's Ben took up space when he moved and sat in order to maintain his dominant status.

Second, using a *commedia* approach with its heavy reliance on physical humor seemed to free the actors to explore and interject comic bits and physical shtick in what might otherwise have been regarded as a 'sacred' text. Since the emphasis was already on the movement, once we incorporated the dialogue, the actors quickly found bits of business to flesh out their characters, add dimension to the dialogue, and uncover the latent humor in the text. For example, the second time Ben reads one of his newstory harangues from the paper could typically be played with the blunt surface level of the lines. Ben reads the story of a child of eight who killed a cat:

BEN. It's a fact. What about that, eh? A child of eight killing a cat!

GUS. How did he do it?

BEN. It was a girl.

GUS. How did she do it?

BEN. She—

[He picks up the paper and studies it.]

It doesn't say.

GUS. Why not?

BEN. Wait a minute. It just says—Her brother, aged eleven, viewed the incident from the toolshed (1110).

Although the lines are funny as written in their vaudevillian back-and-forth rapid fire patter, in our production the comedy went even further. Gus had made a finger puppet from a bit of newspaper and mouths his short lines back at Ben with his puppet. When Ben reaches the line, "She—," he searches for the conclusion of the story by rifling angrily through his paper only to find (on the line, "It doesn't say,") that a huge chunk of his paper is torn out—Gus' finger puppet. Only by snatching up the puppet and unfolding it can Ben finish his account. The physical bits and the entire exchange were played quickly—the movement was not permitted to slow down the rhythm of the exchange. The shtick added a dimension to the characters' relationship, with Gus' inanity having an uncomfortable intensity that added an extra edge to Ben's impatience and anger. But the business also demonstrated the complementarity of the two characters and how their almost ritualistic aggression is something they enjoy and understand on a deeper level: i.e., both of them enjoyed sharing the story of an eight-year-old cat-killer.

In addition to the physicality, humor in our production was no longer embedded only in the dialogue, but had—through the exercise of *commedia*'s stock comic prototypes—found its way back into the characters themselves. When Ben remarks that the toilet doesn't fill properly due to a "deficient ballcock," Gus reacts overtly, comically and—most important for his *commedia* characterization—unsubtly, taking this Pinter moment from its dark, unspoken and possibly erotic undertow to a bawdy moment of pornographic Zanni-ism. Gus, ever the peasant, seems incredulous that one word could be so outstanding as to contain both "ball" and "cock."

Moreover, the physicality and the open door to comic business provided by the *commedia* choice enhanced our actors' timing and ability to feel and read the audience's reaction to a script that can be somewhat opaque. For example, the insatiable "Pinter pause" can become a deadly, uncomfortable dry zone for a college or amateur actor. With the *commedia* style choice, pauses were naturally filled with business based upon the demands of the *zanni*. Pauses in dialogue became time to explore through *zanni* protocols some equally obscured aspects of Pinter's dramaturgical universe: empty matchbooks found inside shoes and mysterious notes left in dumb waiters are rich fodder for *commedia* formulas. Actors were freed through the demands of *commedia* to explore physical bits, emotional interactions, and how far they could play with the audience.

For the audience, the filling of the Pinteresque pause relieved them of one discomfort and provided them amply with another. It was as if an animalistic brain stem had been put in charge of the cerebral cortex of Pinter's patter. Here, the action and body language of the actors amplified the relentlessness of the script. This was not just an unsettling and dark Pinter: pushing the comic, physical envelope had the effect of making this world even more perverse, more unsettling, and always "in your face."

The *commedia* approach also forced the actors to abandon some of their own inclinations and whatever training methods might induce them to develop and analyze their characters internally. These actors would probably not have helped themselves by asking "What would Gus do?" or "What would Ben do?" as a way of forming their characters' motivations or objectives. But the question "How would my *zanni* play this?" always had a likely answer: *commedia* is not a method of internalization or analysis, but one of ready stock solutions to dramatic challenges designed to produce reliable audience responses. The actor playing Ben was particularly married to the comforts of psychological realism—the *commedia* style left him no choice but to seek out and assume external acting techniques and to free himself, at least in this exercise, from the necessity of psychological motivation and to simply embody the character and the language in large and non-realistic ways.

The integration of *commedia* voices and the *commedia* technique of "playing to the pit" were less successful. The carnivalesque barks and grunts worked for the actor playing Gus when they were used to accompany comic business and provided an appropriate lowness to the character. Barking and grunting and other vocal extremities did not work so well for Pinter's dialogue, especially since it placed Gus in a different play, stylistically, from the actor playing Ben.

How ultimately did this one experiment reflect on the *commedia* approach and its effect on the text and how the audience sees the play? Did the heavy stylization inherent in *commedia* undercut the believability of the characters? Would the stakes of the play remain as high at the end of the day? Or would the experiment simply come off as a forced, inappropriate performance style choice?

Even with the use of *commedia* acting choices, the concluding moments of *The Dumb Waiter* must unearth the play's dark side and the audience must have some investment in the characters and their world, however constructed, for that dark side to be more than a grotesquery. At the end of the play, Gus exits to get a glass of water, while Ben receives word that the person to be killed will be entering right away. As Ben calls for Gus to return and help with the hit, Gus enters and is obviously the intended victim.

From an audience perspective, the assertion of the play's serious import was, in this case, not a matter of if, but when. The craft and control in Pinter's dialogue was a formidable force that often tried to walk off with an actor's voice no matter what his body was doing. Gus' impassioned "tested" passage was a quick segue to the play's climactic moments that transformed the meaning of *commedia* body vocabulary. As the last moments of the play emerge, the *zanni* movements of Gus transformed him from a comic stock character to a paranoid trapped in a comic stock character. The quick Zanni head motions from left to right were still those of the most sympathetic character, but it was one we now sympathized with as a victim, and one whose *commedia* stereotype made him seem all the more trapped, his fate truly sealed. At the same time, the play's final moments of rupture between Gus and Ben, when Ben, for example, now comments on his paper without even telling Gus what he is reading, give that actor an opportunity to make Ben even more the *commedia* Brighella, a loud, brash prototype fulfilling his amoral function—again all the more horrific for the Stepford-like trap the *commedia* formulas have set up for this pair. Although using a commedia approach was questionable at the start, the end results indicated that the project was successful, not only for the actors' development, but for the audience.

NOTES

[1] I am grateful to my students Ari Gratch, who played Gus in this production, and Finn Kelley, who played Ben. Both are talented, intelligent actors who consistently brought a tremendous amount of enthusiasm and ideas to rehearsal, making this project a joy.

[2] Elin Diamond compares Ben and Gus in *The Dumb Waiter* to Laurel and Hardy, commenting that the comedy comes from their relationship—that Hardy (Ben) bullies and blames Laurel (Gus) for their catastrophes while Laurel pauses and then resumes choreographed mischief (Diamond 96). Francesca Coppa identifies the repartee between Ben and Gus as the "strutting rhythm of polished comedy routines" (Coppa 44). Coppa also comments on the extensive use of physical farce in the scenes with the dumb waiter.

[3] John Rudlin emphasizes that the *commedia* present in vaudeville is more Italian humor that melded into the vaudeville pot" (Rudlin 7).

WORKS CITED

Almansi, Guido, and Simon Henderson. *Harold Pinter.* New York: Methuen, 1983.

Cave, Richard Allen. "Body Language in Pinter's Plays." *The Cambridge Campanion to Harold Pinter.* Ed. Peter Raby. Cambridge UP, 2001. 107-129.

Coppa, Francesca. "The Sacred Joke: Comedy and Politics in Pinter's Early Plays." *The Cambridge Companion to Harold Pinter.* Ed. Peter Raby. Cambridge: Cambridge U P, 2001. 44-56.

Diamond, Elin. *Pinter's Comic Play.* Cranbury, NJ: Associated University Presses, 1985.

Duchartre, Pierre Louis. *The Italian Comedy.* 1929. London: Dover, 1966.

Gordon, Mel, ed. *Lazzi.* New York: PAJ Publications, 1983.

Hall, Peter. "Directing the Plays of Harold Pinter," *The Cambridge Companion to Harold Pinter.* Ed. Peter Raby. Cambridge: Cambridge UP, 2001. 145-154.

Lea, K. M. *Italian Popular Comedy.* 1934. Oxford: Russell and Russell, 1962.

Oreglia, Giacomo. *The Commedia dell'Arte.* London: Methuen, 1968.

Pinter, Harold. *The Dumb Waiter. Drama: Classical to Contemporary.* Ed. John C. Coldewey and W.R. Streitberger. Rev. ed. Upper Saddle River: Prentice Hall, 2001.

Pinter, Harold. Jacket notes. Celebration *and* The Room. New York: Grove, 1999.

Prentice, Penelope. *The Pinter Ethic: The Erotic Aesthetic.* New York: Garland, 1994.

Rudlin, John. *Commedia dell'Arte: An Actor's Handbook.* London: Routledge, 1994.

Whyte, Angus. E-mail to the author. 23 Sept. 2003.

Directing *No Man's Land*, Playing Spooner

SIDNEY HOMAN AND SHAMROCK McSHANE

In February 2005, the Acrosstown Repertory Theatre in Gainsville, Florida, staged a production of Harold Pinter's *No Man's Land*. We offer here a perspective on that production and the play from the experiences of its director and lead actor.

Profiting from the Critics

Critics are very divided on this play. Some provide an allegory or grid to make sense of its complex characters, nonlinear form, and dialogue that is alternately specific and allusive, casual and abstract. The play's organizing principle is "a cricket match" (Gale, 203), one where "fantasy and memory" battle each other (Gabbard, 252). The play dramatizes our attempts at "creative recollections," or "a manipulation of the past" (Almani 98, 89). Spooner has been variously identified as the figure of Death or a "spurious savior" (Burkman 143), or "a potential agent of change" (Batty 83). Michael Billington establishes a series of contrasts in the work: genius/lack of talent, success/failure, drunk/sober, elegance/uncouthness, smoothness/roughness, politeness/violence, fixed/fluid, past/present, memory/reality, town/country (246). We are in a "homosexual household" where Spooner is the intruding heterosexual (Orr 89).

Other commentators point instead to the pervasive ambiguity of the play. The reviewer Peter Thompson dismissed the play as an "elaborate spoof," inviting but ultimately frustrating and parodying anyone seeking a clear meaning (Hinchliffe, in Gale, 1986 153). *No Man's Land* is marked by a "pervasive discontinuity in the action," offering only a "depiction of lived experience as an aggregate of discontinuous moments" (Quigley 36, 51). For Elin Diamond, by the end "Action and words eventually exhaust themselves." What begins as a comedy does not end so because of the "thoroughness of [Spooner's} rejection."

Given such antithetical responses, I struggled mightily to develop my director's concept before rehearsals started. In moments of weakness, I thought to myself, "Well, I'll just have to learn about the play, to come to grips with it, during rehearsals!" But what if that moment of revelation, *if* there were to be such a moment, came late—too late?

The actor I had cast as Spooner, a talented Irishman with the delightful name of Shamrock McShane, came to my rescue, albeit inadvertently. A student of David Mamet, when asked during rehearsal for *As You Like It* to speak about the life offstage of his character Jacques, McShane shocked us with, "There is no 'young' Jacques, and I don't really know what his favorite color might be. Because he hasn't told me. All that Jacques is ... are his lines in the play. There's no other dimension to him than that." There followed an enlightening correspondence between us on this issue: what constitutes the dramatic character? Is the approach actor-centered (the actor's filling out the playwright's outline) or playwright-centered, the character's being no more or less than what the author has given us, what he or she has allowed the character to say and do in the play itself?

We continued this debate after I had asked McShane to play Spooner and, invariably, it fed into my inability to establish a clear director's concept. On one hand, there seems to be an enormous sense of the past in *No Man's Land*, a bow to the very sort of material on which the Method actor could stake a claim. Hirst and Spooner have known each other since Oxford; their lives were tangled further when Hirst had an affair with Spooner's wife, Emily. The immediate source of the evening is their having met the night before at Jack Straw's Castle, a local pub, and both offer histories of the place: Hirst of the time it was frequented by Jack Straw himself, a noted highwayman, Spooner of an encounter with a Hungarian émigré in the same place, an encounter that "changed [his] life" (23), or so he claims. Yet all this history, this earlier life of the characters, seemed terribly fake, contrived, less like facts than the purposeful creation of a past, part of the antithesis of "fantasy and memory" that one of the scholars had noted (Gabbard 252).

I also recalled Pinter's own response to someone who asked him to spell out the meaning of his plays: "It is entirely taking place before your very eyes" and the characters, therefore, "are sharing something in the present" so that "the past is not past." For the playwright himself, the issue is "who's feeling what at what time" (Pinter, in Gussow 42-43).

What if *No Man's Land* enacted the attempt by all four characters to create an evening, to impose through their delivery and gestures (the twin poles of the actor's craft) a personal play, one in competition with the plays fashioned by others? Appropriately, during an evening and a morning, followed by a second evening, involving a host and guest, we witness the unreal atmosphere of a cocktail party, an arena of play where guests and hosts present themselves, engage in self-fashioning (to use Stephen Greenblatt's term) for the benefit of others—to impress them, outplay them, perhaps seduce or at least interest them. Spooner, in fact, monopolizes the conversation, with only occasional and cryptic comments from Hirst, for the first half of Act 1, and it is only when he finally takes a seat (designated by Pinter's stage direction) that he and Hirst engage in anything resembling conversation, or stage dialogue. Excluded from the conversation at one point, Foster launches into a monologue describing the vicissitudes of his life, imposing himself, reducing to a silent audience the two men who had been establishing contact without him. This is to say that the characters, each in his own way, do what the actors do—entertain, fashioning a life, a past, a present, perspectives, emotions, out of those words, words, words that Mamet claims are all we really have. The play is thus about creation at the present moment, despite Hirst's claim to have written poems in the past, or Spooner's reference to his companion Hugo who once translated his verse. Characters try to "win" the evening, to best their opponents. The effort is simultaneously theatrical and woefully human.

Spooner may dismiss others whose self is nothing more than a "calculated posture" (16) but he too is posing, a poseur. The first topic on which the men agree is that "All we have left is the English language" (18-19), and in his concurrence with the guest, Hirst reworks the line as "its salvation rests in you"—to which Spooner reluctantly adds "and you too." The present, or in the phrase Spooner and Hirst share, "as it comes" (22), is "truly unscrupulous" (20). Spooner, author of the curious adjective, knows all too well that the past ultimately means nothing, that (in the actor's term) sub-text is just that, something below or beneath the text and not the immediate issue. Like an actor in live theatre, Spooner is interested only in "where [he is] eternally present and active" (20). It is "what is taking place before your very eyes," to revisit Pinter's own phrase, the present that is demanding, that defines the game, and is the source of tension and creation.

At various times in the rehearsals, the actors speculated that Spooner wants to replace Hirst or, by displacing Foster and Briggs, become Hirst's sole companion, in a "happy household" (50) of two rival but compatible poets. Spooner puts his finger on the issue when he claims to be a "poet" not of dreams or the past but of what is present (20). Spooner full well understands the difficulty of his task, and his description of "an imaginative leap [which] few can do" (86), while aimed sarcastically at Foster, seems no less self-referential.

At the cocktail party we craft an evening with words, as we move about, drink in hand, chatting, telling stories, laughing, showing interest (whether genuine or faked), playing the "game" for the occasion. And when we leave, the evening is "over," just as it is in the theatre when the actors take their bows and the audience departs the house.

Spooner and Hirst

This concept, once established, and one which did not come exclusively from the director's head, allowed us in turn to shape the four characters, the players in this evening's game. I look here at the two main characters.

If Spooner is possibly the figure of death, as has been claimed (Burkman 140), he is surely an intruder, a fresh player, and, as such, one of which both spectator and fellow characters must be wary. His name may invoke the word "spoonerisms" or even the adage, "When you sup with the devil sup with a long spoon"; one cannot relax and take what he says on face value. Quite often, in fact, his self-characterization seems a ruse, or a "pitfall and a snare," as he himself claims life to be (18). He boasts of his "indifference" (10), of his never having been loved, and insists that anyone's showing an "interest" in him would cause the "acutest alarm" (17), and yet he pursues Hirst like a lover. At first claiming to be a "free man" (21), by the end of the play he wants nothing so much as to be Hirst's servant or "secretary," his "chevalier" (89) who will accept "death's challenge" in the name of his master. Defining himself as a "betwixt twig peeper," that is, a voyeur, someone content to be an audience, he really wants to be a player onstage, if not the lead character. When Hirst crawls out of the room halfway through the first act, Spooner is triumphant, even, in our production, taking Hirst's chair in his conversation with Briggs that follows shortly after the exit. Little wonder, he is thrown when Hirst re-enters toward the end of the act, nervous, excited, as lively and full of spirits as he was depressed and rude earlier. At one point, Spooner decries "psychological interpreters," the denizens of the "wet dream world" (20), and yet he boasts of being the person who was drowning in "[Hirst's] dream" (47), that revelation leading to Hirst's collapse onstage.

Spooner is a protean creation, the figure of both his conscious and unconscious efforts. While this may literally be his first time in Hirst's home, he has also been here before: "I have known this before," as he says, recalling the lines of T. S. Eliot's Prufrock (6). "Known before," I should add, in a way parallel to the actor who has performed the same play, said the same lines, the day before. Differential, overplaying the perfect guest when he tells Hirst three times that his host is "kindness itself," Spooner also has a massive ego, a sense of the self, as he recasts Descartes's "I think therefore I am " with "I am I" (89). Actually, the philosopher's relative assertion of self may be more accurate in Spooner's case, in his world where thinking through language makes it so. If he is a poet, or at least a friend of the arts, the very subject of his toast, he is very much the would-be artist this evening. Spooner wants Hirst to "see [him] in a different light" (88). Trying to impose his reality (one where the guest either displaces or joins the host) on the "fixed" (17) reality of Hirst's living room, he is like Iago who attempts to impose his reality, a sordid tale of adultery, on the happy marriage of Othello and Desdemona. Our Spooner was crushed when, after his long speech seeking to be the host's secretary, companion, chevalier, agent, representative to the press, Hirst, after taking a long sip from his glass, announces, "Let us change the subject" (91). Spooner slumped on the couch, Briggs and Foster, standing behind it, gloating over his apparent defeat. Thus Spooner's own melodramatic description of "those who have almost lost hope" (90) turns on him. He has only his language, his only weapon or "wedge" (50) to gain entrance to this world; literally, his part is by far the largest in the play. More than that, given his protean nature, it is not *what* he says—which we cannot ever fully trust—but *how* he says it, his style, and this is precisely what he remembers about the encounter with the Hungarian émigré. Indeed, he is annoyed at Hirst for asking if he can recall "what" the drinking companion had said (25).

Most of the commentators on the play see Spooner at the end as excluded from Hirst's world, his mission having failed. We took a somewhat different option in our production, allowing him a partial victory. Spooner joined Hirst downstage, at the table holding liquor and glasses, but when Hirst insists that there is "nothing" in his world, that the dead body in the water, even the memory of walking to the lake, were only illusions, "nothing," Spooner corrects him. And in that correction he recognizes the fixity of Hirst's hermetically sealed world, indeed, echoes Hirst's own description of the world just before he falls to the floor in Act 1. If Spooner cannot enter Hirst's world, he can at least recognize it, define it: "No. You are in no man's land. Which never moves, which never changes, which never grows older, but which remains forever, icy and silent" (95).

Thus Spooner acknowledges, speaks about what cannot be his. In an imagined scene we might project, the next day he will meet someone else, perhaps at a bar, be taken into their house as a guest, try to become part of that world, and be rebuffed again. But here, for the moment, his description is so penetrating that Hirst is reduced to the cliché "I'll drink to that."

Spooner has such sad clarity at the end, at least as we staged it, and it is perhaps a curious coincidence that Hirst's earlier response to Spooner's appeal that he "live with [him] and be [his] secretary," is "Is there a big fly in here? I hear buzzing" (88). In a play bursting with literary allusions, this looks like one to Ms. Dickinson's "I Heard a Fly Buzz when I Died." There, as the narrator on the verge of death tries to imagine the passage from out of this life, she is almost comically interrupted by a fly which suddenly starts buzzing, intervening between her and the fading light and distracting her from her task.

Hirst is mostly silent during Spooner's opening monologue, one that extends for thirteen pages, and yet his interjections, for that is what they are, prove the equal for his guest's loquaciousness. Our audiences learned to cherish Hirst's questions and observations, finding them that much more valuable because of their rarity. Pinter elsewhere speaks of his dialogue as "the weasel under the whiskey cabinet" (Pinter, in George 33). We approach the cabinet to perform the quite mechanical action of opening the glass door, taking out a bottle, and then shutting the door. But this routine action cannot remain so because we know a weasel lives just underneath the cabinet. We never see the creature but knowing it is there proves unsettling, this "unseen presence" that complicates, deepens, make mysterious, even terrifying the otherwise mundane action. Hirst's dialogue serves that function in the first half of Act 1. His clichés, the pleasantries of the genial host—"As it is?" or even "Cheers" (17)—seem to bear a weight, implications beneath the surface. A single "no" from him, when Spooner asks if he "hang[s] around Hampstead Heath," throws the guest who immediately qualifies the question with "excursions," then "rare excursions" before taking refuge in the theoretical possibility of their meeting: "you hardly expect to run into the likes of me? I take it?" (18). Hirst's single "hardly" is clearly not the answer Spooner had wished. The adjective "infelicitous" (Hirst's one-word equivalent of Spooner's "A most clumsy construction, I thought") sends Spooner in paroxysms of joy: "My Christ you're right." And the sarcastic rejoinder, "what a wit," is taken by the overeager guest as positive: "You're most acutely right." At this point he tries to bind himself with Hirst as two artists who have nothing left "but the English language." (18) And when Hirst "edits" his four lines to "You mean in what rests its salvation" (19), like a teacher correcting a student's paper, Spooner is irritated, in our production muttering a somewhat petulant "more or less" (19). From Spooner's perspective, Hirst is a difficult audience that he tires to win over, to impress. But when Spooner seeks confirmation that he hasn't said too much, hasn't "gone to far," Hirst's reply is prophetic, as if he knew the end of the play: "I'm expecting you to go very much further," a reply that always elicited a nervous laughter from our audience (20). Having claimed that his strength lies in the indifference of others, Spooner asks, "That doesn't mean I interest you, I hope?" and on Hirst's comforting negative, "Not in the least," the host spun on his heel and waltzed upstage, leaving Spooner in the lurch.

If Spooner plays an offensive game, Hirst's is mostly defensive, as if he were occupying a fortified position. In fact, seconds after this exchange Spooner makes reference to the German military strategist Von Kleist, whose manual on how to retreat and hold a defensive position is considered a classic of the literature of military strategy. Spooner's reference may simply be part of his bluffing a self-image of the erudite reader, yet it also accurately describes Hirst's equal, if not superior position in the evening's game. A standard rule in military maneuvers is that the offense must outnumber the defense by at least two to one. Spooner's nervous energy in these opening thirteen pages may be a sign of his own suspicions, perhaps not even conscious ones, that the battle is at best a stalemate. Appropriately, in their war stories, Hirst worked with Military Intelligence, while Spooner occupied the inferior position of manning a torpedo boat (71).

Spooner makes a toast to Hirst's "impotence" (33), doubting if he ever had a wife, while boasting about the parts—teeth, buttock, breasts—of his own wife. And he mocks Hirst's sexual relations, if he had them, with innuendos borrowed from cricket: "Tell me with what speed she swung in the air. With what velocity she came off the wicket ... In other words, did she google?" (30) Confronted by Hirst's silence (a literal stage direction in Pinter's text), Spooner wonders if he ever "truly caressed her ... truly did husband her" (31). An offensive player, Spooner rejoices in what Hirst calls his "physical condition" (70), boasting to Briggs that he is both "young" and a "poet."

If Spooner's poetry, his verbal assault, both to define himself and put the host in his place, is aggressive, physical, improvised at the present moment, Hirst's poetry, more rare, indeed almost absent until he returns late in the first act, is linked with the past, and with death. His first sustained speech, which leaves Spooner "enraptured," describes the village church festooned with garlands for young men and women—and old men, he adds in response to Spooner's question, who died "maiden" (29). Compared to Spooner's, his is a short speech, capped with a "There is no more" in response to Spooner who, "enraptured," begs him to continue (30). Hirst's art is already finished; he is "past [his] best now." (72). His most sustained poetry describes the tennis balls, "under the twigs, the dead leaves" (81), and we will recall it was Spooner who peeped through twigs, not looking directly at the lovers, as he is careful to add, but only at the "whites of [their] eyes" (19). Hirst's is a world of his youth, a period "fixed" in his memory (45), one that is "solid," petrified, though the lovers in his photograph album were once "transformed by light, while being sensitive ... to all the changing light." These photographs are his "true friends." His art celebrates "the good ghost," caught in the photo, the emotions "trapped," and if the figures there are "fixed, imprisoned," Hirst, by a sort of necrophilic poetry, confers the illusion of life on them so that they seem to "respond to your touch, to your look" and, so acknowledged, express a "joy [that is] ... unbounded." It is this dead art, this art of the dead, an art locked in the past like the lovers on Keats's Grecian urn, that he *tenders*, and the verb admits the pun on both cherish and cultivate or grow. When Briggs dismisses Hirst's past as "blank," he receives a blunt "nonsense," and on this exchange Briggs, like a bad angel, threatens to revolt, refusing to fetch the bottle for his master. But Briggs knows he can't be dismissed because, an integral part of Hirst's world, having chosen to abandon the real world outside the confines of this "large room in a house in North West London" (9), he simply "won't go." (80) Hirst well knows he and his attendants must "consort with the society to which [they are] attached." (85) Along with Keats, another poet comes to mind, one already invoked in Spooner's four "I have known this before"—T.S. Eliot of *The Four Quartets*. In the rose garden, the still, unchanging, fraudulent world of art, nothing grows old, nothing decays, and yet the children laughing in the bushes will never materialize. Art, as for Keats, is permanent, and hence all we know of "truth and beauty," but it is also dead, an illusion. Spooner, in our production, made an assault on this art world, this closed society, but rather than penetrating it, let alone overthrowing Hirst, could only acknowledge its power in these final words in the play.

Drinking and Speaking

A veritable "feast" of words, its language running from the mundane to the surreal, *No Man's Land* is no less a highly physical play, mostly notably in its props. At various times the characters drink beer, gin, whiskey, scotch, champagne, and coffee, and our small glass table downstage center was usually overflowing with bottles and glasses of various sorts. Drinks are also brought onstage—one moment a whiskey, the next coffee, the next a fresh champagne bottle. Indeed the consumption of alcohol makes demands on the actors; one reviewer wondered how the actors managed to hold their bladders. And the drinking, as it progresses during the evening, affects the speech and movement of the characters. My notes to the actors raised a series of questions: how well do you hold your liquor? How do you hold a glass? How do you ingest your drink? To what degree do you use the glass as an extension of your hand while talking? How do you pour drinks, for yourself, for others—as the evening progresses? In larger measure, what is your character's attitude toward drinking? With the drink table placed so far downstage, a mere two feet from the first rows on audience left and right, the actors were under close surveillance, and we experimented at length in getting just the right color and texture for the *faux* liquors. At one point, Hirst even shocks Spooner when he asks for a whiskey. "Weren't you drinking vodka?" Spooner questions, and Hirst's "I'd prefer a whiskey" was delivered a bit harshly, as if he resented this challenge from a guest (22). Of course, the play literally begins and ends with drinks. Hirst's opening "As it is?" (15) is later reworked by Spooner into "As it comes?" (22). When Spooner mocks Hirst's "hazel shit," the host hurls a glass at him (32—"ineffectually" in Pinter's stage direction). Clearly, the drinks constitute a "presence" in the play, both the lubricant and centerpiece of the cocktail party, an element in Hirst's hosting, and yet something more. That weasel under the whiskey cabinet comes into play when, say, Spooner declines Hirst's offer of "some hot refreshment" (22), or Foster tries to decline Briggs's offer of champagne. While they will be used later, the two empty coffee mugs on the table bother Spooner, for, spotting them, the visitor asks if there is another "free man" in the house, besides himself, or perhaps besides Hirst.

Momentarily confused by Hirst's "another what?," Spooner restates his question with "People. Person." Hirst remains enigmatic ("What other?"), and when Spooner points out the obvious, "There are two mugs on that shelf," Hirst offers only the noncommittal "The second is for you." Spooner then presses the point, asking for whom the first mug is intended, but is confused further with Hirst's evasive, "Would you like to use it?" (21-22) In the best sense of the cliché, the drinks and the drinking "take on a life of their own," attaching themselves in some mysterious way to the dialogue and the characters.

An Actor's Adventure in *No Man's Land*

I leapt at the chance to play a part in Sidney Homan's production of Harold Pinter's *No Man's Land*. It was not a leap of faith; I knew what I was getting into, having worked on half a dozen plays with Sid, including *The Threepenny Opera*, *Julius Caesar*, and *As You Like It*. I knew what the stakes were, that once again we would be attempting to make a work of art.

Sid plans things long in advance. That's good. When you're attempting a play as difficult as *No Man's Land* it's essential to know the play. I ended up knowing this play very well. Sid asked me to think about playing Hirst in the late spring of 2004 and I studied the part over the summer. In the fall, however, after casting Spooner became problematic, I took on Spooner instead. The play opened on February 10, 2005.

As I studied my lines I became aware that I'd been here before—in David Shelton's graduate acting class in the University of Florida Theatre Department in 1984. In fact, it was Pinter that showed the way. Two of my classmates were doing a scene from *The Homecoming*, the scene where Teddy and Ruth arrive in the dark house while everyone is asleep. As a caprice, my classmates decided to play the scene as if they were drunk. There was nothing in the lines, *per se*, to contradict them. It was very funny. But it was not Pinter's play.

Up until then I had been very much on the rebel's side of the argument, that what was presented on stage, whatever that was, that *was* the play. And you could make whatever you wanted on stage, and if people liked it or thought about it or hated it, then that was the thing, and it had nothing to do with whose *property* it was, or being faithful to some sacred text—there were no sacred texts.

That's the way we had played the game in Chicago in the seventies, fast and loose, whether it was Brecht's *Caucasian Chalk Circle* or Giraudoux's *Electra* or Shakespeare's *Romeo and Juliet* or Chekhov's *Three Sisters* or Genet's *Deathwatch*. You had to make the plays your *own*. Playwright be damned. It was the only way to get any attention at all. Unless you wanted to write your own plays, as David Mamet was doing with the Saint Nicholas Theater Company in New Town.

Then I started writing plays, and I came to realize that it has to be the way it has to be. This is the meaning of the word, that it is this word and not any other word.

For me, and I dare say for Pinter and Mamet, acting and playwriting are inseparable. It was probably that way for Shakespeare too. That is why, even though he is prone to put Stanislavsky down nowadays, Mamet was once inclined to credit Old Stan, as he was wont to call him, with crafting the best guide ever for playwriting. Stanislavsky's fundamental discovery of the objective shows not only a method of acting but, more importantly, how to construct dramatic action, propelling the plot in a wave of "I Wants" until it is either achieved or annihilated.

Pinter's text has been crafted in such a way that the words can only be spoken properly when the logic of the *text* is followed. You can replace that logic with something else, but then the words are not an exact fit, and you are playing a kind of jazz, a variation on a theme, which is fine in its own way, but, let's be honest: it's not the play.

My first task as an actor is to write my lines and cues, what Shakespeare called your *sides*, in longhand on sheets of looseleaf, and to parse them into the smallest beats, so that it ends up looking like one long ribbon of poetry, which I then study as such, reading and re-reading, closely, habitually, until I internalize this poem. I call this Learning the Lines.

As an actor, I believe what you do is you learn your lines and then you act them and the audience learns them too. So, in effect, you are both student and teacher. If the play is any good, the performance then becomes lifelike, and, like life, teaches everyone its lessons.

Coming into Pinter, I knew from Mamet (and Shakespeare) that the only way to make every beat work was to hit each word exactly on the mark. A good performance of *Oleanna*, say, (to use an example common to both Mamet and Pinter, who directed *Oleanna* in London) would be based on a letter-perfect line reading, which, I can attest, is nearly impossible. It is much the same with Pinter; part of the daredevil act is to get the words just right, and that requires absolute knowledge of them, and then *trust.* You've got to trust in the words and in yourself to say them, as naturally as breathing. There are commonalities in the rhythms, the breathing patterns of Shakespeare, Pinter, and Mamet, shared iambics, and if you relax and stick to the channel, you will find your way.

The play begins with a question from a man we will come to know (albeit only by the playbill, not the play) as Hirst: "As it is?" (15). And the man who will call himself Spooner replies: "As it is. Absolutely as it is."

It Is Fantasy Versus Memory. Which Is More True, More False?

It is 1975. John Gielgud and Ralph Richardson are Spooner and Hirst. In twenty years Mamet will write his treatise on acting, *True and*

False, wherein he will describe an approach to acting he calls practical aesthetics. It will go beyond Stanislavsky's notion of sense memory into a realm of knowledge. It comes down to Learning the Lines. Mamet and Pinter are aligned.

Plays are present tense. They unfold before our eyes. They are to be performed and not narrated, as Aristotle observed. The theater is a temporal art. You can only experience it at eight o'clock when we put on the play. That makes it different from a book or a painting. In a play, everything exists in time.

In the unconscious there is no time.

The Freudian word "wish" appears again and again in Spooner's speech: "I leave experience to psychological interpreters, the wet dream world. I can do any graph of experience you *wish* to suit your taste or mine. Child's play." (20)

As we know from Freud, nothing could be more serious than child's play.

"Temperamentally, I can be what you *wish*" (89—this and all subsequent italics in Pinter's text are my own).

"A form of an affair. She had no *wish* for full *consummation*. She was content with her particular predilection: *consuming* the male member" (76).

Note too the play on "consume" and "consummation," with "consumption" always waiting in the wings, hovering above, flooding the stage only to empty it, like the ocean and the shore.

Full consummation is an approximation of wish fulfillment.

"A consummation devoutly to be wished." We are doing a Freudian tango here that leads to Oedipus and Hamlet. "I looked up into my mother's face once ...." (26)

"Unless of course you positively *wished* on such an occasion to speak...." (91)

There are all these wishes.

Spooner is Hirst's death wish come to life. He invites Death into his house, and then the game is played out in something perversely like the chess match between Death and the Knight in Bergman's *The Seventh Seal.* What makes it perverse is the humor.

One critic likened the play to a cricket match (Gale, 203). Consider the list of sporting cum sexual terms that Spooner throws at drunken Hirst, implicating Hirst's wife—if there is or ever was such a person. "... with what speed she swung in the air, with what velocity did she come off the wicket, whether you could bowl a shooter with her, or an offbreak with a leg break action. In other words, did she google?" (30)

In this Age of Google, would this line still resonate with the sexual intent Pinter meant? Oh, yes.

"Ever painted a beer mug?" (40)

"You must come and see my collection any time you *wish*." (41)

The landlord of the Bull's Head, like the Hungarian émigré, parallels Hirst. Spooner enjoins Hirst to "never disdain a *helping hand*." (33) He offers his friendship to Hirst. In the second act he will indeed go much further. He will embody Von Kleist's *Retreat from the Caucasus*. He will retreat from friendship to servitude, even to worship.

Moments later Spooner is telling Briggs and Foster: "The landlord's a friend of mine. When he's shorthanded I give him a *helping hand*." (37)

Spooner says, "I was one of the golden of my generation. Something happened. I don't know what it was. Nevertheless, I am I, and have survived insult and deprivation. I am I." (89)

David Mamet contends that there is really no such thing as "character," that, instead, the illusion of a character is produced. In *No Man's Land* Pinter had produced an equation to demonstrate the principle.

Spooner offers himself to Hirst, as Kent does to Lear. "I come to you as a warrior. I would be happy to serve you as my master. I bend my knee to your excellence." (89) Spooner's long speech of solicitation, his final appeal, is a mirror to Kent's: "I do profess to be no less than I seem; to serve him truly that will put me in trust; to love him that is honest; to converse with him that is wise and says little ... ."

When the play opens, Hirst and Spooner have presumably just arrived at Hirst's house. They have been discussing strength as they arrived at Hirst's door, or, at least Spooner was discussing strength.

It later develops in the dialogue that the two just met at the bar of Jack Straw's Castle.

Pinter's Spoonerisms revolve around thinking, knowing, and wondering: "Have you any *idea* from what I derive my strength?" (26) "You will want to *know* what I had done to provoke such hatred in my own mother." (26) "You will *wonder* of course what he translated." (63) "Let us content ourselves with the *idea* of an intimate reading in a pleasing and conducive environment." (91)

"Silence is an alternative form of meaning," wrote one critic (Rayner 90-91). What silence can mean is a laugh. Witness the silence observed before Hirst says, "Let us change the subject." (91) The line follows that long speech by Spooner, his impassioned monologue wherein he seeks a haven in Hirst's home. After a couple of performances in which he paused only briefly before saying his line, Jay Lay decided to let the awkward silence stand on its own until it collapsed. When he finally said his line, it was greeted with a laugh. What had happened in the pause was the dismissal of Spooner's proposition. What happened in the pause was dramatic choice. The audience's laughter was its means of assuring itself that Hirst's conclusion had been perceptibly reached.

When Hirst finally eclipsed the silence with his line ("Let us change the subject"), a large laugh burst in the audience like a bubble popping. Truth be told, the timing never worked that well again, although Lay experimented by varying the length of that particular pause throughout the rest of the run. But as for the laugh, regardless of size, Pinter surely knew it would happen. The laugh is in response to neither Spooner's plea nor Hirst's rejection of it, but rather to the silence which has filled the house with tension.

The new subject is darkly laughable, a kind of cosmic joke, as the dialogue devolves into stichomythia. Those lines are the hardest to learn, because they are made of interplay. The hardest lines for me to learn were those revolving around Stella to Winstanley, the clever contest between Hirst and Spooner to see which of them can spin a Wildean web faster and tighter. Seeing the allusion Pinter was making to Stella and Stanley in *Streetcar Named Desire* didn't help because it didn't play. I had to construct the relationships of Bunty and Stella Winstanely, Rupert, Arabella Winscott and her father, Muriel Blackwood, Doreen Busby, Geoffrey Ramsden, and my supposed wife, Emily Spooner, and to call them forth in rapid fire.

Michael Billington describes the play as exploring moods rather than ideas (p 242). This can be seen in the reflexive language of the play, the dialogue that is continually turning on itself, not proceeding forward in syllogistic fashion, but instead circling regressively, constantly retreating to "As it is," stuck in No Man's Land.

"But on your excursions, however rare ... on your rare excursions, you hardly expect to run into the likes of me, I take it." "Hardly." (18)

The mood was heightened, the gloom intensified by the lighting scheme, finding the evening sun shrinking from view through the upstage window. Is that the "global despair" that Billington refers to, filling the stage itself (247)? It is opposed by the "localized activity" (247)—drinking, which is also anaesthetizing.

Billington also sees *No Man's Land* as a "profoundly personal play," perhaps because the two main characters, as writer and would-be writer, characterize all writers as The Writer. There is a "sense of umbilical connection between Hirst and Spooner" (244-45). It is almost as if they are the same person. And they are. They are both Harold Pinter.

That's the way dialogue works. As Mamet has pointed out, playwriting basically comes down to sitting around and talking to yourself.

So, the play begins with the playwright's question to himself: "As it is?"

The words mirror each other, but they also occur in time, so the repetition can come a beat later, or half a beat later, or several major beats down the road. Mamet has said he knows of dozens of definitions of the dramatic term "beat," but I will stick to the strictly Stanislavskian notion of a Unit of Dramatic Action, which involves choice and objective.

"I remain capable of *undertaking* the gravest and most daunting responsibilities." A moment later: "It is my task as a gentleman to remain amiable in my behavior, courageous in *undertakings* ...." (89)

"I shall regard it as *incumbent* upon me to keep a clear countenance and a clean conscience." (89) This hearkens back to: "I do feel it *incumbent* upon me to make one thing clear: I do not peep on sex." (19)

No Man's Land is composed of matching couplets to the end, and easy to learn finally, once the actor has established the tone, the feeling, as opposed to the idea, to inhabit the fact and not the idea.

Once we got the play on its legs, I found that I needed an internal geography to get the lines right. I needed to know the layout of the public house where the landlord is a friend of mine. The poetry readings are held on the second floor. The private room for the board meeting is on the first floor.

God? There's precious little difference between God and anybody who can lord it over you. And there is a Lord in the play—Lord Lancer, whose name is evoked to impress the land*lord*.

"Think before you speak."

"Before you reply ..."

"But that is by the by and would in no sense be a condition. Let us *con*tent ourselves with the *idea* of an intimate reading, in a pleasing and *con*ducive envir*on*ment. Let us *con*sider an evening to be remembered by all who take part in her."

"Let us change the subject." (90-91)

Let us pray.

The play has come full circle, like *Finnegans Wake*, and maybe the beginning is actually somewhere in the middle.

Billington sees Hirst and Spooner as "antithetical and yet interdependent" (246). That is because they are one soul, Pinter's, divided. And then they are sub-divided into Foster and Briggs.

The "shark in the harbor" (60) might also describe Spooner's circling of Hirst in the opening scene.

Is Hirst a man who appears to be strong but who inhabits "the idea and not the fact"? (16) The play itself is an idea that becomes fact; that is the way of all plays, moving from page to stage. Hirst inhabits an idea and then a fact, a *house* that is like a fortress.

Is Spooner sticking "a needle through that posture" and discerning "the essential flabbiness of the stance"? (16) It would seem so, when Hirst crawls on his belly offstage and Spooner lifts not a finger to help him. This will contrast sharply with Spooner's intervention on Hirst's behalf, after Foster and Briggs have arrived and Hirst has collapsed again.

What all four characters inhabit is an idea. They inhabit Pinter's idea of the play. They people it.

Pinter constructs a plot out of parallels, like "the former and the latter."

"You are kindness itself" is repeated three times. It is as if the playwright in composition is *constructing* a quality rather than a character.

"My only security, you see, my true comfort and solace, rests in the confirmation that I elicit from people of all kinds a constant and common level of indifference. It assures me that I am as I think myself to be, fixed, concrete." (17) Spooner is like a definition in a dictionary.

Spooner, reflecting on peeps and twigs, seems to have it backward. Wouldn't one's peep rest on a twig and not the other way around? And yet Spooner says, "When my twigs happen to, shall I say, rest their peep on sexual conjugations, however periphrastic, I see only whites of eyes so close they glut me. And when you can't keep the proper distance between yourself and others, when you can no longer maintain an objective relation to matter, the game's not worth the candle, so forget it." (19)

Like the language of the play itself—like the offer and the act of Spooner's proposition of friendship—things are themselves and their opposites. The language teases. It can sound simultaneously clinical and lurid.

It will be seen that Spooner cannot keep the proper distance between himself and Hirst; he insinuates himself into Hirst's life. As for maintaining an objective relation to matter, this is what Pinter has been attempting all along. That is what makes it so difficult to decide whether the play is Hirst's or Spooner's (Gale 220).

And whatever game is being played is not worth the candle, so forget it, which is exactly what Pinter does when he reaches the final lines of the play, those about *No Man's Land* that circle back to Hirst's first exit from the scene by way of belly and floor.

Learning the lines I would find a natural progression: "Your health. Your good health. Your very good health."

"... the like of which—" "What was he drinking?" "... [He] possessed a measure of serenity the like of which I had never encountered." (25)

"The command from an upper floor." (68) As in God.

Spooner's refrain is: "I've known this before." That is because it has all happened before.

"You've guessed, I would imagine, that he was an erstwhile member of the Hungarian aristocracy." (24) How it glides off the tongue.

You have to create the Hungarian émigré in the person of Hirst. You have to create the scene outside the café by the canal in Amsterdam, and the Whistler sitting very still at a table nearby.

My line readings edged closer to Lay's, and I began to steal his phrasing. The comical way he confided to Spooner, "You will find *tennis balls*!"

(81) I parodied Lay with my reading of: "It is essential that the meeting be private, you see, as we shall be discussing *policy*." (65)

"Tennis balls." "Policy." The same rhythm.

"Live as one already dead" goes a Chinese proverb. *No Man's Land* embodies that idea. Hirst is the one in his dream who has drowned. He is already dead, recalling his life, as through a glass darkly, a whiskey glass.

The Audience in the Parking Lot

We were all gratified to hear the audience talking about the play both during intermission and, what is more, in the parking lot after the show. Let one of their number have the last word, with a comment I overheard after the show the night before the run ended: It's confusing. Sure. I'm confused. But maybe that's not a bad thing. There's no plot, but ... hell ... life doesn't have a "plot." We just ... are. Know what I mean? Way I see it, tonight we spent some time with some very interesting people—almost real ones.

NOTES:

The text for *No Man's Land* is that printed by Grove Weidenfeld, New York, 1975.

No Man's Land was staged at the Acrosstown Repertory Theatre, Gainesville, Florida, in February, 2005. **Cast:** Hirst–Jay Lay, Spooner–Shamrock McShane, Foster–Lyndsay Cox, Briggs–Kathleen Monahan. **Staff:** Director–Sidney Homan, Stage Manager–Emily Holbrook, Set Designer–Michael McShane, Lighting Designer–Michael McShane, Assistant to the Director-Clarence Ray, Musical Score–Daniel Homan, Make-Up Artist–Dawniece Tims, Costume Designer–Rachael Teague, House Manager–Armando Davilla.

WORKS CITED:

Almansi, Guido. *Harold Pinter.* London: Methuen, 1983.

Batty, Mark. *Harold Pinter.* Plymouth, England: Northcote House, 2000.

Billington, Michael. *The Life and Work of Harold Pinter.* London: Faber, 1996.

Burkman, Katherine H. "Death and the Double in Three Plays by Harold Pinter," in *Harold Pinter: You Never Heard Such Silence*, ed. Alan Bold. London: Vision Press, 1984: 131-145.

Diamond, Elin. *Pinter's Comic Play.* Lewisburg, Pa.: Bucknell UP, 1985.

Gabbard, Lucina Paquet. *The Dream Structure of Pinter's Plays: A Psychoanalytic Approach.* Rutherford, N.J.: Fairleigh Dickinson UP, 1976.

Gale, Steven H. *Butter's Going Up: A Critical Analysis of Harold Pinter's Work.* Durham, N.C.: Duke UP, 1977.

Greenblatt, Stephen. *Renaissance Self-Fashioning: From More to Shakespeare.* Berkeley: U of California P, 1980.

Hinchliffe, Arnold P. "After *No Man's Land*: A Progress Report," in *Harold Pinter: Critical Approaches*, ed. Steven H. Gale. Rutherford, N.J.: Fairleigh Dickinson UP, 1986: 153-163.

Orr, John. *Tragicomedy and Contemporary Culture: Play and Performance from Beckett to Shepard*. Ann Arbor: U of Michigan P, 1991.

Pinter, Harold. "A Conversation with Harold Pinter," by Mel Gussow. *New York Times Magazine* (5 December 1971): 42-43, 126-36.

—. "Interview," *Sunday Times* (London, 4 March 1962), quoted by Kathleen George, *Rhythms in Drama*. Pittsburgh: Pittsburgh UP, 1980): p. 33.

Quigley, Austin. "Time for Change in *No Man's Land*," in *Harold Pinter: A Casebook*. Ed. Lois Gordon. New York: Garland Publishers, 1990: 33-60.

Rayner, Alice. "Image and Attention in Harold Pinter," in *Pinter at* Sixty, ed. Katherine H. Burkman and John L. Kundert-Gibbs. Bloomington: Indiana UP, 1993: 90-99.

The New World Order in Poland

***Nowy Ład Świata* (*The New World Order*) by Harold Pinter. Stefan Żeromski Theatre, Kielce, Poland, December 2006.** Trans. Bolesław Taborski. Directed by Piotr Szczerski. Set design by Jerzy Sitarz. Lighting design by Krzysztof Sendke. Cast: Beata Pszeniczna, Aneta Wirzinkiewicz, Maria Wójcikowska, Mirosław Bieliński, Hubert Bronicki, Marcin Brykczyński, Janusz Głogowski, Edward Janaszek, Krzysztof Mateusiak, Paweł Sanakiewicz, Dawid Żłobiński, Maciek Bieliński.

For the audience, the beginning of the quadruple bill directed by Piotr Szczerski is as uncomfortable as uncomfortably political are three of the pieces comprising the performance: *One for the Road*, *Mountain Language*, the sketch *The New World Order* (the fourth one is *Victoria Station*). The spectators are kindly asked to wait in front of the enormous metal double doors on which the words: NOWY ŁAD ŚWIATA, HAROLD PINTER have been welded. About ten minutes before the performance starts a group of men dressed in black let the people into the lamp-lit corridor leading to the inner yard of the theatre's building. While checking the tickets the men staple to them black, white, or red cards. The meaning of this becomes clear when the audience reach the end of the corridor where three men—in black from head to toes—hold black, white and red clubs at the level of their waists. Suddenly, the voice from the loudspeaker orders the people to form groups based on the colour of their stapled cards. One realizes that while it is not the performance yet, it is not real life either. A randomly selected group of people is asked to enter an old lift, which instantly brings to mind the title contraption from *The Dumb Waiter*. In a dignified upward pull, the lift groans, squeaks and takes them up to some unknown part of the theatre. The audience is gently forced to enter "the new world order" of the theatre. And Pinter.

From this time on the spectators are guided through the theatre's corridors and staircases by the guides in black who carry the respective clubs. The bill begins with *One for the Road* in which all the spectators take part, but afterwards while one group is watching *Victoria Station*, the others—arranged in two rows as if during a roll call in a prison—witness the fates of the characters in *Mountain Language*. In the interval between the two plays, when the people are passing one another in the foyer, they suddenly realize that somehow "the reds" have disappeared. In answer to the unexpressed doubt, one of the guides shouts out: "The reds are no more!" After they have seen both plays, the audience is united once more for the title sketch which forms the pregnant punchline of the performance. The actor playing Nicolas in *One for the Road* is now the one who is sitting blindfolded on the chair while the Sergeant and the Officer from *Mountain Language* wallow in his fear of "any one of the number of things that [they] might do to him" (271). It becomes clear that in this world the changes are sudden and frequently unconditional. And no questioning of them is allowed. This really is "the new world order" captured at the moment of its birth.

Of all the cast in *One for the Road*, Paweł Sanakiewicz (Nicolas) is the most memorable. Each time he pours whiskey into his glass, he carefully wipes the neck of the bottle with one swift movement of his finger and licks off the remaining drop, managing to save it before it can mingle with the dust on the table in the interrogation room. His voice is soft, the tone of it friendly and encouraging. But the words he says are merciless, spiteful, and full of ideological jabber with which he has been brainwashed. When he goes past the table to come up to the interrogated family members, tension soars. Nicolas' monologue becomes even more suave and it transforms into a test for how much hatred can the couple bear before they go at their persecutor. Beata Pszeniczna (Gila) and Marcin Brykczyński (Victor) play all these emotions out with highly controlled twitches of fingers and lips together with clandestine eye-blinking. These are the only things they can do, as Pinter did not give Gila, Victor, and Nicky much to say. So to maintain the theatrical tension they have to craft their apprehensive gestures and glances in such a way that they react to what Nicolas is saying subtly enough to show what is going on inside them and accurately enough not to reveal any unwanted contempt for him, which would make his monologue improbable and pitifully funny. Although there are rare moments when theatrical illusion is on the verge of being broken, Beata Pszeniczna, Marcin Brykczyński, and Maciek Bieliński (Nicky) manage to do it well and skillfully. The most arresting moment comes at the end of the play. Victor, dressed in a neat suit which covers his tattered clothes, enters Nicolas' room and they both have a toast. The last look that Victor gives Nicolas, after he learns that Nicky "*was* a little prick" (247; emphasis mine), changes the meaning of the toast into a celebration of the death of innocence. Lights fade on the final tableau of the two main characters facing each other, emotions boiling behind their unmoving stares.

The audience becomes more wary of the authority which the guides of respective groups impose on them as they are led onto the stage where they are left standing in two rows to watch *Mountain Language*.

Wire-mesh prison doors clang and rattle as the Sergeant and the Officer announce the prohibition of mountain language and recite absurd laws about dogs being required to give their names prior to biting. Each part of the play takes place in a separate section of a symbolic prison created by an almost three-metre-high wire-mesh partition which divides the stage into two parts. In "Visitors Room" and "Voice in the Darkness," contrary to the stage directions in the text of the play, lights fade on the guards and spotlights carve out the silhouettes of the prisoners and their loved ones. Instead of voices over, the actors deliver their lines themselves, which renders the scenes more intense while the light etches the experience of the imprisonment in the lines on the actors' faces. Mirosław Bieliński as the Sergeant underlines the contempt in which he holds the visitors and prisoners by chewing gum and exaggerating the movements of his square jaw as he barks questions at the helpless, but proud Young Woman (Aneta Wirzinkiewicz). The Sergeant's manner is at the same time relaxed and threatening. Bieliński's acting focuses on drawing attention to the power that the Sergeant—an intermediary between the people and the Officer—is able to exercise while his superiors are not watching. The source of this power lies in the way Bieliński stares the visitors and prisoners into silence; it is as though he was saying, "I have seen this a thousand times and I know that however hard you try you won't achieve what you've come here for. So keep trying, because I like it."

The next stop-over in the journey along the dimly-lit, as if taken from Kafka's *The Trial*, corridors of the Żeromski Theatre is the upper circle. There the spectators can sit down again. A pool of light fades-in slowly to reveal the Controller's office and a moment later the Driver emerges from the darkness, at the opposite end of the balcony, his facial features illuminated from below his chin. They begin to kill time arguing about the location of Victoria Station and calling each other through the microphones. They cease and then start again to uncover their dreams and fantasies to the faceless voice at the other end of the line, "trying to make sense out of our lives" (198). Although the actors (Krzysztof Mateusiak and Edward Janaszek) do not always manage to observe all the pauses and quick replies which give *Victoria Station* its sleepy rhythm of a late night conversation, they craftily succeed in distancing the audience for a while from the disturbing atmosphere of prison walls and interrogation rooms. The inclusion of *Victoria Station* among overtly political Pinter plays has an eerie effect on the whole performance in that it unexpectedly enhances the perspective from which we look at the Driver and the Controller. As a result, questions are bound to be asked. One wonders whether the Driver could be the Hooded Man from *Mountain Language* in the past. Maybe what the audience are participants of is the beginning of a love affair which led to the marriage with the P.O.B. who fell asleep at the back of his car? And maybe the Controller and the Driver are to become two future prisoners, sharing the same cell, with no communication devices at hand to maintain contact with the outside world?

These and other questions resound when the last act of the performance commences. *The New World Order* brings back the actors who are already familiar. Now, however, roles have changed significantly. The Sergeant from *Mountain Language* is Des—an expert leader and most probably a torturer. The Officer becomes Lionel—a young, inexperienced adherent of "democracy"—and Nicolas from *One for the Road* sits silently, blindfolded and helpless. Taking into account merely the title of the sketch, the use of the actors who have been seen in different contexts earlier the same evening is nothing short of intriguing. Thus, all the plays which make up the whole performance are connected not only by thematic interrelationships. What is also suggested is the unity of their author's artistic vision. What we have already learnt at the beginning of Pinter's playwriting career from *The Room* and *The Birthday Party* is that names and ranks are frequently subject to unsuspected changes. On the one hand, thus, it should not come as a surprise that the person who once was the Officer is now a determined and enthusiastic lower-rank advocate of "the new world order." It should also not be unexpected that the one who once interrogated is now being questioned. On the other hand, "disturbing" is one of the weakest words one can use to describe the juxtaposition of Hubert Bronicki's (Lionel) almost manic and childlike enthusiasm with Sanakiewicz's defenceless silence.

Des and Lionel shake hands in mutual understanding of their ideological principles; there is a blackout and suddenly the performance is over. The guides with coloured clubs are gone, the spectators have to usher themselves to the cloakroom. No one knows which world order is now the official one and this uncertainty is the most disconcerting feeling that remains. All the four pieces are performed with great fidelity to the texts. Apart from minor slips, Pinter's pauses and silences are diligently followed and emphasized. It is a fact of life that every theatrical performance of the same play/plays is different, but in the case of *The New World Order* by the Żeromski Theatre this is doubly so. As the audience is divided into groups, and although the beginning and ending of the performance is the same, what can follow *One for the Road* is either *Victoria Station* or *Mountain Language*. Therefore, if one does not know beforehand (and one should not) the organizational patterns behind the stapled white, black and red cards, the reception of the performance can be at least twofold. But is not this sign of arbitrariness in fact one of the inherent features of "the new world order"?

Łukasz Borowiec
John Paul II Catholic University of Lublin, Poland

Old Times in Hamburg

University Players, Hamburg University

Directed by Jasper Koch. Cast: Madeleine Lange (Kate), Johannes Scott-Weijers (Deeley), Stephanie Arapian (Anna). Stage design by Kai Cassuben and Moritz Schulte

During the German World Cup euphoria, when the collective festival mood had people dancing in the streets and even usually fairly reserved North German locals suddenly developed a great enthusiasm for Brazilian dance groups, the "University Players" student theatre at Hamburg University had to move to a smaller stage for their performance of Pinter's *Old Times* so that thousands of students could watch a World Cup game on a widescreen TV in the huge auditorium. In spite of the almost tropical weather conditions and the prevailing World Cup mania, there was quite a strong interest in this play.

Perhaps Pinter's focus on political aspects in recent years, his strong attacks on American foreign policy and especially on the Iraq war which were widely acclaimed here, resulted in focusing on the more political plays and rather rare performances of *Old Times* during the last years. Plays like *Mountain Language*, *Ashes to Ashes*, and *One for the Road* were staged here fairly regularly, whereas Pinter classics like *The Caretaker*, *The Homecoming* or *The Birthday Party*, which dominated the German stage thirty years ago, were neglected.

Hans Schweikart, the grand old theatre director and German specialist for Pinter's plays, directed *Old Times* in 1972 at the Hamburg Thalia Theater (with Ingrid Andree, Ursula Lingen and Boy Gobert). Since I had the privilege of attending the complete rehearsal period of several weeks until opening night at that time and had the chance to admire that brilliant, outstanding production, I was afraid that this still very vividly remembered "benchmark production" might now, 35 years later, distort my evaluation of this production. I don't think it did since these events are hardly comparable.

Jasper Koch, the young director of the "University Players," has just finished his M.A. thesis about Pinter's influence on the plays of Patrick Marber. While he watched various Marber plays in London, he also saw a performance of *Old Times* and was struck by the fascinating way in which Pinter dealt with past events. "I think it's a great memory play which confronts you with the past as a sort of patchwork pattern to rearrange the present," explains Jasper Koch, who was also fascinated by the competitive character of speech patterns: "In Marber's *Dealer's Choice*, for instance, you have this struggle for domination which of course is a typical Pinter phenomenon. It is also obvious in *Old Times* where the manipulation of past events is used in a very subtle way to gain access on an emotional level and revitalize old memories and a past love affair."

Jasper Koch had also directed some Shakespeare plays, which were always a dominant feature in the repertoire of the "University Players." The student group gained national acclaim with a heavily "updated" *Macbeth* a few years ago, when they showed similarities between the mysterious death of a local politician who was found drowned in the bathtub of a Swiss hotel and the intrigues and machinations of Macbeth. No wonder then that the dramatic aspects of the forever debating trio Kate, Deeley and Anna and their different memories of postwar London are expertly tuned and dramatically put into effect. Memories of meeting in a cinema during an *Odd Man Out* performance, living together in crammed flats until Deeley married Kate, which left Anna the odd one out, are also subtly used instruments in an individual power struggle and a battle for strengthening emotional positions in this memory game.

What a relief to find a stage which is conventionally designed: No TV screens, no video installations, no hi-tech distractions. Just a plain sitting-room scenario with a sofa, a small table with various bottles and two armchairs, the background indicating windows—exactly as stated in the play's stage directions. Similarly, the direction also catches the pure Pinter spirit. The famous opening scene with Anna standing quietly at the window in the background, not facing the audience and only beginning to talk after Deeley and Kate had discussed preparations for her imminent visit at great length, is well timed and appears to be a natural process. When Anna suddenly intervenes with her recollections of "queuing all night" and of idealised postwar London episodes, she drifts unobtrusively into the discussion of Kate and Deeley—almost like another instrument in an ongoing performance of chamber music.

The surprising introduction of Anna as a visible, yet not quite present character in 1971, when *Old Times* was first shown in Peter Hall's famous production at the Aldwych Theatre, was of course quite an ingenious novelty which resulted, as Michael Billington pointed out in his Pinter biography, from Pinter's treatment of characters in his film scripts. Instead of tedious references or an introductory ritual announcing a new character, he lets Anna simply turn from the window to move down to the other two characters—a simple but effective movie technique which worked very smoothly in this production. The American actress Stephanie Arapian, a rather stout lady, managed in her own very subtle way to demonstrate Anna's ambivalent character: As the intervening outsider who topples the delicate balance in Deeley's marriage with Kate, she appears to be emotionally vulnerable. Yet her manoeuvres of manipulating past events in order to claim Kate's friendship again vividly show her strong position in an almost Machiavellian power game. With an intriguing, powerful impact, she delivers the main theme of the play: "There are some things one remembers even though they may never have happened. There are things I remember which may never have happened but as I recall them so they take place." When Deeley finally feels he might be losing Kate and he has to fight for her, he stalks in circles around Anna in the aggravated macho-style of a Spanish matador, accusing her of distorting the truth. Yet she can hold her own and she fights back effectively. The intensity and the aggravation of this scene is one of the highlights of the production.

Johannes Scott-Weijers as Deeley appears at times exaggerating his emotional upheaval and thereby losing the soft, artistic touch of the movie director required of his role. But on the whole he is a credible character who presents his version in this memory game convincingly. Madelaine Lange as Kate is quite a surprise: With a subtle smile and a coy look she acknowledges Anna's claim for a renewal of their friendship while she manages to rebuke her obvious attempts at reconstructing past memories with a vicious and bitchy turn of the head and the deadly and cynical reference to the shared London period, remembering a strange encounter with Anna: "I remember you lying dead. You didn't know I was watching you. I leaned over you. Your face was dirty. You lay dead..."

"The past is a foreign country, they do things differently there" was the motto of L.P. Hartley's novel *The Go-Between* and Pinter's marvelous film script which he wrote in 1969. Of course the ramifications of past events and their distortions fascinated Pinter in almost all his plays and in his intense preoccupation with the Proust project. This successful performance of *Old Times,* applauded by an enthusiastic audience, demonstrated convincingly how emotionally gripping and disturbing this powerful memory play still is.

Peter Münder
Hamburg

Endgame with Spools: Harold Pinter in *Krapp's Last Tape*

The Royal Court's small Theatre Upstairs holds only eighty seats spread over long benches, so it was not surprising that all ten performances of Pinter's *Krapp* were sold out within seventeen minutes. You actually felt like a successful gold digger once you were allotted a ticket after a tedious waiting-list period.

The audience's apprehensions prior to this remarkable evening were quite tangible. Would Harold Pinter, suffering from throat cancer since 2002, be able to move around the stage freely and fool around with the famous bananas as the constipated 69-year-old Krapp? Would he repeat the comical stints of famous German actors like Bernhard Minetti or Martin Held, who inserted a few hilarious circus scenes and even slipped over the banana skin in Beckett's own famous Berlin production of 1969? And in what light would Ian Rickson, artistic director at the Royal Court, show the failed writer Krapp in this moving and disturbing monologue ridiculing his commercial failure to sell more than seventeen copies of his opus magnum, "eleven of which at wholesale prices to public libraries overseas"?

When the dim light over Krapp's table illuminates Harold Pinter at the beginning of the play, we can just watch him sitting behind the old tape recorder and a collection of tin boxes containing the spools. He is staring straight into the audience brooding with a grim, angry expression. And when after nearly two minutes of this silent staring the tension has grown almost unbearably, he starts his electric wheelchair and rolls into his archive filled with racks of manuscripts where you hear him filling a glass with water. Only then does he roll back behind his table to start looking for "the old rascal"—box three, spool five, pronouncing "spool" with great relish. Having found this particular spool, he sweeps the remaining lot to the floor in a furious burst of energy. Surely this introspective Krapp, listening to his reminiscences of thirty years ago, is not only fed up with his memories and his own past, but with the whole state of affairs.

Black and bleak—these are the dominating first impressions. The walls surrounding the stage constructed by Hildegard Bechtler are totally black, the archive's racks on the lefthand corner in the back are feebly lit while Pinter wears a black robe sitting in a black wheelchair. So it is not surprising that he cuts the comical banana-act. There is simply no room for fun and games or singing (prescribed in Beckett's text) in this grim endgame with spools.

One year after he was awarded the Nobel Prize for Literature, Harold Pinter wanted to pay his tribute to his old friend and mentor Samuel Beckett (1906-1989), whom he always admired. The young actor Pinter had discovered the puzzling fascination of Beckett's prose in *Murphy* during his famous Irish tour with the well-known theatre impresario and actor Anew MacMaster and had instantly developed a keen appetite for Beckett's later novels and his plays which influenced his own work. When you watch Peter Hall's production of *Waiting for Godot* at the New Ambassador Theatre, as I did the night before this "Krapp-noir" performance, you are instantly confronted with various aspects which are also blended into *The Caretaker*: The irregular, circular speech patterns, the humour in spite of the desolate atmosphere and simple things like the preoccupation with the shoes or pulling carrots out of a shabby coat which Aston is repeating in a similar fashion when he suddenly takes a sandwich or a salt-cellar from his pocket offering it to Davies.

Beckett's work appears to be an "oscillating hall of mirrors" at first, Pinter remarked about the great Irish master, but after getting your bearings you would finally be confronted with basic truths and the heart of the matter, however grim and sinister this appears to be. The verdict pronounced in *Godot*, namely that birth is a process delivered astride a grave, seems to be the same sinister view shared by Pinter in this harsh version of *Krapp's Last Tape*. Whatever he evokes during his confrontation with his alter ego—"that stupid bastard I took myself for thirty years ago"—recalling the memory of floating in a boat with a girlfriend or playing with a dog - he finds it abominable or disgusting. Instead of a yearning for a romantic episode, we witness the furious outburst of indignation: "Everything there, everything on this old muckball, all the light and dark and famine and feasting of the ages! Never knew such silence. The earth might be uninhabitated." What initially might have appeared to be a harmless look back at the playing fields of the "young whelp" now turns out to be a shattering vision of an apocalyptic endgame behind a spool.

The only moment which showed Krapp in an almost sentimental mood with an emotional touch was connected with "Effie", referring to his past girlfriend avidly reading the German novel *Effie Briest* (by Theodor Fontane) which causes Krapp to collect the book from the shelf, touching it tenderly, pressing it to his cheek and then throwing it on the floor.

When Pinter ended this impressive, albeit one-dimensional, grim performance, grumpily and offhandedly stating "Perhaps my best years are gone. But I wouldn't want them back. Not with the fire in me now", there is a stunned long silence in the audience—including Pinter's famous friend and director Sir Peter Hall—followed by an outbreak of an overwhelming enthusiastic applause. When Harold Pinter finally got out of his wheelchair to take a bow we certainly realized we had witnessed a great performance of an outstanding actor and playwright and a historical moment of contemporary theatre. A bleak and grim performance it certainly was—but it was perfectly rendered in Sam's spirit and true to Samuel Beckett's almost nihilistic *Weltanschauung*.

Peter Münder
Hamburg

Report from Britain
Harold Pinter 2005-2006

LINDA RENTON AND MARK TAYLOR-BATTY

2005 proved to be quite a year for Harold Pinter. The already happy double celebration of both his 75th birthday and the 25th anniversary of his and Lady Antonia Fraser's wedding was further embellished by a range of unexpected awards, not least being the Nobel Prize for Literature. The year had begun well with the award of the Wilfred Owen Prize for Poetry in April, and, in addition to this and the Nobel Prize, Pinter found himself the recipient of the Franz Kafka Prize (received on his behalf by Václav Havel) on 26 October, and of the tenth European Theatre Award on 12 March 2006.

On stage, 2005 began on a high with Lindsay Posner's excellent production of *The Birthday Party*, which opened at Birmingham Repertory Theatre on 11 March before transferring to London on 25 April, and which is reviewed separately in this edition of *The Pinter Review*. In conjunction with the performance, *Front Row* (BBC Radio 4, 28 February) was given over entirely to an interview with the author, who spoke about the play's initial failure, the influence of Kafka and the Gestapo, and his real-life encounter with 'Stanley' in a seaside boarding house, which was the genesis of the play. In this interview he went on to speak about the nature of drama, its ambiguity, saying that if a play 'states its meaning [...] the life goes out of [it]', whereas 'a political poem [...] about war [...] you just write it as it is.' Significantly, it was in this interview that Pinter stated that he thought he had stopped writing plays now. 'I've written about twenty-nine plays, isn't that enough?' he asked, provocatively. Now, he asserted, his energy was going into different directions, into poetry and politics. Interviewed by Lawrence Pollard on *The Culture Show* (BBC 2 television, 21 April 2005) prior to the London opening of *The Birthday Party,* Pinter was asked why he now chose to employ poetry to address political issues (rather than plays). Pinter replied that he did not like to repeat himself, and had 'probably come to an end' of the subject (the abuse of power and authority) 'in that form.' Pollard referred to the Sikh play *Behzti*, which had led to violent protests among the Sikh community in Birmingham and had its run cancelled by the city's Repertory Theatre before opening night in December 2004, and asked whether Pinter defended the right of theatre to offend. Pinter said that in this case he did, since 'it was clearly a very intelligent, objective account of a state of affairs which was [...] undermined by mob rule.' 'Theatre,' he said, 'is essential to our social and political life' because it possesses 'an independence' which is 'being eroded before our very eyes in this country and many others.'

◆ ◆ ◆

Public celebrations for Pinter's 75th birthday began on 5 October when Radio 3 broadcast the 1990 recording of *Betrayal*, directed by Ned Chaillet, with Pinter as Robert, Sir Michael Gambon as Jerry and Patricia Hodge as Emma, in a production of this 'incontrovertibly great play' which 'could not be bettered' (David Sexton, *Sunday Telegraph Review*, 16 October, p.9). Curiously, no London theatre chose to participate in the celebrations of Pinter's milestone birthday, and for staged performances the focus moved abroad to the Pinter Festival at the Gate Theatre, Dublin. This was the fourth Pinter Festival organised by the Gate (one of which was held at the Lincoln Center in New York in 2001), and included performances of *Old Times* (30 September–8 October), directed by Michael Caven and starring Stephen Brennan, Jamie Dee and Donna Dent, and *Betrayal* (14 October–19 November), directed by Robin Lefèvre and starring Cathy Belton, Risteárd Cooper, Nick Dunning and Gary Murphy. Michael Billington describes Michael Caven's 'meticulous production' of *Old Times* where the 'political implications', never far away in the drama of Irish life, are made clear as Deeley and Anna fight for possession of Kate 'like two territorial opposites fighting over a neutral buffer state'. It reminds us, says Billington, 'that the Irish have a peculiar affinity with Pinter and respond instinctively, as with Shakespeare, both to his linguistic rhythms and resonant images of oppression' (Billington, *Guardian,* 3 October 2005).

The central focus of the celebrations was the birthday weekend of 7–9 October, when a group of distinguished actors, including Sir Michael Gambon, Sir Derek Jacobi, Jeremy Irons, John Hurt, Stephen Rae, and Penelope Wilton, flew to Dublin to appear in the weekend's celebrations and stayed on for the birthday dinner at the Unicorn restaurant, which was also attended by playwrights Sir Tom Stoppard, Frank McGuinness, and Conor McPherson. Performances over the weekend included readings of *Family Voices* and *Celebration,* and a selection from 'a lifetime' of Pinter's poetry and prose, after which, Billington notes, the audience rose spontaneously 'to honour the man and his work' (*The Guardian,* 14 October).

As invited guest of the festival, Pinter very much enjoyed his weekend in Dublin, and greatly appreciated the performances and the investments in them that the actors, directors, and designers had given. The weekend, however, ended unpleasantly. On his way to the airport, on the eve of his birthday, he met with an accident. Over the last twelve months he had begun to lose some of the power in his legs, and was now walking with the aid of a stick. Getting out of his car at the airport, he planted his stick on the pavement to gain a hold before raising himself out of the car. Unfortunately it had been raining, his walking stick slipped on the wet pavement and he fell and knocked his head so violently on the curb that he cut his forehead open, spilling alarming quantities of blood around him. He was dashed to hospital, where he was obliged to stay overnight before returning home with his wife in the morning.

◆ ◆ ◆

***Voices* (BBC Radio 3)**

Music composed by James Clarke.

Voices: Harry Burton, Andy de la Tour, Gawn Grainger, Gabriel Hamilton, Anastasia Hille, Douglas Hodge, Roger Lloyd-Pack, Harold Pinter and Indira Varma.

Music: Apartment House; Eileen Aagaard; Prometheus Ensemble; Rolande van der Paal; Etienne Siebens; the BBC Symphony Orchestra, conducted by Martyn Brabbins and David Porcelijn; Fatma Mehralieva.

Produced by Ned Chaillet and Phillip Tagney.

This specially commissioned work, a collaboration between Pinter and the composer James Clarke, was broadcast to mark the day of Pinter's 75th birthday on 10 October 2005. Created from passages from Pinter's later political plays (*One for the Road, Mountain Language, The New World Order, Party Time,* and *Ashes to Ashes*), with their haunting images of torture and oppression, voices, threads of music, rise and fall out of silence and darkness. Pinter describes the play as about 'the hell that we all share here and now' (Alice Jones, *Independent,* 7 October). And through radio, which operates directly on the individual imagination, we are led to share the experience of the dispossessed, becoming other prisoners, in other rooms.

The form of the work is intrinsically poetic. Released from a narrative line, these passages from Pinter's plays, which are already poetry, form a greater poetic whole, which is further extended by the music. For example, the lines of the mother and son in *Mountain Language* contain a world of suffering, deprivation, and injustice that is not just this mother's or this son's, but universal. Clarke's use of the Azeri singer (Fatma Mehralieva) to underscore the mother's lines points to the fact that although we understand the words in English, they move beyond nationality to a shared humanity. Equally important is the way the music takes up the suggestion of transcendence. For example, all we hear of the prisoner in the extract from *New World Order* is his breathing. But this is followed by soft cymbals and shivering strings, and a singer's high note which merges with the music. In this way Clarke opens out the earthly plane into a soundscape that invokes the steely light of stars, and the greater cosmos. The note comes again after the interrogation of the woman in *One for the Road*. Like Jimmy's speech from *Party Time*, where the central passage is given in silence, these voices, which emerge from darkness and silence, continue beyond the physical plane, and we understand that whatever degradation they have suffered, even if it is death, something of them survives which cannot be destroyed. That is what Pinter brings out in his poetry and Clarke in his music. No-one is lost. Something always survives.

Some critics had reservations. Sue Arnold (*Observer*, 16 October 2005) felt the piece didn't allow enough time 'to develop a theme as serious as torture' and felt that 'the dialogue was superfluous' since 'James Clarke's extraordinarily powerful music said it all', while David Sexton (*Sunday Telegraph Review*, 16 October 2005, p. 9) felt that 'in comparison with *Betrayal* and Pinter's many other great plays' it was 'little more than a fragmentary farrago'. But these critics overlook the overwhelming sense of transcendence which operates in both theme and form.

Although Clarke said in an interview following the broadcast that he did not write music to 'deliberately go with the words', there are times when the music seems to illustrate the language, with the sound of a whip cracking, or a chord suggesting a blow, or the ugly panting rhythm of a rape. What both Clarke and Billington emphasise in the same interview is the musicality of Pinter's text, which lends itself to such a treatment. Clarke quotes an early critic who likened Pinter's work to that of Webern with its 'extreme clarity, and precision and economy', and, as Billington notes, the use of silence. Pinter's text is used almost word for word although Clarke said he had added one or two repetitions. 'But apart from that it's exactly how he constructed it with a very clear musical form.' Clarke refers to the work as a new form, one in which text and music can be united 'in a different way so that the text is pure and the clarity of the words is uncompromised.'

◆ ◆ ◆

The award of the Nobel Prize for Literature, 13 October 2005

On the morning of 13 October 2005, Harold Pinter opened his copy of *The Guardian* at the breakfast table, thinking that perhaps he might read the name of the recipient of the Nobel Prize for Literature. He was curious to know whether it might have gone to Orhan Pamuk, the celebrated Turkish writer. Of course, the announcement of the recipient of the prize was yet to be made. Shortly after 11:30 he received a phone call from his agent Judy Daish, who was ringing to inform him that he was about to receive a call from a representative of the Nobel Prize committee in Stockholm. His immediate response to this news was a genuinely baffled 'Why?' Five minutes later the chair of the Nobel committee rang him to clarify that he had in fact won the 2005 Nobel Prize for Literature, and that this was to be announced to the world a quarter of an hour later. Pinter recalls his response as being rendered speechless.

In receiving this most prestigious of international awards, Pinter joins the ranks of other illustrious recipients, among them Samuel Beckett, Alexander Solzhenitsyn, Pablo Neruda, Wole Soyinka and Seamus Heaney. The award by the Swedish Academy not only recognises Pinter's stature as a dramatist but also alludes to his political concerns, as one 'who in his plays uncovers the precipice under everyday prattle and forces entry into oppression's closed rooms'. Speaking the same day on a special edition of *Front Row* (BBC radio 4), Pinter described himself as 'deeply honoured' by the award 'and rather flabbergasted', later telling *Newsnight* (BBC2 television) that it had never occurred to him that the award would go to him. He was visibly delighted in this interview with Kirsty Wark and when asked about the timing of this award, considering his recent anti-war stance, he was clearly glad of the opportunity to speak on the BBC's flagship news programme of his disdain for 'the mendacity and the corruption and the injustice of so many of the actions taken by what are called the freedom-loving democracies' and called for Tony Blair to 'be arraigned as a war criminal before the international Court of Justice,' before quipping with charm that he was still expecting a congratulatory bunch of flowers from the Prime Minister.

During that interview, and in all the photographs taken early that day outside his Holland Park home which were to appear on front pages around the world, Pinter, who rarely sports headgear, wore a black sailor's cap that covered the bruising caused by his rude meeting with a Dublin pavement earlier that week. The dressing covering his stitches was visible on his right temple, and this unfortunate and unexpected arrangement combined to add an enigmatic quality to those photographs of Pinter smiling, an attitude in itself so rarely seen in photographs of the artist.

Congratulations flooded in from the theatrical world, among which were those from fellow playwrights Sir Tom Stoppard, Sir David Hare, and Michael Frayn. Stoppard described Pinter as altering the language of drama, redefining 'the flow of information that goes from the stage to the audience', while Frayn praised Pinter as 'a courageous man with a generous heart, who has repeatedly stood up for the persecuted' (*Guardian*, 14 October). Hare, whose play *Stuff Happens* is about the US and UK political manoeuvres prior to the Iraq war, said the Academy had made 'a brilliant choice' (Dalya Alberge, *The Times*, 14 October). Alberge notes that the prize has been awarded to 'a radical and unrelenting critic of America and its war in Iraq and of the government of Tony Blair', and as *The Times* leader the same day also notes, this may be one of the reasons for the award, that 'Pinter is just about the biggest and sharpest stick with which the Nobel committee can poke America in the eye'. However, it takes issue with Pinter's political anger which, it says, 'only occasionally verges on the coherent', failing to note the devastating clarity in Pinter's careful enumeration of atrocities, injustices and corrupt regimes. With the exception of this critical outburst, and the conservative *Daily Mail* referring to the decision as a 'shock', the British press on the whole tended to either play down the political aspect or embrace it, as did *The Independent*, which capitalised on it as part of its ongoing criticism of the British government's handling of the Iraq conflict.

Not unnaturally, perhaps, there were detractors from America, one of whom was Roger Kimball, editor of the American magazine *The New Criterion*. Kimball is reported by the *Guardian* as saying that he considered Nobel prizes in general to be ridiculous, and this one was 'not only ridiculous but repellent', adding that Pinter's 'anti-American rantings have been saved from being merely outrageous by their insanity' (*Guardian*, 14 October 2005). This is not only a clear example of the way unpalatable truths are sidelined by labelling them insane, but a fine example of the style he seeks to castigate.

In Sweden, where a jury member (one not involved in the Pinter decision) had resigned a week prior to the announcement (stating that the previous year's selection of Elfriede Jelinek had damaged the award's reputation) (*Svenska Dagbladet*, 12 October 2005), there was an understandably greater investment in the international reputation of the prize, and the political implications were debated immediately. Interestingly, for example, only Swedish newspapers made any reference to Pinter's earlier call for Slobodan Milosevic to have a neutral trial as an example of his outspokenness on European politics. A journalist for Sweden's largest circulating tabloid, *Aftonbladet*, was dismissive of Pinter's worthiness, stating that 'there were certainly much more exciting choices'[1] (*Aftonbladet*, 14 October 2005). Zurich's conservative *Tages-Anzeiger* was even more disapproving of the award, unkindly dismissing Pinter as 'Beckett's harmless younger brother'[2] (*Tages-Anzeiger*, 14 October 2005) and criticising the Nobel jury for the manner in which their 'strange, contestable, grotesque decisions accumulate; the list of overlooked worthy writers becoming ever longer.'[3] In the Netherlands, referencing the recent resignation from the Nobel committee, *Die Volkskrant* wondered if 'the choice of Harold Pinter was a compromise: not easy to disagree with, but an avoidance of any real decision'[4] (*Die Volkskrant*, 13 October 2005). In France, where Pinter is highly revered, Brigitte Salino considered how the Nobel Academy was 'pursuing the praise of a certain radicalism' (*Le Monde*, 14 October 2005), relating Pinter's award to those made to Dario Fo in 1997 and Jelinek the previous year. In the same edition, the celebrated French director Roger Planchon applauded the award, describing Pinter as 'one of the world's greatest writers and one of its most politically engaged citizens'.[5]

Back in the UK, Michael Billington recognised that Pinter's involvement in politics is seen by many 'as an unfortunate aberration' (*Guardian,* 14 October). A similar point was made by Joan Smith in the *Independent on Sunday* (16 October, p. 39), who felt that Pinter's position in Britain 'says something about the status of the engagé intellectual in this country, where literary success and political commitment sit uncomfortably together'. She notes that her friend Orhan Pamuk, a writer of 'controversial political novels' who was at that time facing trial in Turkey for insulting his country's national character, inspires a high degree of popular affection in his own country, as does the Syrian poet 'Adonis' (Ali Ahmad Sa'id) in his adopted country of Lebanon. But in Pinter's home country there has been little official response to his award, although *The Telegraph* quoted the 'PM's official spokesman' as saying 'Of course, we would congratulate Harold Pinter on the recognition he has received.' Tessa Jowell, the Culture Secretary, said 'Harold Pinter has been a colossal figure in British literature for nearly fifty years' (Nigel Reynolds, 14 October).

Even those commentators who are less than complimentary about Pinter's political activities pay tribute to his stature in the literature of the twentieth century. For example, Charles Spencer (*Telegraph,* 14 October) finds a worrying approach to politics in the apparent equivalence Pinter draws between the morals of George W. Bush and Adolf Hitler. Nevertheless, he acknowledges the 'haunting poetry' of Pinter's drama, concluding that 'For once the Nobel Committee has got it right' in awarding these 'richly deserved Nobel laurels'. Mary Riddell (*The Observer*, 11 December 2005, p. 28) also takes issue with Pinter's politics, particularly as they emerged in the acceptance speech he recorded for Stockholm (when he was too ill to travel). And yet she too concludes by saying 'All he has tried to do, besides writing some of the best plays of the last century, is to rail against injustice.'

Robert McCrum in *The Observer* (16 October, p.4) describes Pinter as 'that very rare creature in British cultural life, a public intellectual with unrivalled rhetorical gifts'. In evident support of Pinter's views, *The Independent* of 14 October reprinted his speech on being awarded the Wilfred Owen Prize for Poetry earlier in the year, under the heading 'Torture and Misery in the Name of Freedom.' In the speech Pinter points out that 'we have learnt nothing. Nearly 100 years after [Owen's] death the world has become more savage, more brutal, more pitiless'. It is this commitment to speaking out that *The Guardian* leader (14 October) cites as part of 'a grand, often hidden tradition of dissent in English culture', akin to that of Bunyan, Milton, and Auden, poets who 'breathe something like divine fire into the literature of revolution'.

On 20 October 2005, the revised version of ***Various Voices*** was launched at the Royal Court Theatre with readings from the work, followed by a conversation between Pinter and the Royal Court's artistic director, Ian Rickson.

Extracts from the prose pieces, read by Harry Burton, included Pinter's first youthful encounter with the work of Samuel Beckett and their later drunken spree in Paris. But the majority of readings were extracts from Pinter's political writings, both prose and poetry, the latter read with moving resonance by the poet Tony Harrison. These included 'The Disappeared', 'God Bless America', 'Democracy' and 'Death'. Particularly poignant is 'Meeting', in which 'The long dead look out towards/The new dead/Walking towards them'. The poem invokes Wilfred Owen's 'Strange Meeting', and the irony of Pinter's title is that such meetings between those killed in war are no longer strange, but endlessly repeated; only the language which describes them has changed. Throughout the political writings, and in Pinter's conversation with Ian Rickson, a theme emerged in the distance between the words that are spoken and the actions that are taken by the body politic, particularly America. Pinter explained how the words 'Freedom', 'Democracy' and 'Liberation' are translated by Bush and Blair into 'Death', 'Destruction' and 'Chaos'. And in relation to Britain's own politics he quoted Tom Stoppard's statement of two weeks earlier, as he was leaving Belarus to return to England. Stoppard had said 'At least I am going to a country where I can publicly call the PM a liar'. Pinter pointed out that soon after this, at the Labour Party Conference, an elderly man had been ejected by force for doing just that. He called upon whichever 'little shit' the Home Office might have sent to the theatre to convey a message directly back to Tony Blair; 'that I, and millions of other people, hold him in contempt', an invitation which received sympathetic laughter and applause.

When asked whether he had heard from the Prime Minister on the subject of the Nobel Prize, Pinter said he had heard nothing, but he had once written an open letter to him in the *Guardian*—so the PM might write an open letter back. (The Prime Minister did send a letter of congratulations, but later, in January 2006.)[6] Pinter's letter in the *Guardian*, reproduced in *Various Voices,* notes American belligerence around the world since 1945 in the name of 'democracy'. But while Pinter castigated American policies he made it clear that he is not talking about every single person in the country, since he knows that 'There's a whole body of people in America horrified by what the country is doing'.

In the same way, he added, although he rails against this country's policies, he has a deep love of England, its language and poetry.

Pinter appeared frailer on this occasion than he ever had before at a public event. It was slightly disarming, for example, to witness his need of a hand to get out of his chair at the end of his interview. Although physically frail, Pinter's voice was as strong as ever, despite a slight hoarseness in its tone. He received a particularly warm reception from the audience, most of whom queued for signed copies of the new edition. After an hour of signing, Pinter retired to join his wife for a glass of wine before leaving the bar area. His friend Ian Smith joined them temporarily and, when they were all ready to leave, Ian offered his hand in support for Pinter to lift himself from his seat. Instead of pulling on the proffered arm, though, Pinter jokingly tugged at it in a spirited miniature tug of war, attempting to drag Smith lower before finally rising. Recognising the game, Smith used his other arm to tug Pinter's wrist upward. For those who witnessed this small friendly interaction, there was the heart-warming sight of a kind of typical Pinter playfulness, and one that was dismissive of his current ailments.

The week before the Royal Court appearance, Pinter had been asked by Mark Lawson (*Front Row Special*, 13 October) if there would be a political content to his Nobel acceptance speech. In reply, the writer said 'I have a deep suspicion that I might mention politics.' When asked about his speech by Ian Rickson, Pinter declared that it was to be called 'Art and Politics.' This was to be the longest public speech that Pinter had ever been requested to give, and he applied his undivided attention to constructing it in October and November. However, his health was to prove problematic as it took an unpleasant turn in November and December, eventually contributing to his doctor's insistence that he should not travel to Sweden to receive the Nobel Prize in person. He had become afflicted by a persistent skin irritation and, following tests, was discovered to have a mysterious condition which, he was told, had its origins in the Brazilian rain forests. He received treatment for this obscure affliction and, one day, while at work putting the final touches to his Nobel lecture, his doctor rang, having been examining his blood tests, to insist that he be taken immediately into hospital. Within an hour he found himself in intensive care with severe breathing difficulties. Once over this trauma, Pinter had to remain in hospital for further treatment and observation. The condition affected him significantly, and at its worst made it near-impossible for him to eat or drink. To record his Nobel lecture he had to come out of hospital for a few hours, arriving at the studios in a wheelchair, in which he delivered his address, and returned to his hospital room as soon as the recording was complete. Anyone who has watched the speech will recall how Pinter seemed slowly to be energised and vivified by the content of his lecture, his determined, focussed, unfaltering delivery in stark contrast to the image of a frail gentleman in a wheelchair, his lap covered by a blanket.

That speech, video-taped to be projected before the assembled Academy in Börssalen, Stockholm, on the evening of 7 December, was described by Barry Gray of the World Socialist Website (9 December) as 'passionate, truthful and courageous' offering 'a blistering critique of the entire course of US foreign policy in the period since World War II, and indicting Britain for its role as Washington's junior partner and accomplice.' As Billington also noted, this was a 'passionate and astonishing speech, which mixed moral vigour with forensic detail' (Billington, *Guardian,* 8 December). The speech, which began with a definition of two truths, the artistic truth that is constantly elusive, and truth in the real world, ended with a call for us all to seek the real truth for ourselves and our societies. Politicians, he said, are not interested in truth, only in the maintenance of power, and they manipulate language to that end, to obscure what is really going on. We all, therefore, have a 'crucial obligation' to seek the truth underneath that language because otherwise 'we have no hope of restoring what is so nearly lost to us—the dignity of man'.

Curiously—suspiciously even—the BBC made no reference to Pinter's speech in the evening news broadcasts of 7 December. Even *Newsnight*, which two months earlier had rushed to gain an interview with Pinter the day his laureateship was announced, made no reference to the speech broadcast by Britain's latest Nobel Prize winner just a few hours earlier. That no British terrestrial TV station ran the speech live seemingly added insult to this apparent injury. Channel 4 had gained the rights to show the lecture, but did so at midnight, having broadcast Pinter's video live on their digital current affairs channel, More4.

As part of the celebrations to mark the 50th anniversary of independent television, on 27 and 30 November the National Film Theatre showed two of Pinter's plays: *The Lover* (1963) made by Associated-Rediffusion, and *The Collection* (1961) produced by Granada TV in 1976. These plays were part of a highly-regarded series of works by new and important writers who came into television drama from the mid 1950s to the 1980s. By the time *The Lover* came to the small screen in 1963, Pinter had proved himself at the forefront of contemporary writing across a variety of media with his first screenplay, *The Servant*, released later the same year. These two short works, with their stellar casts, Vivien Merchant (Sarah), Alan Badel (Richard), Michael Forrest (John) in *The Lover*, directed by Joan Kemp-Walsh, and Alan Bates (James), Malcolm McDowell (Bill), Helen Mirren (Stella), Laurence Olivier (Harry) in *The Collection,* directed by Michael Apted, have lost none of their sexual potency in the years since they first appeared on television, and played to packed and highly appreciative audiences.

◆ ◆ ◆

The celebrations to mark Pinter's 75th birthday and the award of the Nobel Prize continued in December (1-3), when an all-star cast assembled to give a reading of *Celebration* (2000) at the *Albery Theatre* in London.

This staged reading, directed by Alan Stanford, was originally performed at the Gate Theatre, Dublin, as part of Pinter's birthday celebrations in October, in which many of the current actors also appeared. Those taking part in London were Sir Michael Gambon (Lambert), Kenneth Cranham (Matt), Penelope Wilton (Julie), Sinéad Cusack (Prue), Jeremy Irons (Russell), Janie Dee (Suki), Charles Dance (Richard), Joanna Lumley (maitre d') and Stephen Rea as the all important waiter.

Sam Marlowe describes how the cast relished 'the rhythms and shifts of the writing' and notes Gambon's 'wonderfully rumpled and uncouth' Lambert, and Dee's 'ripe sensuality that switches in a breath to penetrating *froideur*'. Marlowe quotes Dee's line: 'I want you to be rich so that you can buy me houses and panties, and I'll know that you really love me.' It suggests, he says, 'both sexual promise and threat and is typical of Pinter at his best' in a play which is 'full of such moments' (*The Times,* 3 December 2005). Michael Billington describes these diners as 'gold-plated philistines', 'displaced people' who, 'shorn of any inherited values [...] live in an eternal present of sex, food and conspicuous consumption'. And in this context, it is the waiter who 'has access to a world of family and feeling denied to the grandstanding diners' (*Guardian,* 2 December 2005). More than that, through the shade of his grandfather the waiter has access to a larger world inhabited by the famous names of the twentieth century, now past, but, like the memory of his grandfather, still vital and alive. It is this continuum of the past into the present which is stated quite clearly by Suki, who says 'I sometimes feel that the past is never past'. The lines directly echo a statement that Pinter made in 1971: 'I certainly feel more and more that the past is not past, that it never was past. It's present.' (Gussow, *Conversations,* 1994, p. 38). And past, present, and future are all contained in this particular celebration as Lambert assures us: 'Plenty of celebrations to come. Rest assured.'

◆ ◆ ◆

On 12 March 2006 Pinter was in Turin to receive the European Theatre Award, the highlight of a three-day symposium on his work chaired by Michael Billington. He was in a much improved state of health, and clearly enjoyed the events. Roger Planchon's troupe of actors from Paris brought a special compilation of Pinter's political plays, run as one long uninterrupted performance entitled *The New World Order*. It began with the sketch *The New World Order*, segued into *Press Conference* and *Precisely,* which led then into *One for the Road*, *Mountain Language* and concluded with *Party Time*. Continuity between roles permitted a sense of structural unity to the compilation that was compelling. For example, the victim of *New World Order* was performed by the same actor who played the hooded husband in *Mountain Language*, Victor in *One for the Road* and Jimmy in *Party Time*. As a tribute to Pinter, it was a most fitting production, and wholly apt to his recent concerns.

The symposium included both academic papers and testimonies by artists, actors and directors from around Europe and concluded, after Pinter's receipt of the award, with readings by Michael Gambon, Penelope Wilton and Jeremy Irons, in a tribute prepared by the Gate Theatre, Dublin. As part of the celebrations Pinter spoke on stage to Billington about his recent illnesses, his political concerns, America's power and Britain's subservience to that power, and his regard for Robin Cook, the labour MP who 'had the courage to speak out and to resign over Iraq.' And he cited his concern over political theatre in Britain and America, particularly in the case of *My Name is Rachel Corrie*, which was withdrawn from performance in New York as part of the 'suppression of dissent and truth' which is happening in these two countries. But beyond all this, he retained 'a shaky faith in the act of theatre' and its ability to capture, like no other medium, that intense moment 'that passes between the stage and the auditorium' (Pinter in conversation with Michael Billington, *Guardian,* 14 March 2006). On receipt of the award, he stood downstage centre on the platform of the Teatro Carignano, and spoke of how he hoped Europe might one day come together as a unified force strong enough to oppose or resist the influence of US political will.

On 27 March–6 May 2006, The Gate Theatre, Notting Hill, London, presented *In Celebration of Harold Pinter: A Slight Ache* and *A Kind of Alaska,* directed jointly by Claire Lovett and Thea Sharrock in what Charles Spencer describes as a 'cleverly selected double bill' (*Telegraph,* 3 April). (Pinter, although still recovering his health, had also attended some rehearsals at this tiny theatre close to his home.) Spencer praises Anna Calder-Marshall's 'understated emotion' as Deborah, supported by Niall Buggy as the doctor and Diana Hardcastle as the sister (the Flora of *A Slight Ache*, with Michael Byrne as Edward). Michael Billington (*Guardian,* 31 March) sees a development in the writing between these two plays, from the earlier work to the later, which Spencer describes as a 'beautiful, pity-filled' work, 'blessed with delicate precision'. And *Time Out* describes how the play makes the audience laugh 'even as the piece ambushes them with its

reflections on lost lives and the tragedy of ageing'. Together with *A Slight Ache* ('menacing, gripping, and very funny') it is proof, says Sam Marlowe, 'that Pinter is an artist we should never need an excuse to celebrate' (*The Times,* 1 April 2006).

Spencer welcomed this celebration, noting that 'the British theatre has been signally slow to honour Harold Pinter since he received the Nobel Prize for Literature last year', adding that although there 'has been a massive Euro-junket in Turin and much rejoicing ... in Dublin [...] in London there has been only the sound of silence'. This is a point made by other critics including Mary Riddell ('Prophet Without Honour', *Observer,* 11 December 2005), and particularly Billington, whose article 'A Gulf in Appreciation' notes the different responses to Pinter's work at home and abroad (*Guardian,* 14 October 2005). In a recent article on the National Theatre Billington notes that Pinter is not alone among 'senior living dramatists' (Hare, Stoppard and Bond) in their lack of attention from that central theatre (*Guardian,* 24 March 2006, pp. 12-13).

Nevertheless, Pinter is not without honour in this country. Made a Companion of Honour by the Queen in 2002 for his services to literature, his work continues to be a potent cornerstone of contemporary British theatre. One only has to note the range of works produced over the last year, from the fifty-year celebrations of the English Stage Company at the Royal Court, where *The Room* and *The Dumb Waiter* were presented as 'key moments in the development of modern drama' (Royal Court Theatre), to the new work, new form that is *Voices,* presented by the BBC to celebrate his 75th birthday, to see that Pinter's work continues to engage, and enrage, audiences and critics, who honour it with their constant attention.

NOTES

[1] "visst hade det funnits mer spännande val", 'Pinter—Pyspunka!', Pelle Andersson, *Aftonbladet,* 14 October 2005.

[2] "als kleiner, harmloser Bruder von Beckett, seinem Vorbild", *Tages-Anzeiger,* 14 October 2005.

[3] "Die seltsamen, anfechtbaren, ja grotesken Entscheide häufen sich, die Liste der großen Übergangenen wird immer länger", Ibid.

[4] "Er zijn talrijke prozaïsten en dichters wier bekroning meer voor de hand had gelegen, maar waarover de Zweedse Academie kennelijk geen overeenstemming heeft kunnen bereiken." 'Harold Pinter wint Nobelprijs voor Literatuur,' Michaël Zeeman, *Die Volkskrant,* 13 October 2005.

[5] "l'un des plus grands écrivains du monde et l'un de ses citoyens les plus politiquement engages". 'De Roger Planchon aux pacifistes, un hommage appuyé', *Le Monde,* 14 October 2005.

[6] That letter, which arrived on 27 January 2006, and Pinter's reply, are given in Michael Billington, *Harold Pinter,* rev. edn, London: Faber & Faber, 2007. 425-26.

Harold Pinter's Politics: A Silence Beyond Echo

Charles Grimes
Cranbury, NJ: Farleigh Dickinson, 2005.

Since the late eighties, Pinter's politics have taken center stage in Pinter studies and in London newspapers. Despite his prestige as a playwright, his political views are not as well documented by the American press. Such an oversight could be the result of Pinter's anti-American stance, the US's isolationism, illiteracy, or apathy, but it also reflects a fundamental difference between the US and the rest of the civilized world in terms of the relationship between art and politics. To put it bluntly, simply, and with a bit of bias thrown in for good measure, the US tends to view its artists as unruly children who are tolerated while they occupy their assigned playpens, but they are ridiculed, dismissed, or ignored once they begin to speak, quoting Teddy from *The Homecoming*, outside their "province."

Charles Grimes's book is one scholarly attempt to blur the artificially imposed boundaries between American art and politics. He examines not only the strategies of oppression in Pinter's plays, strategies that isolate and marginalize individuals, as the US does to its artists and dissidents, but he also argues that Pinter's political theatre is ultimately pessimistic: the revolutionaries are all silenced, and "their opponents" are "articulate, ruthless, and impregnable" (32). Grimes, for example, finds his subtitle from a 1964 Pinter comment that bears repeating: "When true silence falls we are still left with echo but are nearer nakedness." Grimes suggests that Pinter's political dramas illustrate a "silence beyond echo," a silence "purer and more absolute—more real" than the silence prior to the echo (217). For postmodernists, of course, any "real" or "pure" theory, ideology, or sound sends up the red flags, but in the case of Grimes's argument, which addresses the postmodernist agenda nicely, this perception of silence is appropriate.

The specific works he examines, for example, are, with some exceptions, some of the darker dramas, those that highlight fascism and oppression: *The Birthday Party*, *The Dumb Waiter*, *The Hothouse*, *Precisely*, *One for the Road*, *Mountain Language*, *Celebration*, *Press Conference*, *New World Order*, *The Comfort of Strangers*, *Victory*, *Reunion*, Pinter's direction of Ronald

Harwood's *Taking Sides*, Pinter's direction of Jean Giraudoux's *The Trojan War Will Not Take Place*, and *Ashes to Ashes*. As Grimes notes, in all these works, the oppositional voice is silenced, thereby reflecting the tremendous power of the oppressors, as well as the ineffectiveness of the opposition.

Grimes, of course, addresses the fact that Pinter continues to write, speak, direct, and act. Referencing Beckett's "I can't go on, I must go on" as well as the work of Kenneth Burke, Grimes illustrates that while Pinter's works do not present optimistic outcomes, they serve as exempla for political action. Political resistance may make no change, but the alternative, to do nothing, is immoral. As Grimes succinctly summarizes Pinter's vision, "ethics must exist without any assumption of efficacy" (49).

The book is an important and well-researched one, one that addresses many issues regarding Pinter's politics, life, and theatre. If, for example, readers are unfamiliar with the Albigensenist heresy, mentioned by McCann in *The Birthday Party*, Grimes has done the homework. Overall, his argument is compelling, particularly in the light of the plays he has chosen to discuss in this volume.

It is, however, difficult to forget Pinter's most successful revolutionary at this juncture, Ruth of *The Homecoming*. Despite the male attempts to silence and marginalize her, she speaks, ironically reminding them that silence may have more power than words: my "lips move.... Perhaps the fact that they move is more significant ... than the words which come through them." Like many of the characters in his political plays, Pinter continues to speak out against oppression, but he has also, to some extent like Ruth, decided to be silent by his discontinuation of playwriting, which may create, to use Grimes's image, a silence beyond echo that speaks for all.

Ann C. Hall,
Ohio Dominican University

Harold Pinter: A Bibliographical History

Comp. William Baker and John C. Ross.
London, Eng. and New Castle, DE:
The British Library and Oak Knoll Books, 2005.
323 pp.

The product of over seven years of collaborative research, *Harold Pinter: A Bibliographical History* is a colossal addition to scholarship on Harold Pinter and an invaluable resource for scholars of modern and contemporary British literature, theater, and film. Compiled jointly by bibliographical historians William Baker, Presidential Research Professor of English and the University Libraries at Northern Illinois University (DeKalb, IL), and John C. Ross, a research fellow at Massey University (Palmerston North, New Zealand), this fortuitously-timed, meticulously-detailed descriptive bibliography, completed in October 2004 and published just a month before the October 2005 announcement that Pinter had won the Nobel Prize in Literature, augments and updates previous standard bibliographies of Pinter's *oeuvre*. It covers mostly Pinter's "print-published writings" and some versions of his "texts in other media which he has wholly or partly authored" (book jacket).

As its co-compilers acknowledge (xxii), they draw upon *Harold Pinter: An Annotated Bibliography* (Boston: G.K. Hall, 1978), compiled by Steven H. Gale, and upon other more-recent bibliographical publications. These include my "Harold Pinter Bibliography," compiled for the *Pinter Review* since 1987; my article "The Harold Pinter Archive in the British Library" (*The Pinter Review: Annual Essays 1994* [1994]: 14-53), which focuses mostly on Pinter's plays, poetry, prose, and other miscellaneous manuscript holdings in the British Library (BL), with selected examples from unpublished drafts of Pinter's screenplays; Gale's and Christopher C. Hudgins' follow-up article, "The Harold Pinter Archives: II: A Description of the Filmscript Materials in the Archive in the British Library" (*The Pinter Review: Annual Essays 1995 and 1996* [1997]: 101-42); related archival manuscripts published with introductory notes or in articles by Francis Gillen in other volumes of *The Pinter Review*; and other bibliographical resources from various libraries, archives, other institutions, and individuals (xxii-xxv). As its subtitle "*A Bibliographical History*" indicates, this volume also serves as an historical account of Pinter's life as a writer. As such, it complements the updated edition of another source that Baker and Ross acknowledge, Michael Billington's *The Life and Work of Harold Pinter*, re-titled *Harold Pinter* (London: Faber and Faber, 2007).

The front matter of the volume includes an informative "Introduction" of just over 14 pages (vii-xxi), readily accessible as the "Book Excerpt" posted online at *oakknoll.com* (<http://www.oakknoll.com/bookexcerpt.php?booknr=86929>); four pages of "Acknowledgements" (xxii-xxv); a list of "Abbreviations" (xxvi); a "List of Illustrations" (xxvii); those 24 "Colour illustrations of dust jackets" (non-paginated); and a detailed "Chronology" (xxiii-xl). By their "*terminus ad quem*" (October 2004), Baker and Ross observe, "if one takes into account his published juvenilia, from 1947 onward, Pinter's authorial career already extends fifty-seven years" (vii). Anticipating the Swedish Academy's Nobel Prize tribute, Baker and Ross point out that he "is widely regarded as the outstanding English dramatist of the later twentieth century; and one can affirm that his major stature owes much to the sheer cumulative magnitude of his *oeuvre*, over this period, as well as to its often very high quality" (vii).

On the basis of their bibliographical study of Pinter's *oeuvre*, Baker and Ross hypothesize "that Harold Pinter may well have derived from his writing of poetry in the 1950s, before he came to the writing of plays, a degree of confidence and competence in the constituting of texts from a concatenation of disjunctive utterances and verbally-evoked images, held together by complex rhythms" and that "[f]rom his early experiences as an actor he derived a sense of what can be made in the theatre, together with much reading, notably of Samuel Beckett" (xx). "Thereafter," they observe, "while his manifold activities as a director of, or actor in, numerous stage-plays, television and radio dramas, or films, scripted by other writers can be noticed here, when at all, only in the *Chronology*, nonetheless, a recognition of the extent to which he has been, and to some extent continues to be, a man of the theatre, in a broad sense, is vital for an adequate appreciation of the progress of his own dramatic writings" (xx). Recognizing Pinter's "increasing eminence," to which they attribute his being "able to select which projects he would direct or act in," and "his gift for engaging with the spirit of works by other authors" and "for respecting and seeking to preserve their integrity" in his adaptations of their works to television and film, they attest to Pinter's having "developed his own distinctive authorial 'voice'" while staying "open to the challenges and stimuli deriving from such engagement." In their retrospective viewpoint on Pinter's writing career, echoing Gale's thematic and stylistic "critical analysis" of the late '70s (*Butter's Going Up* [Durham: Duke UP, 1977]) and anticipating Charles Grimes' sophisticated critical perspective in *Harold Pinter's Politics: A Silence Beyond Echo* (Madison & Cranbury, NJ: Fairleigh Dickinson

UP/Associated U Presses, 2005), Baker and Ross propose that "Shifting ideas and techniques have advanced dialectically through such engagement and openness" (xx). As items in this volume indicate, Pinter's "progressive engagements with political and humanitarian causes" since 1973 ("Introduction" xx) followed his activities in the anti-apartheid protest of playwrights (H2), as well as in the Campaign for Nuclear Disarmament (CND) protests in the early 1960s (K23). Letters and news accounts published from that era are sometimes difficult to find, but Baker and Ross enable later scholars to locate them with greater ease through their assembling them so deftly in this single volume.

Among the many great strengths of *Harold Pinter: A Bibliographical History* is its foundation in the collection of books and related published materials owned by Baker and Ross, most particularly, Baker's valuable collection of Pinter's works "amassed" over four decades (xxiv), upon which their most-detailed descriptions of items draw. A true bibliophile, he provides evidence throughout the book of precise first-hand examination of his own limited and special (often signed) editions of works that he and Ross are describing. Their bibliographical information and their cumulative scholarly knowledge, training, and skill in communicating it for a volume of this magnitude are crucial to the success of this work, in the scaffolding that they provide neophyte scholars and in the special embellishments that they offer its most sophisticated readers. Both kinds of readers will reap rewards from owning and consulting this book. For advanced Pinter scholars and for academic libraries, it is, of course, an essential resource.

Each of the eleven sections (A-K) in the "main sequence" (1-222) includes a useful headnote. Some sections are extended, with reference to unpublished archival materials, in the 54-page "Appendix One: *Individual Literary Works* (223-77) and, to a lesser degree, in the much-briefer, six-page "Appendix Two: *Textual Revisions and Promptbooks* (278-83). Both indices, "Index I: *Works by Harold Pinter*" (285-96) and "Index II: *General Index*" (297-323), are important components of this work and designed to be useful to scholars. There are some errors in them. "Index II" lists the name of Pinter's only son (with first wife Vivien Merchant) as "[Pinter], David" ($A35a^1$, G123). But his actual first name is Daniel, as the dedication quoted in $A35a^1$ indicates (71; cf. xxix in "Chronology," though not indexed), and his current surname is no longer Pinter. After Merchant's death in 1980, Daniel changed his surname to Brand, the maiden name of his maternal grandmother. (I correct a few other errors that I noticed in context later.)

Regarding what constitutes "publication" for their volume, Baker and Ross follow "the narrow definition of publication as print-publishing for public sale" and consider "a published entity ... constituted by its containing the text of just one particular work, or by its containing the texts of a particular combination of works, whether two, or three, or many" (x). For their purposes, "[a]ny such published entity may have concrete forms in a number of manifestations, either as different editions or reprintings of the same textual version(s), or including editions to some extent revised, incorporating different versions of one or more of the one or more texts contained." In cases "[w]here the entity contains the text of a single work, other manifestations of this entity can include an appearance in print of the text within a serial, or within an anthology, along with works by other authors." While their bibliography "primarily" documents "such published entities in their various manifestations," they identify "substantially different versions of the text of each work," but they do not "notice the presence of minor textual variations" (x-xi). Departing occasionally from that general definition of "publication" in practice, Baker and Ross do list some photocopied materials; e.g., the "*Distributed typescript* [1965]" of Pinter's otherwise-unpublished screenplay "The Compartment" (B1; cf. W27), for reasons cited below.

Section A: "*Plays and Sketches for the Stage, Radio, and Television*" (1-109), the longest section in the book, covers a period of 43 years, beginning with the "*first edition (Encore [Magazine]) (1959)*" of *The Birthday Party* (A1) and concluding with the "*Acting edition (2002)*" of Pinter's most-recent full-length play, *Celebration* (A57). This section is perhaps the most important one to most readers, and it is appropriately listed first. It describes mostly published editions of Pinter's dramatic works in meticulous detail. The entries often incorporate pertinent notes about publishers' variant editions and revisions (some developed further in the two appendices). Especially interesting in the entry for the "first edition" (1966) of Samuel French's acting edition of *The Homecoming* (A20j) is "*Note One*" (49-50). It describes unauthorized "amendments" (46) and "bowdlerized stage directions" (50), made by someone working for Samuel French, Ltd., who Pinter recognized to be silently censoring his actual text, changing and/or omitting or refusing to change passages that were to be restored after the abolition of the Lord Chamberlain's office. This note cites "a series of letters between Pinter and the responsible employee of Samuel French Ltd., from 23 January to 24 February 1969" (49), but does not identify its location. (Ross recalls that they would be in a box on *The Homecoming* in the Pinter Archive [e-mail message of 1 Apr. 2008]; that would seem to be current Box 24].)

Section B focuses on the "*Screenplays*" (111-26), beginning with B1, the "*Distributed typescript [1965]*" of "The Compartment," which, though "only ... informally published, in duplicated typescript," Baker and Ross include "because of its great interest as Pinter's only original screenplay and one of his earliest efforts in the genre" (xiv). The section ends with B9, which includes separate entries for each of the three volumes of Pinter's

"*Collected Screenplays*" (124-26). They list these volumes "within [Section B], rather than in the *Collections* section (I). Of the screenplays included in this collected edition, only *The Dreaming Child* had not been previously published" (xiv). The cross-referenced Appendix One augments Section B, ending with the British Library Harold Pinter Archive's typescript drafts of his screenplay for Shakespeare's *The Tragedy of King Lear* (2000), commissioned by Tim Roth for a projected film (to be directed by Roth), which, they point out, "has not yet been filmed or published" (xiv).

Section C: "*Poetry*" (127-32) "deals with publishings of individual poems first published separately" (127). The first nine items, covering from Spring 1947 through January 1953, document pertinent variations in the "Author's name given as 'Harold Pinter'" and the "Author's name given as 'Harold Pinta'" (C1-9). These begin with his first published poem "Dawn" (C1), published in *Hackney Downs School Magazine* (161 [Spring 1947]: 27). Section C concludes with entry C49, the 2003 Iraq War-inspired poem "The 'special relationship'" (published in the *Guardian* 9 Sept. 2004, G2: 4). Thus, this section comprises the period of 57 years mentioned in the "Introduction" to the volume.

In their headnote for Section C, Baker and Ross observe that Section I, subsection 2 ("*Editions of Collected or Selected Works*") lists collections of Pinter's poems: "*Poems* (1968), *Poems*, second edition, extended (1971), *Poems and Prose 1949–1977* (1978), *I Know the Place* (1979), *Collected Poems and Prose* (Methuen edition of 1986 and Faber editions of 1991 and 1996), *Ten Early Poems* (1992), *Various Voices* (1998), and *War* (2003)," pointing out parenthetically that "for some of these there is a corresponding American edition" (127). In "all but the latest of these collections," Pinter published "some poems ... for the first time," so to identify such poems, readers must "see the entries for these volumes." For the poem "Restaurant" (C26) in *Collected Poems and Prose* (*CP&P*), Baker and Ross list the first publication date, in the *Daily Telegraph*, from the (unverified) credits acknowledged at the end of that volume: "In *CP&P*, etc. dated 1989. No more specific date of first publication is given" (129). Not included is the date of composition ("1987"), which follows "Restaurant" on page 51 of the 1996 Grove Press paperback edition of *CP&P*, described (on the back of its title page) as "an expanded version of *Collected Poems and Prose*, first published in 1986 by Methuen London Ltd., being an expanded version of *Poems and Prose 1949–1977*, first published in 1978 by Eyre Methuen" (Cf. I7b [204-05]).

In "The Harold Pinter Archive in the British Library" (*The Pinter Review: Annual Essays 1994*), I describe Box 61 ("Poems"), which includes "a finished typescript draft of the poem 'Restaurant' (in a plastic binder)" and "a [transcribed] holograph list of names to receive it, with those to whom it was sent checked off" (33; cf. 31-34 for the rest of its contents).

Box 61 also includes "one [poem] dedicated movingly 'to my unborn son' [Daniel] and a typescript (uncorrected first draft?) of 'American Football'" (33), other unpublished correspondence not listed in the BL photocopied on-site or online finding lists, and non-poetic manuscripts. Some of the correspondence pertains to publishing collections, including the 1991 Faber edition of *Collected Poems and Prose* (I7).

Box 68 ("Poems BL") was originally unnumbered (as late as 1999) but later assigned that number. As I describe in the 1994 *Pinter Review* article, it includes Pinter's unpublished manuscripts, typescripts, and correspondence pertaining to many of the poems published in *CP&P*, among them a fascinating collection of items pertaining to both "American Football" (C29a), whose publication was highly controversial, and "Death" (C37), which Pinter read toward the end of his 2005 Nobel Lecture, "Art, Truth & Politics" and which concludes Faber's updated and expanded edition of *Various Voices: Prose, Poetry, Politics 1948–2005* (*VV* [2005]), *Death etc.* (2005), and *The Essential Pinter: Selections from the Work of Harold Pinter, Including 'Art, Truth & Politics,' Harold Pinter's Nobel Lecture* (New York: Grove P, 2006). (Pinter's poem "Death" is also incorporated in George Tokaya's art installation *Face the Dead* [2000] mentioned further below.)

Baker and Ross do not refer to my published discussion of the contents of Box 61 ("Poems") and do not cite the contents of Box 68 at all in either Section C or Section I, subsection 2 (covering Pinter's poems in the afore-mentioned "*Editions of Collected or Selected Works*"), or in Appendix One, on Pinter's "*Individual Literary Works*," which is confined to "the annals of Harold Pinter's more substantial or significant literary works in the genres of drama (including screenplays) and prose fiction (including only those short stories with a relatively complex 'history')" (223). As its headnote continues, Appendix One "does not cover unpublished items, in the main sequence, although a few of these are noticed at the end." (I consider both appendices further in order below.)

The headnote to Section C concludes by observing that "Some more recent poems have also appeared on the website www.haroldpinter.org but only one of those listed here ["Justin Faulkus" (C 31)] has so far appeared only on that site, and such appearances are not normally noted" (127). (Also not noted in C31 is additional information about the poem "Justin Faulkus" found in Box 68 of the BL Pinter Archive.) In Section C Baker and Ross include the first "publishings" of the individual poems collected in *War* (2003) (I12). They do not include "Death May Be Ageing" (April 2005), first published in the *Guardian* (19 April 2005), in "Harold Pinter's Poetry" on his official website (<http://www.haroldpinter.org/poetry/deathmaybeageing.html>), and reprinted in *Various Voices: Prose, Poetry, Politics 1948–2005* (*VV* [2005] 180). As Pinter wrote and published them even more recently, other poems not included are: "Lust" (22 Jan. 2006), also published in "Harold Pinter's Poetry" (<http://www.haroldpinter.org/poetry/lust.html>); "Laughter" (10 Nov. 2006), first published as the "The Saturday Poem" in the *Guardian* (25 Nov. 2006, Guardian Review sec.: 23); and "The Watcher," first published in the *Guardian* (9 Apr. 2007, G2: 3).

Though its Universal Resource Locator (URL) is not noted in Section C, "The Special Relationship" (sic) ("August 2004") is published online on Pinter's official website, *haroldpinter.org*, and accessible via a direct link featured on its home page (<http://www.haroldpinter.org/home/thespecialrelationship.html>); as "The 'Special Relationship' (US/UK)" in the collaborative authors' website, *Another America* (<http://www.anotheramerica.org/new_pinter_poem.htm>), established in 2004 by Pinter's friend Donald Freed; and, as "The 'Special Relationship'" in Faber and Faber's updated *Various Voices* (*VV* [2005] 261) and in Grove Press's *Death etc.* ([2005] 83). "Meeting" (C41; erroneously listed as C40 in "Index I" [293]; I12) and "After Lunch" (C42; I12) are also both featured on the cover of the 2004 volume of *The Pinter Review*. Although Baker and Ross cite some reprinted poems published in 2003 and 2004 (e.g., in the collection *War* [I12] and the periodical *Red Pepper* ["*Note*"] on 211-12), they do not cite some other related URLs with "individual publishings" that became accessible before their announced cut-off date of October 2004 (vii) and that I would consider "significant" reprints.

Notably, they do not acknowledge *Scent of Disorder*, a series of seven art installations, by Indonesian/Dutch artist George M. Tokaya. These art installations are documented on Tokaya's website (<http://home.hetnet.nl/~f2htokaya/documentation.html>). They are also featured in a special section of Pinter's official website entitled "Poetry in Art" (<http://www.haroldpinter.org/poetry/poetry_inart.shtml>), which states that "Pinter's work is an inspiration for [Tokaya] to design installations, make videos, paintings and graphics." *Face the Dead* (Installation 7) incorporates the complete text of Pinter's 1997 poem "Death" (C37) and could be considered a "publishing" of the poem, although it is not "print-published," according to the "narrow definition of publication" (x) already cited. It was exhibited first separately at the Pinter in London conference in June 2000 and later as part of the whole series at Borg Rusthoven, in the Netherlands. *Current Revenge* (Installation 5) was inspired by Pinter's 1995 poem "Don't Look" (C32), and the titular *Scent of Disorder* (Installation 6) by his 1996 poem "Order." Toyaka provides audio clips of Pinter's own readings of these poems as voiceovers accompanying videos of these installations in the artist's online website.

"*Fiction*" is the subject of section D (133-37), a relatively-short section whose headnote notices that "A few of the items in this section have a sufficiently complex history to also be given separate notice in

Appendix One" but that only "One item, the novel *The Dwarfs*, merits a full-scale entry here" (133). This section begins with "The Examination" (D1a), published in *Prospect* (Summer 1959): 21-25, and also includes several other interesting first publications of such works as "The Black and White" (D2a-D2b), "Tea Party" (D3a-D4), "Kullus" (D4), "The Coast" (D5), "Lola" (D6), and "Problem" (D7) in various magazines and their reprint information in *Poems and Prose 1949-1977* (London: Eyre Methuen, 1978) (133-34), abbreviated as "*P&P*." The remaining 4 (partial) pages provide a separate entry listing for each of four published editions of the novel *The Dwarfs* (D8a-d) and additional separate entries (D9-14) for "Short Story" (D9), "Girls" (D10a-b), "Latest Reports from the Stock Exchange" (D11), "Sorry About This" (D12), "Tess" (D13), and "Voices in the Tunnel" (D14). This section's headnote also states that "The short fiction pieces have been included in a series of collections, with only the first of these being noted" and refers readers to the headnote for Section C ("*Poetry*"), which mentions that for some of the collections listed "there is a corresponding American edition" and that "In all but the latest of these collections, some poems were published for the first time," referring further to "the entries for these volumes" and that they only "refer to sites of first publication" (127). The entries for "Sorry About This" (D12 [1999]) and "Tess" (D13 [2000]), however, refer to them as "Reprinted in *VV* [*Various Voices*] (Grove, 2000), an edition not listed in Section I ("*Collections*"). Box 60 ("Prose") in the British Library Pinter Archive contains unpublished typescripts with significant holograph revisions pertaining to some items listed in Section D, but Baker and Ross do not provide cross-references to it. Box 60 is mentioned briefly in Appendix One (W64) (276), where only a "few items" listed under the rubric "*Unperformed or Uncompleted Sketches, or Short Stories*" appear to "have a sufficiently complex history to also be given separate notice" (133).

Even though this *Bibliographical History* does not account for most "print-published" items appearing after its announced cut-off date of October 2004 (vii), it does cite URLs for some subsequently-dated entries described in Section E: "*Prose Non-Fiction: Essays, Articles, and Published Speeches*"(138-48) published electronically in *haroldpinter.org*, as well as some URLs of some other electronic publications of these works and also the *Harold Pinter Society Newsletter* (distributed to subscribers through the U.S. Postal Service and, more recently, electronically). It does not, however, cite the online publication of "Harold Pinter's Turin Speech" ("The American administration is a bloodthirsty wild animal," *Daily Telegraph* 11 Dec. 2002), which, Pinter also "submitted" for electronic publication in Donald Freed's collaborative *Another America* (<http://www.anotheramerica.org/Pinter_On_Bush.htm>), launched in 2004..

"*Published Letters to Newspapers, Magazines, etc.*" are listed in Section F (149-54), which includes Pinter's published "letters to editors" but "excludes letters for which he is only one of the signatories, and which are covered in *Section H*" (xv). The short headnote states: "In some cases, the item has been seen in the serial in which it is printed. In others it has not yet been examined, and the reference used may not provide the heading or the page number. Nonetheless, in the interests of comprehensiveness, where an item is known to exist, as much information is provided about it as is currently available" (149). This section begins with "A Letter to the Editor" by Harold Pinter (F1), published in *The Play's the Thing* (Oct. 1958: 10-11), and concludes with "Bush and Blair 'terrorists'" (F54), published in *The Spectator* (30 Oct. 2004: 38). The penultimate item (F53) has an error in its title. A letter written from Pinter to his friend Mick Goldstein, it is not entitled "'Waiting for Godot': an unpublished letter" as listed (154; cf. 295); but rather it is entitled "Waiting for *Waiting for Godot*: an Unpublished Letter," as published in issue 14 (Spring/Summer 2004) of *Areté* (88-90). The same letter to Goldstein about Beckett's play was published also as "Letter from Harold Pinter to His Friend, Mick Goldstein, regarding *Waiting for Godot*" in the 2004 *Pinter Review* (5-6). In both of these published versions (88 & 5, respectively), Pinter dates it: "Friday August 1955 from Portstewart, County Londonderry" (not noted by Baker and Ross).

As pertains to some entries listed in previous sections, Section F does not always identify the sources of "currently available" information being cited (149). In their "Introduction," Baker and Ross state: "In compiling listings of items, especially in non-literary categories, we have been much assisted by several existing enumerative bibliographies which cover Pinter's writings (as well as secondary sources), notably Rüdiger Imhof's *Pinter: A Bibliography* (London: TQ Publications, 1975), Steven H. Gale's *Harold Pinter: An Annotated Bibliography* (Boston, MA: G. K. Hall & Co., 1978), and, from 1989 [sic] onward, Susan Hollis Merritt's bibliographies in the annual volumes of *The Pinter Review*" (viii). They add that "Malcolm Page's *File on Pinter* (London: Methuen Drama, 1993) has also been useful" (viii). Later, in their "Acknowledgements," they suggest that they may have "drawn upon" my "Harold Pinter Bibliography" since its inception, as they note that it has been published in *TPR* "since 1987" (xxii). In some entries for items which apparently they have not examined themselves, they do provide citations to such sources (especially in Sections H, J, and K, and in the appendices); but, in other entries, they do not. Therefore, it is not always possible to trace where their information comes from and to verify it in order to avoid perpetuating possible errors that might originate with some of those publications (or their compilers' sources).

Section G lists "*Interviews Printed in Newspapers or Magazines*" (155-66). In their "Introduction," Baker and Ross state that the "magazine" category "comprises articles by journalists which do not have a question-response structure, and yet incorporate substantial passages of direct speech, deriving from an interview with Pinter, rather than merely being reproduced from some previously published source" (xv); they add that in Section G: "Undoubtably, some printed interviews or interview-based articles exist that have not been identified or located" (155). This section begins with the important anonymous interview "Mr. Harold Pinter: Avant-Garde Playwright and Intimate Review" (G1), published in the London *Times* (16 Nov. 1959: 4), and concludes with Kate Kellaway's interview with Pinter entitled "Theatre of War" (G125), whose lead is: "The Iraq war has energised dramatists with David Hare's new play the latest in a surge of political drama. Pinter, Frayn and others on the front line talk to Kate Kellaway" (*Observer* 29 Aug. 2004, Arts: 5).

The entry for item G18: "Interview with Harold Pinter. *Daily Mirror* (*ca.* 20 March 1965) (clipping seen, but not traced)" may not at first glance seem particularly useful or easily verifiable. Yet if it had been excluded entirely on that basis, all record of such an ephemeral newspaper interview might disappear forever. Such items published in the "pre-electronic age" (Baker's phrase qtd. in his institution's press release, "Pinter's Nobel Prize Shines Light On Work of NIU Researcher," *Northern Illinois U* 19 Oct. 2005, 31 Oct. 2005 <http://www.niu.edu/PubAffairs/RELEASES/2005/oct/bakerbook.shtml>) must be located in research libraries with such holdings (usually on microfilm or microfiche), or in a newspaper's or broadcasting network's own archives (not always publicly accessible to scholars). There is a typographical error in the entry for Lawrence M. Bensky's often-cited interview with Pinter, entitled "The Art of the Theatre III: Harold Pinter: An Interview" (G20), first published in *The Paris Review* (10.39) in Fall 1966 and now readily accessible electronically from the website of *The Paris Review* (<http://www.theparisreview.com/viewinterview.php/prmMID/4351>). It is reprinted in the volume *Writers at Work: The Paris Review Interviews* (among its various editions cited on 156-57), edited by George (not "Charles") Plimpton (an error requiring correction in Index II [317] as well).

Section H, "*Miscellaneous: Minor Pieces, Collaborative Writings, Editing, etc.*" (167-83), "covers a wide range of kinds of items," including Pinter's "brief contributions to various publications, letters to newspapers or petitions with multiple signatures, volumes edited by Pinter, and so forth" (xv). It includes less familiar items that may not be listed at all in previously-published bibliographies. The first entry (H1) is Pinter's "Foreword" to *Two Plays by Eugene Labiche*, published by Dramatists Play Service in 1962 (167), an item not listed by Gale. The third from-the-last item (H69) is

"The Catch: A Correspondence" (with Alan Wilkinson), published by the Evergreen Press in 2003, whose very-detailed description is based on Baker's own "'special edition' copy numbered '19/500' and a 'standard edition' copy numbered '223/500'" (181-83). "*Note one*" about a source for this item cites "an e-mail to William Baker dated 11 March 2004," in which "Alan Wilkinson, the publisher" gives the history of its publication (182-83). According to "*Note three*, "The text concern[s] a fine catch Pinter made while playing for the Gaieties Cricket Club. Wilkinson had heard about it over a drink and on 21 January 2002 wrote to Pinter asking a number of questions about the catch. Pinter replied on 24 and 31 January 2002. The main text consists of Wilkinson's questions and Pinter's answers, followed by the complete text of the letter of 31 January 2002" (183).

Section I: "*Editions of Collected or Selected Works*" (184-212) "is divided into two sequences, one of collected plays (but with the volumes including also some short prose pieces) and the other of volumes of poetry and prose" (xv). The first "Subsection" (I1) on "Plays and Prose" (184-95) is divided further into two additional "sequences" (or sub-subsections). (Arabic numeral "1" throughout the book are typeset as the letter "I"; to avoid confusion I am rendering the numeral as "1.") The first sub-subsection lists editions published in the UK (Cf. xvii), and includes "Plays: One [-Four] 1976-81": both the "*Methuen edition, in four volumes (1976–81)*" (I1a.) and the "*Faber edition (1991–93)*" (I1b.). The second sub-subsection, headed "[American Edition] [sic] Complete Works 1977-81" (I2), includes the Black Cat edition in four volumes published by Grove Press (1977–81) (I2a.) and the Grove edition in four volumes (1990) (I2b.). "Subsection 2: Poetry and Short Prose Works" (196-212), begins with Pinter's collection entitled *Poems* (1968) (I3), including two editions, published by Enitharmon Press: the "*First edition, first issue*" ($I3a^1$.) and the "*First edition, second issue (1970)*" ($I3a^2$.), followed by the "*Second edition, with nine added poems (1971)*" (I3b.), including both an "*Ordinary bindings issue*" (b[i]) and a "*Special copies issue*" (b[ii]). The items described here (196-99) include several elegant (and expensive) limited and signed editions collected by Baker or added to his collection from other collections which he purchased, such as that of Gerald Berkowitz ("Acknowledgements" xxiv). Section I ends with *War* (I12), published by Faber and Faber in 2003 (211-12). *Death etc.* was not published in time for inclusion; if it had been, it might have been listed and/or cross-referenced in both subsections, as it contains plays, poetry, and prose, unlike *Various Voices* (I9), which contains no plays and no other dramatic works, and *The Essential Pinter* (2006), which includes only plays and poetry.

For the 1999 American (hardback) edition of *Various Voices: Prose, Poetry, Politics: 1948–1998*" (I9b.), published by Grove Press (ISBN 0-8021-1643-4), Baker and Ross describe its "*Contents*: As for the British edition"

(209), first published in hardback by Faber and Faber in 1998 (I9a.). But the first British and American *paperback* editions do contain items not included in the first British and American hardback editions and not accounted for by the subtitle ("*1948–1998*") or by copyright dates on the back of their title pages. In 2000, then Faber Drama editor Peggy Paterson responded to my e-mail query about this discrepancy by acknowledging that there had been a mistake in not updating the date of the Faber paperback collection's subtitle and copyright information from "1998" to "2000"–the first publication date of "Tess"–and assured me that subsequent editions would correct that error, which the 2005 edition does. The back of the title page for the (unlisted) 2005 revised (paperback) Faber and Faber edition of *Various Voices* (ISBN 0-571-23009-1; 978-0571-23009-9) indicates that *Various Voices* was "First published in 1998"; its "Paper edition first published in 1999"; and "This revised edition first published in 2005," thus correcting previous errors brought to Peggy Paterson's attention.

In contrast to Section G, both Section J and Section K include interviews broadcast on radio or television but "not published in print" (155). They list "*Sound Items*" (213-18) and *Audio-Visual Materials*" (219-22) that "are not broadcastings of works also published in print (which are dealt with in *Appendix One*)" (xv). These sections are both considerably shorter than the earlier ones dealing with print publications, due to limitations acknowledged in their headnotes. For example, Section J takes account of Pinter's "radio talks ... radio interviews, and various other programmes or events in which he participated and for which he may have generated some text, either for a radio broadcast or for a stand-alone sound recording" (213). It "covers those items for which there is no corresponding print-publication item." But when there is such a printed publication, "the item is normally covered in the relevant section, with a note about radio broadcasting and/or, as appropriate, in *Appendix One*," with the exception of the sound recording of parts of the first (hardback) edition of *Various Voices* (J49), deemed "a major sound-recording item of special interest" and thus "included" in Section J. This set includes "excerpts read by Pinter, platform performance, Lyttleton [Lyttelton] Theatre, 1998" (Baker and Ross 217) from the Faber and Faber first (hardback) edition of *Various Voices* (1998), its book launch. (*Lyttelton* is misspelled elsewhere in the book and in "Index II.")

Otherwise, Section J on "*Sound Items*" (213-18) does exclude "items for which he was clearly simply an actor, narrator, or director, although where doubt exists an item is included rather than excluded," occasionally omitting "precise dates of broadcast"; "in the interests of comprehensiveness, these items are listed with whatever data are presently available" (213). As the headnote states about the items listed in Section J, as sources of such data, Baker and Ross refer readers to "material in the British Broadcasting Corporation's Written Archives Centre (*WAC*), in the *Radio Times* (*RT*), and in the National Sound Archives in the British Library (NSA)." From my own work in such archives, I know how difficult it is to document these materials and how "knowing" where they are physically located in the handwritten or typed records of non-digitized archives requires on-site research, as, serendipitously, one discovers items about which one lacks advance knowledge. The headnote for Section J concludes by also pointing to the lack of adequate bibliographical information in the "on-line National Sound Archives catalogue (accessible via www.cadensa.bl.uk)," which "includes some further items that may be worthy of inclusion, but does not provide sufficient detail, nor, in many cases, dating (many of the items are, in any case, recordings of Pinter's plays or poems or Pinter's reading the works of other authors and hence not eligible for inclusion here)" (213). This advance information is very helpful to other scholars planning to visit or to access these archives.

Section K on "*Audio-Visual Materials*" (219-22) acknowledges some limitations on bibliographers similar to those Baker and Ross already observe in the previous section: "This section covers television and film items for which there is no print-publication equivalent, so that they are not given notice in other sections or in *Appendix One* (e.g., it does not include transmissions or recorded forms of Pinter's screenplays or television plays)" (219). Moreover, like Section J, this section "does not normally include Pinter's participation as an actor, narrator, or director unless he is also the author of some feature of the text" (Cf. "Introduction" vii-viii; 213). As for sources for materials described in this section, its headnote states that "[i]n many cases, copies of films or video cassettes are available at the British Film Institute, London (*BFI*)." The headnote concludes: "As with *Section J*, some items are included with available information, although all the relevant details are not known" (219). These caveats in Sections J and K (and the corresponding points in the "Introduction" xi) suggest some possibly-fruitful directions for future researchers interested in exploring and documenting Pinter's work produced for and/or broadcast on the various audio-visual and electronic media.

Their headnote to "Appendix One: *Individual Literary Works*" (223-77) establishes that, with respect to "performance, presentation, or publication," Baker and Ross are concerned "only with the first occurrence. For stage-productions, this means that the British première is normally the only one to be noticed. Likewise for publication, only the British edition in which a work appeared has always been noticed" (223-24). Making "no attempt ... to document the subsequent reproduction of films in video cassettes or, more recently, in DVD videodiscs," they direct readers to "appropriate databases, such as *WorldCat* ... [to] discover that most of the films for which Pinter supplied screenplays have been reproduced in one or both of these forms" (224).

The "Introduction" establishes that a "bibliographical history goes beyond the scope of a descriptive author bibliography, in seeking to offer a kind of documentary biography of the author, in terms of his or her published writings, to signal connections between these writings, and (as appropriate) to document the history of each of them" (viii). Baker and Ross stress that "In approaching this task, for Harold Pinter's works," applying "the concepts of authorship, text and publication" raises problems, and they explain in considerable detail, with useful examples, why that is so. Pertaining to Pinter's "works in dramatic modes, for live theatre, radio or television," while "his authorship is usually clear-cut, with only a few, clearly acknowledged cases of explicit collaboration," they add this important qualification:

> However, presentations in the various media naturally involve significant dimensions of collaboration and social production; and these cuts and re-writings have sometimes manifestly resulted from experience within the production process, as can be seen from promptbooks, especially when Pinter himself was involved as the director, or was working closely with a director, with a particular cast of actors, and evaluating audience response. Thus some degree of indirect influence from other agents cannot be wholly ruled out. (viii-ix)

Baker and Ross delineate further the complexities and limitations of bibliographical history as these pertain to publishing work by a writer who is a playwright, actor, director, and screenwriter as it is affected by such collaborative "agents" (ix). Since "a dramatic text comprises not only lines of dialogue, but also stage directions, and other 'apparatus,'" they note further that "in the American acting editions especially, where these features sometimes diverge from those of the standard [published] editions, the variants may well have originated from some director's notations in a script being used as a copy-text, perhaps with Pinter's approval" (or perhaps not, I might add). Sometimes (if at all) one can determine the origin and authoritativeness of such changes only through interviews with the playwright and/or those involved in the productions. For example, during rehearsals that he attended for Carey Perloff's 1989 CSC Repertory production of *The Birthday Party* (in a double bill with the New York première of *Mountain Language*), although, according to Perloff, "he never intended there to be a staircase on the set," to accommodate its prominent inclusion, Pinter "added a line"–"What a lovely flight of stairs."–and "made some cuts.... All the way through" (Merritt, "A Conversation with Carey Perloff [et al.]," *Pinter Rev.* [1989]: 61-62). (Such changes that Pinter makes for specific productions may not enter subsequent published editions.) "Still," Baker and Ross stress, "the most extensive re-writing and re-formatting have come about when Pinter himself has adapted a work initially designed for one medium for one of the others, responding to its differing exigencies" (ix).

Their point applies especially to "Pinter's screenplays," where "the authorship situation is more complex than for his works in other modes" (ix). Users of this bibliography must recognize that such complexity of authorship pertains both to the published screenplays listed in Section B and to the unpublished and/or unproduced screenplays listed in Appendix One: "*Individual Literary Works*" (223-77), which draws upon previously-published accounts of the Harold Pinter Archive in the British Library (currently being catalogued) for descriptions of some items which Baker and Ross may not have been able to examine.

That qualification also applies to Appendix Two: "*Textual Revisions and Promptbooks*" (279-83), a much-shorter section. Its textual and interpretive accuracy might be enhanced by specific interviews with Pinter and other actors and directors and others involved in productions, such as interviews with Susan Engel, James Severns, Auriol Smith, and Henry Woolf about the production of Pinter's first play, *The Room*, being compiled through the *Theatre Archive Project* (2003–2008), a collaboration of staff of the British Library and Sheffield University sponsored by The Arts and Humanities Research Council (AHRC), as listed in my current "Harold Pinter Bibliography" (Cf. <http://www.bl.uk/projects/theatrearchive/theroom.html>). Baker and Ross provide examples from the film scripts to illustrate their own admonitions. Examples from "promptbooks" or from "textual revisions" detailed in previously-published criticism and listed in Appendix Two also illustrate similar "complexities" of "the authorship situation" pertaining to Pinter's works written and/or produced for the stage and other audio-visual media (radio, television, cinema, and electronic resources). In addition to citing the British Library's Harold Pinter Archive and previously-published articles about it as primary and secondary sources of their information about "*Textual Revisions and Promptbooks*" in Appendix Two, Baker and Ross also cite the National Theatre (NT) Archive in Salisbury House, Brixton Road, London, which houses video recordings of stage productions and printed programs and press cuttings relating to them. My own experience exploring the NT Archive confirms that it is, as Daniel Rosenthal writes, "an invaluable collection of documents, artwork and recordings, open to students, scholars and other interested parties" (<http://www.nationaltheatre.org.uk/An%20Invaluable%20Collection+9810.twl>): a major repository of press clippings, programs, and production statistics, as well as promptbooks. It houses the NT's video recordings of its own stage productions, a useful repository to consult if one has missed seeing any of them live on stage or wants to re-experience them for further study or production preparation. (In their "main sequence" [e.g., Section A], Baker and Ross do not list or refer otherwise to these video recordings of NT productions of Pinter's plays or to their accession numbers, as they do for the NT promptbooks that they list in Appendix Two.)

Baker and Ross also explain why they have not included "theatre programmes" in their bibliographical history, describing the program as "a genre" which, like others already noticed, includes "grey areas of mixed, shared or implied authorship," yet still wondering "what ... one is to make of the contents of theatre programmes for stage productions for which Pinter was the director." "While not necessarily their author," they observe, Pinter "may be assumed to have authorised them," yet they encountered and list "only one instance in which a programme note was signed" and that is "for the 1980 first production of his own play *The Hothouse*" (ix). "Otherwise," they have "disregarded" entirely "this genre" of notes in theater programs or playbills.

With respect to unpublished materials in archives (which are accounted for in Appendix One), in their "Introduction," Baker and Ross observe that in this Appendix they adopted "an ad hoc [sic] format ... to provide summary information about the composition, live performance or presentation via radio, television or film, and publication, of the various works" (xviii). Given "that for the films later reproductions are of the nature of copies with a different technology," Baker and Ross give "no attention to ... video cassettes or DVD videodiscs" (xviii). They single out, "Outstandingly, ... the Pinter Archive (*PA*), lodged as Loan 110 [A] in the British Library" (xviii) and observe, "The contents of the collection have been listed in the British Library finding list" and are "the subject of two substantial articles in *The Pinter Review*" by me and by Gale and Hudgins already cited above.

The British Library finding list (even the periodically-updated online versions: (<http://www.bl.uk/catalogues/manuscripts//HITS0001.ASP?VPath=arevhtml/62484.htm&Search=Loan.+110+A&Highlight=F>), currently listing 80 boxes (24 Dec. 2007), does not list fully the contents of the boxes already accessible in the Pinter Archive. On 11 December 2007, the British Library announced that it has acquired over 150 boxes of Pinter's Archive, nearly doubling the size of the Archive's 80 boxes currently listed in the BL's online finding list and now including also "over 12,000" letters, as well as "manuscripts, scrapbooks, photographs, programmes and emails of Harold Pinter" ("Pinter Archive Saved for the Nation," press release, 11 Dec. 2007 <http://www.bl.uk/news/2007/pressrelease20071211.html>). This "thrilling" acquisition offers new kinds of material not previously accessible to researchers at all. It completes Pinter's literary archive (in its current state) and enables the Library to sort and to catalogue what the current head of Modern Literary Manuscripts, Jamie Andrews, describes as a "wonderful collection that sheds new light on each stage of Harold Pinter's unparalleled career over the past 50 years." Andrews assures scholars that he and his colleagues at the British Library "look forward to making the material accessible to researchers, and to playing our part in celebrating his life and work," with a "small display" called "His Own Domain: Harold Pinter, A Life in Theatre" featuring "a range of unique manuscripts, letters, photographs, and sound recordings" from the Archive, exhibited in The Sir John Ritblat Gallery: Treasures of the British Library, from 10 January through 13 April 2008. Andrews expects cataloguing the recently-acquired Archive to take about a year, until the end of 2008. (See BL press release <http://www.bl.uk/news/2008/pressrelease20080109.html> and hyperlinked *Front Row* interview with Jamie Andrews; Arikfa Akbar, "British Library Acquires Pinter Archive for £1.1m," *Independent* 12 Dec. 2007, 14 Dec. 2007 <http://news.independent.co.uk/uk/this_britain/article3244698.ece>; and BL "Reader Bulletin[s]" for Jan. and Apr. 2008 <http://www.bl.uk/services/reading/bulletin2008jan.html> and <http://www.bl.uk/services/reading/bulletin2008apr.html>.)

Until the British Library sorts through the new materials and properly catalogues them, they will likely remain inaccessible to researchers, although an updated finding list may be constructed for the interim. One must also keep in mind that the British Library's organization and thus presentation of the entire Pinter Archive will change considerably after it is properly catalogued (Sally Brown, personal telephone conversation, 17 Dec. 2007). The cataloguer of the Pinter Archive, Kate O'Brien, who began working at the British Library in January 2008, is in the process of reorganizing, reclassifying, rearranging, and renumbering Boxes 1 to 80 and specific materials within them. According to Andrews and O'Brien, all of the materials will moved into upgraded archive-quality boxes, and, for purposes of continuity with previously-published accounts of the Archive, the new catalogue will cross-list the previous corresponding box number locations of the temporary finding list (personal telephone conversations, 19 & 20 Feb. 2008). On 29 February 2008, the BL Web Editor launched the "Harold Pinter Archive Blog" (<http://britishlibrary.typepad.co.uk/pinter_archive_blog/>), whose principal author is Kate O'Brien, reporting on the cataloguing process, with occasional related postings from her colleagues (O'Brien, e-mail message of 1 Apr. 2008). The formal British Library manuscripts catalogue (or "registry") will supersede all such previous reference locations and become standard for future citations to the Harold Pinter Archive in the British Library.

The British Library press release and Andrews' interview comments about this acquisition cited in news accounts single out Pinter's unpublished autobiographical prose memoir "Queen of all the fairies" as a particular highlight of the collection, along with correspondence with other major literary figures like Samuel Beckett and "a collection of poignant letters" to his "inspirational" Hackney Downs School English teacher Joseph Brearley. In their headnote to Appendix One, Baker and

Ross briefly mention "Queen of all the fairies," referring to it as "Queen of All the Fairies" and describing it as Pinter's unpublished prose "reminiscences of his youth in Hackney, of which a carbon copy, 8 typed pages [rectos only], is in the Pinter Archive, Box 60, along with several drafts or fragments of unpublished short stories and sketches" (223). They do not refer to Pinter's explanation of the origin of the title in a letter to me dated 17 October 1994 or my quotations from the memoir published with his permission in my 1994 *Pinter Review* article on the BL Pinter Archive. According to Pinter, as I quote him there, the title "Queen of all the fairies" derives from a line of "'a bawdyish song we sang as boys' in which 'Queen of the Fairies is the central character'" entitled "Chanson Populaire" and the pertinent excerpt is: "'Twenty-one, never been done,/Queen of all the Fairies.//Oh what a pity/She's only one titty/To feed the baby with/Poor little bugger/He'll never play rugger...' (Letter)" ("The Harold Pinter Archive in the British Library" 28n11; 45-46). At the end of Appendix One, Baker and Ross list some other items from Box 60 which are "short stories" or "dramatic pieces" (276-77), but they omit such significant non-fiction prose as "Queen of all the fairies," as they have excluded both that genre and poetry from entries in this appendix.

A reference in Appendix One (W65:1.): "Manuscripts in *PA* [Pinter Archive] Boxes 65, 66: not seen" (276) pertains to Pinter's (unpublished) screenplay adaptation of Nabokov's *Lolita* (W65); that entry misspells the surname of the director of the released film, Adrian Lyne (not "Lynne" [276, 312]). It appears that they may not have examined some other boxes in the Pinter Archive. Both Boxes 61 and 68 contain poetry-related manuscripts; but, as mentioned earlier, whereas they do refer directly to materials in Box 61, they do not cite Box 68 or mention several poetry manuscript materials located in it at all, either in Section C or Section I (in additional notes, for instance) or in the appendices, which both exclude the poetry. According to Baker, however, they did have to make substantial cuts from the appendices due to press constraints (personal conversation, MLA Convention, Hyatt Regency, Chicago, IL, 30 Dec. 2007).

Baker and Ross cite the contents of some other archives containing unpublished Pinter manuscripts in Appendix One. The Lilly Library owns three of the earliest known unpublished typedrafts of *The Caretaker* (the stage play), which contain significant holograph revisions by Pinter. Baker and Ross list these unpublished typedrafts as Item W14: "Manuscripts, etc., in Inu-L, 'Pinter mss.' (not seen; citing information and quoted from the on-line catalogue)" (237). (They do not provide the URL of that catalogue listing; it is <http://www.indiana.edu/~liblilly/lilly/mss/html/pinter.html#xtocid2610938>.) Their "Abbreviations" page gives "Lilly Library (University of Indiana [Indiana University], Bloomington, Indiana)" (xxvi).

One of these drafts held by the Lilly Library is the "first draft" typedraft of *The Caretaker*, with Pinter's earliest holograph revisions. A key difference between this earliest archived typedraft of *The Caretaker* and the published play is a female character whom Pinter deleted in later typedrafts held in the British Library (Box 6, as discussed in "The Harold Pinter Archive in the British Library" 34), making it a play with only three male characters. A similar change occurred later, when Pinter converted the unpublished manuscript of his only novel *The Dwarfs* (41; begun in 1952 [xxviii]) into a play (for radio and stage) (Cf. Boxes 11-14 and 40 in BL Pinter Archive). Pinter excised or further "cast out" the already-"outcast" female character "Virginia" for the "distinctly all-male" dramatic version of *The Dwarfs* (Elizabeth Sakellaridou, *Pinter's Female Portraits* [London: Palgrave Macmillan, 1988] 12-13, 18, 45), written in the late 1950s and first broadcast on radio on 2 December 1960 (A12 [31]). That broadcast occurred just a few months before Pinter was readying *The Caretaker* ("a major all-male play ... a strong masculine interlude" [Sakellaridou 13]) for its first productions and publication (A2ff.). Baker and Ross list the first publication of *The Caretaker* in *Encore* magazine as "[May? 1960]" (A2 [9]). These early typedrafts in the Lilly Library offer significant additional glimpses into Pinter's process of composition and revision which could have been noted in the entries for *The Caretaker* in Appendix One had Baker and Ross examined them. Baker and Ross cite Pinter's "Author's Note" concerning his omission of "the essential character of Virginia" from his "short play "extracted" from *The Dwarfs* (224-25). They do not note previous scholarly references to Pinter's deletion of the character of Virginia from the published novel *The Dwarfs* (D8) in his radio and stage play versions (A12, 13); or that Kerry Lee Crabbe restored Virginia in his new stage adaptation of the novel directed by Christopher Morahan at the Tricycle Theatre, London, in April/May 2003, and published by Faber and Faber in April 2003 (H68).

In their Appendix Two, Baker and Ross provide a "*Note*" stating: "Promptbooks and other documents not yet available in the NT Archive for: *Remembrance of Things Past* (directed by Di Trevis; opened 23 November 2000 [through 4 April 2001]), adapted by Pinter and Di Trevis [Cf. A54; <http://www.nationaltheatre.org.uk/Remembrance%20of%20Things%20Past+1224.twl>]; or for *No Man's Land* (directed by Harold Pinter; opened 6 December 2001)" (283). Such items may be available by now either in the NT Archive in Salisbury House or in the BL Pinter Archive. Pinter has added many materials to his Archive since October 2004, including programs, promptbooks, correspondence, photographs, and related documents, so that the situation that Baker and Ross describe already has changed considerably, as the Archive has been ongoing, as they clearly acknowledge (Cf. vii, xvii, xxi), with Pinter periodically adding, rearranging, and/or removing materials and having sold the vastly-expanded entire archive to the British Library.

Relying on Gale's account previously published in *The Pinter Review*, Baker and Ross do cite and note some unpublished manuscripts by Pinter pertaining to his screenplays in "The Harold Pinter Collection" at the Harry Ransom Humanities Research Center (HRC), at the University of Texas at Austin (<http://research.hrc.utexas.edu:8080/hrcxtf/view?docId=ead/00108.xml>), which consists of only two boxes. Baker and Ross do not refer to (cite or otherwise note) unpublished materials from and relating to Harold Pinter and his published works and American and British productions listed in the registries (catalogues) of archival collections of the papers of other writers–such as his friends and fellow playwrights Tom Stoppard (<http://research.hrc.utexas.edu:8080/hrcxtf/view?docId=ead/00179.xml>) and David Hare (<http://research.hrc.utexas.edu:8080/hrcxtf/view?docId=ead/00267.xml>), also held at the HRC, in Austin–and of Pinter's directors, such as Alan Schneider, who directed the New York premières of several of Pinter's plays. Among Schneider's papers, owned by the University of California, San Diego, where he held an appointment at the time of his accidental death in Paris on 5 May 1984 (while his production of *Victoria Station*, *One for the Road*, and *A Kind of Alaska* was still in production in New York), one finds listed programs and promptbooks (some of them autographed by Pinter) and a folder of correspondence between Schneider and Pinter ("The Register of Alan Schneider Papers: 1937–2001," <http://orpheus.ucsd.edu/speccoll/testing/html/mss0103a.html>). Another Schneider manuscript collection not mentioned by Baker and Ross is the "Alan Schneider Papers, 1923-1984" (T-Mss 1985-002) on deposit in the Billy Rose Theatre Division at the New York Public Library (68-page "Guide" accessible at <http://www.nypl.org/research/manuscripts/the/theschne.xml>). It contains such materials as programs, correspondence, and bound scripts relating to Schneider's productions of *The Dumb Waiter* and *The Collection*, a 1962 double bill (18), and *Pieces of Eight*, which included Pinter's sketch "The Black and White" (33, 38, 40, 54), and "Of particular note are scripts for *The Homecoming* (ca. 1964) [Signed and inscribed by Mr. Schneider: 'Original version sent to me by HP in response to my wanting to option it'] and *Landscape* (ca. 1968) [Bound signed 'from HP' and 'Alan Schneider' both by Mr. Schneider] by Harold Pinter" with Schneider's handwritten explanatory notes (47-48).

Although Harold Pinter is widely regarded as an "international" playwright, and although his website emphasizes that by listing foreign productions of his plays in its periodically-updated "Calendar" section, Baker and Ross state in their "Introduction":

> Generally, we have excluded translations into languages other than English from the body of the bibliography, although, where known

> of, they are noticed in *Appendix One* (designated the letter 'W'). That is, we have not sought to offer a full coverage of them, but have provided it where the data has been readily available. However, items with the texts in English, print-published in non-Anglophone countries, are included in the relevant sections. (viii)

Since Steven H. Gale's 1978 G. K. Hall publication *Harold Pinter: An Annotated Bibliography*, which provides some translations, no subsequent bibliography comprehensively compiles translations of Pinter's plays into other languages. In the headnote to Appendix One, Baker and Ross state that "translations into other languages, where they occur [in this appendix], are provided as the last part of each entry, in a separate temporal sequence" (223). For some works, they have listed such translations; for others, they have not. In that manner, in "*Appendix One*," they list published translations of *The Birthday Party*, *The Caretaker*, and *The Homecoming* and some of Pinter's other dramatic works variously into Czech, Danish, Dutch, French, German, Greek, Italian, Japanese, Polish, Portuguese, Serbo-Croatian, Spanish, Swedish, and Turkish.

There are a few typographical errors relating to published translations of Pinter's works duplicated by Baker and Ross. For example, while the title for *The Caretaker* in Czech translation (apparently adopted from Gale) is correct (*Správce*) (W14:16.), the title for *The Birthday Party* in Czech translation is not "*Norozeniny*" (W6:14.) but rather "*Narozeniny*"; the title for *The Homecoming* in Czech translation is not "*Navrat domu*" (W24:12.) but rather "*Návrat domů*"; and the Czech translator cited is Milan Lukeš not "Lukěs" (W14:16.); such discrepancies alter proper Czech pronunciation. Those errors appear to emanate from Gale's original entry 93 (12), which is not cited directly (Cf. general acknowledgment in the headnote to Appendix One on 223), and they lead to associated errors in "Index II" (312) in this volume by Baker and Ross. This appendix does not list more recent (unpublished) Czech translations of Pinter's plays by František Fröhlich: *Betrayal* (*Zrada*), translated in 1993; *The Homecoming* (translated again as *Návrat domů*), for a Prague revival in 1994; *Moonlight* (*Měsíční svit*), also staged in 1994, in Kříž's Czech première; and *Ashes to Ashes* (*... a v prach se obrátíš*), for its Czech première, and *The Lover* (*Milenec*), both for Kříž's Prague double bill. These translations have been listed in the "Harold Pinter Bibliography" and cited in performance reviews and other articles published in *The Pinter Review* prior to 2000. (A bibliography of Fröhlich's Czech translations is accessible in the database of the *Czech Literary Translators' Guild* (<http://www.obecprekladatelu.cz/F/FrohlichFrantisek.htm>, [up]dated 2 June 2006.)

In 1996 *Mountain Language* (1988) was performed by Kurdish actors in London (Cf. Harold Pinter, "A Pinter Drama in Stoke Newington," Letter to the *Guardian* 9 July 1996, rpt. in *Various Voices* [2005] 213), and it had already been presented in Kurdish translation in 1993 by "the Kurdish [theater group] *Tiyatora Botan* in Cologne to audiences of immigrants from Turkey, where Kurds were long called 'mountain Turks' (*dağli Türkler*), by the government" (Stephen Blum and Amir Hassanpour, "'The Morning of Freedom Rose up': Kurdish Popular Song and the Exigencies of Cultural Survival," *Popular Music* 15.3 [Oct. 1996]: 325). That Kurdish translation of *Mountain Language* (*Zimanê çiya*), by Mehmet Uzun, was published in "Programme books distributed by the *Tiyatora Botan*," according to Blum, who "attended one of the group's performances in Vienna on 1 June 1994" (Blum and Hassanpour 340n1).

In June 1998 I saw the production of *Ashes to Ashes* staged in Dutch translation by Janine Brogt (with English surtitles) by Toneelgroep Amsterdam, performed by Pierre Bokma (Devlin) and Lineke Rijxman (Rebecca), in a double bill with *Buff*, by Gerardjan Rijinders, directed by Titus Muizelaar at Riverside Studios, Hammersmith, a production to which I refer in "Harold Pinter's *Ashes to Ashes*: Political/Personal Echoes of the Holocaust" (*TPR* [2000]: 73-74; 83; cf. "Harold Pinter Bibliography" 203). Notably, prior to the London première of *Ashes to Ashes* at the Royal Court, on 12 September 1996, Pinter had given Toneelgroep permission to stage the play's world première in Brogt's Dutch translation in Amsterdam (Cf. <http://www.toneelgroepamm.nl/default.asp?path=bktnx647>). Yet Baker and Ross omit this Dutch translation of *Ashes to Ashes*.

They do list an unpublished Italian translation (*Ceneri alle Ceneri*), by Alessandra Serra, staged in Italy in 1997 (W60:5.) (Cf. "Harold Pinter Bibliography" 203) and a French translation (no title given), by Eric Kahane, described as "Stage play presented in France, 1998, translated by Eric Kahane, directed by Harold Pinter" (W60:6.). (Kahane translated and adapted *Betrayal* as *Trahisons*; its French premiere was directed in 1982 by Raymond Gérome at the Théâtre Montparnasse in Paris, where I saw it in June 1983, and it was first published as *Trahisons: une pièce d'Harold Pinter* in the journal *L'Avant-Scène* in 1987 and in *Trahisons; Un pour la route [One for the Road]: et autres pièces* [Paris: Gallimard, 1987].)

In the interview about *Harold Pinter: A Bibliographical History* published in his university's press release cited earlier, Baker observes:

> The book on Pinter was much more difficult than the [2002] bibliographical history of George Eliot [on which he also collaborated with Ross].... With Eliot, you had the publishers' records of volumes produced. With Pinter, whose career began in the 1940s, we were dealing with the pre-electronic age. Publishers' archives, especially in this country [the U.S.], have disappeared because of the changes in technology. Ours is the age of tragically disappearing information, often deleted in technological transformations.... There were other challenges as well.... Early in his career, Pinter published plays, poems,

> fiction and non-fiction in small magazines that no longer exist. (Qtd. in "Pinter's Nobel Prize")

Overcoming such daunting challenges defined throughout this volume, yet never appearing to be overwhelmed by them, William Baker and John C. Ross do supreme "justice to Pinter's manifold works," succeeding in accomplishing their stated goals of documenting his "greatness" and making "accessible" much of their own personal "fascination" with his creations (xxv). Harold Pinter's own response attests to their monumental collaborative achievement. Echoing enthusiastically Len's refrain in the stage play *The Dwarfs*—"What a piece of cloth." (*Three Plays* [New York: Grove Press, 1962] 89), he wrote Baker: "What a piece of work! I'm staggered.... Apart from anything else, it gives shape to my own life" (Letter of 23 Aug. 2005, qtd. in "Pinter's Nobel Prize"). *Apart from that*, their work gives shape to our own lives as scholars.

Susan Hollis Merritt
Bluff Point, New York

BIBLIOGRAPHY

Harold Pinter Bibliography: 2002–2004

With a Special Supplement on the 2005 Nobel Prize in Literature, October 2005 – May 2006*

Compiled by Susan Hollis Merritt, Bibliographical Editor

Bibliographical Works

[*N.B.*: The entry for *Harold Pinter: A Bibliographical History*, comp. William Baker and John C. Ross, which went to press in October 2004 for publication in 2005, is listed below in "**Forthcoming Publications, Upcoming Productions, Conferences, and Other Works in Progress**," prior to the "***Special Supplement.***"]

Carpenter, Charles A., comp. *Harold Pinter, 1930- : A Descriptive Chronology of His Plays, Theatrical Career, and Dramatic Theories.* "Harold Pinter" section of *Twelve Modern Dramatists: With Selective Bibliographies.* 23 Apr. 2007. 8 Feb. 2008 <http://bingweb.binghamton.edu/~ccarpen/Pinter.htm>. ["Excerpted with additions and other modifications from Charles A. Carpenter, comp., *Modern British, Irish, and American Drama: A Descriptive Chronology, 1865-1965*"; "Introduction" includes "explanation of principles and limitations"; "A selective bibliography of books by and about the dramatist is appended." A downloadable document file "of about 160 pages, continuously updated" available for purchase from Carpenter (<E-mail: ccarpen@binghamton.edu>), according to on-site instructions; "Periodic updates sent free of additional charge."

—. *Modern British, Irish, and American Drama: A Descriptive Chronology, 1865-1965.* 23 Apr. 2007. 17 Aug. 2007 <http://bingweb.binghamton.edu/~ccarpen/>. (Cited in *Modern Drama* 46. 1 (Spring 2003): back page: "This is the equivalent of a 350-page reference book which traces the development of modern dramatic literature and theory in Great Britain, Ireland, and the United States from year to year and month to month beginning in 1865 and ending in 1965.")

* Listed here are items published or produced from 2002 through 2004, with selected items from 2005 and 2006 relating to Pinter's Nobel Prize in Literature, and some items prior to 2002 included in the *British Humanities Index*, *Film Index International*, *Humanities Index*, *MLA International Bibliography* (online & print), and *The Year's Work in English Studies*, and in databases listed below but not included in the "Harold Pinter Bibliography: 2000-2002" (*The Pinter Review: Collected Essays 2002 and 2003*: 242-300), published in 2004 and abbreviated throughout as "*TPR* (2004)." This list also includes references from a variety of other databases available on *Dialog*, *FindArticles.com*, *FirstSearch*, *Informe*, *InfoTrac*, *Lexis-Nexis*, *Literary Reference Center* (*EBSCO*), *NewsBank*, *Project Muse*, *ProQuest Direct*, and *Uncover*. URLs of other online resources, such as *HaroldPinter.org*, are identified within angle brackets throughout. Some listed items published before 2005 are also based on references selected from Charles A. Carpenter, comp., *Harold Pinter, 1930– : A Descriptive Chronology of His Plays, Theatrical Career, and Dramatic Theories*, and from Carpenter's downloadable document file *The Plays and Filmscripts of Harold Pinter: A Selective, Classified International Bibliography of Publications about Pinter and His Literary Works*, as cited throughout with immense gratitude for his collegial generosity.

—. *The Plays and Filmscripts of Harold Pinter: A Selective, Classified International Bibliography of Publications about Pinter and His Literary Works.* 3 Apr. 2007. Downloaded 4 Apr. 2007. (Courtesy of compiler.) [Downloadable document file available for purchase from Carpenter following on-site instructions described in the section *Harold Pinter* and other sections of *Twelve Modern Dramatists*, as listed above.]

Original Works by Harold Pinter

"American Football." 80 in *101 Poems Against War.* Ed. Matthew Hollis and Paul Keegan. Afterword Andrew Motion. London: Faber and Faber, 2003. [Rev. by Patterson.]

"Aqui esta. (Dos poemas). (Poema)." and "Paris. (Dos poemas). (Poema)." *Nexos: Sociedad Ciencia, Literatura* 25.301 (Jan. 2003): 47-49. [Spanish translations of "It Is Here (to A.)" and "Paris."]

Celebration. New York: Samuel French, Inc., 2002. (Acting ed.)

"Democracy." *Spectator* 15 Mar. 2003. 14 Mar. 2003 <http://www.spectator.co.uk . . .>. [Print version contains poem.]

The Disappeared and Other Poems. Selected by Harold Pinter and Stephen Stuart-Smith. With Images by Tony Bevan. London: Enitharmon P, 2003. 11 Feb. 2008 <http://www.enitharmon.co.uk/books/viewBook.asp?BID=216 >. [The images consist of "12 full-colour plates in the text, reproducing paintings by Tony Bevan made between 1986 and 2002 ... [and] printed by Expression Printers Ltd." Two eds. available: a regular limited ed., of 100 signed and numbered copies; and a deluxe ed., of 75 numbered copies, signed by Harold Pinter and Tony Bevan, each with "a signed and numbered original etching by Tony Bevan—Violet Interior—printed at Hope Sufferance Press on 350gsm Zerkall natural white." Both eds. bound and slipcased by The Fine Bindery in Northamptonshire and printed by Sebastian Carter at the Rampant Lions P, Cambridge.]

"God Bless America." *Guardian* 22 Jan. 2003. *Guardian Online* 20 Mar. 2003 <http://www.guardian.co.uk/0,3858,4588393,00.html>.

"Pinter on War." *Red Pepper: Raising the Political Temperature* Feb. 2004, Culture. 20 Jan. 2008 <http://www.redpepper.org.uk/article554.html>. Archived at <http://www.redpepper.org.uk/rubrique65.html>. [Inc. "Weather Forecast," "Democracy," "The Bombs," and "God Bless America."]

Press Conference. London: Faber and Faber, 2002.

"Real Lives: Cancer Cells." *Guardian* 14 Mar. 2002, sec. G: 5. Rpt. in *Guardian Online* 14 Mar. 2002). 23 Jan. 2008 <http://books.guardian.co.uk/departments/poetry/story/0,,666973,00.html>. [Updated URL (previously listed in *TPR* (2004): 242.]

"Sorry About This." *Areté: The Arts Tri-Quart.: Fiction Poetry Reportage Reviews* 1 (Winter 1999): *Poetry Reportage Review* 1 (Winter 1999): 18. (Special thanks for assistance to editor Craig Raine.) [Retroactive entry.]

"The Special Relationship" (Aug. 2004). *Guardian* 9 Sept. 2004, G2: 4. *HaroldPinter.Org* 12 Oct. 2007 <http://www.haroldpinter.org/home/thespecialrelationship.html>.

"Three Scenes from *Lolita.*" *Areté: The Arts Tri-Quart. Fiction Poetry Reportage Reviews* 5 (Spring/Summer 2001): 5-16. (Special thanks for assistance to editor Craig Raine. [Retroactive entry.]

War. London: Faber and Faber, 2003. (Courtesy of author.)

Related Reviews

Armstrong, Robert. "Paperbacks: Granta Offers Outsiders' Views of America." *Star Tribune* (Minneapolis, MN) 12 May 2002, Entertainment: 15F. [Rev. of *Granta 77: What We Think of America* (Spring 2002) and *Perpetual War for Perpetual Peace: How We Got to Be So Hated*, by Gore Vidal.]

Case, Brian. "'Granta 77: What We Think of America' Edited by Ian Jack: Book Reviews." *Time Out* (London) 3 Apr. 2002: 52. (Cf. *TPR* [2004]:242.)

Chrisafis, Angelique, and Imogen Tilden. "Pinter Blasts 'Nazi America' and 'deluded idiot' Blair." *Guardian* 11 June 2003, Guardian Home Pages: 9. 28 Sept. 2007 <http://www.guardian.co.uk/arts/news/story/0,11711,975050,00.html>. (Cited also in Knowles, "Harold Pinter 2002-2004," *TPR* [2004]: 233.)

Finlayson, Iain. "Non-Fiction Shorts." London *Times* 27 Mar. 2002, Features. [Rev. of *What We Think of America*, ed. Ian Jack, *Granta* 77 (London: Granta, 2002).]

Gardner, M. C. "Harold Pinter's *War.*" *Another America Jour.* Lightning Source, Inc. 2003. 18 Sept. 2007 <http://www.anotheramerica.org/harold_pinter's_war.htm>.

"Les Livres – Le Scenario Proust, A la recherche du temps perdu de Harold Pinter; Zapata, recit et Viva Zapata, scenario; Un artiste engagé de John Steinbeck." *Positif* no. 516 [2004]: 102[-3].

Maddocks, Fiona. "Pinter's War Against Bush: Harold Pinter Has Beaten Cancer[,] Now He's Battling 'the nightmare of US belligerence'." London *Evening Standard* 5 June 2003: 43. [Cited also in Knowles, "Harold Pinter 2002-2004" 233.]

Malcolm, Noel. "Stanzas and Sound-bites: Noel Malcolm Compares the Poetry of Harold Pinter with the Poeticism of Donald Rumsfeld." Rev. of *War*, by Harold Pinter. London *Sunday Telegraph* 6 July 2003: 11. (Cited in Knowles, "Harold Pinter 2002-2004," *TPR* [2004]: 234.)

"No War on Iraq, British Artists Urge Blair in Letter." *Agence France Presse* 18 Sept. 2002, International News. ["Signatories included playwright Harold Pinter. . . ."]

Notebook: ... A Slight Ache, or Beyond Idiocy." *New Republic* 15 Apr. 2002: 8. [Brief rev. of Pinter's contribution to *What We Think of America*.]

Patterson, Christina. "The Threat of War: Literature: Anthology of Peace Poetry Rushed Out." London *Independent* 19 Feb. 2003. Rpt. in *FindArticles.com* 11 Feb. 2008 <http://findarticles.com/p/articles/mi_qn4158/is_20030219/ai_n12675565>.

Report on "War." *Guardian* 11 June 2003: 9. (Cited in Knowles, "Harold Pinter 2002-2004," *TPR* [2004]: 223.) [On "Pinter's speech at the National Theatre."]

"RUSHES – Harold Pinter Screenplays; Chris Evans Returns; Locarno and Karlovy Vary Festivals; Mr Busy." *Sight and Sound* (London) 12.10 (2002): 4[-11]. (8 pages.)

Wetzsteon, Rachel. "Lyric Gestures." *American Theatre* 20.2 (Feb. 2003): 60-67. *Literary Reference Center*. 24 Aug. 2006. (8 pages.) [Inc. rev. of *Various Voices: Prose, Poetry, Politics*, by Harold Pinter (New York: Grove P, 2001).]

Unpublished Screenplays by Harold Pinter

"Sleuth." [For a film to be directed by Kenneth Branagh and starring Michael Caine and Jude Law. Final revised draft completed in 2005 and filming completed in 2007 for wide release in fall 2007, as listed below in "**Forthcoming ....**"]

Essays, Speeches, and Correspondence by Harold Pinter

Birnberg, Ben, Bruce Kent, Yael Lotan, Harold Pinter, Andrew Wilski, and Susannah York. "Comment & Analysis: Letter: Time to Free Vanunu." *Guardian* 29 Oct. 2002, Guardian Leader Pages: 17. [Letter from members of the Campaign to Free Vanunu.]

"Introduction" to "The Kurdish Human Rights Project 10th Anniversary Lecture given by Noam Chomsky at St Paul's Cathedral on 9th December 2002." 21 Dec. 2002 <http://www.haroldpinter.org/politics/introtochomskyspeech.html>.

"Letter from Harold Pinter to His Friend, Mick Goldstein, regarding *Waiting for Godot*." "Friday August 1955 from Portstewart, County Londonderry." *Pinter Rev.* (2004): 5-6.

Letter to President George W. Bush. 2 in "While We Have Your Attention Mr. President. . . : It's Not Often That We Get the Chance to Speak Directly to the Most Powerful Man in the World. So As George Bush Lands in Britain for His First State Visit, We Asked 60 Brits and Americans to Make the Most of It." *Guardian* 18 Nov. 2003, G2: 2-17. 1 Nov. 2007 <http://books.guardian.co.uk/departments/politicsphilosophyandsociety/story/0,,1087685,00.html>. In four parts. Page 1 of part one (8 pages). ["Dear President Bush, I'm sure you'll be having a nice little tea party with your fellow war criminal, Tony Blair. Please wash the cucumber sandwiches down with a glass of blood, with my compliments. Harold Pinter Playwright."]

"Letters from Harold Pinter to Henry Miller." 18 Oct. 1949; 20 Jan. 1950. *Pinter Rev.* (2004): 1-4.

Mahon, Alice, MP Tony Benn, Jeremy Corbyn, MP Tam Dalyell, MP Carol Naughton, Harold Pinter, Mohamed Sawalha. "Comment & Analysis: Letter: Hard Choices about War." *Guardian* 12 Nov. 2002, Guardian Leader Pages: 21.

"On Prisons in the United States: Extract from a Speech Delivered to the Confederation of Analytical Psychologists, London, 25 June 1999." 67-68 in *Captive Audience: Prison and Captivity in Contemporary Theater*. Part II. Ed. Thomas Fahy and Kimball King. New York and London: Routledge, 2003.

Pinter, Harold, and Arnold Wesker. "In the Fray: War's the Thing: Playwrights Argue Over Iraq." *Wall Street Jour.* 4 Mar. 2003, Leisure & Arts: D8, col. 1. [See also "War on Iraq: Pinter v Wesker," as listed below.]

"Speech at Hyde Park [F]ebruary 15 2003." *HaroldPinter.org*. 22 Feb. 2003. <http://www.haroldpinter.org/home/hydeparkspeech.html>.

"'The US and UK don't care about Iraqis—they've been killing them for years'." Pinter's response featured in "What Would You Do? You Don't Want War. But How Do We Stop Saddam Doing This Again? In Recent Weeks, It Has Become the Hawks Favourite Reposte to Mounting Anti-War Sentiment. But Should Critics of Military Action Have to Answer It? And, If So, Can They Offer Any Real Alternative? We Asked 30 High-Profile Opponents of the War to Tackle the Question." *Guardian* 27 Feb. 2003, Guardian Features Pages: 2. "Special Report: The Anti-War Movement." 11 Feb. 2008 <http://www.guardian.co.uk/antiwar/story/0,,903863,00.html>. ["'What should we do? The question should be: 'What have we done?'" Other responses in this online version are by Julian Barnes, Mohamed Heikal, Noam Chomsky, Margaret Drabble, JG Ballard, Michael Atiyah, Woody Harrelson, Ken Livingstone, and Terry Eagleton.]

"Waiting for *Waiting for Godot*: An Unpublished Letter." *Areté: The Arts Tri-Quart.: Fiction Poetry Reportage Reviews* 14 (Spring/Summer 2004): 88-90. (Special thanks for assistance to Editor Craig Raine.)

"War on Iraq: Pinter v Wesker." *BBC News* 24 Feb. 2003. 7 Mar. 2003 <http://news.bbc.co.uk/1/hi/world/middle_east/2793739.stm>. [Announcement of program; transcript of remarks by Pinter and Arnold Wesker. "All this week, the BBC World Service's World Today programme is bringing the views of various people on the case for war with Iraq. Here, playwrights Harold Pinter and Arnold Wesker present contrasting opinions." See also Pinter and Wesker, "In the Fray," as listed above in **"Essays, Speeches ...."**]

Interviews with Harold Pinter

Pinter, Harold. Interview. Broadcast on *Today*. BBC 4. 11 June 2003. (Cited also in Knowles, "Harold Pinter 2002-2004," *TPR* [2004]: 234.) 29 Sept. 2007 <http://www.bbc.co.uk/radio4/today/listenagain/zwednesday_20030611.shtml>. ["Harold Pinter on his call for Tony Blair to step down over Iraq."]

—, and Peter Florence. "Conversation" with author. Orange Word ser., The British Library, London. 11 Mar. 2004. [See account by Toby Moore, as listed below in **"Biographical Profiles ...."**]

—, and Ronald Harwood. "Old Times." *RLS* [Royal Society of Literature] *2003* (Feb. 2003): 6-7. [Full published version of conversation recorded in Pinter's West London study.] Listed at <http://www.rslit.org/publications.htm#2003>. Excerpted in "When Harold Met Ronald: Harold Pinter and Ronald Harwood Have Known Each Other, As Actors and Playwrights, for 50 Years. Here They Discuss Celebrity Casting, Musicals at the National Theatre, and the Critics." London *Independent* 6 Feb. 2003, Features: 13. Rpt. in *FindArticles.com* 8 Feb. 2008 <http://findarticles.com/p/articles/mi_qn4158/is_20030206/ai_n12674933>. Brief excerpt in "Quote of the Month." *Theatre Record* 23 (2003): 3, col. 2.

Stanford, Peter. "Interview: Harold Pinter: Between the Lines: Harold Pinter Can Tell You What He Thinks of Blair ('deluded') and [the US ('stark raving mad')]." London *Independent on Sunday* 13 Apr. 2003, Sunday Rev.: 8-9. (Cited also in Knowles, "Harold Pinter 2002-2004," *TPR* [2004]: 232.)

Taylor, Kate. "Fighting Words: Harold Pinter Has Spent a Lifetime Charting the Abuse of Power–Which Hasn't Always Endeared Britain's Greatest Living Playwright to the Establishment at Home." Toronto *Globe and Mail* 13 Oct. 2001, Weekend Rev.: R3. [Retroactive entry.]

Biographical Profiles, Letters, and Features about Harold Pinter

Allen, Richard. "UK News: Pinter Leads Comics' Attack on Iraq Conflict." London *Evening Standard* 24 Feb. 2003. *No War On Iraq Liaison* 11 Mar. 2003 <http://www.no-war-on-iraq.freeserve.co.uk/uknews025.html>.

"Artists Speak Out on Iraq." *St. John's Telegram* 21 Sept. 2002, Arts & Entertainment: E16. ["Playwright Harold Pinter, actress Jemma Redgrave and filmmaker Ken Loach were among 100 artists who petitioned British Prime Minister Tony Blair to pull back from war with Iraq."]

Associated Press (Londres). "Harold Pinter a un cancer." *Cyberpress.ca* 1 Feb. 2002. 7 Feb. 2002 <http://www.cyberspace.ca>. [French-Canadian news.]

Billen, Andrew. "Television: Small Rooms Are Perfect: A Tribute to Harold Pinter on

BBC2." *New Statesman* 4 Nov. 2002: 49.

Billington, Michael. "Look Back in Hackney." *Guardian* 16 Apr. 2004, G2: 14-15. (Cited in Knowles, "Harold Pinter 2002-2004," *TPR* [2004]: 232.) 29 Sept. 2007 <http://arts.guardian.co.uk/critic/feature/0,,937737,00.html>. [Feature relating to Kerry Lee Crabbe's adaptation *The Dwarfs* (Tricycle Theatre), as cited below in **"Theatre Performances of Plays by Pinter**."]

Bowley, Martin. "Letter: Theatres Lost Its Roots." *Guardian* 21 Feb. 2002, Guardian Leader Pages: 19.

Braithwaite, Tom. "The Core: Arts: Fancy a Pinter?" *Warwick Boar* 11 Mar. 2002 [24.18] (Spring 2002). ["The best playwright of his generation? Maybe. Harold Pinter's skill and artistic flair have made him one of Britain's biggest players in the thespian world. Tom Braithwaite looks at the hardest working man in the business."]

"Briefly: Pinter Ill." *USA Today* 4 Feb. 2002, Life: 2D. (Final Ed.)

"British Press Report Says Harold Pinter Has Cancer." *Deutsche Presse-Agentur* 1 Feb. 2002, Miscellaneous, 12:19 Central European Time.

Brooks, Richard. "Harold Pinter." London *Sunday Times* 3 Feb. 2002, Features. [Concerns Pinter's having written "a new sketch ... called Press Conference."]

Brown, David. "Harold Pinter Is Treated for Throat Cancer." London *Times* 1 Feb. 2002, Home News.

Campling, Chris. "Radio Choice: Classical Serial–New Grub Street." London *Times* 7 Sept. 2002, Feature; Play: 41. [Pinter as narrator of *New Grub Street*, by George Gissing, broadcast on Radio 4.]

Chancellor, Alexander. "Footnote." London *Daily Telegraph* 23 Jan. 2003: 29.

Charter, David. "Blair Is a Hypocrite, Says Pinter." London *Times* 22 Jan. 2003, Home News: 4.

Coleman, Mark. "Celebrities Take Sides Over War on Saddam." *Scotsman* 28 Sept. 2002: 7.

"Court Circular." London *Times* 7 Nov. 2002, Features: 45. ["Mr Harold Pinter was received by The Queen when Her Majesty invested him with the Insignia of a member of the Order of Companions of Honour."]

"Curmudgeon of Honour." London *Daily Telegraph* 29 Aug. 2002: 25. [Concerns Pinter's appearance at the Edinburgh International Book Festival on 25 Aug. 2002.]

Ellis, Samantha. "Theatre: Curtain Up: No 4: The Birthday Party, Pinter's First Major Play, a Spectacular Flop When It Opened in London in 1958." *Guardian* 2 Apr. 2003, Guardian Features Pages: 11.

Evans, Martin. "Pinter Has Cancer." *Press Association* 1 Feb. 2002, Home News.

Ezard, John. "Accolade for Pinter at Anniversary Awards." *Guardian* 14 Dec. 2004: 6.

—. "Pinter Awarded Wilfred Owen Prize for Poetry Opposing Iraq Conflict." *Guardian* 4 Aug. 2004: 9.

"Fast News: ... Cancer Diagnosis." *Courier Mail* 2 Feb. 2002, World: 20.

Flintoff, John-Paul. "Rebel without a Pause." London *Financial Times* 15 Feb. 2003: 1. (Saturday London Ed.) ["Harold Pinter doesn't write many plays these days but, as John-Paul Flintoff discovers, his appetite for agitating those in power remains."]

Gibbons, Fiachra. "Pinter Back on Stage Despite Cancer Diagnosis." *Guardian* 2 Feb. 2002, Guardian Home Pages: 8.

Gilbert, Jenny, with portrait by Richard Ansett. "How We Met: Kathy Lette and John Mortimer." London *Independent on Sunday* 3 Nov. 2002, Features: 5, 6. [Mortimer mentions how he and Kathy Lette first met "at a meeting of the 20th of June Group," a group of "left-wing, pro-Labour writers" which he formed with Pinter and others.]

Ginsburg, David R. "Letters: Pinter Was There First." *Los Angeles Times* 14 Apr. 2002, Sunday Calendar (Calendar Desk), Part 6: 87. [Corrects Stephen Farber's reference to "writer-director Christopher Nolan's ... overlapping flashbacks that kept pushing backward in time" as "something novel" (in "The Writing Was on the Wall in the '60s" [7 Apr. 2002]) by pointing out Pinter's use of "exactly the same device ... in exquisite service of the drama" in his play *Betrayal*.]

"Harold Pinter." In Vol. 1, Part 1 of *Jewish Writers of the Twentieth Century*. Ed. Sorrel Kerbel. New York and London: Fitzroy Dearborn (An Imprint of Taylor & Francis Books, Inc.), 2003. (This ed. published in the Taylor & Francis e-Library, 2006). <http://www.eBookstore.tandf.co.uk>.

"Harold Pinter Has Cancer." Glasgow *Herald* 2 Feb. 2002: 5.

"Harold Pinter 'Treated for Cancer'." London *Independent* 1 Feb. 2002, News: 6.

Higgins, Charlotte. "Pinter's Poetry? Anyone Can Do It." *Guardian* 30 Oct. 2004: 1. [Previews annual T.S. Eliot lecture, by Don Paterson.] (See Paul and reply by Swift.)

Hill, Claire. "Think Again About Iraq, Blair Warned." *Western Mail* 27 Aug. 2002. [Concerns Pinter's remarks at the Edinburgh International Book Festival on 25 Aug. 2002.]

James, Canon Eric. "Letters – Archbishop Rivals Pinter." *New Statesman* 24 June 2002.

Kelbie, Paul. "Pinter Back in the Spotlight at Edinburgh Book Festival." London *Independent* 13 June 2002, News: 9.

Kerevan, George. "What an Odd Coalition the Peace Party Is." *Scotsman* 15 Feb. 2003: 1.

King, Robert L. "News Plays and a Modern Master." *North American Rev.* 287.2 (Mar.-Apr. 2002): 45 +. (6 pages.) [Feature focusing in part on Pinter's performance in *One for the Road* in 2001 and the Royal Court's concurrent prods. of *Mountain Language* and *Ashes to Ashes*.]

Kirby, Terry. "Sidelined in the US, the Left's Greatest Thinker Finds Warm Welcome in Britain." London *Independent* 7 Dec. 2002, News: 8. [Feature on lecture by Noam Chomsky at St. Paul's Cathedral, London, 8 Dec. 2002, to be "given the full star treatment–introductions by one of Britain's foremost intellectual dissidents, playwright Harold Pinter, and prominent civil rights barrister Michael Mansfield, QC." The event, which "sold out rapidly" to "2,000 people," marks "the 10th anniversary of the Kurdish Human Rights Project, a charity which supports Kurds in Iraq."]

—. "The Threat of War: Doves on the Warpath: A Million Ordinary Britons Prepare to Demonstrate for Peace: The London March." London *Independent* 13 Feb. 2003, News: 3.

Kirkup, James. "Obituary: Bernard Fresson: Popular French Actor Hampered by His Assets." London *Independent* 23 Nov. 2002, First Ed.: Obituaries: 24.

Leitch, Luke. "Pinter Says His Battle Against Cancer Was Like 'dark dream'." London *Evening Standard* 28 Aug. 2002: 17. [At the Edinburgh International Book Festival on 25 Aug. 2002.]

Levy, Geoffrey, and Gordon Rayner. "Revealed: The Haunting Story behind Harold Pinter's Confession This Week That He Has Not Seen His Only Son for 11 Years." London *Daily Mail* 10 July 2004: 16.

Lister, David. "Media: The Fight for Hearts and Minds: Their Different Stances on War against Iraq Have Started a Battle of [Circulation and Ideas in the Sunday Newspaper Market]." London *Independent* 4 Mar. 2003, Features: 12. [Concerns the "head-to-head confrontation" between the anti-War Independent on Sunday and the pro-War Observer, "not just causing some big name defectors from the latter's readership, including a number of anti-war big names such as Harold Pinter, but creating a new battle of both circulation and ideas in the (Sunday newspaper) market."]

"A Little Tension Goes a Long Way: Answer the Questions! Indira Varma: Learning the Art of Chain-Smoking for Her New Role." *Independent on Sunday* 24 Nov. 2002, Features: 7. [Interview.]

Livingstone, Ken. "Threat of War: Stars Turn Up Heat at Park Rally." *Guardian* 17 Feb. 2003, Guardian Home Pages: 4. [Inc. quotation of Pinter's words.]

Lorenzo, Ronald. "Letter: Axis of Good." *Guardian* 14 Jan. 2003.

Louie, Rebecca, Suzanne Rozdeba, Dakota Smith, and Ben Widdicombe. "Casey on Call for Ben-Jen Nuptials? ... Pinter on the World Stage." *Daily News* (New York, NY) Dec. 2002, Gossip: 28. [Reports on Pinter's 2002 Turin speech.]

McLean, Terry. "Surf City: Weird Harold, Harold Pinter, Harold Lloyd, Harold Budd, Harold Park." Melbourne *Herald Sun* 9 Dec. 2002, Features: 65. [Websites pertaining to "harold."]

Mead, Walter Russell. "The United States: Granta 77: What We Think of America, edited Ian Jack. London: Granta Books, 2002, 257 pp. 12.95 (paper)." In "Recent Books [on International Relations]." *Foreign Affairs* Sept.-Oct. 2002, Books: 195.

Millar, Frank. "Blair Defines Peace Marchers with Call for Regime Change." *Irish Times* 17 Feb. 2003, World News; Iraq Crisis: 10. (City Ed.) ["To deafening cheers, playwright Harold Pinter claimed that American barbarism would 'destroy the world' and described the US as a country 'run by a bunch of criminals ... with Tony Blair as a hired Christian thug.'"]

Miller, Phil. "Pinter Heads Line-Up for Book Festival: Playwright to Make His First Public Appearance in Edinburgh following Treatment for Throat Cancer." Glasgow *Herald* 13 June 2002: 4.

Moore, Toby. "I Don't Do Happy: Harold Pinter Relishes the Ugly Side of Life, But That Doesn't Mean He Can't Raise a Smile." London *Financial Times* 13 Mar. 2004, FT Weekend Mag. – The Performance: 10. 28 Aug. 2007 <http://www.ft.com> (Searchable archive). [Account of interview with Harold Pinter by Peter Florence, Hay Festival director, as "part of the Orange Word series of 'conversations' with screenwriters" at the British Library.]

"My Election: Harold Pinter." *Guardian Unlimited* 14 May 2001. 20 Jan. 2003 <http://politics.guardian.co.uk/redbox/comment/0,9408,490527,00.html>. [Retroactive entry.]

"Names in the News: Cancer Strikes." *Philadelphia Inquirer* 2 Feb. 2002, Domestic News.

O'Neill, Phelim. "The Guide: Out on Video and DVD: Buy This!" *Guardian* 5 Oct. 2002, The Guide: 20. [DVD of *Straw Dogs*, dir. Sam Peckinpah, includes "letters between Peckinpah and Harold Pinter–who turned down a scripting job saying, 'I detest it with unqualified detestation.'"]

Paul, Adrian. "Comment & Analysis: Letters: Poets at War over Pinter and Politics: [2]. *Guardian* 2 Nov. 2004: 25. (See Higgins and Swift.)

Peachey, Paul. "Theatreland Elite Voices Chorus of Dissent As War Draws Closer." London *Independent* 15 Feb. 2003. 6 Mar. 2003 <http://news.independent.co.uk/low_res/story.jsp?story=378420&host=3&dir=65>. ["Figures from the artistic community featured prominently in two full-page advertisements listing hundreds of high-profile personalities against the war over the past two days (13 and 14 Feb. 2003). They include the musicians Craig David, Damon Albarn and Jarvis Cocker; the writers Nick Hornby, Harold Pinter and David Hare; the filmmakers Mike Leigh and Terry Gilliam; the artists Sam Taylor-Wood and Damien Hirst and the actors Dustin Hoffman and Sinead Cusack. ... Other anti-war events include Poets Against the War at the Bloomsbury Theatre in London, where all 550 tickets were sold out before last night's performance."]

Peschek, David. "Pop: Manic street Preachers: NEC, Birmingham +++ - -." *Guardian* 5 Dec. 2002, Guardian Leader Pages: 22. [Rev. of concert by Manic Street Preachers ("The Manics"); "Faster (a hit single that references 'Plath and Pinter') remains remarkable."]

"Pinter Honour." London *Times* 7 Nov. 2002, Home News: 4. [Companion of Honour conferred on Pinter for his services to literature by Queen Elizabeth II at Buckingham Palace on 6 Nov. 2002.]

"Pinter Honoured by the Queen." *Montreal Gazette* 9 Nov. 2002, Entertainment; In Brief: D14.

"Pinter Marks the End of an Era." *BBC Bristol* 13 Jan. 2003. 18 Sept. 2007 <http://www.bbc.co.uk/bristol/content/goingout/2003/01/09/pinter.shtml>.

"Pinter's Dramatic Impact." *BBC News* 14 June 2002, Arts. 19 June 2002 <http://news.bbc.co.uk/2/hi/entertainment/2045367.stm>.

Plain Dealer. "People Watch: ... Pinter Honored." Cleveland *Plain Dealer* 9 Nov. 2002, Arts & Life: E2.

"Playwright Harold Pinter Has Throat Cancer: Paper." *Agence France Presse* 1 Feb. 2002, International News.

"Playwright Harold Pinter Treated for Cancer." *AP Worldstream* 1 Feb. 2002, International News. (Distribution: Europe; Britain; Scandinavia; Middle East; Africa; India; Asia; England.)

"Playwright Harold Pinter Treated for Cancer." *Associated Press* 1 Feb. 2002, International News, BC cycle.

"Playwright Pinter Treated for Cancer." *AP Online* 1 Feb. 2002, International News.

Randall, David, Severin Carrell, Andrew Johnson, and Jonathan Thompson. "Millions Britons Turn Out to Vote with Their Feet: UK Marches." London *Independent on Sunday* 16 Feb. 2003, News: 3.

Reynolds, Nigel. "Pinter Writes Poem on His Cancer Fight." London *Daily Telegraph* 15 Mar. 2002: 5. ["Cancer Cells."]

Reynolds, Nigel. "Pinter Determined to Keep Working Despite Cancer." London *Daily Telegraph* 1 Feb. 2002: 3.

Robinson, David. "Cancer Battle Author Determined to Attend Event." *Scotsman* 13 June 2002: 3. [Edinburgh Book Festival.]

—. "Pinter and Bennett Book In for Literary Feast." *Scotsman* 13 June 2002: 3. [Edinburgh Book Festival.]

Rosen, Steven. "Pinter's Brilliance Lights Screen, Too: Playwright Began Film Run in '60s." *Denver Post* 26 Apr. 2002, Weekend: F8. [Feature article about Pinter on occasion of Denver Center Theatre Company prod. of *Betrayal*.]

"Roundup: Doyen of British Playwrights Harold Pinter Has Cancer." *Deutsche Press-Agentur* 1 Feb. 2002, Miscellaneous, 14:36 Central European Time.

"Royal Honour for Pinter." London *Daily Telegraph* 7 Nov. 2002: 17. [Companion of Honour.]

Rush, George, and Joanna Molloy. "Chance of a Lifetime for O'Toole? ... Starry, Starry Fight." *Daily News* (New York, NY) 18 Feb. 2003, Gossip: 18.

Schlesinger, Michael. "Letters: 'Merrily' Got There First." *Los Angeles Times* 21 Apr. 2002, Sunday Calendar (Calendar Desk), Part 6: 83. [Response to article on *Memento*, by David R. Ginsburg, who "suggests that Harold Pinter originated the story-told-backward gimmick in his 1978 play 'Betrayal' (Letters, April 14).... No less than George S. Kauman and Moss Hart used the device earlier in their bittersweet romance 'Merrily We Roll Along,' which opened on Broadway in the fall of 1934, and was recently musicalized by the equally distinguished Stephen Sondheim and George Furth."]

Swift, Todd. "Comment & Analysis: Letters: Poets At War Over Pinter and Politics." *Guardian* 2 Nov. 2004: 25. (Reply to Higgins.)

Syal, Rajeev, Andrew Alderson, and Catherine Milner. "One Million March Against War: There Were Politicians, Playwrights, Lending Names from Showbusiness–and Hundreds of Thousands of Ordinary Britons, All Intent On Delivering a Stark Message to Tony Blair." London *Sunday Telegraph* 16 Feb. 2003: 2.

Szalwinska, Max. "G2: Edinburgh: Harold Pinter Is Famous: Ask the Audience." *Guardian* 9 Aug. 2004: 8.

Walker, Tim. "Arnold vs Harold." London *Sunday Telegraph* 16 Feb. 2003.

Wesker, Arnold. "Opinion & Letters: Letters: Threat of War: Tyrants Win." *Guardian* 15 Feb. 2003, Guardian Leader Pages: 23.

Worrington, Margaret. Letter to the Editor. Sydney *Sunday Telegraph* 29 Sept. 2002, Features: 100. [Questions validity of Pinter's imagery in "Cancer Cells."]

Other Pertinent News Reports and Features

Aaronovitch, David. "G2: Saddam Has the Last Word." *Guardian* 27 July 2004: 5. ["Saddam's poem on Bush."]

Adilman, Sid. "Canadian Content Rules Fuzzy." Toronto *Star* 27 Apr. 2002, Arts:

J15. [Rejection by the Canadian Television Fund of Rhombus Media, an award-winning specialist in internationally selling arts specials, for a program based on Harold Pinter's play *Celebration*, which was proposed by director Patricia Rozema, "who wanted to direct a TV version ... with Pinter playing all the roles. Rhombus Media enthusiastically offered to be the producer. All agreed. Bravo! And CBC got TV rights for Canada. A British co-production with BBC was arranged. ... But though the rules of the Canadian Television Fund allow for co-productions with the United Kingdom, it refused to invest on the grounds that Celebration would not be 'visibly Canadian'."]

[Agence France Presse (La Haye, 9 fev.).] "Les défenseurs de Milosevic, un groupe heteroclite (DOSSIER – ENCADRE)." *Agence France Presse*, Information Generales.

"Anniversary Show for Arts." *The Stage* 26 Sept. 2002: 2. [Announces special celebration at the Arts Theatre marking its 75th anniversary.]

"Anti-War March: What the Speakers Said." *Guardian* 15 Feb. 2003. *Guardian Online* 20 Feb. 2003 & 31 Jan. 2008 <http://www.guardian.co.uk/antiwar/story/0,,896437,00.html>. [Inc. excerpts from Harold Pinter's remarks.]

"The Art of Berlusconi: Boulevard." London *Financial Times* 13 Mar. 2002, Observer: 13.

"The Art of War." London *Daily Telegraph* 7 Mar. 2003: 29. ["Harold Pinter, Andrew Motion and other prominent poets" presented "10,000 anti-war poems ... to Downing Street."]

Associated Press. "Karel Reisz, 76: Director Helped Reshape British Cinema." *Boston Globe* 28 Nov. 2002, Obituary: B5.

"Award-winning Play to Get UT [University of Tampa] Reading." *St. Petersburg Times* (Florida) 23 Oct. 2003, City & State: 2B. [*Manifest*, by Brian Silberman, winner of "the first Pinter Review Prize for Drama."]

"Barcelona: London: Theatre." *Financial Times* 5 Feb. 2002, The Arts: 13. (USA Ed. 1.) [Announcement of National Theatre prod. of *No Man's Land*, dir. Harold Pinter, "until March 3."]

"Bailey Acting Up Again." *Department of History Newsletter*, U of Manitoba, Can. 10 Jan. 2003. 7 Feb. 2003 <http://www.umanitoba.ca/faculties/arts/history/news/news-jan10.html>.

Barnes, Anthony. "Van der Valk Actor Dies." *Press Association* 11 Feb. 2002, Home News. [Obituary of actor Barry Foster.]

Barnett, Correlli. "End Britain's relationship with America." London *Daily Telegraph* 12 Dec. 2002, Features: Letter to the Editor: 27.

Barnett, Nick. "Busy with Berkoff." Wellington *Dominion* 4 Apr. 2002, Features, Arts (Arts on Thursday): 17. [Feature about (potent pause) Productions 2002 staging of Pinter's *Old Times*; mentions influence of Pinter on name of this Auckland (New Zealand) theater company, which "grew out of actor Michael Lawrence's long-standing love for Pinter's writing"; its first production was *The Birthday Party* in 1996.]

Barrow, Andrew. "A Peculiarly Outrageous Act to Follow: Once Lovingly Uncleaned, Crammed and Untidy: Quentin Crisp's Chelsea Bedsit Has Been Transformed." London *Daily Telegraph* 9 Nov. 2002: 5. [Feature about the Beaufort Street home of Quentin Crisp; Pinter later acknowledged that his visit to the once "broken-down room" in the summer of 1955 initially inspired his first play, *The Room.*]

"Barry Foster." London *Times* 12 Feb. 2002, Features. [Obituary; died 11 Feb. 2002, at the age of 74.]

Baskin, Ellen. "Movies: A Method to the Madness; Ian Holm Evolves from King Lear to Literary 'Nutter' Joe Gould in Stanley Tucci's New Film." *Los Angeles Times* 9 Apr. 2000, Calendar ("Calendar Desk"): 29. [Interview with Ian Holm. Retroactive entry.]

Bedell, Geraldine. "British Stars Rally to Save Italy's Gay Envoy: Artists' Campaign Earns a Rebuke from Rome As PM Silvio Berlusconi Seeks to Fire His Head of Culture in London." *Observer*, 24 Feb. 2002, Observer News Pages: 9. ["Prominent figures in the British arts" led by Colin Firth and inc. Harold Pinter campaign "to save the job of Dr. Mario Fortunato."]

Bergan, Ronald. "Bernard Fresson: French Actor who Underestimated His Talents on Stage and Screen." *Guardian* 5 Dec. 2002, Guardian Leader Pages: 26. [Obituary of French actor who, "in the 1960s ... played–with Delphine Seyrig–in Harold Pinter's *The Collection* and *The Lover.*"]

"Bernard Spear." London *Times* 23 May 2003, Features: 40. [Obituary.]

"Betrayal by Harold Pinter: Harold Pinter Is One of the World's Greatest Living Playwrights. As the BBC Launches a Pinter Season [*Pinter at the BBC*], the Royal Theatre Puts On His 1978 Play about Adultery." *BBC - Northamptonshire - On Stage - Betrayal, bbc.co.uk* 29 Oct. 2002. 2 Feb. 2008 <http://www.bbc.co.uk/northamptonshire/stage/betrayal.shtml>.

Black, Edward. "Memory Loss Forces [Julie] Christie to Quit Acting." *Scotsman* 22 Apr. 2002: 8.

Brown, Craig. "Kylie Down Under: A Symposium." London *Daily Telegraph* 2 Mar. 2002: 27. [Mentions Pinter in spoof re: celebrity Australian pop singer Kylie Minogue; mock-"symposium" on "widespread claims" that she had "cosmetic surgery on her bottom."]

Brown, Mark. "The Favourite Son." *Scotland on Sunday* 7 Apr. 2002: 7. [Feature about *No Man's Land* (Royal National Theatre, London), dir. Harold Pinter, in Edinburgh.]

"Bryan Pringle." London *Times* 22 May 2002, Features. [Obituary; among many other notable roles, Pringle played Stanley in the Royal Shakespeare Company prod. of *The Birthday Party*, dir. Harold Pinter, at the Aldwych Theatre, London, which opened on 18 June 1964 <http://www.haroldpinter.org/directing/directing_bday.shtml>.]

Bunbury, Stephanie, Neil Jillett, and Steven Carroll. "It's a [Wallace] Shawn Thing: ... A Remembrance of Things Past." *Sunday Age* (Melbourne, Austral.) 4 Nov. 2002, Arts & Entertainment: 103. [Brief notice of Melbourne Arts Festival prod. "performed by VCA (Victorian College of the Arts) students past and present ... directed by Di Trevis with whom Pinter collaborated on the stage version"; prod. previously listed in *TPR* (2004): 269.]

Burton, Laurie, and Nadia Saint. "Drama: Pinter's Coming Home: The Homecoming by Harold Pinter, Moser Theatre, May 6-11 [2003]." **** [of five stars]. *Oxford Student* 1 May 2003 <http://www.oxfordstudent.com/2003-05-01/

ox2/27> (Outdated URL). (Page 1 of 4 pages.) 16 Jan. 2008 <http://www.oxfordstudent.com/tt2003wk1/Drama/drama>. [Archived feature.]

Buruma, Ian. “Real Lives: Why Do Some Europeans Express Such Irrational Rage about America and Israel? It Comes Down to Guilt and Fear.” *Guardian* 2 Apr. 2002, Features: 7. [*What We Think of America*, *Granta* 77, listed in *TPR* (2004): 242.]

Calder, John. “Obituary: Professor Martin Esslin.” *Independent* 27 Feb. 2002, Obituaries: 6.

Calvert, Jonathan, and Robert Winnett. “Stars Turn Out for That Vietnam Experience.” London *Sunday Times* 16 Feb. 2003, Home News: 4.

Cavendish, Dominic. “The King and I: Michael Gambon, Tipped As the New Professor Dumbledore, Has Come from a Working-Class Childhood to Playing Edward VII in the BBC Drama, The Lost Prince.” London *Daily Telegraph* 17 Jan. 2003. *Electronic Telegraph* 6 Feb. 2003 <http://www.arts.telegraph.co.uk>.

—. “Priceless Moments Lost for Ever: Our Theatres Are Brimming with Superb Performances–So Why Aren’t We Preserving More of Them, Asks Dominic Cavendish.” London *Daily Telegraph* 30 Nov. 2002: 7. [“Harold Pinter was so impressed by an NVASP (National Video Archive of Stage Performance [Theatre Museum]) recording of *One for the Road* that he allowed it to be broadcast as part of this month’s BBC retrospective,” *Pinter at the BBC.*]

—. “Top Five Moments of Menace in Pinter.” London *Daily Telegraph* 26 Jan. 2002: 6.

Chancellor, Alexander. “Alexander Chancellor’s Diary.” London *Daily Telegraph* 27 Oct. 2003: 21. [“The hallmark of the past week has been betrayal. It is hard to think of anyone who hasn’t been betrayed or done some betraying, and, in the spirit of the times, the playwright Harold Pinter’s play Betrayal has just opened in London.”]

Chow, Clara. “Cutting Up Two Plays about Murder: The Theatre Practice Will Stage Harold Pinter’s The Dumb Waiter and Jean Genet’s The Maids in One Production.” *Straits Times* (Singapore) 10 Mar. 2003, Life!

Cohen, Nick. “Comment: Without Prejudice: The Left Isn’t Listening: The Stop the War Coalition Is the Greatest Threat to Any Hope for a Democratic Iraq.” London *Observer* 16 Feb. 2003, Observer News Page: 31.

—. “Why It Is Right to Be Anti-American: Conservatives Used to Be the Ones Who Hated the US; the Left Looked To It for Inspiration. All That Has Changed – and Justifiably, Argues Nick Cohen.” *New Statesman* 14 Jan. 2002.

“Colchester: Caretaker’s First Night Cancelled.” *Essex County Standard* 15 Feb. 2002. <http://archive.essexcountystandard.co.uk/2002/2/15/166620.html>.

Conradi, Peter, and Bruce Wallace in London; Joe Lauria in New York; and Anne-Sophie Dumetz in Ottawa. “Millions Say ‘No’ to War: Cities around the World Overrun in Biggest Protest in History.” *Ottawa Citizen* 16 Feb. 2003, News: A1.

Cooper, Neil. “A Saga of Old Family Values: Corin Redgrave Is to Appear in Revivals of The Forsyte Saga and Harold Pinter’s No Man’s Land. He Tells Neil Cooper of His Motivation.” Glasgow *Herald* 5 Apr. 2002: 15. [Interview.]

Cornwall, Jane. “Sam I Am.” Melbourne *Sunday Herald Sun* 29 Sept. 2002, Sunday

Mag.: Z15. [Feature about director Sam Mendes.]

Coughlin, Con. "The Peaceniks Are Winning the War in the Studios: Con Coughlin Licks His Wounds After a Series of Bruising Encounters on Air with the Anti-Americans Brigade." London *Sunday Telegraph* 2 Mar. 2003: 23.

Crawford, Wayne. "Willing to Do Bush Bidding." *Mercury* (Hobart, Austral.) 29 Mar. 2003, In Depth: 25. [Quotes Pinter: "The American administration is now a bloodthirsty wild animal. Bombs are its only vocabulary. Many Americans we know are horrified by the posture of their government but seem to be helpless."]

Crew, Robert. "Soulpepper Hires Stratford Star [William] Hutt." *Toronto Star* 4 Mar. 2003, Entertainment: C5. [As Hirst, opposite Peter Donat (as Spooner), in *No Man's Land*.]

Croft, Andy. "Pure Doggerel." *New Statesman* 6 Dec. 2004: 42-43.

Davies, Hugh. "Enter the New Elizabethans: A Poet and a Punk Rocker Feature on the 50-Year Roll of Honour. Hugh Davies Reports." London *Daily Telegraph* 31 Jan. 2002: 6.

Dening, Penelope. "Giant Applause for Pint-sized Pinter Actor." *Irish Times* 29 Sept. 2001, Weekend: 72. (City Ed.) 22 Feb. 2008 <http://www.ireland.com/newspaper/weekend/2001/0929/01092900223.html> (Subscription required for full access). [In Holm in *The Homecoming* (Comedy Theatre).]

"Director's Weekend Shock." *Australian* 18 Dec. 2002, Features: 9. [Obituary of Karel Reisz.]

Dore, Edna. "Alexander Dore: Obituaries." *The Stage* 20 June 2002: 13.

"Double Standard in Assessing Honours." *The Stage* 20 June 2002: 8.

Downs, Gigi. "A Chance to Catch a Pinter Classic." *San Diego Union-Tribune* 14 Mar. 2002, Entertainment, Night & Day: 29. [Feature announcing *The Caretaker* (Renaissance Theatre Company).]

Dudek, Duane. "Acting the Manic 'Joe Gould' Stretched Holm Beyond His Shakespearean Roots." *Milwaukee Jour. Sentinel* 25 Apr. 2000, Cue: 1E. [Feature about Ian Holm.]

Edwardes, Jane. "Stage d'Or: Face to Face: Penelope Wilton." *Time Out* (London) 18 Sept. 2002: 24-25. [Interview.]

"Elizabeth Countess of Longford." London *Times* 13 Feb. 2003, Features: 41. [Lists attendees at Requiem Mass held in Westminster Cathedral on 12 Feb. 2003.]

Elkes, Neil. "Stage Is Set for Bright New Talents." *Global News Wire*, *Europe Intelligence Wire*, *Birmingham Post and Mail*, *Evening Mail* 28 June 2002. [The Sir Derek Jacobi Festival of Drama, held at Sutton Coldfield, resulted in overall winner for Pinter's *One for the Road* and "individual awards for director Michelle Gale, 19, of Perry Barr and actor Tom Hadley, 16, of Sutton Coldfield."]

Ellis, Samantha. "No 4: The Birthday Party, London 1958: Pinter's First Major Play, a Spectacular Flop When It First Opened in London in 1958." *Guardian* 2 Apr. 2003. 16 Jan. 2008 <http://arts.guardian.co.uk/curtainup/story/0,,927919,00.html>.

Entertainment Editors & Theater Writers. "Hollywood Slow-Down Gives LA's Fringe Theatre Scene Boost: Film Industry Pros Re-Stage Harold Pinter's 1960 Play, The Dumb Waiter." *Business Wire* 4 Mar. 2002. Rpt. in *FindArticles.com*. 22 Feb. 2008

<http://findarticles.com/p/articles/mi_m0EIN/is_2002_March_4/ai_83525503>.

Evans, Lloyd. "Diary." *Spectator* 2 Feb. 2002: 9. [About Hackney and Hackney Downs school; cites Pinter's encounter with a mother (Alithea Lahr) and her six-year-old child (Chris Lahr), also the son of *New Yorker* critic John Lahr: the same anecdote recounted by Pinter in his acceptance speech for the David Cohen British Literature Prize. (Cf. 56 in John Lahr, "Demolition Man: Harold Pinter and 'The Homecoming,'" *New Yorker* 24 & 31 Dec. 2007, Onward and Upward with the Arts: 54-69.)]

Farish, William S. "End Britain's Relationship with America." London *Daily Telegraph* 12 Dec. 2002, Features: Letter to the Editor: 27.

Fenton, James. "Saturday Review: Poetry: Masterclass: A License for Drama." *Guardian* 7 Dec. 2002, Guardian Saturday Pages: 28. ["In the Last of the Series, James Fenton Discusses the Poet's Role in the Operatic Tradition," citing his "horror of choruses and 'verse speaking'," as "really a horror of Eliot's choruses in Murder in the Cathedral (1935)," in contrast to "Auden's choruses from the same period" ("the best things in his plays") and "Eliot's unfinished Sweeney Agonistes, which actually plays very well, even when performed by amateurs, and which was rightly said to anticipate much of the spirit of Pinter's (prose) drama."]

"Festival Ticket Sales Up 50 Per Cent." *Edinburgh Evening News* 6 July 2002: 11. [Among four other events, Pinter's event is sold out.]

"Film and Theatre Director Who Once Worked at the Gate: Karel Reisz." *Irish Times* 30 Nov. 2002, Obituaries: 18. (City Ed.)

Fleming, John. "New Company Aims to Challenge." *St. Petersburg Times* 25 July 2002, weekend: 27W.

"Former UN Officials Launch Ad Campaign to End Sanctions on Iraq." *Agence France Presse* 20 Mar. 2002, International News. [Among more than 200 names, Harold Pinter a signatory of "full-page advertisement in Wednesday's (20 Mar. 2002) *International Herald Tribune* to highlight [Iraq's] plight: 'No more economic sanctions. The Iraqi people have suffered enough!'"]

Frankel, Glenn. "In Britain, War Concern Grows into Resentment of U.S. Power: Anxiety over Attack on Iraq Moves to Political Mainstream." *Washington Post* 26 Jan. 2003, Sec. A: A14.

Fraser, Antonia. "Diary." *Spectator* 15 Mar. 2003. 14 Mar. 2003 <http://www.spectator.co.uk/the-magazine/the-week/10947/diary.thtml>.

Fray, Peter. "Angry Young Man No More: Review." *The Age* (Melbourne, Austral.) 17 July 2003, A3: 11. [Features review of *Howard Katz* and interview with its playwright, Patrick Marber, whose "playwriting heroes include David Mamet, Tom Stoppard and Harold Pinter. . . ."]

French, Philip. "Review: Screen: A Scholar of Film: Philip French Pays Tribute to the Late Karel Reisz, Whose Writing Was As Inspirational As His Movies." London *Observer* 1 Dec. 2002, Observer Rev. Pages: 10.

Frois, Emmanuele. "CINEMA: Hommage du XXXe Festival du Film de La Rochelle a une comedienne, amoureuse de la vie; Juliette Binoche ou les vertus du bain moussant." *Le Figaro* 26 June 2002, Culture.

Gardner, Elysa, and Susan Wloszczyna. "Christopher Plummer Earns First Robards

Award." *USA Today* 1 Feb. 2002, Life: 1E. (Final Ed.)

"Going Out: Betrayal." London *Daily Telegraph* 25 Oct. 2003: 11. [Brief announcement of *Betrayal* (Duchess Theatre, London), dir. Peter Hall. "Peter Hall directs an outstanding production of Harold Pinter's greatest and most accessible play, a brilliantly observed deeply painful account of an adulterous romance with the twist that the story is told backwards."]

"Going Out, Staying Out." *Scotsman* 14 May 2002: 15. ["Director Guy Hollands and leading Citz designer Kenny Miller work together on this Citizens' Community Company production of Harold Pinter's rarely performed 1960s play in which a young man called Walter returns home to find that his aunts have let his room to a mysterious young woman. This is the fourth annual show from the community company, whose current members include a disc jockey, a welder, a barmaid, a baker and an ultrasound technician; the evening also includes a selection of Pinter's offbeat review sketches."]

Gray, Alison. "So Who Are the New Protesters?" *Scotsman* 17 Feb. 2003: 2.

Green, Blake. "Holm Again: British Actor Has a 'Homecoming' in Pinter's Play." *Newsday* (New York, NY) 19 July 2001, Part II: B3. (All Editions.) [Interview with Ian Holm. Retroactive entry.]

Grice, Elizabeth. "'She shut her eyes and floated away.'" London *Daily Telegraph* 20 Jan. 2003: 15. ["Lady Longford, who died last year, was passionate about history. Her eldest daughter, Lady Antonia Fraser, and granddaughter Flora have found a way to keep her name and passion alive."]

Griffiths, Gwyn. "Radio." *Morning Star* 3 May 2003.

Grossberg, Michael. "Troupe to Open 10th Season with a Pair of Pinters." *Columbus* (OH) *Dispatch* 7 Nov. 2002, Features–Weekender, Stage Notes: 19. (Home Final Ed.)

—. "Women At Play to Celebrate 10th Season with Pair by Pinter." *Columbus* (OH) *Dispatch* 25 May 2005, Features–Accent & Arts; Stage Notes: 4D.

Grove, Lyndon. "Seeing the World through the Eyes of Art." *Nuvo: Reflections of the Good Life* 4.3 (Autumn 2001): 32, 34. [Concerns "World Leaders: A Festival of Creative Genius" at Harbourfront Festival 2001; includes photograph of Harold Pinter and mentions him. Retroactive entry.]

Gussow, Mel. "Uncovering the Humor in Pinter's Pawn-and-Catalyst Caretaker." *New York Times* 8 Nov. 2003: B11, col. 1, Arts & Ideas/Cultural Desk. [Interview with Patrick Stewart, concerning his performance as Davies in *The Caretaker* (Roundabout Theatre Company, American Airlines Theatre, New York).]

Hawtree, Christopher. "Games: Teaser." London *Independent on Sunday* 10 Feb. 2002, Features: 61. [Sports-related quiz involving poem by Pinter.]

Hayward, Anthony. "Bryan Pringle: Obituary." London *Independent* 22 May 2002. Rpt. in *FindArticles.com*. 2 Feb. 2008 <http://findarticles.com/p/articles/mi_qn4158/is_20020524/ai_n12611337/pg_1>.

Heawood, Jonathan. "Review: Books: Sacrifice of the Innocents: In the Forest by Edna O'Brien Weidenfeld and Nicolson pounds 16.99, pp. 217." *Observer* 28 Apr. 2002, Observer Rev. Pages: 17. ["In the Forest has been welcomed by her (O'Brien's) old friend Harold Pinter as a masterpiece while arousing a critical storm in Ireland."]

Horwitz, Jane. "Hearts and Minds and Voices: Potomac Project's Stage Trio." *Washington Post* 5 Aug. 2003, Style: C1. (Final Ed.)

"Hot Seat: Theatre." *Weekend Australian* 13 July 2002, Review-Column-Hot SeatArts: R14. [Announcement of revival of Harold Pinter's *The Caretaker* (Brink Productions, Belvoir Street Theatre); refers erroneously to its director Hannah Macdougall as starring in it; listed below in **"Theater Performances of Plays by Harold Pinter."**]

Hurwitt, Robert. "Prof. Martin Esslin–Scholar of the Theater." *San Francisco Chronicle* 28 Feb. 2002, News, Obituaries: A20.

"Jan Kott." London *Times* 10 Jan. 2002, Features. [Obituary.]

Jury, Louise. "Actor Who Played TV Sleuth Van der Valk Dies at 70." *Independent* 12 Feb. 2002, News: 4. [Obituary of Barry Foster.]

"Karel Reisz: Director Who Spearheaded the Sixties Film Revolution and Later Changed Course to Find a New Raison d'Être in the Theatre." London *Times* 28 Nov. 2002, Features: 44. ["Karel Reisz, film and theatre director, was born in Octava, Czechoslovakia, on July 21, 1926. He died of a blood disorder in London on November 25, 2002, aged 76."]

Kilroy, Ian. "Interview: All Things Come Holm: You Recognise His Face, and You Know He's Been in Lots of Films–But What's His Name Again? Ian Holm, Appearing in Harold Pinter's The Homecoming at the Gate Theatre This Month, Talks to Ian Kilroy about His Life and Career As a Character Actor." *Irish Times* 2 June 2001, City Ed., Weekend: 64.

—. "Theatre: Before and Afterplay: With Pinter, Beckett and Now Friel Productions, Actress Penelope Wilton Has Made Her Mark on Theatre and Film in London and Dublin Over the Past Few Decades." *Irish Times* 2 Mar. 2002, City Ed., Weekend: 53. [Interview-based feature; Kilroy mistakenly refers twice to Wilton as "the thinking man's crumpet," an epithet actually "initially bestowed by humorist Frank Muir" not on Wilton but on Pinter's former lover Joan Bakewell (David Pickering, "Bakewell, Joan: British Broadcast Journalist," *The Museum of Broadcast Communications.* 23 Jan. 2008 <http://www.museum.tv/archives/etv/B/htmlB/bakewelljoa/bakewelljoa.htm>).]

Lewis, John. "Music–Album Reviews: Various Artists; Music." *Time Out* 6 Feb. 2002: 112. ["A wonderful sketch on Armando Iannucci's show," *When Love Speaks* (EMI Classics), "had African villagers raising money for cashstrapped British fringe theatre companies: 'Desperate people like Harold Pinter no longer have the chance to say challenging things about the human condition,' mourned a young Kenyan boy. We must help him'."]

"Listings: Theatre Fringe." *Time Out* 29 May 2002: 171-72. [List includes Pinter's play *The Dumb Waiter*, presented by North London TC; "comic interpretation of the Pinter classic."]

"Londoner's Diary." London *Evening Standard* 28 July 2003. [Announcement of closing down of Harold Pinter's and Antonia Fraser's "favourite Notting Hill restaurant Orsino in Portland Road."]

Lyman, Rick. "Karel Reisz, Director of Film Including 'The French Lieutenant's Woman,' Dies at 76." *New York Times* 28 Nov. 2002, sec. C (The Arts/Cultural Desk): 11, col. 1.

"Martin Esslin." London *Times* 27 Feb. 2002, Features. [Obituary.]

Martin, Mick. "The Guide: Preview Theatre: Betrayal Northampton." *Guardian* 2 Nov. 2002, The Guide: 36. [Announcement.]

Martland, John. "Nunn and Miller Lead Honours List." *The Stage* 20 June 2002: 12.

McGarry, Patsy. "Theatre World Mourns Pauline Flanagan." *Irish Times* 1 July 2003, Home News: 5. (City Edition.)

McKie, David. "Comment & Analysis: Elsewhere: Poetry in Motion." *Guardian* 4 Nov. 2004: 26.

McMillan, Joyce. "Rebel with Cause to Celebrate." *Scotsman* 10 Apr. 2002: 8.

Methven, Charlie. "Italians Puzzled by Pinter, Says Greta Scacchi." London *Daily Telegraph* 17 July 2004, FeaturesSpy: 20.

Milne, Tom. "Obituary: Karel Reisz: The Director of Saturday Night and Sunday Morning and The French Lieutenant's Woman, His Focus Was Characters on the Margins." *Guardian* 28 Nov. 2002.

"Milosevic Should Get a Lawyer, Defense Committee Says." *Agence France Presse* 30 Jan. 2002. [Canadian lawyer Christopher Black, head of "the legal branch of the International Committee for the Defense of Slobodan Milosevic," to be in London in first week of Feb. 2002 "to hold a support rally for Milosevic with English playwright Harold Pinter."

Moncrieff, Chris. "Honours List: Knighthoods for Robson and Jagger." *Financial Times, Global News Wire, Europe Intelligence Wire, Western Mail* 12 June 2002. [Inc. "playwright Harold Pinter (Companion of Honour)."]

Moore, John. "Three Old Pros Uncover Pinter DCTC's Stars Tackle 'Betrayal'." *Denver Post* 12 Apr. 2002, Weekend: FF1. [Interview-based feature article about prod. of *Betrayal* (dir. Anthony Powell); cf. *TPR* (2004): 260-61.]

"Music and Arts Guide." *PAP Polish Press Agency: PAP News Wire* 27 Mar. 2002, General. [Theatre: Production of *Old Times* (*Dawne czasy*), by Harold Pinter, dir. Agnieszka Lipiec-Wroblewska, "with guest appearance by Grazyna Szapolowska, the Norodowy theatre, Scena przy Wierzbowej, Wierzbowa St. Wed. March 27, 2002, 19:30."]

Newey, Adam. "A Howl of Disapproval." *New Statesman* 14 July 2003, the back half: 54-55.

Newley, Patrick. "Martin Esslin." *The Stage* 7 Mar. 2002: 11. [Obituary.]

—. "Ray Stricklyn: Obituaries." *The Stage* 20 June 2002: 13.

—. "Robert Whitehead: Obituaries." *The Stage* 4 July 2002: 11.

"New Venue Hails Beckett." *The Stage* 11 Apr. 2002: 2. [John Calder to "open a new venue in Waterloo," The Samuel Beckett Studio, "a 50-seat theatre behind Calder Bookshop across from the Young Vic Theatre," in the summer of 2002, to stage "Established playwrights such as Beckett, Harold Pinter and Jean-Paul Sartre ... alongside new work by emerging talent."]

Nightingale, Benedict. "Bard of Broken Spirits: Benedict Nightingale Welcomes David Mamet's Brutal Vision of Everyday Life Back to the Westend." London *Times* 6 May 2003, Features, Times2: 17. [Quotes David Mamet's description of how Pinter's dramatic sketches inspired Mamet's play *Sexual Perversity in Chicago*."]

—. "Joan Littlewood, British Theater Pioneer of 'Oh What a Lovely War,' Dies at 87." *New York Times* 24 Sept. 2002: B8.

Nosowicz, Dorota. "Iraq Crisis: The Peace Marches: Marching Facts and Figures." London *Observer* 16 Feb. 203, Observer News Pages: 2.

"Obituary of Bryan Pringle: Actor Who Excelled as Glum Comic Characters in Plays by Harold Pinter, Samuel Beckett and Jack Rosenthal." London *Daily Telegraph* 21 May 2002: 23.

Obituary: Karel Reisz. London *Daily Telegraph* 28 Nov. 2002: 31.

"Obituary: Karel Reisz." *Scotsman* 28 Nov. 2002: 16.

"Obituary of Philip Heslop[, QC]: Barrister Who Specialised in Company Law, Took Silk at the Early Age of 36 and Became a Friend of Harold Pinter." London *Daily Telegraph* 17 July 2003: 25. ["Outside work, Heslop loved his family, his dogs and his farm at Toller Porcorum in Dorset, where he cultivated his garden. It was here that, late in life, he formed an unlikely but enduring friendship with the Left-wing playwright Harold Pinter and his wife Lady Antonia Fraser, who holidayed nearby."]

O'Mahony, John. "Review: Profile: Publishing's One-Man Band: John Calder." Manchester (UK) *Guardian* 20 July 2002: 16. ["Born into a brewing dynasty, he worked as a timber merchant before setting up an imprint that published some of the great avant garde writers of the 20th century. Taciturn and independent, he has also weathered a turbulent private life."]

"Opening This Week." *Daily News* (New York, NY) 14 July 2002, Showtime: 5. (Sports Final Ed.) [*Langrishe, Go Down* at Film Forum on 17 July 2002.]

Paton, Maureen. "Cooking Up Controversy." *The Stage* 9 May 2002: 9. [Feature about Arnold Wesker; comparisons with Pinter; cites Wesker's perspective on comparisons.]

Patridge, Des. "Exiled Director Now on a Different Watch List." *Courier Mail* 10 July 2002, Features: 44. ["The most comprehensive retrospective of films by Joseph Losey, whose career spanned 4 1/2 decades, ... featuring at this year's [2002] Brisbane International Film Festival": ten films, including two based on screenplays by Pinter, *The Servant* and *Accident*, but not *The Go-Between*, "his third collaboration with Pinter," for which, in 1970, Losey received the highest honour of his long and troubled career, winning the Palme D'Or at the Cannes Film Festival. . . ."]

Peralman, Jonathan. "Spotlight: Openings: ... Theatre." *Sydney Morning Herald* 24 July 2002, Metropolitan: 16. [*The Caretaker* (Belvoir Street Theatre, Surry Hills, Sydney, Austral.), on 24 July 2002.]

"Performers Take Centre Stage." *Global News Wire – Europe Intelligence Wire, Birmingham Post and Mail, Evening Mail* 11 June 2002. ["Overall winner" of the Sutton Coldfield College (UK) drama contest "was One for the Road," which also won "awards for director Michele Gale and actor Tom Handley."]

Perrier, Jean Louis. "Raymond Gerome: Acteur distingué et metteur en scène prise." *Le Monde* 8 Feb. 2002, Carnet. [Obituary.]

Pesca, Mike. "Remembering George Plimpton: Writer, 'Paris Review' Founder Dies at Age 76 in New York Apartment." *Day to Day*, National Public Radio 26 Sept. 2003. 16 Jan. 2008. <http://www.npr.org/templates/story/story.php?storyId=1447605>. [Inc. links to related NPR news articles.]

Peter, John. "His First Act's Been Running for 50 Years Now–At 72, He's Still Going Strong. So Take a Bow, Peter Hall, the Great British Enabler." London *Sunday Times* 22 June 2003, Features; Culture: 14.

Petkovic, John. "Time Out: Enduring Tale of Survival Fascinates Filmmakers Today: Heralding Harold." *Plain Dealer* 7 Apr. 2007, Sunday Arts: J2. (Final/All.) [Brief sec. of feature announcing prod. of *Betrayal* (Cleveland Play House).]

Pilger, John. "Society: John Pilger Takes On Martin Amis: Martin Amis Represents a Problem: That Some of the Most Acclaimed and Privileged Writers in the English Language Fail to Engage with the Most Urgent Issues of Our Time." *New Statesman* 17 June 2002: 13-14. 22 Aug. 2007 <http://www.newstatesman/200206170006>. ["Not a single English writer commanding the celebrity that provides an extraordinary public platform has written anything incisive and worthy of memory about the meaning and exploitation of September 11, 2001—with the exception, as ever, of Harold Pinter." Comments on Martin Amis' "long essay … entitled 'The voice of the lonely crowd'" (*Guardian* 1 June 2002).]

Plimmer, Martin. "The Monday Book: 25 Years As a One-Man Humour Factory Is No Joke for Craig." London *Independent* 17 Feb. 2003, Features: 12.

"Pole Grasped Bard Vibes: Obituary: Jan Kott." *Australian* 22 Jan. 2202, Features: 16.

Pond, Elizabeth. "European Shock and Awe." *Washington Quart.* 26.3 (Summer 2003): 191-203. 22 Aug. 2007 <http://www.twq.com/03summer/docs/03summer_pond.pdf>. [After observing that "Underlying all other European worries is fear of U.S. hubris in playing God in the Middle East" and noting the "deep anxiety" indicated by "the anti-Iraq war sentiment of an overwhelming 82 percent of the European public," cites "playwright Harold Pinter's blistering poem 'God Bless America' in *The Guardian*, January 22, 2003," as an "example" of "the derision of U.S. policies in some British media" (193, n. 7; 202).]

Portman, Jamie. "Actor Finds a Role Crazy Enough for Him: Ian Holm Plays a Panhandler Who Wanders around Manhattan Writing a Masterpiece in His Head." *Ottawa Citizen* 13 May 2000, Arts: J2. (Final.) [Feature interview-based article about Ian Holm. Retroactive entry.]

"Production News: Corin Redgrave." *The Stage* 10 Jan. 2002: 51. [Announcement of *Pinter Sketches I* and *Pinter Sketches II.*]

Purser, Philip. "Obituary: Barry Foster: Versatile Actor Best Known for His Portrayals of Orde Wingate and a Dutch Detective." *Guardian* 12 Feb. 2002, Guardian Leader Pages: 20.

"Queen's Birthday Honours." *Financial Times*, *Global New Wire*, *Europe Intelligence Wire*, *Edinburgh Evening News* 15 June 2002: 5. [Inc. Harold Pinter, Companion of Honour.]

"Queen's Birthday Honours: Let's Spend Together The Knight." *Global News Wire*, *Europe Intelligence Wire*, *Birmingham Post and Mail*, *Evening Mail* 15 June 2002. [Cites Harold Pinter, Companion of Honour.]

"Queen's Birthday Honours: National Awards." *Financial Times*, *Global News Wire*, *Europe Intelligence Wire*, *Newsletter* 15 June 2002. [Inc. Harold Pinter, Companion of Honour.]

"Queen's Jubilee Birthday Honours: Arise Sir Bobby and Arise Sir Mick … Honours for the Masters of Their Game." *Global News Wire*, *Europe Intelligence Wire*,

Birmingham Post and Mail, *Evening Mail* 15 June 2002. [Inc. Harold Pinter, Companion of Honour.]

Radoszkowicz, Abigail. "What's On: ... Pinteresque Hebrew." *Jerusalem Post* 12 Nov. 2002, Arts: 7. [Announces "A double bill of two short, Pinter thrillers – his very early The Dumb Waiter and the [later] Victoria Station. . . ."]

Radz, Matt. "Dunsmore Hits with Wit: Actress Takes Top Honours for Her Role As a Cancer Patient." Montreal *Gazette* 4 Feb. 2002, Arts & Life: E6. (Final Ed.) [In addition to Rosemary Dunsmore's award for her role in *Wit*, "Saidye Bronfman Centre's Betrayal by Harold Pinter was named the best English-language production as Quebec's top theatre awards were handed out during a three-hour cemerony at Monument National on St. Laurent Blvd."]

Rawson, Christopher. "PICT Builds '03 Season On an Ambitious Quartet." *Pittsburgh Post-Gazette* 13 Mar. 2003, Arts & Entertainment: B-1.

Remnick, David. "Postscript: George Plimpton." *New Yorker* 3 Oct. 2003. 16 Jan. 2008. <http://www.newyorker.com/archive/2003/10/06/031006ta_talk_remnick>.

Rizzo, Frank. "As He Likes It: One of Theater's Towering Figures, Sir Peter Hall, Discusses the Past, Present and Future, Which Includes Directing His Daughter [Rebecca Hall] at Shubert in One of Shakespeare's Most Popular Plays [*As You Like It*]." *Hartford Courant* (CT) 19 Oct. 2003, Arts: G1. (Statewide ed.)

"Robert Whitehead." London *Times* 4 July 2002, Features: 34. [Obituary. Theatrical producer born in Montreal on 3 Mar. 1916; died in Pound Ridge, New York, on 15 June 2002.]

Rosenthal, Daniel. "Holm Sweet Homecoming." London *Times* 10 Sept. 2001, Features. [Interview with Ian Holm.]

"Ruth Cracknell." London *Times* 17 May 2002, Features. [Obituary.]

Ryan, Phyllis. "The Awards." *Irish Times* 12 Feb. 2002, City Ed.; Home News; ESB Theatre Awards: 10. [Nominated for "Best Actor" included "Ian Holm for the Gate Theatre prod. of *The Homecoming* by Harold Pinter."]

Santini, Laura. "Vecchi tempi, un duello." Mentelocale.it: diretto da Guglielmi 14 Dec. 2004, Feb. 2008 <http://www.menteleocale.it/teatro/contenuti/index_html/id_contenuti_varint_11581>. (In Italian.)

Scatena, Dino, Barry Morris, Michael Bodey, Tim Morrissey, and Elizabth Fortescue. "24 Hours–The Best of What's on This Weekend." Sydney *Daily Telegraph* 14 Dec. 2002, Features-Type-Review-Column-24 HOURS Weekend confidential Sydney Confidential: B14.

Schama, Simon. "Saturday Review: Lives & Letters: A World of Their Own: From Dickens and Kipling to de Beauvoir and Koestler, Simon Schama Continues His Two-Part Survey of European Attitudes to America." *Guardian* 5 Apr. 2003, Guardian Saturday Pages: 34. ["In the most extreme polemics American freedom is itself a disingenuous fraud, coercion with a smiley face; Harold Pinter's 'monster out of control'."]

Senter, Al. "Playing His Part." *The Stage* 10 Oct. 2002: 8. [Feature about John Normington, who performed Sam in *The Homecoming* in both 1965, when he was "aged just 28," and in "the 1991 West End revival when he was a youthful 54."

Shorter, Eric. "Obituary: Bryan Pringle: Warm-hearted Actor with a Lugubrious Style."

Guardian 22 May 2002, Guardian Leader Pages: 20.

Sierz, Aleks. "Peter Hall." London *Sunday Times* 22 June 2003, Features; Culture: 14. [Quotations by colleagues, inc. Harold Pinter.]

Smith, Michelle. "University Theatre Season Opens with Harold Pinter's *The Homecoming*." Sidebar in U of Georgia guide (column). 19 Sept. 2007 <http://www.uga.edu/columns/041011/guide.html>. [About 2004-2005 season.]

"Snap Shot." *Houston Chronicle* 31 Oct. 2002: 1.

Stephen, Chris. "Anti-War Voices Unite for Protest." *Scotland on Sunday* 16 Feb. 2003: 5. [Reports on March and rally in Hyde Park, at which Pinter spoke.]

Steyn, Mark. "Stanza to Reason, As the Group Calls Itself, Marks the First Time Britain's Top Versifiers Have Worked Together." London *Daily Telegraph* 25 Jan. 2003: 24.

"Student Listings–Regular Happenings: Theatre Bargains; Student." *Time Out* 23 Jan. 2002: 129. [Announcement of *No Man's Land* (Lyttelton Theatre, Royal National Theatre).]

"Taking the Lead." *Entertainment Design* Mar. 2002, Bizwireprojectnews, ISSN: 1520-5150. [Describes the lighting designed by Paul Mathiesen for "The World Leaders Festival, a five-week show hosted by American Express celebrating creative individuals such as Harold Pinter, Joni Mitchell, Peter Gabriel, and Stephen Sondheim, who have reshaped the world as we know it, ... held recently at Liberty Grand in Toronto."]

Taylor, Paul. "Theatre: The Kind of Misery That Makes You Happy to Be Alive." London *Independent* 11 Feb. 2002, Features: 10.

—, Rhoda Koenig, and Stuart Price. "The Best Plays: ... Betrayal (Old Vic, Bristol)." London *Independent* 28 Feb. 2003, Features: 25.

—, and Stuart Price. "Theatre: The Best Plays: ... Betrayal (Royal Theatre, Northampton)." London *Independent* 22 Nov. 2002, Features: 25.

Taylor, Ros. "Rage against the War Machine." *Guardian* 27 Feb. 2003. 20 Mar. 2003 <http://politics.guardian.co.uk/redbox/story/0,9029,904435,00.html>.

"Theater: Harold and Mel." *Washington Times* 26 July 2003, Arts: Notable and New: D1.

"Theatre: Preview–Cues: On the Move." *Time Out* 30 Jan. 2002: 30. [Concerns Nick Starr's appointment to executive director of the Royal National Theatre; previously executive director of the Almeida, where he opened "a new Harold Pinter" before leaving.]

"Theatre: West End–Now Booking." *Time Out* 30 Jan. 2002: 134, 135. [Announcement of "Sketches by Harold Pinter, directed by Gari Jones, with Patrick Marber, Corin Redgrave, Penelope Wilton and Harold Pinter, at the National Theatre, Lyttelton ... Feb. 8 & 11."]

"Two Share Cohen Prize." *Irish Times* 29 Mar. 2003, City Ed., Weekend, Loose Leaves: 60. [Pinter presented Thom Gunn and Beryl Bambridge with their shared David Cohen British Literature Prize.]

Tysome, Tony. "Pinter Plays Sought to Plug Archive Gap." *Times Higher Education Supplement* 29 Oct. 2004: 8. ["Reports on the loss of literary works of playwrights including the plays of Harold Pinter from a British Library archive in Great Britain.

Ignorance of the Theatre Arts amendment; Danger of losing an essential part of artistic heritage; Benefits of students. Theatre, workers, writers and cultural and social historians from the comprehensive and accessible archives."]

Vallance, Tom. "Obituary: Karel Reisz: Director of Saturday Night and Sunday Morning." London *Independent* 28 Nov. 2002, Obituaries: 22.

Vestey, Michael. "Religious Conviction: Radio." *Spectator* 24 Aug. 2002: 45. [Concerns BBC Radio 4's program *Thought For The Day* opposed in "a letter" signed by "100 prominent atheists," including Harold Pinter, "sent by the British Humanist association, the National Secular Society and the Rational Press Association. . . ."]

"War on Iraq: U.S. Ups the Pressure: Stars in Plea for Peace." *Mirror* 19 Sept. 2002.

"War Protesters On Hand As President Bush Arrives in London." *Knight Ridder Tribune Business News* 19 Nov. 2003: 1.

Waterhouse, Rosie, Toby Helm, and Andrew Sparrow. "Protest 'will end Blair's legitimacy as leader of nation'." London *Daily Telegraph* 15 Feb. 2003: 7.

Webb, Paul. "Give This Man a Knighthood: Alan Bates's Talent Is Burning as Brightly as Ever. So Why, Asks Theatre Historian Paul Webb, Has He Not Had the Honour He Deserves?" London *Daily Telegraph* 15 Apr. 2002: 17.

Welsh, Anne Marie. "The Faithful: Globe Director Staunchly Believes in Pinter." *San Diego Union-Tribune* 31 Jan. 2002, Entertainment: Night & Day: 28. [Interview with Karen Carpenter, associate director of Globe Theatres, Balboa Park, San Diego, CA; concerns upcoming prod. of *Betrayal* (Cassius Carter Centre Stage).

—. "Renaissance Man: Surgeon 'Retires' to San Diego to Produce Cutting-Edge Plays." *San Diego Union-Tribune* 18 Mar. 2002, Lifestyle: D1. [George Flint, founder of Renaissance Theater Company, on occasion of prod. of *The Caretaker*, dir. Rosina Reynolds.]

Wheatcroft, Geoffrey. "Milton Shulman: Jovial Film and Theatre Critic with a Curmudgeonly Reputation." London *Independent* 24 May 2004. Rpt. in *Encore Theatre Mag.* (Online) 24 May 2004. 16 Sept. 2007 <http://encoretheatremagazine.blogspot.com/Shulman.htm>. [Obituary.]

With Files from the Star's Wire Services [byline]. "Last of the Famous Projectionists." *Toronto Star* 3 Feb. 2002, Entertainment: D6. (Sunday Ontario Ed.)

Wintle, Angela. "The Longford Legacy: The Writer Judith Kazantzis, Daughter of Lord and Lady Longford, Talks Frankly to Angela Wintle about Her Turbulent Relationship with Her Sister, Lady Antonia Fraser." London *Sunday Telegraph* 19 Jan. 2003: 2.

Wolf, Matt. "Legit: Strands: 'Birthday' Boy." *Variety* 25-31 Oct. 2004: 62. ["Actor Henry Goodman, who played Max Bialystock in the Broadway musical 'The Producers' in 2002 before departing the production prematurely, signed to perform in a production of Harold Pinter's 'The Birthday Party' that will make tour stops in both Birmingham and Bath, England, before opening in London's West End on April 11, 2005."] (See "**Forthcoming . . .**" below.)

Woodward, Will [Education ed.]. "Pounds 2 m Aids Rebirth of 'Worst School.'" *Guardian* 17 Jan. 2002, Guardian Home Pages: 12. [Concerns Hackney Downs comprehensive school becoming a city academy.]

Wroe, Nicholas. "Review: Profile: The History Woman: Antonia Fraser." *Guardian* 24 Aug. 2002: 16. ["Before biography was fashionable, she made the past popular.

Her private life has been a source of fascination. But the former Tory MP's wife who converted to Catholicism and votes Labour knows what it means to be an outsider, she tells Nicholas Wroe."]

Via, Dan. "Answering 'the Call': 'Ionesco – Stoppard – Pinter': Through Sept. 1 Longacre Lea Productions 202/316-1659." *Washington Post* 16 Aug. 2002. [Feature incorporating interview with Longacre Lea director Kathleen Akerley.]

Vitello, Paul. "These Words Can Only Begin to Define Conflict." *Newsday* (New York, NY) 3 Apr. 2003, News: A34.

Zekas, Rita. "Peter in Pinterland." *Toronto Star* 1 Aug. 2003, Entertainment: E4.

Theater Performances of Plays by Harold Pinter

L'Anniversaire (*The Birthday Party*). In French. Dir. Marcel Delval. Perf. Maryse Dinsart, John Dobrynine, Bernard Graczyk, Philippe Jeusette, Nicole Valberg, and Jean-Michel Vork. Théâtre Varia, Brussels, Belgium. Season 2002-2003. 7 Nov. 2002 <http://www.varia.be/navigationframe.htm>. Hyperlinked prod. summary in "Archives pour 2002-2003." 2 Feb. 2008 <http://www.varia.be/fr/archives/2002/#goto>.

Anniversario and *La Stanza* (*Celebration* and *The Room*). In Italian. Trans. Alessandra Serra. Dir. Roberto Andò. Perf. Guiseppe Battiston ("Cameriere" [Server]), Flavio Bonacci (Richard), Giovanna Di Rauso (Sonia), Paolo Graziosi (Matt), Lorenza Indovina (Suki), Caterina Sylos Labini (Julie), Carlo Valli (Lambert), Jean Claude N'Guessan ("Altro cameriere" [Other Server]); and [Marina Confalone?] (Prue). Scene and Lighting Giovanni Carluccio. Costumes Nanà Cecchi. ERT: Emilia Romagna Teatro Fondazione, Teatro Stabile Publicco Regionale, Modena, Italy [permanent Public Theatre of the Emilia-Romagna Region, founded in1977]. 2003. 2 Feb. 2008 <http://www.haroldpinter.org/plays/frn_celebration_it03.shtml>. Italian première, Festival di Palermo. 13 Oct. 2000 until Nov. 2000. 2 Feb. 2008 <http://www.emiliaromagnateatro.com/produzione.asp?P_Spt_CID=423>. Cf. <http://www.apriteilsipario.it/archivio/panoramica02-03/schede/sch100.htm>.

Ashes to Ashes. Dir. Robert Mann. Perf. Gloria Mann Craft (Rebecca) and Warren Kelder (Devlin). Stage Manager Rebecca Zuber. Prod. Manager Linda Woznicki. Fashion Designer Michael Boris. Sets Ryan James. Lighting Mark Simmons. Sound John Bashew. Mannatee Films, WalkerSpace Theater, TriBeCa, New York City. December 2003. (Rev. by Hampton.)

Ashes to Ashes. Dir. Tobin A. Maheras. Perf. Amy Fleetwood (Rebecca) and Steven Sturm (Devlin). A Theatre Under the Influence (in association with Joseph E. Boling). The Union Garage, Seattle, WA. 15 Feb.-2 Mar. 2002. (Brief rev. by Fetzer.)

Ashes to Ashes and *A Kind of Alaska.* Wimbleton Studio Theatre, London. 28 Apr.-3 May 2003. [Listed in "Upcoming Events for the Year 2003" at *haroldpinter.org.*]

Betrayal. Dir. Gareth Machin. Perf. Simon Shepherd (Robert), Lesley Vickerage (Emma), and Jay Villiers (Jerry). Bristol Old Vic, Bristol, Eng. 31 Jan.-1 Mar. 2003. 19 Nov. 2002 <http://www.bristol-old-vic.co.uk/betrayal.html>. [Outdated URL; the theater's website at <http://www.bristol-old-vic.co.uk> became "SaveOldVic," at least temporarily devoted to raising funds for its refurbishment.] (See Koenig, Price, "Pinter Marks End of an Era," and Taylor, as listed above in "**Other Pertinent News Reports . . . .**")

Betrayal. Dir. Ian Hastings. Perf. Timothy Deenihan (Jerry), Sally Mais (Emma), Marco

Rossi (Waiter), and Keith Woodason (Robert). Decor Paul Kondras. Lighting Brent Lees. Sound Julie Washington. Duke's Theatre, Lancaster, Eng. 11 Mar.-2 Apr. 2005. (Rev. by Hickling.)

Betrayal. Dir. Jerry Finn. Perf. David Breitbarth, V. Craig Heidenreich, Tessie Hogan, and Bradford Wallace. Banyan Theater Company, Sainer Pavilion at the New College of Florida, Sarasota, FL. 31 July-11 Aug. 2002. (See announcement by Fleming, as listed above in "**Other Pertinent News Reports . . . .**")

Betrayal. Dir. Karen Carpenter. Cassius Carter Centre Stage, Globe Theatre, San Diego, CA. 31 Jan. 2002-10 Mar. 2002. (See interview of Carpenter by Welsh, as listed above in "**Other Pertinent News Reports. . . .**"; rev. by Braunagel.)

Betrayal. Dir. Leslie A. Kobylinski. Perf. Larry Danièle (Robert), Sheri S. Herren (Emma), and David Sher (Jerry). Port City Playhouse, Alexandria, VA. 28 Feb.-2 Mar. 2003. (Rev. by Toscano.)

Betrayal. Dir. Mark Ingram. Perf. Matthew Gibson (Robert), Mark Ingram (Jerry), John Sweet (Waiter), and Linda Worsley (Emma). Rogue & Peasant Theatre Company, Princess Court Theatre, Kingston, Ont., Can. 7-16 Feb. 2002. "Performances," Rogue & Peasant Theatre Co. 14 Jan. 2002 <http://www.roguetheatre.org/index.cfm?page=showplay&play=10>.

Betrayal. Dir. Peter Hackett. Perf. Paul Vincent Black (Robert), Andrew May (Jerry), and Anne Torsiglieri (Emma). Cleveland Play House, Cleveland, OH. (Rev. by Tony Brown.)

Betrayal. Dir. Rupert Goold. Perf. John Lloyd Fillingham (Jerry), John McAndrew (Robert), and Paula Stockbridge (Emma). Royal Theatre, Northampton, Eng. 8-23 Nov. 2002. (See "Betrayal by Harold Pinter" and Taylor & Price, as listed above in "**Other Pertinent News Reports. . . .**")

Betrayal. Dir. Sarah Denhardt. Perf. Charlotte Akin (Emma), Bryan Davis (Waiter), Jim Jorgensen (Robert), and Dan Via (Jerry). Theatre on the Run. Fountainhead Theatre and The Keegan Theatre, Arlington, VA. 14 Aug.-11 Sept. 2004. 2 Oct. 2007 <http://www.keegantheatre.com/scripts/runisa.dll?s7:gp::11843+betrayal/>.

Betrayal. Dir. Scott Edmiston. Perf. Jason Asprey (Robert), Anne Gottlieb (Emma), and Joe Pacheco (Jerry). Scenic design Janie Howland. Costumes Gail Astrid Buckley. Lighting design Karen Perlow. Sound design Dewey Dellay. Nora Theatre Company, Boston Playwrights' Theatre, Boston, MA. Through 30 Mar. 2003. (Rev. by Byrne.)

Betrayal. Dir. Terry Hands. Perf. Vivien Party (Emma), Robert Perkins (Robert), Steffan Rhodri (Jerry), and Johnson Willis (Waiter). Emlyn Williams Theatre, Clwyd Theatr Cymru, Mold, Flintshire, North Wales. May 2002. (Rev. By Hallett.)

Betrayal. Dr. Tom McDermott. Richard Fancy (Robert), Suzanne Ford (Emma), and Stephen Hoye (Jerry). Set design John Berger. Music Keith Stevenson. Pacific Resident Theatre, Venice, CA. Aug. 2002. (Rev. by Shirley.)

Betrayal. (In repertory with *The Fight for Barbara*, by D. H. Lawrence, and *Design for Living*, by Noel Coward.) Dir. Peter Hall. Perf. Janie Dee (Emma), Aden Gillett (Jerry), Hugo Speer (Robert), and James Supervia (Waiter). Decor John Gunter. Lighting Peter Mumford. Sound Gregory Clarke. Peter Hall Company. Theatre Royale, Bath. 9 July-Aug. 2003. (Rev. by Billington, Brown, Coveney, Gross, Hewison, Kellaway, Koenig, Macaulay, Nightingale, Spencer, Taylor, and Woodis.

Rpt. in *Theatre Record* 23 (2003): 908-14.) *Betrayal* transferred to the Duchess Theatre, London. 8 Oct. 2003-31 Jan. 2004. (Rev. by Billington, Coveney, Nathan, Shenton, and others rpt. in *Theatre Record* 23 [2004]: 1375-79.) Online posting of some prod. details. 18 Mar. 2003 <http://www.theatreroyal.org.uk/main/betrayal.html> (no longer accessible).

The Birthday Party. Dir. Erica Whyman. Perf. Anna Calder-Marshall (Meg), Robert East (Goldberg), John Lloyd Fillingham (Stanley), John Nettleton (Petey), and Robert Patterson (McCann). Stage design Soutra Gilmour. Crucible Theatre, Sheffield, Eng. Until 2 Mar. 2002. (Rev. by Gardner; Koenig; Shuttleworth; and Taylor.)

The Birthday Party. Dir. Guy Hollands. Perf. Jill Freer (Lulu), Alec Heggie (Petey), Bryan Larkin (McCann), Ronnie Simon (Stanley), and Katherine Stark (Meg). [Goldberg?] Decor Neil Warmington. Tag Theatre, The Tron. Glasgow, Scotland. 20-27 Sept. 2003. (Rev. by Mark Brown, Cramer, Cooper, Cramer, McEwan in Cooper and McEwan. Rpt. in *Theatre Record* 23 (2003): 1291-2.

The Birthday Party. Dir. Joanne Akalaitis. Perf. Remo Airaldi (McCann), Thomas Derrah (Stanley), Elizabeth Laidlaw (Lulu), Will LeBow (Goldberg), Maren MacDonald (Meg), and Terence Rigby (Petey). Scenic Designer Paul Steinberg. Costume designer Gabriel Berry. Lighting designer Jennifer Tipton. Composer and sound designer Bruce Odland. Sound engineer David Remedios. Stage Manager M. Pat Hodge. Associate dramaturg Ryan McKittrick. American Repertory Theatre (ART), Cambridge, MA. 6-27 Mar. 2004. 22 Aug. 2007 <http://www.amrep.org/birthday/ >. (Rev. by Clay, Fanger, Gorfinkle, Kennedy, Lowe, and Siegel; see also program notes and interview by McKittrick, as listed below in "**Related Articles . . . .**")

The Caretaker. Dir. Adrian Stokes. Perf. Victor Gardener (Mick), Ian Kirkby (Aston), and Nigel Terry (Davies). Set design David Thomas. Mercury Theatre, Colchester, UK. Opened 16 Feb. 2002. (See "Colchester: Caretaker's First Night Cancelled," as listed above in "**Other Pertinent News Reports . . .**"; rev. by Redman.)

The Caretaker. Dir. Dave Bond. Perf. Owen Garmon, John Kearney, and Keith Woodason. The Torch Theatre, Milford Haven. 5-16 Feb. 2002. Followed by a short tour of Wales from 20 Feb. to 9 Mar. 2002. (Listed in "Forthcoming events for the year 2002," 5 Feb. 2002 <http://www.haroldpinter.org/home/index.shtml>, and in *TPR* [2004]: 262.)

The Caretaker. Dir. David Jones. Perf. Aidan Gillen (Mick), Kyle MacLachlan (Aston), and Patrick Stewart (Davies). Sets John Lee Beatty. Costumes Jane Greenwood. Lighting Peter Kaczorowski. Sound Scott Lehrer. Production stage manager Matthew Silver. Technical supervisor Steve Beers. Roundabout Theatre Company, American Airlines Theatre, New York. 24 Oct. 2003-25 Jan. 2004. 20 Sept. 2007 <http://www.roundabouttheatre.org/03-04.htm#caretaker>. (See interview with Patrick Stewart by Shewey and David Jones, "Travels," as listed below in "**Related Articles . . .**"; rev. by Brantley, Gillen, Isherwood, Rich, Simon, and Teachout.)

The Caretaker. Dir. Glynis Leyshon. The Vancouver Playhouse Theatre Company, Vancouver, BC, Can. 40th anniversary season (2002-2003). 5 Apr.-3 May 2003. 4 Oct. 2002 <http://www.vancouverplayhouse.com . . .> (dedicated page no longer accessible). 2 Feb. 2008 <http://www.vancouverplayhouse.com/about-us/company-history.php>.

The Caretaker. Dir. Hannah Macdougall. Perf. William Allert (Mick), David Mealor

(Aston), and Anthony Phelan (Davies). Set design Geoff Cobham. Belvoir Street Theatre, Surry Hills, Sydney, Austral. Until 4 Aug. 2002. (See announcement in "Hot Seat," as listed above in ""**Other Pertinent News Reports . . .**"; rev. by Bodey, Dunne, McCallum, and Rose.)

The Caretaker. Dir. James Mango. Perf. Kirk Brown (Mick), Allan Byrne (Aston), and Reuben Silver (Davies). Charenton Theater Company, Studio 210, Playhouse Square, Cleveland, OH. Through 9 Mar. 2002. (Rev. by Tony Brown.)

The Caretaker. Dir. John Stephens. Perf. Hugh Adams (Aston), David Milford (Davies), and Brandon O'Dell (Mick). Set design Kat Conley. Theatre in the Square, Marietta, GA. Through 10 Nov. 2002. (Rev. by Brock.)

The Caretaker. Dir. Lindsay Posner. Perf. Simon Kunz (Aston), Terence Rigby (Davies), and Paul Ritter (Mick). Decor Christopher Oram. Lighting Hartley T. A. Kemp. Bristol Old Vic, Bristol, Eng. 9-23 Sept. 2003. (Rev. by Gardner and Peter.)

The Caretaker. Dir. Michael Cabot. Perf. Nicholas Gasson (Mick), Richard Stemp (Aston), and Benjamin Warren (Davies). Designer Geraldine Bunzl. London Classic Theatre Company. Ten-week tour of the UK and Ireland. 15 Sept.-26 Nov. 2004. 2 Oct. 2007 <http://www.londonclassictheatre.co.uk/>. (Rev. by Sierz.)

The Caretaker. Dir. Patrick Marber. Comedy Theatre. Previewed 8 Nov. 2000; opened 15 Nov. 2000; closed 3 Feb. 2001. *Albermarle of London: London West End Theatre Guide*. 20 May 2002 <http://www.albemarle-london.com/caretaker.html>. [Inc. "Excerpts from the reviews"; cf. entry in *TPR* (2004): 263.]

The Caretaker. Dir. Paula Suozzi. Perf. Ted Tyson (Davies), Jonathan West (Aston), and Jeremy Woods (Mick). Off-Broadway Theatre, Milwaukee, WI. Through 17 Mar. 2002. (Rev. by Jaques.)

The Caretaker. Dir. Rosina Reynolds. Perf. Bryan Bevell (Aston), Ron Choularton (Davies), and Jeffrey Jones (Mick). Set Marty Burnett. Lighting Karin Filijan. Renaissance Theatre Company. 6th @ Penn Theatre, Hillcrest, San Diego, CA. 16 Mar.-14 Apr. 2002. (Rev. by Welsh.)

The Collection and *The Lover*. By Harold Pinter. Part of "Travesía escénica por la literatura dramática del siglo XX." *Salamanca, European Capital of the Culture in 2002. European Commission, Europa* (Updated) 15 May 2007. 20 Sept.. 2007 <http://ec.europa.eu/culture/eac/ecocs/present_cap/salamanque_en.html>. [Announcement of production of *The Collection* and *The Lover*, by Harold Pinter, as part of "the first of the projects supported by the European Commission's Culture 2000 programme," involving "five theatrical creations, each of which was directed by five Spaniards who are very different but united in their strong commission to contemporary theatre."]

The Dumb Waiter. Dir. Brian Eatwell. St. Stephens Theater, Los Angeles. 9 Mar.-7 Apr. 2002. [See Entertainment Editors & Theater Writers, as listed above in "**Other Pertinent News Reports . . . .**"]

The Dumb Waiter. Dir. Frances Johnston. Perf. Stuart Duffield (Gus) and Stephen Peacock (Ben). [No venue listed.] Newcastle, Austral., 21, 22, 24 & 25 May 2002. (Rev. by Longworth.)

The Dumb Waiter. Dir. Graham Price. Perf. Devin Charlebois (Gus) and James Richardson (Ben). Ottawa Third Wall Theatre Company. Ottawa Fringe Festival, U of Ottawa Theatre (Unicentre), Ottawa, Can. 28-30 June 2002. (Rev. by Mazey.)

The Dumb Waiter. Dir. Liz Chance. Perf. Anthony Martin (Gus) and Danny Nash

(Ben). Cat and Fiddle Hotel, Balmain. Until 7 July 2002.

The Dumb Waiter. Dir. Brian Eatwell. Perf. Derrick O'Connor (Gus) and Michael O'Hagan (Ben). Set design Brian Eatwell. Lighting design Don Fauntleroy. Sound design Tyler Bowe. St. Stephen's Church, Hollywood, CA. Through 7 Apr. 2002. (Rev. by Brandes and Foley.)

The Dumb Waiter. Dir. Casey Lim (Joint dir. of the English-language Checkpoint Theatre). In "Waterloo Murders," a double bill with *The Maids*, by Jean Genet, performed simultaneously in Mandarin. The Theatre Practice's Hall, Stamford Arts Centre, Singapore, Malaysia. (See Chow, as listed above in "**Other Pertinent News Reports ... .**"; rev. by Yee, who observes that the plays were staged "simultaneously, in about 1 1/2 hours," with "two sets of actors," who shared the same performance room.)

The Dumb Waiter. Dir. Richard Murray. Perf. Derek Fisher (Gus) and Richard Murray (Ben). Part of "a varied 2002 edition of Replay." Newcastle Rep. (Rev. by Longworth.)

"*The Dumb Waiter* and Other Pieces." Dir. Douglas Hodge. Perf. in *The Dumb Waiter*: Toby Jones (Gus) and Jason Watkins (Ben). ["Other Pieces" included *The Black and White*; *Precisely*; *Trouble in the Works*; *Last To Go*; *That's Your Trouble*; and *Victoria Station*.] Set & Costume Designer Miriam Buether. Lighting Designer Johanna Town. Composer Nick Bicât. Sound Designer John Leonard. Oxford Playhouse, Oxford, Eng. 17-28 Feb. 2004. (Rev. by Billington, Coveney, Marlowe, Roddam, Spencer, and Wood. Rpt. in *Theatre Record* 24 [2004]: 248-49.)

The Dumb Waiter and *Victoria Station*. Dir. and trans. Leona Schectman and Michal Badani. Perf. Ronen Yifrah and Erin Boham. ZOA House, Rehov Daniel Frisch 1, Tel Aviv, Israel. Nov. 2002. (See Radoszkowicz, as listed above in "**Other Pertinent News Reports . . . .**"]

The Dwarfs. Adapt. by Kerry Lee Crabbe from the novel by Harold Pinter. Dir. Christopher Morahan. Perf. Ben Caplan (Mark), Daisy Haggard (Virginia), Jamie Lee (Pete), and Mark Riche-Oxley (Len). Decor Eileen Diss. Costumes Dany Everett. Lighting Mick Hughes. Sound John Leonard (for Aura). Tricycle Theatre, London. 23 Apr. -31 May 2003. (See Billington, "Look Back in Hackney," as listed above in "**Biographical Profiles . . .**"; bev. By Bassett, Billington, Brown, Cavendish, Clapp, de Jongh, Edwardes, Evans, Foss, Gross, Hemming, Marmion, Morley, Nathan, Nightingale, Reynolds, Sierz, Taylor [2], Thaxter, and Woodis. Rpt. in *Theatre Record* 23 [2003]: 527-34.)

The Homecoming. Dir. Ed Baierlein. Perf. Ed Baierlein (Max), Jamie Powers (Ruth), John Seifert (Sam), Augustus Truhn (Lenny), and others. Germinal Stage Denver. Through 5 May 2002. (Rev. by Bows.)

The Homecoming. Dir. Elinor Renfield. Set Dan Joy. Costumes Mary Jo Horner. Lights Christopher Ostrom. Perf. James Doerr (Max), Kim Dooley (Ruth), Leo Kittay (Joey), Robert Kropf (Lenny), Dafydd Rees (Sam), and Jeff Zinn (Teddy). Set Dan Joy. Costumes Mary Jo Horner. Lights Christopher Ostrom. The Wellfleet Harbor Actors Theatre, Wellfleet, MA. Through 22 June 2002. (Rev. by Fanger.)

The Homecoming. Dir. Greg Hersov. Perf. Eamon Boland (Sam). Michael Higgs (Teddy), James Hillier (Joey), Paul Hilton (Lenny), Simone Lahbib (Ruth), & Pete Postlethwaite (Max). Designer Laurie Dennett. Lighting Designer Bruno Poet. Sound Designer Steve Brown. Fight Director Renny Krupinski. Dialect

Coach Tim Charrington. The Royal Exchange Theatre, Manchester, Eng. (25th Anniversary Season.) 23 Jan.-2 Mar. 2002. [Previously listed in *TPR* (2004): 264; rev. by Cavendish; Kingston, in Kingston and Potton; and Nightingale.]

The Homecoming. Dir. Imogen Russell Williams. Perf. Ting Ting Judy Hu (Ruth), Martin Malinowski (Max), Andrew Mortimer (Lenny), and others. Moser Theatre, Wadham College, U of Oxford, Oxford, Eng. 6-11 May 2003. (Feature by Burton and Saint, as cited above in "**Other Pertinent News Reports . . . .**")

The Homecoming. Dir. Ray Paolino. Perf. inc. Cheryl Binnie (Ruth), Blake Bowen (Lenny), and David Pollack (Max). Cellar Theatre, Fine Arts Building, University Theatre, U of Georgia. 13-15 Oct., 17 Oct. 2004. 2004-2005 season. (Announcement by Smith, as cited above in "**Other Pertinent News Reports . . . .**")

The Homecoming. Dir. Robin Lefèvre. Perf. Nick Dunning (Teddy), Ian Hart (Lenny), Ian Holm (Max), John Kavanagh (Sam), Jason O'Mara (Joey), & Lia Williams (Ruth). Decor Eileen Diss. Costumes Dany Everett. Lighting Mick Hughes. The Gate Theatre, Dublin. Through 30 June 2001. Comedy Theatre, London. Sept. 2001. [Previously listed in *TPR* (2004): 265; rev. by Billington, "Saturday Review."]

The Hothouse. Perf. Peter Bailey (Roote) and others. Part of Pinter Fest 2003. Black Hole Theatre, Gas Station Theatre, Manitoba, Can. 15-18, 19, and 21-25 Jan. 2003. (See "Bailey Acting Up Again," as listed above in "**Other Pertinent News Reports . . . .**"; and "Pinter Fest 2003," as listed below in "**Other Related Programs and Reviews**.")

"JMK: Party Time and One for the Road." Dir. Bijan Sheibani, Winner of the JMK (James Menzies Kitchin Memorial Trust Award). Designer Paul Burgess. Lighting Guy Kornetzki. Battersea Arts Centre, London. 18 July-17 Aug. 2003. <http://www.bac.org.uk/>.

A Kind of Alaska. Pint-sized Theatre, Warwick U. C Central, Edinburgh Fringe Festival, Edinburgh, Scotland. Until 24 Aug. 2003. (Rev. by McEwan in Cooper and McEwan.)

A Kind of Alaska, in a double bill with *Me and My Friend*, by Gillian Plowman. Dir. by Svetlana Dimcovic. Perf. John Cunningham (Dr. Hornby), Fiz Marcus (Deborah), and Louise Yates (Pauline). Design Sam Dowson. Lighting Sam Akester. Movement Richard Ryan. Orange Tree Theatre, London Borough of Richmond Upon Thames, Eng. 13-30 June 2002. 22 Feb. 2008 <http://www.jghonline.co.uk/orangetree/whats_on_archive.asp?ID=34&ArchiveYear=2002> and <http://www.haroldpinter.org/plays/plays_alaska5.shtml>. (Rev. by Stearn and Thaxter.)

The Lover. Dir. Mark Kilmurry. Perf. Felicity Price (Sara) and Richard Sydenham (Richard/Max). Sheebang Productions, Belvoir Downstairs, Belvoir Street Theatre, Surry Hills, Sydney, Austral. 4-22 Dec 2002. (See Scatena, et al., as listed above in "**Other Pertinent News Reports . . .**"; rev. by Low, Low & Dunne, Simmonds, and "The Week's Best.")

The Lover. Gobo Theatre. Krater Comedy Club, Brighton, Eng. 14 Apr. 2002. [Listing in "Showcase." *Komedia* 14 Apr. 2002. 17 Apr. 2002 <http://www.komedia.co.uk/0204/200204141930_t_theloverby.shtml> (outdated URL). Archived via *The Internet Archive: The Wayback Machine*. Last updated 14 Feb. 2002. 23 Jan. 2008 <http://web.archive.org/web/20020503102412/http://www.komedia.co.uk/0204/200204141930_t_theloverby.shtml>.]

The Lover. Perf. Jane Huxley and Saul Ware. ThinkTank Theatre. The Mill Studio, Yvonne Arnaud Theatre, Guilford. July 2004. The Priority Playhouse, Arundel, West Sussex. 11-15 Jan. 2005. Announcement in "The Harold Pinter Community Forum." 8 Dec. 2004. 12 Oct. 2007 <http://p079.ezboard.com/ftheharoldpintercommunityfrm1.showMessage?topicID=433.topic>.

The Lover. The White Bear Theatre Club. Artistic Dir. Mike Kingsbury. 26-31 Aug. 2003. "Upcoming Events for the Year 2003." 1 Sept. 2003 <http://www.haroldpinter.org/home/index.shtml>.

The Lover and *The Collection*. Dir. Anthony Caldarella. Perf. [in *The Lover*:] Henry Olek (Richard/Max) and Susan Priver (Sarah); [in *The Collection*] Yvette Brooks (Stella), Brian Foyster (Bill), Colin McCabe (James), and David Purdham (Harry). Hudson Backstage Theatre, Hollywood, CA. Through 29 Sept. 2002. (Rev. by Shirley.)

Monologue. Dir. Gari Jones. Perf. Henry Woolf (Man). Scenic Designer Eileen Diss. Costume Designer Mick Hughes. Almeida Theatre Company. Cottesloe Theatre, Royal National Theatre Platforms, London. 14, 15, 16, 23, & 24 Jan. 2002. Online posting. 11 Jan. 2002 <http://www.nationaltheatre.org.uk/Monologue+1194.twl> (Archived.) (Previously listed in *TPR* [2004]: 266.)

Mountain Language and *Ashes to Ashes*. Storytellers Reading Series, Pittsburgh Irish and Classical Theater (PICT), Pittsburgh, PA, 18-19 May 2003. (See Rawson, as listed above in "**Other Pertinent News Reports . . . .**")

"Nightschool by Harold Pinter": *Night School*, and selected review sketches. Dir. Guy Hollands. Citizens' Community Company. Citizens' Theatre, Glasgow. 14-18 May 2002. "Citizens Learning and TAG: Community Company: Performance Projects to Date." 22 Feb. 2008 <http://www.citz.co.uk/?page=new&node_id=1.7.4>. (See announcement in "Going Out, Staying Out," as listed above in "**Other Pertinent News Reports . . . .**")

No Man's Land. Dir. Albert Schultz. Perf. Peter Donat (Spooner) and William Hutt (Hirst). Premiere Dance Theatre, Harbourfront Centre, Toronto. 10 July-23 Aug. 2003. (See announcement by Crew, as listed above in "**Other Pertinent News Reports . . . .**")

No Man's Land. Dir. Dana Burns-Westberg. Perf. Geoffroy Bateman, Nicholas Calderbank, Damian Corcoran, and Mike Norris. Sudden Théâtre, Paris, France. 24 Sept.-27 Oct. 2002. (In English.) 28 Sept. 2002 <http://www.theatreonline.com/guide/detail_piece.asp?i_Region=25&i_Programmation=5916&i_Genre=&i_Origine=&i_Type=>.

No Man's Land. Dir. Harold Pinter. King's Theatre, Edinburgh. [Touring prod. of Lyttelton Theatre, London prod. listed in *TPR* (2004): 267-68.] (See announcement in "Barcelona" and feature by McMillan, as listed above in "**Other Pertinent News Reports . . . .**"; rev. by Devine and McMillan.)

No Man's Land. Dir. Richard Romagnoli. Perf. Richard Pilcher (Hirst) and Alan Wade (Spooner). Potomac Theatre Festival, Olney Theatre Center, Olney, Maryland. July-August 2003. Post-play discussion moderated by Mel Gussow, after the 7:45 p.m. performance. 26 July 2003. (See Horwitz; "Theater: Harold and Mel"; and Zekas, as cited above in "**Other Pertinent News Reports ...**"; rev. by Blanchard, McCauley, and brief rev. by Horwitz in "Our Picks.")

Old Times. Dir. Mark Rhoda. Costume & set design Misha Kachman. Bruce Davis Theater, Montgomery Hall Fine Arts Center, Department of Theater, St. Mary's College of Maryland, St. Mary's City, MD. 10-12, 14 Dec. 2003 (five performances). (See announcement in "Calendar of Events: December [2003] – January 2004," *River Gazette* <http://lepmfi.gsfc.nasa.gov/mfi/lepedu/herrero_speaker.pdf>.)

Old Times. Dir. Roger Curtis. Perf. Karen J Fairbrook (Kate), Greg Michaels (Deeley), and Cynthia White (Anna). Golden Fish Theatre, Seattle, WA. Nov. 2002. (Rev. by Green.)

Old Times. Dir. Roger Michell. Perf. Helen McCrory (Anna), Gina McKee (Kate), and Jeremy Northam (Deeley). Decor William Dudley. Lighting Rick Fisher. Donmar Warehouse Theatre, London. 7 July-4 Sept. 2004. (Rev. by Bassett, Billington, Brantley, G. Brown, deJongh, Edwardes, Gross, Halliburton, Kellaway, Letts, Miller, Morley, Nathan, Nightingale, Segal, Shenton, Spencer, Taylor, Thaxter, Wolf [2], and Woodis; "Reviews," rpt. in *Theatre Record* 24 [2004]: 890, 900-05, 1002-05.)

"A Pair of Pinters" – *The Room* & *Victoria Station.* Dir. Teri McCaskill. Studio Theatre, Raven Theatre, Chicago, IL. 19 Jan.-23 Feb. 2003. 9 Feb. 2003 <http://www.raventheatre.com/current/current.html> (since updated). Cf. <http://www.raventheatre.com/current.shtml>.

Party Time/One for the Road. Dir. Bijan Sheibani ["winner of this year's James Menzies-Kitchen Award for Young Directors"]. Perf. Jason Barnett (Jimmy / Victor), Paul Cawley (Douglas), Maria Charles (Melissa), Clare Francis (Liz), Bettrys Jones (Dusty), Kristin Hutchinson (Charlotte / Gila), Colin McCormack (Gavin / Nicolas), and Robert Styles (Fred). Prod. Abigail Gonda. Decor Paul Burgess. Lighting Guy Kometzki. Sound Emma Laxton. Presented by The James Menzies-Kitchin Memorial Trust Award for Young Directors. BAC 1, Battersea Arts Centre, London. 22 July-17 Aug. 2003. (Rev. by Bassett, Chappell, Halliburton, and Logan. Rpt. in *Theatre Record* 23 (2003): 963.)

"Pinter Briefs": "The Black and White," "Precisely," "Request Stop," "Victoria Station," and "A Kind of Alaska." "*Potomac Theatre Project Evening A.* Dir. Richard Romagnoli. The Potomac Theatre Project: Potomac Theatre Festival 2002: Awakening/Awareness Festival. Olney Theatre, Olney, MD. 16 July-11 Aug. 2002. (In rep. with Evening B: *The After-Dinner Joke*, by Caryl Churchill). (Rev. by Pressley.) (Cf. *TPR* [2004]: 268–69.)

"Seductions: A Classic Quartet of Short Plays, by George Bernard Shaw, Harold Pinter, Tennessee Williams and Anton Chekhov." Inc. *The Lover.* Perf. Lillian Care and Sean Ferratt. Theater Southwest, Houston, TX. Through 23 Nov. 2002. (See "Snap Shot," as listed above in "**Other Pertinent News Reports . . . .**")

Sketches I and *Sketches II.* Lyttelton Theatre, Royal National Theatre, London. 11 Feb. [*Sketches I*] and 8 Feb. [*Sketches II*] 2002. [Listed in *TPR* (2004): 269.] (*Sketches II*: Rev. by Billington.)

"Two by Harold Pinter": *The Room* and *Celebration.* Dir. Katherine Burkman; co-dir. Jane Cottrell; and assistant dir. Karin Maresh. Perf. (in *The Room*:) William Dancey (Mr. Kidd), Kenny Johnson (Mr. Sands), David Fawcett (Bert Hudd), Richard Mason (Riley), Christina Sidebottom (Rose Hudd), Aili Vcelka (Mr. Sands); (in *Celebration*:) Michael Detmold (Matt), Penny Donahue (Pru), David Fawcett (Lambert), Heather Hodnett, David Richard, Stephen Woosley (the Waiter), and others. Women At Play, Van Fleet Theatre, Davis Discovery Center, Columbus, OH. 11, 12, 15-17 Nov. 2002. (See announcements and rev. by Grossberg.)

Vecchi Tempi (*Old Times*). In Italian. Trans. Alessandra Serra. Dir. Roberto Andò. Perf. Umberto Orsini (Deeley), Greta Scacchi (Anna), and Valentina Sperlì (Kate); alternative cast: Umberto Orsini (Deeley), Elena Ghiaurov/Galatea Ranzi (Anna), and Valentina Sperlì (Kate). Set and lighting Gianni Carluccio. Video Luca Scarzella. Costumes Nanà Cecchi. Emilia Romagna Teatro Fondazione—CTB Teatro Stabile di Brescia. Opened at the Teatro Storchi di Modena, Italy, 14 Jan. 2004. Also produced at Teatro Duse, 14-23 Dec. 2004. Perf. Umberto Orsini, Valentina Sperli (Kate), and Galatea Ranzi (Anna). *CanvasManagement.com* 2 Feb. 2008 <http://www.canvasmanagement.com/production.php?id=336&lang=e&artist=67>, <http://www.emiliaromagnateatro.com/produzione.asp?P_Spt_CID=111>, <http://www.mentelocale.it/teatro/contenuti/index_html/id_contenuti_varint_11581>, and <http://www.teatrostabilegenova.it/t_cartellone.asp?MeseCorrente=0&SelStagione=63&chkProduzionePropria=2&selCriterioRicerca=3&txtCerca=Vecchi+tempi&txtCercaCognome=&txtCercaNome=&TipoRicerca=0&itemID=12&livello=2&label=archivio&invia+il+modulo.x=14&invia+il+modulo.y=7>. (See feature by Methven and Santini, as listed above in "**Other Pertinent News Reports ...**")

Performance Reviews of Plays by Harold Pinter

Bassett, Kate. "Theatre: Watch Out, This One Bites Hard; After Mrs Rochester Lyric Hammersmith London The Dwarfs Tricycle." Rev. of *The Dwarfs* (Tricycle Theatre, London). London *Independent on Sunday* 27 Apr. 2003, Features: 12. Rpt. in *Theatre Record* 23 (2003): 527. ["'After Mrs Rochester' hits the spot, while 'The Dwarfs', below, isn't as interesting as its writer, Harold Pinter."]

—. Rev. of *Old Times* (Donmar Warehouse, London). London *Independent on Sunday* 11 July 2004. Rpt. in *Theatre Record* 24 (2004): 903.

—. "Theatre: All Washed Up (on a Shore of Wet Jumpers)." Rev. of *Party Time / One for the Road* (BAC1 [BAC Studio], Battersea Arts Centre, London). London *Independent on Sunday* 3 Aug. 2003, Features: 12. Rpt. in *Theatre Record* 23 (2003): 963.

Billington, Michael. "*Betrayal*: 4 Stars Duchess Theatre, London." *Guardian* 9 Oct. 2003. (10 Oct. 2003 version cited in Knowles, "Harold Pinter 2002-2004," *TPR* [2004]: 232.) 29 Sept. 2007 <http://arts.guardian.co.uk/critic/review/0,,1059202,00.html>.

—. "Review: The Main Event: Theatre: *Old Times*: Donmar Warehouse, London 4/5." *Guardian* 9 July 2004: 22. *Guardian* 8 July 2004. Rpt. in *Theatre Record* 24 (2004): 901.

—. "Review: Theatre: Odd Theatrical Affinities: Theatre: Design for Living / Betrayal: Royal, Bath 4/5." Rev. of *Betrayal* (Theatre Royal, Bath). *Guardian* 10 July 2003, Guardian Leader Pages: 26. Rpt. in *Theatre Record* 23 (2003): 909. (Cited also in Knowles, "Harold Pinter 2002-2004," *TPR* [2004]: 232.)

—. "Review: Theatre: The Dark Imagination of Harold Pinter: *The Dumb Waiter* and Other Pieces: Playhouse, Oxford 3/5." *Guardian* 16 Feb. 2004: 20. Rpt. in *Theatre Record* 24 (2004): 248.

—. "Review: Theatre: The Dwarfs: Tricycle Serves Up a Filleted Pinter: Tricycle, London 3/5." *Guardian* 24 Apr. 2003, Guardian Leader Pages: 28. Rpt. in *Theatre Record* 23 (2003): 530.

—. "Reviews: Theatre: Pinter Delivers a Short, Sharp Shock: Sketches: National Theatre, London 4/5." *Guardian* 11 Feb. 2002, Guardian Leader Pages: 19. ["A version of this review appeared in later editions of Saturday's [9 Feb. 2002] paper"; listed in *TPR* (2004): 271; cf. <http://arts.guardian.co.uk/critic/review/0,,671747,00.html>.]

—. "Saturday Review: Arts: The King of the Jungle: Ian Holm Brings Epic Majesty to Pinter's *Homecoming*." *Guardian* 16 June 2001.

Blanchard, Jayne. "Funny and Scary 'Land' of Lost Souls: Production of Pinter Play Balances Humor, Bleakness." *Washington Times* 26 July 2003, Arts, Theater: D2. (Final ed.).

Bodey, Michael. "Ten Days to Turn Into a Bull Artist." Sydney *Daily Telegraph* 27 July 2002, Features-Type-Feature-Column-Around TownInside [sic] Edition: 26.

Bows, Bob. "*The Homecoming* and *Betrayal*." *ColoradoDrama.com* (Archives). 22 Feb. 2008 <http://coloradodrama.com/pinter.html>.

Boyd, Chris. "Selective Memory: A Triumph." Melbourne *Herald Sun* 4 Nov. 2002, Arts & Entertainment: 103. [Rev. of *No Man's Land* (Victorian College of the Arts), dir. Di Trevis, previously listed in *TPR* (2004): 269.]

Brandes, Philip, and F. Kathleen Foley. "Theater Beat: 'First Lady Suite': Marrying Into History: ... 'The Dumb Waiter' Serves Up Humor, Terror." *Los Angeles Times* 15 Mar. 2002, Calendar (Calendar Desk), Part 6: 33.

Brantley, Ben. "London Notebook: Pinter Is Still Pointing the Way, with Shadows and Darkness." *New York Times* 13 July 2004, Arts and ideas/Cultural Desk: E1, 5. (Late Ed., East Coast.) 20 Sept. 2007 <http://query.nytimes.com/gst/fullpage.html?res=9F0CE1DD1E3BF930A25754C0A9629C8B63&sec=&spon=&pagewanted=all>. [Rev. of *Old Times* (Donmar Warehouse, London).]

—. "Theatre Review: Forces Cruel, Kindly and Shifty in Pinterland." *New York Times* 10 Nov. 2003. 29 Aug. 2007 <http://theater2.nytimes.com/mem/theater/treview.html?res=9F00EFD71039F933A25752C1A9659C8B63>.

Braunagel, Don. "Theater Review: Effectively Rounding Out Harold Pinter and His Pauses." *Los Angeles Times* 5 Feb. 2002, Calendar, Part 6 (Calendar Desk): 10.

Brock, Wendell. "Theater: Theatre in the Square Poses a Pinter Puzzler Well Worth Mulling Over." *Atlanta Jour. and Constitution* 4 Oct. 2002, Preview: 4Q.

Brown, Georgina. Rev. of *Betrayal* (Theatre Royal, Bath). London *Mail on Sunday* 13 July 2003. Rpt. in *Theatre Record* 23 (2003): 910.

—. Rev. of *The Dwarfs* (Tricycle Theatre, London). London *Mail on Sunday* 27 Apr. 2003. Rpt. in *Theatre Record* 23 (2003): 527-28.

—. Rev. of *Old Times* (Donmar Warehouse, London). London *Mail on Sunday* 11 July 2004. Rpt. in *Theatre Record* 24 (2004): 902.

Brown, Mark. Rev. of *The Birthday Party* (Tag Theatre, The Tron, Glasgow, Scotland). *Scotsman* 24 Sept. 2003. Rpt. in *Theatre Record* 23 (2003): 1292.

Brown, Tony. "Pinter Work Rendered with Surgical Precision." Cleveland *Plain Dealer* 15 Apr. 2002, Arts & Life: C1.

Byrne, Terry. "Theater Review: Details Intensify Pain of 'Betrayal.'" *Boston Herald* 11 Mar. 2003, Arts & Life: 39.

Catlett, Mallory. "Madness and Method in *This Room Is Moving*." *Canadian Theatre Rev.* 119 (Summer 2004): 35-39. [Theatrical production by Screaming Flea Theatre Company, Vancouver, British Columbia, Can. Re: *The Dwarfs*.]

Cavendish, Dominic. "The Seeds of Pinter's Genius." Rev. of *The Dwarfs* (Tricycle Theatre, London). London *Daily Telegraph* 25 Apr. 2003. Rpt. in *Theatre Record* 23 (2003): 527.

—. "Postlethwaite's Return Is Just the Ticket." London *Daily Telegraph* 30 Jan. 2002: 20. Rpt. in *Theatre Record* 22 (2002): 91. [Expanded retroactive entry.]

Chappell, Helen. Rev. of *Party Time / One for the Road* (BAC1, Battersea Arts Centre, London). *What's On* 6 Aug. 2003. Rpt. in *Theatre Record* 23 (2003): 963.

Clapp, Susannah. "Dramatis Interruptus." *Observer* Apr. 2003: 11. Rpt. in *Theatre Record* 23 (2003): 529. (Cited also in Knowles, "Harold Pinter 2002-2004," *TPR* [2004]: 232.) [Inc. brief rev. of *The Dwarfs* (Tricycle Theatre, London).]

Clay, Carolyn. "Theater: Vintage Avant-Garde: *The Birthday Party* at the ART, *What the Butler Saw* at the Huntington." *Boston Phoenix* 19-25 Mar. 2004. 22 Aug. 2007 <http://72.166.46.24/boston/arts/theater/documents/03678.242.asp>.

Cooper, Neil. Rev. of *The Birthday Party* (Tag Theatre, The Tron, Glasgow, Scotland). *Herald* 25 Sept. 2003. Rpt. in *Theatre Record* 23 (2003): 1292.

Cooper, Neil, and Louisa McEwan. "Ambitious Adaptation Lacks Imagination and Verve: ... A Kind of Alaska." [Rev. by Louisa McEwan.] Glasgow *Herald* 6 Aug. 2003: 14.

Coveney, Michael. Rev. of *Betrayal* (Duchess Theatre, London). London *Daily Mail* 9 Oct. 2003. Rpt. in *Theatre Record* 23 (2004): 1375.

—. Rev. of *Betrayal*. London *Daily Mail* 11 July 2003. Rpt. in *Theatre Record* 23 (2003): 914-15.

—. Rev. of "*The Dumb Waiter* and Other Pieces." London *Daily Mail* 20 Feb. 2004. Rpt. in *Theatre Record* 24 (2004): 248.

Cramer, Steve. Rev. of *The Birthday Party* (Tag Theatre, The Tron, Glasgow, Scotland). *List* 2 Oct. 2003. Rpt. in *Theatre Record* 23 (2003): 1291.

de Jongh, Nicholas. "Passionate Pinter." Rev. of *The Dwarfs* (Tricycle Theatre, London). London *Evening Standard* 24 Apr. 2003: 49. Rpt. in *Theatre Record* 23 (2003): 528. (Cited also in Knowles, "Harold Pinter 2002-2004," *TPR* [2004]: 233.)

—. Rev. of *Old Times* (Donmar Warehouse). London *Evening Standard* 8 July 2004. Rpt. in *Theatre Record* 24 (2004): 900.

Devine, Rachel. "No Man's Land." London *Sunday Times* 14 Apr. 2002, Features.

Dunne, Stephen. "All Care, No Transportability, for a Pre-Indulgence Classic." *Sydney Morning Herald* 26 July 2002, Metropolitan: 12.

Edwardes, Jane. "'Old Times' Donmar Warehouse O-WE: Theatre: Preview." *Time Out* (London) 14 July 2004: 139.

—. Rev. of *The Dwarfs* (Tricycle Theatre, London). *Time Out* (London) 30 Apr. 2003. Rpt. in *Theatre Record* 23 (2003): 530-31.

Evans, Lloyd. "Disorganised Dossier: ARTS Theatre." Rev. of *The Dwarfs* (Tricycle Theatre, London). *Spectator* 3 May 2003: 55-56. Rpt. in *Theatre Record* 23 (2003): 531.

Fanger, Iris. "Pinter's Parlor: *The Homecoming* Shines in Wellfleet." *Boston Phoenix* 6-13 June 2002. 22 Feb. 2008 <http://www.bostonphoenix.com/boston/arts/theater/documents/02299100.htm>.

—. "This Week's Picks: After Endgame: Joanne Akalaitis Throws a *Birthday Party.*" *Boston Phoenix* 5-11 Mar. 2004. 22 Aug. 2007 <http://72.166.46.24/boston/events/theater/documents/03644284.asp>.

Fetzer, Brett. "Stranger Suggests; Thursday Feb 28: Ashes to Ashes." *The Stranger.com* 28 Feb.-6 Mar. 2002. 22 Aug. 2007 <http://cgi.thestranger.com/2002-02-28/stranger_suggests.html>.

"The Five Best: Plays." London *Independent* 28 Feb. 2002, Features: 13. (First Ed.) [Inc. *No Man's Land* (Oxford Playhouse from 26 Feb. to 2 Mar. 2002).]

Foss, Roger. Rev. of *The Dwarfs* (Tricycle Theatre, London). *What's On* 30 Apr. 2003. Rpt. in *Theatre Record* 23 (2003): 530.

Fricker, Karen. "Dublin Fests Short on New Work But Tied Up in 'Knots.'" *Variety* 24-30 Oct. 2005, Legit: 39.

Gardner, Lyn. Rev. of *The Caretaker* (Bristol Old Vic). *Guardian* 11 Sept. 2003. Rpt. in *Theatre Record* 23 (2003): 1211.

—. "Review: Theatre: The Birthday Party: Crucible Theatre, Sheffield 3/5." *Guardian* 13 Feb. 2002, Guardian Leader Pages: 18.

Gillen, Francis. "*The Caretaker* in New York." *Pinter Rev.* (2004): 171-74. (Illus.)

Gorfinkle, Constance. "Archives: Theater Preview: Rigby Has Long History with Harold Pinter." Boston *Patriot Ledger* 2 Mar. 2004. 22 Aug. 2007 <http://ledger.southofboston.com/articles/2004/03/02/life/life02/txt>.

Green, Leah B. "'Old Times' Is Up to Audience to Figure Out." *Seattle Times* 27 Nov. 2002, ROP Zone, Northwest Life: F2.

Gross, John. "A Fine Pair of Love Triangles: Theatre." London *Sunday Telegraph* 13 July 2003: 8.

—. Rev. of *Old Times* (Donmar Warehouse). London *Sunday Telegraph* 11 July 2004. Rpt. in *Theatre Record* 24 (2004): 901-02.

—. "Theatre." Rev. of *The Dwarfs* (Lyric, Hammersmith). London *Sunday Telegraph* 4 May 2003: 22.

—. "Theatre." Rev. of *The Dwarfs* (Tricycle Theatre, London). London *Sunday Telegraph* 27 Apr. 2003. Rpt. in *Theatre Record* 23 (2003): 529-30.

Grossberg, Michael. Theater Review: Two by Harold Pinter: Production Among Year's Best." *Columbus* (OH) *Dispatch* 11 Nov. 2002, Features – Accent & Arts: 7C.

Hallett, Victor. "Betrayal; Theatre Review: Mold." *The Stage* 9 May 2002: 14.

Halliburton, Rachel. "Elusive Reality." Rev. of *Old Times* (Donmar Warehouse, London). *Spectator* 24 July 2004: 42. Rpt. in *Theatre Record* 24 (2004): 905.

—. Rev. of *Party Time / One for the Road* (BAC1). London *Evening Standard* 28 July 2003. Rpt. In *Theatre Record* 23 (2003): 963.

Hampton, Wilborn. "A Rocky Marriage Channels the World's Woes." *New York Times* 18 Dec. 2003: E3. (Late Ed., East Coast.)

Harris, Timothy. "Japan: Timothy Harris: in Tokyo." *Plays International* July-Aug. 2004: 42-43, 58. ["Abstract: Summer 2004 Tokyo stage productions are reviewed, including: two versions of Harold Pinter's 'The Dumb Waiter,' Sam Shepard's 'True West,' and the musical 'Hedwig and the Angry Inch.'"

Hemming, Sarah. "Early Rites of Passage Revisited: Theatre: The Dwarfs (Tricycle Theatre, London). London *Financial Times* 25 Apr. 2003. Rpt. in *Theatre Record* 23 (2003): 529.

Hewison, Robert. Rev. of *Betrayal* (Theatre Royal, Bath). London *Sunday Times* 20 July 2003. Rpt. in *Theatre Record* 23 (2003): 915-16.

Hickling, Alfred. Rev. of *Betrayal* (Duke's Theatre, Lancaster, Eng.) *Guardian* 21 Mar. 2005. Rpt. in *Theatre Record* 25 (2005): 379.

Horwitz, Jane. "Our Picks." *Washington Post* 1 Aug. 2003, Weekend: T3. [Inc. Jane Horwitz's brief rev. of *No Man's Land* (Olney Theatre Center, Potomac Theatre Festival).]

Isherwood, Charles. "The Caretaker." Rev. of *The Caretaker* (Roundabout Theatre Company, American Airlines Theatre, New York). *Variety* 17 Nov. 2003: 44.

Jaques, Damien. "Human Nature Takes Center Stage in 'The Caretaker'." *Milwaukee Jour. Sentinel* 3 Mar. 2002, News: 7B.

Jillett, Neil, and Steven Carroll. "Melbourne Festival." *Sunday Age* (Melbourne) 3 Nov. 2002, Agenda: 9. [Rev. of *No Man's Land* (Victorian College of the Arts), dir. Di Trevis, previously listed in *TPR* (2004): 269.]

Kellaway, Kate. "Review: Critics: Theatre: I Can't Menage without You: Three Plays from the Peter Hall Company Look At Love, Lust, Loss–and the Eternal Triangle." *Observer* 13 July 2003, Observer Rev. Pages: 10. [Inc. rev. of *Betrayal* (Theatre Royal, Bath).]

—. Rev. of *Old Times* (Donmar Warehouse). *Observer* 11 July 2004. Rpt. in *Theatre Record* 24 (2004): 900.

Kennedy, Louise. "ART Director, Celebrates Simplicity in Pinter's Complex 'Birthday Party'." *Boston Globe* 5 Mar. 2004. *Boston.com* 22 Aug. 2007 <http://www.boston.com/news/globe/living/articles/2004/03/05/art_director_celebrates_simplicity>.

K[ingston], J[eremy] and Ed Potton. "The Best Shows Nationwide." London *Times* 26 Jan. 2002, Features.

Koenig, Rhoda. "Reviews: Theatre: The Birthday Party Crucible Theatre Sheffield." London *Independent* 14 Feb. 2002, Features: 12. (First Edition.)

—. "Theatre: Design for Living / Betrayal Theatre Royal Bath: Designed for Betrayal: Janie Dee and Hugo Speer Get Shirty in Bath." London *Independent* 14 July 2003, Features: 17. Rpt. in *Theatre Record* 23 (2003): 910-11.

Letts, Quentin. Rev. of *Old Times* (Donmar Warehouse, London). London *Daily Mail* 9 Sept. 2004. Rpt. in *Theatre Record* 24 (2004): 904.

Logan, Brian. Rev. of "*Party Time / One for the Road*". *Time Out* 30 July 2003. Rpt. in *Theatre Record* 23 (2003): 963.

Longworth, Ken. "Ambiguous Pinter Production." *Newcastle Herald* 21 May 2002, News: 46.

Low, Lenny Ann. "A Bit on the Side, a Lot Left Unsaid." *Sydney Morning Herald* 13 Dec. 2002, Metropolitan: 18.

—, and Stephen Dunne. "Performance: ... The Lover." *Sydney Morning Herald* 14

Dec. 2002, Metropolitan: 16.

Lowe, Leah. "Performance Review: 'The Birthday Party.'" *Theatre Jour.* 56 (2004): 508-10.

Macaulay, Alastair. "Design for Living / Betrayal: Theatre Royal, Bath. London *Financial Times* 11 July 2003. Rpt. in *Theatre Record* 23 (2003): 911.

Marlowe, Sam. Rev. of "*The Dumb Waiter* and Other Pieces." London *Times* 16 Feb. 2004. Rpt. in *Theatre Record* 24 (2004): 248.

Marmion, Patrick. Rev. of *The Dwarfs* (Tricycle Theatre, London). London *Daily Mail* 25 Apr. 2003. Rpt. in *Theatre Record* 23 (2003): 528.

Mazey, Steven. "Audience Turnout Picks Up." *Ottawa Citizen* 24 June 2002, Arts: B1.

McCallum, John. "Modern Parallels in Pinter's Tale of Loss." *Australian* 26 July 2002, Features: 14.

McCauley, Mary Carole. "Dramas Offer Gritty Lessons of Life's Trials at Olney Fest: Cutting-Edge Plays Are Not Light Fare." *Baltimore Sun* 5 Aug. 2003, Today: 1E. (Final Ed.)

McMillan, Joyce. "Review: No Man's Land: King's Theatre, Edinburgh." *Scotsman* 17 Apr. 2002: 5.

Miller, Keith. "ARTS - *Old Times* (Donmar Warehouse, London). [By] Harold Pinter. *The Old Masters* (Comedy Theatre). [By] Simon Gray." *TLS, The Times Literary Supplement* 23 July 2004: 16.

Morley, Sheridan. "Arts – Theatre – Top Hats and No Trousers – Georges Feydeau Succeeds Where Harold Pinter Fails." Rev. of *The Dwarfs* (Tricycle Theatre, London). *New Statesman* 12 May 2003: 46. 24 Feb. 2008 <http://www.newstatesman.com/200305120042>. Rpt. in *Theatre Record* 23 (2003): 533.

—. Rev. of *Old Times* (Donmar Warehouse, London). Rpt. in *Theatre Record* 24 (2004): 903.

Nathan, John. Rev. of *Betrayal* (Duchess Theatre, London). *Jewish Chronicle* 17 Oct. 2003. Rpt. in *Theatre Record* 23 (2004): 1375.

—. "Rev. of *The Dwarfs* (Tricycle Theatre, London). *Jewish Chronicle* 9 May 2003. Rpt. in *Theatre Record* 23 (2003): 534.

—. Rev. of *Old Times* (Donmar Warehouse, London). *Jewish Chronicle* 16 July 2004. Rpt. in *Theatre Record* 24 (2004): 904.

Nightingale, Benedict. "The Homecoming." London *Times* 31 Jan. 2002, Features.

—. "Pinter among the Little People." Rev. of *The Dwarfs* (Tricycle Theatre, London). London *Times* 24 Apr. 2003. Rpt. in *Theatre Record* 23 (2003): 530.

—. Rev. of *Betrayal* (Theatre Royal, Bath). London *Times* 11 July 2003: 908-09.

—. Rev. of *Old Times* (Donmar Warehouse, London). London *Times* 9 July 2004. Rpt. in *Theatre Record* 24 (2004): 900-01.

O'Connor, John Courtney. "Pinter's Brave Rite of Passage." *Morning Star* 1 May 2003: 21.

Peter, John. Rev. of *The Caretaker* (Bristol Old Vic). London *Sunday Times* 14 Sept. 2003. Rpt. in *Theatre Record* 23 (2003): 1211.

—. Rev. of *The Dwarfs* (Tricycle Theatre, London). London *Sunday Times* 27 Apr.

2003. Rpt. in *Theatre Record* 23 (2003): 529.

Pressley, Nelson. "Olney's One-Act Plays: A Mixed Bag of Brevity." *Washington Post* 24 July 2002, Style: C4. [Rev. of "Pinter Briefs."]

Redman, Mary. "The Caretaker: Theatre Review: Colchester." *The Stage* 14 Mar. 2002: 17.

"[Reviews:] London: 'Old Times'" and "More on Previous Productions." *Theatre Record* 24 (2004): 890, 900-05, 1002-05. [Revs. of *Old Times*, dir. Roger Michell, Donmar Warehouse, London.]

Reynolds, Oliver. Rev. of *The Dwarfs* (Tricycle Theatre). *Times Literary Supplement* 2 May 2003: 20. (Cited in Knowles, "Harold Pinter 2002-2004," *TPR* [2004]: 233.)

Rich, Joshua. "The Caretaker." Rev. of *The Caretaker* (Roundabout Theatre Company, American Airlines Theatre, New York), *Entertainment Weekly* 21 Nov. 2003: 94.

Roddam, Victoria. "The Dumb Waiter & Other Pieces by Harold Pinter." The Oxford Playhouse 17-28 Feb. 2004. *BBC - Oxford Stage - The Dumb Waiter Review* Feb. 2004. 29 Aug. 2007 <http://www.bbc.co.uk/Oxford/stage/2004/02/dub_witer_review.shtml>.

Rocamora, Carol. "Theater: Yuri Gagarin Rides Again." *Nation* 25 Feb. 2002: 34, 36. [Rev. of *No Man's Land* (Royal National Theatre, London); prod. details previously listed in *TPR* (2004): 267-68.]

Roddam, Victoria. "Review: The Dumb Waiter" (The Oxford Playhouse, Oxford, UK). *BBC – Oxford Stage – The Dumb Waiter Rev.* Feb. 2004. 29 Aug. 2007 http://www.bbc.co.uk/oxford/stage/2004/02/dumb_waiter_review.shtml>.

Rose, Colin. "More Punch, Less Pillow." Sydney *Sun Herald* 28 July 2002, Metro: 6.

Segal, Victoria. Rev. of *Old Times* (Donmar Warehouse, London). London *Sunday Times* 11 July 2004. Rpt. in *Theatre Record* 24 (2004): 902-03.

Shenton, Mark. Rev. of *Betrayal* (Duchess Theatre, London). London *Sunday Express* 12 Oct. 2003. Rpt. in *Theatre Record* 23 (2004): 1375.

—. Rev. of *Old Times* (Donmar Warehouse, London). London *Sunday Express* 11 July 2004. Rpt. in *Theatre Record* 24 (2004): 900.

Shirley, Don. "Theater Review: A Winding Ramble in 'The Country': Martin Crimp's Play, in Its American Premiere at La Jolla Playhouse, Can't Manage to Rise Above a Garden-Variety Domestic Drama." *Los Angeles Times* 6 Aug. 2003, Calendar, Part 5 (Calendar Desk): 5.

Shuttleworth, Ian. "Perfectly Out of Synch with Reality and Realism: Theatre: The Birthday Party." *Financial Times* 14 Feb. 2002, The Arts: 16.

Siegel, Ed. "Stage Reviews: ART's 'Party' Celebrates the Surreal." *Boston Globe* 12 Mar. 2004. *Boston.com.* 22 Aug. 2007 <http://www.boston.com/news/globe/living/articles/2004/03/12/arts_party_celebrates_the_surreal/>. [Rev. of *The Birthday Party* (American Repertory Theatre, Cambridge, MA).]

Sierz, Aleks. "Laugh Out Loud Darkness." *Times Educational Supplement* 24 Sept. 2004: 20. [Rev. of *The Caretaker* (Dir. Michael Cabbot).]

—. Rev. of *The Dwarfs* (Tricycle Theatre, London). London *Tribune* 2 May 2003. Rpt. in *Theatre Record* 23 (2003): 531.

Simmonds, Diana. "Westies Return in Triumph: ... Lovers' Appeal an Enduring Appeal." Sydney *Sunday Telegraph* 15 Dec. 2002, Features-Column-Arts: 132.

Simon, John. "Bum Rap." Rev. of *The Caretaker* (Roundabout Theatre, American Airlines Theatre). *New York* 24 Nov. 2003: 131.

Spencer, Charles. Rev. of *Design for Living / Betrayal* (Theatre Royal, Bath). London *Daily Telegraph* 9 July 2003. Rpt. in *Theatre Record* 23 (2003): 911-12.

—. Rev. of "*The Dumb Waiter* and Other Pieces." London *Daily Telegraph* 17 Feb. 2004. Rpt. in *Theatre Record* 24 (2004): 248-49.

—. Rev. of *Old Times* (Donmar Warehouse, London). London *Daily Telegraph* 8 July 2004. Rpt. in *Theatre Record* 24 (2004): 901.

Stearn, Richard. "'A Kind of Alaska'/'Me and My Friend' Orange Tree O-WE; Theatre: Review." *Time Out* 19 June 2002.

Taylor, Paul. "Arts Reviews: An Un-Seemly Form of Betrayal: Theatre: The Dwarfs Tricycle Theatre London 00999: Power Play: Ben Caplan As Mark, and Mark Rice-Oxley As Len, in The Dwarfs." London *Independent* 25 Apr. 2003, Feature: 20.

—. "First Night: A Stilted, Clumsy Exercise That Is Best Left to Pinter Fanatics: The Dwarfs Tricycle Theatre, London." London *Independent* 24 Apr. 2003, News: 8; 25 Apr. 2003, Review: 21. Rpt. in *Theatre Record* 23 (2003): 528-29. (Cited also in Knowles, "Harold Pinter 2002-2004," *TPR* [2004]: 233.)

—. "The Five Best Plays in London ... and Beyond." London *Independent* 2 Mar. 2002, Features: 40. [Rev. of *The Birthday Party* (Sheffield Crucible), dir. Erica Whyman.]

—. Rev. of *Old Times* (Donmar Warehouse, London). London *Independent* 18 July 2004. Rpt. in *Theatre Record* 24 (2004): 904-05.

—. "Theatre: The Five Best Plays in London: ... and Beyond: Design for Living / Betrayal (Theatre Royal, Bath)." London *Independent* 2 Aug. 2003, Features: 38.

Teachout, Terry. Rev. of *The Caretaker* (Roundabout Theatre Company, American Airlines Theatre, New York). *Wall Street Jour.* 14 Nov. 2003. *Breaking News.* 29 Aug. 2007 <http://www.artspass.com/news.asp?bn=true&bb=3464>.

Thaxter, John. "The Dwarfs: Theatre Review: Tricycle." *The Stage* 1 May 2003: 14.

—. "A Kind of Alaska/Me and My Friend: Theatre Review: Richmond." *The Stage* 27 June 2002: 14.

—. Rev. of *Old Times* (Donmar Warehouse, London). *What's On* 14 July 2004. Rpt. in *Theatre Record* 24 (2004): 904.

—. Rev. of *Old Times* (Donmar Warehouse). Rpt. in *Theatre Record* 24 (2004): 904-05.

Thomson, Helen. "A Sense of Erotic Possibility." *The Age* (Melbourne), 29 Oct. 2002, The Culture: 4. [Rev. of *No Man's Land* (Victorian College of the Arts), dir. Di Trevis, previously listed in *TPR* (2004): 269.]

Toscano, Michael. "'Betrayal' a Compelling Affair." *Washington Post* 27 Feb. 2003, Alexandria-Arlington Extra: T8.

"The Week's Best: Nov 29-Dec 5." *Sydney Morning Herald* 29 Nov. 2002, Metro: 2.

Welch, Anne Marie. "Renaissance Man: Pinter's 'Caretaker' Gets an Up-to-Date Staging." *San Diego Union-Tribune* 18 Mar. 2002, Lifestyle: D1.

Wolf, Matt. "Legit Reviews: Abroad: *Old Times* (Donmar Warehouse; 251 Seats; £29 [$54] Top)." *Variety* 19-25 July 2004: 64-65.

—. "Old Times Donmar Warehouse, London. [Matt Wolf: The Critics.]" London *Financial Times* 9 July 2004: 13. (London 1st Ed.) Rpt. in *Theatre Record* 24 (2004): 902.

Wood, Peter. "The Dumb Waiter and Other Pieces" (Oxford Playhouse, and Touring). *The British Theatre Guide 2004.* 29 Aug. 2007 <http://www.britishtheatreguide.info/reviews/dumbwaiter-rev.htm>.

Woodis, Carole. Rev. of *Betrayal* (Theatre Royal, Bath). London *Herald* 11 July 2003. Rpt. in *Theatre Record* 23 (2003): 909-10.

—. Rev. of *The Dwarfs* (Tricycle Theatre, London). London *Herald* 8 May 2003. Rpt. in *Theatre Record* 23 (2003): 534.

—. Rev. of *Old Times* (Donmar Warehouse, London). London *Herald* 12 July 2004. Rpt. in *Theatre Record* 24 (2004): 905.

Yee, Esther. "Playing Ping Pong with One-Act Plays." *Strait Times* (Singapore) 17 Mar. 2003, Life!

Plays Directed by Harold Pinter and Reviews

The Old Masters

The Old Masters. By Simon Gray. Dir. Harold Pinter. Perf. Peter Bowles (Joseph Duveen), Sally Dexter (Nicky Mariano), Edward Fox (Bernard Berenson), Barbara Jefford (Mary Berenson), and Steven Pacey (Fowles). Decor Eileen Diss. Costumes Dany Everett. Lighting Mick Hughes. Sound John Leonard for Aura. Assistant Dir. Katie Read. Presented by Greg Ripley-Duggan with Duveen Productions and Ted Tulchin. Comedy Theatre. 1 July-28 Aug. 2004. (Revs. rpt. in *Theatre Record* 24 (2004): 877-82, 889; see also Shuttleworth.

Reviews of *The Old Masters*

Bassett, Kate. London *Independent on Sunday* 11 July 2004. Rpt. in *Theatre Record* 24 (2004): 877.

Billington, Michael. *Guardian* 2 July 2004. Rpt. in *Theatre Record* 24 (2004): 880.

Brown, Georgina. London *Mail on Sunday* 4 July 2004. Rpt. in *Theatre Record* 24 (2004): 879.

Clapp, Susannah. London *Observer* 4 July 2004. Rpt. in *Theatre Record* 24 (2004): 881.

de Jongh, Nicholas. London *Evening Standard* 2 July 2004. Rpt. in *Theatre Record* 24 (2004): 877.

Edwardes, Jane. *Time Out* (London) 7 July 2004. Rpt. in *Theatre Record* 24 (2004): 878.

Foss, Roger. London *What's On* 7 July 2004. Rpt. in *Theatre Record* 24 (2004): 879.

Gross, John. London *Sunday Telegraph* 4 July 2004. Rpt. in *Theatre Record* 24 (2004): 877-78.

Halliburton, Rachel. *Spectator* 24 July 2004. Rpt. in *Theatre Record* 24 (2004): 882.

Hewison, Robert. London *Sunday Times* 11 July 2004. Rpt. in *Theatre Record* 24 (2004): 878.

Letts, Quentin. London *Daily Mail* 2 July 2004. Rpt. in *Theatre Record* 24 (2004): 880.

Macaulay, Alastair. London *Financial Times* 3 July 2004. Rpt. in *Theatre Record* 24 (2004): 879-80.

—. "Theatre: [SURVEYS EDITION]." London *Financial Times* 26 June 2004: 38.

—. "Why Playing with Time Should Be Left to an Old Master." London *Financial Times* 9 July 2004, Alastair Macaulay–London Theatre: 10. (USA 1st Ed.)

Miller, Keith. "ARTS - *Old Times* (Donmar Warehouse, London) Harold Pinter. *The Old Masters* (Comedy Theatre). [By] Simon Gray." *TLS, The Times Literary Supplement* 5285 (2004): 16.

Morley, Sheridan. London *Express* 3 July 2004. Rpt. in *Theatre Record* (2004): 878.

Nathan, John. *Jewish Chronicle* 9 July 2004. Rpt. in *Theatre Record* (2004): 877.

Nightingale, Benedict. London *Times* 3 July 2004. Rpt. in *Theatre Record* 24 (2004): 880.

Shenton, Mark. London *Sunday Express* 4 July 2004. Rpt. in *Theatre Record* 24 (2004): 877.

Shuttleworth, Ian. "Prompt Corner: ... Juggling Halibut." *Theatre Record* 24 (2004): 875-76. [Brief ed. commentary on the prod., particularly "Edward Fox's portrayal of Beranard Berenson in *The Old Masters*," dir. Harold Pinter, and on prod. revs. rpt. in *Theatre Record* (as listed herein).]

Spencer, Charles. London *Daily Telegraph*. Rpt. in *Theatre Record* 24 (2004): 880-81.

Taylor, Paul. London *Independent* 5 July 2004. Rpt. in *Theatre Record* 24 (2004): 879.

Wolf, Matt. "Legit Reviews: Abroad: 'The Old Masters.'" *Variety* 12-18 July 2004: 34.

—. Rev. of *The Old Masters. International Herald Tribune* 21 July 2004. Rpt. in *Theatre Record* 24 (2004): 881-82.

Woodis, Carole. London *Herald* 5 July 2004. Rpt. in *Theatre Record* 24 (2004): 881.

Films and Videos/DVDs

American Film Theatre Series (1973-75). Prod. Ely Landau. "30th Anniversary digitally re-mastered 35mm colour films" by 3DD Entertainment (UK) in association with Lorber Media (PAL/Region 2, Europe & Japan). (Courtesy of Sarah Andersen, Publicity Officer, 3DD Entertainment.) VHS/DVD box sets of the 14 newly digitally remastered films in North America (NTSC/Region 1, U.S./Canada). Press release. Online posting. 18 Feb. 2003 <http://www.kino.com/video/news.html>. Available: 1 Apr. 2003. Box Set 1 (Spring 2003): *The Iceman Cometh* (1973, dir. John Frankenheimer); *Rhinoceros* (1974, dir. Tom O'Horgan); *Butley* (1973, dir. Harold Pinter); *Luther* (1973, dir. Guy Green); & *The Maids* (1974, dir. Christopher Miles). Box Set 2 (Summer 2003): *A Delicate Balance* (1973, dir. Tony Richardson); *The Man in the Glass Booth* (1975, dir. Arthur Hiller); *In Celebration* (1974, dir. Lindsay Anderson); *The Homecoming* (1973, dir. Peter Hall); & *Three Sisters* (1970, dir. Laurence

Olivier). Box Set 3 (Fall 2003): *Galileo* (1974, dir. Joseph Losey); *Lost in the Stars* (1974, dir. Daniel Mann); *Jacques Brel Is Alive and Well and Living in Paris* (1975, dir. Denis Héroux); & *Philadelphia, Here I Come* (1975, dir. John Quested). [Special features : theatrical trailers, essays (by Michael Feingold, Chief Theatre Critic, *The Village Voice,* also printed within package insert); the AFT cinebills; stills galleries; an interview with Edie Landau, Exec. in Charge, The American Film Theatre; AFT Promotional Reel: "Ely Landau: In Front of the Camera" (1974); "The American Film Theatre Trailer Gallery," inc. a complete list of the AFT films; "The American Film Theatre Scapbook." Letterboxed (1.85:1) & enhanced for 16x9 TVs. Copyright 1974 by AFT Distributing Corp. All rights reserved. Special Contents copyright 2003 Kino International Corp. DVD packaging copyright 2003 Kino International Corp. All rights reserved.] (Courtesy of Brian Shirey, Dir. of DVD & Video Operations; additional information available from Rodrigo Brandão, Dir. of Publicity, Kino International Corp.) Cf. "American Film Theatre Series (1973-75)." *TPR* (2004): 297. (Rev. by Cashill, Horowitz, and Schickel.)

Pinter, Harold. Script Coordinator. *The Heroes of Telemark.* Screenplay by Ivan Moffat and Ben Barzman. Dir. Anthony Mann. Release: 1965. Copyright: 1965. Country: Great Britain. [Film.] *Film Index International.* (See "Remote Control: Rwd." as listed below; Maasz as listed in "**Articles . . . .**")

Film and Video/DVD Feature Articles and Reviews

Billington, Michael. "And You Thought His Plays Were Great … ." *Guardian* 4 Oct. 2002, Guardian Friday Pages: 14. " *Guardian Unlimited* 4 Oct. 2002. 26 Sept. 2007 <http://arts.guardian.co.uk/critic/feature/0,,804140,00.html>. ["Harold Pinter is so famous as a playwright that people tend to overlook the enormous contribution he has made to cinema. They don't know what they're missing."]

Brown, Geoff. "New Videos and DVDs." London *Times* 24 Oct. 2002, Features; Times2: 18. [*The Caretaker* (BFI, PG, 1963) on video (PAL) and DVD (Region 2).]

Cashill, Robert. Rev. of *The American Film Theatre Collection. Cineaste* 1 Apr. 2004: 75-77.

Dalton, Stephen. "Film Guide: Reviews: The Quiller Memorandum [1966]." London *Times* 11 Jan. 2003, Features: Play: 32. [Broadcast on Channel 4 on 16 Jan. 2003.]

"DVDs & Videos to Buy: Films–DVD and Video." *Time Out* 13 Mar. 2002: 71. [*The Servant* (dir. Joseph Losey, 1963), GB.]

Harris, Mark. "Video Review: Beckett on Film (2002)." *Entertainment Weekly* 13 Sept. 2002. 23 Feb. 2008 <http://www.ew.com/ew/article/0,,349380,00.html>.

—, Scott Brown, Karen Valby, Michael Sauter, Josh Wolk, Monica Mehta, and Alice King. "What to Watch: A Comprehensive Guide to What's New Tape and DVD – Blockbusters, Classic Picks, Genre Flicks, and Much More: New to DVD." *Entertainment Weekly* 13 Sept. 2002, Video & DVD/What to Watch: 133. [*Beckett on Film* (Ambrose, 2002), 647 mins., unrated, 4 discs, $149.95.]

Holden, Stephen. "Film: Before They Were Stars, They Were Star-Quality." *New York Times* 14 July 2002, sec. 2 (Arts and Leisure Desk): 11, col. 1. (Late Edition–Final.)

[*Langrishe, Go Down.*]

Horowitz, Marc. "Movies Movies Movies Movies." *Sound and Vision* 69. 3 (Apr. 2004): 93. [Rev. of vol. 2 of producer Ely Landau's landmark American Film Theatre series.]

James, Caryn. "Filming Beckett, for Education or Excitement." *New York Times* 15 Sept. 2002: 33. (Late Ed.) [*Stage on Screen: Beckett on Film* (PBS), 90-min. special broadcast on 15 Sept. 2002.]

Jay, David. "Face Off." *Sight and Sound* 12.10 (Oct. 2002): 4-5. [Discusses the "Harold Pinter Weekend" (Barbican Cinema, London): "The jagged intrusions of his (Pinter's) own work include the bafflingly visceral aristocratic pastimes in 'Accident', but also unexpectedly free-wheeling verbal attacks in 'The Pumpkin Eater.'"]

Krebs, Josef. Rev. of *The Dirk Bogarde Collection. Sound and Vision* 67.4 (May 2002): 97. Inc. *The Mind Benders* (1963); *The Servant* (1963), and *Accident* (1967).

Macnab, Geoffrey. "Home Movies: Reviews." *Sight and Sound* 13.9 (Aug. 2003): 66. [Rev. of *Accident* (film).]

Martin, Adrian. "Perverse Film Acts." *The Age* (Melbourne) 27 Nov. 2002, The Culture: 7. [Feature article on William Friedkin, mentioning the "claustrophobic rendition of Harold Pinter's *The Birthday Party* (1968)."]

Patridge, Des. "Exiled Director Now on a Different Watch List." *Courier Mail* 10 July 2002, Features: 44. [Concerns "The most comprehensive retrospective of films by Joseph Losey, whose career spanned 4 1/2 decades, ... featuring at this year's [2002] Brisbane International Film Festival." Program inc. ten films, two based on Pinter screenplays, *The Servant* and *Accident* but not *The Go-Between*, Losey's "third collaboration with Pinter," for which Losey received the highest honour of his long and troubled career, winning the Palme D'Or at the Cannes Film Festival. . . ."

Perry, George. "All in the Delivery." London *Sunday Times* 14 Apr. 2002, Features. [Rev. of *The Go-Between* (1971).]

—. "Shattered Dreams of Lost Love." London *Sunday Times* 5 May 2002, Features. [Rev. of *The Remains of the Day* (dir. James Ivory). Adapt. of novel by Kazuo Ishiguro, for which Pinter had "optioned the film rights and wrote a screenplay for Mike Nichols to direct, but, eventually, it passed to Merchant Ivory Productions, Ruth Prawer Jhabvala rewrote it, although much of Pinter's uncredited material was retained."]

Peters, Patrick. "Rwd." *Empire* 169 (July 2003): 140.

"Remote Control: Rwd." *Empire* 174 (Dec. 2003): 173.

Rosen, Steven. "Video Pick: Beckett Boxed Set Is Great Cinema." *Denver Post* 6 Dec. 2002, SCN: F7. (1st Ed.) [*Beckett on Film: 19 Films X 19 Directors.*]

Schickel, Richard. "Theater: Famous Plays, Famous Players, Forgotten Films." *New York Times* 13 Apr. 2003, sec. 2 (Arts & Leisure): 5, 23. [Feature article on the American Film Theater VHS and DVD boxed sets (14 films) (Kino). Positive revs. of *The Homecoming* and *Butley* (dir. by Pinter).]

Scott, A. O. "Film Review: A Foolish Affair in a Frustrated life." *New York Times* 17 July 2002, sec. E (The Arts/Cultural Desk): 5, col. 1. (Late Edition-Final). [*Langrishe, Go Down.*]

S.R. "The Guide: Screen Talks: Harold Pinter and Alan Sillitoe, London." *Guardian*

5 Oct. 2002, The Guide: 18. [Re: Billington's Barbican Screen Talk on Harold Pinter, and other parts of the "Harold Pinter Weekend," previously listed in *TPR* (2004): 287.]

Stratton, David. "Great and the Good: Film: Brisbane International Film Festival: Various Venues, Ended Yesterday." *Australian* 22 July 2002, Features: 15. ["This year's Joseph Losey program, which included his Harold-Pinter-scripted masterpieces *The Servant* and *Accident*, both with Dirk Bogarde, was a highlight."]

Sun, Perry. "DVD Video: Drama: *The Servant*." *Widescreen Review* 61 (June 2002): 84. (Illus.)

Television Productions/Programs and Reviews

Jury, Louis. "Film Theatre Revisits the Golden Era of the Television Play." London *Independent* 3 Mar. 2003, News: 8. [*The Lover* (ITV [Associated-Rediffusion], 1963): "one of the highlights of a new season at the National Film Theatre, London, dedicated to the glory days of the television golden era of Armchair Theatre and the Wednesday Play in the 1960s and 1970s was over. About four years ago, when Pinter offered the BBC his latest work, Ashes to Ashes, the corporation didn't even call back. 'I have a good record with the BBC. But these were totally different people from ones I dealt with before,' he said."]

McLean, Gareth. "Pause for Reflection: Close Encounter ... Indira Varma and Harold Pinter in One for the Road, BBC2." *Guardian* 28 Oct. 2002, Guardian Features Pages: 22. [Rev. of *Pinter at the BBC*, previously listed in *TPR* (2004): 284-85.]

Redmond, Camilla. "Satellite; Cable & Digital: Pick of the Day: General." *Guardian* 31 Oct. 2002: 17; 21. [*Pinter at the BBC*: *Celebration*; *The Basement*.]

Radio Productions and Reviews

"Beckett." *Breakfast*. Radio National, Austral. (ABC: Australia Broadcasting Corp.) 7 Jan. 2003. [Introd. to interview with Herbert Blau and Ruby Cohn on "Summer Breakfast," in conjunction with the Samuel Beckett Symposium, which, in 2003, included a RealAudio link to the program (no longer provided). 16 Jan. 2003; redirected 1 Feb. 2008 <http://www.abc.net.au/rn/talks/brkfast/stories/s758865.htm>.

Bennett, Vanora. "Radio: ... Pinter at the BBC: Friday Play: A Slight Ache, Radio 4, 9 pm." London *Times* 15 Nov. 2002, Features; Times 1: 25.

Gilbert, Jenny. "Preview: Radio; Jenny Gilbert Tunes In to the Sound of Silence." London *Independent on Sunday* 10 Nov. 2002, Features: 51. [Announcement of BBC Radio 4 broadcast of *A Slight Ache* (*The Friday Play*) at 9 p.m.; perf. Harold Pinter (Edward) and Jill Johnson (Flora), followed by broadcast of "the original 1964 recording" of Pinter and Geoffrey Bayldon performing "Last To Go."]

Hodgkinson, Will. "The Guide: Saturday: Radio: Sound Bits." *Guardian* 2 Nov. 2002, The Guide: 61. [Announces the broadcast of 1970 BBC Radio 4 production of *The Birthday Party* on *The Saturday Play* as part of *Pinter at the BBC*.]

"Tribute's Poetry and Emotion." *The Stage* 19 Sept. 2002: 22. [Inc. brief rev. of *New Grub Street*, by George Gissing, adapt. Tony Ramsay (R4, from 8 Sept. 2002); narrator: Harold Pinter.]

Pinter, Harold. "What We Think of America." *Radio Eye*, Radio National, Austral. (ABC: Australia Broadcasting Corp.) 30 Mar. 2002. 16 Jan. 2008 <http://www.abc.net.au/rn/arts/radioeye/stories/s515871.htm>. [Recorded in the London studio of the ABC for broadcast on *Radio Eye*; Pinter's contribution to *What We Think of America*, ed. Ian Jack, *Granta* 77 (London: Granta, 2002); listed in *TPR* (2004): 242.]

Other Related Programs and Reviews

After Beckett: d'après Beckett: Samuel Beckett Symposium. U of Western Sydney in association with Sydney Festival 2003. Sydney Theatre Company. Sydney, Austral. 6-9 Jan. 2003. <http://pubsites.uws.edu.au/conferences/beckett/index2.html>. [Previously listed in *TPR* (2004): 297.]

"Archive Hour–Theatre of the Absurd." Radio 4. 10 July 2003, 8 p.m. [Focusing on the life and work of Martin Essin; see announcement by Griffiths, as listed above in "**Other Pertinent News Reports . . . .**"]

Collateral Damage–Responses to War. Lyttelton Circle Foyer, National Theatre, London. 7, 14, 21, and 28 Mar. 2003 at 5:15 p.m. (45 mins.) E-mail subscription announcement from marketing@nationaltheatre.org.uk 28 Feb. 2003.

Dwyer, Carmel. "Beckett Festival Days." *Australian Financial Rev.* 29 Nov. 2002, Mag.: 101. [*Waiting for Godot*, *Endgame*, *Beckett on Film*.]

Endgame. Dir. Benedict Andrews. Perf. Peter Carroll, Jacek Koman, Lynne Murphy, and Matthew Whittet. Sydney Theatre Company (STC), Wharf 1, Wharf Theatre Complex, Sydney, Austral. Previews from 28-31 Dec. 2002; 2 Jan.-2 Feb. 2003. 3 Feb. 2008 <http://pubsites.uws.edu.au/conferences/beckett/endgame.html>.

Evans, Lloyd. "Review: Pinter the Performer Outdoes Pinter the Poet." London *Daily Telegraph* 4 Mar. 2003: 21. [On Pinter's performance in *Promises to Keep* reading his poem "It Is Here (to A)" and other poems by Auden, Donne, Wilfred Owen, and George Barker.]

Hinden, Michael. "The Legacy of Beckett: Stoppard and His Contemporaries." After Beckett: d'après Beckett: Samuel Beckett Symposium. Wharf 1, The Wharf Theatre Complex, Sydney, Austral. 7 Jan. 2003.

Lambert, Gavin. "The Rebel Inside: Gavin Lambert Remembers Karel Reisz, the Gentleman Director Who Revolutionised British Cinema." *Guardian* 20 June 2003. 30 Sept. 2007 <http://arts.guardian.co.uk/fridayreview/story/0,,980636,00.html>.

Memorial tribute for Karel Reisz. Co-sponsored by the National Film Theatre and *Variety*. National Film Theatre, London. 25 June 2003. (The program "showcased Reisz's 1966 comedy 'Morgan: A Suitable Case for Treatment' and the 1978 dramatic thriller 'Who'll Stop the Rain'. ... Friends and colleagues spoke about the director, who was also the first programming director of the National Film Theater in the early 1950s. Reisz also played a pivotal role in the development of British cinema as one of the founders of the Free Cinema movement. ... Speakers included playwright-screenwriter-actor Harold Pinter, director Stephen Frears, director Roger Spottiswoode, 'Rain' screenwriter Judith Rascoe and Variety executive editor Steven Gaydos. Also on hand: John Lahr, thesp Bill Nighy, NFT founder Denis Forman, Film London chair Sandy Liberson and chief Adrian Wootton, plus vet art director Philip Harrison, whose credits include the original 'Avengers' TV series and 'Morgan'.")

Not in Our Name. *Action: Events*: No War on Iraq Liaison City Hall benefit and Mayor's reception. The Council Chamber (6-8 p.m.) and The Living Room, City Hall (8-9:30

p.m.), London. 23 Feb. 2003. [An evening of poetry, performance, acoustic sets, and witness accounts in London's City Hall with Harold Pinter, Ken Livingstone (Mayor of London), Jeremy Hardy, Adrian Mitchell, Jean Binta–Breeze, John Hegley, Michael Rosen, Richard Bradbury, with Alice Mahon MP, and others.]

No War on Iraq. National demonstration organized by the Stop the War Coalition, CND (Campaign for Nuclear Disarmament), and Muslim Association of Britain, London. 15 Feb. 2003. 18 Feb. 2003 <http://www.no-war-on-iraq.freeserve.co.uk/action.html>. [Harold Pinter addressed rally.]

Onič, Tomaž "Translating Register in Pinter's Drama." 20 in *English Language and Literature Studies in the Context of European Language Diversity: Book of Abstracts.* First International Conference of the Slovene Association for the Study of English. Slovene Association for the Study of English: Faculty of Arts, Department of English, 2004. [Conference paper on register shifts in the Slovene translation of *The Caretaker* and *The Birthday Party.*]

Pinter Fest 2003. Annual program: Master Playwright of the 20th-Century. 9-25 Jan. 2003. Manitoba Theatre Centre. Winnipeg, Manitoba, Can. <http://www.pinterfest.com/fest.html>. 8 Jan. 2003 <http://www.haroldpinter.org/plays/frn_pinterfestival_ca03.shtml> (Official site of Pinter Fest: no longer active). [Previously listed in *TPR* (2004): 299.] (See "Winnipeg Celebrates Playwright Harold Pinter," listed below.]

Promises to Keep: A poetry evening celebrating youth and promise with readings from Harold Pinter, Harriet Walter, and others. Duke of York's Theatre, London. 1 Mar. 2003. (See rev. by Evans, listed above, and "Saturday Review: Events," listed below.)

"Saturday Review: Events: Promises to Keep." *Guardian* 1 Mar. 2003, Guardian Saturday Pages: 39.

Sheehan, Paul. "Still Waiting for Godot." *Australian Mag.* 4 Jan. 2003, Mag.-Type-Feature-Biog-Samuel Beckett: 6. [Re: anniversary prod. of *Waiting for Godot* (Sydney Festival 2003), as listed below.]

"Speak!" "Actor's Church," Covent Garden, London. 23 Oct. 2003. 2 Oct. 2007 <http:www.refugeecouncil.org.uk>. (Courtesy of "evesigourney" in "Speak with Harold Pinter at our London event!" in the *Harold Pinter Community Discussion Forum* 10 Sept. 2003. 2 Oct. 2007 <http://p079.ezboard.com/ftheharoldpintercommunityfrm1.showMessage?topicID=355.topic>.) [Hosted by The Refugee Council (UK); an evening of readings by: Harold Pinter; Beverly Naidoo (Carnegie Medal Winner); Monica Ali (listed for 2003 Booker Prize); and Harry Kunzru (shortlisted for 2002 Whitbread First Novel Award).]

Thomas, Archie. "Brits Unspool Reisz Tribute." *Variety* 30 June-13 July 2003, News: 51.

20th Century Masters Tribute Series: A Tribute to Samuel Beckett. PEN American Center, The Town Hall, New York City. 9 Dec. 2002. *PEN American Center: Events.* 10 Dec. 2002 <http://www.pen.org/events.htm>. Updated link: <http://www.pen.org/page.php/prmID/508>. Selection of talks published in: *PEN America 5: Silences: Silences Tributes* <http://www.pen.org/page.php/prmID/483>. [Inc: Mel Gussow, "Uproarious Pessimism"; Richard Seaver, "The Terror of the Words"; Jeannette Seaver, "Evenings in Paris"; Edward Albee, "Pure Magic"; Paul Auster, "Laughter in the Dark"; Christopher Rickes, "Deranged Punctilio"; Israel Horovitz, "Father of Choice"; Tom Bishop, "Language Barriers."]

Waiting for Godot. By Samuel Beckett. Dir. Neil Armfield. Perf. John Gaden and Max Cullen. After Beckett: d'après Beckett: Samuel Beckett Symposium, Company B, Belvoir Street Theatre, Surry Hills, Sydney, Austral. 5 Jan.-23 Feb. 2003. 3 Feb. 2008 <http://pubsites.uws.edu.au/conferences/beckett/godot.html>. (Rev. by Sheehan.)

"War." Reading by Harold Pinter. Olivier Theatre, Royal National Theatre, London. 10 June 2003. 6:00 p.m. Program description "Harold Pinter: War." *Royal National Theatre* 30 Apr. 2003. 28 Sept. 2007 <http://www.nt-online.org/?lid=4429>. ["Pinter's response to world events is always pure and simple: he writes with an economy that throws the stark light of truth onto any given subject. There is no fudge, no dallying, no compromise. On the set of *Henry V*, Pinter marks the publication of *War* and reads eight poems and one speech that testify to the strength and lucidity of his unwavering view on war and provide a declaration for humanity. Afterwards he will answer questions about his work. Chaired by Michael Billington."] (Rev. by Malcolm, as listed above in "**Related Reviews**." Cited also in Knowles, "Harold Pinter 2002-2004," *TPR* [2004]: 233.)

Warren, Marcus, and Sally Pook. "American Poets in Anti-War Protest." London *Daily Telegraph* 6 Mar. 2003: 7. [Poets against the War projects.]

"Winnipeg Celebrates Playwright Harold Pinter." *CBC.ca.* Last updated 9 Jan. 2003. 2 Feb. 2008 <http://www.cbc.ca/arts/story/2003/01/09/pinterfest090103.html>. (Hyperlinked official site of Pinter Fest 2003 no longer active.)

Related Articles, Books, and Parts of Books

Aragay, Mireia. "Possessing Jane Austen: Fidelity, Authorship, and Patricia Rozema's *Mansfield Park.*" *Literature/Film Quart.* 31.3 (Sept. 2003): 177-85.

Batty, Mark. "Staged Dialogues with Authorship: Pinter and Beckett as Directors." *TPR* (2004): 48-60.

Begley, Varun. "The Aesthetics of Refusal: Pinter among the Radicals." *Modern Drama* 45.4 (Winter 2002): 628-45.

—. *Harold Pinter and the Twilight of Modernism.* Toronto: U of Toronto P, 2005.

—. "The Modernist as Populist: Pinter's *Betrayal* and Mass Culture." *TPR* (2004): 83-102.

—. "A Poetics for Thugs." 11-21 in *The Art of Crime.*

Branam, Harold. "The Dumb Waiter." *Cyclopedia of Literary Places.* Pasadena, CA: Salem P, 2003. *Literary Reference Center.* 24 Aug. 2006. (2 pages.)

Bryden, Mary. "*The Caretaker* and *Betrayal.*" *TPR* (2004): 202-06.

Burch, Steven Dedalus. "*Ashes to Ashes.*" *Reference Guide to Holocaust Literature.* Ed. Thomas Riggs. Farmington Hills, MI: St. James P, 2002. 365-66. (Courtesy of author.)

—. "Harold Pinter." *Reference Guide to Holocaust Literature.* Ed. Thomas Riggs. Farmington Hills, MI: St. James P, 2002. 245-48. (Courtesy of author.)

Burkman, Katherine H. "The Contamination of Birth by Sex and Death in the Plays of Beckett and Pinter." *TPR* (2004): 39-47.

—. "A Kind of Alaska." *Masterplots II: Drama Series.* Rev. ed. Pasadena, CA: Salem P, 2004. *Literary Reference Center.* 24 Aug. 2006. (5 pages.)

Caponi, Paolo. *Adultery in the High Canon: Forms of Infidelity in Joyce, Beckett and Pinter*. Milan: UNICOPLI, 2002. (Cited in Carpenter, "Plays and Filmscripts" 17, 49, 51; 77-107; "77-107: 'Betrayal(s)' ... stresses the play, but gives some attention to others.")

Castagnino, Maria I. "Harold Pinter y los múltiples aspectos de una traición." 21-34 in Dubatti. [On *Betrayal* (play).] (Cited in Carpenter, "Plays and Filmscripts" 64.)

Catlett, Mallory. "Madness and Method in *This Room Is Moving*." *Canadian Theatre Rev*. 119 (Summer 2004): 35-39. (Version of the *The Dwarfs* by Screaming Flea Theatre Company in Vancouver, British Columbia, Can.) (Cited in Carpenter, "Plays and Filmscripts" 92).

Cho, Sookhee. "A Study of the Matchseller in *A Slight Ache*." *Jour. of Modern British and American Drama* (Seoul) 17.1 (2004): 5-30. [Treatment of intruder; relationship to the double.]

Combs, Richard. "Joseph Losey – Exiled to Europe by the Hollywood Blacklist, Joseph Losey Enjoyed a High-Profile Yet Unclassifiable Art-House Career Spanning 30 Years. A Look at the Contradictions, Reversals, and Doublings of a Filmmaker Equally at Home with Harold Pinter and Elizabeth Taylor." *Film Comment* 40.2 (2004): 44[-49].

Connor, Kathleen, and Signey Homan. "Tears and an Actor's Discovery: Playing Kate in *Old Times*." *TPR* (2004): 156-70.

Crawford, Nicholas. "Staging Authorship: Pinter's *No Man's Land* and Shepard's *True West*." *Comparatist Jour. of the Southern Comparative Literature Association* 27 (May 2003): 138-64.

Dubatti, Jorge, ed. *Estudios críticos sobre Harold Pinter*. Buenos Aires: Nueva Generacíon / CIHTT, 2002. (Cited in Carpenter, "Plays and Filmscripts" 12.)

Dukore, Bernard. "Remembering": "To Martin [Esslin]." *TPR* (2004): 235-36. (Memorial tribute.)

Fahey, Joseph. "An Interview with Pavel Dobrusky and Peter Hackett." *TPR* (2004): 178-86. [Designer and artistic director of *Betrayal (*Cleveland Playhouse), Spring 2002.]

Fahy, Thomas, and Kimball King, eds. *Captive Audience: Prison and Captivity in Contemporary Theater*. Studies in Modern Drama. General ed., Kimball King. New York and London: Routledge, 2003. [Introd. by Fahy; ed. note by King.]

Fernández Monterde, Cristina. "Una aproximación pragmática al estudio del texto literario: Propuesta de análisis de *Betrayal* desde las teorías de la cortesía y de la relevancia." *ELIA: Estudios de Linüística Inglesa Aplicada* 1 (2000): 107-17. [Linguistic approach; on *Betrayal*.]

Forceville, Charles. "The Conspiracy in *The Comfort of Strangers*: Narration in the Novel and the Film." *Language and Literature* 11 (2002): 119-35. (Cited in Carpenter, "Plays and Filmscripts" 145.)

Foster, Verna A. "Pinter: *The Caretaker* and *No Man's Land*." 187-97 in *The Name and Nature of Tragicomedy*. Aldershot, Hampshire, UK: Ashgate, 2004. (Cited in Carpenter, "Plays and Filmscripts" 80, 118.)

Gale, Steven H. "In Memoriam: Martin Esslin, Mark W. Estrin, and Albert Wertheim." *TPR* (2004): 238-41.

—. *Sharp Cut: Harold Pinter's Screenplays and the Artistic Process*. Lexington: UP of

Kentucky, 2002. (Courtesy of publisher.) ["Choice Outstanding Academic Title" for 2003; e-mail correspondence from author dated 28 Apr. 2006.]

Gardey, Mariana. "Ideologia y discurso dramático: una puesta a en escena de *The Homecoming* (*De vuelta al hogar*)." 68-82 in Dubatti. (Cited in Carpenter, "Plays and Filmscripts" 100.)

Gardner, Colin. "Harold Pinter's Time-Image: *The Servant* (1963), *Accident* (1967) and *The Go-Between* (1970)." 134-79 in *Joseph Losey*. Manchester, Eng.: Manchester UP, 2004. (Cited in Carpenter, "Plays and Filmscripts" 142.)

Gauthier, Brigitte. *Harold Pinter et les dramaturges de la fragmentation: Antonin Artaud, Peter Brook, Samuel Beckett, Tom Stoppard, Peter Shaffer, Dennis Reardon, le Living Theatre, David Mercer, Bob Wilson, David Edgar, Harold Pinter*. Paris: Harmattan, 2002. (Also cited in Carpenter, "Plays and Filmscripts 21, 82, 106, 108. Inc.: "Pinter et ses schizodrames" 35-78, with 35-53 on *The Caretaker*; 53-66 on *A Kind of Alaska*, and 66-78 on *The Hothouse*.)

—. *Harold Pinter, le maître de la fragmentation*. Paris: Harmattan, 2003. (Cited in Carpenter, "Plays and Filmscripts" 21. Incorporates parts of Gauthier's *'The caretaker' of the Fragments of Modernity: Étude de l'oeuvre de Pinter*. Paris: Ellipses, 1996.)

—. "Harold Pinter scénariste: Débat avec Michel Climent et Eric Kahane animé par Brigitte Gauthier au Cinéma L'Entrepôt." 99-122 in *Dramaturges et cinéastes de l'anti-psychiatrie: Entretiens sur l'ère de la fragmentation*. Paris: Harmattan, 2003. (Cited in Carpenter, "Plays and Filmscripts" 144.)

Giberti, Karina. "La traducción de Pinter en Argentina: El caso de *Betrayal / Traicôn*." 83-88 in Dubatti. (Cited in Carpenter, "Plays and Filmscripts" 67.)

Gilleman, Luc. "Het Pinterfenomeen en Harold Pinters Pintereske politiek." *De Vlaamse Gids* (Antwerp, Belgium) 76.3 (May-June 1992): 12-20. (Retroactive entry from *MLA International Bibliog.* [2004].)

Gillen, Francis, and Steven H. Gale. "Introduction." *TPR* (2004): x-xii.

Gordon, Lois, and William Baker. "Harold Pinter." *Cyclopedia of World Authors*. 4th rev. ed. Pasadena, CA: Salem P, 2004. *Literary Reference Center*. 23 Aug. 2006.

Gordon, Robert. "*Family Voices*: Pirandello and Pinter." *Pirandello Studies: Jour. of the Society for Pirandello Studies* 23 (2003): 22-34. [Comparison of the playwrights' dramatic technique; comparision of Pinter's *Family Voices* with Pirandello's *Sei personaggi in cerca d'autore* (*Six Characters in Search of an Author*.]

Grimes, Charles V. "Harold Pinter's *Ashes to Ashes*: The Criminality of Indifference and the Failure of Empathy." 49-60 in Kane, *The Art of Crime*.

—. "Process and History in Harold Pinter's *Reunion* Screenplay." *TPR* (2004): 144-55.

Hall, Ann C. "Challenging Theatre: The Cleveland Playhouse's Production of Harold Pinter's *Betrayal*." *TPR* (2004): 174-77.

—. "Harold Pinter's Prison House: The Screenplay of Kafka's *The Trial*." 69-80 in Fahy and King.

—. "Lost in the Funhouse: Crime and Spectacle of Kafka's *The Trial*." 72-81 in Kane.

—. "Making Spaces: Women At Play's Production of Harold Pinter's *The Room* and *Celebration*." *TPR* (2004): 207-09. (Illus.)

"Harold Pinter." *British Writers: Retrospective Supplement I.* Ed. Jay Parini. New York: Charles Scribner's Sons, 2002.

Hribar, Darja Darinka. "Harold Pinter in Slovene Translations." *English Language Overseas Perspectives and Enquiries* (ELOPE) [Published by the Slovene Association for the Study of English in Ljubljana, a member of ESSE (European Society for the Study of English) 1.1/2 (2004): 195-208. COBISS.SI-ID 13220360. (Courtesy of Tomaž Onič.)

—. "Rewriting the Dramatic Convention of the Theatre of the Absurd in Slovene Translation. 141-49 in *On the Relation Theory and Translation Practice.* Ed. Jean Peeters. Studien zur romanischen Sprachwissen-schaft und interkultwiellen Kommunikation, vol. 19. Frankfurt am Main: P. Lang, 2005. COBISS.SI-ID 229046016. (Courtesy of Tomaž Onič.) [Includes a discussion of problems in translation register; deals with various levels of formality and their translation; based on translation of swearwords in *The Homecoming.*]

—. "Some General Notions on Translating the Absurd Drama for the Stage and Harold Pinter's Plays in Particular: A Slovene Perspective." 299-312 in *Crossing Borders: Interdiscipinary Intercultural Interaction.* Eds. Bernhard Kettemann and Georg Marko. Buchreihe zu den Arbeiten aus Anglistik und Americanistik, vol. 15. Tübingen: G. Narr., 1999. COBISS.SI-ID 9097736. (Courtesy of Tomaž Onič.)

Hudgins, Christopher C. "Harold Pinter's *The Handmaid's Tale*: Freedom, Prison, and a Hijacked Script." 81-108 in Fahy.

Hutchings, William. "The Birthday Party." *Cyclopedia of Literary Places. Literary Reference Center* 24 Aug. 2006. (2 pages.)

Jones, David. "Robards and Plummer: Partners in 'No Man's Land.'" *TPR* (2004): 237-38.

—. "Travels with Harold: David Jones['s] Staging of *The Caretaker* for Roundabout Culminates a 40-Year Career Acting and Directing the Work of Harold Pinter." *Front & Center Online: The Online Version of Roundabout Theatre Company's Subscriber Mag.* (Fall 2003). (3 pages.) 20 Sept. 2007 <http://roundabouttheater.org/fc/fall03/jones.htm>.

Jones, Gari. (Staff Dir. for *No Man's Land.*) *No Man's Land* [by] *Harold Pinter.* NT Education Workpack. Ed. Dinah Wood. Coordinator Simon Kenwright. <http://www.nationaltheatre.org.uk>. (11 pages.)

Kane, Leslie, ed. and introd. *The Art of Crime: The Plays and Films of Harold Pinter and David Mamet.* Studies in Modern Drama. Series Ed. Kimball King. New York and London: Routledge, 2004.

Kang, Hee-Kyung. ["A Portrait of an Old Artist: Self-Consciousness of *No Man's Land.*"] *Jour. of Modern British and American Drama* 17.2 (Aug. 2004): 5-22. [In Korean; English summary. Treatment of the double; relationship to self-knowledge.]

—. ["A Text of Desire and Seduction: Self-Reflexivity in *Old Times.*" *Jour. of Modern British and American Drama* 15.2 (Aug. 2002): 37-55. [In Korean; English summary.]

Karwowski, Michael. "Harold Pinter – A Political Playwright?" *Contemporary Rev.* 283 (Nov. 2003): 291-96. 22 Oct. 2005 <http://www.highbeamcom/library>. ["The writer analyzes Harold Pinter's recent reinterpretation of some of his stage plays in political terms. Focusing specifically on *The Caretaker*, he argues that Pinter's political revisions are contradicted by the plays themselves."]

Knowles, Ronald. "London Report: Harold Pinter 2002-2004." *TPR* (2004): 221-34.

Koenig, Gaspard. "Proust / Pinter." *Magazine Littéraire* 422 (2003): 90-94. (Cited in Carpenter, "Plays and Filmscripts" 156.)

Lavers, Norman, as updated by Thomas J. Taylor, and Patrick Adcock. "Harold Pinter." *Critical Survey of Drama*. 2nd rev. ed. Pasadena, CA: Salem P, 2003. *Literary Reference Center*. 24 Aug. 2006. (12 pages.)

Leiton, Gabriela. "*Landscape* de Pinter y *Play* de Samuel Beckett: la historia inverifiable." 102-10 in Dubatti. (Cited in Carpenter, "Plays and Filmscripts" 52.)

Levy-Daniel, Héctor. "Harold Pinter, dramaturgia de la amenaza." 110-30 in Dubatti. (Cited in Carpenter, "Plays and Filmscripts" 38, 74, 92, 133. Also in *Dramateatro Revista Digital* 12 May-Aug 2004 [internet journal; n. pag.]; on *The Room*, *The Birthday Party*, and *The Dumb Waiter*.]

Lounsberry, Barbara. "Family Voices." *Masterplots II: Drama Series*. Rev. ed. Pasadena, CA: Salem P, 2004. *Literary Reference Center*. 24 Aug. 2006. (5 pages.)

Lorenz, Janet E. "Betrayal." *Masterplots II: Drama Series*. Rev. ed. Pasadena, CA: Salem P, 2004. *Literary Reference Center*. 24 Aug. 2006. (5 pages.)

Lussana, Pierandrea. "Sincerity at Risk: Psychoanalysis, Applied to the Child and to Art or Dedicated to Extended Metapsychology?" *International Forum of Psychoanalysis* 10.1 (Feb. 2001): 5-11. (Rev. of *Sincerity: A Study in the Atmosphere of Human Relations*, by D. Meltzer.)

Maasz, Ronnie. "You Never Saw That on Screen." *British Cinematographer* 13 (Feb. 2005): 37. ["Ronnie Maasz talks about filming particular sequences on location for the film *The Inspector* and *The Heroes of Telemark* that went awry."]

Mackean, Ian. "Harold Pinter: Winners and Losers in the Plays of Harold Pinter." *English Literature* n.d. <http://www.english-literature.org/essays/pinter.html> 17 May 2002.

Mansour, Wisam. "Pessimism in Pinter's Drama: A Philosophical Perception." *Forum Modernes Theater* 15.2 (2000): 174-77. ["*The Birthday Party*. Treatment of isolation; relationship to pessimism."]

Margarit, Lucas. "Pinter y Beckett o la enuciación desde el vacío." 131-36 in Dubatti.

McKittrick, Ryan. "Party Politics." *American Repertory Theatre* (ART) 20 Dec. 2003. 22 Aug. 2007 <http://www.amrep.org/articles/2_3b/party.html>. [Interview with Joanne Akalaitis, dir. of *The Birthday Party* (ART).]

—. "Preparing for the Party." Program notes for *The Birthday Party* (American Repertory Theatre prod. of Mar. 2004). *ART: American Repertory Theatre* 2 Mar. 2004. 22 Aug. 2007 <http://www.amrep.org/articles/2_3b/preparing.html>. *Articles Online* 2.36 (Mar. 2004).

Meltzer, D. *Sincerity: A Study in the Atmosphere of Human Relations*. ["A previously unpublished book, appearing in D. Meltzer's Collected papers" as described in Lussana (as listed above); "Explores *The Dwarfs*, *The Birthday Party* and *The Homecoming* by Harold Pinter, both the capacity to communicate genuine emotion and its limitation by the subject's inability to say-what-he-means, because of rigidity and coldness, and to mean-what-he-says, because of an integrated narcissistic structure.

. . ." (Taylor & Francis Group). Retroactive entry.]

Mennemeier, Franz N. "Harold Pinter." 162-69 in *Das moderne Drama des Auslandes.* 4th ed. Berlin: Weidler, 2003.

Merritt, Susan Hollis. "*Betrayal* in Denver." *TPR* (2004): 187-201. (Illus.)

—. "'HURRY UP PLEASE IT'S TIME': Pinter Past, Pinter Present, and Pinter Future." *TPR* (2004): 61-82.

—, comp. "Harold Pinter Bibliography: 2000-2002." *TPR* (2004): 242-300.

Moore, John Noell. "Teaching and Writing Poetry." *English Jour.* 91.3 (Jan. 2002): 44-50. ["Harold Pinter's very short play *The Black and White* presents a minimalist approach to the questions these other texts raise and also sets up a provocative conversation with Edward Albee's *The Sandbox.* Both plays are easily dramatized in the classroom."]

Morgan, Chris. "The Caretaker." *Cyclopedia of Literary Places.* Pasadena, CA: Salem P, 2003. *Literary Reference Center.* 24 Aug. 2006. (2 pages.)

Moussa, Hiba. "*Mansfield Park* and Film: An Interview with Patricia Rozema." *Literature / Film Quart.* 32.4 (Dec. 2004): 255-60. [Patricia Rozema talks about her version of *Mansfield Park.*]

Nadel, Ira B. "Lie Detectors: Pinter / Mamet and the Victorian Concept of Crime." 119-36 in Kane.

Nyusztay, Iván. "The Faces of the Other: Configurations of Alterity in Emmanuel Levinas and Harold Pinter." *[The] Ana Chronis T* (2002) n. pag. [Treatment of sameness; otherness compared to Emmanuel Lévinas, *Totalité et Infini.*]

Oeder, Horst G. *Die Philosophie in Harold Pinters Frühwerk: Verbindungen zur Neuplatonismus der italienischen Renaissance.* Schriftenreitik Studien zur Anglistik und Amerikanistik, Bd. 5. Hamburg: Kovač, 2004. [Bibliog. refs. 463-73.] (Also cited in Carpenter, "Plays and Filmscripts" 76, 103, 135; Inc.: 103-04 on *The Room,* 105-213 on *The Birthday Party*; and 341-452 on *The Homecoming.*]

Oh, Kyungshim. "The Multiple Functions of Storytelling in *Ashes to Ashes.*" *Jour. of Modern British and American Drama* (Korea) 15.3 (Dec. 2002): 103-26. [In Korean; English summary. Treatment of storytelling; by female characters; relationship to political power.]

Onič, Tomaž. "Mutacíje kot najradi-kalnejš pomenski premiki med iz-virnikom in prevodom Pinterjevega Hišnika." *Vestnik-Društvo za tuje jezike in Književnosti* 38.1/2 (2004): 273-81. In Slovene. ("Mutations as the Most Radical of the Shifts between the Original and the Translation of Pinter's *The Caretaker.*") CORBISS. SI-ID 13754632. (Courtesy of author.)

—. "Problematikia prevajanja Komičnega v dramskih bhsedelih, specifika iger Harolda Pinterja. *Vestnik – Društvo za tuje jezike književnosti* 37.1/2 (2003): 391-405. In Slovene. ("The Problems of Translation of the Comical in Drama Texts, Specifically in Plays by Harold Pinter.") COBISS SI-ID 13047560. (Courtesy of author. "*Vestnik* is a local journal published by the Slovene Society for Foreign Languages and Literatures; as far as I know, it is not in any important international database.")

—. "Reviewer Response to Pinter's 'The Caretaker'" on the International and Slovene Stage." *Acta Neophilogica* (Faculty of Arts, U of Ljubljana) 37.1/2 (2004): 87-94. CORBISS.SI-ID 27838818.

"Other Wars, the Same Wars." *World Press Rev.* 48.12 (Dec. 2001): 35-36. (2 pages.)

["Abstract: Issues concerning the literary representations of war by Sarah Kane and Harold Pinter are discussed. Particular attention is given literary techniques used by the two writers in portraying the ways in which political instabilities affects human interrelations."]

Paiva de Oliveira, Ubiratan. "The Presence of Music in Pinter's Works." *Pinter Rev.* (2004): 109-22.

Parrill, Sue. "Not the Bluebird of Happiness: Bird Imagery in the Film *Mansfield Park.*" *Literature / Film Quart.* 31.3 (Sept. 2003): 186-92. (Illus.)

Pdrez [sic] Ríu, Carmen. "An Interview with Karel Reisz." *Literature / Film Quart.* 31.2 (Aug. 2003): 156-60. (Interview conducted at the Gijn Film Festival in Nov. 1998. Dir. Karel Reisz discusses his involvement in the Free Cinema Movement; the relationship between *The French Lieutenant's Woman* and the novel; and directorial practice.)

Peithman, Stephen. "The Bard and the Boys." *Stage Directions* 15.10 (Oct. 2002): 98-99. [Inc. revs. of *The Life and Work of Harold Pinter*, by Michael Billington, and *Harold Pinter: A Celebration*, ed. Richard Eyre.]

Pérez [sic] Ríu, Carmen. "An Interview with Karel Reisz." *Literature / Film Quart.* 31.2 (Aug. 2003): 156-60. (Interview conducted at the Gijn Film Festival in Nov. 1998. Dir. Karel Reisz discusses his involvement in the Free Cinema Movement; the relationship between *The French Lieutenant's Woman* and the novel; and directorial practice. Also cited in Carpenter, "Plays and Filmscripts" 150.) Rpt. in *FindArticles.com* 12 Sept. 2007 <http://findarticles.com/p/articles/mi_qa3768/is_200301/ai_n9213013/pg_1>.

Perloff, Carey. "Harold Pinter's 'Mountain Language'." Aug. 2001. *Crimes of War: Cultural Supplement.* 31 Oct. 2003 <http://www.crimesofwar.org/cultural/pinter-print.html>.

Pilard, Philippe. "Joseph Losey et Harold Pinter: Une collaboration exemplaire? (*The Servant*; *Accident*; *The Go-Between*)." 118-27 in Denitza Batcheva, ed. *L'univers de Joseph Losey.* Condé-sur-Noireau: Corlet, 2000. Also published in *Avant-Scène Cinéma* 495 (2000): 82-91; *CinemAction* 96.3 (2000): 118-27. (Cited in Carpenter, *Plays and Filmscripts* 145).

—. "Losey / Pinter: un collaboration exemplaire? *CinemAction* 96.3 (2000): 118-27.

"Pinter: por el camino de Proust: en 1971, Pinter hizo la adaptación cinematográfica de En busca del tiempo perdido. La editorial Gallimard acaba de publicar el guión original." *Nexos: Sociedad, Ciencia, Literatura* 25.309 (Sept. 2003): 92-93.

The Pinter Review: Collected Essays 2003 and 2004. Ed. and introd. Francis Gillen and Steven H. Gale. Tampa: U of Tampa P, 2004.

Prentice, Penelope. "Comedy and Crime: Pinter's Primal Power." 61-71 in Kane.

Price, Steven. "Harold Pinter's 'Before the Law.'" 38-48 in Kane.

Propato, Cecilia. "Pinter y la otra comunicación." 144-49 in Dubatti. (Cited in Carpenter, "Plays and Filmscripts" 67. On *Betrayal.*)

Pruner, Michel. *Les théâters de l'absurde.* Paris: Nathan, 2003. (Rev. By Fletcher.)

Ranson, Nicholas. "*The Homecoming.*" *Masterplots II: Drama Series.* Rev. ed. *Literary Reference Center.* Pasadena, CA: Salem P, 2004. 12 Sept. 2007.

Reitz, Bernhard. "'I Just Wouldn't Want to Be at the Other End of His Anger': Harold

Pinter's Political Plays of the Nineties." *Anglistik and Englisch-unterricht* 64 (2002): 165-80. [Treatment of protagonist; as victim.]

Renton, Linda. *Pinter and the Object of Desire: An Approach through the Screenplays.* Oxford, Eng.: European Humanities Research Centre, U of Oxford, and Modern Humanities Research Association, 2002. (Courtesy of author and publisher.)

Russell, Dennis. "The Theater of Hyperrealism: The Political Plays of Harold Pinter." *Mind's Eye: A Liberal Arts Jour.* (Fall 2003): 48-57. (Cited in Carpenter, "Plays and Filmscripts" 44.)

Shepherd-Barr, Kirsten. "Reconsidering Joyce's *Exiles* in Its Theatrical Context." *Theatre Reearch International* 28 (2003): 169-80. (Cited by Carpenter, "Plays and Filmscripts" 47; "the 1970-71 revival directed by Pinter.")

Shewey, Don. "In Command: Patrick Stewart Takes Charge in Roundabout's Revival of *The Caretaker.*" *Front and Center Online: The Online Version of Roundabout Theatre Company's Subscriber Mag.* (Fall 2003). 20 Sept. 2007 <http://roundabouttheater.org/fc/fall03/stewart.htm>. (3 pages.)

Silverstein, Marc. "'You'll Never Be without a Police Siren': Pinter and the Subject of Law." 22-37 in Kane.

Smith, Susan Harris. "'Pinteresque' in the Popular Press." *TPR* (2004): 103-08.

Sofer, Andrew. "The Cheese-Roll under the Cocktail Cabinet: Pinter's Object Lessons." *TPR* (2004): 29-38.

"Staging Pinter: From Pregnant Pauses to Political Causes." Transcribed (with the assistance of Sean Donnelly) and ed. by Susan Hollis Merritt. *TPR* (2004): 123-43. [Panelists: Patricia Rozema, Henry Woolf, and Hersh Zeifman. Moderator: Jeanne Colleran.]

Stone, Leonard A. "Harold Pinter and the Fragmentation of Working-Class Consciousness." *Cultural Logic: An Electronic Jour. of Marxist Theory and Practice* 6 (2003). 23 Feb. 2008 <http://clogic.eserver.org/2003/stone.html>. (30 paragraphs.) [Archived in "Back issues" sec. Treatment of working class.]

Taborda, Marta. "Lenguaje y comunicación en Harold Pinter: Notas sobre La lengua de la montaña." 155-61 in Dubatti.

Trussler, Simon. "Pinter, Harold." 764-66 in *Continuum Encyclopedia of British Literature.* New York: Continuum International Publishing Group Ltd, 2003.

Uchman, Jadwiga. "Harold Pinter's Specific Brand of the Theater of the Absurd and His Anti-Totalitarian Plays." 309-18 in Anna Kedra-Kardela, et al., eds. *Perspectives on Literature and Culture.* Lublin: Maria Curie-Skłodowska U, 2004. (Cited in Carpenter, "Plays and Filmscripts" 32.)

"Visconti leyendo a Proust: En busca del tiempo perdido acompañó a Visconti desde 1922, desde la tarde en que descubrió a su padre, totalmente absorto, leyendo a Proust en la biblióteca familiar." *Nexos: Sociedad, Ciencia, Literatura* 25.309 (Sept. 2003): 90-91.

Waterman, David. "Le terrorisme d'état et le contrôle social: *One for the Road* et *Mountain Language* de Harold Pinter." *Forum Modernes Theater* 18.1 (2003): 86-93. [Treatment of oppression; relationship to audience response; social change.] (Also cited in Carpenter, "Plays and Filmscripts" 116, 129.)

Wixson, Christopher. "'I'm Compelled to Ask You Questions': Interrogative Comedy and Harold Pinter's *Ashes to Ashes.*" *TPR* (2004): 7-28.

Wyllie, Andrew. "Harold Pinter (1930-)." *The Literary Encyclopedia* 20 June 2002. Rev. 10 Dec. 2005. 12 Sept. 2007. <http://www.litencyc.com/php/speople.php?rec=true&UID=4985>. (Subscription required for full access.)

Yagi, Naoki. "From Proust to Pinter: Colour, Sound, Movement, and Montage." *English Literature* (Tokyo, Japan) 84 (2002): 126-42. (Cited in Carpenter, "Plays and Films" 157.)

Related Book Reviews

Adler, Thomas P. Rev. of *The Cambridge Companion to Harold Pinter*, ed. Peter Raby (New York & Cambridge, Eng.: Cambridge UP, 2001). *TPR* (2004): 210-13.

Baker, William. Rev. of *The Cambridge Companion to Harold Pinter*, ed. Peter Raby. *Choice* 39.8 (Apr. 2002): 1419. [Cf. rev. listed below; the texts are mostly the same.]

—. Rev. of *Harold Pinter* [*The Cambridge Companion to Harold Pinter*], ed. Peter Raby. *Reference Reviews* 16.3 (2002): 26. [Cf. rev. listed above; the texts are mostly the same.]

Bean, Kellie. Rev. of *Pinter At 70: A Casebook*, ed. Lois Gordon, 2nd rev. ed. (1990; New York & London: Routledge, 2001), and *The Pinter Ethic: The Erotic Aesthetic*, 2nd ed. (1994; New York & London: Routledge, 2000), by Penelope Prentice. *Modern Drama* 46 (2003): 127-30.

Fletcher, John. Rev. of *Les théâters de l'absurde*, by Michel Pruner (Paris: Nathan, 2003). *Theatre Research International* 29.3 (Oct. 2004): 287. [Abstract: "... focuses primarily on French drama and theater of the absurd but has a short section on Harold Pinter," which Fletcher believes misreads the playwright.]

Hall, Ann C. Rev. of *Pinter and the Object of Desire: An Approach through the Screenplays*, by Linda Renton. *TPR* (2004): 214-15.

Hudgins, Christopher C. Rev. of *Sharp Cut*, by Steven H. Gale. *TPR* (2004): 216-20.

Menta, Ed. Rev. of *The Cambridge Companion to Harold Pinter*, ed. Peter Raby. *Theatre Survey* 44.1 (2003): 124-25.

Rev. of *Harold Pinter*, by Mark Batty. *Forum for Modern Language Studies* (U of St. Andrews, Fife, Scotland) 39.1 (2003): 88. *Oxford Journals* (Oxford UP). 14 Sept. 2007 <http://fmls.oxfordjournals.org/cgi/reprint/39/1/88-b>.

Other Articles, Books, Parts of Books, Interviews, and Reviews of Interest

Aragay, Mireia, and Pilar Zozaya. "The State of British Theatre Now: An Interview with Michael Billington. *Atlantis, revista de la Asociación Española de Estudios Anglo-Norteamericanos* 26.1 (June 2004): 89-100.

Aronson, Arnold. Rev. of *Playing Underground: A Critical History of the 1960s Off-Off Broadway Movement*, by Stephen J. Bottoms. *Modern Drama* 48 (2005): 611-13.

Ayckbourn, Alan. *The Crafty Art of Playmaking*. London: Faber and Faber, 2002. (Rev. by Sierz.)

Bakewell, Joan. *The Centre of the Bed*. London: Hodder & Stoughton, 2003. (Rev. by Byrnes, MacGregor, and Patterson.)

Blacker, Terence. "The Secretive World of Sex outside Marriage: Usually When Adultery

Is Exposed in the Lives of Public People, It Can be a Surprising Business." London *Independent* 15 Oct. 2003, Comment: 16.

Bottoms, Stephen J. *Playing Underground: A Critical History of the 1960s Off-Off Broadway Movement.* Theater: Theory/Text/Performance. Ann Arbor: U of Michigan P, 2004. Rev. of Aronson.

Broughton, Philip Delves. "'I thought it was too unoriginal to write': Natasha Fraser-Cavassoni Comes from a Glittering Literary Dynasty – So Why Did Her First Book Take So Long? Philip Delves Finds Out." London *Daily Telegraph* 19 Mar. 2003: 19.

Burnett, Allison. Rev. of *The Diaries of Kenneth Tynan*, ed. John Lahr. *Variety* 11 Jan. 2002. 5:01 p.m.(PT).

Byrnes, Sholto. "Pandora." London *Independent* 22 Oct. 2003, Features: 15. ["In her new memoir, The Centre of the Bed, Joan Bakewell describes how she was sent a manuscript of Harold Pinter's 1978 play, *Betrayal*, and realised it was all about her love affair with him. When Bakewell wrote her memoir, she returned the favour. 'I sent him a copy of the manuscript. ... we are in touch. He said he was very interested by all the early stuff, which he didn't know. And he told me about the current production of *Betrayal* [at the Duchess Theatre]. He's really pleased with it so he wanted me to see it.' But has he been as understanding about the book as she once was about the play? 'Well, he has a very different temperament,' explains a revealingly diplomatic Bakewell."]

Dirda, Michael. "The Books a Critic Turns to When, for the First Time in Years, He Can Actually Read What He Wants: Readings by Michael Dirda." *Washington Post* 10 Nov. 2002, Book World: T15. [Inc. rev. of *Journals, 1987-1989*, by Anthony Powell: "Day-to-day reflections by the author of the acclaimed Dance to the Music of Time. Shrewd, sometimes acerbic comments on books, literary visitors (Naipaul, Pinter). . . ."]

Evans, Everett. "All the Stage Is a World; Biographer Tells Unvarnished Story of John Gielgud." *Houston Chronicle* 8 Sept. 2002, Zest: 19.

Fraser-Cavassoni, Natasha. *Sam Spiegel: The Biography of a Hollywood Legend.* Boston: Little, Brown, 2003. (See Broughton; rev. by French and Kaufman.)

French, Philip. "Review: Books: Sam the Sham: He was a Liar, Cheat and Conman, But Sam Spiegel Deserves a Place in Movie History: Sam Spiegel by Natasha Fraser-Cavassoni Little, Brown pounds 22.50, pp512." London *Observer* 16 Mar. 2003, Observer Rev. Pages: 15.

Giannachi, Gabriella. *Virtual Theatres: An Introduction.* London and New York: Routledge, 2004. (Rev. by Saltz.)

Gibbons, Luke. "In Conversation with Stephen Rea." *Yale Jour. of Criticism* 15.1 (Spring 2002): 5-19.

Haring-Smith, Tori. "Dramaturging Non-Realism: Creating a New Vocabulary." *Theatre Topics* 13.1 (Mar. 2003): 45-54. [Considers the effect of reversed chronology on "[s]pectators of Harold Pinter's *Betrayal*" (48).]

Hribar, Darja Darinka. "Vplivi estetiko absurda na slovenskega dramatika Draca Jančarja." *Vestnik-Društvo za tuje jezike in književnosti* (Slovene Society for Foreign Languages and Literatures) 38.1/2 (2004): 241-49. ["The Influence of the Absurd Aesthetic on the Slovene Playwright Drago Jančar."] (Courtesy of Tomaž Onič.)

Jones, Catherine. "Interview with Timothy West." *Theatre Archive Project: The British Library, U of Sheffield and AHRC* [Arts & Humanities Research Council (UK)]. Conducted 5 Jan. 2004. 17 Sept. 2007 <http://www.bl.uk/projects/theatrearchive/west.html>.

Kaufman, Gerald. "An Oscar for Obnoxiousness: Gerald Kaufman Enjoys This Life of Sam Spiegel, the Unpopular But Successful Hollywood Producer." London *Sunday Telegraph* 16 Mar. 2003: 13.

MacGregor, Sue. "Review: Memoirs: Joan Bakewell Conquered Hurdles, Both Professional and Emotional, Yet Never Lost Her Integrity, Says Sue MacGregor: The End of the Affair." *Guardian* 1 Nov. 2003, Guardian Saturday Pages: 10. (Final Ed.)

Majer, Thomas. "Klingende Angelschnüre: Chorhappenings, Installationen, Punkklänge und Daumenkinos bein Festival Rümlingen." *Neue Zeitschrift für Musik* 163.6 (Nov.-Dec. 2002): 66-67. ["Twanging Fishing Lines: Choir Happenings, Installations, Punk Sounds, and Flip-Books at the Festival Rümlingen."]

Mangan, Michael. *Staging Masculinities: History, Gender, Performance.* New York: Palgrave Macmillan, 2003.

Miller, Susan. *A Map of Doubt and Rescue.* Tampa: U of Tampa P, 2004. [Winner of the 2004 Pinter Review Prize for Drama.]

Morley, Sheridan. *John Gielgud: The Authorized Biography.* New York: Simon & Schuster, 2002. (Rev. by E. Evans.)

Patterson, Christina. "Books: Having Your Crumpet and Eating It: The Centre of the Bed by Joan Bakewell Hodder & Stoughton Pounds 20." London *Independent* 24 Oct. 2003.

Phillips, Tom. "Fifty Years of British Theatre." *Contemporary Rev.* 281 (Aug. 2002): 100-06.

Powell, Anthony. *Journals, 1987-1989.* 1996. Toronto: Random House of Canada, Ltd., 1997. (Rev. by Dirda.)

Raley, Rita. "E Empires." *Cultural Critique* 47 (Spring 2004): 111-50.

Rea, Stephen. "Stephen Rea: Select Film and Stage Credits." *Yale Jour. of Criticism* 15.1 (Spring 2002): 21.

Rogoff, Gordon. "Auden Country and the Search for the Perfect Play." *Theater* 32.1 (Winter 2002): 48-61.

Roof, Judith. *All about Thelma and Eve: Sidekicks and Third Wheels.* Urbana: U of Illinois P, 2002.

Saltz, David Z. Rev. of *Virtual Theatres: An Introduction*, by Gabriella Giannachi. *Modern Drama* 48 (2005): 629-31.

Sierz, Aleks. "The Wednesday Book: Alan Ayckbourn Proves He Is a Dramatist to Be Taken Seriously." London *Independent* 9 Oct. 2002. 23 Feb. 2008 <http://www.independent.co.uk/arts-entertainment/books/reviews/the-crafty-art-of-playmaking-by-alan-ayckbourn-613607.html>. [Rev. of *The Crafty Art of Playwriting*, by Alan Ayckbourn.]

Silberman, Brian. *Manifest: A Play.* Tampa: U of Tampa P, 2003. ["Winner of the 2003 Pinter Review Prize for Drama."]

Tredell, Nicholas. "Simpson, N[orman] F[rederick]." *Continuum Encyclopedia of British Literature.* New York: Continuum International Publishing Group,

2003. 913-14.

Tynan, Kenneth. *The Diaries of Kenneth Tynan*. Ed. John Lahr. London and New York: Bloomsbury, 2001. (Rev. by Burnett.)

Dissertations and Theses Recently Completed or in Preparation

Al-Hamdany, Alia Mohammad Saleh. "Irrationality and Aggressive Behavior in the Major Recent Plays of Harold Pinter: A Critical Study." M.A. thesis. Department of English, U of Mosul, Iraq, 20 Dec. 2005. Supervisor: Assistant Professor Kannan Abdullah Mohammed. [Requirements for M.A. completed 20 Dec. 2005.] (E-mail correspondence with author of 21 Jan. 2006; copy of abstract courtesy of author in e-mail correspondence of 16 Feb. 2006.)

Bergfeldt, Perrilla. "Insiderism in Pinter: Problems in the Translation of Pinter's Formulaic Expressions into Swedish." Diss. U of Surrey, 2002.

Donahue, Linda. "Doctoral Projects in Progress in Theatre Arts, 2004." *Theatre Jour.* 56.2 (May 2004): 275-79.

Farahani, Maryam Dolatabadi. "Manipulation of Power: *A Slight Ache*, *Ashes to Ashes*, and *One for the Road*." M.A. thesis. [Faculty of Humanities, Karaj Azad University, 2004. Thesis Advisor: Dr. Reza Didari. Thesis Reader: Dr. Jalai Sokahnvar. Thesis Examiner: Dr. Kourosh Lachini. (E-mail correspondence with author of 24 Feb. 2004.)

Ferreira de Castro, Carla. "As Vozes do Silêncio nos dramas de Harold Pinter e nas encenacöes de Peter Brook." Ph.D. diss. [Institution?] Supervisor: Prof. Yvette K. Centeno. (In Portuguese.) (In progress according to e-mail message sent via *Harold Pinter Community Discussion Forum.*)

Hribar, Darja Darinka. "Sestavine sloga Harolda Pinterja v slovenskih prevodih: vpliv slogovnih posebnosti na speje manje na Slovenskem." Ph.D. diss. Faculty of Arts, U of Ljubljana, 1999. COBISS SI-ID 8442888. ("Components of Harold Pinter's Style in Slovene Translations: The Influence of Stylistic Characteristics on the Reception in Slovenia." Courtesy of Tomaž Onič.)

Ibrahim, Areeg Abdel-Hamid. "Masks of Ontology: A Comparative Study of Representative Contemporary British and Egyptian Drama." *Dissertations Abstracts International* (Section A: The Humanities and Social Sciences) 64.8 (Feb. 2004): 2876. Diss. U of Connecticut, 2003. DA 3101692. ["And Tom Stoppard; treatment of social problems; cultural identity, cultural change compared to Alfrid; Dirbālah, 'Abd al-Latif. Dissertation abstract.]

Juntunen, Jacob M. "Late Twentieth Century Mainstream Theatre as Political Critique in the United States." Diss. Northwestern U. Interdisciplinary Ph.D. in Theatre and Drama. [Advisor:] Tracy C. Davis. Expected date of completion: 2009.

Liu, Yan. "The Mother as the Other: A Psychoanalytic and Feminist Reading of Motherhood in Ibsen, O'Neill and Pinter." *Dissertations Abstracts International* (Section A: The Humanities and Social Sciences) 64.7 (2004): 2479. Chinese U of Hong Kong, 2003. DA 3099292. [Treatment of mother; relationship to patriarchy compared to Eugene O'Neill; Henrik Ibsen.]

Mohammad, Marwa Ghazi. "The Social and Political Awareness in Selected Plays by Harold Pinter." M.A. thesis in English literature. Department of English, College of Education for Women, U of Baghdad, Apr. 2007. Supervisor: Dr. Muayad E. Jajo. [Thesis submitted Apr. 2007; Viva completed 8 Oct. 2007.] (E-mail correspondence with author; copy of thesis courtesy of author received on 19 Dec. 2007.)

Nygaard, Thomas Lie. "Speech Rhythm as a Comic Device in Plays by Harold Pinter, in Particular *Old Times* and *Ashes to Ashes.*" M.A. thesis. Department of English, U of Bergen, Norway. Advisor: Stuart Sillars. 17 Dec. 2002. (E-mail correspondence with author of 24 May 2005.)

Onič, Tomaž. "Drama Harolda Pinterya Hišnik v slovenskem kulturnem prostoru." Master's thesis. Factuly of Arts, U of Ljubljana, 2002. ("*The Caretaker* by Harold Pinter in the Slovene Cultural Space." COBISS SI-ID 18579554. (Courtesy of author.)

—. "Harold Pinter's *The Caretaker* and Its Slovene Translation." Faculty of Education, U of Maribor, 1999. COBISS(Undergraduate thesis.) (Courtesy of author.)

Santiroprapai, Anthony. "Brutal Space(s): Political Discourse in the Late Plays of Harold Pinter, 1980-1999." Diss. Saint Louis U. English. Advisor: Tom Adler. Date of expected completion: 2004.

Taylor-Herbert, Saranne. "The Effects of Theatre Translation Problems on the Production of Selected Plays by Harold Pinter in West and Post-Unification Germany." Ph.D. diss. Performing Arts Department, De Montfort U, Leicester, UK. Supervisor: Michael Patterson. (E-mail correspondence with author of 8 Dec. 2005; 3 Aug. 2006.)

Forthcoming Publications, Upcoming Productions, Conferences, and Other Works in Progress

Artist and Citizen: 50 Years of Performing Pinter. Conference organizer: Mark Taylor-Batty. Workshop Theatre, U of Leeds, Eng. 12-14 Apr. 2007. 24 Feb. 2008 <http://www.leeds.ac.uk/theatre/pinter/index.html> ("Home"); <http://www.leeds.ac.uk/theatre/pinter/papers.html> ("Papers").

Baker, William, and John C. Ross, comps. *Harold Pinter: A Bibliographical History.* New Castle, DE: Oak Knoll Press and London: The British Library, 2005. (Courtesy of publisher.) [Reviewed in this vol. of *TPR.*]

Batty, Mark. *About Pinter: The Playwright and the Work.* London: Faber and Faber, 2005. (Courtesy of publisher.) [Reviewed in this vol. of *TPR.*]

Bean, Kellie. "Scenes from a Marriage: Lyotard, Pinter, and the Theatre of Gender." Chap. 6 (85-100) in *Gender after Lyotard.* Ed. Margret Brebowicz. SUNY Series in Gender Theory. Albany: SUNY P, 2007.

Begley, Varun. *Harold Pinter and the Twilight of Modernism.* Toronto: U of Toronto P, 2005. (Courtesy of publisher.)

Betrayal. Perf. Barbara Gulam (Emma), Stephen Webber (Robert), and Rex Young (Jerry). Actors Theatre of Louisville, Louisville, KY. 4-29 Jan. 2005. (E-mail correspondence, dated 28 Apr. 2006, with Steven H. Gale, who "served as a consultant during pre-production and then as a featured speaker at several pre- and post-performances.")

Billington, Michael. *Harold Pinter.* Rev. and updated ed. of *The Life and Work of Harold Pinter.* 1996. London: Faber and Faber, 2007. (Courtesy of author.)

The Birthday Party. By Harold Pinter. Dir. Lindsay Posner. Perf. Eileen Atkins, Henry Goodman, Geoffrey Hutchings, Sinead Matthews, Paul Ritter, and Finbar Lynch. Duchess Theatre, London. May 2005.

Brewer, Mary Francis, ed. "Harold Pinter's *The Dumb Waiter.*" Amsterdam (Neth.)

and New York: Rodopi. [Collection of paired essays on the play. In preparation.]

Celebration. By Harold Pinter. Dir. Alan Stanford. Staged reading. Perf. Joanna Crumley, Kenneth Cranham, Sinéad Cusack, Charles Dance, Janie Dee, Michael Gambon, Jeremy Irons, Stephen Rea, and Penelope Wilton. The Gate Theatre, Albery Theatre, London. 1-3 Dec. 2005. [Celebrating his Nobel Prize in Literature and his 75th birthday.]

Celebration. Dir. John Crowley. Perf. James Bolam, Janie Dee, Colin Firth, James Fox, Michael Gambon, Julia McKenzie, Sophie Okonedo, Stephen Rea, and Penelope Wilton. *More 4*. Channel Four (UK). First broadcast Feb. 2007. <http://www.channel4.com/more4/drama/c/celebration.html>. (DVD courtesy of Matthew [Harry] Burton.)

Celebration and *The Room*. By Harold Pinter. Dir. Neil Pepe. Perf. (in *The Room*:) Beth Peil (Rose), Thomas Ray Ryan (Bert), Peter Maloney (Mr. Kidd), Kate Blumberg (Mrs. Sands), David Pittu (Mr. Sands), Earle Hyman (Riley); (in *Celebration*:) Patrick Breen (Lambert), Betty Aidem (Julie), Thomas Jay Ryant (Matt), Carelyn McCormick (Prue), Brennan Brown (Russell), Kate Blumberg (Suki), Philip Goodwin (Richard), Christa Scott-Reed (Sonia), David Pittu (Waiter). 20th anniversary season (2005-2006). Atlantic Theatre Company, New York. Previews from 16 Nov. 2005. Opening 5 Dec. 2005. Through 21 Jan. 2006.

"Citation at Academic Convocation 2007: Lois Gordon: Professor of English, Metropolitan Campus: Distinguished Professor of English." Press release. Fairleigh Dickinson U, Teaneck, NJ. 26 Sept. 2007. [Resolution conferring honor "reserved for those who have set the standard for scholarly eminence in their fields of inquiry. . . ."]

The Collection. By Harold Pinter. Dir. Joe Hytner. Perf. Ade O'Brien (Bill), Okey Nzelu (James), James Sharpe (Harry), and Claire Wells (Stella). Prod. Josh Sutton. Lighting Designer James Lawson and Mike Fletcher. Stage Manager Peter Johnson. Assistant Stage Manager Meg Atkinson. Set Designer Louise Barker. Costume Designer Hannah Love. Master Carpenter Phil Norris. Costume Consultant Georgia Artus. Sound Engineer Louise Barker. Fitzpatrick Hall, Queen's College, University of Cambridge, Cambridge, Eng., UK. 7-10 Nov. 2007. [*Camdram.net* (Association of Cambridge Theatre Societies). 23 Jan. 2008. <http://www.camdram.net/shows/07/collection>.]

The Dumb Waiter. By Harold Pinter. Dir. Harry Burton. Perf. Lee Evans (Gus) and Jason Issacs (Ben). Trafalgar Studios, London. 2 Feb.-24 Mar. 2007. <http://www.theambassadors.com/trafalgarstudios/sp_p3494.html>. Sonia Friedman Productions press release. 3 Jan. 2007. 2 Oct. 2007 <http://www.soniafriedman.com/news_press_releases/dumb_waiter_limited_run>. (Courtesy of Matthew [Harry] Burton.)

The Dumb Waiter. By Harold Pinter. Perf. Keith Farquhar (Gus) and Alex Laube (Ben). Event during Viva Pinter: Spectacle Lyon 3. Auditorium Malraux. 19 Mar. 2007. (See "Viva Pinter," as listed below.)

"The Dumb Waiter and Other Pieces." By Harold Pinter. Dir. Simon Reade. Perf. Jonathan Broadbent (Ben) and Ferdy Roberts (Gus) [and all the other characters and personae]. Bristol Old Vic Studio, Bristol, UK. Inc.: "Press Conference" (2001); "American Football" (1991); "Precisely" (1983); "The Coast" (1975); "That's Your Trouble" (1964); "The Black and White" (1959); and *The Dumb Waiter* (1957). April 2006.

Festival of Harold Pinter. Dir. Rush Rehm. Stanford Summer Theater. Pigott Theater, Drama Department, Stanford U, Palo Alto, CA. 11 July-8 Aug. 2005. Inc. *The Lover* and "Night," dir. Jeffrey Bihr; "Applicant" and *The Collection*, co. dir. Rush Rehm and Ed Iskandar; and five film screenings: *The Handmaid's Tale*, *Turtle Diary*, *The French Lieutenant's Woman*, *The Go-Between*, and *Accident*.

Fortune's Fool: A Life of Joe Brearley: The Man Who Taught Harold Pinter. Ed. G. L. Watkins. Introd. Harold Pinter. Dinton, Aylesbury, Buckinghamshire, Eng.: TwigBooks (in association with The Clove Club), 2008. (Courtesy of the editor.)

Fractured Narratives: Pinter, Postmodernism and Diasporic Writing. (Working title.) Pinter Centre for Performance and Creative Writing. Goldsmiths College, U of London. May or June 2009. (E-mail correspondence with Pinter Centre Director Robert Gordon, 31 Oct. 2007. For updates, please see: <http://www.goldsmiths.ac.uk/pinter-centre/>.)

Le Gardien (*The Caretaker*). D'Après la pièce d'Harold Pinter . Scénario Harold Pinter. Réalisateur Clive Donner. Avec Alan Bates [Mick], Donald Pleasence [Davies] et Robert Shaw [Aston]. DVD-9 Vidéo. Doriane Films (BFI; with the support of the CNC), 2008. Traduction Française Phillippe Djian. Sous-Titres Anglais et Français. Noir et Blanc, 126 min. Copyright © 1962-1963 – Caretaker Films Ltd. and Taylor Productions Inc. (Courtesy of Cécile Farkas, Doriane Films.) [French DVD, region 9 (PAL format), in black and white, in French translation, with English and French subtitles.]

Gordon, Lois. *Nancy Cunard: Heiress, Muse, Political Idealist*. New York: Columbia UP, 2007.

Grimes, Charles. *Harold Pinter's Politics: A Silence Beyond Echo*. Madison and Teaneck, NJ: Fairleigh Dickinson UP, 2005. Cranbury, NJ: Associated U Presses, 2005. (Courtesy of publisher.) [Reviewed in this vol. of *TPR*.]

Harold Pinter and Jazz: An Evening of Celebration. With Henry Woolf and Susan Williamson. CBC Saskatchewan, Canada. 7 Apr. 2007. (Radio program.)

The Homecoming. By Harold Pinter. Dir. Daniel Sullivan. Perf. Eve Best (Ruth), Raul Esparza (Lenny), Michael McKean (Sam), Ian McShane (Max), and Gareth Saxe (Joey). Set Design Eugene Lee. Costume Design Jess Goldstein. Lighting Design Kenneth Posner. Sound Design John Gromada. Cort Theatre, New York. Previews from 23 Nov. 2007. Opening 9 Dec. 2007. Through 13 Apr. 2008. (For updates, reviews, and related features, see official prod. website: <http://www.thehomecomingonbroadway.com>.)

The Hothouse. By Harold Pinter. Dir. Ian Rickson. Perf. Leo Bill (Lamb), Finbar Lynch (Gibbs), Stephen Moore (Roote), Peter Pacey (Lobb), Paul Ritter (Lush), Lea Williams (Miss Cutts), and Henry Woolf (Tubb). Set design Hildegard Bechtler. Lighting design Peter Mumford. Music Stephen Warbeck. Sound design Ian Dickinson. Lyttelton Theatre, Royal National Theatre, London, Eng. 11 July 2007–27 Oct. 2007.

Hribar, Darja. "Rewriting the Dramatic Convention of the Theatre of the Absurd in Slovene Translation." 141-49 in *On the Relationships between Translation Theory and Translation Practice*. Ed. and fwd. Jean Peeters. Frankfurt, Germany: Peter Lang, 2005.

A Kind of Alaska. By Harold Pinter. In a double bill with *Reunion*, by David Mamet. Dir. Cate Blanchett. Sydney Theatre Company, Sydney, Austral. (Announcement in Matthew Westwood, "Cate's Husband Revelling in Family Dramas," *Australian* 19 Dec. 2005, Local: 3.)

A Kind of Alaska and *Moonlight*. Dir. Andy Arnold. Perf. (*A Kind of Alaska*:) Stephen Clyde (Hornby), Jill Redford (Deborah), and Morag Stark (Pauline); (*Moonlight*:) Joe Arbley (Jake), Andy Arnold (Andy), Stephen Clyde (Ralph), Ben Hitchins (Fred), Jill Riddiford (Maria), and Jackie Wylie (Bridget). Decor Sarah Pauley. Costumes Fi Carrington. Lighting Trane-house-red. Assistant dir. Laura Bissell. Arches Theatre Company, Glasgow, Scotland. 30 Sept.-15 Oct 2005.

Madagascar. By J. T. Rogers. Perf. Kathryn Lee Johnson (June), Angie Radosh (Lillian), and Bill Schwartz (Nathan). New Theatre, Coral Gables, FL. 9 Sept.- Oct. 2005.

Münder, Peter. *Harold Pinter*. Reinbek beiHamburg (Germ.): Rowohlt Taschenbuch Verlag, 2006. (Courtesy of author and publisher.) Biographical study. (In German.)

Murray, Craig. *Murder in Samarkand: A British Ambassador's Controversial Defiance of Tyranny in the War on Terror*. Edinburgh: Mainstream Publishing, (Feb.) 2007. ["A fearless book by a fearless man. Craig Murray tells the truth whether the 'authorities' like it or not. I salute a man of integrity." – Harold Pinter.]

One Day Conference on Harold Pinter. VMV College and Department of Fine Arts, Rashtrasant Tukdoji Maharaj Nagpur U. Hotel Sunny International, Nagpur, India. 2 Dec. 2006. [Staff Reporter, "Meet Throws Light On Pinter's Works," *The Hitavada* (Nagpur, India) 3 Dec. 2006; clipping courtesy of participant Dr. Chillaranjan Misra.)

Onič, Tomaž. "Ohranjanje registra v dramskem prevodu." *Vestnik-Društvo za tuje jezike in Književnosti* 39.1/2 (2005): 271-81. COBISS SI-ID 14460424. In Slovene. ("Preserving Register in Drama Translation"; courtesy of author.)

—. "Translating Recurrences in Pinter's Plays." *English Language Overseas Perspectives and Enquiries* (ELOPE) (Slovene Association for the Study of English in Ljubljana, member for the European Society for the Study of English [ESSE]) 2.1/2 (2006): 293-99. COBISS.SI-ID 14670856. (Courtesy of author.)

Pinter, Harold. "Apart From That." *Areté: The Arts Tri-Quart.: Fiction Poetry Reportage Reviews* 20 (Spring/Summer 2006). [Dramatic sketch. A dialogue between "*Two people on mobile phones.*" (Special thanks for assistance to editor Craig Raine.)

—. "Laughter." In "Review: Laughter: The Saturday Poem: By Harold Pinter." *Guardian* 25 Nov. 2006, Guardian Review Pages: 23.

—. "Lust." 22 Jan. 2006. In "Harold Pinter's Recent Poetry." *HaroldPinter.org*. 15 Dec. 2007 <http://www.haroldpinter.org/poetry/lust.html>.

—. "Poem." *Spectator* 23 Apr. 2005: 13.

—. *Six Poems for A*. London: Faber and Faber, 2007.

—. "The Watcher: A New Poem by Harold Pinter." *Guardian* 9 Apr. 2007: 3.

—, and James Clarke. *Voices*. Collaborative dramatic work for radio with music. Words by Harold Pinter. Music by James Clarke. BBC Radio 3. 10 Oct. 2005. 9:30 p.m. (UK). Première. Also re-broadcast on 30 Dec. 2006. 8:45-9:30 p.m. (UK). 45 mins. 17 Sept. 2007 <http://www.bbc.co.uk/radio3/speechanddrama/voices_pinter.shtml>. "Programme Information: Network Radio Week 1: Saturday 30 December 2006." 17 Sept. 2007 <http://www.bbc.co.uk/pressoffice/proginfo/radio/wk52/sat_01.shtml>. (See also: Phil Daoust, "G2 Radio:

Monday: Pick of the Day." *Guardian* 10 Oct. 2005: 33.) "Sound Byte of 'Voices,'" with Harry Burton as Jimmy, aired 10 Oct. 2005, on BBC Radio 3, excerpt broadcast in Michele Norris, "Harold Pinter's 'Voices,'" *All Things Considered*, National Public Radio 13 Oct. 2005, 9:00 a.m. EST.

Pinter and Other Playwrights (Session 99), Pinter and Politics (Session 123), and Pinter Beyond the Stage (Session 158). Program arranged by the Harold Pinter Society. Coordinators: Christopher M. Wixson, Eastern Illinois U; Steven Dedalus Burch, U of Alabama; and Craig N. Owens, Drake U. Annual Convention of the Midwest Modern Language Association. The Pfister Hotel, Milwaukee, WI. 12 Nov. 2005.

Pinter and Others (Session 137) and Pinteresque Trans/Media(tions) (Session 180); and a staging of *Landscape* (dir. Craig N. Owens) (192). Program arranged by the Harold Pinter Society. Coordinators: Craig N. Owens, Drake U; Christopher M. Wixson, Eastern Illinois U. Annual Convention of the Midwest Modern Language Association. Palmer House Hilton, Chicago, IL. 11 Nov. 2006.

Pinter: Passion, Poetry, Politics. International symposium held in conjunction with the Europe Theatre Prize. Turin, Italy. 8-12 Mar. 2006. Organizer: Michael Billington. "Introd." *X Premio Europa per il teatro a Harold Pinter*. 6 Oct. 2007 <http://www.premio-europa.org/Premio.nsf/(PagineWWW)/en_pinter_convegno.htm>. [Corrected title of conference.]

Playing Pinter: Performance Pop Culture and Politics in the Works of Harold Pinter (Special Session 252) and The Aftermath: Harold Pinter, the Nobel Prize, and the Iraq War (Special Session 767). Program arranged by the Harold Pinter Society. Presiding: Ann C. Hall, Ohio Dominican U. Annual Convention of the Modern Language Association. Hyatt Regency, Chicago, IL. 28 & 30 Dec. 2007.

Program on the Poetry of Harold Pinter. 140th session of Iran's Literature Foundation. 24 Dec. 2005. (Announcement in: "Poetry of Nobel Laureate Pinter to Be Discussed in Tehran." *MehrNews.com* 19 Dec. 2005. 20 Dec. 2005 <http://www.mehrnews.ir>.)

Rogers, J. T. *Madagascar*. Tampa: U of Tampa P, 2005. [Winner of the 2005 Pinter Review Prize for Drama.]

Rose, Charlie. "A Conversation with Harold Pinter." *The Charlie Rose Show*. WNET-TV (New York City) (Public Broadcasting Service). First broadcast 1 Mar. 2007, 11:00 p.m. ET-12:00 a.m. ET. Also broadcast on PBS affiliate channels at various scheduled times. WXXI-TV (Rochester, New York) (Public Broadcasting Service). Broadcast 1 Mar. 2007 from 11:00 p.m. ET to 12:00 a.m. ET. (52 mins., 21 secs.) 1 Mar. 2007 <http://www.charlierose.com/guests/harold-pinter>. (Full-length streaming video accessible directly from the show's website.)

"Sleuth." Screenplay by Harold Pinter for film *Sleuth* based on his adaptation of 1970 play by Anthony Shaffer. Dir. Kenneth Branagh. Perf. Michael Caine (Andrew Wyke) and Jude Law (Milo Tindle). Prod. Simon Halfon, Jude Law, Simon Moseley, Marion Pilowsky, and Tom Sternberg. Premiere screening at the Venice Film Festival 30 Aug. 2007. Release dates: 12 Oct. 2007 (limited U.S.); 23 Nov. 2007 (limited UK). Sony Classic Pictures official site. 7 Oct. 2007 <http://www.sonyclassics.com/sleuth/>. [Screenplay completed May 2005; revised for 2007 film.] DVD release date 11 Mar. 2008 (USA); 17 Mar. 2008 (UK).

A Slight Ache and *The Lover*. By Harold Pinter. Dir. David Roylance. Perf. John O'Connor (the Matchseller; Richard), Simon Cole (Edward; the Milkman), Caroline

Trowbridge (Flora; Sarah). Set and lighting design Kate McDermott. European Arts Company. 2005 UK Touring production. 4-27 May 2005. Dir. Jonathan Kemp. Perf. Richard Latham, Miriam Cooper, and John O'Connor. Spring 2006 touring prod. 20 Feb.-31 Mar. 2006. (*Harold Pinter Community Discussion Forum.* 15 Dec. 2005. 18 Sept. 2007 <http://p079.ezboard.com/ftheharoldpintercommunityfrm1.showMessage?topicID=559.topic>.) Additional production details: "Previous Productions: 2005" and "Future Productions: Spring 2006," *European Arts Company Web Site* © 2006. 19 Sept. 2007 <http://www.europeanarts.co.uk/Productions.php#slightache2005> and <http://www.europeanarts.co.uk/Productions.php#slightache2006>.

Smith, Ian, comp. and introd. *Pinter in the Theatre.* Fwd. Harold Pinter. London: Nick Hern Books, 2005. (Courtesy of publisher.) Paperback ed., 2006. New York: Theatre Communications Group, 2006.

Theatre Archive Project: British Library, U of Sheffield, AHRC [Arts & Humanities Research Council (UK)]. 17 Sept. 2007 <http://www.bl.uk/projects/theatrearchive/homepage.html>. Companion website for "a five-year project (2003-2008) to reinvestigate British theatre history 1945-1968, from the perspectives of both the theatregoer and the practitioner. The Project Team includes staff from both the British Library and the University of Sheffield." Inc. interviews which mention Harold Pinter and his works, or which discuss them more extensively; see, e.g., Catherine Jones's interview with Timothy West, as listed above in "**Other Articles. . . .**"

Working With Pinter. Dir. Harry Burton. Transmission *More 4*, Channel 4 (UK) 26 Feb. 2007. Repeated 9 Mar. 2007. Subsequent screenings of DVD: Artist and Citizen: 50 Years of Performing Pinter, U of Leeds, Leeds, Eng., 12 Apr. 2007; East End Film Festival, Genesis Mile Cinema, London, 23 Apr. 2007; The End of the Pier International Film Festival, Bognor Regis, West Sussex, Eng., UK, 1 May 2007. (DVD courtesy of Matthew [Harry] Burton.)

Viva Pinter: Hommage à Harold Pinter, Prix Nobel de Littérature, Légion d'Honneur 2007. Organized by the Université Jean Moulin, Lyon 3, and ENGS LSH. Organizer: Brigitte Gauthier, Université de Lyon 3. March 2007. Events: 2-21 Mar. 2007; International Colloquium 22, 23, 24 Mar. 2007. 14 Sept. 2007 <http://www.vivapinter.org>. Program is accessible online. (Photocopy of printed program courtesy of William Baker.)

Special Supplement on the 2005 Nobel Prize in Literature, October 2005 – May 2006

The 2005 Nobel Prize in Literature

News Announcements and Related Features

"Activist Who 'cleaned the gutters of the English langauge'." *Sunday Independent* (Zaire) 15 Oct. 2005.

Agence France-Presse (AFP) English. "British Writer Hornby Has No Time for Germany's 'Maggie'." *HighBeam Research* 20 Oct. 2005.

Agencies. "'The foremost representative of British drama': Excerpts from the Swedish Academy's Citation Awarding the Nobel Prize for Literature to British Playwright Harold Pinter." *Guardian Unlimited* 13 Oct. 2005. 14 Oct. 2005 <http://books.guardian.co.uk/nobelprize/story/0,,1591412,00.html>.

Alberge, Dalya. “Recognition for Pinter’s World–Slippery and Very, Very English: Highest Honour for the Man Who Made Silence an Art Form.” London *Times, Times Online* 14 Oct. 2005. <http://entertainment.timesonline.co.uk/tol/arts_and_entertainment/books/article578404.ece>.

Allen-Mills, Tony. “This Pinter Guy Could Turn into a Pain Belatedly, Americans Are Wising Up to a Nobel Menace, Says Tony Allen-Mills.” London *Sunday Times* 6 Nov. 2005. 3 Oct. 2007 <http://www.timesonline.co.uk/tol/news/article586943.ece>.

“Als Kleiner, Harmloser Bruder von Beckett, Seinem.” *Tages-Anzeiger* 14 Oct. 2005. (Cited in Renton & Taylor-Batty in this vol. of *TPR*.)

Al-Solaylee, Kamal. “Playwright Pinter Shocked by Nobel Win: Works of the ‘permanent public nuisance’ Combine Evasions, Menace and Comedy.” *Globe and Mail* (Toronto) 14 Oct. 2005. 15 Oct. 2005 <http://www.theglobeandmail.com>.

Andersson, Pelle. “Pinter – Pyspunka!” *Aftonbladet* 14 Oct. 2005. [“Visst Hade det funnitsmerspännande val.”] (Cited in Renton and Taylor-Batty in this vol. of *TPR*.)

Ansen, David. “Periscope: Nobels: A Pinter Perfect Recipient.” *Newsweek* 24 Oct. 2005: 10.

Anti-war Playwright Awarded Nobel.” *Herald Sun* (Melbourne, Austral.) 14 Oct. 2005. 13 Oct. 2005 <http://www.heraldsun.news.com.au>.

“ArtNews: Profile: Controversial Master of Suspense Pinter Wins Nobel Crown.” *Monsters and Critics.com* 13 Oct. 2005. 14 Oct. 2005 <http://arts.monsterandcritics.com>.

Associated Press. “Harold Pinter Wins Nobel Prize in Literature.” *New York Times* 13 Oct. 2005, 8:17 a.m. EST. 13 Oct. 2005 <http://www.nytimes.com>.

—. “Lifestyle: Fellow Writers Praise Choice of Harold Pinter.” *Jamaica Observer* 16 Oct. 2005. 16 Oct. 2005 <http://www.jamaicaobserver.com>.

Bancroft, Colette. “In Tampa, a Nobel Celebration.” *St. Petersburg Times Online Tampa Bay* 14 Oct. 2005: 1A. (South Pinellas Ed.)

Barr, Robert (AP, London; International News Agency) “Nobel Winner Pinter Rages against U.S. Arrogance; Calls Blair ‘deluded idiot’.” *cbc.ca* (Canadian Press) 13 Oct. 2005. 13 Oct. 2005 <http://www.cbc.ca/cp/world/051013/w101338.html> (Outdated URL). 23 Feb. 2008 <http://www.internationalnewsagency.org/nobel_winner_pinter_rages_agains.htm>.

Battersby, Eileen. “Pinter Honoured with Nobel Prize for Reshaping Drama.” *Irish Times* 14 Oct. 2005. 23 Sept. 2007 <http://www.ireland.com/newspaper/frontpage/2005/1014/1127148498744.html>.

Bell, Ian. “It Is Harold Pinter’s Morality and Politics, Not His Artistic Genius, That Have Won Him the Nobel Prize for Literature.” London *Sunday Herald* 16 Oct. 2005. 15 Oct. 2005 <http://www.sundayherald.com>.

Bhatia, Shyam (DH News Service London). “Nobel Prize for Literature: Harold Pinter’s Nobel Reward.” *Deccan Herald* (Bangalore, India) 14 Oct. 2005. 13 Oct 2005 [updated URL from *Deccan Herald* archives] 19 Sept. 2007 <http://www.deccanherald.com/archives/oct142005/foreign1738392005101 3.asp>.

Billington, Michael. “Critic’s View: A Gulf in Appreciation.” *Guardian* 14 Oct. 2005: 5. 14 Oct. 2005 <http://books.guardian.co.uk/nobelprize/story/0,,1592229,00.html>.

—, comp. "'They said you've a call from the Nobel committee. I said, why?'" *Guardian* 14 Oct. 2005: 1. 14 Oct. 2005 <http://books.guardian.co.uk/nobelprize/story/0,,1592185,00.html>.

"Biobibliographical Notes." *Swedish Academy* 13 Oct. 2005. 13 Oct. 2005 <http://www.svenskaakademien.se/Templates/Article1.aspx?PageID=572bd425-df9d-4240-8146-261beb6d3f67>. [For Harold Pinter as 2005 Nobel Laureate in Literature.]

Bragg, Melvyn. "'A True Man of the Theatre': Interviews by Sarah Phillips and Nicki Sprinz." *Observer* 16 Oct. 2005. 16 Oct. 2005 <http://books.guardian.co.uk/nobelprize/story/0,,1593030,00.html>.

Brahmbhatt, Preetee. "The Nobel Laureate Who Likes Cricket." *Rediff India Limited* 13 Oct. 2005. 13 Oct. 2005 <http://www.rediff.com/news/2005/oct/13harold.htm>.

Brantley, Ben. "A Creator of Theater That Seizes the Sense: An Appraisal." *New York Times* 13 Oct. 2005. 14 Oct. 2005 <http://www.nytimes.com/2005/10/13/books/13cnd-pinter.html>. (2 pages.)

"British Playwright Wins 2005 Nobel Literature Prize." *Chinaview.cn. Xinhuanet.com* 13 Oct. 2005. 13 Oct. 2005 <http://news.xinhuanet.com/english/2005-10/13/content_3614158.htm>.

Brown, Jeffrey, Emily Reuben, and Ben Brantley. "Literary Laureate." *NewsHour with Jim Lehrer* (*Online NewsHour*) 13 Oct. 2005. 15 Oct. 2005 <http://www.pbs.org/newshour/bb/entertainment/july-dec05/pinter_10-13.html>. (Transcript and streaming video of segment.)

Brown, Stephen. "Update 4–Playwright Pinter Wins Nobel Literature Prize." *Reuters Business Channel, today.reuters.com* 13 Oct. 2005. 13 Oct. 2005 <http://today.reuters.com>.

Byrne, Terry. "Playwright Pinter Wins $1M Nobel Surprise." *Boston Herald* 14 Oct. 2005. 14 Oct. 2005: 8. 14 Oct. 2005 <http://theedge.bostonherald.com/artsNews/>.

Cohen, Joshua. "Harold Pinter, Son of a Tailor and Weaver of the Absurd, Awarded a Nobel." *The Forward* (*The Jewish Forward*) 21 Oct. 2005, News. 20 Oct. 2005 <http://www.forward.com>.

Connors, Greg. "Litbloggers Fill Screens with Gossip." *Buffalo News* 17 Oct. 2005, The Link, Blogarhythms: C1.

Cristobal, Adrian. "The Sounds of Silence." *Manila Bulletin* 22 Oct. 2005, Breakfast Table, Opinion & Editorial.

Crown, Sarah. "Nobel Prize Goes to Pinter: Swedish Academy Confounds Expectations by Naming Harold Pinter as This Year's Laureate." *Guardian Unlimited* 13 Oct. 2005. 14 Oct. 2005 <http://books.guardian.co.uk/nobelprize/story/0,,1591402,00.html>.

"Culture Playday for Pinter." *Australian* 15 Oct. 2005, Features, Editor: 34.

Curry, Ann. "British Playwright Awarded Nobel Prize." *Today*, NBC 13 Oct. 2005, 7:00 a.m. EST.

Dalley, Jan. "Academy Honours Pinter." *Financial Times* 14 Oct. 2005. 14 Oct. 2005 <http://financialtimes.com>.

Daniszewski, John, and Don Shirley. "Pinter, Master of Menacing Drama, Wins Nobel

Prize." *Los Angeles Times* 14 Oct. 2005. 15 Oct. 2005 <http://www.latimes.com>.

"De Roger Planchon aux pacifistes, un hommage appuyé." *Le Monde* 14 Oct. 2005. ["L'un des plus grands écrivains du monde et l'un de ses citoyens les plus politiquement engagés."] (Cited in Renton & Taylor-Batty in this vol. of *TPR*.)

DiCintio, A.J. "Hate, Hypocrisy, and the Nobel Prize for Literature." *MichNews.com* 25 Oct. 2005. 25 Oct. 2005 <http://www.michnews.com/artman/publish/printer_10032.shtml>.

"Did the Right Pinter Win?" *New York Post Online Ed.* 14 Oct. 2005. 14 Oct. 2005 <http://www.nypost.com>.

"Die Seltsamen, Anfechtbaren, ja grotesken Entscheide häufen sich, die Liste der großen Übergangenen wird immer länger." *Tages-Anzeiger* 14 Oct. 2005. (Cited in Renton & Taylor-Batty in this vol. of *TPR*.)

Donahue, Deirdre. "Playwright Pinter Wins Nobel Prize." *USA Today* 13 Oct. 2005, 7:12 a.m.; updated 6:16 p.m. EST. 19 Oct. 2005 <http://www.usatoday.com/life/books/news/2005-10-13-nobel-pinter_x.htm?POE=NEWISVA>.

"Earth to Stockholm. . . ." *New Criterion* 24.3 (Nov. 2005): 1-2.

Engdahl, Horace (The Permanent Secretary of the Swedish Academy). "Prize Announcement" and "Interview." 13 Oct. 2005. In "The Nobel Prize in Literature 2005." Copyright © Nobel Media AB/Nobel Web AB 2005. *Nobelprize.org* 13 Oct. 2005. 25 Sept. 2007 <http://nobelprize.org/nobel_prizes/literature/laureates/2005/announcement.html>. (Video links to formal announcement and interview.) ["Announcement of the Nobel Prize in Literature 2005 by the Permanent Secretary, Horace Engdahl, at the Swedish Academy in Stockholm, October 13, 2005. ... The announcement is followed by an interview with Horace Engdahl about the 2005 Nobel Laureate in Literature. Interviewer is Ola Larsmo, freelance journalist."]

—. "The Nobel Prize in Literature 2005: Harold Pinter." Press release. *Svenska Akademien.* 13 Oct. 2005. 24 Sept. 2007 <http://www.svenskaakademien.se/Templates/Article1.aspx?PageID=64869f13-ddb1-4c4>. ["The Nobel Prize in Literature for 2005 is awarded to the English writer Harold Pinter 'who in his plays uncovers the precipice under everyday prattle and forces entry into oppression's closed rooms'."]

Engelhard, Jack. "Harold Pinter Saved My Life." *ChronWatch* 25 Oct. 2005. 25 Oct. 2005 <http://www.chronwatch.com>.

"Excerpts from the Work of Harold Pinter: Following Are Excerpts from the Work of Harold Pinter, Who Won the Nobel Prize in Literature on Thursday." *New York Times* 13 Oct. 2005. 14 Oct. 2005 <http://www.nytimes.com/2005/10/13/books/pinter-excerpts.html>.

Feingold, Michael. "Theater: Giving Us Pause: Nobel Laureate Harold Pinter: The Silences Demarcate the Warring Lines on the Battlefield of Words." *Village Voice* 14 Oct. 2005. 15 Oct. 2005 <http://www.villagevoice.com>.

Freeman, John. "Books: Pinter Aims His Salvos at U.S. Policy." *Orlando Sentinel* 23 Oct. 2005. 23 Oct. 2005 <http://www.orlandosentinel.com>.

—. "Politics May Have Helped Me Win Nobel, Says Pinter." *Times Online* 13 Oct. 2005. 14 Oct. 2005 <http://www.timesonline.co.uk>.

Galloway, George. "If Jack Wants Immigration, Why Banish Elvis and Co.? (Column)." London *Mail on Sunday* 22 Oct. 2005. 22 Oct. 2005 <http://www.highbeam.com/library>.

Gomez, Edward M. "World Views: What Is Iraq Facing Now?" and "Nobel Prize-Winning Playwright Harold Pinter's Politics." *SFGate.com* 18 Oct. 2005. 18 Oct. 2005 <http://www.sfgate.com>.

Gray, Simon. "When Harold Met Antonia: As the Nobel Jury Honours Harold Pinter, Simon Gray Remembers How His Friend's Passionate Love Affair with Antonia Fraser Threatened to Turn the Original Production of 'Otherwise Engaged' into a Bedroom Farce." London *Sunday Telegraph* 16 Oct. 2005, Review: 5.

Grey, Barry. "British Playwright Harold Pinter Awarded Nobel Prize in Literature." *World Socialist Web Site* 14 Oct. 2005 <http://www.wsws.org/articles/2005/oct2005/pint-o14.shtml>.

Griehsel, Marika. "Harold Pinter: The Nobel Prize in Literature 2005: Interview." Photo by Martin Rosenbaum. *Nobelprize.org* 13 Oct. 2005. 13 Oct. 2005 <http://nobelprize.org/literature/laureates/2005/pinter-telephone.html>. ("Telephone interview with Harold Pinter after the announcement of the 2005 Nobel Prize in Literature, October 13, 2005. Interviewer is Marika Griehsel, freelance journalist.")

Grove Press and Grove/Atlantic, Inc. "Grove Press Congratulates Harold Pinter Author of *Death etc.*, *The Homecoming*, *Betrayal*, and *The Birthday Party*, Winner of the 2005 Nobel Prize in Literature." *New York Times* 25 Oct. 2005, The Arts: E8. (Paid advertisement.)

Hare, David. "'In Pinter you find expressed the great struggle of the 20th century—between primitive rage on the one hand and liberal generosity on the other.'" *Guardian* 14 Oct. 2005. 15 Oct. 2005 <http://books.guardian.co.uk/nobelprize/story/0,,1592186,00.html>. ["Harold Pinter Was Yesterday Awarded the Nobel Prize for Literature. For Once, Says David Hare, the Committee Has Got It Exactly Right."]

"Harold Pinter Wins Nobel Laureate Prize." *Daily Times* 14 Oct. 2005. 13 Oct. 2005 <http://www.dailytimes.com>.

"Harold Pinter Wins the Nobel Literature Prize." *Gulf Times* (Doha, Qatar) 16 Oct. 2005. 15 Oct. 2005 <http://www.gulf-times.com>.

Hedvall, Barbro. "Ett blygsamt förslag." *Dagens Nyheter* 14 Oct. 2005. 1 Jan. 2006 <http://www.dn.se>.

Howard, Jennifer. "Nobel Prize in Literature Goes to Harold Pinter, British Playwright Widely Studied in Academe." *Chronicle of Higher Education* 13 Oct. 2005, Today's News. 13 Oct. 2005 <http://chronicle.com/free/2005/10/2005101301n.htm>.

Hunka, George. "Shakespeare, Beckett, Pinter." *Superfluities: Unnecessary Thoughts from an Unimportant Man* 13 Oct. 2005. 22 Oct. 2005 <http://ghunka.blogspot.com/2007/05/shakespeare-beckett-pinter.html>.

"In Praise of… Harold Pinter." *Guardian*, Special Reports 14 Oct. 2005. 13 Oct. 2005 <http://books.guardian.co.uk/nobelprize/story/0,,1592245,00.html>.

Inskeep, Steve (host), and Neda Ulaby. "Playwright Pinter Wins Nobel for Literature." *Morning Edition*, National Public Radio 13 Oct. 2005, 11:00 a.m. EST.

Isherwood, Charles. "Critic's Notebook: A Pinter Actor Must Know His Between-the-Lines." *New York Times* 16 Oct. 2005, sec. 4, Week in Review: 1, 3.

Italie, Hillel. "Fiery Critic of U.S. Wins Nobel Prize." *Chicago Sun-Times* 14 Oct. 2005 15 Oct. 2005 <http://www.suntimes.com/output/news/cst-nws-nobel14.html>.

— (AP). "Pinter Wins Nobel Prize in Literature." *Star Tribune* (Minneapolis-St. Paul, MN) 13 Oct. 2005. 13 Oct. 2005 <http://www.startribune.com>.

Jack, Ian. "Winning Isn't Everything: Ian Jack on Controversies around Literary Prizes." *Guardian Unlimited* 22 Oct. 2005, Books. 22 Oct. 2005 <http://books.guardian.co.uk/nobelprize/story/0,,1597926,00.html>.

Jh/po/rl. "AFK News Limited: British Playwright Harold Pinter Wins Nobel Literature Prize Update." *Forbes.com* 13 Oct. 2005. 13 Oct. 2005 <http://www.forbes.com/finance/feeds/afx/2005/10/13/afx2275702.html>.

Jones, Kenneth, and Robert Simonson. "Harold Pinter Wins Nobel Prize for Literature." *Playbill* 13 Oct. 2005. 13 Oct. 2005 <http://www.playbill.com/news/article/95651.html>.

Jones, Ryan. "Literature Nobel Laureate Pinter 'Overwhelmed' by Win." *Earth Times* 14 Oct. 2005. 14 Oct. 2005 <http://earthtimes.org/articles/show/4235.html>.

Keegan, Rebecca Winters. "People: Pinter's Progress." *Time* 24 Oct. 2005: 123. (Illus.)

Keillor, Garrison. "The Land of Republican Perfection: Where the Only Mistake You Can Ever Make Is to Confess Your Sins." *Salon.com* 19 Oct. 2005. 19 Oct. 2005 <http://dir.salon.com/story/opinion/feature/2005/10/19/keillor/index.html>.

Kimball, Roger. "The Nobel Prize for What?" *Armarvirumque: Commentary: The New Criterion Weblog* 13 Oct. 2005. 20 Sept. 2007 <http://newcriterion.com:81/weblog/2005/10/nobel-prize-for-what.html>.

Kung, Michelle. "Nobel Efforts: Reviewing Harold Pinter's Other Career." *Entertainment Weekly* 22 Oct. 2005. (List of some of Pinter's adaptations of others' novels in his screenplays.)

Kustow, Michael. "The Jewish Voice of Harold Pinter." *Jewish Chronicle* 30 Nov. 2005, "What's Up in Europe?" Rpt. in *All about the Jewish Theatre.* <http://www.jewish-theatre.com/visitor/article_display.aspx?articleID=1608>.

Laksin, Jacob, and Patrick Devenny. "The Nobel Savage." *FrontPageMag.com* 19 Oct. 2005. 19 Oct. 2005 <http://www.frontpagemag.com/Articles/Read.aspx?GUID={1E069984-F20C-406A-AFC8-0638D6B4CF5B}>.

Lawless, Jill, and Jenn Wiant (Associated Press). "Splenetic British Playwright Harold Pinter, Master of the Pause, Wins Nobel Prize." *AP Worldstream* (Dateline: London) 13 Oct. 2005. 25 Sept. 2007 <http://www.highbeam.com/doc/1P1-114105405.html>.

Lawson, Mark. "Saturday: Comment and Debate: Renaissance for the Nationality That Dared Not Speak Its Name: The Plaudits Heaped on Artists from Harold Pinter to Nick Park Show that Englishness Is No Longer a Handicap." *Guardian* 15 Oct. 2005: 32.

Leith, Sam. "The Childish Urge to Tease Our Greatest Living Playwright Is Much

Too Delicious to Resist." London *Daily Telegraph* 15 Oct. 2005, Features; News Review on Saturday: 23.

Levy, Lawrence. "Asides." *Newsday* (New York, NY) 16 Oct. 2005, Opinion: A47.

Liddle, Rod. "King Harold." *Spectator* 22 Oct. 2005, 26 Mar. 2008. <http://www.spectator.co.uk>.

Liddy, Matt. "The Pinter of Our Discontent." *ABC News* (Australian Broadcasting Corp) 14 Oct. 2005, 17 June 2008 <http://www.abc.net.au/news/art/articulate/200510/s1482261.htm>.

"Luminaries Applaud Pinter's Nobel: Some of the Biggest Names in the Arts Have Applauded the Decision to Award Playwright Harold Pinter the 2005 Nobel Prize for Literature." *BBC News* 13 Oct. 2005. 13 Oct. 2005 <http://news.bbc.co.uk/2/hi/entertainment/4339894.stm>.

Lyall, Sarah. "Pinter Wins Nobel for Dramas of Ominous Power Struggles." *New York Times* 14 Oct. 2005: 1. (Late Ed.) 14 Oct. 2005 <http://www.nytimes.com/2005/10/13/books/13cnd-nobel.html>.

Mahadevan-Dasgupta, Uma. "The Word: The Interpreter of Silences." *Indian Express* 23 Oct. 2005. 23 Oct. 2005 <http://www.indianexpress.com>.

Marr, Oliver. "Pandora: Beleagu[e]red Blunkettt Prefers Not to Discuss the News." London *Independent* 18 Oct. 2005. (Published 17 Oct. 2005.)

Mbeki, Thabo. "Hail the Nobel Laureates – Apostles of Human Curiosity!" *ANC Today: Online Voice of The African National Congress* [5.42] 21-27 Oct. 2005. (6 pages.)

McCrum, Robert. "Books: Pause and Effect: Harold Pinter, Just Awarded the Nobel Prize for Literature, Has Dramatised the Pain of Being Human for Four Decades, Says Robert McCrum, Providing a Voice for Our Times—Even in Its Distinctive Silences." *Guardian* 16 Oct. 2005 <http://books.guardian.co.uk/nobelprize/story/0,,1593032,00.html>.

McMillan, Joyce. "Angry Young Man Has Grown into One of Establishment's Greatest Critics." *Scotsman* 14 Oct. 2005. 13 Oct. 2005; 20 Sept. 2007 <http://news.scotsman.com/topics.cfm?tid=596&id=2084392005>.

"Media: Media Diary": "Happy Harold." London *Independent* 22 Oct. 2005.

Melamed, Ariana. "Culture: A Nobel for Screenwriting." *Ynetnews.com* 23 Oct. 2005 <http://www.ynetnews.com>.

Merwin, Ted. "Into the Abyss: Considering Nobel Laureate Harold Pinter's Oeuvre from a Jewish Perspective." *Jewish Week* 21 Oct. 2005. 21 Oct. 2005 <http://www.thejewishweek.com>.

"A Moment of Reflection amid the Noise of Events." *Asharq Alawsat* 25 Oct. 2005. 25 Oct. 2005 <http://aawsat.com/english/print.asp?artid=id2350>.

Moore, Matt (Associated Press). "Acerbic and Biting Briton Harold Pinter Wins 2005 Nobel Prize in Literature." *AOL News* 13 Oct. 2005.

—. "British Playwright Harold Pinter Wins 2005 Nobel Prize in Literature." *Macleans* 13 Oct. 2005. 13 Oct. 2005 <http://www.macleans.ca>. (7 pages.) *AOL News* 13 Oct. 2005, 11:13 EDT.

—. "Harold Pinter Wins Literary Nobel." *Rediff India Abroad* 13 Oct. 2005. 13 Oct. 2005 <http://in.rediff.com/news/2005/oct/13nobel.htm>.

—. "Pinter Wins Nobel Literature Prize." London *Independent* 14 Oct. 2005. 14 Oct. 2005 <http://enjoyment.independent.co.uk/theatre/news/article319277.ece>.

—. "Pinter Wins Nobel Prize in Literature: British Playwright Harold Pinter Wins Nobel Prize in Literature; Breakthrough Was 'The Caretaker'." *ABCNews* 13 Oct. 2005. 13 Oct. 2005 <http://abcnews.go.com>.

Morgan, Peter. "Look Wider for Laureates." *Australian* 19 Oct. 2005, Features, Higher Education: 43.

Nathan, John. "Harold Pinter Will Not Attend Nobel Prize Ceremony." *Playbill* 24 Nov. 2005. 26 Sept. 2007 <http://www.playbill.com/news/article/96472.html>.

Nightingale, Benedict. "Bard of Our Perilous Era Whose Comedies of Menace Capture the Dark That Stays Beneath." London *Times* 14 Oct. 2005. 23 Sept. 2007 <http://www.timesonline.co.uk/tol/news/uk/article1081345.ece>.

"Nobel Literature Prize Goes to Harold Pinter." *EuroNews* 13 Oct. 2005, News. 23 Sept. 2007 <http://www.euronews.net/create_html.php?page=detail_info&article=314002&lng=1>.

"Nobelpreisträger Pinter: 'Ich muss jetzt aufhören, sprachlos zu sein.'" *Spiegel Online* 13 Oct. 2005. 23 Sept. 2007 <http://www.spiegel.de/kultur/literatur/0,1518,379606,00.html>. (In German.)

"Nobel Prize for Pinter." *Hackney Gazette* 20 Oct. 2005. 20 Oct. 2005. <http://www.hackneygazette.co.uk>. 23 Sept. 2007 <http://www.hackneygazette.co.uk/content/hackney/gazette/news/story.aspx?brand=HKYGOnline&category=news&tBrand=northlondon24&tCategory=newshkyg&itemid=WeED20%20Oct%202005%2012%3A51%3A04%3A250>.

"Nobel Prize for Playwright Pinter." *Manchester Online: Manchester Arts Literature* 13 Oct. 2005. 23 Sept. 2007 <http://www.manchesteronline.co.uk/entertainment/arts/literature/s/177/177848_nobel_prize_for_literature.html>.

"Nobel Prize Media Links." Official website of the Harold Pinter Society. *Pintersociety.org* 13 Oct.–11 Dec. 2005. 3 Nov. 2007 <http://www.pintersociety.org/links/nobellinks/nobellinks.html>. (Comp. Mark Taylor-Batty with some assistance from Susan Hollis Merritt.)

Nolan, Tanya (reporter), and Peter Cave. "AM–Harold Pinter Wins Nobel Prize for Literature." *ABC Online* 14 Oct. 2005. 23 Sept. 2007 <http://www.abc.net.au/am/content/2005/s1482078.htm>. (Transcript of radio broadcast with RealAudio link.)

Nooryani, Bunny. "Britain's Harold Pinter Wins Nobel Literature Prize (Update 2)." *Bloomberg.com* 13 Oct. 2005. 13 Oct. 2005 <http://www.bloomberg.com>.

Norris, Michele. "British Playwright Pinter Receives Nobel." *All Things Considered*, National Public Radio 13 Oct. 2005, 9:00 a.m. EDT.

Notes & Comments: November 2005: Earth to Stockholm. . . ." *New Criterion* Nov. 2005: 1-2.

Odone, Cristina. "Cristina Odone's Diary: … Angry Old Man." London *Observer* 16 Oct. 2005. 19 Oct. 2005 <http://observer.guardian.co.uk>.

"Oscar Nominee Pinter Wins Nobel." *Knight Ridder Tribune Business News* 15 Oct.

2005, Jour.: 1.

"Our View: Writer Harold Pinter Is Master of Menace behind a Few Words." *Delaware Online* 15 Oct. 2005. 15 Oct. 2005 <http://www.delawareonline.com>.

Paramuta, Pragya. "Pinter Who?" *Kolkata Newsline* (Kolkata, India). *Cities.expressindia.com* 18 Oct. 2005.

Parini, Jay. "Theater: Pinter's Plays, Pinter's Politics." *Chronicle of Higher Education* 11 Nov. 2005, Chronicle Review: B15. 20 Sept. 2007 <http://chronicle.com/weekly/v52/i12/12b01501.htm>.

"Pause for Thought: Harold Pinter and the Nobel Prize for. . . ." *Times Online* 14 Oct. 2005. 13 Oct. 2005 <http://www.timesonline.co.uk>.

Phillips, Sarah, and Nicki Sprinz. "'A True Man of the Theatre.'" Interviews by Sarah Phillips and Nicki Sprinz with Melvyn Bragg, Susannah Clapp, David Edgar, and Roger Lloyd Pack. *Observer* 6 Oct. 2005. 16 Oct. 2005 <http://observer.guardian.co.uk>.

"Picture of the Week: Harold Pinter: Master of the Dramatic Pause Is Left Speechless by Prize." London *Independent on Sunday* 16 Oct. 2005, News: 63. (First Ed.)

Pilger, John. "The Silence of Writers: On Nobel Prize Winner Harold Pinter." *Znet* 16 Oct. 2005, Mainstream Media. 23 Sept. 2007 <http://www.zmag.org/content/showarticle.cfm?ItemID=8941>.

"Pinter: A Cry in the Wilderness!" *The Times of India Online* (Times Internet Network) 13 Oct. 2005, 08:31:19 p.m. 13 Oct. 2005. 23 Sept. 2007 <http://timesofindia.indiatimes.com/articleshow/1261595>.

"Pinter's Dramatic Impact: Harold Pinter, Who Has Won the Nobel Prize for Literature, Is Widely Regarded as the UK's Greatest Living Playwright." *BBC News* 13 Oct. 2005. 23 Sept. 2007 <http://news.bbc.co.uk/2/hi/entertainment/4324562.stm>.

"Pinter's Prize." *Boston Globe* 14 Oct. 2005, Globe Editorial. 24 Sept. 2007 <http://www.boston.com/news/globe/editorial_opinion/editorials/articles/2005/10/14/pinters_size>.

"Pinter's World." *Khaleej Times Online* 16 Oct. 2005, Editorial. 16 Oct. 2005 <http://www.khaleejtimes.com/DisplayArticleNew.asp?section=editorial&xfile=data/editorial/2005/october/editorial_october42.xml>.

"Pinter Wins Nobel Literary Prize: Controversial British Playwright and Campaigner Has Won the 2005 Nobel Prize for Literature." *BBC News* 13 Oct. 2005. 19 Nov. 2005 <http://news.bbc.co.uk/go/pr/fr/-/1/hi/entertainment/arts/4338082.stm>.

"Pinter Wins Nobel Literature Prize: London, England (CNN)–British Playwright Harold Pinter Has Been Awarded the 2005 Nobel Prize in Literature." *CNN.com* 13 Oct. 2005. 24 Sept. 2007 <http://edition.cnn.com/2005/WORLD/europe/10/13/nobel.pinter/index.html>.

Prasad, G. J. V. "Op-Ed: Pinter: Poet-Playwright of Peace and Violence: Celebrating the 2005 Nobel Laureate for Literature, Harold Pinter." *Indian Express* 15 Oct. 2005. 15 Oct. 2005 <http://www.indianexpress.com>.

Pryce-Jones, David. "How Low Can They Go? II: Harold Pinter Wins the Nobel Prize in Literature." *National Rev.* 7 Nov. 2005. *Benador Associates website.* 9 Nov. 2007 <http://www.benadorassociates.com/article/18793>.

Rérolle, Raphaëlle, and Brigitte Salino (with A.F.P.). "De Roger Planchon aux pacifistes, un hommage appuyé." *Le Monde.fr* 14 Oct. 2005. 16 Oct. 2005 <http://www.lemonde.fr>.

"Revue de presse: Théâtre–Harold Pinter, un engagé couronné." *Courrier International.com* 14 Oct. 2005 <http://www.courrierinternational.com/>.

Reynolds, Nigel. "Pinter Left 'Speechless' After Winning Nobel Prize at 75." London *Daily Telegraph* 14 Oct. 2005. 13 Oct. 2005 <http://www.telegraph.co.uk>.

Rifkind, Hugo. "People with Hugo Rifkind: Nobel Thoughts from Harold." London *Times* 14 Oct. 2005. 24 Sept. 2005 <http://www.timesonline.co.uk/tol/news/uk/article578219.ece>.

Roberts, Robin. Announcement of Harold Pinter's Nobel Prize. *Good Morning America*. ABC News 13 Oct. 2005, 7:00 a.m. ET., ABC News Transcripts.

Robinson, David. "Pinter Wins Nobel Prize, Then Exits Stage Left." *Scotsman* 14 Oct. 2005 ("Last updated ... 01:54 BST"). 24 Sept. 2007 <http://living.scotsman.com/index.cfm?id=2084312005>.

Roy, Nilanjana S. "Pinter's Birthday Party: Speaking Volumes." *Business Standard* (India). *Business-standard.com* 17 Oct. 2005. 18 Oct. 2005 <http://www.business-standard.com>. Rpt. in <http://www.armeniandiaspora.com/forum/showthread.php?t=39869>.

Schottenius, Maria. "Hårt, rått och macho." *Dagens Nyheter* 13 Oct. 2005. 1 Jan. 2006 <http://www.dn.se/DNet/jsp/polopoly.jsp?a=473881>. (In Swedish.) ["Harold Pinter säger vad han vill. Inte Harry Potter - men Harold Pinter. För andra året i rad får Svenska Akademien kristallkronorna att svaja till i de gyllene salarna."]

Schwartz, Stephen. "And the Winner Is ... The Nobel Prize in Literature Goes to: A Bush-hating Leftist!" *Weekly Standard* 14 Oct. 2005. 25 Sept. 2007 <http://weeklystandard.com/Content/Public/Articles/000/000/006/208tcruy.asp>. Rpt. as "Nobel Leftist." *CBS News* 14 Oct. 2005, Opinion. 24 Sept. 2007 <http://www.cbsnews.com/stories/2005/10/14/opinion/main944151.shtml>.

Shenton, Mark. "A Pinteresque Pause for a Pinter Honour. . . ." *The Stage Online* 14 Oct. 2005, Newsblog. 14 Oct. 2005 <http://www.thestage.co.uk/shenton/2005/10/a_pintersque_pause_for_a_pinter_hon.php>.

Sheward, David. "Pinter, Master of Menace and Pauses, Wins Nobel Prize." *BackStage.com* 21 Oct. 2005. 24 Sept. 2007 <http://www.backstage.com/backstage/features/article_display.jsp?vnu_content_id=1001349669>.

Shteir, Rachel. "Culture Box: The Nobel Fool: Harold Pinter's Strident Politics." *Slate* 17 Oct. 2005. 24 Sept.. 2007 <http://www.slate.com/id/2128206/>.

Siegel, Ed. "Pinter, Theater's Explorer of Menace, Awarded Nobel." *Boston Globe* 14 Oct. 2005. 24 Sept. 2007 <http://www.boston.com/news/nation/articles/2005/10/14/pinter_theaters_explorer_of_menace_awarded_nobel/>.

Simon, Scott. ""Harold Pinter's 'Betrayal'." *Weekend Edition Saturday*. National Public Radio 15 Oct. 2005, 1:00-2:00 p.m. [Profile of Nobel Laureate with excerpts from *Betrayal*; NPR player.]

Sisario, Ben, comp. "Arts, Briefly: The Poet's Voice." *New York Times* 30 Nov. 2005,

The Arts: E2.

Sitoy, Lakambini A. "Letters from the Outlands." *ABS-CBN News.com* (ABS-CBN Interactive [Philippines]) 19 Oct. 2005. 25 Sept. 2007 <http://www.abs-cbnnews.com/storypage.aspx?StoryId=19213>.

[Smith, Joan.] "Joan Smith: Pinter Is Angry, Touchy and Aggressive. But Good Luck to Him." London *Independent* 16 Oct. 2005, Comment.

Smith, Neil. "'Political element' to Pinter Prize." *BBC News* 13 Oct. 2005 ("Last updated ... 16:33 GMT, 17:33 UK"). 25 Sept. 2007 <http://news.bbc.co.uk/2/hi/entertainment/4339096.stm>.

Spencer, Charles. "Happy Birthday Party for Harold Pinter." London *Daily Telegraph* 14 Oct. 2005, Opinion. 25 Sept. 2007 <http://www.telegraph.co.uk/opinion/main.jhtml?xml=/opinion/2005/10/14/do1402.xml>.

Stoppard, Tom, Christopher Hitchens, Corin Redgrave, Roger Kimball, Michael Colgan, and Michael Frayn. "Harold Pinter's Surprise 75th Birthday Present." *Guardian* 14 Oct. 2005, News: 5. *Guardian Unlimited* 14 Oct. 2005. 15 Oct. 2005 <http://www.guardian.co.uk>.

"Strange Thoughts on the Road from Sidcup." *Australian* 27 Oct. 2005, Editorial: 1. (All-round Country ed.) 26 Oct. 2005 <http://www.theaustralian.news.com.au/printpage/0,5942,17045810,00.html>.

Suroor, Hasan. "Pinter to Continue Anti-War Campaign: Acceptance Speech to Deal with the 'state of the world' in the Light of Iraq and Afghanistan." *The Hindu* 15 Oct. 2005, International. 25 Sept. 2007 <http://www.thehindu.com/2005/10/15/stories/2005101504171400.htm>.

Taheri, Amir. "Saddam Hussein and the Winner of the Nobel Prize of the Nobel Prize for Literature." *Asharq Alawsat* 21 Oct. 2005. 24 Sept. 2007 <http://aawsat.com/english/news.asp?section=2&id=2277>.

Teachout, Terry. "Leisure and Arts: Another Left Turn in Stockholm: An American-hating Playwright Wins a Nobel. Surprisingly, He Deserves It." *Wall Street Jour.* 16 Oct. 2005, Editorial Page. 25 Sept. 2007 <http://www.opinionjournal.com/la/?id=110007414>.

Traub, James. "Their Highbrow Hatred of US: How Did Virulent Anti-Americanism Become So Respectable?" *New York Times Mag.* 30 Oct. 2005, The Way We Live Now: 15-16.

Turki, Fawaz. "Reflections on Harold Pinter." *Arab News* ("The Middle East's Leading English Language Daily") 19 Oct. 2005 (16 Ramadhan 1426). 18 Oct. 2005 <http://www.arabnews.com>.

Tyrrell, Fiona. "Celebrating Pinter Power." *Irish Times* 15 Oct. 2005, Weekend, Arts: 8. [Actors' comments on Pinter at a celebratory dinner after the Gate Theatre's Pinter 75 festival at the Unicorn restaurant in Dublin.]

United Press International. "Harold Pinter Wins Nobel Literature Prize." *Science Daily.com* 13 Oct. 2005. 14 Oct. 2005 <http://www.sciencedaily.com>.

"UT Professor Nominated Nobel Winner." Press release. *University of Tampa* 13 Oct. 2005. 25 Sept. 2007 <http://static.ut.edu/public_info/UT-Professor-Nominated-Nobel-Winner.cfm>.

Wagner, Erica. "Early Reviewers Left Baffled by Shock of the New." London *Times Online* 14 Oct. 2005. 14 Oct. 2005 <http://www.timesonline.co.uk>.

Walker, Martin. "Walker's World: Pinter's Anti-U.S. Nobel." *United Press International* 14 Oct. 2005, 9:56 a.m., International Intelligence–Analysis. 14 Oct. 2005 <http://www.upi.com/International_Intelligence/Analysis/2005/10/13/walkers_world_pinters_antius_nobel/3053/>.

Walters, Caroline, and Lianne Vella. "Surprisingly Nobel Pinter." *Independent Student Voice* (University of Edinburgh Student Newspaper) 17 Oct. 2005. 18 Oct. 2005 <http://www.studentnewspaper.org>. Rpt. in *Armenian Diaspora News Forum* 25 Oct. 2007. 25 Sept. 2007 <http://www.armeniandiaspora.com/forum/showthread.php?t=39867>.

Wark, Kirsty. "Newsnight Review 14 October, 2005." With guests Sarah Churchill, Michael Gove, Hardeep Singh Kohli, and Rachel Campbell-Johnson. *Newsnight Review*, *BBC News* 14 Oct. 2005. 25 Sept. 2007 <http://news.bbc.co.uk/2/hi/programmes/newsnight/review/4338384.stm>. [Brief clips from interview with Harold Pinter.]

Wennö, Nicholas. "Nobel 2005: Pinters talande tystnad: Teatrala favoritvapen effektiva på film." *Dagens Nyheter* 13 Oct. 2005. 25 Sept. 2007 <http://www.dn.se/DNet/jsp/polopoly.jsp?a=473879>. (In Swedish.) [Provides links to articles in English and to ten Pinter-related articles in Swedish.]

Winer, Linda. "Pinter's Surprise Prize: The British Playwright Who 'forces entry into oppression's cold rooms' Wins Nobel for Literature." *Newsday* (New York, NY) 14 Oct. 2005, News: A26. (Nassau and Suffolk Ed.)

Winn, Steven. "Pinter Tapped for Nobel: Enigmatic British Playwright Has Unnerved Audiences for Half a Century." *San Francisco Chronicle* 14 Oct. 2005. 25 Sept. 2007 <http://sfgate.com/cgi-bin/article.cgi?file=/c/a/2005/10/14/MNGC0F88JV1.DTL>.

"Winner Questions Nobel Glory." *News24.com* (South Africa) 14 Oct. 2005. 15 Oct. 2005 <http://www.news24.com/News24/Entertainment/Abroad/0,6119,2-1225-1243_1816941,00.html>.

Yglesias, Matthew. "Barbarians at the Gate." *TPM Cafe* 14 Oct. 2005. 20 Oct. 2005 <http://yglesias.tpmcafe.com/story/2005/10/14/151529/22>. Comments on Schwartz, listed above.

—. "Goes Both Ways." *TPM Cafe* 17 Oct. 2005. 20 Oct. 2005 <http://yglesias.tpmcafe.com/story/2005/10/17/104533/97>. [Further commentary.]

Zeeman, Michaël. "Harold Pinter wint Nobelprijs voor Literatuur." *Die Volkskrant* 13 Oct. 2005. ["Er zijn talkrijke prozaïsten en dichters wier bekroning meer voor de hand had gelegen, maar waarover de Zweedse Academie Kennelijk geen overeenstemming heeft kunnen bereiken."] (Cited in Renton & Taylor-Batty in this vol. of *TPR*.)

Related Letters

Davey, Peter. "Pinter's Ideals Fail the Test of War." Letter to the editor. London *Daily Telegraph* 17 Oct. 2005, Features, Leading Article: 19.

Inlow, Robert J. "Letter: Pinter, a Playwright and Peace Promoter." London *Independent* 17 Oct. 2005, Comment: 32. (First Ed.)

Kane, Terence. "Letters: Don't Give Pinter a Pass." *Newsday* (New York, NY) 21 Oct. 2005, Opinion: A53. (Nassau and Suffolk ed.)

Matza, Peter. "Letter: Pinter and Owen." London *Independent* 15 Oct. 2005, Comment: 40. (First Ed.)

Norman, Terry, Gillian Slovo, Graham Ennis, and Katherine Salahi. "Letters: Pause and Reflect on Pinter's Nobel Win." *Guardian Unlimited* 17 Oct. 2005. 25 Sept. 2007 <http://books.guardian.co.uk/nobelprize/story/0,,1594013,00.html>.

Art, Truth an Politics: The Nobel Prize Lecture

Pinter, Harold. "Art, Truth and Politics: Excerpts from the 2005 Nobel Lecture." *World Literature Today* 80.3 (May 2006): 21-27.

—. *Art, Truth and Politics: The Nobel Lecture.* London: Faber and Faber, 2006. (1000 copies printed for private circulation. Courtesy of Dinah Wood, Faber and Faber.)

—. "Art, Truth and Politics: Nobel Lecture 2005." *PMLA* 121 (2006): 811-18.

—. "Art, Truth and Politics: The Nobel Lecture." 431-42 ("*Appendix*") in Michael Billington, *Harold Pinter.* Rev. updated ed. London: Faber and Faber, 2007.

—. *Harold Pinter: Art, Truth and Politics: The Nobel Prize Lecture.* © Copyright 2006 Illuminations. All Rights Reserved. Transmission by Channel 4, United Kingdom, 7 Dec. 2005. DVD. 46 mins. 8 Sept. 2007 <http://www.illuminationsmedia.co.uk/ourfilms/product/6/harold_pinter_art,_truth__politics.html>. Digital video disc and VHS video recording. "Programme and Film Production, London, UK: Harold Pinter: Art, Truth & Politics." (Courtesy of Illuminations.) [Commercially-produced DVD of Harold Pinter's Nobel Lecture: "Harold Pinter: Art, Truth and Politics.]

—. "Harold Pinter Delivers His Nobel Prize Acceptance Speech." Introd. David Hare. *More4*, Channel 4, UK. 7 Dec. 2005, 4:30 p.m. – 5:30 p.m. BT. (Live transmission.) Edited version, 8:30 p.m. – 9:00 p.m. BT.

—. "Nobel Lecture: Art, Truth and Politics." Presented on video at the Swedish Academy, Stockholm, Sweden. 7 Dec. 2005. In "Harold Pinter: The Nobel Prize in Literature 2005." *Nobelprize.org.* Copyright © 2005, The Nobel Foundation. 25 Sept. 2007 <http://nobelprize.org/nobel_prizes/literature/laureates/2005/pinter-lecture-e.html>. (HTML and PDF versions accessible in English, Swedish, French, and German.)

—. "The Nobel Lecture: Art, Truth and Politics." *Guardian Unlimited* 8 Dec. 2005. 27 Sept. 2007 <http://arts.guardian.co.uk/comment/story/0,,1662113,00.html>. ["In his video-taped Nobel acceptance speech, Harold Pinter excoriated a 'brutal, scornful and ruthless' United States. This is the full text of his address."]

The Presentation Speech of the 2005 Nobel Prize in Literature to Harold Pinter

Wästberg, Per. "Presentation Speech: By Writer Per Wästberg, Member of the Swedish Academy, Chairman of its Nobel Committee, December 10, 2005." In "Harold Pinter: The Nobel Prize in Literature 2005." Stockholm Concert Hall, Stockholm, Sweden. 10 Dec. 2005. *Nobelprize.org.* Copyright © 2005, The Nobel Foundation. (In English; also accessible in Swedish.) <http://nobelprize.org/nobel_prizes/literature/laureates/2005/presentation-speech.html>. [The Nobel Medal and Certificate were accepted on behalf of Harold Pinter by Stephen Page, publisher, Faber and Faber. In delivering the final paragraph, Mr. Wästberg added the word "regrettable" before "absence," saying "In the [regrettable] absence of this year's Nobel Laureate in Literature . . . ."]

News Announcements and Related Features

Abramowicz, Susanna. "Pinter's Attack on US Policy." *Ejpress.org* 14 Dec. 2005.

AFP [Agence France-Presse]. "Playwright Harold Pinter Hospitalised." *ABC [Australia Broadcasting Corporation] News Online* 5 Dec. 2005, 11:38pm (AEDT). 26 Sept. 2007 <http://harold-pinter-news.newslib.com/story/5775-3056204/>.

Associated Press [AP]. "Pinter's Role for Leaders of Coalition: Terror Defendants." *Australian* 9 Dec. 2005, World: 8.

Atchia, Michael. "Live 'N' Learn: Harold Pinter and the Search for Truth." *L'Express Outlook: The Weekly Review* 20 Dec. 2005. 25 Sept. 2007 <http://www.lexpress.mu/display_search_result.php?news_id=56328>.

Bernstein, Richard. "Rice's Visit: Official Praise, Public Doubts." *New York Times* 11 Dec. 2005, sec. 1, col. 1 (Foreign Desk): 18. (Late Edition–Final.)

Billington, Michael. "Devil's Advocate: 4 Stars Mercury, Colchester." *Guardian* 14 Nov. 2005. 25 Sept. 2007 <http://arts.guardian.co.uk/critic/review/0,,1641945,00.html>.

—. "Fine Art: When Pinter Let Fly." London *Mail and Guardian Online* 23 Dec. 2005. 25 Sept. 2007 <http://www.chico.mweb.co.za/art/2005/2005dec/051223-fly.html>.

—. "Passionate Pinter's Devastating Assault on US Foreign Policy: Shades of Beckett As Ailing Playwright Delivers Powerful Nobel Lecture." *Guardian* 8 Dec. 2005, Guardian Home Pages: 7. 25 Sept. 2007 <http://books.guardian.co.uk/nobelprize/story/0,,1662009,00.html>.

Bond, Paul. "Harold Pinter's Artistic Achievement." *World Socialist Web Site* 29 Dec. 2005. 25 Sept. 2007 <http://www.wsws.org/articles/2005/dec2005/pint-d29_prn.shtml>.

Bradley, Mike. "OTV: Thursday 15 December: Screengrabs." *Observer* 11 Dec. 2005, Observer Mag. Pages: 117.

Brown, Stephen. "Pinter Attacks US Policies in Nobel Lecture." *Reuters* 7 Dec. 2005. 17 Dec. 2005 <http://today.reuters.com>.

BWW News Desk. "Harold Pinter, For Health Reasons, Cancels Nobel-Related Appearances." *Broadway World.com* 1 Dec. 2005. 25 Sept. 2007 <http://broadwayworld.com/viewcolumn.cfm?colid=6159>.

Byrne, Ciar. "Of Bandits and Terrorists: Pinter's Broadside." London *Independent* 8 Dec. 2005, News: 3. (First Edition.)

"The Buzz: Pinter Extension." *Newsday* (New York, NY) 9 Dec. 2005, News: A13. (All editions.)

Carroll, Vincent. "On Point: Not-so-free Speech: ... Hark! A Harold Angry Sings." *Rocky Mountain News* 9 Dec. 2005, Commentary/Editorial: 48A. (Final Edition.)

Clark, Bob. "Reconstucting Pinter: Nobel Lecture Explores Writer's Elusive Plays." *Calgary Herald* (Alberta, Can.) 12 Mar. 2006: C3. [See Gale, listed above.] (E-mail correspondence from Gale dated 28 Apr. 2006.)

"Comment: They Said What?" *Observer* 11 Dec. 2005, *Observer* News Pages: 30.

Correction. *New York Times* 10 Dec. 2005, sec. A, col. 3 (Metropolitan Desk: Corrections): 2. (Late Edition–Final.)

"Corrections." *International Herald Tribune* 12 Dec. 2005, World News: Europe: 3. ["An article Thursday (8 Dec. 2005) about the playwright Harold Pinter's criticism of American foreign policy in his acceptance speech for the Nobel Prize in Literature described it incompletely. He said that both President George W. Bush and Prime Minister Tony Blair–and not just Blair–should be tried before the International Criminal Court of Justice for the invasion of Iraq."]

"Corrections and Clarifications." *Guardian* 12 Dec. 2005, Guardian Leader Pages: 28. (Final Edition.) [Correction of transcription of Harold Pinter's Nobel Lecture.]

Cosic, Miriam. "So Much Talk and So Few People Listening." *Australian* 9 Dec. 2005, Features, Arts: 17. (All-round Country Edition.)

"The Culture Show." London *Independent* 15 Dec. 2005. ["A highlights package from the past year which includes the Nobel Prize winner Harold Pinter (right) on the future of the theatre, Martin Scorsese on Caravaggio and the Mercury Prize winners. . . ."]

Deutsche Press-Agentur (DPA). "Arts News: Harold Pinter to Miss Out on Nobel Prize Ceremony." Rpt. in *Monsters and Critics.com* 24 Nov. 2005. 30 Nov. 2005 <http://arts.monstersandcritics.com>.

Dyer, Gwynne. "One of the Last Great Anti-American Rants." *Japan Times* 18 Dec. 2005. 19 Dec. 2005 <http://www.japantimes.co.jp>.

El Khazen, Jihad. "To Whom Do You Read Your Psalm [sic] 'Doctor'?" *Dar al hayat* 19 Dec. 2005. 20 Dec. 2005 <http://www.daralhayat.net>.

Farrell, Gerard. "Reply Letters and Emails: Masterful Pinter." *Guardian* 9 Dec. 2005, Guardian Leader Pages: 35. (Final Ed.)

Ferguson, Niall. "Harold Pinter Should Stick to Writing Plays." *Australian* 12 Dec. 2005, Features, Opinion/Op Ed: 8. (All-round Country Ed.) (Replies by Falconer, Joel, and Robertson, as listed below in "**Related Letters**.")

"Furthermore." *Omaha World-Herald* 16 Dec. 2005, Editorial, 6B.

Gale, Steven H. "Humanities Nobel Lecture: Butter's Going Up: Harold Pinter and the Artistic Process." U of Calgary, Alberta, Can. 13 Mar. 2006. [See Williamson, listed below.] (E-mail correspondence from author dated 28 Apr 2008; U of Calgary "What's On" for 3-19 Mar. 2006.)

Goodley, Simon. "People." *Guardian* 7 Dec. 2005, Guardian Home Pages: 7.

Green, John. "Reply: Letters and Emails: Masterful Pinter." *Guardian* 9 Dec. 2005, Guardian Leader Pages: 35. (Final Edition.)

Hari, Johann. "Pinter Does Not Deserve the Nobel Prize." London *Independent* 6 Dec. 2005, Comment: 35. (First Edition.) (Replies by Allen, Connell, and Niven, as listed below in "**Related Letters**" below.)

"Harold Pinter Cancels Nobel Trip." *Sveriges Radio* 30 Nov. 2005. 26 Sept. 2007 <http://www.sr.se/cgi-bin/isidorpub/PrinterFriendlyArticle.asp?ProgramID=2054&Nyheter=&artikel=744745>.

"Harold Pinter Taken to Hospital: Playwright Harold Pinter, Winner of This Year's Nobel Prize for Literature, Has Been Admitted to Hospital." *BBC News* 6 Dec. 2005, 09:52 GMT. 27 Sept. 2007 <http://news.bbc.co.uk/2/hi/entertainment/4502430.stm>.

Heawood, Sophie. "The Best and Worst of 2005: From Harold Pinter's Nobel Prize to Strife at ENO, Our Panel Pick the Highlights and Lowlights of the Arts

Year. Interviews by Sophie Heawood." *Guardian Unlimited* 22 Dec. 2005. 26 Sept. 2007 <http://arts.guardian.co.uk/features/story/0,,1672450,00.html>. [Inc. interview with David Hare: "**Low**: The shaming indifference of the political class to Harold Pinter winning the Nobel prize. Most of us are past being scandalised by the omissions of the BBC, which appears to have lost all interest in literature and the performing arts, but it seems astonishing that the BBC did not broadcast the statement by a Nobel prize-winning author. Such things used to be their bread and butter. Worse, they censored all mention of the speech from their TV news. Astonishing, too, that not one party leader congratulated Pinter or commented on what he had to say. Politicians want us to be interested in them. But why should we be, when they're not interested in anything but sport and themselves?"]

Honigsbaum, Mark. "Publisher to Stand In for Pinter at Nobel Ceremony." *Guardian Unlimited* 24 Nov. 2005. 26 Sept. 2007 <http://books.guardian.co.uk/news/articles/0,,1649326,00.html>.

"In Praise of ... 2005." *Guardian Unlimited* 31 Dec. 2005. 26 Sept. 2007 <http://www.guardian.co.uk/leaders/story/0,,1675665,00.html>. "... Liverpool won the European championship and Harold Pinter a Nobel Prize."

Jewish Telegraphic Agency (JTA). "Pinter Wins Nobel Literature Prize." *Cleveland Jewish News* 20 Oct. 2005. 12 Oct. 2007 <http://www.clevelandjewishnews.com/articles/2005/10/20/news/world/bpinter1021.prt>.

Johnson, Boris. "Quotes of the Week: Playwright, in a Message Accepting Nobel Literature Prize." London *Independent on Sunday* 11 Dec. 2005, Comment: 37. (First Edition.)

Jones, Alice. "Arts: The Angry Brigade: A New Exhibition Celebrates the Era When British Burst into Life." London *Independent* 15 Dec. 2005.

Jones, Chad. "A Gallon of Pinter." In "Theater Losses: Wilson, Miller; Gains: Pinter's Nobel." *Inside Bay Area* (CA) 23 Dec. 2005. 24 Dec. 2005 <http://www.insidebayarea.com>.

"Just Jim: Prizewinning Hatred." *Outdoor Life* Apr. 2006: 31+.

Kilarski, Sharon. "The Laureate Goes to Brutality." *Epoch Times International* 21 Oct. 2005. 21 Oct. 2005 <http://www.theepochtimes.com/tools/printer.asp?id=33566>.

"Leading Article: Harold Pinter–Portrait of the Artist as Activist." London *Independent* 8 Dec. 2005, Comment: 32. (First Edition.)

Leiter, Robert. "Media Clippings: Literary Genius." *Jewish Exponent* (Philadelphia, PA) 5 Jan. 2006. 26 Sept. 2007 <http://www.jewishexponent.com/ViewArticle.asp?ArtID=2015>.

Leys, Nick. "Don't Try It at Home, Nobel Winner Jokes." *Australian* 12 Dec. 2005, Local: 5. (All-round Country Edition.) [Re: Barry Marshall. Comment re: Pinter not attending not fully accurate.]

Lyall, Sarah. "A Nobelist's Cri de Coeur: Accepting Award, Pinter Lashes Out at U.S." *New York Times* 7 Dec 2005. Rpt. in *International Herald Tribune* 7 Dec. 2005. 4 Aug. 2008 <http://www.iht.com/articles/2005/12/07/news/nobel.php>. [See correction in *New York Times* of 8 Dec. 2005 listed directly below and "Corrections" listed above.]

—. "Playwright Takes a Prize and a Jab at U.S.: Accepting Nobel, Pinter Says Lies Were Used to Justify War." *New York Times* 8 Dec. 2005, International (Foreign Desk): A3, col. 1. (Late Edition–Final.) [Correction appended.]

Maxwell, Andrew. "Inspired by Pinter." In "Hong Kong Should Be Testing Ground for Democracy." *South China Morning Post* 15 Dec. 2005, News, Letters: 18.

"More Pauses, Please." London *Daily Telegraph* 9 Dec. 2005, Features, Leading Article: 21. (London ed.)

"Nobel Prize Media Links." Official website of the Harold Pinter Society. *Pintersociety.org* 13 Oct.–11 Dec. 2005. 3 Nov. 2007 <http://www.pintersociety.org/links/nobellinks/nobellinks.html>. (Comp. Mark Taylor-Batty, with some assistance from Susan Hollis Merritt.)

"Nobel Prize-Winning Playwright Harold Pinter in London Hospital." *Yahoo! News* 5 Dec. 2005. 19 Dec. 2005 <http://news.yahoo.com>.

Organ, Maggie. "Saturday: Reply: Letters & Emails: Jesus in the Picture." *Guardian* 17 Dec. 2005, Guardian Leader Pages: 35.

Pilger, John. "Blair Criminalizes His Critics." *Anti-War.com* 6 Jan. 2006. 6 Jan. 2006 <http://www.antiwar.com/orig/pilger.php?articleid=8350>.

—. "The Death of Freedom." *New Statesman* 9 Jan. 2006. 26 Sept. 2007 <http://www.newstatesman.com/200601090004>.

"Pinter Drops Out of Nobel Lecture: Harold Pinter Has Been Forced to Pull Out of the Lecture Given by Winners of the Nobel Prize for Literature Due to Poor Health." *BBC News* 30 Nov. 2005, 14:18 GMT. 27 Sept. 2007 <http://news.bbc.co.uk/2/hi/entertainment/4485250.stm>.

"Pinter Pulls Out of Nobel Events Due to Ill Health." *Reuters UK* 30 Nov. 2005, 5:56 p.m. GMT.

"Pinter's Harsh Words Don't Tell the Whole Story." *South China Morning Post* 9 Dec. 2005, News, Editorial : 18.

Pitts, Jonathan. "Nobelists Use Event to Assail Bush: Attacks on Policies of the U.S. Administration Have Become Common in Past Few Years." *Baltimore Sun* 11 Dec. 2005, Telegraph: 23A. (Final Ed.)

Portillo, Michael. "Chattering Classes." *New Statesman* 12 Dec. 2005: 45.

"Primary Addresses Dec. 4-10: [. . .] Stockholm." *New York Times* 11 Dec. 2005, sec. 4, col. 1 (Week in Review Desk: The Week): 2. (Late Ed.–Final.)

Reuters (Oslo). "The World: No Need for Nuclear Arms, Laureate Says." *Los Angeles Times* 11 Dec. 2005, Main News, Foreign Desk, Part A: 28. (Home Ed.)

Reynolds, Nigel. "Pinter Rails against US in Nobel Prize Speech." London *Daily Telegraph* 8 Dec. 2005, News: 12.

Riddell, Mary. "Comment: Prophet without Honour: Harold Pinter Can Be Cantankerous and Puerile. But He Is a Worthy Nobel Winner." London *Observer* 11 Dec. 2005, Observer News Pages: 28. (Reply by Rosenthal, as listed below in "**Related Letters**.")

"A Round-up of Today's Other Stories in Brief: Pinter Attacks U.S. Foreign Policy." *Irish Times* 8 Dec. 2005, World: Other World Stories: 12.

Rowlands, Nanw. "Special Honour for Pinteresque Pretensions." *Cherwell Online* 21 Oct. 2005, 12:57:57. 22 Oct. 2005 <http://www.cherwell.org>.

Rummonds, James. "James Rummonds: 145 Million Dead Disprove Pinter." *Santa Cruz Sentinel* 25 Dec. 2005. 25 Dec. 2005 <http://www.santacruzsentinel.com/archive/2005/December/25/edit/stories/05edit.htm>.

Rush, George, and Joanna Rush Molloy, with Jo Piazza and Chris Rovzar. "Eminem, Who Often Gave Ex a Bad Rap, Aims to Rewed Her: ... Pinter: Jail to the Chief." *Daily News* (New York, NY) 8 Dec. 2005, Gossip: 38. (Sports Final Ed.)

Russell, Michael. "Driving Our Culture up a Cul-de-Sac." *Herald* (Glasgow) 12 Dec. 2005, Features: 14.

"Saturday: Web Page: Guardian.co.uk: Top Stories." *Guardian* 10 Dec. 2005, Guardian Saturday Comment Pages: 34. (Final Ed.)

Seaquist, Carla. "Harold Pinter's Pen Betrays His Normalcy." *Christian Science Monitor* 7 Dec. 2005, Opinion: 9.

Siegel, Robert, and Michele Norris. "Nobel Laureate Pinter Lashes Out at US Policy." *All Things Considered*, National Public Radio 9 Dec. 2005, 9:00 a.m. EST.

Taylor, James C. "Theater: Perspective: When Pinter Should Have Paused for Effect: Dishing Off a Rambling Recorded Rant for His Nobel Recognition, the Ailing Writer Misses a Chance to Say So Much More." *Los Angeles Times* 1 Jan. 2006, Sunday Calendar: Calendar Desk, Part E: 34. 5 Jan. 2006.

"A Terrible Rendition." *Irish Times* 10 Dec. 2005, News Features: Other Stories: 2.

"They Think." London *Independent* 8 Dec. 2005, Features: 80.

Van Gelder, Lawrence, comp. "Mussels Enlisted for Art Project." *New York Times* 9 Dec. 2005, Sec. E, Pt. 1, col. 1 (Movies, Performing Arts/Weekend Desk: Arts, Briefly): 7. (Late Edition–Final.)

Walsh, John. "Hamlet without the Prince: The Glittering Ceremony to Present Harold Pinter with a Nobel Prize." London *Independent on Sunday* 11 Dec. 2005, News: 18.

Weales, Gerald. "The State of Letters: Harold Pinter and the Nobel Prize." *Sewanee Rev.* 114.4 (Fall 2006): 603-09.

Welsh, Anne Marie. "A Wrecking Ball: Playhouse Goes Out in Style." *San Diego Union-Tribune* 12 Dec. 2005, Lifestyle: D-2. (Correction appended.)

"What Is True?: In His Video-taped Nobel Acceptance Speech Thursday to the Swedish Academy in Stockholm, British/Screenwriter Harold Pinter Excoriated a 'brutal scornful and ruthless' United States. Here Is What He Had to Say in that Speech about Truth." *Ottawa Citizen* 11 Dec. 2005, The Citi[z]en's Weekly: B3. (Final Ed.)

Williamson, Molly. "KSU [Kentucky State U] Professor Is Authority on Nobel Prize Winner: Revealing Ambiguity." *State Jour.* (Frankfort, KY) 27 Oct. 2005: A1, 7. [See Gale, listed above.]

Wilson, Peter (MAT P). "Nobel Groupies Go Hunting for Laureate Autographs." *Australian* 9 Dec. 2005, World: 8. (All-round Country Ed.)

Xinyl, Hong. "We've Come a Long Way–Maybe: In 2005, Full-Frontal Nudity in Quills Was Approved by the Authorities, But the References to the Death Penalty in Human Lefts Were Not. What Gives?" *Strait Times* (Singapore) 13 Dec. 2005. [Brief comment on Pinter's Nobel Lecture.]

Related Letters

Allen, Les. “Reply: Letters and Emails: Masterful Pinter.” *Guardian* 9 Dec. 2005, Guardian Leader Pages: 35. (Final Ed.) (Reply to Hari, as listed above in “**News Announcements and Related Features**.”)

Connell, Andy. “Before You Attack Pinter–Pause.” London *Daily Telegraph* 18 Dec. 2005, Features, Letter to the Editor: 24. (Reply to Hari, as listed above in “**News Announcements and Related Features**.”)

Dunn, Alexander. “Unfair to Americans.” *South China Morning Post* 13 Dec. 2005, News, Letters: 14.

Edwards, A. J. S. “Pinter and Point-scoring.” *Australian* 14 Dec. 2005, Features, Letters: 13. (All-round Country Ed.).

Falconer, Noel. “Before You Attack Pinter–Pause.” London *Daily Telegraph* 18 Dec. 2005, Features, Letter to the Editor: 24. (Reply to Ferguson, as listed above in “**News Announcements and Related Features.**”)

Friedman, Dan. “Dear Mr. Pinter.” *Zeek*, Jan. 2006. 1 Jan. 2006 <http://www.zeek.net/politics_0601.shtml>. (3 pages.)

Joel, J. F. “Before You Attack Pinter–Pause.” London *Daily Telegraph* 18 Dec. 2005, Features, Letter to the Editor: 24. (Reply to Ferguson, as listed above in “**News Announcements and Related Features**.”)

Klotz, Marvin, Bill Waung, and Mauricio D’Tejada. “Pinter’s Take on History Has Some Merit.” *Los Angeles Times* 14 Dec. 2005, California, Metro, Editorial Pages Desk, Part B: 12. (Home Ed.)

Mascall, Lesley. “Entertainment Needs Redeeming Value.” *Christian Science Monitor* 12 Dec. 2005, Opinion, Letters: 8. [Re: Carla Seaquist’s Dec. 7, 2005, Opinion piece on Harold Pinter’s lecture: “Harold Pinter’s Pen Betrays His Normalcy.”]

McKinlay, Morag. “There Is Indeed a Clear Cultural Direction.” *Glasgow Herald* 13 Dec. 2005, Features: 13.

Niven, Alastair. “Letter: Writer Who Shaped Modern Drama.” London *Independent* 7 Dec. 2005, Comment: 32. (First Edition.) (Reply by president of English PEN to Hari, as listed above in “**News Announcements and Related Features**.”)

Peacock, John N. Letter to the Editor. London *Mercury* 17 Dec. 2005: 29.

Penrith, John Green. “Masterful Pinter.” *Guardian Online* 9 Dec. 2005. 27 Sept. 2007 <http://www.guardian.co.uk/letters/story/0,,1663125,00.html>.

Pincus-Roth, Zachary. “Theater: Directions: Enter, Stage Left: ‘The Room,’ ‘Celebration’ and ‘The Homecoming.’” *New York Times* 18 Dec. 2005, Sec. 2 (Arts & Leisure Desk): 4, col. 1. 27 Sept. 2007 <http://www.nytimes.com/2005/12/18/theater/18pinc.html>.

Robertson, James C. “Before You Attack–Pause.” London *Daily Telegraph* 18 Dec. 2005, Features, Letter to the Editor: 24. (Reply to Ferguson, as listed above in “**News Announcements and Related Features**.”)

Rosenthal, Stan. “Precious Pinter.” Letters to the Editor. London *Observer* 18 Dec. 2005. 7 Jan. 2006 <http://observer.guardian.co.uk/print/0,3858,5358598-102277,00.html>. (Reply to Riddell, as listed above in “**News Announcements and Related Features**.”)

Related New Editions and Other Publications

"Harold Pinter: Recent Publications and the Nobel Prize." *Contemporary Theatre Rev.* 16.1 (2006): 129-43.

Pinter, Harold. *The Birthday Party*, *No Man's Land*, *Mountain Language*, and *Celebration*. 4 vols. London: Faber and Faber, 2005. [Box set; a "celebratory collection" marking Pinter's 2005 Nobel Prize in Literature.] (Courtesy of Dinah Wood, Faber and Faber.)

—. *Death etc.* New York: Grove P, 2005. (Courtesy of Eric Price, Grove Press.)

—. *The Dwarfs.* New York: Grove P, 2006. (Courtesy of Eric Price, Grove Press.)

—. *The Essential Pinter: Selections from the Work of Harold Pinter.* New York: Grove P, 2006. (Courtesy of Eric Price, Grove Press.)

—. *Harold Pinter: Plays Four.* 2nd expanded ed. 1998. London: Faber and Faber, 2005. [*Betrayal*, *Monologue*, *One for the Road*, *Mountain Language*, *Family Voices*, *A Kind of Alaska*, *Victoria Station*, *Precisely*, *The New World Order*, *Party Time*; *Moonlight*, *Ashes to Ashes*, *Celebration*.] (Courtesy of Dinah Wood, Faber and Faber.)

—. *Various Voices: Prose, Poetry, Politics 1948-2005.* Rev. ed. 1998. London: Faber and Faber, 2005. (Courtesy of Dinah Wood, Faber and Faber.)

Note to Readers

Citations and preprints, offprints or photocopies of publications and programs pertaining to the categories listed above (or categories of previous annual Harold Pinter bibliographies) are welcome. Please direct all such information about pertinent recent and forthcoming publications, upcoming productions, and works in progress (including relevant URLs or links) to:

Susan Hollis Merritt
Bibliographical Editor
The Pinter Review
PO Box 95
Keuka Park, NY 14478-0095
E-mail: shmerritt@aol.com
URL: http://www.susanhollismerritt.org

Notes on Contributors

William Baker is Distinguished Research Professor of English and University Libraries, Northern Illinois University. His "Harold Pinter" was published in the Continuum Writers' Lives series in 2008 and his and J. C. Ross' *Harold Pinter: A Bibliographical History* (British Library and Oak Knoll, 2005), the recipient of a CHOICE Book of the Year Award, is reviewed in the current issue.

Mardia Bishop holds a Ph.D. from Ohio State University. She presents and publishes on popular culture and contemporary theatre. She is co-editor of *PopPorn: Pornography in American Pop Culture* and the forthcoming *Mommy Mania: Motherhood in Pop Culture.* In addition, she writes and directs children's theatre. Currently she teaches at the University of Illinois, Urbana and Champaign.

Łukasz Borowiec is a Ph.D. student at the John Paul II Catholic University in Lublin, Poland. His MA thesis was entitled "Function of Objects and Props in Harold Pinter's One-Act Comedies of Menace: A Semiological Approach" (2004). His Ph.D. thesis is going to be a scholarly translation of Harold Pinter's novel *The Dwarfs.* His main interests are literary translation, modern British and Polish drama (especially radio drama), with an emphasis on functions of objects and props in drama and theatre.

Katherine Burkman is Professor Emeritus from The Ohio State University Department of English. She has published widely on Harold Pinter, Samuel Beckett, and other modern dramatists. After retiring, she spent many years as Artistic Director of *Women at Play*, a group in Columbus, Ohio, who wrote and performed both their own plays and those of Pinter, Beckett, and others from 1994 until 2006. She is presently editing a memoir written by Elbert Lenrow entitled *Kerouac Ascending* and a book on the figure of the double in drama, fiction, and film.

Richard Corballis is Professor of English at Massey University, New Zealand. Modern drama is one of his chief research interests, and he has written a book (*Stoppard: The Mystery and the Clockwork*) and several articles on Tom Stoppard. His interest in drama is not solely theoretical; he has at various times been an actor, a director (of *One for the Road,* among other plays), and a theatre critic. More recently his articles have drifted beyond the theatre and have been largely focused on the literatures of New Zealand and Ireland (especially the work of James Joyce). He is currently preparing a biography of the New Zealand playwright Bruce Mason, and a book on the uses and abuses of national female symbols.

Ariel Dorfman is a Chilean-American poet, novelist, playwright, human rights activist, and a Distinguished Professor at Duke University. He has received numerous international awards including the Sudamericana Award for a novel, the Laurence Olivier for Best Play (*Death and the Maiden*, which has been made into a feature film by Roman Polanski), and two theatre awards from the Kennedy Center. His books, written both in Spanish and English, have been translated into more than forty languages and his plays staged in over 100 countries. His memoir, *Heading South, Looking North,* was the basis for Peter Raymont's award-winning documentary film, "A Promise to the Dead: The Exile Journey of Ariel Dorfman." He contributes regularly to the major newspapers of the world.

Luc Gilleman teaches in the English Department and the Comparative Literature program at Smith College. He is the author of *John Osborne: Vituperative Artist* (Routledge, 2002) and articles on British, American, and European drama.

Francis Gillen is Dana Foundation Professor of English at The University of Tampa and recipient of the University's Louise Loy Hunter Award as outstanding teacher. He is broadly published in modern drama, including numerous essays on Pinter, as well as essays on Tennessee Williams, Tom Stoppard, Anthony Shaffer and Arthur Miller. He also writes on the modern novel, with essays on Woolf, Forster, James, Heller, Updike, Barthelme and McCarthy. He is a playwright as well. *Home* received a staged reading at the Players' Theater in Sarasota; *You Look Wan* at the annual Last Frontier Theatre Conference in Valdez, Alaska. His play on Florida's migrant workers was produced on video. He has finished a new play on the British artist Eric Gill.

Robert Gordon is Professor of Drama at Goldsmiths College, University of London. His scholarly research includes critical writing on post-war British theatre, Strindberg, Wilde, Pirandello and Arthur Miller, Shakespeare in performance and South African theatre. His monograph, *Stoppard: Text and Performance,* was published by Macmillan. *The Purpose of Playing: Modern Acting Theory in Perspective* was published by the University of Michigan Press in 2006. He has worked as an actor, playwright, and director in Britain, the UK, South Africa, the USA, Italy, and Ireland. He is currently working on a book on Harold Pinter for the Michigan Modern Dramatists series.

Ann C. Hall is the current president of the Harold Pinter Society. She is a professor of English at Ohio Dominican University. She has just edited a collection of essays called *Making the Stage: Essays on the Changing Nature of Theatre, Drama, and Performance* (Cambridge Scholars Press). She has recently been named a Theatre Series editor for Palgrave-Macmillan. Her theatre series invites books on the nature of theatre, drama, and performance in contemporary culture.

Sidney Homan is Professor of English at the University of Florida and author of ten books on Shakespeare and the modern playwrights. He is also an actor and director in professional and university theatres. His *Fish in the Moonlight: Growing Up in the Bone Marrow Unit*, which appeared in June 2008, collects stories of his growing up in Philadelphia in the 1940s and '50s and relates his experience telling them to young patients on his university hospital's Bone Marrow Unit in his role as Artist-in-Residence.

Christopher C. Hudgins, after many years as Chair of the Department of English at the University of Nevada, Las Vegas, is now the Dean of the College of Liberal Arts at UNLV. He still finds a bit of time, amidst bureaucratic tasks and fundraising and planning activities, to continue his work on a long-stewing book on Pinter's filmscripts. Hudgins is particularly pleased that the graduate programs in creative writing he launched twenty years ago as English Department Chair have now been ranked by *The Atlantic Monthly* as among the top five in the United States.

Susan Hollis Merritt is the author of *Pinter in Play: Critical Strategies and the Plays of Harold Pinter*, published by Duke University Press, and numerous articles, reviews, and parts of books on Pinter and contemporary drama, criticism, theory, and theater. She has served as the Bibliographical Editor of *The Pinter Review* since 1987. Her travels to Prague and London for research on "Global Politics: Contemporary Drama and the Media," investigating connections among virtual literary communities, cultural media, performance, celebrity, politics, social activism, and philanthropy, has been supported by grants and stipends from the International Research & Exchanges Board, the National Endowment for the Humanities, the Fulbright Senior Scholar Program, and Marist College. As a plenary speaker at the conference "Artist and Citizen: 50 Years of Performing Pinter" at the University of Leeds in April 2007, she spoke about "Pursuing Pinter," the subject of her research for over forty years.

Peter Münder is a journalist based in Hamburg, Germany. His enthusiasm for Pinter's plays originated in 1963, when he watched a production of *The Caretaker* by a group of Oxford University students in a rundown Dublin cinema. He is the author of *Harold Pinter und die Problematick des Absurden* and he has recently written a biography of Harold Pinter published by Rowohlt/Hamburt.

Shamrock McShane was born in Oak Park, Illinois, in 1951. He worked in the theater in Chicago in the 1970s and then formed the Everyday Theater in Key West in 1980. He now lives in Gainesville, Florida, teaching at Westwood Middle School and making movies.

John Peter is a longtime Chief Drama Critic for the *Sunday Times* of London, and author of *Vladimir's Carrot: Modern Drama and the Modern Imagination.*

Linda Renton teaches film studies, including film adaptation, at Bath Spa University, England. Her book, *Pinter and the Object of Desire: an approach through the screenplays,* was published by Legenda, Oxford, in 2002.

Elizabeth Sakellaridou is Professor of Theatre Studies in the Department of English of Aristotle University in Thessaloniki, Greece. She has written extensively on Harold Pinter and other contemporary British dramatists, with special emphasis on gender, culture, and politics. Her interest in the phenomenology of the stage has expanded to include issues of performativity of the dramatic discourse and the interaction of the new technologies. Her current research project explores contemporary forms of the tragic and its relation to melancholia. Her latest book is *Contemporary Women's Theatre; From Post-Brechtian to Post-Feminist Representations* (Athens: Ellinika Grammata, 2007).

Mark Taylor-Batty is a senior lecturer in Theatre Studies at the Workshop Theatre, University of Leeds, UK. He is the author of Harold Pinter (Northcote House, 2001) and *About Pinter* (Faber and Faber, 2005) and co-author, with his wife Juliette Taylor-Batty, of *Samuel Beckett's Waiting for Godot* (Continuum, 2009).